The Rough Guide to

Wales

There are more than one hundred and fifty Rough Guide titles
covering destinations from Amsterdam to Zimbabwe

Forthcoming titles include
Argentina • Croatia • Ecuador • Southeast Asia

Rough Guide Reference Series
Classical Music • Country Music • Drum 'n' Bass • English Football
European Football • House • The Internet • Jazz • Music USA • Opera
Reggae • Rock Music • Techno • Unexplained Phenomena • World Music

Rough Guide Phrasebooks
Czech • Dutch • Egyptian Arabic • European Languages • French • German
Greek • Hindi & Urdu • Hungarian • Indonesian • Italian • Japanese
Mandarin Chinese • Mexican Spanish • Polish • Portuguese • Russian
Spanish • Swahili • Thai • Turkish • Vietnamese

Rough Guides on the Internet
www.roughguides.com

ROUGH GUIDE CREDITS

Text editor: Polly Thomas
Series editor: Mark Ellingham
Editorial: Martin Dunford, Jonathan Buckley, Jo Mead, Kate Berens, Amanda Tomlin, Ann-Marie Shaw, Paul Gray, Helena Smith, Judith Bamber, Orla Duane, Olivia Eccleshall, Ruth Blackmore, Sophie Martin, Geoff Howard, Claire Saunders, Gavin Thomas, Alexander Mark Rogers, Joe Staines, Lisa Nellis, Andrew Tomičić, Claire Fogg, Richard Lim, Duncan Clark, Peter Buckley (UK); Andrew Rosenberg, Mary Beth Maioli, Don Bapst, Stephen Timblin (US)
Production: Susanne Hillen, Andy Hilliard, Link Hall, Helen Ostick, Julia Bovis, Michelle Draycott,

Katie Pringle, Robert Evers, Niamh Hatton, Mike Hancock, Robert McKinlay
Cartography: Melissa Baker, Maxine Repath, Nichola Goodliffe, Ed Wright
Picture research: Louise Boulton, Sharon Martins
Online editor: Kelly Cross (US)
Finance: John Fisher, Gary Singh, Edward Downey, Mark Hall, Tim Bill
Marketing & Publicity: Richard Trillo, Niki Smith, David Wearn, Jemima Broadbridge (UK); Jean-Marie Kelly, Myra Campolo, Simon Carloss (US)
Administration: Tania Hummel, Charlotte Marriott, Demelza Dallow

ACKNOWLEDGEMENTS

The Rough Guide to Wales owes a great deal to many friends and acquaintances, Welsh or otherwise, who happily shared their knowledge, voiced their opinions and expressed an enthusiasm for Wales which we hope is evident throughout this book.
Special thanks are due to staff at tourist offices throughout the country, particularly Eurwyn Thomas, and at Rough Guides to Paul Gray for the overview, Ed Wright and Melissa Baker for patient cartography, Helen Ostick for cool typesetting, Sharon Martins for fabulous pictures, Russell Walton for proofreading, and Diana Jarvis for painstaking extra books research.

Mike Parker would like to thank: Nathan, Nick, Gruffudd Rowland Williams, Lucie, Les and Sue, Gini,

the Dragon Collective crew, Nigel, Carol and Steve, Toby, Tasha and the bump, Ulrike and Owen, Tony and the generous boozers of Caernarfon, Billy, Debs and Matty, Gwilym Morus and all at Maen Alaw and the Môn Eisteddfod, Carlos, Jan and Elizabeth Morris, Kate and Peter, Adam Price, John Barnie and Francesca Rhydderch, Paul and Polly, Annie and the new bab, the Wendy bus and faithful hound Patsy for making so many Welsh walks such fun. Most of all, *diolch yn fawr* to the wonderful people and places of Wales for such effortless inspiration.

Paul Whitfield would like to thank: Andy and Jelly for restful breaks in between bursts of frenetic research, and Irene Gardiner whose forbearance through long research trips is always appreciated.

PUBLISHING INFORMATION

This third edition published June 2000 by
   Rough Guides Ltd, 62–70 Shorts Gardens,
   London WC2H 9AB.
Distributed by the Penguin Group:
Penguin Books Ltd, 27 Wrights Lane, London W8 5TZ
Penguin Putnam, Inc., 375 Hudson Street, NY 10014, USA
Penguin Books Australia Ltd, 487 Maroondah Highway, PO Box 257, Ringwood, Victoria 3134, Australia
Penguin Books Canada Ltd, 10 Alcorn Avenue, Toronto, Ontario, Canada M4V 1E4
Penguin Books (NZ) Ltd, 182–190 Wairau Road, Auckland 10, New Zealand
Typeset in Linotron Univers and Century Old Style to an original design by Andrew Oliver.
Printed in England by Clays Ltd, St Ives PLC.
Illustrations in Part One and Part Three by Edward Briant.

Illustrations on p.1 & p.439 by Henry Iles
© Mike Parker and Paul Whitfield, 2000
No part of this book may be reproduced in any form without permission from the publisher except for the quotation of brief passages in reviews.
528pp – Includes index
A catalogue record for this book is available from the British Library
ISBN 1-85828-543-7

The publishers and authors have done their best to ensure the accuracy and currency of all the information in *The Rough Guide to Wales*, however, they can accept no responsibility for any loss, injury, or inconvenience sustained by any traveller as a result of information or advice contained in the guide.

The Rough Guide to

Wales

written and researched by

Mike Parker and Paul Whitfield

ROUGH
GUIDES

THE ROUGH GUIDES

TRAVEL GUIDES • PHRASEBOOKS • MUSIC AND REFERENCE GUIDES

 We set out to do something different when the first Rough Guide was published in 1982. Mark Ellingham, just out of university, was travelling in Greece. He brought along the popular guides of the day, but found they were all lacking in some way. They were either strong on ruins and museums but went on for pages without mentioning a beach or taverna. Or they were so conscious of the need to save money that they lost sight of Greece's cultural and historical significance. Also, none of the books told him anything about Greece's contemporary life – its politics, its culture, its people, and how they lived.

So with no job in prospect, Mark decided to write his own guidebook, one which aimed to provide practical information that was second to none, detailing the best beaches and the hottest clubs and restaurants, while also giving hard-hitting accounts of every sight, both famous and obscure, and providing up-to-the-minute information on contemporary culture. It was a guide that encouraged independent travellers to find the best of Greece, and was a great success, getting shortlisted for the Thomas Cook travel guide award,

and encouraging Mark, along with three friends, to expand the series.

The Rough Guide list grew rapidly and the letters flooded in, indicating a much broader readership than had been anticipated, but one which uniformly appreciated the Rough Guide mix of practical detail and humour, irreverence and enthusiasm. Things haven't changed. The same four friends who began the series are still the caretakers of the Rough Guide mission today: to provide the most reliable, up-to-date and entertaining information to independent-minded travellers of all ages, on all budgets.

We now publish more than 150 titles and have offices in London and New York. The travel guides are written and researched by a dedicated team of more than 100 authors, based in Britain, Europe, the USA and Australia. We have also created a unique series of phrasebooks to accompany the travel series, along with an acclaimed series of music guides, and a best-selling pocket guide to the Internet and World Wide Web. We also publish comprehensive travel information on our web site:

www.roughguides.com

HELP US UPDATE

We've gone to a lot of effort to ensure that the third edition of *The Rough Guide to Wales* is accurate and up-to-date. However, things change – places get "discovered", opening hours are notoriously fickle, restaurants and rooms raise prices or lower standards. If you feel we've got it wrong or left something out, we'd like to know, and if you can remember the address, the price, the time, the phone number, so much the better.

We'll credit all contributions, and send a copy of the next edition (or any other Rough Guide if you prefer) for the best letters. Please mark letters: "Rough Guide Wales Update" and send to:
Rough Guides, 62–70 Shorts Gardens, London WC2H 9AB, or Rough Guides, 4th Floor, 345 Hudson St, New York, NY 10014.
Or send email to: mail@roughguides.co.uk
Online updates about this book can be found on Rough Guides' Web site at www.roughguides.com

THE AUTHORS

At the age of twelve, **Mike Parker** bought himself a Teach Yourself Welsh book and was hypnotized by this ancient land and its diverse culture. Since he started shaving, he has written books on four UK cities and the gay scenes in northern England, Ireland and Scotland, but it is to Wales that he always returns, as much for its pumping nightlife and rural cosmopolitanism as its crags and castles. At home in Birmingham, England, he combines travel writing with stand-up performing and the odd bit of broadcasting.

Born in England, **Paul Whitfield** spent childhood holidays secreting plastic toys in the sands of Welsh coastal resorts and failing to find them again. Twenty years later, after spending formative years in New Zealand, he returned to Britain and spent numerous weekends hiking the hills, climbing the crags and paddling the whitewater rivers of Snowdonia. Inspired by the Rough Guides he'd used through extensive travels he decided to jack in a life making biscuits in Liverpool and write this guide to Wales. He has now been lured back to New Zealand but makes frequent return trips to Wales in between Rough Guide assignments around New Zealand and to Alaska, California and Mexico.

READERS' LETTERS

Thanks to the readers of the last edition who wrote in with helpful comments and suggestions: Pat Andringa, Joy and Bob Barrell, Louisa Beall, Ikki Bhogal, Roger Brickell, Fran Brughera, Lisa Brughera, Toeja Gerson-Lohman, Mrs G.P. Hirst, Timothy J. Horgan, Judy Hutchings, Eirian Ifan, Anthony R. Johnson, Bruce Jones, Ruth Lambert, Pamela Littman, J. Murgatroyd, Hugh Prichard, Gabrielle Rivers, Ian Ross, Joel Rubenzahl, Gyla Smith, Jackie Smith, Sonja Soehnel, Richard Watkins, Linda Webb, Yvonne and Rob Westwood and Jodie Young.

Apologies to anyone whose name has been spelt incorrectly, and to those whose signatures could not be deciphered.

CONTENTS

Introduction ix

• CHAPTER 4: THE CAMBRIAN COAST

• CHAPTER 5: SNOWDONIA & THE LLŶN

• CHAPTER 6: THE NORTH COAST & ANGLESEY

PART THREE CONTEXTS

LIST OF MAPS

MAP SYMBOLS

══	Motorway	♦	Point of interest
══	Major road	⚑	Golf course
──	Minor road	◒	Cave
-----	Path	▲	Mountain peak
▬▬	Railway	⅄	Pass
▬▬	Wall	𝄐	Waterfall
──	Ferry route	⌇	Cliff
∿∿	Waterway	ⓘ	Tourist office
▬ ▬ ▬	Chapter division boundary	⊠	Post office
▬▪▬▪	Welsh border	★	Bus stop
✗	Airport	■	Building
△	Youth hostel	⊞	Church
Ⓧ	Campsite	⊡	Cemetery
♨	Castle	▒	Park
🏛	Stately home	▨	National Park
⌂	Abbey	▢	Forest
♟	Museum	▦	Marsh
✿	Country park	░	Sand/beach
P	Parking	▨	Nature reserve

INTRODUCTION

P erched on the rocky fringe of western Europe, **Wales** often gets short shrift in comparison to its Celtic cousins of Ireland and Scotland. Neither so internationally renowned nor so romantically perceived, the country is usually defined – if it is known at all – by its male voice choirs and tightly-packed pit villages. But there's far more to the place than the hackneyed stereotypes, and at its best, Wales is the most beguiling part of the British Isles. Even its comparative anonymity serves it well: where the tourist dollar has swept away some of the more gritty aspects of local life in parts of Ireland and Scotland, reducing ancient cultures to misty Celtic pastiche, Wales remains brittle and brutal enough to be real, and diverse enough to remain endlessly interesting.

Within its small mass of land, Wales boasts some stunning physical attributes. Its mountain ranges, ragged coastline, lush valleys and old-fashioned market towns all invite long and repeated visits. The culture, too, is compelling, whether in its Welsh- or English-language manifestations, its Celtic or its industrial traditions, its ancient cornerstones of belief or its contemporary chutzpah. Recent years have seen a huge and dizzying upsurge in Welsh self-confidence, a commodity no longer so dependent upon comparison with its big and powerful neighbour of England. Popular culture – especially music and film – has contributed much to this revival, as has the arrival of a National Assembly in 1999, the first all-Wales tier of government for six hundred years.

WALES AND ITS SHIFTING COUNTY BOUNDARIES

Wales is a small and thinly populated country, and most of the 2.8 million inhabitants congregate in the southern quarter of this land, which stretches 160 miles from north to south and 50 miles from east to west. Only 8000 square miles in all, it is smaller than Massachusetts and only half the size of The Netherlands.

After Henry VIII's Acts of Union in 1536 and 1543, when the Welsh administrative system became formally linked with England's, Wales was divided into thirteen counties or shires, their borders predominantly reflecting those of the baronial domains (or Marcher lordships) they replaced. These counties held fast for hundreds of years: ancient divisions and names familiar to all. In 1974, however, the Local Government Act brought wholesale reorganization of county divisions throughout Britain; in Wales, the original thirteen were streamlined into eight, four of which covered the industrialized southeast (including three separate divisions of Glamorganshire).

Throughout Britain, the "new" counties were never highly regarded, and this was true too of Wales, even though new county boundaries and names – Dyfed, Clwyd, Gwent – corresponded largely with ancient Welsh provinces and kingdoms. In the early 1990s, after twenty years of public discontent, the whole structure of local government was yet again up for grabs, with Wales and Scotland the first to change. After extensive consultation and frequent changes of heart, 22 new unitary authorities came into being, replacing the previous two-tier county and district council structure. Thus, we see the re-emergence of old county names like Denbighshire, Flintshire, Pembrokeshire and Monmouthshire (if not often within the same boundaries as before 1974), the maintenance of post-1974 names such as Powys and Gwynedd, and the creation of a whole new set of "county boroughs" (such as Cardiff, Neath-Port Talbot, Blaenau Gwent, Caerphilly) in the heavily populated south. Throughout the book, new divisions are used, although some institutions and venues still use the names from the 1974–96 period.

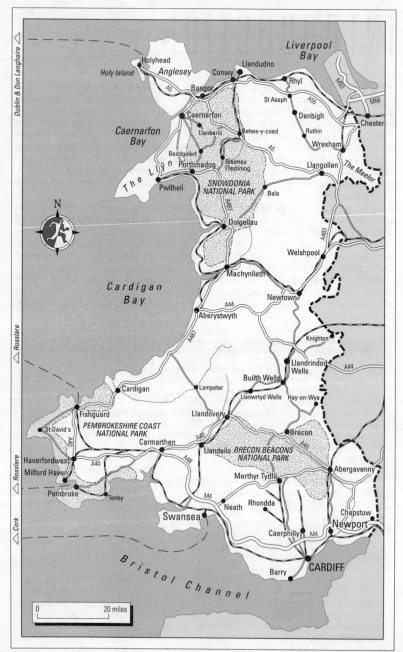

© Crown copyright

After centuries of enforced subjugation, the national spirit is undergoing a remarkable renaissance. The ancient symbol of the country, *y ddraig goch* or the red dragon, seen fluttering on flags everywhere in Wales, is waking up from what seems like a very long slumber.

Once you've crossed the border from England into Wales, the differences in appearance, attitude and culture between the two countries are immediately obvious. Wales shares many physical and emotional similarities with the other Celtic lands – Scotland, Ireland, Cornwall, Brittany and even Asturias and Galicia in northwest Spain. A rocky and mountainous landscape, whose colours are predominantly grey and green, a thinly scattered, largely rural population, a culture rooted deeply in folklore and legend and the survival of a distinct, ancient language are all hallmarks of Wales and its sister countries. To the visitor, it is perhaps the Welsh language, the strongest survivor of the Celtic tongues, that most obviously marks out the country. Tongue-twisting village names and vast bilingual signposts point to a glorious tale of endurance against the odds, slap next to the heartland of English language and culture, the most expansionist in history. Everyone in Wales speaks English, but nearly a quarter of the population also speak Welsh: TV and radio stations broadcast in it, all children learn it at school and visitors too are encouraged to try speaking at least a fragment of the rich, earthy tones of Europe's oldest living language.

Although it's often the older aspects of Welsh and Celtic culture, from stone circles to crumbling castles, that bring visitors here in the first place, contemporary Wales is also worthy of indulgent inspection. The cities and university towns throughout the country are buzzing with an understated youthful confidence and sense of cultural optimism, while a generation or two of so-called "New Age" migrants have brought a curious cosmopolitanism to the small market towns of mid-Wales and the west. Although conservative and traditional forces still sporadically clash with these more liberal and anarchic strands of thought, there's an unquestionable feeling that Wales is big enough, both physically and emotionally, to embrace such diverse influences. Perhaps most importantly of all, Welsh culture is underpinned by an iconoclastic democracy that contrasts starkly with the establishment-obsessed divisions of England, or even, to some extent, of Scotland or Ireland. Wales is not – and never has been – so absorbed by matters of class and status as its near neighbours. Instead, the Welsh character is famously endowed with a musicality, lyricism, introspection and sentimentality that produces far better bards and singers than it does lords and masters. And Welsh culture is undeniably a popular expression, arising from an inherently democratic impulse. Anything from a sing-song in the pub to the grandiose theatricality of an Eisteddfod involves everyone – including any visitor eager to learn and join in.

Where to go

Like all capital cities, **Cardiff** is atypical of the rest of the country, but as the first major stop on both rail and road routes from England into south Wales, it's a good place to start. Most national institutions are based here, not least the new National Assembly, currently in a temporary home but soon to be housed in purpose-built splendour amidst the massive regeneration projects of Cardiff Bay. The city is also home to the National Museum and St Fagans Folk Museum – both are excellent introductions to the character of the rest of Wales – and the brand-new Millennium Stadium, which hosted the 1999 Rugby World Cup. The only other centres of appreciable size are dowdy **Newport** and breezy, resurgent **Swansea**, lying respectively to the east and west of the capital. All three cities grew as ports, mainly exporting millions of tons of coal and iron from the **Valleys**, where fiercely proud industrial communities were built up in the thin strips of land between the mountains.

Much of Wales' appeal lies outside the towns, where there is ample evidence of the warmongering which has shaped the country's development. Castles are everywhere, from the hard little stone keeps of the early Welsh princes to Edward I's incomparable series of thirteenth-century fortresses at **Flint**, **Conwy**, **Beaumaris**, **Caernarfon**, **Harlech** and **Rhuddlan**, and grandiose Victorian piles where grouse were the only enemy. Fortified residences served as the foundation for a number of the stately homes that dot the country, but many castles were deserted and remain dramatically isolated on rocky knolls, most likely on spots previously occupied by prehistoric communities. Passage graves and stone circles offer a more tangible link to the pre-Roman era when the priestly order of Druids ruled over early Celtic peoples, and later religious monuments such as the great ruined abbeys of **Valle Crucis**, **Tintern** and **Strata Florida** lend a gaunt grandeur to their surroundings.

Whether you're admiring castles, megaliths or Dylan Thomas's home at **Laugharne**, almost everything in Wales is enhanced by the beauty of the countryside, from the lowland greenery of meadows and river valleys to the inhospitable heights of the moors and mountains. The rigid backbone of the **Cambrian Mountains** terminates in the soaring peaks of **Snowdonia** and the angular ridges of the **Brecon Beacons**, both superb walking country and both national parks. A third national park follows the **Pembrokeshire Coast**, where golden strands come separated by rocky bluffs overlooking offshore bird colonies. Much of the rest of the coast remains unspoilt, though seldom undiscovered, with long sweeps of sand often backed by traditional British seaside resorts: the **north Wales coast**, the **Cambrian coast** and the **Gower peninsula** display a notable abundance.

When to go

The English preoccupation with the weather holds equally for the Welsh. The climate here is temperate, with Welsh summers rarely getting very hot and nowhere but the tops of mountain ranges ever getting very cold, even in midwinter. Temperatures vary little from Cardiff in the south to Llandudno in the north, but proximity to the mountains is a different matter: Llanberis, at the foot of Snowdon, gets doused with more than twice as much rainfall as Caernarfon, seven miles away, and is always a few degrees cooler. With rain never too far from the mind of any resident or visitor, it is easy to forget that throughout much of the summer, Wales – particularly the coast – can be bathed in sun. Between June and September, the Pembrokeshire coast, washed by the Gulf Stream, can be as warm as anywhere in Britain. The bottom line is that it's impossible to say with any degree of certainty that the weather will be pleasant in any given month. May might be wet and grey one year and gloriously sunny the next, and the same goes for the autumnal months – November stands an equal chance of being crisp and clear or foggy and grim. Obviously, if you're planning to lie on a beach, or camp in the dry, you'll want to go between June and September – a period when you should book your accommodation as far in advance as possible. Otherwise, if you're balancing the likely fairness of the weather against the density of the crowds, the best time to get into the countryside or the towns is between April and May or in October. If outdoor pursuits are your objective, these are the best months for walking, June to October are warmest and driest for climbing, and December to March the only times you'll find enough water for kayaking.

PART ONE

THE BASICS

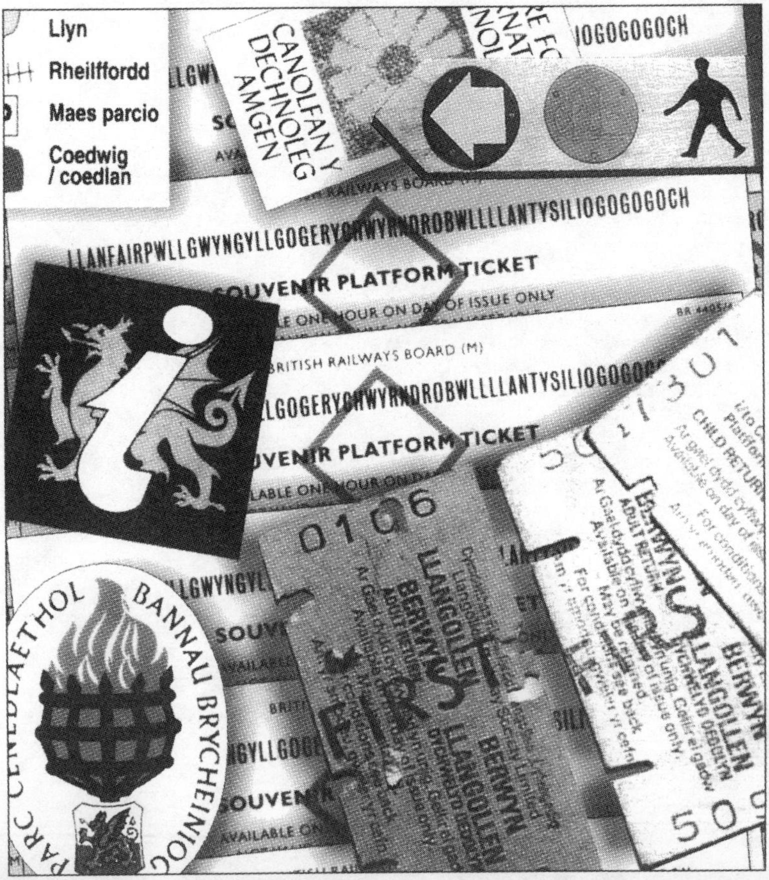

GETTING THERE FROM THE UK AND EUROPE

Crossing the border from England into Wales is straightforward, with train and bus services forming part of the British national network. High costs and minimal time savings mean flights within Britain are of little use, with the possible exception of those from Scotland. If you're driving from England, you'll probably be using one of the half-dozen or so roads which all run east to west through Wales. The two providing the quickest access into the heart of the country run along opposite coasts: the M4 motorway in the south, and the A55 dual carriageway in the north. These are both fast and busy roads, but minor routes are more appealing if you aren't in too much of a hurry.

If you're travelling from Ireland, **ferries** are by far the cheapest and easiest way of getting to Wales. From the rest of Europe, there's the choice of flying from various destinations to Cardiff International Airport, or using either the traditional cross-Channel ferry services or the Channel Tunnel to England and making your way onwards from there.

BY PLANE

The only airport of any size in Wales is **Cardiff–Wales International** (☎01446/711111, fax 711675, *www.cial.co.uk*), ten miles southwest of the capital, at which scheduled flights arrive from selected Northern European capitals and a few British destinations. The main international carrier is KLM (UK information on ☎08705/074074,

www.klmuk.com), which flies into Cardiff from Amsterdam. The only other main carriers flying into Cardiff are British Airways (☎0345/222111, *www.british-airways.com*), for flights to and from Belfast, Brussels, Edinburgh, Glasgow, Aberdeen, Guernsey and Paris; Ryanair (☎0870/333 1239, *www.ryanair.ie*) for flights to Cardiff from Dublin; and Manx Airlines (☎0345/256256, *www.manx-airlines.com*), which operates services from Jersey and the Isle of Man to Cardiff – these are mostly business flights, timed and priced accordingly, and often not operating at weekends.

In general, from Europe and Ireland you are better off flying into London, Birmingham or Manchester and moving on by bus or train. There are no worthwhile scheduled flights from England to Wales or within Wales.

BY TRAIN

After centuries of dreams and plans, the **Channel Tunnel** finally opened for business in 1995, with two operators using the tunnel. **Eurostar** (☎0990/186186, *www.eurostar.co.uk*) runs hourly **passenger trains** between London Waterloo, Paris and Brussels. Two direct daily connections from Waterloo run along the Alpha Line to Newport and Cardiff, one of which continues to and from stations en route to Swansea and Carmarthen. The least expensive return fares to London (which must be booked three days in advance and span a Saturday night) are £89 from Paris, £79 from Brussels and £69 from Lille. Full fares with no restrictions are £249 from Paris and Brussels and £210 from Lille. Youth tickets (for under-26s) have no restrictions attached and cost £79 from Paris, £69 from Brussels and £65 from Lille. Eurostar also offers frequent promotional fares. The other Channel tunnel operator, **Eurotunnel**, runs a frequent **car-carrying train service** that crosses from Calais in northern France to Folkestone in southern England. Buses, cars and motorbikes are loaded onto a freight train, known as Le Shuttle (☎0990/353535, *www.eurotunnel.com*), which takes 35 minutes to get between the loading terminals at Calais and Folkestone. You can just turn up on the day you want to travel, but booking is advised, especially at weekends; tickets are fully flexible. A five-day return for a car and four passengers travelling

TRAIN FARES AND SAVINGS

Ordinary standard-class **fares** on UK trains are high, and first-class costs an extra 33 percent, but there are six types of reduced fare ticket.

Savers are return tickets that can be used on all trains on Saturdays, Sundays and bank holidays, on most weekday trains outside the morning rush hour for the outward journey, and all trains for the return leg. If you buy a return ticket at any station outside the morning rush hour, you'll routinely be issued with a Saver ticket. Guaranteeing you a seat, an **Advance** ticket costs the same as a Saver and permits travel on most services over 150 miles, but must be bought before noon on the day before travel, and numbers are limited. **SuperSavers**, cheaper still, cannot be used on Fridays nor on half a dozen other specified days of the year, normally Saturdays during July and August. A **SuperAdvance** ticket costs much the same as a SuperSaver, has the same limitations as the Advance ticket and numbers are even more limited; again, the only advantage to booking a SuperAdvance ticket is that you're guaranteed a seat. Saver and SuperSaver tickets are valid for one month (outward travel has to be within two days of the date on the ticket), and allow a break in the return (but not outward) leg of the journey.

Like the Advance and SuperAdvance tickets, the even cheaper **Apex** tickets are issued in limited numbers on certain journeys of 150 miles or more, but these have to be bought at least seven days before travelling and you must specify your outward and return departure times. They include a seat reservation in the price. In addition, there is a **Leisure First** ticket which is more expensive than a Saver, but allows travel on any train, must be booked before 4pm on the day before you travel and requires outward and return journeys to be separated by a Saturday.

In practice, you can buy Saver, SuperSaver and Leisure First tickets to just about anywhere, but other tickets are only available in limited numbers on long, popular journeys. For Wales, that means journeys between London and the main stations on the north and south coast lines.

Children under five travel free, while those aged 5–15 inclusive pay half the adult fare on most journeys – though there are no discounts on Apex tickets. In an apparent effort to dissuade people from using their services, the rail companies now regard skis and large musical instruments as children and charge you for them accordingly. Most long-distance trains now have limited space for **bicycles** and you are required to reserve a place before you travel and pay £3 for each journey.

At weekends, many long-distance services have a special deal whereby you can convert your standard-class ticket to a first-class one by paying a £5 supplement. This is seldom worthwhile within Wales, but vital if you are travelling to London after a Rugby International match at Cardiff and don't want to stand up. As a guide to **prices**, a standard class return ticket on the London–Cardiff route can cost anything from £23 (Apex) and £87 (open ticket), with Savers (£45.60), SuperSavers (£37) and SuperAdvance tickets (£32) in between.

off-peak costs £169–215 in peak season. Travelling between 10pm and 6am brings the price down to £139.

Despite the tunnel, **car ferries** remain well and truly in business, often undercutting the tunnel prices and, in the case of the Calais–Dover service, not taking much longer (see box, for more details).

FROM ENGLAND AND SCOTLAND

Ongoing **rail privatization** has seen numerous changes in a very short space of time, not all of them positive. Now that all of the old British Rail network has been split amongst competing companies, services have proved decidedly sketchy on the less profitable routes – something particularly relevant to parts of rural Wales. In theory, though, this fragmentation shouldn't impact upon passengers – **through-ticketing** was enshrined in the privatization legislation, and you should not have any trouble in booking a journey on trains run by two or more operators. In practice, though, the national rail helpline (see below) has been heavily criticized for giving only partial information; however, the situation does seem to be improving, and the phone line should be your first port of call for all enquiries regarding train travel.

TRAIN INFORMATION

National rail enquiries ☎0345/484950
Minicom service ☎0845/605 0600

Two main lines provide frequent, fast services **to Wales from London**: the south Wales line from London Paddington via Reading, Swindon and Bristol to Newport, Cardiff and Swansea; and the north coast line to Bangor and Holyhead. Very few direct trains from England go beyond Swansea, although connections at either Cardiff or Swansea link up with services to Carmarthen and stations in Pembrokeshire. **From other cities in England and Scotland**, you'll probably need to change en route – at Bristol or Bath for the south coast line, at Crewe for the north coast – though for south Wales, a semi-fast shuttle runs between Manchester or Birmingham and Cardiff via Hereford or Gloucester.

Mid-Wales is best reached via Birmingham and Shrewsbury, with two lines plunging deep into the heart of the country. The faster route heads through Welshpool, Newtown and Machynlleth, beyond which it divides at Dyfi Junction. The southern spur goes a few miles to Borth and Aberystwyth, the northern one crawls up the coast through Tywyn, Barmouth, Harlech and Porthmadog to Pwllheli. Even slower (but very picturesque) is the second route from Shrewsbury, the Heart of Wales line, which limps four or five times daily into Wales, through Knighton, Llandrindod Wells, Llanwrtyd Wells, Llandovery, Llandeilo and a host of tiny halts on the way to Llanelli and Swansea.

Journey times between main centres are remarkably short: London–Cardiff takes under two hours and London–Swansea around three hours. Heading for the north coast, expect the London–Holyhead service to take just over four hours.

BY BUS

Inter-town **bus** services duplicate a few of the major rail routes, often at half the price of the train or less. Buses are reasonably comfortable and often have drinks and sandwiches available on board on longer routes. By far the biggest national operator is **National Express**, whose network covers England and sends half a dozen tendrils into Wales. The chief routes are from London to Cardiff, Swansea and on to Pembroke and Milford Haven; London to Wrexham; London to Aberystwyth; London along the north Welsh coast to Holyhead and Pwllheli, both via Birmingham; Birmingham to Cardiff and Swansea; Birmingham to Haverfordwest; Manchester along the north coast to Llandudno, Bangor and Holyhead; and a cross-country trek from Great

BUS INFORMATION

National Express coach enquiries
☎0990/808080

National line to identify local ticket agencies
☎0990/010104

National Express on the Internet:
www.nationalexpress.co.uk

Yarmouth via the East Midlands and Birmingham to south Wales. National Express services are so popular that for busy routes and services during weekends and holidays, it's a good idea to buy a reserved journey ticket, which guarantee a seat.

One-way tickets are usually little cheaper than an **economy return** ticket, which is good for travel on any day except Friday and is valid for three months. If you travel on Friday, expect to pay around thirty percent more. Typical economy return **journey costs** to Cardiff are £25 from London; £49 from Edinburgh, Glasgow or Newcastle; £29 from Manchester; and £17 from Birmingham. A Manchester–Holyhead return costs £15.

If you're planning to travel extensively throughout Britain by bus, the various National Express **discount passes** may save you a lot of money. UK residents under 25, in full-time education or of retirement age can buy a National Express **Discount Coach Card** (£8), which is valid for one year and entitles the holder to a thirty percent discount on any fare. All passengers are entitled to buy a **Tourist Trail Pass**, which offers unlimited travel on the National Express network. Covering two days' travel out of any three, a Tourist Trail Pass costs £49 for adults, £39 for students and under-26s; five days' travel in ten cost £85 or £67 respectively; eight days in sixteen cost £120 or £95; and fifteen days in thirty will set you back £187 or £149. In Britain, you can buy Tourist Trail Passes from major travel agents, at Gatwick and Heathrow airports, at the British Travel Centre in London (see p.24), or at the main National Express offices. The main Welsh offices are at Cardiff and Swansea, but tickets are available through a broad network of travel agents – contact the number in the box above for local details. In North America, these passes should be available through any travel agent or direct from British Travel International (see box on p.12 for address).

For more on bus passes that can be used within Wales and the rest of Britain, see "Getting around", p.30.

BY ROAD: DRIVING

Travelling to Wales by car from England, the main roads into **the north** are the upgraded coastal **A55** route, a dual carriageway all the way from Chester via Holywell, St Asaph and Colwyn Bay, through a tunnel under the Conwy Estuary and on to Bangor, where it connects with the old trunk route, the A5. Although the A5 is still single carriageway across Anglesey to Holyhead, the final stretch of the A55 dual carriageway will cross the island by 2002. The **A5** is still the major road into north Wales from the Midlands and the south of England, best approached from the **M6** just north of Wolverhampton, via the fast **M54** and new Shrewsbury bypass. Much of the A5 has been improved in recent decades, although there are still bottlenecks at Llangollen and Betws-y-Coed.

The Shrewsbury route is also the best for access into **mid-Wales** as far south as Newtown and Aberystwyth, using the **A458** to Welshpool from the Shrewsbury bypass. Further south, the **A456** from Birmingham, via Kidderminster and Leominster, is occasionally slow when passing through towns, but generally easier than the route through Worcester and Hereford to reach the A44 in Radnorshire and, to the south, the A438/470 to Brecon. This road connects with the swift westbound A40 at the Brecon bypass, best for routes from the Midlands and north of England to southern Cardiganshire and northern Carmarthenshire. An alternative route from the Midlands is via the **M50** "Ross Spur", a quiet motorway off the M5 south of Worcester, meeting the A449 dual carriageway at Ross-on-Wye. The road continues south, dividing at Raglan into the quick A40 for Brecon and the A449 down to Newport, the M4 and all destinations west.

The **M4 from London** makes the most dramatic entry into Wales, across the twin River Severn Bridges. Stay on the M4 and you'll be ushered into Wales across the **Second Severn Crossing** (£4.25 toll), a graceful bridge a few miles south of the M48 and the original **Severn Bridge** (same toll), rising high over the mud flats as it descends towards Chepstow. Both motorways reconnect just west of Caldicot. The M4 coasts quickly westwards, although tailbacks are hardly a rarity around Cardiff and Newport. Thankfully, the spectacular new river crossing at Swansea is now open, ending the hideous queues on the old A48 stretch. At Pont Abraham, a few miles north, the M4 mutates into the A48 dual carriageway, connecting with the excellent A40 at Carmarthen and coursing west to Haverfordwest for connections to Pembrokeshire and southern Cardiganshire.

HITCHING AND LIFT-SHARING

The extensive motorway network and the density of traffic makes long-distance hitching through England and Scotland to the Welsh border and along the M4 to Cardiff and Swansea relatively easy. Key junctions on the edge of metropolitan areas and motorway service stations are the favoured hitching spots, and standing with a sign at the exit produces the best results.

However, **hitching is not generally advised**, especially if you are a woman travelling alone. A way around this impasse is offered by the **lift-sharing** advertisements in the small-ads paper *Loot*, available daily in London, Manchester and Bristol, with private individuals offering and seeking lifts around Britain. There's no British lift-share agency currently in operation: the "Connections" small ads in *Wanderlust* magazine (☎01753/620426, fax 620474, *www.wanderlust.co.uk*) are probably your best bet, and it's also worth checking notice boards in health food shops and other "alternative" establishments.

BY FERRY

Wales has three main ferry ports all serving boats **from Ireland** (see box, opposite). Ferries from Dublin, and both ferries and high-speed catamarans from Dun Laoghaire (six miles south of Dublin), arrive at Holyhead on the northwest tip of Wales, while Rosslare, just outside Wexford, is the departure point for ferries and catamarans to Fishguard, and ferries to Pembroke Dock, both in southwest Wales.

Stena Line (☎08705/707070, *www.stenaline.com*) operates ferries and cats from Dun Laoghaire to Holyhead, and services from Rosslare to Fishguard; Irish Ferries (☎08705/171717, *www.irishferries.ie*) runs ferries from Dublin to Holyhead and from Rosslare to Pembroke Dock. **Ferry prices** for the two companies are almost identical, whichever ports you travel between, though for cars, winter fares tend to be a little cheaper from Rosslare, as are high-summer fares to Holyhead. One-way foot passenger fares range from £20 in winter to £29 on summer sailings from Friday to Sunday. Cars

FERRY CONNECTIONS

	Company	Frequency	Duration
From Belgium			
Ostend–Dover	Hoverspeed (SeaCat)	4–7 daily	2hr
Zeebrugge–Hull	P&O North Sea Ferries	1 daily	14hr
From Denmark			
Esbjerg–Harwich	Scandinavian/Stena	3–4 weekly	18hr
From France			
Boulogne–Folkestone	Hoverspeed (SeaCat)	April–Sept 4 daily	55min
Caen–Portsmouth	Brittany	Jan–mid-Nov 2–3 daily	6hr
Calais–Dover	P&O Stena	30–35 daily	75min
Calais–Dover	Hoverspeed (Hovercraft/SeaCat)	6–20 daily	35min/50min
Cherbourg–Poole	Brittany	Jan–mid-Nov 1–2 daily	4hr 15min
Cherbourg–Portsmouth	P&O Portsmouth	1–5 daily	3–5hr
Dieppe–Newhaven	P&O Stena	2 daily	4hr
Dieppe–Newhaven	Hoverspeed (Super SeaCat)	April–Sept 3 daily	2hr
Le Havre–Portsmouth	P&O Portsmouth	2–3 daily	5–8hr
Roscoff–Plymouth	Brittany	Jan–mid-Nov 1–3 daily	6hr
St Malo–Poole (via Jersey)	Condor	May–Oct 1 daily	5hr 40min
St Malo–Portsmouth	Brittany	Jan–mid-Nov 1–7 weekly	8hr 45min
St Malo–Weymouth (via Jersey)	Condor	May–Oct 1 daily	5hr
From Germany			
Hamburg–Harwich	Scandinavian	3–4 weekly	19hr
Hamburg–Newcastle	Scandinavian	May–Sept 2 weekly	22hr
From Holland			
Amsterdam–Newcastle	Scandinavian	2–7 weekly	14hr
Hook of Holland–Harwich	Stena (Catamaran)	2 daily	3hr 40min
Rotterdam–Hull	North Sea	1 daily	14hr
From Ireland			
Cork–Swansea	Swansea–Cork Ferries	mid-March–Nov 4–6 weekly	10hr
Dublin–Holyhead	Stena/Irish Ferries	2–6 daily	1hr 50min/3hr 15min
Dublin–Liverpool	Isle of Man Steam Packet	March–Sept 1–2 daily	3hr 45min
Dun Laoghaire–Holyhead	Stena (Catamaran)	4–5 daily	99min
Rosslare–Fishguard	Stena/Stena Sea Lynx	2–6 daily	1hr 35min–3hr 30min
Rosslare–Pembroke	Irish Ferries	2 daily	4hr
From Norway			
Bergen–Lerwick	Smyril	mid-May–mid-Sept 1 weekly	12 hr
Kristiansand–Newcastle	DFDS Scandinavian	2 weekly	18hr
Stavanger/Bergen– Newcastle	Fjord Line	4–6 weekly	20–27hr
From Spain			
Bilbao–Portsmouth	P&O	2 weekly	29–40hr
Santander–Plymouth	Brittany	March–mid-Nov 1–2 weekly	24hr
From Sweden			
Gothenburg–Newcastle	Scandinavian	Feb–Dec 2 weekly	26hr

with up to five people cost from £88. To save money, avoid weekend sailings from mid-July to mid-September and travel during the day rather than at night. **Catamarans** cost about £5 more as a foot passenger and £10–30 more for a car depending on season. There is also a ferry from Cork to Swansea, operated by Swansea–Cork Ferries (☎01792/456116, *www.swansea-cork.ie*). Most are ten-hour night sailings costing £24–34 for foot passengers and £95–190 for a car and up to four passengers, with special offers for returns also available.

There's a much greater choice of **ferries from Europe** to ports in England, the most convenient of which are listed in the box overleaf. Competitive pricing, especially since the Channel Tunnel opened, means that unless you are in a hurry lower prices may lure you onto a boat rather than into the tunnel. There are regular crossings with Hoverspeed, Stena Line and P&O from Calais to Dover, the shortest route, for which the lowest fare for a small car and two adults is around £70. For full details of ferry routes and prices, call the ferry companies direct.

GETTING THERE FROM THE US AND CANADA

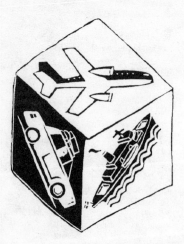

of direct flights into Manchester or Birmingham airports, both of which are directly linked to the rail network. If you want to avoid England altogether, it is possible to arrive at Cardiff Airport via flights from Glasgow in Scotland, Dublin in Ireland or Amsterdam in Holland, all of which receive transatlantic flights. See p.3 for full details on flights to Cardiff.

SHOPPING FOR TICKETS

Given the enormous volume of air traffic crossing the Atlantic, you should have no problem finding a seat – the problem will be sifting through all the possibilities. Basic fares, especially to London, are kept very reasonable by intense competition, and discounts by bulk agents and periodic special offers from the airlines themselves can drive prices still lower. Any local travel agent should be able to access airlines' up-to-the-minute fares, although in practice they may not have time to research all the possibilities – you might want to call a few airlines direct (see box on p.10).

There are no regular scheduled transatlantic flights into Wales, so you're best off flying into an English airport and continuing overland. For visitors from the US and Canada, the range of options will always be greatest – and the fares will usually be lowest – flying into London, Britain's busiest gateway city. Two of London's airports – Heathrow and Gatwick – handle transatlantic flights, and in terms of convenience for onward travel they're about equal. For quicker access to mid or north Wales, you might consider one of the growing number

Barring special offers, the cheapest of the airlines' published fares is usually an **Apex** ticket, although this will carry certain restrictions: you have to book – and pay – at least 21 days before departure, spend at least seven days abroad (maximum stay one month), and you tend to get penalized if you change your schedule. There are also winter **Super Apex** tickets, sometimes known as "**Eurosavers**" – slightly cheaper than

DISCOUNT AGENTS, CONSOLIDATORS, TRAVEL CLUBS AND COURIER BROKERS

Air Brokers International, 150 Post St, Suite 620, San Francisco, CA 94108 (☎1-800/883-3273, *www.airbrokers.com*). Consolidator.

Air Courier Association, 15000 W 6th Ave, Suite 203, Golden, CO 80401 (☎303/278-8810, *www.aircourier.org*). Discount travel club offering courier flights.

Airtech, 588 Broadway, Suite 204, New York, NY 10012 (☎1-800/575-TECH, *www.airtech.com*). Standby seat broker (mainly from Northeastern US cities) with discounted confirmed flights from cities throughout the US.

Council Travel, 205 E 42nd St, New York, NY 10017 (☎1-800/2-COUNCIL, *www.counciltravel.com*), plus branches in many other US cities. Primarily a youth/student travel organization that also offers consolidated flights to everyone.

Educational Travel Center, 438 N Frances St, Madison, WI 53703 (☎1-800/747-5551, *www.edtrav.com*). Discount agent for students and teachers with consolidated rates for everyone.

Last Minute Travel Club, 100 Sylvan Rd, Suite 600, Woburn, MA 01801 (☎1-800/LAST-MIN). Travel club specializing in standby deals.

Moment's Notice, 7301 New Utrecht Ave, Brooklyn, NY 11204 (☎212/486-0500, *www.moments-notice.com*). Discount travel club.

New Frontiers/Nouvelles Frontières, 12 E 33rd St, New York, NY 10016 (☎1-800/366-6387, *www.newfrontiers.com*); 1180 Drummond St, Suite 330, Montréal, PQH3G 2R7 (☎514/871-3000); plus other branches in Los Angeles, San Francisco and Québec City. French discount travel firm.

Now Voyager, 74 Varick St, Suite 307, New York, NY 10013 (☎212/431-1616, *www.nowvoyagertravel.com*). Discount broker with some courier flights.

Preferred Traveler's Club, 4501 Forbes Blvd, Lanham, MD 20706 (☎1-800/444-9800, *www.emitravel.com*). Discount travel club.

STA Travel, 10 Downing St, New York, NY 10014 (☎1-800/777-0112, *www.sta-travel.com*) and other branches nationwide. Worldwide specialist in independent travel with special emphasis on student/youth fares.

Student Flights, 5010 E Shea Blvd, Suite 104A, Scottsdale, AZ 85254 (☎1-800/255-8000, *www.isecard.com*). Committed to finding the cheapest student/teacher/youth fares – if you find one for less they issue a $50 rebate to ID cardholders.

Travac, 989 6th Ave, 16th Floor, New York, NY 10018 (☎1-800/872-8800, *www.travac.com*). Consolidator and charter broker.

Travel Avenue, 10 S Riverside, Suite 1404, Chicago, IL 60606 (☎1-800/333-3335, *www.travelavenue.com*). Consolidator.

Travel CUTS, 187 College St, Toronto, ON M5T 1P7 (☎416/979-2406, *www.travelcuts.com*) plus other branches all over Canada. Student/youth travel organization with discounted rates for others.

Travelers Advantage, 3033 S Parker Rd, Suite 1000, Aurora, CO 80014 (☎1-800/548-1116, *www.travelersadvantage.com*). Discount travel club.

UniTravel, 11737 Administration Drive, Suite 120, St Louis, MO 63146 (☎1-800/325-2222, *www.flightsforless.com*). Consolidator.

Worldtek Travel, 111 Water St, New Haven, CT 06511 (☎1-800/243-1723, *www.worldtek.com*). Discount travel agency.

---

an ordinary Apex, but limiting your stay to between seven and 21 days. Some airlines also issue **Special Apex** tickets to people younger than 24, often extending the maximum stay to a year. Many airlines offer **youth** or **student fares** to under-26s (a passport or driving licence are sufficient proof of age), though these tickets are subject to availability and can have eccentric booking conditions. It's worth remembering that most cheap return fares involve spending at least one Saturday night away and that many will only give a percentage refund if you need to cancel or alter your journey – make sure you check the restrictions carefully before buying a ticket.

Whatever the airlines are offering, however, any number of specialist travel companies should be able to beat it. These are the outfits you'll see advertising in the Sunday newspaper travel sections, and they come in several forms. **Consolidators** buy up large blocks of tickets that airlines don't think they'll be able to sell at their published fares, and then sell them at a discount. Many advertise fares on a one-way basis, enabling you to fly into one city and out from another without penalty. Besides being cheap, consolidators normally don't impose advance purchase requirements (although in busy times you'll want to book ahead just to be sure of getting a ticket), but they often charge very stiff fees for date changes; note also that airlines generally won't alter tickets after they've gone to a consolidator, forcing you to make changes only through the consolidator. Lastly, as these companies' margins are pretty tiny, they make their money by dealing in volume – don't expect them to entertain lots of questions.

Discount agents also wheel and deal in blocks of tickets off-loaded by the airlines, but they tend to be most worthwhile to students and under-26s, who can often benefit from their special fares and deals. Agents can also offer a range of other travel-related services such as travel insurance, rail passes, youth and student ID cards, car rental, tours and the like. Some specialize in charter flights, which may be even cheaper than any available scheduled service, but again there's a trade-off: departure dates are fixed and cancellation penalties are high.

Discount travel clubs are another option for those who travel a lot – most charge an annual membership fee, which may be worth it for discounts on air tickets, car rental and the like.

Incidentally, don't automatically assume that tickets purchased through a travel specialist will be the least expensive on offer – once you get a quote, check with the airlines and you may turn up an even cheaper promotional fare. Be advised also that the pool of travel companies is swim-

---

MAJOR NORTH AMERICAN AIRLINES AND ROUTES

Only direct routes are listed below; many other routings are possible through these "gateway" cities.

Aer Lingus (US ☎1-800/223-6537, www.aerlingus.ie). New York, Newark, Los Angeles, Chicago and Boston via Dublin or Shannon to London and Manchester.

Air Canada (Canada ☎1-800/555-1212 for local toll-free number; US ☎1-800/776-3000, www.aircanada.ca). Calgary, Edmonton, Halifax, Montréal, Ottawa, Toronto and Vancouver to London; Toronto to Manchester and Glasgow.

American Airlines (US ☎1-800/433-7300, www.aa.com). Boston, Chicago, Dallas-Fort Worth, Los Angeles, Miami, Newark, New York and Raleigh-Durham to London; Chicago to Manchester and Birmingham, plus Glasgow in summer.

British Airways (US ☎1-800/247-9297, www.british-airways.com). Atlanta, Baltimore, Boston, Charlotte, Chicago, Denver, Dallas-Fort Worth, Detroit, Houston, Los Angeles, Miami, Montréal, New York, Orlando, Philadelphia, Phoenix, San Diego, San Francisco, Seattle, Tampa, Toronto, Vancouver and Washington DC to London (with extensive connections on to other UK destinations); also New York to Manchester.

Canadian Airlines (Canada ☎1-800/665-1177; US ☎1-800/426-7000, www.cdnair.ca). Calgary, Ottawa, Toronto and Vancouver to London.

Continental Airlines (☎1-800/231-0856, www.flycontinental.com). Houston, Newark and Cleveland to London, Newark to Manchester and Birmingham.

Delta Air Lines (☎1-800/221-1212, www.delta-air.com). Atlanta to London and Manchester; Cincinnati to London.

Kuwait Airways (☎1-800/458-9248). New York to London.

Northwest Airlines (☎1-800/447-4747, www.nwa.com). Detroit, Minneapolis, Los Angeles and Seattle to London.

TWA (☎1-800/221-2000, www.twa.com). St Louis to London.

United Airlines (☎1-800/538-2929, www.ual.com). Chicago, Denver, Los Angeles, Newark, New York, Seattle, San Diego, San Francisco and Washington DC to London (with many other onward connections possible through a co-operative agreement with British Midland).

Virgin Atlantic Airways (☎1-800/862-8621, www.fly.virgin.com). Boston, Chicago, Los Angeles, Miami, Newark, New York, Orlando, San Francisco and Washington DC to London (with many onward connections possible through a co-operative agreement with British Midland).

ming with sharks – exercise caution with any outfit that sounds shifty or impermanent, and never deal with a company that demands cash up front or refuses to accept payment by credit card.

Regardless of where you buy your ticket, the price will depend on when you travel. Fares to Britain are highest from around early June to mid-September; they drop during the shoulder seasons (mid-September to early November and mid-April to early June), and you'll get the best deals during the low season (November through April, excluding Christmas). The Christmas–New Year holiday period is a law unto itself – if you want to travel at this time, book at least two or three months ahead, and be prepared for fares even higher than those in summer.

If Britain is only part of a longer journey, you might want to consider buying a **round-the-world (RTW)** ticket. Some travel agents can sell you an "off-the-shelf" RTW ticket that will stop in about half a dozen cities, of which London is usually one; connections to other parts of Britain will probably have to be added on separately. Others will assemble a route for you, which can be tailored to your needs but is apt to be more expensive. Prices start at around $2000 ($1600 if travelling in summer) for a simple RTW ticket stopping in London.

A further possibility is to see if you can arrange a **courier flight**, although the hit-or-miss nature of these makes them most suitable for the single traveller with the minimum of luggage and a very flexible schedule. In return for shepherding a parcel through customs and possibly giving up your baggage allowance, you can expect to get a highly discounted ticket. A couple of courier brokers are listed in the box on p.9; for more options, consult *A Simple Guide to Courier Travel* (Pacific Data Sales Publishing).

Prices quoted in the sections below are based on the lowest typical Apex fares, exclusive of tax (which is around $50–100). Youth/student and consolidator tickets will usually be cheaper on high-volume routes, but not necessarily on the more obscure ones. Flying at weekends ordinarily adds $20–60.

FLIGHTS FROM THE US

Dozens of airlines fly from New York to London, and a few fly direct from other East Coast and Midwestern cities. The best low-season fares

from New York to London hover around $500 round-trip. Low-season fares to London can also start as low as $470 from Boston, $380 from Washington DC and $410 from Chicago; Delta flies from Atlanta starting from around $420; Virgin and British Airways from Miami or Orlando for $660; and Continental from Houston for about $430. For high-season fares, add $150–340.

Don't assume you'll have to change planes when flying from the West Coast – American, British Airways, United and Virgin all fly nonstop from Los Angeles. Several carriers connect with flights to London from LA or San Francisco, with low-season midweek fares from both cities starting at around $460. Northwest offers a direct service from Seattle to London for as low as $468. High-season fares will be at least $200 more.

Several airlines fly direct to a few of Britain's regional airports, notably Manchester (from New York with British Airways, from Chicago with American Airlines, from Newark with Continental, and from Atlanta with Delta), Birmingham (British Airways from New York and American from Chicago) and Glasgow (American Airlines from Chicago during summer only); for onward connections, British Airways has the greatest selection of destinations. These airports are "common rated" with London, which means that Apex fares should be the same as to London. However, it's much harder to find discounted fares to regional airports (consolidators and discount agents tend to deal only in high-volume destinations), and there are far fewer direct flights to these destinations than there are to London. If you fly to London on a discounted ticket, expect to pay $100–150 each way for an onward connection within Britain.

FLIGHTS FROM CANADA

In Canada, you'll get the best deal flying to London from the big gateway cities of Toronto and Montréal, where low-season midweek fares start at around CAN$650 round-trip; direct flights from Ottawa and Halifax will usually cost only slightly more. From Edmonton, Calgary and Vancouver, London flights start at $1020. High-season travel can add a premium of $300–400 to all these fares.

Only Air Canada flies nonstop to Manchester and Glasgow (both from Toronto), but you can pick up direct or connecting flights from many Canadian cities to Birmingham, Manchester and

SPECIALIST OPERATORS

Bargain Boating (☎1-800/637-0782). Self-crewed boat rentals for canal trips.

BCT Scenic Walking (☎1-800/473-1210, *www.bctwalk.com*). Extensive line-up of walking trips (7–16 days) in regions including the Pembrokeshire Coast, Snowdonia, mid Wales and other destinations in England and Scotland.

British Travel International (☎1-800/327-6097, *www.britishtravel.com*). Agent for independent arrangements: rail, bus passes, and hotels, with a comprehensive cottage rental and B&B reservation service; also apartment rentals in London.

CIE Tours International (☎1-800/243-8687, *www.cietours.com*). All-inclusive coach tours, independent travel arrangements, accommodation and car rental deals.

Contiki Tours (☎1-800/CONTIKI, *www.contiki.com*). Organized tours with a party-like atmosphere geared toward 18–35-year-olds.

English Experience Travels Limited (☎1-800/892-9317, *www.english-experience.com*). Small group tours focusing on British life; some homestay options.

Especially Britain (☎1-800/869-0538, *www.expresspages.com/e/especiallybritain*). Fly-drives and independent rail tours built around accommodation in B&Bs, country houses and castles.

Home at First (☎1-800/5CELTIC, *www.homeatfirst.com*). Independent travel packages including airfare, ground transportation and cottage, house, or apartment rental.

Insight International Tours (☎1-800/582-8380, *www.insightvacations.com*). Fully escorted coach tours.

Le Boat (☎1-800/922-0291, *www.leboat.com*). Inland waterway travel on hotel boats, self-crewed boats and yacht charters; also golf cruises.

Select Travel Service (☎1-800/752-6787, *www.selecttravel.com*). Customized history, literature, theatre, horticulture, and other specialized tours.

Sterling Tours (☎1-800/727-4359, *www.sterlingtours.com*). Offers a variety of independent itineraries and some packages.

All these tours can be booked through a travel agent at no extra cost.

Newcastle (usually via London), and to Glasgow from Vancouver, often at no extra cost over the fare to London. Again, British Airways is the best source for onward connections, including the Glasgow–Cardiff run.

PACKAGES AND ORGANIZED TOURS

Although you may want to see Wales at your own speed, you shouldn't dismiss the idea of a package deal. Many agents and airlines put together very flexible deals, sometimes amounting to nothing more restrictive than a flight plus accommodation and car or rail pass, and these can actually work out cheaper than making the same arrangements yourself on arrival – this is particularly true for car rental, which is expensive in Britain. A package can also be great for your peace of mind, if only to ensure a worry-free first week while you're finding your feet for a longer tour.

There are hundreds of tour operators specializing in travel to the British Isles. Most can do packages of the standard highlights, but of greater interest are the outfits that help you explore Britain's unique points: many organize walking or cycling trips through the countryside, boat trips along canals, and any number of theme tours based around Britain's literary heritage, history, pubs, gardens, theatre, golf – you name it. A few of the possibilities are listed in the box above, and a travel agent will be able to point out others. For a full listing, contact the Wales representative at the British Tourist Authority or the Wales tourist board directly (see box on p.29).

Be sure to examine the fine print of any deal, and bear in mind that everything in brochures always sounds great. Choose only an operator that is a member of the United States Tour Operator Association (USTOA) or has been approved by the American Society of Travel Agents (ASTA).

GETTING THERE FROM AUSTRALIA & NEW ZEALAND

As there are no direct flights to Wales from anywhere in Australia or New Zealand, the easiest way of getting there is to route through Britain's main entry point, London, and then travel onward either overland or by connecting flight; there are also a few direct flights from Australia or New Zealand to Manchester in northern England. For all onward details, see "Getting there from the UK and Europe", pp.3–8.

The route from Australia and New Zealand to London is a highly competitive one, with flights via Southeast Asia generally being the cheapest option. Fares are **seasonally adjusted** – low season is October to mid-November and mid-January to February; high season is May to August and December to mid-January; the rest of the year is classed as shoulder season. Tickets purchased direct from the airlines tend to be expensive; travel agents offer much better deals on fares and have the latest information on limited special deals and stopovers with some of the best discounts through Flight Centres and STA, who can also advise on visa regulations.

FLIGHTS FROM AUSTRALIA

Fares from Australia's **eastern cities** are common rated while flights from Perth via Asia and Africa are around A$200 less, and via the Americas about A$400 more. The cheapest **scheduled flights** are via Asia with Garuda, Gulf Air, Korean Air, Japan

Airlines (JAL) and Royal Brunei; costing from A$1350, these usually involve a transfer in the carrier's hub city. For a little more, Virgin Atlantic or Malaysian Airlines can get you to London via Kuala Lumpur from A$1600. In the mid range are Cathay Pacific, Malaysian Airlines, Thai Airways and Singapore Airlines, all at roughly A$1650–1850. British Airways and Qantas both quote direct-flight fares from A$1700 in low season up to A$2500 in high season. Many of the airlines also offer **free stopovers** in their hub cities; JAL flies from Brisbane, Cairns and Sydney several times a week including an overnight hotel stopover in Osaka or Tokyo. British Airways and Qantas offer fares through to Edinburgh for A$1750. Otherwise, the cost of an add-on flight from London to Glasgow or Edinburgh will be anything from A$150 to A$300, depending on the season.

Currently, the best fares on offer are the Airtours/Britannia Airways **charter flights** to London and Manchester via Singapore and Bahrain, which run several times a month between November and March. Fares start at A$1100 in low season, hover around the A$1500 mark in the shoulder season, and range up to A$1800 in high season.

The lowest fares for routes **via Africa** are with Qantas or British Airways through Johannesburg or Harare, returning via Southeast Asia from around A$2000. South African Airways have a route stopping over in Johannesburg which starts at about A$2230 from Sydney and A$2200 from Perth.

Flights are generally pricier **via North America**, with United Airlines offering the cheapest deal via Los Angeles and either Chicago, New York or Washington (A$1950–2430), while Air New Zealand fly via Auckland and Los Angeles – and Canadian Airlines via Toronto or Vancouver – for around A$1975–2450.

FLIGHTS FROM NEW ZEALAND

The most direct route from New Zealand is **via North America**. Air New Zealand offer the best value – a return flight via Los Angeles costs NZ$2200 in low season and NZ$2900 in high season, while United Airlines has a similar deal for NZ$2275–2975. Canadian Airlines flies via Vancouver or Toronto, starting at NZ$2095.

AIRLINES IN AUSTRALIA AND NEW ZEALAND

Air New Zealand (New Zealand ☎09/357 3000 or 0-800/737000, *www.airnz.co.nz*; Australia ☎132476, *www.airnz.com.au*). Daily flights to London from Brisbane, Melbourne and Sydney (code share with Ansett from other major cities in Australia) via Asia and from New Zealand via Los Angeles.

Airtours & Britannia Airways (Australia ☎02/9247 4833; New Zealand ☎09/308 3360). Several flights per month (Nov–March only) from Adelaide, Auckland, Brisbane, Perth and Sydney to London, and once a week to Manchester via Singapore and Bahrain.

British Airways (Australia ☎02/8904 8800, *www.britishairways.com/regional/australia*; New Zealand ☎09/356 8690). Daily direct flights from Brisbane, Melbourne, Perth and Sydney. Code share with Qantas (part owners of the company) from other major cities to London via Los Angeles and Singapore and twice weekly via Harare or Johannesburg from Sydney; daily from Auckland via Los Angeles. Onward connections to other destinations in Britain.

Canadian Airlines (Australia ☎1-300/655 767; New Zealand ☎09/309 0735; *www.cdnair.ca*). Several flights per week from Auckland, Melbourne and Sydney to London via Toronto or Vancouver.

Cathay Pacific (Australia ☎131747; New Zealand ☎09/379 0861; *www.cathaypacific.com/australia*). Several flights per week from Auckland, Brisbane, Cairns, Melbourne, Perth and Sydney to London and Manchester via Hong Kong.

Garuda (Australia ☎1-300/365 330; New Zealand ☎09/366 1855 or 0-800/128 510; *http://151.196.75.122/garuda*). Several flights weekly from Australia and New Zealand to London via Denpasar or Jakarta.

Gulf Air (Australia ☎02/9244 2199; New Zealand ☎09/308 3366, *www.gulfairco.com*). Several flights weekly from Sydney to London via Singapore and Bahrain or Abu Dhabi.

Japanese Airlines (JAL) (Australia ☎02/9272 1111; New Zealand ☎09/379 3202; *www.jal.co.jp*). Daily flights from Brisbane and Sydney to London via Osaka or Tokyo, and several weekly from Auckland and Cairns, also via Osaka and Tokyo. Code share with Air New Zealand. Onward connections to Edinburgh.

KLM (Australia ☎02/9231 6333 or 1-800/505 747, *www.klm.com.au*). Twice weekly flights from Sydney to London via Singapore and Amsterdam.

Korean Air (Australia ☎02/9262 6000; New Zealand ☎09/303 0166; *www.koreanair.com*). Several flights weekly via Seoul from Auckland, Brisbane and Sydney to London, and once a week from Christchurch.

Malaysia Airlines (MAS) (Australia ☎132627; New Zealand ☎09/373 2741 or 008/657 472; *www.malaysiaairlines.com.my*). Several flights a week from Auckland, Melbourne, Perth and Sydney to London via Kuala Lumpur. Onward connections to the northwest of England.

Qantas (Australia ☎131313; New Zealand ☎09/357 8900 or 0-800/808 767; *www.qantas.com.au*). Daily flights from major Australasian cities to London via Bangkok or Singapore. Onward connections with British Airways to regional UK airports.

Royal Brunei Airlines (Australia ☎02/3221 7757, *www.bruneiair.com*). Several flights weekly from Brisbane, Darwin and Perth to London via Singapore or Abu Dhabi.

Singapore Airlines (Australia ☎131010, *www.singaporeair.com.au*; New Zealand ☎09/303 2129 or 0-800/808 909, *www.singaporeair.co.nz*). Daily flights from Auckland, Brisbane, Christchurch, Melbourne, Perth and Sydney and several weekly from Adelaide and Cairns to London and Manchester via Singapore.

South African Airways (SAA) (Australia ☎02/9223 4402, *www.sairways.com.au*; New Zealand ☎09/379 3708). Four flights a week to London from Sydney and Perth via Johannesburg.

Thai Airways (Australia ☎1-300/651 960; New Zealand ☎09/377 3886; *www.thaiair.com*). Several flights a week from Auckland, Brisbane, Melbourne, Perth and Sydney to London Heathrow via Bangkok.

United Airlines (Australia ☎131777; New Zealand ☎09/379 3800; *www.ual.com*). Daily flights from Auckland, Melbourne and Sydney to London and Manchester via Los Angeles and Chicago, New York or Washington.

Virgin Atlantic (Australia ☎02/9244 2747 or 1-800/646 747, *www.fly.virgin.com.au*; New Zealand ☎09/308 3377). Daily flights from Sydney and several weekly from Melbourne to London via Kuala Lumpur. Code-share with Malaysia Airlines for the first leg.

DISCOUNT TRAVEL AGENTS

Anywhere Travel, 345 Anzac Parade, Kingsford, Sydney, NSW 2032 (☎02/9663 0411, *anywhere@ozemail.com.au*).

Budget Travel, 16 Fort St, Auckland; plus branches around the city (☎09/366 0061 or 0-800/808 040).

Destinations Unlimited, 87 Albert St, Auckland (☎09/373 4033).

Flight Centres Australia: 82 Elizabeth St, Sydney, NSW 2000 (☎13/1600, *www.flightcentre.com.au*), plus branches nationwide. New Zealand: 350 Queen St, Auckland (☎09/358 4310), plus branches nationwide.

Northern Gateway, 22 Cavenagh St, Darwin, NT 8000 (☎08/8941 1394, *oztravel@norgate.com.au*).

STA Travel, Australia: 855 George St, Ultimo, Sydney, NSW 2007; 256 Flinders St, Melbourne, VIC 3000; plus branches nationwide (nearest branch ☎131776; telesales ☎1300/360 960). New Zealand: 10 High St, Auckland (☎09/309 0458; telesales ☎09/366 6673, *www.stratravel.com.au*), plus branches nationwide.

Student Uni Travel, 92 Pitt St, Sydney, NSW 2000 (☎02/9232 8444); plus branches in Brisbane, Cairns, Darwin, Melbourne and Perth.

Thomas Cook Australia: 175 Pitt St, Sydney, NSW 2000; 257 Collins St, Melbourne, VIC 3000; plus branches nationwide (local branch ☎131771; telesales ☎1800/801 002; *www.thomascook.com.au*). New Zealand: 191 Queen St, Auckland (☎09/379 3920).

Trailfinders, 8 Spring St, Sydney, NSW 2000 (☎02/9247 7666, *www.trailfinders.com.au /australia*) plus branches in Brisbane and Cairns.

Travel.com, 76–80 Clarence St, Sydney, NSW 2000 (☎02/9262 3555, *www.travel.com.au*).

UK Flight Shop, 7 Macquarie Place, Sydney, NSW 2000 (☎02/9247 7833, *www.ukflightshop.com.au*); plus branches in Melbourne and Perth.

USIT Beyond, corner of Shortland St and Jean Batten Place, Auckland (☎09/379 4224 or 0-800/788 336, *www.usitbeyond.co.nz*); plus branches in Christchurch, Hamilton, Palmerston North and Wellington.

SPECIALIST AGENTS

Adventure Specialists, 1st Floor, 69 Liverpool St, Sydney, NSW 2000 (☎02/9261 2927, *www.adventurespec.citysearch.com.au*). A selection of walking and cycling holidays throughout Britain and Wales.

Adventure World Australia: 73 Walker St, North Sydney, NSW 2060 (☎02/9956 7766 or 1-800/221 931, *www.adventureworld.com.au*). New Zealand: 101 Great South Rd, Remuera, Auckland (☎09/524 5118). A wide variety of tours around Wales.

Best of Britain, 352a Military Rd, Cremorne, Sydney, NSW 2090 (☎02/9909 1055). Flights, accommodation, car rental, tours, canal boats and B&Bs.

Explore Holidays, 55 Blaxland Rd, Ryde, NSW 2112 (☎02/9857 6200). Organizes accommodation throughout Britain, as well as special interest and rambling trips.

YHA Travel Centre Australia: 422 Kent St, Sydney, NSW 2000 (☎02/9261 1111); 205 King St, Melbourne, VIC 3000 (☎03/9670 9611, *www.yha.com.au*). New Zealand: corner of Shortland St and Jean Batten Place, Auckland (☎09/379 4224, *www.yha.co.nz*). Organizes budget accommodation and backpacker-type tours throughout Britain and Wales for Hostelling International members.

Garuda, JAL, Korean Air and Thai Airways fly to London **via Asia**, with either a transfer or stopover in the airlines' home city, for NZ$1900–2300; for a little more money and comfort, Qantas and British Airways fly via Sydney and Bangkok to London from NZ$2175 or NZ$2475 respectively, including onward connections to other destinations in Britain.

As with Australia, the cheapest fare is Airtours or Britannia Airways' **charter flights** from Auckland to London and Manchester, running several times a month from November to March; fares are from NZ$1620 low season, NZ$1850 shoulder season and NZ$2110 high season.

ROUND-THE-WORLD FARES

If you're planning to visit Wales as part of a long trip, a **round-the-world ticket (RTW)** that includes London, from where you can travel on to Wales – see "Getting there from the UK (pp.3–8) can be very good value. Currently the best deals on offer are the "Global Explorer" and "One World" tickets (Qantas and British Airways), and the "Star Alliance" deal (United, Air New Zealand, Thai, Lufthansa, Air Canada, SAS, ANA, Ansett and Varig) – all of which allow a minimum of four stopovers on several continents on a mileage basis; these cost A$2400/NZ$3000 to A$2700/NZ$3400. Note that while it's easy enough to include London on your itinerary, a stop in Cardiff may involve backtracking and can be harder to arrange.

VISAS, CUSTOM REGULATIONS AND TAX

Citizens of all European countries – other than Albania, Romania, Bulgaria, and the republics of the former Soviet Union (with the exception of the Baltic States) – can enter Britain with just a passport, generally for up to three months. US, Canadian, Australian and New Zealand citizens can travel in Britain for up to six months with just a passport. All other nationalities require a visa, available from the British Consular office in the country of application.

For stays longer than six months, **US, Canadian, Australian and New Zealand citizens** should apply to the British Embassy or High Commission (see box opposite). If you want to extend your stay, you should write, before the expiry date given on the endorsement in your passport, to: The Under Secretary of State, Home Office, Immigration and Nationality Dept, Lunar House, Wellesley Rd, Croydon CR9 2BY (☎020/8686 0688), enclosing your passport or National Identity Card and form IS120 (if these were your entry documents).

CUSTOMS

Since the inauguration of the EU Single Market, travellers coming into Britain directly from another EU country do not have to make a declaration to **customs** at their place of entry, and can effectively bring almost as much wine or beer across the Channel as they like. The guidance levels are ninety litres of wine and 110 of beer, which should be enough for anyone – any more than this, and you'll have to provide proof that it's for personal use only. If you're travelling to or from a non-EU country, you can still buy duty-free goods, but within the EU, this perk no longer exists. The duty-free allowances are as follows:

Tobacco: 200 cigarettes; or 100 cigarillos; or 50 cigars; or 250g of loose tobacco.

Alcohol: Two litres of still wine, **plus** one litre of drink over 22 percent alcohol, or two litres of alcoholic drink not over 22 percent, or another two litres of still wine.

Perfumes: 60ml of perfume plus 250ml of toilet water.

You're also allowed **other goods** to the value of £136.

There are **import restrictions** on a variety of articles and substances, from firearms to furs derived from endangered species, none of which should bother the normal tourist. However, if you need any clarification on British import regulations, contact HM Customs and Excise, Dorset House, Stamford St, London SE1 9PY (☎020/7202 4227), or their Web site at *www.hmce.gov.uk*. You are not allowed to bring **pets** into Britain without

BRITISH EMBASSIES AND HIGH COMMISSIONS ABROAD

Australia British High Commission, Commonwealth Ave, Yarralumla, Canberra, ACT 2600 (☎02/6257 1653, fax 6257 5857, *www.uk.emb.gov.au/*).

Canada British High Commission, 80 Elgin St, Ottawa, ON K1P 5K7 (☎613/237-1530, fax 237-7980, *www.britain-in-canada.org/*).

Ireland 29 Merrion Rd, Ballsbridge, Dublin 4 (☎01/205 3822, fax 205 3890.

Netherlands Lange Voorhout 10, 2514 ED, The Hague (☎070/427 0427, fax 427 0345, *www.britain.nl*).

New Zealand British High Commission, 44 Hill St, Wellington (☎04/472 6049, fax 471 1974, *www.brithighcomm.org.nz*).

USA 3100 Massachusetts Ave NW, Washington, DC 20008 (☎202/588-6500, fax 588-7850, *www.britainusa.com/embassy*).

OVERSEAS REPRESENTATION IN BRITAIN

Australia High Commission, Australia House, Strand, London WC2B 4LA (☎020/7379 4334, *www.australia.org.uk*); Consulate, Chatsworth House, Lever St, Manchester M1 2QL (☎0161/228 1344).

Canada High Commission, 1 Grosvenor Square, London W1X 0AB (☎020/7258 6600, *www.canada.org.uk*).

Ireland Embassy, 17 Grosvenor Place, London SW1X 7HR (☎020/7235 2171, *www.irlgov.ie*); Consulate, Brunel House, 2 Fitzalan Rd, Cardiff CF24 0EB (☎029/2066 2000).

Netherlands Embassy, 38 Hyde Park Gate, London SW7 5DP (☎020/7590 3200).

New Zealand High Commission, New Zealand House, 80 Haymarket, London SW1Y 4TQ (☎020/7930 8422, *www.newzealandhc.org*).

USA Embassy, 24 Grosvenor Square, London W1A 1AE (☎020/7499 9000); Consulate, 3 Regent Terrace, Edinburgh EH7 5BW (☎0131/556 8315, *www.usembassy.org.uk*).

subjecting them to prohibitively long periods of quarantine.

VAT

Most goods in Britain, with the chief exceptions of books and food, are subject to **Value Added Tax** (**VAT**), which increases the cost of an item by 17.5 percent and is usually included in the quoted price. Visitors from non-EU countries can save money through the **Retail Export Scheme**, which allows a refund of VAT on goods to be taken out of the country. Savings will usually be minimal for EU nationals, because of the rates at which the goods will be taxed upon import to the home country. Note that not all shops participate in this scheme (those doing so display a sign to this effect) and that you cannot reclaim VAT charged on hotel bills or other services.

WORKING IN WALES

Unless you're a resident of an EU country, you need a permit to work legally in Wales, which, in this regard, maintains the same laws as the rest of the UK. Without the backing of an established employer or company, such a permit can be very difficult to obtain. Persons aged between 17 and 27 may, however, apply for a Working Holiday-Maker Entry Certificate, which entitles you to a two-year stay in the UK during which it is permitted to undertake work of a casual nature (ie, not in a profession, or as a sportsperson or entertainer). The certificates are only available abroad, from British embassies and consulates, and when you apply you must be able to convince the officer you have a valid return or onward ticket, and the means to support yourself while you're in Britain without having to claim state benefits of any kind. Note, too, that the certificates are valid from the date of entry into Britain – you won't be able to recoup time spent elsewhere in the two-year period of validity.

In **North America**, full-time college students can get temporary work permits through BUNAC, 30 Southbury, CT 06488 (☎1-800/GO-BUNAC, *www.bunac.org*). Permits are valid for up to six months and cost $225; send an application form, college verification form and two passport photos to the above address; allow two to three weeks to process the application.

Other visitors entitled to work in Britain are **Commonwealth citizens** with a parent or grandparent who was born in the UK. If you fall into this category, you can apply for a Certificate of Entitlement to the Right of Abode. If you're unsure about whether or not you may be eligible for one of these, contact your nearest British Mission (embassy or consulate), or the Foreign and Commonwealth Office in London (☎020/7270 1500 or 7238 4633).

The **kind of work** you can expect to find in Wales as a visitor is generally unskilled employment in hotels, restaurants, cleaning companies and on farms. Working conditions may not be up to much, and as a casual employee you can be fired at short notice. Pay is poor, too (£3–4 per hour), and will bring in barely enough to survive. So unless you're desperate, try to save at home before travelling. With voluntary work, the choice of jobs improves considerably, ranging from farm camps to placements with service organizations. Scores of useful addresses are featured in a guide called *Working Holidays*, published by the Central Bureau for Educational Visits and Exchanges (CBEVE), available from 10 Spring Gardens, London SW1A 2BN (£9.99). *Summer Jobs in Britain* by David Woodworth (£8.99) gives comprehensive information on paid seasonal work in the UK.

If you're between 17 and 27, and don't have kids, you might also consider working as an au pair. This enables you to live for a maximum of two years with an English-speaking family. In return for your accommodation, food and a small amount of pocket money (say £40 per week), you'll be expected to help around the house and to look after the children for a maximum of five hours each day. The easiest way to find au pair work is through a licensed agency. The Federation of Recruitment and Employment Services (FRES), 36–38 Mortimer St, London W1N 7RB (☎0800/320558, *www.fres.co.uk*), will send you a list of reputable agents (ie, those that are vetted annually by the government) for £3.75.

COSTS, MONEY AND BANKS

The British pound sterling (£; *punt* in Welsh, and widely referred to as "a quid") is a decimal currency, divided into 100 pence (p; in Wales, c for *ceiniogau*). Coins come in denominations of 1p, 2p, 5p, 10p, 20p, 50p, £1 and £2. Notes come in denominations of £5, £10, £20 and £50. Shopkeepers will carefully scrutinize any £20 and £50 notes tendered, as forgeries are widespread, and you'd be well advised to do the same (though few people do). The quickest test is to hold the note up to the light to make sure there is a thin wire filament running through the note from top to bottom; this is by no means foolproof, but will catch most fakes.

You may also come across Scottish banknotes which are legal tender in England and Wales, though often refused by traders. They come in the same denominations and have the same value as the British notes but are issued by three different banks; the Bank of Scotland, the Royal Bank of Scotland and the Clydesdale Bank.

CREDIT CARDS AND TRAVELLER'S CHEQUES

Most hotels, shops and restaurants in Wales are happy to accept the major **credit and charge cards** – Access/MasterCard, Visa/Barclaycard, American Express and Diners' Club – although they're less useful in the most rural areas, and smaller establishments all over the country, such as B&B accommodation, will often accept cash

only. Your card will also enable you to get cash advances from most ATMs, though there will often be a standard fee which makes it more cost effective to withdraw one large sum rather than several small amounts – call the issuing bank of your credit card company to get a list of Welsh locations. In addition, you may be able to make withdrawals from your home bank account using your ATM cash card via the international Cirrus and Plus networks – your international banking department should be able to advise of this. Make sure you have a personal identification number (PIN) that's designed to work overseas.

The safest, if not the most convenient, way to carry your money is in **traveller's cheques** (in sterling), available for a small commission (normally one percent) from any major bank. The most widely accepted traveller's cheques are American Express (Amex), followed by Visa and Thomas Cook – most cheques issued by banks will be one of these three brands. You'll usually pay commission again when you cash each cheque, normally another one percent or so, or a flat rate – though no commission is payable on Amex cheques exchanged at Amex branches (see box, overleaf). Traveller's cheques issued in sterling are not usually accepted as currency and will need to be converted to cash at a bank or through the issuing agency. Keep a record of the cheques as you cash them, and you can get the value of all uncashed cheques refunded immediately if you lose them.

There are no exchange controls in Britain, so you can bring in as much cash as you like and change traveller's cheques up to any amount.

BANKS AND BUREAUX DE CHANGE

Banks are almost always the best places to **change money and cheques**, and in every sizeable town in Wales you'll find a branch of at least one of the big five: NatWest, Halifax, HSBC, Barclays and LloydsTSB. As a general rule, **opening hours** are Monday to Friday 9.30am to 3.30pm, though branches in larger towns and cities are often open an hour later in the afternoons and on Saturday mornings. Outside banking hours, you're best advised to make your way to a **bureau de change**, found in most city cen-

American Express only operates two offices in Wales; also listed are the most convenient English offices.

Bristol, 74 Queens Rd, Clifton BS8 1QU (☎0117/906 5105).

Cardiff, 3 Queen St, CF1 4AF (☎029/2066 8858).

Chester, 12 Watergate St, CH1 2LA (☎0870/600 1060).

London, 1 Savoy Court, Strand, WC2R 0EZ (☎020/7240 1521).

Shrewsbury, 27 Claremont St, SY1 1QG (☎01743/236387).

Swansea, 28 Kingsway, SA1 5JY (☎01792/455006).

THOMAS COOK OFFICES

Cardiff, 16 Queen St, CF1 4UW (☎029/2042 2500).

Llandudno, 51 Mostyn St, LL30 2NN (☎01492/613900).

Newport, 144 Commercial St, NP9 1LN (☎01633/207000).

Pontypridd, 25 Taff St, CF37 4UP (☎01443/493221).

Swansea, 3 Union St, SA1 1PJ (☎01792/332000).

Wrexham, 20–21 Hope St, LL11 1BG (☎01978/207000).

tres, often at train stations or airports. Commissions at such places can be high, though you are still much better off than changing money or cheques in hotels, where the rates are normally the poorest on offer.

If, as a foreign visitor, you run out of money, or there is some kind of emergency, the quickest way to get **money sent out** is to get in touch with your bank at home and arrange for them to wire the cash to the nearest bank. Alternatively, you can have cash sent through Western Union (☎1-800/325-6000 in North America; ☎0800/833833 in the UK) or through the MoneyGram service used by American Express (cardholders only) and Thomas Cook travel agents: contact the nearest office (see box, above) or in the US call ☎1-800/543-4080. In all cases, the fees charged don't depend on source or destination, and only depend on the amount being transferred: wiring US$1000, or equivalent, to Wales will cost US$75. The funds should be available for collection at the company's local office within minutes of being sent.

COSTS

With the current strength of the pound, Wales has become an expensive place to visit, though if you're coming from England, particularly London, prices will seem reasonable in comparison. The **minimum expenditure**, if you're camping and preparing most of your own food, would be in the region of £20 per day, rising to around £25–30 per day if you're using the hostelling network, some public transport and grabbing the odd take-away or meal out. Couples staying at budget B&Bs, eating at unpretentious restaurants and visiting a fair number of tourist attractions are looking at around £30–40 each per day – if you're renting a car, staying in comfortable B&Bs or hotels and eating well, you should reckon on at least £50 a day. Single travellers should budget on spending around sixty percent of what a couple would spend, mainly because single rooms tend to cost more than half the price of a double. For more detail on the cost of accommodation, transport and eating, see the relevant sections.

YOUTH AND STUDENT DISCOUNTS

Various official and quasi-official youth/student ID cards are widely available, and most will pay for themselves in savings pretty soon. Full-time students over the age of 16 are eligible for the **International Student Identity Card** (**ISIC**, *www.istc.org*), which entitles the bearer to special fares on local transport and discounts at museums, theatres and other attractions; for Americans and Canadians there's also a health benefit (see opposite). The card costs US$20 for Americans, CAN$16 for Canadians, A$15 for

Australians, NZ$17 for New Zealanders and £6 in the UK, and is available from branches of Council Travel, STA and Travel CUTS around the world (see pp.9 & 15).

The only requirement for the Travel CUTS **Go-25 Card** is that you are aged 25 or younger; it costs about the same as the ISIC and carries the same benefits. It can be purchased through Council Travel in the US, Travel CUTS in Canada and STA in Australia (see boxes on pp.9 & 15). STA also sells its own ID card that's good for some discounts, as do various other travel organizations. A university photo ID might open some doors, too.

INSURANCE AND HEALTH

Wherever you're travelling from, it's a good idea to have some kind of travel insurance to cover you for loss of possessions and money, as well as the cost of any medical and dental treatment. If you're visiting from elsewhere in Britain, you may well be covered by your existing home contents policy, but should you need extra cover, Endsleigh is about the cheapest British insurer, offering a month's cover for around £25 – Frizzell and Columbus are also good value. Whatever your policy, if you have anything stolen, get a copy of the police report, as this is essential to substantiate your claim.

US and **Canadian** citizens should also carefully check their existing insurance policies before taking out a specific travel policy. You may discover that you're already covered for medical and other losses while abroad. **Canadian provincial health plans** typically provide some overseas medical coverage, although they are unlikely to pick up the full tab in the event of a mishap.

Holders of official **student**, **teacher** or **youth cards** are entitled to accident coverage and hospital inpatient benefits – the annual membership is far less than the cost of comparable insurance. **Students** may also find that their student health coverage extends during the vacations and for one term beyond the date of last enrolment. Bank and credit cards (particularly American Express) often provide certain levels of medical or other insurance, and travel insurance may also be included if you use a major credit or charge card to pay for your trip. **Homeowners' or renters'** insurance often covers theft or loss of documents, money and valuables while overseas.

For specialist travel policies, the best **premiums** are usually to be had through student/youth travel agencies – ISIS policies, for example, cost $48–69 for fifteen days (depending on level of coverage), $80–115 for a month, $149–207 for two months, $510–700 for a year. If you're planning to do any "dangerous sports" (skiing, mountaineering, etc), be sure to ask whether these activities are covered, as some companies levy a surcharge.

Most North American travel policies apply only to items lost, stolen or damaged while in the custody of an identifiable, responsible third party – hotel porter, airline, luggage consignment, etc. Even in these cases you will have to contact the local police within a certain time limit to have a complete report made out so that your insurer can process the claim.

Travel insurance policies in **Australia and New Zealand** tend to be put together by the airlines and travel agent groups such as UTAG, AFTA, Cover-More and Ready Plan in conjunction with insurance companies. They are all similar in premium and coverage, although Ready Plan

TRAVEL INSURANCE COMPANIES

In the UK

Columbus ☎020/7375 0011.
Endsleigh ☎020/7436 4451.

Frizzell ☎01202/292333.
Worldwide ☎01892/833338.

In the US and Canada

Access America US☎1-800/284-8300; Canada ☎1-800/654-1908.
Carefree Travel Insurance US☎1-800/323-3149.
Desjardins Travel Insurance Canada only ☎1-800/463-7830.
International Student Insurance Service (ISIS) – sold by STA Travel US & Canada ☎1-800/777-0112.

Travel Guard US☎1-800/826-1300; Canada ☎715/345-0505.
Travel Insurance Services US☎1-800/937-1387.
Worldwide Assistance US☎1-800/821-2828.

In Australia and New Zealand

AFTA Australia☎02/9956 4800.
Cover-More Australia☎02-9202 8000 or 1-800/251 881, *email@cover-more.com*; NZ ☎09/377 5958 or 0-800/657 744.

Ready Plan Australia☎03/9791 5077 or 1300/555 017; NZ ☎09/300 5333.
UTAG Australia☎1-800/809 462.

gives the best value. A typical policy for the UK covering medical bills, lost baggage and personal liability will cost around A\$110/NZ\$140 for two weeks, A\$170/NZ\$200 for one month, A\$265/NZ\$330 for two months

HEALTH

No vaccinations are required for entry into Britain. Citizens of all EU countries are entitled to free medical **treatment** at National Health Service hospitals; citizens of other countries are charged for all medical services except those administered by accident and emergency units at National Health Service hospitals. Thus a US citizen who has been hit by a car would not be charged if the injuries simply required stitching and setting in the emergency unit, but would be if admission to a hospital ward were necessary. Health insurance is therefore strongly advised for all non-EU nationals.

Pharmacists (known generally as chemists in Britain) can dispense only a limited range of drugs without a doctor's prescription. Most pharmacies are open during standard shop hours, though in large towns some may stay open as late as 10pm – local newspapers carry lists of late-opening pharmacies. Doctor's surgeries tend to be open from about 9am to noon and then for a couple of hours in the evenings; outside surgery hours, you can turn up at the casualty department of the local hospital for complaints that require immediate attention – unless it's an **emergency**, in which case ring for an ambulance on ☎999.

EMERGENCIES AND POLICE

As in any other country, Wales' major towns have their dangerous spots, but these tend to be inner-city housing estates where you're unlikely to find yourself. The chief risk on the streets – though still minimal – is pick-pocketing, so carry only as much money as you need, and keep all bags and pockets fastened. Should you have anything stolen or be involved in an incident that requires reporting, go to the local police station; the

☎999 number should only be used in emergencies.

Although the traditional image of the friendly British "Bobby" has become tarnished by stories of corruption and crooked dealings, the **police** continue to be approachable and helpful. If you're lost in a major town, asking a police officer is generally the quickest way to get help – alternatively, you could ask a **traffic warden**, a much-maligned species of law enforcer responsible for parking restrictions and other vehicle-related matters. They're distinguishable by their flat caps with a yellow band, and by the fact that they are generally armed with a book of parking-fine tickets; police officers on street duty wear a distinctive domed hat with a silver top, and are generally armed with just a truncheon.

EMERGENCIES

For **Police** (*heddlu*), **Fire Brigade** (*brigad dan*), **Ambulance** (*ambiwlans*) and, in certain areas, **Mountain Rescue** or **Coastguard** (*gwyliwr y glaaunn*), dial ☎**999**.

INFORMATION AND MAPS

If you want to do a bit of research before arriving in Britain, contact the British Tourist Authority (BTA) in your country – the addresses are given in the box on p.24. The BTA will send you a wealth of free literature, some of it just rose-tinted advertising copy, but much of it extremely useful – especially the maps, city guides and event calendars. If you want more hard facts on a particular area, you should approach the Wales Tourist Board offices, also listed on p.24. In general, they are helpful and will provide glossy brochures worth scanning before you set out.

TOURIST OFFICES

Tourist offices (usually called Tourist Information Centres) exist in virtually every

BRITISH TOURIST AUTHORITY HEAD OFFICES

The worldwide BTA Web site is at *www.visitbritain.com*

Australia Level 16, Gateway, 1 Macquarie Place, Sydney, NSW 2000 (☎02/9377 4400, fax 9377 4499).

Canada 5915 Airport Rd, Suite 120, Mississauga, ON L4V 1T1 (☎1-888/VISIT-UK or 905/405-1840, fax 405-1835).

Ireland 18–19 College Green, Dublin 2 (☎01/670 8000, fax 670 8244).

New Zealand 17th floor, 151 Queen St, Auckland (☎09/303 1446).

USA 551 5th Ave, 7th floor, New York, NY 10176 (☎1-800/462-2748 or 212/986-2200 or 986-2266).

WALES TOURIST BOARD OFFICES

Written requests for information should be sent to: WTB, Dept GN, PO Box 1, Cardiff CF1 2XN (☎029/2047 5226).

Mid Wales Tourism, The Station, Machynlleth SY20 8TG (☎0800/273747, fax 01654/703855, *info@brilliantbreaks.demon.co.uk*).

North Wales Tourism, 77 Conway Rd, Colwyn Bay LL29 7LN (☎01492/531731, fax 530059, *www.nwt.co.uk*).

Tourism South Wales, Dept WM99, Charter Court Enterprise Park, Swansea SA7 9DB (☎01792/781212, fax 781300).

Tourism West Wales, Old Bridge, Haverfordwest, Pembrokeshire SA62 2EZ (☎01437/766388, fax 766008).

Wales Tourist Board, Britain Visitor Centre, 1 Regent St, London SW1Y 4XT (☎020/7808 3838, *www.visitwales.com*).

Wales Tourist Board, Head Office, Brunel House, 2 Fitzalan Rd, Cardiff CF24 0UY (☎029/2049 9909, *www.visitwales.com*).

Welsh town – you'll find their phone numbers and opening hours in the relevant sections of the Guide. The average opening hours are much the same as standard shop hours, with the difference that in summer they'll often be open on a Sunday and for a couple of hours after the shops have closed on weekdays; opening hours are generally shorter in winter, and in more remote areas the office may well be closed altogether. All centres offer information on accommodation (which they can often book – see p.34), local public transport, attractions and restaurants, as well as town and regional maps. In many cases all of this is free, but a growing number of offices make a small charge for their accommodation list or the town guide with accompanying street plan.

Areas designated as National Parks (the Brecon Beacons, Pembrokeshire Coast and Snowdonia) also have a fair sprinkling of **National Park Information Centres**, which are generally more expert in giving guidance on local walks and outdoor pursuits.

WALES ONLINE

Weaving your way in and out of the numerous Web sites before leaving for Wales is a good way to familiarize yourself with the place, book up accommodation and arm yourself with tips and information. We've indicated relevant Web sites throughout this chapter, but listed here are some useful general sites.

WALES-SPECIFIC SITES

Total Wales
www.totalwales.com
First stop for the latest in Welsh news and extensive links.

Castles of Wales
www.castlewales.com
Essential site covering over 400 Welsh castles with photos, history, ground plans and direct links to Ordnance Survey location maps.

Everything Celtic on the Net
og-man.net
Everything Celtic on the Web with direct links to all manner of Welsh sites, Celtic and otherwise.

Centre for Alternative Technology
www.cat.org.uk
Homepages for the Centre for Alternative Technology's pioneering ecological centre.

This Week
www.thisweek.co.uk
Sign up for e-newsletters for north, mid-, south-east or southwest Wales.

A Welsh Course
www.cs.brown.edu/fun/welsh
Learn to speak Welsh online with a basic course which includes good cultural links.

Welsh Witchcraft
www.tylwythteg.com/dynionmwyn
Druidry, benign witchcraft and festival listings.

Welsh Choirs on the Web
www.choir.demon.co.uk/choirs.htm
Listings of male voice choirs throughout Wales with links to the homepages of some.

North Wales Index
www.northwalesindex.co.uk
Excellent set of North Wales links, many relevant to Wales in general.

GENERAL BRITISH SITES

UK Online
www.ukonline.co.uk
A guide to events throughout Britain, sport, up-to-the-minute news and access to telephone books.

British Travel International
www.britishtravel.com
Details hotel accommodation, cottage rental, bus and rail information.

Knowhere
www.knowhere.co.uk
Self-styled user's guide to Britain, with up-to-date information, readers' comments and best-of/worst-of sections.

UK Mountain Sports Community
www.mtn.co.uk
Information on mountaineering courses, holidays, gear and books.

Ordnance Survey
www.ordsvy.gov.uk
Details the full range of Ordnance Survey maps, including digital maps.

Seaview ferries
www.seaview.co.uk/ferries.html
Comprehensive ferry information on services from and to Britain.

MAPS

Most bookshops will have a good selection of **maps of Wales** and Britain; the best can be found in specialist travel bookshops (see box overleaf). Of the many North American outlets, the British Travel Shop in New York, in particular, stocks a phenomenal array of maps, and Rand McNally is also a good bet.

Virtually every service station in Britain stocks one or more of the large-format **road atlases** produced by the AA, RAC, Collins, Ordnance Survey (OS) and others, which cover all of Britain at around three miles to one inch and include larger-scale plans of major towns. The best of these is the Ordnance Survey road atlas, which handily uses the same grid reference system as their accurate and detailed folding maps – the one inch to four mile *Travelmaster 7* covers Wales and the West Midlands.

If you want more detail, the most comprehensive maps are again produced by the **Ordnance Survey**, a series renowned for its accuracy and clarity. The 204 maps in its 1:50,000 (a little over one inch: one mile) Landranger series cover the whole of Britain in enough detail to be useful for most walkers. The 1:25,000 Pathfinder series is more detailed, but most serious hikers favour the same-scale Outdoor Leisure maps which cover only the most frequently walked areas. Each is sensibly designed to take in a specific area, and even shows fencelines and field boundaries to aid navigation. There are seven Outdoor Leisure maps for Wales, three covering Snowdonia from the north coast down to Cadair Idris, two large double-sided ones spanning the Brecon Beacons and Black Mountains, and another two charting Pembrokeshire. OS maps are widely available in bookshops, but in any walking district of Wales you can be sure to find the relevant maps on sale locally.

MAP OUTLETS

AUSTRALIA AND NEW ZEALAND

Adelaide: The Map Shop, 6–10 Peel St, SA 5000 (☎08/8231 2033, *mapshop.net.au*).

Auckland: Speciality Maps, 46 Albert St (☎09/307 2217).

Brisbane: Worldwide Maps and Guides, 187 George St (☎07/3221 4330, *enterprise.powerup.com.au/~wwmaps*).

Christchurch: Mapworld NZ, 173 Gloucester St (☎03/374 5399, *www.maps@mapworld.co.nz*).

Hamilton: Map Shop, 544 Grey St (☎07/856 4450).

Melbourne: Map Land, 372 Little Bourke St (☎03/9670 4383, *mapland@lexicon.net.au*); Melbourne Map Centre, 738–740 Waverley Rd, Chadstone (☎03/9569 5472, *melbmap.com.au*).

Perth: Perth Map Centre, First Floor, Shaft Lane, 884 Hay St, WA 6000 (☎09/8322 5733, *www.q-net.net.au/~perthmap*).

Sydney: Dymocks, 350 George St, (☎02/9223 5974); Travel Bookshop, Shop 3, 175 Liverpool St (☎02/9241 3554).

Wellington: Map Shop, 193 Vivian St, PO Box 22-185 (☎04/385 1462, *www.mapshop.co.nz*).

US AND CANADA

Rand McNally (*www.randmcnallystore.com*) have a total of 24 stores across the USA; call ☎1-800/333-0136 (ext 2111) for the location of your nearest store, or for direct-mail maps.

Chicago: The Savvy Traveller, 310 S Michigan Ave, Chicago, IL 60604 (☎312/913-9800, *www.thesavvytraveller.com*).

Los Angeles: Map Link Inc, 30 S LaPatera Lane, Suite 5, Santa Barbara, CA 93117 (☎805/692-6777).

Montréal: Ulysses Travel Bookshop, 4176 St-Denis, PQ H2W 2M5 (☎514/843-9882, *guidu-ly@ulysses.ca*).

New York: BritRail's British Travel Shop, 551 5th Ave, NY 10176 (☎212/490-6688); The Complete Traveler Bookstore, 199 Madison Ave, NY 10016 (☎212/685-9007); Traveler's Choice Bookstore, 2 Wooster St, NY 10013 (☎212/941-1535).

San Francisco: The Book Passage, 51 Tamal Vista Drive, Corte Madera, CA 94925 (☎415/927-0906); The Complete Traveler Bookstore, 3207 Fillmore St, CA 94123 (☎415/923-1511); Sierra Club Bookstore, 85 2nd St, San Francisco, CA 94105 (☎415/977-5600); Phileas Fogg's Books & Maps, Stanford Shopping Center, Suite 87, Palo Alto, CA 94304 (☎1-800/233-FOGG in California; ☎1-800/533-FOGG elsewhere in US).

Seattle: Elliot Bay Book Company, 101 S Main St, WA 98104 (☎206/624-6600).

Toronto: Open Air Books and Maps, 25 Toronto St, ON M5C 2R1 (☎416/363-0719).

Vancouver: International Travel Maps and Books, 552 Seymour, BC V6B 3J5 (☎604/687-3320).

ENGLAND AND SCOTLAND

Glasgow: John Smith and Sons, 57–61 St Vincent St, G2 5TB (☎0141/221 7472).

London: Daunt Books, 83 Marylebone High St, W1M 3DE (☎020/7224 2295) and 193 Haverstock Hill, NW3 4QL (☎020/7794 4006); National Map Centre, 22–24 Caxton St, SW1H 0QU (☎020/7222 2466, *www.mapsworld.com*); Stanfords, 12–14 Long Acre, WC2E 9LP (mail order on ☎020/7836 1321, *sales@stanfords.co.uk*), 52 Grosvenor Gardens, SW1W 0AG (☎020/7730 1314) and within the British Airways offices at 156 Regent St, W1R 5TA (☎020/7434 4744); The Travel Bookshop, 13–15 Blenheim Crescent, W11 2EE (☎020/7229 5260, *www.thetravelbookshop.co.uk*).

WALES

Cardiff: Blackwell's, 13–17 Royal Arcade, CF1 2PR (☎029/2039 5036).

Swansea: Uplands Bookshop, 27 Uplands Crescent (☎01792/470195).

IRELAND

Dublin: Easons Bookshop, 80 Middle Abbey St, Dublin 1 (☎01/873 3811); Fred Hanna's Bookshop, 27–29 Nassau St, Dublin 2 (☎01/677 1255); Hodges Figgis Bookshop, 56–58 Dawson St, Dublin 2 (☎01/677 4754).

Belfast: Waterstone's, Queens Building, 8 Royal Ave, Belfast BT1 1DA (☎028/9024 7355).

GETTING AROUND

The large cities and densely populated valleys of south Wales support comprehensive train and bus networks, but the more thinly populated areas of mid- and north Wales have to make do with skeletal services. That said, it is rare to find somewhere that isn't reached by an occasional bus, even if it also picks up the local mail. As elsewhere in Britain, the removal of public transport subsidies and the privatization of the rail and bus networks has left a system that is one of the most expensive in Europe and one of the most confusing when it comes to timetables and ticketing. Government policy through much of the 1990s has seen new roads carved through the countryside regardless of the environmental cost. However, this does mean that getting about by car is easy, and unless you are planning to spend all your

The **Wales Bus, Rail and Tourist Map and Guide** is an essential source of timetable information, showing all public transport routes along with the details of who runs the service and a rough idea of frequency. It's available from transport and tourist operators in Wales, and in advance from the Wales Tourist Board (see p.24). To help cut through the confusion, there's also a **Train, Bus & Coach National Enquiry Number** (☎0906/550 0000) though since the call is charged at £1 a minute you may prefer to go direct to operators: we've listed the major ones over the next few pages.

time in Cardiff and Swansea, sheep and agricultural equipment are likely to be a more persistent problem than other road users.

If you're using public transport, one basic rule is to make sure you're aware of all the passes and special deals on offer. An equally simple strategy for drivers is to try and take the more scenic back-roads unless you're in a real hurry. Cyclists should skip to the outdoor pursuits section, p.50.

TRAINS

A chronic lack of investment and a foolhardy privatization process have thrown **rail travel** in Wales – and throughout Britain – into confusion. Britain's train tracks and stations are now owned and maintained by Railtrack, while trains and services are run by a tangle of private companies, each printing separate timetables and issuing their own tickets (though this shouldn't cause problems even if you're booking a journey that involves two or more train operators; see box, overleaf).

Services in Wales cover all the main cities and a seemingly random selection of rural towns and wayside halts. The two **major lines** are at opposite ends of the country and are connected only by routes though England. In the north, long-distance and local services ply the coastal strip from Chester in England through Conwy, Bangor and on to Holyhead for the Irish ferries. Along the south coast, Newport, Cardiff and Swansea are joined by a fairly fast service extending to London in the east and Fishguard (where you can also pick up boats to Ireland) in the west. Wales & West (credit card booking line ☎0870/900 0773) operate most services along these routes, with First Great Western (credit card booking line ☎0345/000 125) running an express service from London and Bristol to Cardiff, Swansea, Pembroke Dock and Fishguard. Services on the remainder of Wales' train lines are infrequent, and are occasionally replaced by buses on Sunday: quieter lines include the Heart of Wales from Swansea to Shrewsbury, also run by Wales & West. The equally infrequent mid-Wales line from Shrewsbury to Aberystwyth and Pwllheli has services run by Central Trains (credit card booking line ☎0870/000 7070). Local services around Cardiff are run by Valley Lines, for which there is no credit card booking.

RAIL INFORMATION AND BOOKING IN WALES

All **rail timetable enquiries** are now directed through a central agency reached on ☎0345/484950 (☎0845/604 0500 for a Welsh-language service). Calls are charged at the local-call rates – at peak times you may have to wait ten minutes or more for a reply. They'll tell you the operator's credit card booking number (or see overleaf) and advise you of the cheapest of the many tickets usually on offer. Once you've decided which service you need, you can make debit or **credit card bookings** (Amex, Visa,

MasterCard, Diners' Club and Switch) with one of the many train operating companies: tickets can be mailed to a UK address (allow five days) or you can pick them up at the station. For more information on UK train services, go to the national Web site (*www.rail.co.uk*).

You can also book tickets online at *www.thetrainline.com*. If you're in Britain, they'll be sent to you in a couple of days. Otherwise, you pick up your tickets at the station on the day of your journey.

For all its inconveniences, the train is nonetheless one of the best ways to get around Wales: the views are superb and the engineering often impressive. In addition to the mainline network, there are over a dozen volunteer-run train lines (see box on p.30). All run steam trains, most on narrow-gauge tracks and predominantly as tourist attractions.

You can buy **tickets** for trains at stations or from major travel agents – details of the **different types of fare** available are given on p.4. At many smaller stations, the ticket offices are closed at weekends, and in a lot of minor towns they've shut for good. In these instances, there's sometimes a vending machine on the platform. If there isn't a machine, you can buy your ticket on board – but if you've boarded at a station with a machine or ticket office and haven't bought a ticket, you're liable for an on-the-spot fine of £10.

RAIL PASSES

If Wales is only a part of your wider British travels, foreign visitors might find a **BritRail Pass**, which must be bought before you enter the country, a wise investment. The standard **BritRail Classic Pass** is available from BritRail's British Travel Shop (see box opposite) and many specialist tour operators outside Britain (see pp.12 & 15). It gives unlimited travel in England, Scotland and Wales for eight days (US$265, CAN$333), fifteen days (US$400, CAN$500), 22 days (US$505, CAN$633) or a month (US$600, CAN$750). The **BritRail Flexipass** is good for travel on four days in a two-month period (US$235, CAN$293), eight days in two months (US$340, CAN$425) or fifteen days in two months (US$515, CAN$643). Note that both these passes allow further dis-

counts of 10–15 percent for those under 26 (BritRail Youth Passes), and that one child can travel free on each adult pass (other children aged 5–15 years travel at half price). In North America, you can get up-to-date information and book online at *www.raileurope.com*. **Australians** and **New Zealanders** can buy BritRail passes from branches of Thomas Cook at equivalent prices, and those aged between 16 and 25 get a fifty percent discount if the passes are bought in conjunction with a Youth Eurail or Europass.

There are a number of passes and discount cards available only in Britain itself, to foreign visitors and British nationals alike, from main train stations and some travel agents. The best source of **online** information is at *www.railinfo. freeserve.co.uk/railtravel/rovers*. The **All-Line Rail Rover** gives unlimited travel on the entire network throughout England, Scotland and Wales for seven (£260) or fourteen consecutive days (£430). Several train passes cover the Welsh lines specifically, the most comprehensive being the **Freedom of Wales** ticket, allowing travel throughout Wales – and the connecting services through England – for a period of seven days (£69 June–Sept; £59 Oct–May). Additional benefits are discounts on some of the narrow-gauge railways and a flat fare of £1 on certain long-distance buses. Its more adaptable counterpart is the **Flexi-Pass**, good for rail travel throughout Wales for four days in eight (£49 June–Sept; £39 Oct–May), and for eight days in fifteen (£92 June–Sept; £75 Oct–May), both Flexi-Passes cover unlimited bus travel throughout the validity of the pass.

The **North and Mid-Wales Flexi-Rover**, available for seven days (£46.30) or three days out

RAIL OFFICES AND AGENCIES ABROAD

NORTH AMERICA

BritRail's British Travel Shop, 551 5th Ave, New York, NY 10176-0799 (☎212/490-6688). All British rail passes, rail-drive and multi-country passes and Channel Tunnel tickets.

CIT Rail, 9501 W Devon Ave, Suite 502, Rosemont, IL 60018 (☎1-800/248-7245). Eurail Passes and BritRail passes.

Rail Europe (*www.raileurope.com*) US: 500 Mamaroneck Ave, Suite 314, Harrison, New York, NY 10528 (Rail Europe ☎1-800/438-7245; BritRail ☎1-800/677-8585); Canada: 2087 Dundas E, Suite 105, Mississauga, ON L4X 1M2 (Rail

Europe ☎1-800/361-7245; BritRail ☎1-800/555-2748). Eurail, BritRail passes, ferry passes between UK and Ireland, Netherlands, Channel Tunnel passes.

Student Flights, 5010 E Shea Blvd, Suite 104A, Scottsdale, AZ 85254 (☎1-800/255-8000, *www.isecard.com*). Free shipping and $20 discount for BritRail and Eurail passes for everyone.

AUSTRALIA AND NEW ZEALAND

Rail Plus, Level 8, 114 William St, Melbourne 3000 (☎03/9642 8644 or 1300/555 003); Level 6, 76 Symonds St, Auckland (☎09/303 2484).

of seven (£26.30), covers Welsh routes north of Aberystwyth as well as the English lines linking them. Tickets also allow free travel on the Ffestiniog Railway (see box overleaf) and almost all buses in the area. The same region is covered by the **North and Mid-Wales Day Ranger** (£16.90; valid after 9am), and if you aren't interested in the north coast, you might want to restrict yourself to the **Mid-Wales Day Ranger** (£16.30; valid after 8.30am, not valid Sat in July & Aug), the yet more restricted **Cambrian Coast Day Ranger** (£6; valid after 7.50am), and the bargain **Cambrian Coast Evening Ranger** (£3.35; valid after 4.30pm). In south Wales, there's the **South Wales Flexi-Rover** (£32 June–Sept; £27 Oct–May), valid for three days of bus and rail travel out of seven. Lastly, there's the **Cardiff Valleys Day Ranger** (£5.40), which includes several of the local bus services as well as all train journeys throughout the Valleys.

If a rail pass doesn't seem economical, you may be eligible for a discount card: available to full-time students and those from sixteen to 25 years, the **Young Persons Railcard** costs £18, is valid for a year and gives 33 percent reductions on most rail fares. A **Seniors Railcard**, also £18 and offering 33 percent reductions, is available to those aged sixty or over. The **Family Railcard** costs £20, and gives discounts of between 20 and 33 percent for up to four adults travelling with children. It also allows up to four children aged five to fifteen to travel anywhere in Britain for a flat fare of £2 each (which includes a seat reservation).

STEAM RAILWAYS

With the rising demand for quarried stone in the nineteenth century, quarry and mine owners were forced to find more economical ways than packhorses to get their products to market, but in the steep, tortuous valleys of Snowdonia, standard-gauge train tracks proved too unwieldy. The solution was rails, sometimes less than a foot apart, plied by steam engines and dinky rolling stock. The charm of these railways was recognized by train enthusiasts, and long after the decline of the quarries, they banded together to restore abandoned lines and locos. Most lines are still largely run by volunteers, who have also started up new services along unused sections of standard-gauge bed. All the lines run steam engines alongside the more economical diesels which tend to predominate during the off-season.

Although run primarily as tourist attractions, several of the **steam railways** operate as public transport and are detailed as such in the text. Tickets are generally sold separately, but eight railways – under the umbrella name of The Great Little Trains of Wales (designated by "GLT" in the box overleaf) – offer a Wanderer Ticket, allowing either four days' travel within an eight-day period (£32), or eight days in fifteen (£42). Some discounts are also available with mainline rail passes (see above). Wanderer Tickets are valid all year, but since services are limited outside the summer season, you might not find it that worthwhile to buy one if you're visiting during the winter. For more information, check the GLT Web site (*www.whr.co.uk/gltw*).

WALES' STEAM RAILWAYS

The steam railways are listed north to south.

Welsh Highland Railway, Caernarfon (☎01766/512340). Not to be confused with the line of the same name in Porthmadog, this new line, along an old trackbed from Caernarfon to Dinas, will eventually link Caernarfon to Porthmadog via Beddgelert, 25 miles in all. 24-inch gauge. See p.371.

Llanberis Lake Railway, Llanberis (☎01286/870549). A short, waterside section of the former slate line to Port Dinorwig on the Menai Strait. 24-inch gauge. GLT. See p.334.

Snowdon Mountain Railway, Llanberis (☎01286/870223). Wales' only rack-and-pinion railway, climbing from Llanberis to the summit café and post office atop Snowdon. 31.5-inch gauge. See p.337.

Ffestiniog Railway, Porthmadog (☎01766/512340, www.festrail.co.uk). Wonderful thirteen-mile twisting climb from Porthmadog through the Vale of Ffestiniog to the slate mining town of Blaenau Ffestiniog. Links two standard gauge lines. 23.5-inch gauge. GLT. See p.351.

Welsh Highland Railway, Porthmadog (☎01766/513402, www.whr.co.uk). Flat, three-quarter-mile section of what was once the longest and the least profitable of Wales' narrow-gauge lines. 24-inch gauge. GLT. See p.351.

Llangollen Railway, Llangollen (☎01978/860951). Rejuvenated eight-mile section of the former Ruabon–Barmouth line, running through a gorge-like section of the Dee Valley. Standard 56.5-inch gauge. See p.253.

Bala Lake Railway, Bala (☎01678/540666). Four-mile lakeside run using the bed of the former Corwen–Barmouth standard-gauge line. 24-inch gauge. GLT. See p.260.

Talyllyn Railway, Tywyn (☎01654/710472, www.tallyllyn.co.uk). Slow-climbing one-time quarry line, revived in 1951. The original and one of the best of the volunteer-restored lines, running seven miles at the foot of Cadair Idris. 27-inch gauge. GLT. See p.297.

Welshpool and Llanfair Railway, Llanfair Caereinion (☎01938/810441). An eight-mile-long descent to the River Banwy with locos used by the German army and a West Indian sugar plantation. 30-inch gauge. GLT. See p.243.

Corris Railway, near Machynlleth (☎01654/761624). Former slate railway using just over half a mile of track, but with the rights to extend most of the two miles to the Centre for Alternative Technology. 27-inch gauge. See p.295.

Fairbourne & Barmouth Railway, Fairbourne (☎01341/250362). Diminutive former tramway which brought building materials for the construction of Fairbourne town. Arrivals are linked with the passenger ferry to Barmouth. 12-inch gauge. See p.301.

Vale of Rheidol Railway, Aberystwyth (☎01970/625819). Stunning twelve-mile run intended primarily to take tourists to Devil's Bridge. BR's only narrow-gauge and last steam line until it was sold off in 1988. 13.5-inch gauge. GLT. See p.286.

Teifi Valley Railway, near Newcastle Emlyn (☎01559/371077). A short strip of narrow gauge track along a former standard-gauge route. 23-inch gauge. See p.275.

Brecon Mountain Railway, Merthyr Tydfil (☎01685/722988). Two-mile narrow-gauge line, mostly on the bed of the Brecon and Merthyr Railway which closed in 1963. 24-inch gauge. GLT. See p.211.

BUSES AND COACHES

With the skeletal nature of the train system in Wales, you're going to find yourself relying on buses, which provide a much deeper penetration into the countryside. There are a limited number of inter-town buses (known as "**coaches**" in Britain) run by **National Express** (see p.5), but for travel within Wales you'll be using the **local bus services** run by a bewildering array of companies. In many cases, timetables and routes are well integrated, but as private companies compete with each other on the busiest routes, far-flung spots are becoming neglected. Though services are more expensive and less frequent in the rural areas, there are very few places without any service, even if it's only a private minibus on market day or one of the "**postbuses**" (see opposite) that also pick up mail.

In the **northern** half of Wales, Llandudno-based Arriva Cymru (Llandudno ☎01492/596969; Bangor ☎01248/750444; Aberystwyth

☎01970/617951) run the majority of local services as well as a few scenic long-distance runs. Its network is extensive enough to merit buying a one-day **Explorer ticket** (£5), purchased on the bus and valid for unlimited travel on all Arriva buses except the #701 service between Holyhead and Bristol. Throughout the west Wales counties of Carmarthenshire, Ceredigion and Pembrokeshire, you can make use of the **West Wales Rover Ticket** (£4.60 a day), though for longer periods, you're better off with one of the **Flexi-Rover** rail passes (see p.28) which also allow bus travel.

In the **southern** section of the country, the system is far less unified and only a couple of passes are likely to be of much use. Services west of Cardiff and south of Carmarthen are mostly run by the Swansea-based First Cymru (☎01792/580580), which offers the one-day **Swansea Bay Day-out** pass (£3.30) and the weekly **Swansea Bay Rider** (£10.30); both cover Swansea and the Gower. Bws Caerdydd (☎029/2039 6521), the major company serving Cardiff and the Vale of Glamorgan, offers a wide range of day, evening and weekly tickets; prices depend on the number of zones involved (see p.96). For a short visit, you'll probably get better value from the **Cardiff Card** (see p.97), which also gives access to the major sights. All regions have their own detailed local **timetable**, easily obtained from tourist offices, libraries and stations.

POSTBUSES

In parts of west and mid-Wales, bus services and mail delivery are combined in a network of **postbuses** which cover some of the most remote and beautiful Welsh regions. Few postbuses service destinations of interest to most visitors, but as a way of seeing quiet countryside

---

If you're on a budget and fancy travelling in a group, **Hairy Hog Backpacker Adventures**, 98 Neville St, Riverside, Cardiff CF1 8LS (☎029/2066 6900, fax 2066 6464, *www.hairyhog.co.uk*) offers two-day (£49) and five-day (£125) **minibus tours** around Wales' highlights. Itineraries are flexible, but most focus on the core territory of the Brecon Beacons and Snowdonia, extending out into Pembrokeshire and Anglesey on the longer trips. Beds in **hostels** are booked in advance but are not included in the cost.

---

at low cost (comparable with other bus fares for similar distances), and gaining a small insight into life in rural Wales, they can't be beaten. There are currently sixteen postbus routes – the northernmost based at Machynlleth and the most southerly running from Pembroke Dock – usually plied by a morning delivery and an afternoon collection run.

DRIVING

If you want to cover a lot of the countryside in a short time, or just want more flexibility, you'll need your own transport. England's busy but comprehensive motorway system means that getting to Wales is fairly straightforward, but over the border, you'll find there's just the one M4 **motorway**. This is the main westbound route from London, which enters Wales across the new Severn Bridge and skirts Newport, Cardiff and Bridgend before petering out just beyond Swansea. You can also cross from England to Wales from the M48 via the older Severn Bridge; both bridges carry a £4.20 toll on the westbound journey only. An extensive network of dual carriageways and good quality A roads link the major centres, but in rural areas you'll often find yourself on steep, winding, single-track (but usually asphalt) lanes with mini-laybys for vehicles to pass each other – with this in mind, you might want to select a compact rental car. In very remote areas, you may still occasionally have to open gates designed to keep sheep from straying.

In order to **drive in Britain**, you must have a current **driving licence**; most foreign nationals will get by with their licence from home, but if you're in any doubt, you can supplement this with an **international driving permit**, available from national motoring organizations for a small fee. If you're bringing your own vehicle into the country, you should also carry vehicle registration or ownership documents at all times. Furthermore, you must be adequately **insured**, so be sure to check your existing policy.

As in the rest of the UK, you **drive on the left** in Wales, and this can lead to a few tense days of acclimatization. **Speed limits** are 30–40mph (50–65km/h) in built-up areas, 70mph (110km/h) on motorways (freeways) and dual carriageways, and 50mph (80km/h) on most other roads. As a rule, assume that in any area with street lighting, the speed limit is 30mph (50km/h) unless stated otherwise. Road signs are pretty

MOTORING ORGANIZATIONS

American Automobile Association (AAA), 1000 AAA Drive, Heathrow, FL 32746 (☎1-800/222-4357, www.aaa.com).

Australian Automobile Association. Each state has its own club – check the phone book for the local address and phone number (www.aaa.asn.au).

Automobile Association, Norfolk House, Priestly Rd, Basingstoke, Hants RG24 9NZ (☎0990/500600, www.theaa.co.uk).

Canadian Automobile Association. Each province has its own club – check the phone

book for the local address and phone number (www.caa.ca).

National Breakdown Green Flag, Green Flag House, Cote Lane, Leeds LS28 5GF (☎0800/000111, www.greenflag.co.uk).

New Zealand Automobile Association, 99 Albert St, Auckland (☎09/377 4660, fax 309 2745, www.aa.co.nz).

Royal Automobile Club, RAC House, 1 Forest Rd, Feltham, Middlesex TW13 7RR (☎020/8917 2500 or 0800/550055, www.rac.co.uk).

CAR RENTAL FIRMS

UK

Avis ☎0990/900500, www.avis.com

Budget ☎0800/181181, www.budget.com

Europcar BCR ☎08457/222525, www.europcar.com

Hertz ☎0870/844 8844, www.hertz.com

Holiday Autos ☎0990/300400, www.holidayautos.co.uk

National Car Rental ☎01895/233300, www.nationalcar.com

Thrifty ☎0990/168238, www.thrifty.co.uk

US AND CANADA

Alamo (www.goalamo.com) ☎1-800/354-2322

Avis ☎1-800/331-1212

Budget ☎1-800/527-0700

Dollar (www.dollarcar.com) ☎1-800/421-6868

Enterprise (www.pickenterprise.com) ☎1-800/325-8007

Hertz US ☎1-800/654-3131; Canada ☎416/620-9620

Holiday Autos ☎1-800/422-7737

National (www.nationalcar.com) ☎1-800/CAR-RENT

Payless (www.paylesscar.com) ☎1-800/729-5377

Rent-A-Wreck (www.rent-a-wreck.com) ☎1-800/535-1391

Thrifty ☎1-800/367-2277

AUSTRALIA

Avis ☎1-800/225 533

Budget ☎1-300/362 848

Hertz ☎133039

National ☎131045

NEW ZEALAND

Avis ☎0-800/655 111 or 09/526 2847

Budget ☎0-800/652 227

Hertz ☎0-800/655 955

National ☎0-800/800 115

much international ("Give Way" means "Yield"), and road rules are largely common sense: unlike in some American states, you are not permitted to make a kerbside turn against a red light. Another trick for North American drivers is dealing with **roundabouts**, circular islands used at an intersection in place of traffic lights: you negotiate the roundabout clockwise, always giving way to traffic already on the roundabout.

Fuel is sold in litres (a UK gallon = 4.56 litres, a US gallon = 3.8 litres), and is expensive in comparison with North American prices – unleaded petrol (gas) costs in the region of 72p per litre (roughly $4.40 per US gallon), leaded four-star and diesel both slightly more. Prices are generally lowest in the suburbs of cities, where competition is fiercest, and highest at motorway service stations and in remote rural areas.

The Automobile Association (AA), the Royal Automobile Club (RAC) and Green Flag National Breakdown all operate 24-hour emergency **breakdown** services. The AA and RAC also provide many other motoring services, as well as a reciprocal arrangement for free assistance through many overseas motoring organizations – check the situation with yours before setting out. On motorways, the AA and RAC can be called from roadside booths; elsewhere ring ☎0800/887766 for the AA, ☎0800/828282 for the RAC or ☎0800/400600 for Green Flag (calls to all of these lines are free). You can ring these emergency numbers even if you are not a member, although a substantial fee will be charged.

CAR AND MOTORBIKE RENTAL

Compared to rates in North America, **car rental** in Britain is expensive; you'll probably find it cheaper to arrange things in advance through one of the multinational chains, or opt for a fly-drive deal. If you do rent a car from a company in Britain, the least you can expect to pay is around £135 a week for a small hatchback; reckon on paying £40 a day direct from one of the multinationals, £10 or so less at a local firm. Rental agencies prefer you to pay with a credit card; otherwise you may have to leave a deposit of at least £100. There are very few automatics at the lower end of the price scale – if you want one, you

should book well ahead. To rent a car, you'll need to show your driving licence: few companies will rent to drivers with less than one year's experience and most will only rent to people between 21 and 70 years of age.

Motorbike rental is ludicrously expensive if you go to a specialized agent such as Scootabout, 1 Leeke St, London WC1X 9HZ (☎020/7833 4607), which charges around £300 per week for a Deauville, or £365 for a Pan-European ST1100. These prices include insurance cover, 250 free miles (after which it's 10p per mile), and the bikes are kept in top condition. However, you'll save a fortune by taking a chance on an **ex-dispatch machine**; these can be rented from as little as £50 per week from London-based courier companies such as World's End (☎020/8746 3595), Banjax (☎020/7729 5228) and Mike's Bikes (☎020/8983 4896). At the time of writing, Mike's Bikes were offering the best deals, with a Honda CB350 going for £55 per week (plus a £55 deposit), and NTV650s for £85 per week (£200 deposit). They also have CG125s at £50 per week, and offer very competitive insurance deals, including short-term third-party policies from around £50 per month. You don't have to be a dispatch rider to rent from these companies, although you'll need a full bike licence, and some places will only rent to riders aged 23 or over.

ACCOMMODATION

Welsh tourist accommodation has changed notably in recent decades, from the fearsome guesthouses for English holidaymakers in the postwar years, to top-rank international hotels, farmhouse accommodation, hostels and ubiquitous bed and breakfast (B&B) establishments. The change has been for the better, bringing a far greater variety, and considerably better standards, than ever before.

Wales has traditionally been a holiday centre for the millions of English who live within striking distance – particularly those in Birmingham and the Midlands or Manchester, Liverpool and the northwest. This is evident at some of the more faded, tackier seaside resorts in the shape of vast and ugly caravan parks and row upon row of tawdry guesthouses. However, with the lower cost of the foreign package holiday, more English people are choosing to fly abroad for their fortnight of sun and sand, freeing up Wales – its spectacular countryside as much as its coastline – for a rapidly increasing number of international visitors.

HOTELS AND B&BS

The **Wales Tourist Board** (WTB) operates a grading scheme for all kinds of accommodation, **hotels** and **B&Bs** included, using between one and five stars. Unlike the stars used by motoring organisations such as the RAC and AA, the WTB's do not indicate a particular level of amenities or, indeed, price. Rather, they indicate the level of service and quality of a place – its rather more subjective attributes – within its particular category. Each category relates to a type of accommodation, namely Hotel, Country Hotel, Country House, Guest House, Bed & Breakfast, Inn, Restaurant with Rooms, Farm, Lodge, Campus Accommodation, Activity Centre, Castle, Hostel/Bunkhouse/Camping Barn and Conference Centre. The dividing lines between categories are somewhat blurred – you may, with good reason, wonder whether a four-star B&B is better than a two-star hotel or a three-star guesthouse and emerge none the wiser. However, once you decide which kind of accommodation you are looking for, the star-rating system makes it easier to find the better quality establishments within your chosen category. The number of stars does not necessarily reflect a price structure.

To make matters even more complicated, the distinction between hotels, B&Bs and, indeed, most of the other serviced accommodation categories above is also blurring all the time. A bad, fully fledged hotel (so called because of its licensed status) can be vastly inferior to a similarly priced or even cheaper B&B or guesthouse. This is especially the case amongst the growing army of farmhouse B&Bs and country houses, which quite often outstrip any hotel for the sheer

---

ACCOMMODATION PRICE CODES

Throughout this guide, hotel and B&B accommodation is priced on a scale of ① to ⑨, the number indicating the **lowest price** you could expect to pay per night in that establishment for a **double room in high season**. The prices indicated by the codes are as follows:

① under £40	④ £60–70	⑦ £110–150
② £40–50	⑤ £70–90	⑧ £150–200
③ £50–60	⑥ £90–110	⑨ over £200

warmth of welcome and quality of home cooking. B&Bs range from ordinary private houses with a couple of bedrooms set aside for paying guests and a dining room for a rudimentary breakfast, to rooms as well furnished as those in hotels costing twice as much, with delicious home-prepared breakfasts, and an informal hospitality that a larger place couldn't match. Tourist offices throughout Wales will book local accommodation for you, though you'll have to pay them 10 percent of the cost on the spot, which will then be knocked off your bill at the hotel. However, they will only book you into places that they verify (see below) and, in theory at least, you might get a better deal if you do the booking yourself

The WTB produces a comprehensive Farm Holidays brochure, or consult the Welsh Rarebits and Great Little Places lists of top hotels, many of which are in old country mansions or rambling farmhouses. These brochures can be obtained free from Prince's Square, Montgomery, Powys SY15 6PZ (☎01686/668030, fax 668029, www.welsh.rarebits.co.uk), and there are complete lists of accommodation throughout Wales available from the WTB (see p.24).

Official **tourist offices** will only ever give you lists of accommodation that has been "verified" by WTB inspectors, which does at least ensure that you shouldn't be short-changed. However, they can sometimes be reluctant to give information about places that haven't paid to advertise in the official local guide: if you don't see something suitable in the guide, don't be afraid to ask if there is anywhere else that matches your requirements for price and location. There are some wonderful establishments well outside of the official verification system; as far as possible we've mentioned such places in the text.

HOSTELS

The network of the **Youth Hostels Association** comprises some 45 properties in Wales, offering bunk-bed accommodation in single-sex dormitories or smaller rooms. A few of these places are spartan establishments of the sort traditionally associated with the wholesome, fresh-air ethic of the first hostels, but many have moved well away from this institutional ambience. Welsh hostels range from some remote, unheated barns in the wilds of mid-Wales and Snowdonia to more cosmopolitan, purpose-built centres in places such as Cardiff. The greatest concentration of hostels, by far, is in Snowdonia, with smaller clusters in Wales' other two national parks, around the Pembrokeshire coast and in the Brecon Beacons. All cost under £10 a night per person. For a list of all Welsh YHA hostels, contact YHA Wales/Cymru, Floor 4, 1 Cathedral Rd, Cardiff CF11 9HA (☎029/2039 6766, fax 2023 7817, www.yha.org.uk).

Membership of the YHA, which is open only to residents of England and Wales, costs £11 per year (£5.50 for under-18s), and can be obtained either by writing to the YHA (see box below) or in person at any YHA hostel. Members are issued with a directory of all YHA hostels and gain

---

YOUTH HOSTEL ASSOCIATIONS

Australia Australian Youth Hostels Association, Level 3, 10 Mallet St, Camperdown, Sydney (☎02/9565 1325, www.yha.org.au).

Canada Hostelling International/Canadian Hostelling Association, Room 400, 205 Catherine St, Ottawa, ON K2P 1C3 (☎613/237-7884).

England and Wales Youth Hostels Association (YHA), Trevelyan House, 8 St Stephen's Hill, St Albans, Herts AL1 2DY (☎01727/855215, www.yha.org.uk). London shop and information office: 14 Southampton St, London WC2E 7HY (☎020/7836 1036).

Ireland Youth Hostel Association of Northern Ireland, 2 Donegall Rd, Belfast BT12 5JN

(☎028/9032 4733); An Oige, 61 Mountjoy St, Dublin 7 (☎01/830 4555, fax 830 5808, www.irelandyha.org).

New Zealand Youth Hostels Association of New Zealand, PO Box 436, Christchurch 1 (☎03/379 9970, fax 365 4476, www.yha.org.nz).

Scotland Scottish Youth Hostels Association, 7 Glebe Crescent, Stirling FK8 2NE (☎01786/891400, fax 891333, www.syha.org.uk).

USA Hostelling International/American Youth Hostels, 733 15th St NW, Suite 840, Washington, DC 20036 (☎202/783-6161, fax 783-6171, www.taponline.com).

automatic membership of the hostelling associations of the sixty countries affiliated to the International Youth Hostels Federation (IYHF). Foreign visitors who belong to any IYHF association correspondingly have membership of the YHA; if you aren't a member of such an organization, you can join the IYHF at any English or Welsh hostel for a £11 fee.

At any time of year it's best to **book your place** well in advance, and it's essential at Easter, Christmas and from May to August. Most hostels accept payment by MasterCard or Visa; if not, you should confirm your booking in writing, with payment, at least seven days before arrival. Bookings made less than seven days in advance will be held only until 6pm on the day of arrival. If you're tempted to turn up on the spur of the moment, bear in mind that very few hostels are open year-round, many are closed at least one day a week even in high season, and several have periods during which they take group bookings only. To give the full details of opening times within this guide would be impossibly unwieldy, so **always phone** – we've given the number for every hostel mentioned. Most hostels are closed from 10am to 5pm, with an 11pm curfew.

Independent hostels and **bunkhouses** – simple affairs close to the mountains designed for walkers, usually providing mattresses and occasionally bedding in communal dormitories – are becoming a more common feature in Wales and, where relevant, are mentioned in the text of the Guide. A good resource for these is *The Independent Hostel Guide*, published by The Backpackers' Press, 2 Rockview Cottages, Matlock Bath, Derbyshire DE4 3PG, England (☎ and fax 01629/580427). There's also an international Web site (*www.hostels.com*) detailing both YHA and independent hostels worldwide.

CAMPING, CARAVANNING AND SELF CATERING

There are hundreds of **campsites** in Wales, charging from £4 per tent per night to around £10 at the plushest sites, where you'll find amenities such as laundries, shops and sports facilities. Some YHA hostels (see p.35) have small campsites on their property, for which you'll pay half the indoor fee. In addition to these official sites, farmers may offer pitches for as little as £2 per night, but don't expect tiled bathrooms and hairdryers for this kind of money. Even farmers without a reserved camping area may let you pitch in a field if you ask first, and may charge you nothing for the privilege; setting up a tent without asking is an act of trespass and won't be well received. Note that rough camping is illegal in national parks and nature reserves. That said,

---

SELF-CATERING ACCOMMODATION COMPANIES

Brecon Beacons Holiday Cottages, Brynoyre, Talybont-on-Usk, Brecon, Powys LD3 7YS (☎01874/676446; fax 676416, *www.breconcottages.com*). Around 250 cottages and other buildings, some decidedly quirky, in the Brecon Beacons National Park and Wye Valley.

Coastal Cottages of Pembrokeshire, 2 Riverside Quay, Haverfordwest, Pembrokeshire SA61 2LJ (☎01437/767600, fax 769900, *www.coastalcottages.co.uk*). 500 cottages, chalets, flats and houses – some with impressive leisure and activity facilities – around or near the Pembrokeshire coast.

Gwyliau Cymreig (Welsh Holidays), Snowdonia Tourist Services, Ynys Tywyn, High St, Porthmadog, Gwynedd LL49 9PG (☎01766/513829, fax 513837, *www.snowdoniatourist.com*). Best, and cheapest, of the many companies representing around 200 self-catering properties in Snowdonia and the north.

North Wales Holiday Cottages & Farmhouses, Station Rd, Deganwy, Conwy LL31 9DF (☎01492/582492, fax 572504, *www.northwalesholidaycottages.co.uk*). Nearly 200 cottages in the Snowdonia National Park and throughout north Wales, both coast and countryside.

Powell's Cottage Holidays, Dolphin House, High St, Saundersfoot, Pembrokeshire SA69 9EJ (☎01834/812791, fax 811731, *www.powells.co.uk*). About 250 properties, mainly in south Wales and the Gower.

Quality Cottages, Cerbid, Solva, Haverfordwest, Pembrokeshire SA62 6YE (☎01348/837871, fax 837876, *www.qualitycottage.co.uk*). Around 200 coastal cottages throughout Wales.

Wales Cottage Holidays, Bear House, Broad St, Newtown, Powys SY16 2QZ (☎01686/625267, fax 622465, *www.wales-holidays.co.uk*). A varied selection of 500 properties all over Wales.

there are a growing number of informal sites in some of Wales' most beautiful spots. These are free to use and have no facilities; details are given in the text of the Guide.

The problem with most accredited campsites in Wales is that tents have to share the space with **caravans**. Some of Wales' most popular areas – Pembrokeshire, the Wye Valley, the Gower, Snowdonia, the Brecon Beacons – seem to be permanently clogged with these slow-moving, low-tech mobile homes, rumbling inexorably from one park to the next.

As a hangover from the days when thousands of Midland and northern English holiday-makers decamped to the Welsh coast for a fortnight, many of the traditional seaside resorts are infested with camp upon camp of **permanently sited caravans**, rented out for self-catering holidays. Although these can certainly be cost-effective, with facilities such as bars, shops and discos thrown in, many people prefer to take more robust

self-catering holidays in self-contained **cottages, farms, town houses, apartments** or even purpose-built estates. The usual minimum rental period is a week, though long-weekend breaks can often be arranged out of season. In midsummer, or over Christmas and New Year, prices start at around £300 for a place sleeping four or six, although in winter, spring or autumn they can dip below £100 for the same property. Some companies specializing in Welsh holiday cottages are listed in the box opposite; the British Sunday papers generally have exhaustive lists of self-catering holiday companies in their small ads sections.

Detailed, annually revised **guidebooks** to Wales' camping and caravan sites include the AA's *Camping and Caravanning in Britain and Ireland*, which lists their inspected and graded sites, and *Cade's Camping, Tourings and Motor Caravan Site Guide*, published by Marwain. WTB produces self-catering and camping directories, available free from its Cardiff address.

FOOD AND DRINK

improved British fare and an eclectic range of international options, has turned eating and drinking throughout Wales into an interesting and enjoyable part of any stay in the country.

EATING

Indigenous British cuisine has taken an upturn in recent years. The pies, cheeses, puddings and meat from all of the regions are being offered in increasing numbers of establishments. Popular British dishes – steak and kidney pies, the ubiquitous fish and chips, cuts of meat with potatoes and vegetables, and stews, for example – are available everywhere in Wales.

Native **Welsh cuisine** is also making something of a comeback. Not surprisingly, such food is frequently rooted in economical ingredients, although this does not mean that it is of a poor quality. Traditional dishes, such as the delicious native lamb (best served minted or with thyme), fresh salmon, sewin and other trout can be found on an increasing number of menus, frequently combined with the national vegetable, the leek. Specialities include laver bread (*bara lawr*), a thoroughly tasty seaweed and oatmeal cake often

For many centuries, Welsh cuisine has been considered to be little more than a poor relation of the English culinary art, itself hardly well-regarded on the international scene. Restaurants were on the whole uninteresting and the pubs were strictly male-dominated and cheerless. Times have now changed to some extent, for traditional Welsh cuisine is now climbing a slope of resurgence, and this, combined with

fried with a traditional breakfast of pork sausages, egg and bacon. Other dishes well worth investigating include Glamorgan sausages (a vegetarian combination of local cheese and spices), cawl (a chunky mutton broth), and cockles, trawled from the estuary north of the Gower.

Dairy products, in a predominantly rural country, feature highly, especially in the range of Welsh **cheeses**. Best known is Caerphilly, a soft, crumbly, white cheese that forms the basis of a true Welsh Rarebit when mixed with beer and toasted on bread. Creamy goat's cheeses can be found all over the country. Also stemming from the cheapness of their ingredients are some traditional **sweets and cakes**: Welsh Cakes are flat pancakes of sugared dough, and *bara brith*, a popular accompaniment to afternoon tea, literally translates as "speckled (with dried fruit) bread". Menus comprising Welsh dishes can be found in numerous restaurants, hotels and pubs, many of which are part of the **Taste of Wales** (Blas ar Gymru) scheme to encourage native cuisine. Such establishments generally display a sticker in their windows. Welsh Food Promotions, co-ordinator of the Blas ar Gymru scheme, publishes a national directory of hotels, restaurants, cafés and shops where indigenous Welsh cuisine can be sampled. Pick it up from tourist offices or bookshops, or direct from them at the Welsh Development Agency, Cardiff Business Technology Centre, Senghennydd Rd, Cardiff CF24 4AY (☎029/2082 8984, fax 2082 8998, *www.foodwales.co.uk*).

WHERE TO EAT

If you're staying in a hotel, guesthouse or B&B, a cooked breakfast will usually be offered as part of the deal. These are generally served between 8am and 9am, with variations according to the establishment in question. A hearty breakfast is usually enough to see most people through the day, with maybe a lunchtime snack around 1pm. Lunch is generally between noon and 2pm, and evening meals from 6pm to 10pm.

Cafés, found absolutely everywhere, are generally the cheapest places to eat, providing hearty, if cholesterol-laden, breakfasts, a solid range of snacks and full meals for lunch and, in a few instances, evening meals as well. Wales' steady influx of hippies and New Agers over the past thirty years has seen the **wholefood café** become a standard feature of most mid- and west Welsh towns. Cheap and usually vegetarian, these rely extensively on fresh local produce.

Food in **pubs** varies as much as the establishments themselves. In recent years, intense competition has required that they sharpen up their act, and many pubs now offer more imaginative dishes than standard microwaved lasagne and chips. Most places serve food at lunchtime and in the evening (usually until 8.30 or 9pm), and in many towns, the local pub is the most economical place to grab a filling evening meal. Recommendations are given throughout the book.

The growth in upmarket **restaurants** has mirrored Wales' increasing sophistication and attraction to the outside world. People of all nationalities have settled in Wales and few towns are without their Indian and Chinese restaurants, joined over recent years by Japanese, French, Thai, American, Mexican, even Belgian- and New Zealand-style establishments. In the larger and more cosmopolitan centres, **bistros** and **brasseries** have sprung up, many offering superb Welsh and international cuisine at thoroughly affordable prices.

Our restaurant listings include a mix of high-quality and good-value establishments, but if you're intent on a culinary pilgrimage, you'd do well to arm yourself with a copy of the *Good Food Guide* (Hodder), which is updated annually and includes detailed recommendations. Throughout this book, we've supplied the phone number for all restaurants where you may need to book a table. Generally speaking, in pubs and cafés you can expect to pay under £10 per head; in most restaurants and bistros it should be between £10 and £30; only exceptionally will you pay over £30.

DRINKING

As much as in any other part of the British Isles, the **pub** reigns supreme in Wales. Many people imagine that the puritanical "dry" Welsh Sunday is still commonplace: in fact, the last area to remain alcohol-free on the Sabbath was Dwyfor, covering the Welsh heartland of the Llŷn peninsula. Even this bastion crumbled in the mid 1990s, making all of Wales "wet" for the first time in hundreds of years.

Pubs in Wales vary as much as the landscape, from opulent Edwardian palaces of smoked glass, gleaming brass and polished mahogany in the larger towns and cities, to thick-set stone barns in wild, remote countryside. Where the church has faltered as a community focal point, the pub still holds sway, with those in smaller towns and villages, in particular, functioning as community centres as much as places in which to drink alcohol. Live music (occasionally improvised) and (this being Wales) singing frequently round off an evening. As a rule of thumb, if the pub has both a **bar** and a **lounge**, the bar will be more basic and frequently very male-dominated, the lounge plusher, more mixed and probably a better bet for a passing visitor. **Opening times** are fairly standard: Monday to Saturday 11am to 11pm, Sunday noon to 10.30pm (with many quieter places closed between 3pm and 6pm throughout the week), with "last orders" called by the bar staff about fifteen minutes before closing time. In general, you have to be sixteen to enter a pub unaccompanied, though some places have special family rooms for people with children, and beer gardens where younger kids can run free. The **legal drinking age** is eighteen.

Beer, sold by the pint (£1.50–2.20) and half-pint, is the staple drink in Wales, as it is throughout the British Isles. Many pubs are owned by large, UK-wide breweries who sell only their own **bitter** (an uncarbonated, deep-flavoured beer, best when hand-pumped from the cellar), together with a stock of **lagers**, a chilled, fizzy and light drink that corresponds with European and American ideas of beer. Despite being hard to find in England, mild, or **dark** as it is usually known in Wales, is quite common. This is a cheap, very dark and quite sweet beer that tends to pack a bit more of a punch than would be guessed from its taste. Even stronger, sweeter and darker is **porter**, making a welcome comeback in many Welsh pubs. Irish **stout** (Guinness, Murphy's or Beamish), although never as good as it is in Ireland, is widely available and, if well kept, very tasty.

Among beers worth looking out for are the heady brews produced by Cardiff-based **Brains**, mainly found in the southeastern corner of Wales. Their Dark is a superb, rich mild, whilst their Bitter and SA Best Bitter are amongst the best pints to be had anywhere in the UK. Llanelli-based **Felinfoel** covers the whole southern half of Wales, with Double Dragon Premium bitter the aromatic ace in their pack. **Crown Buckley**, also based in Llanelli, produces three excellent bitters and a distinctive mild. The best resource for any serious alehead is the **CAMRA** (Campaign for Real Ale) annual *Good Beer Guide*, which should steer you around the best pubs. If you see a recent CAMRA sticker in a pub window, chances are the beer will be well worth sampling.

Pubs and off-licences (liquor stores) increasingly stock the growing range of Welsh **whiskies** and other spirits. With Celtic cousins Ireland and Scotland having cornered the market in whisky, the Welsh have hit back with the standard Swn-y-mor and a wonderful malt, the Prince of Wales. Welsh gin and Taffski vodka can also be found, as can a number of Welsh **wines**, to be sampled more out of curiosity than anything else. Be warned that wine sold in pubs tends to be slop of the worst order, with the notable exception of pubs serving decent food. Even so, in these establishments and in dedicated **wine bars**, the cost of a bottle can be outrageous.

Pubs are gradually shedding their booze-only image, as more of them serve **tea** and **coffee**, as well as a heavily marked-up range of soft drinks. In more touristy areas, **teashops** have sprung up like fungus, serving tea, snacks and cakes in the daytime. Less twee are the few continental-style **brasseries**, still a rarity out of the main towns, where decent coffee (rarely found in more basic cafés), other drinks and snacks are on offer.

POST AND PHONES

Virtually all post offices (*swyddfa'r post*) are open Monday to Friday 9am to 5.30pm, Saturday 9am to 12.30/1pm. In small communities, you'll find sub-post offices operating out of a shop, but these work to the same hours even if the shop itself is open for longer. Stamps can be bought at post office counters, from the increasingly rare vending machines outside, or from a large number of newsagents and other shops, although often these sell only books of four or ten stamps. A first-class letter to anywhere in Britain (up to 60g; 2.1oz) costs 26p and should – in theory – arrive the next day; second-class letters cost 19p, taking two to four days to arrive. Airmail letters of less than 20g (0.7oz) cost 30p to EU countries, and anything under 10g costs 44p to everywhere else. Pre-stamped aerograms conforming to overseas airmail weight limits of under 10g cost 37p from post offices.

Almost all public **payphones** (*teleffon*) are operated by BT (formerly British Telecom), and there should be one within ten minutes' walk of wherever you're standing, unless you're in the middle of a moor. Some BT payphones take only coins (from 10p upwards), but an increasing proportion are being replaced by a new range of sophisticated machines with an LCD instruction panel displaying in six languages, including Welsh. These phones are designed to accept

On April 22, 2000, the UK's telephone-numbering system will change. Alongside four other regions, London and Cardiff will be given **new area codes**, and special-rate numbers will be **reconfigured**.

Until September 16, 2000, if phoning **from outside an affected area**, you can use either the old number or the new one. However, there is no change-over period for **locally dialled numbers**: the new local numbers won't work until April 22, 2000, and only those numbers will work after that.

The numbers for the affected areas will be reconfigured as follows:

Cardiff:
(01222) xxx xxx becomes **(029) 20**xx xxxx

London:
(0171) xxx xxxx becomes **(020) 7**xxx xxxx
(0181) xxx xxxx becomes **(020) 8**xxx xxxx

The process of reconfiguring **special-rate numbers** (numbers with four-digit prefixes starting 08 or 09) started in autumn 1999, but the latest information is that old and new numbers should work side by side until at least autumn 2000. Mobile phone and pager numbers will all, ultimately, begin with the prefix 07, followed by nine digits (eleven in all). Premium rate numbers (see opposite), will ultimately all begin 09.

OPERATOR SERVICES AND PHONE CODES

Domestic operator (freecall) ☎100

International operator (freecall) ☎155

Domestic directory assistance ☎192 (free from payphones, otherwise 35p)

International directory assistance ☎153 (free from payphones, otherwise 80p)

inland and international calls are cheapest during the **reduced rate periods**: 6pm to 8am on weekdays and all day at weekends and on Bank Holidays. Throughout the Guide, every telephone number is prefixed by the area code, followed by an oblique slash. The prefix can be omitted if dialling from within the area covered by that prefix. Numbers with the prefix ☎0500, ☎0800, and several less intuitive combinations, are free to the caller; ☎0345, ☎0845, ☎01399 numbers (and others) are charged at the local rate; while ☎0891 numbers (information services) and ☎0898 numbers (usually salacious entertainment lines) are charged at the exorbitant "premium rate". A reconfiguration of these telephone numbers is currently taking place, and is not due to be completed until late in 2000; see box opposite.

cash, credit cards (with a minimum call charge of 50p) and phonecards available in denominations of £3, £5, £10 and £20 from post offices and newsagents displaying BT's green logo.

Depending on the time of day, calls from payphones cost between two and four times the price of those from residential phones, but generally follow the same charging pattern. Both

THE MEDIA

The media that you will encounter in Wales is a predictable hybrid of Welsh and Britain-wide information. Although the London-based UK media attempts to cover life in the other corners of Britain, few people would agree that Wales, Scotland and the northern regions of England receive a fair share of coverage in any medium. Of all the solely Welsh media, newspapers are probably the weakest area, and radio or TV coverage the strongest and most interesting.

NEWSPAPERS AND MAGAZINES

Of the **British daily newspapers**, all available in Wales, the vast majority are fearsomely right-wing and Londoncentric – news of Wales is not terribly well covered. In most ordinary weeks, for instance, you could count on the fingers of one hand the number of stories in the UK national papers that have emanated from, say, the new Welsh Assembly in Cardiff, let alone any other area of Welsh life. As devolution bites, however, there is the likelihood that an increasing number of the English papers will produce targeted Welsh editions, although this may amount to little more than them displaying a special dragon or daffodil masthead and the odd football report on Wrexham or Swansea City. The London-based

tabloid newspapers – known otherwise, and with good reason, as the "gutter press" – are the papers you are most likely to see read in any part of Britain. Specializing in prurient gossip and scandal, the two leaders in this field are Rupert Murdoch's trashy *Sun* and the damply leftish *Daily Mirror*. This latter paper is sold in Wales as the *Welsh Mirror*, and incorporates a significant amount of Welsh news and sport in its pages, making it by far the most popular of the specifically Welsh titles. Slightly more upmarket, adding in a bit more news but always filtered through a severely right-wing analysis, are the *Daily Mail* and *Daily Express*. Best of the quality broadsheet papers are the vaguely left-leaning *Guardian*, the right-wing *Daily Telegraph* and the generally robust *Independent*. The only quality **Welsh daily** is the *Western Mail*, an uneasy mix of local, Welsh, British, and a token smattering of international news coupled with populist competitions and features on TV stars. It does, however, maintain an upbeat Welsh slant on everything, although this can sometimes be little more than a ludicrous angle given to a British story on the strength of some tenuous Welsh connection. However, with a few honourable exceptions, the quality of writing and analysis veers too readily towards the lightweight. More perturbing in the long run is that a recent (1999) takeover has seen one company (Trinity Mirror) take control of all three of Wales' significant daily papers: the *Western Mail*, the *Welsh Mirror* and the *Daily Post*, which hardly augurs well for independent examination of fledgling Welsh democracy. The *Daily Post* is by far the best of the **regional dailies**, aimed principally at north Wales, but with an ever-expanding catchment area and a fairly decent spectrum of news and features that marks it out from other local dailies. Of these, the *Wrexham Evening Leader* is parochially newsworthy, as are the *South Wales Echo* in the Cardiff area, the evening *South Wales Argus* in Gwent, and, out in Swansea and the southwest, the *Swansea Evening Post*, Dylan Thomas' old sheet, a lively, community-centred read. All areas have their own long-standing **weekly papers**, generally an entertaining mix of local news, parish gossip and events listings. Wales' national **Sunday paper**, *Wales on Sunday*, from the same family as the *Western Mail*, has descended somewhat into tabloid trivia, but it's still worth buying for its bright, colourful take on Welsh life and occasional hard-hitting exposés and campaigning journalism. It's also very good on Welsh sport.

Go into any bookshop in Wales, and you'll be surprised by the profusion of Welsh **magazines**, in both English and Welsh. For a broad overview of the arts, history and politics, it is hard to beat *Planet*, an English-language bimonthly that takes a politically irreverent line, combining Welsh interest with a wider cultural and international outlook. The more serious English-language monthly *New Welsh Review* is steeped in Wales' political, literary and economic developments, while *Poetry Wales* is an excellent publication of new writing. The bi-monthly glossy *Cambria* subtitles itself as the "national magazine of Wales", an epithet that it's doing its best to fulfil with sparky writing about all matters Cymric, together with superb photography. For a wider view of Welsh social issues, with insights into "alternative" culture and news untouched by the papers, together with creative writing and a hearty infusion of cynical humour, pick up the weekly *Big Issue Cymru*, sold by homeless vendors on the streets of major towns and cities. It's the little sibling of England's *Big Issue* magazine, launched to runaway success in 1991. A new entrant to the satire scene, with some vicious takes on Welsh political life, is *Black Sheep* magazine. Slightly more moderate,

but a good humorous take on Wales nonetheless, is the online magazine Wales Watch, at *http://freespace.virgin.net/wales.watch*. If you're half-proficient in Welsh, the weekly news digest *Y Cymro* is an essential read, or, if you're attempting to master the language, try *Prentis* magazine, aimed at learners, and the weekly news file *Golwg*.

For **listings** and news of arts events, pick up free copies of *Buzz!* or *finetime* in Cardiff and Newport, *What's On* in and around Swansea, *Meter* in west Wales, and the quarterly *This Week Wales* in the north. The Pembrokeshire National Park also produces an excellent free newspaper, *Coast to Coast*, covering events in the region.

TELEVISION AND RADIO

It is in TV and radio that the Welsh media becomes most distinct from its London-based counterparts. Cardiff is the home of Britain's second-largest concentration of TV and radio stations, both Welsh arms of devolved broadcasting organizations like the mighty BBC and indigenous Welsh operators such as S4C and HTV. The wholehearted way in which UK-wide TV and radio has moved out of southeast England is in marked contrast to the Londoncentric print media.

On terrestrial television, the state-funded British Broadcasting Corporation (BBC) operates two **TV** channels in Wales – the mainstream **BBC Wales on 1** and the more esoteric **BBC Wales on 2**. Although these official titles make the stations sound avowedly Welsh, the vast majority of programming is UK-wide, with Welsh programmes, principally news and sport but also features, political and education programmes, slotted into the regular schedules of documentaries, soaps, arts and music shows, quizzes, quality drama and imports. This is even more the case with **HTV** (Harlech Television), the Welsh holder of the licence to broadcast on the commercial, and determinedly populist, ITV network. The principal Welsh channel is **S4C** (*Sianel Pedwar Cymru*, verbally abbreviated to "*ess pedwar eck*"), whose existence is owed to the protesters (including the Plaid Cymru president) who refused to allow the government to renege on its commitment to a Welsh fourth channel alongside the planned UK-wide Channel 4. The station has grown from these shaky beginnings in the early 1980s to become a major player in the European media network, and a sponsor of diverse projects including Welsh animation and feature films, notably the 1994 Oscar-nominated *Hedd Wyn* and the terrifically tasteless prehistoric cartoon *Gogs*. It broadcasts Welsh-language programmes at lunchtime and for five or six hours every evening, although nearly all of them are subtitled in English for those with the Teletext system. In between, the output is in English, culled from the robust minority-aimed programming that Channel 4 broadcasts in England, Scotland and Ireland. S4C's programming is slick, confident and occasionally controversial, and includes a nightly dose of the BBC's longest-running TV soap, *Pobol y Cwm* (*People of the Valley*).

Augmenting the terrestrial stations, **satellite** dishes are an increasingly familiar sight on the side of houses, pubs and hotels in Wales. These tune into a vast array of European pap networks and Rupert Murdoch's **British Sky Broadcasting** (BSkyB) – numerous channels of consumer-oriented dross interspersed with expensive sports programming and a surprisingly good 24-hour news service. **Digital television** services are gaining strength too: the BBC operates a number of channels, ITV has a second outlet and there's even S4C 2. Like much of the digital programming in Britain, the staple diet of such channels is mainly re-runs of past glories.

The BBC is also a major player in **radio**, with five UK networks, all broadcasting in Wales: Radio One combines pop with a slick interpretation of youth and dance culture, Two is dull easy-listening, Three classical, Four a passionately loved ragbag of magazine shows, current affairs, drama, arts and highbrow quizzes, and Five Live a constant, entertaining mix of news and sport. It also operates two stations in Wales alone: **BBC Radio Wales**, a competent, if gentle, English-language service of news, features and music, with occasional dashes of élan, and **BBC Radio Cymru**, which has made great efforts of late to become the voice of Welsh-speaking youth, much to the disapproval of older listeners, many of whom haven't warmed to the brash style of some of its presenters. Like so many radio stations, Radio Wales and Radio Cymru alike can often be a more entertaining option in the evening or at weekends, away from the daytime tyranny of rolling news, sport, weather and traffic congestion.

Of the commercial stations, the brashest is Radio One soundalike **Red Dragon FM**, serving Cardiff and around, together with **Capital Gold**, its twin for news, features and easy-listening music. Better in the capital is **Bay FM**, a laid-back multicultural community station from Cardiff Bay, currently on a restricted licence but aiming for permanence. **Swansea Sound**, whose reception extends west towards Pembrokeshire, is solid and frequently interesting, but the best local station is the bilingual **Radio Ceredigion**, more genuinely community-based than any of the others. Otherwise, there's **Valleys Radio** in – no surprise – the Valleys, **Champion FM** around Caernarfon and Bangor and **Radio Maldwyn,** the cheap and cheerful station for Montgomeryshire. **BBC Radio Clwyd**, **Marcher Coast** (bland pop) and **Marcher Gold** (old pop) battle it out in the north-west corner.

OPENING HOURS AND HOLIDAYS

General shop hours are Monday to Saturday 9am to 5.30/6.00pm, although there's an increasing amount of Sunday and late-night shopping in the larger towns, with Thursday or Friday being the favoured evenings. The big supermarkets also tend to stay open until 8 or 9pm from Monday to Saturday, and open on Sunday from 10am to 4pm, as do many of the stores in the shopping complexes springing up on the outskirts of major towns. Many provincial towns still retain an "early closing day" when shops shut at 1pm – Wednesday is the favourite. Note that not all service stations are open for 24 hours, although you can usually get fuel around the clock in the larger towns and cities. Also, most fee-charging sites are open on Bank Holidays, when Sunday hours usually apply.

> **PUBLIC HOLIDAYS IN WALES**
>
> January 1 Good Friday – late March to mid-April
>
> Easter Monday – late March to mid-April
>
> First Monday in May
>
> Last Monday in May
>
> Last Monday in August
>
> December 25
>
> December 26
>
> Note that if January 1, December 25 or December 26 falls on a Saturday or Sunday, the next weekday becomes a public holiday.

ADMISSION TO MUSEUMS AND MONUMENTS

Many of Wales' most treasured sites – from castles, abbeys and great houses to tracts of protected landscape – come under the control of the privately run UK-wide National Trust or the state-run CADW, Welsh Historic Monuments (see box opposite for addresses) whose properties are denoted in the guide by "NT" and "CADW". Both organizations charge an entry fee for most places, and these can be quite high, especially for the more grandiose NT estates. If you think you'll be visiting more than half a dozen NT places or a similar number of major CADW sites, it's worth taking out annual membership (NT £29, under-26s £14.50; CADW £22, seniors and those 16–20 £15, under-16 £12), which allows free entry to their properties. NT membership covers you throughout Britain, and though CADW sites are restricted to Wales, membership allows half-price entry to sites owned by English Heritage and Historic Scotland. In addition, CADW offers the Explorer Pass, which allows free entry into all CADW sites for three consecutive days (£9), or seven days (£15) and, like the annual passes, are also available with a vast array of family, senior and youth concessions.

A few Welsh **stately homes** remain in the hands of the landed gentry, who tend to charge in the region of £5 for edited highlights of their domain. Many other old buildings, albeit rarely the most momentous, are owned by the local authorities, and admission is often cheaper.

Municipal **art galleries** and **museums** are usually free, though this doesn't hold true for either the National Museum and Gallery or the Welsh Folk Museum, both in Cardiff. Although a donation is usually requested, **cathedrals** tend to be free, except for perhaps the tower, crypt or other such highlight, for which a small charge is made. Increasingly, **churches** are kept locked except during services; when they are open, entry is free. Wales also has a number of ventures exploiting the country's **industrial heritage**, mostly concerned with mining for coal, slate, copper or gold. A short tour supplemented by a video should cost a couple of pounds, while the full underground interactive "experience" can be up to £10.

Entry charges given in the Guide are the full adult rates, but the majority of the fee-charging attractions located in Wales have 25–35 percent **reductions** for senior citizens, the unemployed and full-time students, and 50 percent reductions for children under 16 – under-5s are admitted free almost everywhere. Proof of eligibility is required in most cases. Family tickets are also common, usually priced just under the rate for two adults and a child and valid for up to three kids; those offered by CADW are particularly good value. Most attractions are **open** daily in summer and closed one or two days a week in winter, though major sites are open daily all year – full details of opening hours are given in the Guide.

Finally, foreign visitors planning on seeing more than a dozen stately homes, monuments,

---

THE NATIONAL TRUST AND CADW

The National Trust Head Office, 36 Queen Anne's Gate, London SW1H 9AS (☎020/7222 9251, fax 7222 5097, *www.nationaltrust.org.uk*).

The National Trust (**Wales**), Trinity Square, Llandudno LL30 2DE (☎01492/860123, fax 860233).

CADW Crown Building, Cathays Park, Cardiff CF10 3NQ (☎029/2050 0200, *www.cadw.wales.gov.uk*).

---

castles or gardens might find it worthwhile to buy a **Great British Heritage Pass**, which gives free admission to over five hundred sites throughout the UK. Over sixty of these are in Wales, including Penhow Castle in Chepstow, Tredegar House at Newport and Cardiff Castle, as well as all National Trust and CADW properties. The pass can be purchased for periods of seven days (£30, US$48, CAN$66), fifteen days (£42, US$70, CAN$95) or a month (£56, US$93, CAN$120) from the main air and sea ports, and tourist offices in the largest cities. North Americans can obtain one before leaving home through most travel agents or by calling Rail Europe toll free (☎1-877/456-RAIL in USA; ☎1-800/361-RAIL in Canada). Citizens of other countries should contact their nearest British Tourist Authority office, or consult the list of outlets at *www.information-britain.co.uk/pass/pass.htm*.

ANNUAL EVENTS

The most obviously unique events in Wales are the eisteddfodau (singular eisteddfod), a term that originally meant "a meeting of bards". Nowadays it covers anything from a small village festival, where prizes of a couple of pounds are awarded for poetry and song, to two vast cultural orgies: the International Eisteddfod, held on a pur-

---

EVENTS CALENDAR

The Wales Tourist Board maintains a fairly comprehensive events list on their Web site (*www.visitwales.com*).

February–March: Six Nations rugby championship. Last won by Wales in 1994.

March 1: St David's Day. *Hwyrnos* and celebrations all over Wales.

Early May: Llantrisant Free Festival, Llantrisant Common, Vale of Glamorgan. New Age and music bash.

May–October: Festival of the Countryside, mid-Wales (☎01686/625384). An assortment of events, guided walks, music and demonstrations of rural crafts throughout the summer.

Mid-May: Tredegar House Folk Festival, Newport (☎01633/815612).

Mid-May: Pontrhydfendigaid Eisteddfod, Dyfed. One of the largest, best regional eisteddfodau.

Late May–early June: Hay-on-Wye Festival of Literature (☎01497/821217). London's literati flock to the borders for a week.

Late May: Cardiff International Animation Festival at St David's Hall (☎029/2087 8444). Europe's largest gathering of animators in Britain's liveliest centre of the craft.

End of May–first week in June: St David's Cathedral Festival (☎01437/720271). Superb setting for classical concerts and recitals.

End of May–first week in June: Eisteddfod Genedlaethol Urdd (☎01970/613111). Vast and enjoyable youth eisteddfod – the largest youth festival in Europe – alternating between north and south Wales.

Early June: Gwyl Beaumaris, Anglesey (☎01248/811203). One of Wales' best arts festivals, combined with a regatta and fringe.

Mid-June: Cardiff Singer of the World competition (☎029/2087 8444). Huge, televised week-long festival of music and song held in even-numbered years, with a star-studded list of international competitors.

Mid-June: Man Versus Horse Marathon, Llanwrtyd Wells, Powys (☎01591/610236). A 22-mile race between runners, cyclists and horses. If a human beats a horse (it has come tantalizingly near to happening), he or she stands to pocket around £15,000.

Mid-June: Gwyl Ifan (folk dance festival), various locations in and around Cardiff (☎029/2056 3989).

Late-June: Criccieth Festival (☎01766/522778). Music, theatre and art.

Late June: Drovers' Walk, Llanwrtyd Wells, Powys (☎01591/610236). Waymarked walks recreate the old drovers' routes, with an ex-drovers' inn reopening just for the day.

Last week in June: Gregynog Festival, near Newtown, Powys (☎01686/650224). Classical music festival in the superb country house surroundings of Gregynog Hall.

July 1: Annual commemorative march by nationalists in Abergele, Clwyd, to remember the two inept protesters who accidentally blew themselves up on the occasion of the Investiture of the Prince of Wales in 1969 (see p.365).

Early July: Beyond the Border, the Wales International Storytelling Festival at St Donat's Castle, Vale of Glamorgan (☎01446/794848). Relaxed, entertaining few days in a fabulous setting.

First Friday in July: Fancy Dress Night, Llanidloes, Powys. The thousands of participants create a wonderful atmosphere – the pubs open late, the streets are cordoned off and virtually the whole town gets kitted out.

First or second week in July: Llangollen International Music Eisteddfod (☎01978/861501). Over twelve thousand participants from all over the world, including choirs, dancers, folk singers, groups and instrumentalists.

pose-built fixed site at Llangollen in early July, and the roving Royal National Eisteddfod, in the first week of August. Venues for forthcoming Royal National Eisteddfodau are: Llanelli (2000), Denbigh (2001), St David's (2002), Meifod, near Welshpool in Powys (2003). The similar Urdd Eisteddfod, geared more toward young people, takes place in late May to early June; venues for forthcoming events are: Penrhyn Bay, Llandudno (2000) and Cardiff (2001) dates and locations of 2002–2003 events are listed on the Web site (*www.urdd.org/eisteddfod*). Eisteddfodau

Second weekend in July: Gŵyl Werin y Cnapan, Ffostrasol, near Lampeter, Dyfed (☎01239/858955 or 811433). The best folk and Celtic music festival held anywhere in the world.

Mid-July: Gower Festival (☎01792/390404). Mostly classical music.

Mid-July: Sesiwn Fawr (Big Session), Dolgellau (☎01341/423355, *www.sesiwnfawr.demon.co.uk*). A weekend of Celtic bands and beer all over the town.

Late July: Welsh Proms at St David's Hall, Cardiff (☎029/2087 8444).

Late-July: Royal Welsh Show, Builth Wells, Powys (☎01982/553683). Massive agricultural show and sales fair.

Late July: Ras yr Wyddfa (☎01286/870721). A one-day race from Llanberis up Snowdon, attracting masochists from the world over.

Last week in July–first week in August: Cardiff Street Festival. Includes the Butetown Carnival, a loud, multiracial celebration and party by the bay.

Late July–early Aug: Cardiff Festival (☎029/20873936). Large-scale themed annual festival incorporating music, art, drama, opera and literature.

First week in August: Royal National Eisteddfod (☎029/2076 3777). Wales' biggest single annual event: fun, very impressive and worth seeing if only for the overblown pageantry. Bardic competitions, readings, theatre, TV, debates and copious help for the Welsh language learner.

Mid-August: Brecon Jazz Festival, Powys (☎01874/625557). Widely regarded as one of the best in Britain.

Late August: Pontardawe Music Festival, West Glamorgan (☎01792/830200). Folk, ceilidhs, international music and dance.

Late August: Cilgerran Coracle Races, Dyfed (☎01239/614216).

Late August: Mumbles Beer Festival over two days, showcasing over 30 real ales, plus cider and food. The small entry fee includes a souvenir glass.

Late August: Llandrindod Wells Victorian Festival, Powys (☎01597/823441). A week of family fun, street entertainment and Victorian costumes rounded off with a fireworks display and torchlit procession.

Last week in August: Gwyl Machynlleth (☎01654/703355). Wide-ranging arts festival, with a solid programme of chamber music at its core.

August Bank Holiday Monday: World Bog Snorkelling Championships, Llanwrtyd Wells, Powys (☎01591/610236). Incorporates a mountain-bike bog-leaping contest.

First Saturday in September: Cardiff Mardi Gras, Cardiff (details from the Cardiff Community Safety Partnership, Mon–Fri 10am–5pm (☎029/2087 2632).This lesbian and gay festival first took place in 1999, and consists of live acts and stalls in the grounds of the castle.

Early October: Erddig Apple Festival (☎01978/355314). Two-day festival of all things apple-related – including cider.

October: Swansea Festival of Music and the Arts (☎01792/411570). Concerts, jazz, drama, opera, ballet and art events throughout the city over a three-week period.

Late Oct: Cardiff Beer and Cider Festival (☎029/2066 4132). Three days to sample 120 brews, many of them Welsh.

Mid-November: Welsh International Film Festival, Cardiff (☎029/2049 0034). Art-house films, mostly shown at the Chapter Arts Centre.

December 31: 6km race in Mountain Ash, Mid Glamorgan, in memory of local eighteenth-century shepherd Guto Nyth Brân, who died after running 12 miles in 53 minutes.

December 31: Fancy-dress costume night in New Quay, Dyfed.

December 31: New Year Walk-In, Llanwrtyd Wells, Powys. A boozy stagger round the town.

are the most Welsh of events, incorporating theatre, dance, music (from rock to traditional choirs), debate, ceremony, competitions and exhibitions. However, provision is made throughout for non-Welsh speakers, who are always welcome to what have become Europe's largest indigenous cultural festivals.

Many towns and cities now have annual **arts festivals** of some kind, mentioned throughout the Guide and, in the case of the major events, in the box overleaf. Aside from these, the old working traditions of Wales have spawned such occasions as the annual Cilgerran **coracle races** (see

p.274) and Llanwrtyd's **drovers' runs** (see p.226). Some of Wales' events have a distinctly bizarre background and appearance; for instance the snorkelling competition in peat bogs and the pilgrimages for *Prisoner* fans to the surreal village of Portmeirion. If you want to explore the odd customs and traditions of Britain in greater depth, read Martin Green's *Curious Customs* (Impact Books). Finally, New Age **fairs** and **festivals** are a common feature of summer throughout Wales; these are usually publicized by handbills, posters in wholefood shops and cafés, and by word of mouth. A few, however, have broken through to annual, and permanent, respectability.

OUTDOOR PURSUITS AND SPECTATOR SPORTS

No matter where you are in Wales – even in the more populated valleys and coastline of the south – you're never far from a stretch of countryside where you can lose the crowds on a brief walk or cycle ride. For tougher specimens, there are long-distance footpaths and skyline ridge walks, as well as some of the best rock climbing and potholing (caving) in Britain. Along the coast and at many of the country's inland lakes, you can follow the pursuits of sailing and windsurfing, and there are plenty of fine beaches for less structured fresh-air activities.

WALKING

There isn't a built-up area in Wales that's more than half an hour away from some decent walking country, but three areas are so outstanding they have been designated **national parks**. Most of Wales' northwestern corner is taken up with the **Snowdonia National Park** (see pp.315–348), a dozen of the country's highest peaks separated by dramatic glaciated valleys and laced with hundreds of miles of ridge and moorland paths. From Snowdonia, the Cambrian Mountains stretch south to the **Brecon Beacons National Park**, with its striking sandstone scarp at the head of the south Wales coalfield and lush, cave-riddled limestone valleys to the south. One hundred and seventy miles of Wales' southwestern peninsula make up the third park, the **Pembrokeshire Coast National Park**, best explored by the **Pembrokeshire Coast Path**, one of Wales' increasing number of designated **Long-Distance Paths** (see box on p.50).

Unless you're doing your walking on out-of-season weekdays, don't expect to have trails to yourself. Walking is very popular in all the national parks, and finding solitude can require some effort. Many of the best one-day walks in the country are detailed in this Guide, but for more arduous mountain treks, you'll benefit from bringing a specialist walking guide book, which are widely available in the appropriate walking area. The best are listed in "Contexts" (pp.486–487), and you can get more information from The Ramblers' Association, Britain's main countryside campaigning organization and self-appointed guardian of the nation's footpaths and rights of way. Their main office is at 1/5 Wandsworth Rd, London SW8 2XX (☎020/7339 8500, *www.ramblers.org.uk*), and they maintain a Welsh office at Tw'r Cerddwyr, High St, Gresford, Wrexham, Clwyd LL12 8PT (☎01978/855148, fax 854445).

RIGHTS OF ACCESS

Although they are managed by committees of local and state officials, all three Welsh national parks are, in fact, predominantly privately owned. There is **no general right of access**, but both the National Trust and the Forestry Commission (the principal landowners) normally allow free recreational use of their land.

Access to other land is restricted to **public rights of way**: **footpaths** (pedestrians only) and **bridleways** (pedestrians, horses and bicycles) that have seen continued use over the centuries. Historically, these are often over narrow mountain passes between two hamlets, or linking villages to mines or summer pasture land. Rights of way are marked on Ordnance Survey maps and are indicated with a Public Footpath (*Llwybr Cyhoeddus*) sign; any stiles and gates on the path have to be maintained by the landowner. Some less scrupulous owners have been known to block rights of way by destroying stiles – and with some walkers wilfully straying from official rights of way, some resentment is perhaps understandable. Disputes are still uncommon but your surest way of avoiding trouble is to meticulously follow

the right of way on an up-to-date map. Ordnance Survey maps also indicate routes with **concessionary path** or **courtesy path** status; though these are usually open for public use they can be closed at any time. After years of campaigning, the government has finally passed legislation guaranteeing a general right of access across land. While this is seen as a major victory for land rights activists, in practice, you'll probably still need to abide by the guidelines discussed above.

A relatively new departure by map makers – after years of badgering by The Ramblers' Association – is the latest edition of the "Dolgellau" Landranger map. For the first time, minor tracks – some following ancient drovers' roads – which were previously shown without any right of access, are now included as "other routes with public access". Though no changes have been made to the rights of access, the new awareness has opened up several possible walking and mountain-biking routes, particularly across large tracts of Forestry Commission land.

THE LONG-DISTANCE PATHS

Defined as any route over twenty miles long and waymarked at frequent intervals by a recognizable symbol (an acorn), **Long-Distance Paths** have enjoyed a boom in recent years: with the Landsker Borderlands Trail (see p.173) and the Taff Trail (see p.210) being fairly recent additions. Some of the walks – the Pembrokeshire Coast Path and Offa's Dyke Path in particular – use a strong unifying theme for their route; others are a mite esoteric, though this seldom detracts from the quality of the walk. LDPs are usually well supplied with youth hostels, though you may need a tent for some of the more heroic hikes. *Stilwell's National Trail Companion* (see Books, p.487) currently lists handy accommodation along Glyndŵr's Way, the Offa's Dyke Path and the Pembrokeshire Coast Path.

More LDP information is available from The Ramblers' Association or the Long Distance Walkers' Association (63 Yockley Close, The Maultway, Camberley, Surrey GU15 1QQ, *www.bibloset.demon.co.uk/LDWA/LDWA.htm*).

ROCK CLIMBING AND SCRAMBLING

As well as being superb walking country, Snowdonia offers some of Britain's best rock climbing and several challenging scrambles – ascents that fall somewhere between walks and

THE TOP LDPS

Wales' Long-Distance Paths are detailed where appropriate throughout the Guide. What follows is a brief rundown of the most popular.

Cambrian Way (274 miles). Wales' longest and most arduous path, cutting north–south over the remote Cambrian Mountains.

Dyfi Valley Way (108 miles). A fairly recent creation which traces both sides of the beautiful Dyfi Valley and estuary, described in Laurence Main's path guide (see Books, p.487).

Glyndŵr's Way (128 miles). A lengthy meander amongst the remote mountains and lakes of mid-Wales, from Welshpool to Knighton via Machynlleth.

Landsker Borderlands Trail (60 miles). Slightly contrived circular walk around the Landsker

region, starting from Canaston Bridge in Pembrokeshire.

Offa's Dyke Path (168 miles). From north to south Wales, largely tracing the line of the eighth-century earthwork along the English border.

Pembrokeshire Coast Path (186 miles). Dips into quiet coves and climbs over headlands with sweeping ocean views around the Pembrokeshire Coast.

Wye Valley Walk (107 miles). From Chepstow to Rhayader following the River Wye and partly through England.

---

climbs, requiring the use of your hands. One or two of the tougher walks included in the text have sections of scrambling, but for the most part this is a specialist discipline, well covered in the walking books listed in "Contexts" (see pp.486–487).

In the south of the country, the pick of the crags are the sea cliffs of Gower and the Pembrokeshire Coast, but the vast majority of climbing destinations are to the north in **Snowdonia**. A predominance of low-lying crags combined with easy accessibility make the area particularly popular, and on any sunny weekend you'll spot brightly coloured figures hanging off almost every cliff face. The principal areas to head for are the Llanberis Pass, the Ogwen Valley, Tremadog (near Porthmadog), the sea cliffs around South Stack near Holyhead, and the desperately difficult Pen Trwyn on the Great Orme at Llandudno. The best general guide for experienced climbers, *Rock Climbing in Snowdonia* by Paul Williams (Constable), is stocked in the region's numerous climbing shops.

Beginners should contact Plas-y-Brenin: The National Mountaineering Centre, Capel Curig LL24 0ET (☎01690/720214, *www.pyb.co.uk*), which runs residential courses and two-hour samplers, or the British Mountaineering Council, 177–179 Burton Rd, Manchester M20 2BB (☎0161/445 4747, *www.thebmc.co.uk*), which can put you in touch with climbing guides and folk running courses.

CYCLING

Despite a boom in the sale of mountain bikes, **cyclists** are still treated with notorious disrespect by many motorized road users and by the people who plan the country's traffic systems. There are few proper cycle routes in any of Wales's big towns, so if you're hellbent on tackling the congestion, pollution and aggression of city traffic, get a **helmet** and a secure **lock** – cycle theft is an organized racket. Prospects are brighter in rural areas, where the back roads along river valleys or climbing mountain passes have a sufficient density of pubs and B&Bs to keep the days manageable. Steep gradients can be a problem but ascents are never long, with Wales' highest pass barely reaching 1500ft. Your main problem is likely to be finding spare parts – for anything more complex than a tyre or inner tube, you'll need a specialist shop. The CTC (see opposite) lists places in its annual handbook.

One beacon of hope in the madness of Britain's transport policy is Sustrans, 35 King St, Bristol BS1 4DZ (☎0117/926 8893, *www.sustrans.org.uk*), an organization committed to forming a national cycle network predominantly using existing quiet roads and disused railway lines. The main north–south Welsh leg, **Lôn Las Cymru**, opened in 1996 covering three hundred hilly miles from Anglesey, through Snowdonia, the Brecon Beacons and the industrial valleys of the south, to the Severn Bridge. Sustrans publishes two maps of the route (£6 each; £10 combined), 8a covering Holyhead to Builth Wells and 8b from there to Chepstow and Cardiff. Look out too for their forthcoming Celtic Route across the south of the country to Fishguard.

Off-road cycling is becoming increasingly popular in the highland walking areas, but cyclists should remember to keep to rights of way designated on maps as bridleways, and to pass walkers at considerate speed and with a courteous warning of your presence. Footpaths, unless otherwise marked, are for pedestrian use only. In deference to walkers, access to certain bridleways has been restricted, particularly around Snowdon: bikes are not allowed on the approaches to the summit between 10am and 5pm from June to September. With no book specifically geared to the off-roader in Wales, the best one to buy is the Britain-wide *Fifty Mountain Bike Rides* (Crowood) by Jeremy Evans, featuring ten 2–7hr rides in Wales, complete with sketch maps, riding conditions and details of pubs and cafés along the way.

Transporting your bike by **train** is a good way of getting to the interesting parts of Wales without a lot of stressful pedalling. What with the privatization of the rail network and the profusion of companies running services, it's hard to be specific about what you'll encounter, but in general, bikes are carried free on suburban Valley Lines trains outside the weekday rush hours of 7.30–9.30am and 4.30–6pm. On most inter-town routes in Wales, there is only space for two bikes, so you should reserve in advance: Central Trains (☎0870/000 6060) run from Shrewsbury to Aberystwyth and Pwllheli and don't charge for carriage, but levy a £1 fee for reservations; Wales & West (☎0870/900 0773), who run all the other mainline services, charge £1 for a reservation, but £3 if you turn up unannounced with your bike. **Bike rental** is available at bike shops in most large towns and many resorts, but the specimens are seldom top quality machines – all right for a brief spin, but not for any serious touring. Expect to pay in the region of £10 per day, £50–60 per week.

Britain's biggest **cycling organization** is the Cyclists' Touring Club (CTC), Cottrell House, 69 Meadrow, Godalming, Surrey GU7 3HS (☎01483/417217, *www.ctc.org.uk*), which supplies members with touring and technical advice as well as insurance. Its free sheets for members cover dozens of routes through Wales. Those planning their own touring routes would do well to buy the OS 1:250,000 (4 miles to an inch) Wales and West Midlands maps. These are detailed enough to show relief and almost all tarmacked roads – and you won't find yourself cycling across a whole map in one day. The Ordnance Survey's excellent series of regional *Cycle Tour* guides have now been extended to include Wales: one covers North Wales, the other rest of the country.

If you want a guaranteed hassle-free cycling holiday, various companies offer easy-going tours where you ride from hotel to hotel, and a van carries your bags. Some give you an arranged itinerary, while others guide you. The best of the latter is Bicycle Beano, Erwood, Builth Wells, Powys LD2 3PQ (☎01981/560471, *www.bicycle-beano.co.uk*) which offers weekend or week-long cycling holidays through the Wye Valley, the Cambrian Coast and Snowdonia for around £400 a week including everything except lunch. They're a lot of fun, good value for money and the cooking is vegetarian. Arranged itinerary contenders include PedalAway, Trereece Barn, Llangorron, Ross-on-Wye, Herefordshire HR9 6NH (☎01989/770357, *www.cycling.uk.com/holidays/pedalawa.htm*) based over the border in England but offering itineraries into the Black Mountain, Wye Valley and the Brecon Beacons; and Beics Eryri Cycle Tours, 44 Tyddyn Llywdyn, Parc Yr Hendre, Caernarfon, Gwynedd LL55 2LX (☎01286/676637, *www.cycling.uk.com/holidays/beics.htm*), who run trips in Snowdonia.

BEACHES, SURFING AND WINDSURFING

Wales is ringed by fine **beaches** and **bays**, and many of them are readily accessible by public transport; this, though, does mean that they tend to get very busy in high summer. With most of the Welsh coast influenced by the currents of the North Atlantic Drift, water temperatures are higher than you might expect for this latitude, but only the truly hardy should consider swimming outside the warmer June to October period. For swimming and sunbathing, the best areas to head for are the Gower Peninsula, the Pembrokeshire Coast, the Llŷn Peninsula and the southwest coast of Anglesey. Though it has more resorts than any other section of Wales' coastline, the north coast certainly hasn't got the most attractive beaches, nor is it a place to swim.

Wales' southwest-facing beaches offer the best conditions for either board or kayak surfing, with decent, but by no means Hawaiian-sized, waves at several key spots. In the south, this means Rhossili, at the western tip of the Gower and Whitesands Bay (Porth-mawr), near St David's. The surfing scene in north Wales centres on the long sweep of Porth Neigwl (Hell's Mouth), near Abersoch on the Llŷn, and Rhosneigr on Anglesey. Windsurfers tend to congregate at these major surf beaches and at Barmouth, Borth, around the Pembrokeshire Coast and at Mumbles. For more information, call the Welsh Surfing Federation Surf School, The Barn, The Croft, Llangennith, North Gower, Swansea SA3 1HU (☎01792/386426, *www.britsurf.org/wsf*).

With raw and partly treated effluent still being discharged off many British beaches, it has to be said that they are not the cleanest in Europe, with many falling well below EU standards. Steps are being taken to improve the situation, and Welsh Water, which manages water treatment throughout Wales, is committed to ending the dumping of raw sewage; however, far too many stretches of the coastline remain contaminated by seaborne effluent and rubbish. The EU awards a **Blue Flag** to designated beaches which pass nineteen tests for water quality and 24 land-based criteria for beach facilities. There are a smattering around Wales (all in the areas mentioned above) and numbers are increasing year by year. It is worth remembering, though, that failure to have a blue flag doesn't necessarily mean that the water is bad; it may just be that the beach facilities – parking, toilets, etc – don't meet the criteria.

Don't be fooled by the yellow flags (with deceptively large areas of blue) you'll see on many other beaches. These are awarded to beaches that meet just two of the basic measures of cleanliness by the government's tourist-conscious Tidy Britain Group. For annually updated, detailed information on the condition of British beaches, the *Good Beach Guide*, compiled by the Marine Conservation Society (9 Gloucester Rd, Ross-on-Wye, Herefordshire HR9 5BU, ☎01989/566017), is the definitive source. The Web site is also worth consulting: *www.goodbeachguide.co.uk*.

The loudest voices in the protests against water contamination are recreational users, particularly the Britain-wide campaigning organiza-tion Surfers Against Sewage, 2 Rural Workshops, Wheal Kitty, St Agnes, Cornwall TR5 0RD (☎01872/553001, *www.sas.org.uk*), who maintain a medical database and a clickable map showing conditions around the coast. Additional information on bathing water quality in England and Wales an be gleaned from the environment agency's Web site (*www.environment-agency.gov.uk*).

KAYAKING AND RAFTING

Board riders constantly have to compete for waves with the surf ski riders and kayakers who frequent the same beaches. Paddlers, however, have the additional run of miles of superb coastline, particularly around Anglesey, the Llŷn and the Pembrokeshire coast. The northern coasts are amply detailed in Terry Storry's slightly dated *Snowdonia White Water Sea and Surf* (Cicerone), which also contains maps and notes on Snowdonia's myriad short, steep bedrock rivers, many of which can only be paddled just after a deluge. The same author's more up-to-date *British White Water* (Constable) covers the hundred best rivers in Britain, including all those in his Snowdonia book, plus some in south Wales, though without river maps.

As equipment improves, paddlers have become more daring, and Victorian tourist attractions such as Swallow and Conwy falls, both near Betws-y-Coed, are now fair game for a descent. Most of the kayaking is non-competitive, but on summer weekends you might catch a slalom either on the River Dee at Llangollen or at the National Whitewater Centre on the River Tryweryn, near Bala, where you can also ride the rapids in rubber rafts.

Without your own kayak or canoe, it's still possible to get on the water with tour companies, who can be contacted through the Welsh Canoeing Association, Canolfan Trweryn, Frongoch, Bala, Gwynedd LL23 7NU (☎01678/521199, *www.welsh-canoeing.org.uk*).

PONY TREKKING

Wales' scattered population and large tracts of open land are ideal for **pony trekking**, now a major business with almost 100 approved riding centres and many smaller operations. Don't expect too much cantering over unfenced land: rides tend to be geared towards unhurried appreciation of the scenery from horseback, and are often combined with accommodation on farms. Mid-Wales has the greatest concentration of stables, but there are places all over the country, amply detailed in the brochures supplied by the Wales Trekking and Riding Association, 9 Neville St, Abergavenny, Gwent NP7 5AA (☎01873/858717). Riding schools checked and approved by the WTB get billing in the free *Discovering Wales on Horseback* leaflet; these typically run two-hour morning and afternoon sessions, charging around £8–10 an hour.

RUGBY

Rugby (or more formally, Rugby Union) is a passion with the Welsh, and their national game. Support is strongest in the traditionally working-class valleys of the south Wales coalfields, where the fanaticism has traditionally been fuelled by the national side's success. Welsh rugby saw its glory days in the 1970s, when Wales turned out some of the best sides ever seen. The scarlet jerseys struck fear into their opponents in the **Five Nations Championship** – an annual tournament where Wales, England, Scotland, Ireland and France all played each other (now superseded by the Six Nations Championship with the addition of Italy). That 1970s side won six out of the ten championships – three of them **Grand Slams**, where all four of the Five Nations opponents were beaten individually. The players that made Wales so formidable included fearless fullback J.P.R. Williams, the country's most-capped player; elusive and magical outside-halves Barry John and Phil Bennett; and the world's highest try-scoring scrum-half, Gareth Edwards.

But victories were harder to come by in the 1980s, and by 1991, the national side reached its nadir with its worst-ever international loss of 63–6 at the hands of Australia. That year also saw Wales' highest point scorer, Paul Thorburn, quit the international game disillusioned. Wales' recovery to a dominant side in Rugby Union has been hampered by the loss of many players poached by the rival professional code, Rugby League, chiefly played in northern England and Australasia. It wasn't until 1995 that Rugby Union finally woke up to the fact that amateur status was costing it players, and the code turned professional worldwide, coaxing back key players in the process.

Despite winning the Five Nations Championship in 1994, Wales has generally struggled to keep up with the standards of arch rival England throughout the 1990s, let alone match the power and attacking panache of the all-conquering southern hemisphere sides, Australia, New Zealand and South Africa. Recognizing this southern dominance, the Welsh Rugby Union (*www.wru.co.uk*) enlisted the help of New Zealander, Graham Henry – dubbed "the saviour of the national game" – as coach. After taking over in 1998, he oversaw an astonishing string of victories including one over South Africa in the first game to be played at the brand new 72,500-seater **Millennium Stadium**, built on the site of the legendary Cardiff Arms Park. All this raised hopes of success in the 1999 Rugby World Cup, hosted by Wales, but despite easy progress to the quarter-finals, the Welsh team couldn't match the power and skill of the eventual winners, Australia. However, they were by no means disgraced and in the process of reaching the quarter-finals; Neil Jenkins overtook Australian Michael Lynagh's record for the greatest number of international points scored.

To see an international game, you'll have to be affiliated to one of the Rugby Union clubs or be prepared to pay well over the odds at one of the ticket agencies. Most tickets are allocated months before a match, and touts will often be found selling tickets for hundreds of pounds outside the gates on the day. Away from the international arena, a thriving rugby scene exists at club level, with some 178 clubs and 40,000 players taking to the field most Saturdays throughout the season (September to just after Easter). The four top teams, which usually feature a smattering of international players, are Neath, Swansea, Cardiff and Llanelli, with Pontypridd snapping at their heels. It's often worth going to a match purely for the light-hearted crowd banter – if you can understand the accents. Check with individual clubs for fixtures and ticket prices, which start at well under £10.

FOOTBALL

Compared to rugby, **Welsh football** (soccer) is seen as a minority sport, but in fact there are just as many Welsh footballers who prefer not to pick up the ball and run with it as those who do. The three top sides in the country are Cardiff

City, Swansea City and Wrexham, which all play in the English Football League. In recent years, Wrexham have held their position in the Second Division (behind the Premier and First Divisions) while Cardiff and Swansea have dropped into the Third from time to time. The rest of the clubs play in the lacklustre (but improving) **League of Wales**.

With the retirement of stalwarts such as Ian Rush and Mark Hughes, the national team have had to draft in young blood around key players such as Manchester United's electrifying Ryan Giggs, Newcastle United's Gary Speed and Sheffield United's Dean Saunders. It hasn't been a huge success so far, and, though they've battled valiantly, Wales have again failed to reach the final stages of Euro 2000. For more on the Welsh game, check the Web site of the Football Association of Wales (*www.citypages.co.uk/faw*).

DISABLED TRAVELLERS

Britain has numerous specialist tour operators catering for physically disabled travellers, and the number of non-specialist operators who welcome clients with disabilities is increasing. For information on operators and facilities, get in touch with the Royal Association for Disability and Rehabilitation (RADAR), 12 City Forum, 250 City Rd, London EC1V 8AF (☎020/7250 3222, fax 7250 0212, minicom 7250 4119, *www.radar.org.uk*); or its Welsh equivalent, Disability Wales, Llys Ifor, Crescent Rd, Caerphilly, Mid Glamorgan CF8 1XL (☎029/2088 7325, fax 2088 8702, minicom 2088 7325, *info@dwac.demon.co.uk*). There's also the Holiday Care Service, Floor 2, Imperial Buildings, Victoria Rd, Horley, Surrey RH6 7PZ (☎01293/774535, fax 784647, minicom 776943), which provides extensive lists of inspected accommodation, major sites and caravan parks. Though they're not specifically geared up with visitors in mind, you might also try getting in touch with the Wales Council for the Deaf, Glenview House, Courthouse St, Pontypridd, Mid Glamorgan CF37 1JY (☎01443/485687, fax 408555, minicom 485686), or the Wales Council for the Blind, 3rd floor, Shand House, 20 Newport Rd, Cardiff CF2 1DB (☎029/2047 3954). The Disabled Motorists' Federation (☎01743/761181) will furnish you with a free road route plan and map tailored to your specific needs.

In **North America**, contact Mobility International at PO Box 10767, Eugene, OR 97440 (☎541/343-1284, fax 343-6812, *www.miusa.org*);
the Society for the Advancement of Travel for the Handicapped, 347 5th Ave, Suite 610, New York, NY 10016 (☎212/447-7284, fax 725-8253, *www.sath.org*), a non-profit travel industry referral service that passes queries on to its members; and the Travel Information Service, Moss Rehabilitation Hospital, 1200 W Tabor Rd, Philadelphia, PA 19141 (☎215/456-9600, *www.mossresourcenet.org*), a telephone information and referral service. Undiscovered Britain, 11978 Audubon Place, Philadelphia, PA 19116 (☎215/969-0542, *www.undiscoveredbritain.com*), can organize comprehensive group or independent tours in the UK and Ireland, as well as provide useful information to those travelling independently.

Disabled travellers in **Australia** can get information and advice from ACROD, PO Box 60, Curtin, ACT 2605 (☎06/682 4333, *www.acrod.co.au*); or Barrier Free Travel, 36 Wheatley St, North Bellingen, NSW 2454 (☎02/6655 1733), a fee-based travel access information service; those in **New Zealand** should try the Disabled Persons Assembly, PO Box 10, 138 The Terrace, Wellington (☎04/472 2626).

Should you go it alone, you'll find that Wales is still years behind the advances made in North America and Australasia. **Public transport** companies are only just starting to make any effort to accommodate disabled people; you can find out who is doing this most effectively, and get free travel planning and access information, from Travel Freedom, Unit 2b, St David's Industrial Estate, Pengam NP2 1SW (☎ and minicom 01443/831000, fax 839800).

Some rail services now accommodate wheelchair users in relative comfort, and some assistance is available at stations if you call in advance, preferably 48 hours ahead; call National Rail Enquiries (☎0345/484950, minicom 0845/605 0600) to get the number of the appropriate rail company. Wheelchair users and blind or partially sighted people are automatically given 30–50 percent reductions on train fares. People with other disabilities are eligible for the **Disabled Persons Railcard** (£14 per year), which gives a third off most tickets. There are no bus discounts for the disabled, while, of the major **car rental** firms, only Hertz offer models with hand controls at the same rate as conventional vehicles, and even these are in the more expensive categories. It's much the same story with **accommodation**: modified suites are available at the odd B&B, but mostly only at higher-priced establishments. Exceptions include five wheelchair-accessible YHAs: Broad Haven, Manorbier, Newport, Pen-y-Pass and Conwy.

In some areas of Wales where **public toilets** need to be locked to avoid vandalism, local authorities have joined RADAR's national Key System (☎020/7247 5432), in which disabled people are able to gain access to facilities via a standard key which comes with a booklet detailing locations. Some tourist offices also hold a key which you can borrow.

Access to **monuments and museums** is improving all the time. The National Trust produces its annual *Information for Visitors with Disabilities* guide detailing accessibility to NT sites throughout England and Wales, and CADW allow wheelchair users and the visually handicapped, along with their assisting companion, free entry to all monuments. Access to theatres, cinemas and other public places is slowly improving.

PUBLICATIONS

The most helpful **publication** is the free *Discovering Accessible Wales* booklet, published by the Wales Tourist Board and packed with information covering everything from transport and restaurants to beach access and parking. It also classifies all accredited accommodation into three accessibility grades, and categorizes restaurants and sites using nationally recognized **accessibility symbols**. Even the WTB's guide to *Discovering Wales on Horseback* features riding schools which cater to the disabled.

Other useful publications include RADAR's annually updated *Holidays in the British Isles: A Guide For Disabled People* (£7.50), *Getting There: a Guide to Long Distance Travel* (£5) and *Access to the Skies* (£5). The AA publishes the annual *Disabled Travellers' Guide* (£4.99; free to members). Two helpful **Web sites** are *www.disabilitynet.co.uk* and *www.access-able.com*.

LESBIAN AND GAY WALES

Homosexual acts between consenting males was legalized in Britain in 1967, but it wasn't until 1994 that the age of consent was finally reduced from 21 to 18 (still two years above that for heterosexuals). At the time of writing, legislation to equalise straight and gay ages of consent at 16 has been published for the 1999–2000 parliamentary session, and, although previous attempts have been scuppered, it is likely to finally go through. Lesbianism has never specifically been outlawed, apocryphally owing to the fact that Queen Victoria refused to believe it existed.

With such a rural culture, it's perhaps not surprising that Wales is less used to the lesbian and gay lifestyle than its more cosmopolitan English neighbour. Although Plaid Cymru itself has always supported lesbian and gay rights, there still exists a hard strain of nationalist who believes that gay emancipation is incompatible with true Welsh patriotism. At the 1993 National Eisteddfod in Llanelwedd, Powys, the stall of the national Welsh-speaking lesbian and gay organization, Cylch, was trashed one night – an action that was widely condemned.

The Welsh scene is muted, to say the least. The main centres of population – Cardiff, Newport and Swansea – have a number of pubs and clubs, with Cardiff especially beginning to see a worthy and confident gay scene – a Mardi Gras festival in early September included (see p.109) – more in keeping with the capital's size and status. Details are given in the text of the Guide. Out of the southern cities, however, gay life becomes distinctly discreet, although university towns such as Lampeter and Bangor manage support groups and the odd weekly night in a local bar, while Aberystwyth boasts a gay pub and a significantly homo-friendly milieu. Cardiff's lesbian and gay telephone lines (see p.109) are the most up-to-date source of information on places, events, accommodation and contacts throughout Wales. Alternatively, there are some informal but well-established networks, especially amongst the sometimes reclusive alternative lifestylers found in mid- and west Wales. **Border Women** (who should surely have called themselves Offa's Dykes) is a well-organized network for mid-Wales, with house meetings and monthly discos. They can be contacted via PO Box 42, Ludlow, Shropshire SY8 1WD. **Cylch** organize a variety of events – contact them at Bwlch Swyddfa Bost 23, Aberystwyth, Dyfed SY23. The UK-wide monthly *Gay Times* (£2.75) has thorough listings and contact information, together with the best directory of the half-dozen or so **gay hotels** throughout Wales. Alternatively, there's also a Web site *www.gaywales.co.uk* which details events and venues throughout the country.

ALTERNATIVE, NEW AGE AND GREEN WALES

Possibly more than any other part of Britain, Wales – the mid and west in particular – has become something of a haven for those searching for alternative lifestyles. This process dates back nearly a century, but it was the 1960s that saw mass migration west, something that has continued unabated since. Permanent testimonials to this include the Centre for Alternative Technology (CAT), near Machynlleth, now one of the area's most visited attractions, and Tipi Valley, near Talley, a permanent community in Native American tipis who run a regular public sweat lodge. Both institutions were founded in the idealistic mid-1970s and have prospered through less happy times. For the most part, it's been a fairly smooth process, although antagonism between New Agers and local, established families does break out on occasion.

For visitors, the legacy of this "green" influx is evident throughout Wales. Even in some of the smallest rural towns, you'll often find a health-food shop, wholefood café, somewhere flogging esoteric ephemera or an alternative resource centre. Any of these will give you further ideas and contacts for local happenings, places, groups and individuals. We've tried to give details of such places throughout the Guide. Other manifestations of such prolific non-mainstream activity include a robust free party scene in the rural parts of north, mid- and west Wales. These are often held in spectacularly beautiful settings – by lakes, on beaches – and take place virtually every weekend throughout the summer. Keep your eyes and ears peeled for information and don't hesitate to ask people for guidance. To complement the free events, there's a plethora of good festivals from spring to autumn, ranging from big folk and blues bashes to smaller gatherings in remote fields, with little more than a couple of banging sound systems. Again, information for smaller events travels best by word of mouth, although for larger, more organized and larger events, you'll see adverts and fliers months in advance. Especially in the wake of the vicious 1995 Criminal Justice Act, there are now far stronger laws against trespass and free parties, although their imposition is sketchy. If you run into any problems, there is a Travellers' Legal Advice Service operating in Cardiff (☎029/2087 4580).

For ecologically minded tourists, there are now numerous package deals that include walking, cycling, dancing and healing holidays and retreats in remote centres, usually with vegetarian and vegan food as part of the deal. Some of these are static, many are in temporary sites, while others keep you on the move. Again, we have included many of these within the body of the Guide, and some further ones are listed below.

ORGANIZATIONS RUNNING RETREATS AND HOLIDAYS

Buckland Hall, Bwlch, near Brecon, Powys LD3 7JJ (☎01874/730276). Beautiful hall and gardens hosting many holistic lifestyle courses and workshops.

Centre for Alternative Technology, Machynlleth, Powys (☎01654/703743, www.cat.org.uk). Residential courses on green themes such as self-build homes and organic gardening.

Cerridwen, near Llandysul, Ceredigion (☎01559/370211). Residential courses and breaks, some for women only.

Cwm Bedw Barns, Abbeycwmhir, Llandrindod Wells, Powys LD1 6PH (☎01597/851929). Monthly meditations and regular retreats.

Dreamweavers (☎01974/298920). Residential workshops (on Celtic Shamanism, for instance) at their Morningstar Lodge.

Healing Tao Wales, 7 Miners Lane, Old Colwyn, Conwy LL29 9HG (☎01492/515776). Residential weekend workshops on meditation and Chi Kung.

The Light Centre (☎01267/202264, www.saltrese.freeserve.co.uk). Residential healing retreats and energy workshops in the rural splendour of Carmarthenshire.

Penquoit Centre, Lawrenny, Pembrokeshire (☎01646/651666). Quiet retreat space for individuals or small groups, or hostel accommodation for groups of ten or more.

Vajraloka Buddhist Meditation Centre, Corwen, Denbighshire (☎01490/460406). Regular retreats for men.

DIRECTORY

Drugs It is most unwise to go through customs carrying any illegal substances. Once in the country, being caught in possession of a small amount of marijuana resin, grass, ecstasy or mushrooms will usually get you no more than a fine, though possession of larger quantities or of "harder" narcotics could lead to imprisonment or deportation.

Electricity In Britain, the current is 240V AC. North American appliances will need a transformer and adapter; Australasian appliances will only need an adapter.

Laundry Coin-operated laundries (launderettes) are to be found in Welsh towns of any size, and are open about twelve hours a day from Monday to Friday, with shorter hours at weekends. A wash followed by a spin or tumble dry costs about £2, with "service washes" (your laundry done for you in a few hours) about £1 more.

Smoking The last decade has seen a dramatic change in attitudes towards smoking and a sig-nificant reduction in the consumption of cigarettes. Smoking is now outlawed on most public transport and in just about all public buildings, and many restaurants and hotels have non-smoking areas. That said, establishments are often poorly ventilated so when there are smokers around you really notice it. Smokers are advised, when booking a table or a room, to check that smoking is tolerated there.

Time Greenwich Mean Time (GMT) is in force from late October to late March, when the clocks go forward an hour for British Summer Time (BST). GMT is five hours ahead of New York, ten hours behind Sydney, and twelve hours behind New Zealand.

Tipping and service charges In restaurants a service charge is often included in the bill; if it isn't, leave a tip of 10–15 percent unless the service is unforgivably bad. Some restaurants are in the habit of leaving the "total" box blank on credit-card counterfoils, to encourage customers to add another few percent on top of the service charge – if you're paying by credit card, check that the "total" box is filled in before you sign. Taxi drivers expect a tip in the region of 10 percent. You do not generally tip bar staff – if you want to show your appreciation, offer to buy them a drink.

Toilets Public toilets are found at many train and bus stations and are signposted on town high streets, and are usually free. In urban locations, a fee of 10p or 20p is sometimes charged.

Videos Visitors from North America should note that the UK uses a different and incompatible type of VHS system. Pre-recorded tapes bought here will not play at home unless you have a machine capable of playing both systems.

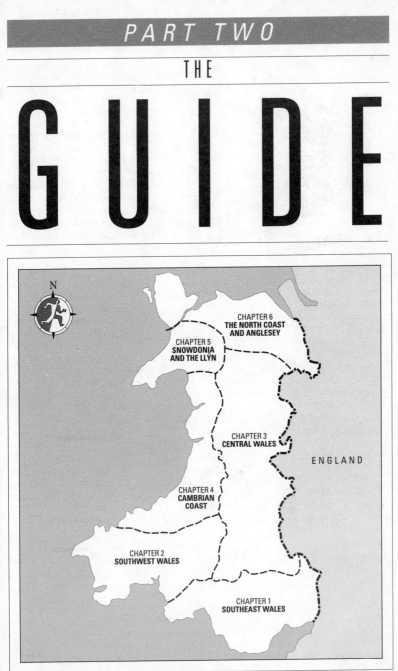

CHAPTER 6
**THE NORTH COAST
AND ANGLESEY**

CHAPTER 5
**SNOWDONIA
AND THE LLYN**

CHAPTER 3
CENTRAL WALES

ENGLAND

CHAPTER 4
**CAMBRIAN
COAST**

CHAPTER 2
SOUTHWEST WALES

CHAPTER 1
SOUTHEAST WALES

© Crown copyright

CHAPTER ONE

SOUTHEAST WALES

H ome to almost 1.8 million people – sixty percent of the country's population – the southeastern corner of Wales, comprising the counties of Monmouthshire and Glamorgan, is one of Britain's most industrialized regions. Both population and industry are most heavily concentrated around the sea ports and former mining valleys; quiet hills and beaches are always just a matter of miles away.

Monmouthshire (formerly Gwent) is the easternmost county in Wales, starting at the English border in a beguilingly rural manner, the **River Wye** crisscrossing between the two countries from its mouth at the fortress town of **Chepstow**; here, you'll find one of the most impressive castles in a land where few towns are without one. In the Wye's beautiful valley lie the spectacularly placed ruins of **Tintern Abbey**, downstream from the old county town of **Monmouth**, which makes a fine base for visiting the craggy ruins of the Three Castles, and even Abergavenny on the fringes of the Brecon Beacons National Park (see Chapter Three, pp.200–224)).

Monmouthshire becomes increasingly industrialized as you travel west, with the **River Usk** meandering through the middle of the county and spilling out into the Bristol Channel at **Newport**, Wales' third-largest conurbation. Although it is hardly likely to feature on a swift tour of Wales, the town has an excellent museum and the remains of an extensive Roman settlement at **Caerleon**, a northern suburb of the town.

To the west and north are the world-famous **Valleys**, once the coal- and iron-rich powerhouse of the nation. This is the Wales of popular imagination: hemmed-in valley floors packed with lines of blank, grey houses, their doors and sills painted in contrasting gaudy brightness, slanted almost impossibly towards the pithead. Although nearly all of the mines have since closed, the area is still one of tight-knit towns, with a rich working-class heritage that displays itself in some excellent museums and colliery tours, such as the **Big Pit** at Blaenafon and the **Rhondda Heritage Park** in Trehafod. The valleys follow rivers coursing down towards the coast, where great ports stood to ship their products all over the world. The greatest of them all was **Cardiff**, once the world's busiest coal port, now Wales' upbeat capital. Excellent museums, a massive castle, exciting rejuvenation projects and Wales' best cultural pursuits make the city an essential stop. Lying to the immediate west, and a world away from the industrial hangover of the city and valleys, is the lush, conservative **Vale of Glamorgan**, dotted with stoic little market towns and chirpy seaside resorts – most notably **Barry** and **Porthcawl**.

ACCOMMODATION PRICE CODES

Throughout this guide, hotel and B&B accommodation is priced on a scale of ① to ⑨, the number indicating the **lowest price** you could expect to pay per night in that establishment for a **double room in high season**. The prices indicated by the codes are as follows:

① under £40	④ £60–70	⑦ £110–150
② £40–50	⑤ £70–90	⑧ £150–200
③ £50–60	⑥ £90–110	⑨ over £200

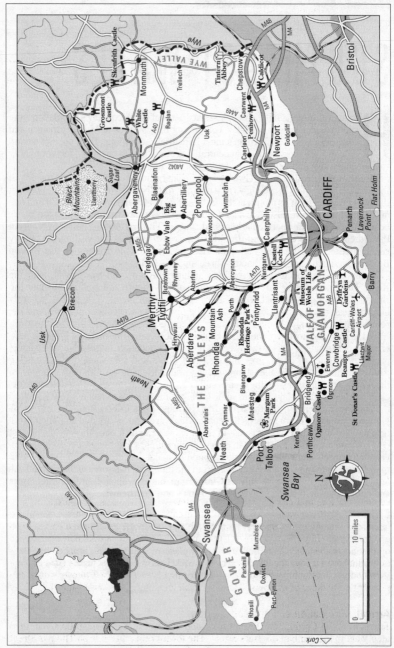

© Crown copyright

The west of Glamorgan is dominated by Wales' second city, **Swansea**, rougher, tougher and less anglicized than the capital. Like Cardiff, Swansea grew principally on the strength of its docks, and sits on an impressive arc of coast that shelves round from the belching steel works of **Port Talbot** in the east to **Mumbles** and **Oystermouth**, holiday towns of amusement arcades, pubs and chip shops, on the jaw of the delightful **Gower peninsula** in the west. Gower – one of the country's favourite playgrounds – juts out into the sea, a mini-Wales of grand beaches, rocky headlands, bracken heaths and ruined castles.

Getting around

Southeast Wales is by far the easiest part of the country to travel around. Swift new dual carriageways connect with the M4, bringing all corners of the region into close proximity. **Public transport** is similarly thorough: this is the only part of Wales with a half-decent train service, and most suburban and rural services interconnect with Cardiff, Newport and Swansea, as well as further afield to Gloucester and the English Midlands; Monmouth was long ago cut off from the train network, although it is easily reached by car and bus. Bus services fill in virtually all of the gaps though often in circuitous and time-consuming fashion.

The Wye Valley

Perhaps the most anglicized corner of Wales, the **Wye Valley** – along with the rest of Monmouthshire – was only finally recognized as part of Wales in the local government reorganization of 1974; before which, the county was officially included as part of neither England nor Wales, so that maps were frequently headlined "Wales and Monmouthshire". Most of the rest of the county is firmly and redoubtably Welsh, but the woodlands and hills by the meandering River Wye have more in common with the landscape over the border. The two main towns are decidedly English in flavour: **Chepstow**, at the mouth of the Wye, with its massive castle radiating an awesome strength; and **Monmouth**, sixteen miles upstream, a spruce, old-fashioned town with the lingering air of an ancient seat of authority.

Six miles north of Chepstow lie the inspirational ruins of the Cistercian **Tintern Abbey**, worth seeing at odd hours when the crowds of coach-trippers have evaporated. Surrounding the abbey are some beautiful walks through the bluebell woods and old oak forests on a spit of land sandwiched by the river bend, rising high above the ruins. Running parallel to the river, albeit on the English side of the border, the southern segments of the **Offa's Dyke** earthworks are closely followed by a long-distance footpath.

Chepstow

Of all the places that call themselves "the gateway to Wales", the old border town of **CHEPSTOW** (Cas-Gwent) has probably the greatest claim, being the first town on the main road into Wales on the immediate Welsh side of the border. Situated on the western bank of the River Wye, just over a mile from where its tidal waters flow out into the muddy Severn estuary, Chepstow is a sturdy place with little of the immediate charm or quirkiness of many other Welsh market towns. This is partly due to the scale of soulless modern developments in the town centre that have combined to overwhelm the remaining buildings in streets still laid out in an identifiably medieval pattern.

Arrival, information and accommodation

Trains between Cardiff and Birmingham stop at Chepstow's **train station**, five minutes' walk to the south of the High Street. The town's **bus station** is on Thomas Street on the other side of the West Gate, and has frequent services to Newport but only one every couple of hours to Tintern and Monmouth. The **tourist office** is located in the castle car park, off Bridge Street (daily: Nov–Easter 10am–1pm & 2–4pm; Easter–Oct 10am–6pm; ☎01291/623772, *www.chepstow.co.uk*). **Bike rental** is available over the border at Pedalabikeaway Cycle Centre in Cannop Valley (☎01594/860065); they'll deliver if they're not too busy. **Accommodation** is not especially abundant, though a few good places do exist.

Afon Gwy, 28 Bridge St (☎ & fax 01291/620158). Comfortable B&B above a good restaurant and bar – some of the spacious, nicely decorated en-suite rooms have river views. ②.

Castle View Hotel, 16 Bridge St (☎01291/620349, fax 627398, *mart@castview.demon.co.uk*). Unexciting but spacious en-suite rooms with satellite TV – some afford views of the castle. ④.

First Hurdle Guesthouse, 9 Upper Church St (☎01291/622189, fax 628421). Rooms in this large B&B have bathrooms, firm beds and attractive decor; full breakfast is included. ②.

George Hotel, Moor St, next to the West Gate (☎01291/625363, fax 627418). Stately, even stiff old place with well-appointed rooms and a ground-floor bar and restaurant. Considerable savings for weekend two-night stays. ⑤.

Mrs Batchlor, 7 Lancaster Way (☎01291/626344). In a modern house around fifteen minutes' walk from the centre of town towards Tintern, this reliable B&B is Chepstow's cheapest. ①.

St Briavels Castle YHA hostel (☎01594/530272, *stbriavels@yha.org.uk*). Superb youth hostel set in a moated Norman castle seven miles northeast of Chepstow, actually over the border in England.

Upper Sedbury House, Sedbury Lane (☎01291/627173). Wonderful, friendly B&B a mile east over the Wye, that's particularly good for long-distance walkers, as the owners will let you leave your car for a small fee, a service even extended to those not staying. ①.

The Town

Chepstow's position as a former river port is evident in the thirteenth-century **Port Wall**, encasing the castle precincts and the town centre in their loop of the river. The fifteenth-century **West Gate** bisects the **High Street**, a handsome thoroughfare sided by Georgian and Victorian buildings and sloping down from the gate towards the river. Here, an elegant five-arch cast-iron **bridge**, built in 1816, is still in use for cross-border traffic into England. A short street with a riverside esplanade, The Back runs southeast from the bridge past a couple of pubs and the *Wye Knot* restaurant, where a plaque commemorates the quay as the site from which the three leaders of Newport's Chartist March of 1839 were dispatched to Van Diemen's Land (Tasmania). Opposite, a Union Jack flag is provocatively daubed on the English side of the river cliffs – a feature since 1935 and regularly repainted.

Bridge Street leads from the old bridge up towards the main entrance of **Chepstow Castle** (April, May & Oct daily 9.30am–5pm; June–Sept daily 9.30am–6pm; Nov–March Mon–Sat 9.30am–4pm, Sun 11am–4pm; £3; CADW). As a strategic siting, the castle can scarcely be bettered. Built tight into a loop of the River Wye, it guards one of the most important routes into Wales. Chepstow was the first stone castle to be built in Britain, with its first Norman incarnation, the Great Tower keep, rising in 1067, just one year after William the Conqueror's victory at Hastings. William had realized the importance of subduing the restless Welsh, creating borderland Marcher Lordships and encouraging the title holders to expand into Welsh territory: a succession of Chepstow's lords attempted this, necessitating renewed and increasingly powerful fortification of their castles over the ensuing two hundred years. Ownership of both title and castle passed to the earls of Norfolk and then Pembroke, who retain the fortress to this day.

The walled castle is comprised of three separate enclosures, the Lower Ward being the largest and dating mainly from the thirteenth century. Here, you'll find the **Great Hall**, home to a wide-ranging exhibition on the history of the castle, incorporating genuine and replica armour from various stages of the castle's past, with particular emphasis on the English Civil War years, when Royalist Chepstow was twice besieged.

Twelfth-century defences separate the Lower Ward from the Middle Ward, which is dominated by the still imposing ruins of the **Great Tower**, whose lower floors include the original Norman keep. Beyond the Great Tower is the far narrower Upper Ward which leads up to the Barbican **watch tower**, from which there are some superlative and vertiginous views looking back over the castle and down the cliff to the mudflats of the river estuary.

Opposite the castle is a crimson-painted Georgian town house containing the **Chepstow Museum** (Mon–Sat 11am–1pm & 2–5pm, Sun 2–5pm; £1). The displays concern themselves with local life, with nostalgic photographs and paintings of the trades supported in the past by the River Wye, and records of Chepstow's brief life in the early part of the twentieth century as a shipbuilding centre. Quality temporary exhibitions change frequently.

Once you've exhausted the charms of Chepstow, you could follow the fairly challenging, two-hour **Wye Valley Walk** to Tintern Abbey (see below), which starts from the castle car park. A map – or a £1 leaflet available from the tourist office – is advisable, as the path tucks and meanders around and above the twisting Wye. You could return along the other side of the river on the Offa's Dyke Path (see p.236), which passes the dramatic viewpoint of Devil's Pulpit (just off the B4228) and reaches its southern end at Sedbury Cliffs, a mile or so east of town on the English side of the border.

Eating and drinking

With a handful of decent **restaurants**, and a host of good **pubs**, some by the river, you'll do fine for a night or two in Chepstow.

Afon Gwy, at 28 Bridge St (☎01291/620158). Smart conservatory restaurant overlooking the river, castle and floodlit bridge, and serving moderately priced meals such as chicken tikka basket with raita or aubergine stuffed with Mediterranean vegetables.

Boat Inn, The Back. Enormously convivial waterside pub with a good, vegetarian-friendly menu.

Caramelle Patisserie & Chocolatier, St Mary's St. First stop for clotted cream fudge, yogurt-coated dates and the wonderful Sidoli's ice cream.

Castle View Hotel (see opposite). Highly rated hotel restaurant serving succulent meals such as pan-fried red snapper for under £10, and also offering lighter lunches.

Five Alls, High St. Genuine local inn with a friendly atmosphere and one of the best pub signs around.

Wye Knot, The Back (☎01291/622929). Chepstow's finest with pricey gourmet meals served on linen tablecloths adorned with fresh flowers. Highlights include grilled goat's cheese with a tapenade dressing or fillet of turbot in sherry cream with wild mushrooms and asparagus.

Tintern Abbey

Six miles north of Chepstow on one of the River Wye's most spectacular stretches, **Tintern Abbey** (April, May & Oct daily 9.30am–5pm; June–Sept daily 9.30am–6pm; Nov–March Mon–Sat 9.30am–4pm, Sun 11am–4pm; £2.40; CADW) has inspired writers and painters for over two hundred years, ever since the Reverend William Gilpin published a book in 1782 extolling the picturesque qualities of the abbey and its valley. On a quiet day, the sight of the soft, roofless ruins is hugely uplifting; the "tall rock/The mountain, and the deep and gloomy wood" written about by Wordsworth are still evident today. Such is the abbey's enormous popularity, however, that in the middle of a summer's day, the magic can all but evaporate: it is better to go out of season or at the beginning or end of the day when the crowds have thinned out.

The abbey lasted as a monastic settlement from its foundation by the Cistercian order in 1131 to its dissolution in 1536, and the original order of monks was brought wholesale from Normandy, its members establishing themselves as major local landholders and agriculturalists. This increased the power and wealth of the abbey, attracting more monks and necessitating a massive rebuilding and expansion plan in the fourteenth century, when Tintern was at its mightiest. Most of the remaining buildings date from this time, after which the influence of the abbey and its order began to wane. Upon dissolution, many of the buildings were plundered and stripped, leaving the abbey to crumble into advanced decay. Its survival is largely thanks to its remoteness, as there were no nearby villages ready to use the abbey stone for rebuilding. From the eighteenth century onwards, travellers searching for a picturesque rather than religious experience have been attracted to the romantically placed, ivy-clad ruins; and a trip to Tintern was essential for the Romantics – Wordsworth and Turner amongst them.

The centrepiece of the complex was the magnificent Gothic **church**, built at the turn of the fourteenth century to encase its more modest predecessor. The bulk of the building remains, with the remarkable tracery in the west window and intricate stonework of the capitals and columns firmly intact; amazingly, these details withstood both the elements and the efforts of plundering raiders over four hundred years. Behind the great east window, the sharply rising slopes of the wooded valley form a perfect backdrop.

Around the church are the less substantial ruins of the **monks' domestic quarters**, mostly reduced to one-storey rubble. Rooms are easily distinguishable, however, including an intact serving hatch in the kitchen and the square of the monks' **cloister**. The course of the abbey's waste disposal system can be seen in the **Great Drain**, an irregular channel that links kitchens, toilets and the infirmary with the nearby Wye. The **Novices' Hall** lies handily close to the Warming House, which, together with the kitchen and infirmary, would have been the only heated parts of the abbey, suggesting that novices might have gained a falsely favourable impression of monastic life before taking their final vows. In the dining hall, you can still see the **pulpit door** that would once have led to the wall-mounted pulpit, from which a monk would read the scriptures throughout each meal.

The best way to appreciate the scale and splendour of the abbey ruins is by taking a walk on the opposite bank of the Wye. Just upstream from the abbey, a bridge crosses the river, from where a path climbs a wooded hillside. Views along the way and from the top are magnificent, framing the gaunt shell of the abbey in its sylvan setting.

Four miles northwest of the ruins, the sleepy hilltop settlement of **TRELLECH** (literally "three stones") was one of the largest boroughs in the vicinity. Reminders of its ancient status abound: there's a thirteenth-century steepled church on a seventh-century site, and, nearby, the curious **Tump**, an ancient mound that, legend has it, cannot be disturbed without deadly reprisal. A few hundred yards further south, by the B4293 Llanishen road, are the three **stones** of the village's name. Also known as Harold Stones, the straining fingers of rock, around 3500 years old and thrusting up in the middle of a sheep-filled field, are thought to be aligned with the Skirrid mountain, Monmouthshire's holiest. Off the lane to Tintern, you'll find the **Virtuous Well**, long a place of pilgrimage, with reputed healing qualities that probably stem from the water's high iron content.

Practicalities

Now cluttered with teashops and overpriced hotels, the tiny village of **TINTERN** (Tyndyrn), immediately north of the abbey, is strung along a mile or so of the A466 around a loop of the river. The principal **visitor centre** (April–Oct daily 10am–5pm; ☎01291/689566) is located another few hundred yards towards Monmouth at the **Old Station** complex. Amongst the amenities here are an interesting exhibition on the old Wye Valley railway and a good selection of leaflets on local walks, including sections of the Offa's Dyke path (see p.236) and cliff rambles above the meandering river. B&B **accommodation** is available locally at the excellent *Wye Barn* on The Quay (☎01291/689456; ②), or slap opposite the abbey, in the sumptuous *Beaufort Hotel*

(☎01291/689777, fax 689727; ④). *Parva Farmhouse Hotel*, on the A466(☎01291/689411, fax 689557; ④), is deservedly renowned for its **food**, while at Trellech, you can eat well at both the *Lion Inn* and the *Village Green* restaurant (☎01600/860119). Those looking to pitch a **tent** can do so in the paddock behind the Old Station in Tintern for a small fee; facilities extend as far as a water pipe and toilets.

Monmouth

Enclosed on three sides by the rivers Wye and Monnow, **MONMOUTH** (Trefynwy) retains some of its quiet charm as an important border post and one-time county town. Now bypassed by the A40 dual carriageway which shoots along the banks of the Wye, Monmouth has few reminders of the twentieth century, save for its occasionally traffic-choked streets.

The centre of the town is **Agincourt Square**, a large and handsome open space at the top of the wide, shop-lined Monnow Street, gently descending to a distinctive thirteenth-century bridge over the River Monnow. The cobbled square is dominated by old coaching inns on either side of the arched Georgian **Shire Hall** – the facade boasts an eighteenth-century statue of the Monmouth-born King Henry V, victor at the 1415 Battle of Agincourt, which brought Normandy (and soon afterwards France) under the rule of the English crown. In front of the Shire Hall is a rather pompous statue of another local, the Honourable Charles Stewart Rolls, who in 1910 became the first man to pilot a double-flight over the English Channel, and also co-founded the Rolls-Royce empire.

Almost opposite Shire Hall is **Castle Hill**, which you can walk up to glimpse some of the ruins of the **castle**, founded in 1068, rebuilt in stone in the twelfth century and almost annihilated in the Civil War. The only notable part of the castle that remains is the Great Tower, in which Henry V is thought to have been born in 1387. Next to the castle, the gracious seventeenth-century **Great Castle House**, built from castle bricks, now serves as the headquarters of the Royal Monmouthshire regiment. Their history is celebrated in the **Regimental Museum** (April–Oct daily 2–5pm; Nov–March Sat & Sun 2–4pm; free) along with material from archeological digs – note the oddly shaped twelfth-century bone dice which definitely wouldn't pass muster in Vegas, and a small kitchen garden arranged around a medlar tree.

Priory Street leads north from Agincourt Square to the market hall complex, which contains the **Nelson Museum** (Mon–Sat 10am–1pm & 2–5pm, Sun 2–5pm; £1), an attempt to portray the life of one of the most successful seafaring Britons through use of the Admiral's personal artefacts – sword, medals, intimate letters and china – together with pictures, prints and naval equipment of the day. Charles Rolls' mother, Lady Llangattock, was an ardent admirer of Nelson and a voracious collector of related memorabilia, and it is her collection now on display in the museum.

At the very bottom of Monnow Street, a couple of hundred yards from Agincourt Square, the road narrows to squeeze into the confines of the seven-hundred-year-old **Monnow Bridge**, crowned with its hulking stone gate of 1262, that served both as a means of defence for the town and a toll collection point. Just over a mile east of Monmouth, a steep road climbs up to **The Kymin** (daily dawn–dusk; free; NT), a fine viewpoint over the town and the Wye Valley. It's crowned by the crenellated Georgian Round House and a Neoclassical **Naval Temple**, built in 1801 to cheer Britain's victories at sea.

Practicalities

Buses operate from the **bus station** behind Kwik Save at the bottom of Monnow Street, and the **tourist office** is in the Shire Hall, Agincourt Square (daily: April–Oct 10am–6pm; Nov–March 9.30am–5.30pm; ☎01600/713899). **Bike rental** is available for around £15 per day from Monmouth Cycle Centre (☎01600/772779) behind the tourist office at 5 Beaufort Arms Court.

Accommodation in town is thin on the ground, though you'll do well at the simple but very competent *Burton Guesthouse* on St James' Square (☎01600/714958, fax 772498; ①), and at the intimate *Riverside Hotel* on Cinderhill Street over the Monnow Bridge (☎01600/715577, fax 712668; ③). Two miles south in the village of Mitchel Troy is the excellent *Church Farm Guesthouse* (☎01600/712176; ②). The nearest tent-friendly **campsites** are both on Drybridge Street (through Monnow Bridge then right): the *Monnow Bridge* (☎01600/714004) is behind the *Three Horseshoes* pub, while the slightly pricier *Monmouth Caravan Park* (☎01600/714745) is a quarter of a mile beyond.

Monnow Street contains an assortment of fast-food joints. For daytime **eating** you're better off at either *The Maltsters Coffee Shop* on St Mary's Street for good coffee and sandwiches, or at *Cygnet's Kitchen*, in White Swan Court off Church Street, which serves more substantial soups and casseroles, and has outside seating. The *French Horn* (☎01600/772733), handsomely situated at 24 Church St, serves French lunch and dinner dishes for around £13, or you can opt for pub grub at the *Punch House* in Agincourt Square; the same sort of fare is cheaper at the *Green Dragon* in St Thomas Square, down by the Monnow Bridge.

Monmouth is also home to a staggering number of **pubs**: worth trying are *The Bull* in Agincourt Square, the young and lively *Nag's Head*, at the bottom of Whitecross Street in St James' Square, and the *Robin Hood*, on Monnow Street near the bridge, where Shakespeare is said to have drunk. If transport is no problem, a superb pub lies three miles south of Monmouth off the A466 in the Wye Valley: to get to *The Boat*, in the English hamlet of Redbrook, cross the border into England, and once at Redbrook, return to Welsh ground via a dizzying footbridge over the River Wye, built on to the side of the disused rail bridge. The bizarre journey is worth it, for the pub is usually home to some amazing characters, liable to strike up a live jazz or folk session at the drop of a woolly hat.

The Three Castles

The fertile, low-lying land north of Monmouth, between the Monnow and the River Usk, was important as an easy access route into the agricultural lands of south Wales, and the Norman invaders built a trio of strongholds here to protect their interests. **Skenfrith**, **Grosmont and White castles** (all CADW) were founded in the eleventh century, and lie within an eight-mile radius of each other.

The size and splendour of the castles demonstrates their significance in protecting the border lands from both the restless English and disgruntled Welsh, who first attacked nearby Abergavenny Castle in 1182, prompting King Ralph of Grosmont to rebuild the three castles in stone. In July 1201, the three were presented as a unit by King John to Hubert de Burgh, who fought extensively on the continent and brought back sophisticated new ideas on castle design to replace earlier models with square keeps. He rebuilt Skenfrith and Grosmont, and his successor as overlord, Walerund Teutonicus ("the German"), worked on White Castle. In 1260, the advancing army of Llywelyn ap Gruffydd began to threaten the king's supremacy in south Wales, and the three castles were refortified in readiness.

Gradually, the castles were adapted more as living quarters and royal administrative centres than military bases, as the Welsh began to adapt to English rule. The only return to military usage came in 1404–05, when Owain Glyndŵr's army pressed down to Grosmont, only to be defeated by the future King Henry V. The castles slipped into disrepair, and were finally sold by the Duchy of Lancaster to the Duke of Beaufort in 1825. The Beauforts sold the three castles off separately in 1902, the first time since 1138 that the three had fallen out of single ownership.

White Castle

Named for its coating of white rendering (a few patches remain on the exterior walls), **White Castle** (Castell Gwyn; May–Sept 10am–5pm; £2; Oct–April unrestricted access) lies about eight miles west of Monmouth, just north of the insignificant village of Llantilio Crossenny. The most awesome of the three castles, it's situated in open, rolling countryside with some superb views over to The Skirrid mountain (see Central Wales, p.218) and the hills surrounding the River Monnow. Entering the grassy Outer Ward, enclosed by a curtain wall with four towers, gives an excellent view over to the brooding mass of the castle, situated neatly in a moat on the Inner Ward. A bridge leads over the moat into the dual-towered Inner Gatehouse, where the western tower, on the right, can be climbed for its sublime vantage point. Here, you can appreciate the scale of the tall twelfth-century curtain walls in the Inner Ward. The arrow slits in the walls are unusually cross-shaped, a distinctive feature of the castle's thirteenth-century rebuilding. Of the domestic buildings within the walls, only the foundations and a few inches of wall remain. At the back of the ward, there are massive foundations of the Norman keep, demolished in about 1260 and unearthed in the early part of the twentieth century. The southern wall that took the place of the keep was once the main entrance to the castle, as can be seen in the postern gate in the centre, on the other side of which a bridge leads over to the Hornwork, one of the castle's three original enclosures, although now no more than a grassy mound.

Skenfrith Castle

Seven miles northeast of White Castle, alongside the River Monnow, the thirteenth-century **castle** (unrestricted access), in the centre of the tiny border village of **SKENFRITH** (Ynysgynwraidd), is dominated by the circular keep that replaced an earlier Norman incarnation. While not as impressive as White Castle, Skenfrith is in a pretty riverside setting on the main street of an attractive village.

The castle's walls are built of a sturdy red sandstone in an irregular rectangle. In the centre of the ward is the 21-foot-high round keep, raised slightly on an earth mound to give archers a greater firing range, and containing the vestiges of the private apartments of the castle's lord on the upper floors; most notable are the huge fireplace and private latrine. Along the west curtain of the wall are the excavated remains of the Hall Range of domestic buildings, including an intact thirteenth-century window, complete with its original iron bars.

Grosmont Castle

Five miles upstream of Skenfrith, right on the English border, the most dilapidated of the Three Castles, **Grosmont Castle** (Castell y Grysmwnt; unrestricted access) sits on a small hill above the village of **GROSMONT**. Entering over the wooden bridge above the dry moat, you first pass through the ruins of the two-stage gatehouse. This leads into the small central courtyard, dominated on the right-hand side by the ruins of a large Great Hall, dating from the first decade of the thirteenth century. The ground-floor rooms were lit by lancet windows with widening stepped sills, as can still be seen. The village **church** is also worth a look, with some impressive Norman features, most notably the nave arches and the font. A memorial in the nave is popularly believed to be of John Kent, a fifteenth-century bard and magician sometimes believed to have been Owain Glyndŵr in hiding.

Practicalities

Though you can drive around all three castles in a couple of hours, the nature of this peaceful countryside makes a more sedate mode of transport preferable. Bikes can be rented in Monmouth (or Abergavenny; see p.215) for a pleasant day-long outing, or you can hike the eighteen-mile circuit of paths detailed in a **booklet** (£3.50 from the tourist offices) which, along with route information, covers the history, points of interest, pubs and accommodation along the way.

Accommodation in the area is largely in farmhouse B&Bs, many of them excellent. Half a mile north of White Castle, in the village of Llanvetherine, is the very friendly *Great Tre-Rhew Farm* (☎01873/821268; ①), and the fractionally cheaper *Brooke Cottage* (☎01873/821315; ①). Of local pubs, pride of place goes to the *Hostry Inn* in Llantilio Crossenny for its excellent **food**.

Mid-Monmouthshire

The confrontational past of the middle tranche of Monmouthshire, long-disputed border country, can be gleaned from the castles that dot the landscape with dependable regularity. This section of the county is noticeably more "Welsh" than the border country of the Wye Valley. Stretching up from the wide-skied marshland that falls gently into the Severn estuary, the land reaches the flat, ugly settlement of **Caldicot**, only notable for its over-restored castle. The A48 runs from the border into south Wales, connecting **Caerwent**, a near-deserted village that was once a great Roman town, and **Penhow**, crowned by a homely fortified manor that guarded the quiet valley.

To the north is an undulating land of forests and tiny villages, crisscrossed by winding lanes that offer unexpectedly delightful views – and quaint hostelries – around each corner. The contours shelve down in the west to the valley of the **River Usk**, the former border of Wales as decreed in the sixteenth century by Henry VIII. Today, the A449 road roars through the valley, bypassing lanes, villages and the peaceful small town of **Usk**, home of the excellent Gwent Rural Life Museum, before joining the A40 near the spectacular ruins of **Raglan** castle.

Caldicot

Sandwiched between the main motorway and rail links between south Wales and London, **CALDICOT** is a sprawling, overgrown village of modern housing and little interest. The only possible exception is the heavily restored **castle** (March–Oct Mon–Sat 10.30am–5pm, Sun 1.30–5pm; £1.50), on the eastern side of the village. Built in the twelfth century as one of the Norman Marcher castles, constructed to keep a wary eye on the Welsh, the buildings crumbled in the years leading up to the 1800s, before being rebuilt by a wealthy Victorian barrister, Joseph Cobb. The only original parts are a large fourteenth-century round tower and elaborate gatehouse, situated either side of a grassy courtyard, whose centrepiece is one of Nelson's battle cannons from his *Foudroyant* flagship. The castle buildings contain exhibitions of local history, together with an impressive furniture collection from the seventeenth to the nineteenth centuries. Rather pricey medieval banquets (☎01291/424447, *www.castle-ents.u-net.com*) take place throughout the summer, and if you decide you need to stay within staggering distance, the en-suite rooms at *Lychgate* (☎01291/422378; ①) at 47 Church Rd (opposite the castle entrance) are an amenable option.

Caldicot is the first sight of Wales for train travellers using the main line from London, and now for drivers using the second Severn bridge crossing (£4.20 toll westbound) from Bristol on the English side of the estuary. Recently constructed access roads have, to some degree, eaten into one of Wales' most unexpected landscapes to the southwest of Caldicot: the pancake-flat lushness of the **Caldicot Levels**, great for gentle cycling, walking and poking around the tiny villages and ancient churches that loom large on the landscape. The best place to appreciate the area's tranquillity is at **Goldcliff**, a straggle of houses petering out by the mudflats of the estuary. Here, you can walk along the sea walls and watch diving sea birds and fishermen competing for the same catch.

Caerwent

Two miles northwest of Caldicot lies the apparently unremarkable village of **CAER-WENT**, from which the former county of Gwent took its name. Almost two thousand years ago, the village was known by the Romans as *Venta Silurum*, the "market town of the Silures", a local tribe forcibly relocated here from a nearby hillfort by the conquering Romans in around 75 AD, after 25 years of battle.

The most complete remnants of the Roman town are the crumbling **walls** which form a large rectangle around the modern village. Access is easiest from the steps next to the *Coach and Horses* pub, leading you up onto stone ramparts that still command melancholic views around the quiet valley. The South Wall is the most complete, still maintaining its fourth-century bastions, and it continues around to the old West Gate. Halfway along, a lane cuts up towards the rather ugly tower of the village **church**: maps and diagrams in the porch explain the site of the village, and you can also see two inscribed stones, one a dedication from the Siluri tribe to their Roman overlord, Paulinus, and another, dedicated to Ocelus Mars, demonstrating the odd merging of Roman and Celtic gods for worship. Opposite the church, on the village's main street, the shin-high, rectangular outline of a Roman temple has been excavated. Nowadays, Caerwent sits on top of an altogether more contemporary military occupation, as the home of Europe's largest American rocket base at the neighbouring RAF station.

Penhow

There's another castle three miles west of Caerwent in the hamlet of **PENHOW**, whose neat church sits next to a fortified moated manor house on top of a grassy hillock. The manor house is known as **Penhow Castle** (Aug Wed–Sun 10am–5.15pm; Easter–July & Sept Wed–Sun 10am–5.15pm; Oct–Easter Wed 10am–4pm; £3.60), and its buildings are an accumulation of styles from the twelfth to the fourteenth centuries. The house is privately owned and claims to be the oldest lived-in castle in Wales, originally built for the St Maur family, a name later corrupted to Seymour. Accompanied only by your choice of headset commentary – historical, social, kids, period music, etc – a tour of the castle begins at the impressive, thick-set Norman keep, the castle's oldest section and the family's private apartments from 1129, now filled with period trimmings such as rush lights and sporting clubs that give a credibly authentic feel. The tour continues through a tiny, narrow passage into the fifteenth-century Great Hall, complete with a minstrel gallery decorated with the Seymour family wings. Steps lead up to the Seymour bedchamber, with one step deliberately built an inch higher than the others, a common ploy in medieval days to trip up intruders. The tour concludes chronologically, passing through some of the Regency-style lodging rooms and finally through into a cluttered Victorian kitchen and nursery.

One seventeenth-century section of the building has been converted into a guest bedroom in period style; rates include breakfast (☎01633/400800, *castles@ compuserve.com*; ⑤).

Usk

Bypassed by the main A449, the peaceful, orderly little town of **USK** (Brynbuga) sits astride the river of the same name. Pastel-painted houses, shops and some great pubs and restaurants line narrow Bridge Street, which leads up from the river and crosses towards the castle, looming up on a hilltop to the left. Opposite the ivy-clad ruins is the hub of the town, **Twyn Square**, where buses stop amongst the copious garish flower boxes that surround the twee restored clock tower. At the top of the square is a thirteenth-century **gatehouse**, once part of a Benedictine nunnery, and now guarding the passage to the impressive twelfth- and thirteenth-century church. There are surviving features from its days as a nunnery in the 1200s, including the nave and the slightly later tower.

Forking to the right off Bridge Street near the river is New Market Street, which runs past the **Gwent Rural Life Museum** (April–Oct Mon–Fri 10am–5pm, Sat & Sun 2–5pm; £1.50), housed in a converted eighteenth-century malt barn and specializing in the period from the early 1800s up until the end of World War II. The enormous collection has been put together over many decades by hundreds of local residents, and it's fascinating. Aspects of farming are explained in a pleasantly haphazard way: everything from animal-castrating implements to re-creations of domestic and farming interiors – including a dairy, brewery, laundry, thatcher's and carpentry workshop – are packed into every available corner, and outdoor barns continue the exhibition with farm carts, stagecoaches and an exhibition about the Great Western Railway. Give yourself a good few hours to take it all in.

Practicalities

Usk is a quiet, enjoyable place to **stay**, with good pubs for evening entertainment. The cheapest **accommodation** is the hostel-style *Usk Centre of Agriculture* (☎01291/672311 ext 25; ①), a mile from town on the A472 Pontypool road. High above this road, three miles west of Usk, *Pentwyn Farm* (☎01495/785249; ②) at Little Mill is a great farmhouse B&B, with superb optional dinners and an outdoor pool. For something a little special try *Glan-yr-Afon House Hotel*, Pontypool Road (☎01291/672302, fax 672597; ⑥), an elegant and gracious country house five minutes' walk west of town. There are **campsites** two miles southeast of Usk at the *Grass Ski Centre* in Llanllowell (☎01291/672652), and four miles north at *Cwm Farm*, in Bettws Newydd (☎01873/840263).

Most of the town pubs serve **food** – the best being *King's Head* on Old Market Street, closely followed by the *Nag's Head* in Twyn Square and the cheap and immensely cheerful *Inn Between* at 53 Bridge St. Otherwise, Bridge Street is lined with small cafés, delis and the excellent, moderately priced *Vineyard at Usk*, at no. 7 (☎01291/672459; closed Sun & Mon), as well as the reasonable *Bush House* at no. 15 (☎01291/672929), serving French, Mediterranean and Welsh dishes, with several vegetarian options. For down-to-earth **drinking**, try the *Inn Between* or the genial *White Hart*, on the corner of Bridge and Maryport streets.

Raglan

Numerous buses leave Usk every day for **RAGLAN** (Rhaglan), seven miles to the north and also easily reached from Monmouth. An unassuming village wallowing in the folds of the hills, Raglan is worth visiting for its glorious **castle** (June–Sept daily 9.30am–6pm; April, May & Oct daily 9am–5pm; Nov–March Mon–Sat 9.30am–4pm, Sun 11am–4pm; £2.40; CADW), whose fussy and comparatively intact style makes a change from so many other crumbling Welsh fortresses. The last medieval fortification built in Britain, Raglan was begun on the site of a Norman motte in 1435 by Sir William ap Thomas, whose design combines practical strength with ostentatious style. Various descendants added to the castle after his death, and building carried on into the late sixteenth century.

The **gatehouse** is still used as the main entrance, and the best examples of the castle's showy decoration appear in its heraldic shields, intricate stonework edging and gargoyles. Inside, stonemasons' marks, used to identify how much work each man had done, can be seen on the walls. Ap Thomas' grandson, William Herbert II, was responsible for the two inner courts, built in the mid-fifteenth century around his grandfather's original gatehouse, hall and keep. The first court is the cobbled **Pitched Stone Court**, designed to house the functional rooms like the kitchen (with two vast double-flued chimneys) and the servants' quarters. To the left is **Fountain Court**, a well-proportioned grassy space once surrounded by opulent residences that included grand apartments and state rooms. Separating the two are the original 1435 **hall**, the **buttery**, the remains of the **chapel** and the dank, cold **cellars** below.

Off Fountain Court, through the South Gate, is the pristine **bowling green**, standing on twelve-foot-high walls above the Moat Walk, and reached by a flight of stone steps from the green. The moated yellow ashlar **Great Tower**, off Fountain Court, demonstrates continental influences in its construction, and gives it a surprisingly contemporary appearance. Two sides of the hexagonal tower were blown up by Cromwell's sidekick Fairfax after an eleven-week onslaught against the Royalist castle in 1646. The tower can still be climbed, however, right to its peak, giving phenomenal views over the green water of the moat, the intricate detail of the castle masonry and the smooth hills beyond.

Newport and around

The westernmost slice of Monmouthshire is wildly varied, from the lofty and windswept peaks of the northern segment around Abergavenny to the grit and industry of the valley towns in the south. Dominating the latter is **NEWPORT** (Casnewydd-ar-Wysg), Wales' third-largest town, a downbeat, working-class place that grew up around the docks at the mouth of the Usk.

The town's rich history has been largely swept away by the twentieth century, and at times, Newport can be thoroughly depressing, but isolated nuggets of antiquity remain, particularly the scant ruins of the riverside **castle** and, high on a hill over the town, the church of St Woolos which was only elevated to cathedral status in 1921. The superb municipal **museum** draws together the strings of the town's vibrant past, including a memorable and informative section on the nineteenth-century **Chartist movement**, formed to fight for universal franchise. The pearl of the district is **Caerleon** – the "old port" on the River Usk – now little more than a northern suburb of the town, although it predates Newport by at least a thousand years. Its well-preserved remains constitute one of the most important Roman military stations in Britain, though some venerate it more for its reputed association with King Arthur.

The Town

Scything the town in two is the River Usk, foul and muddy as the tidal waters flow down to the Severn estuary, three miles away. Wedged in between the rail and main road bridges are the pathetic remains of the town's **castle**, first built in 1191, rebuilt in the fourteenth century, sacked by Owain Glyndŵr in 1402 and refortified later in the same century. Apart from its remarkably uncongenial position, the castle is notable for the sheer drop down to the mudflats of the estuary and the vaulted ceiling still retained in the central tower.

On the other side of the Newport Bridge, a walkway leads along the river bank past Peter Fink's giant red 1990 sculpture, **Steel Wave**, a nod to one of Newport's great industries. The main route into the town centre proper is up the pedestrianized High Street, which shortly meets the main crossroads at Westgate Square. Here stands the **Westgate Hotel** (currently closed for redevelopment), an ornate Victorian successor to the hotel where soldiers sprayed a crowd of Chartist

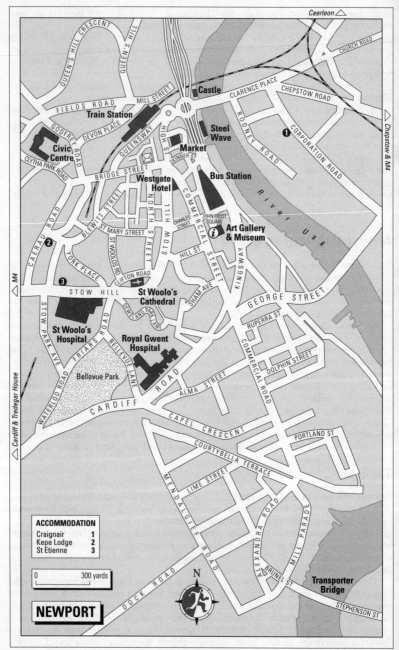

NEWPORT

© Crown copyright

THE CHARTISTS

In an era when wealthy landowners bought votes from the enfranchised few, the struggles of the Chartists were a historical inevitability. Thousands gathered around the 1838 People's Charter that called for universal male franchise, a secret (and annual) ballot for Parliament and the abolition of property qualifications for the vote. Demonstrations in support of these principles were held all over the country, with some of the most vociferous and bloodiest taking place in the radical heartlands of industrial south Wales. On November 4, 1839, Chartists from all over Monmouthshire marched on Newport and descended Stow Hill, whereupon they were gunned at by soldiers hiding in the *Westgate Hotel*, killing around 22 protesters. The leaders of the rebellion were sentenced to death, which was commuted to transportation, by the self-righteous and wealthy leaders of the town. Queen Victoria even knighted the mayor who ordered the random execution.

protesters (see above) with gunfire in 1839, killing at least a dozen – the hotel's original pillars still show bullet marks.

Commercial Street, leading south from Westgate Square, is Newport's main shopping thoroughfare, lined with tatty shops, but beautifully framing the town's famous Transporter Bridge (see below). One hundred yards along Commercial Street, the pedestrianized **John Frost Square** (named after a former mayor and one of the 1839 Chartist leaders) lies to the left. Although no more than an ugly 1960s precinct, the square does contain the distinctly quirky **Newport clock**, originally built for the 1992 Garden Festival at Ebbw Vale. Every hour, the silver mock-temple shudders, shakes, splits, smokes and comes near to apparent collapse, usually drawing an appreciative audience. In front of the clock is the town's library, tourist office and imaginative, well presented civic **museum** (Mon–Thurs 9.30am–5pm, Fri 9.30am–4.30pm, Sat 9.30am–4pm; free). Starting with the origins of Gwent, the displays look at the county's original occupants and their lifestyles, and includes a section on mining with a roll call of those killed in local pit accidents – 3508 men between 1837 and 1927. Newport's spectacular growth from a small Uskside dock in 1801 with a population of 1000 to a grimy port town of 70,000 people by the early twentieth century is well charted through photographs, paintings and contemporary documents. The two most interesting sections deal with the Chartist uprising and the Roman mosaic remains excavated at Caerwent. The top-floor art gallery contains the **Wait Collection** of Edwardian kitsch, most noted for its three hundred-plus teapots in all shapes and sizes. Before leaving John Frost Square, wander across to the far side to see the impressive Chartist mural which outlines their main grievances on banners.

The other road heading south from Westgate Square is **Stow Hill**, one of Newport's few handsome rows of Victorian and Georgian town houses. A ten-minute walk up the hill leads to **St Woolos Cathedral**, a curious jigsaw of architectural styles and periods. The tiny, whitewashed twelfth-century Lady Chapel leads through a superb Norman arched doorway – supported by columns reputedly of Roman origin from Caerleon – into the Norman nave, notable for its clerestory windows, bounded by two fifteenth-century aisles. Sporting a circular east window in a swirl of autumn colours locked in a marbled, round-headed arch that harks back to the Norman features, the modern east end of the cathedral harmonizes well with the rest of the building.

Dominating the Newport skyline is the 1906 **Transporter Bridge** (Mon–Sat 8am–6pm, Sun 1–5pm; car toll 50p, free for cyclists and pedestrians), built to enable cars and people to cross the river without disturbing the shipping channel, hoisting them high above the Usk on a pristine blue dangling platform. Its comical, spidery legs flare out to the ground, connecting Brunel Street on the west bank (reached down Commercial Street and its continuation, Commercial Road) and Stephenson Street opposite. Eccentric it may be, but the ride is smooth and the two-minute crossing has successfully cut commuting times for some since the bridge was reopened in the mid-1990s.

Tredegar House

Buses #15 and #30 go two miles out to the westerly suburbs of Newport and to **Tredegar House** (house Easter–July & Sept Wed–Sun 11.30am–4pm; Aug daily 10.30am–6pm; Oct Sat & Sun 11.30am–4pm; park daily 9am–dusk; house tour & gardens £4, walled gardens & park £1), just off junction 28 of the M4. The home of wealthy local landowners, the Morgan family, from 1402 until 1951, Tredegar and its grounds have been transformed into a recreation park complete with boating and fishing lake and craft workshops. The house itself is an unassuming seventeenth-century pile in warm red brick, built to replace the Morgans' earlier home. Its interior is still in the process of restoration, though some thirty rooms are now open, newly decorated in styles dating from the Victorian era back to the Regency heyday, when Tredegar was one of Wales' most fashionable and exclusive mansions, where royalty and politicians mingled. Of the rooms in the tour, the first-floor Gilt Room is the most memorable: an explosion of glittering fruit bosses, an intricate gilded marble fireplace, mock-walnut panelling and an elaborately painted gold stucco ceiling. The formal walled gardens behind the housekeeper's shop are still in the process of being relaid in patterns culled from eighteenth-century designs.

Practicalities

Newport's **tourist office** is in the museum complex in John Frost Square (daily 9.30am–5pm; ☎01633/842962), a hundred yards from the **bus station** on Kingsway (Newport Transport ☎01633/262914, Stagecoach ☎01633/266336), and a quarter-mile from the **train station** on Queensway.

The range of **accommodation** in Newport is limited, and you might prefer to stay in nearby Caerleon (see opposite). Nonetheless, *Craignair* at 44 Corporation Rd (☎01633/259903; ①) is more than adequate for B&B, and a few pounds cheaper than the genteel *St Etienne*, 162 Stow Hill (☎01633/262341; ②). At the western end of Bridge Street, Caerau Road rises up sharply to the south, passing the relaxed, hospitable *Kepe Lodge* at no. 46a (☎01633/262351; ②). There is a **campsite** at *Tredegar House* (☎01633/815600); see above for bus services.

There are plenty of chain **food** outlets along Bridge and Commercial streets, but downtown is pretty much a culinary desert. For coffee and a light snack, try the *Oriel* café on the top floor of the museum, from where you can view the hourly antics of the Newport Clock. There's more substantial eating by the *Steel Wave* sculpture at *Boyd's*, an American theme restaurant that saves itself with some outside seating by the river. Equally good are the vegetarian *Hunky Dory's* at 17 Charles St, while the *Ristorante Vittorio*, up by the cathedral at 113 Stow Hill (☎01633/840261), is a popular and traditional Italian trattoria – reservations are recommended.

Despite the profusion of **pubs**, none is terribly special: the 1530 *Olde Murenger House*, on the High Street, has a beautiful Tudor frontage spoiled by a tatty interior; the cosy *Lamb*, 6 Bridge St, is popular; and the most spirited pub has to be the *Hornblower* at 127 Commercial St, a raucous biker's pub with some heavy choices of music – not a place for the faint-hearted. Newport is, however, one of the major centres of the buoyant Welsh **rock and dance music** scene. Legendary try-out pub venue is *TJ's*, 14 Clarence Place (☎01633/216608, *www.tjs-newport.demon.co.uk*), where Kurt Cobain proposed to Courtney Love. For a bit of late-night dancing try the youthful *Voodoo* on Bridge Street (☎01633/213138), the older *Zanzibar* (☎01633/250978) at 40 Stow Hill, the studenty *Cotton Club* (☎01633/252973) on Cambrian Road, or *V3*, 18 Stow Hill (☎01633/225555) which occasionally has live music.

Caerleon

Frequent buses wind their way along the three-mile journey north of Newport to **CAERLEON** (Caerllion), whose compact town centre is situated to the immediate northwest of the town bridge over the River Usk. The remnants of the Roman town lie scattered throughout the present-day centre.

It was the Usk (Wysg) that gave Caerleon its old Roman name of Isca, a major administrative and legionary centre built by the Romans to provide ancillary and military services for smaller, outlying camps in the rest of south Wales. Its only near equivalents in Roman Britain were Chester, servicing north Wales and northwest England, and York, dealing with the Roman outposts up towards Hadrian's Wall and beyond. Founded in 74 AD and lasting until its abandonment late in the fourth century, Isca was a garrison housing up to six thousand members of the Second Augustan Legion in a neat, rectangular walled town. Although the settlement fell gradually into decay after the Romans left, there were still some massive remains standing when itinerant churchman and chronicler Giraldus Cambrensis visited in 1188. In his effusive writing about the remains, he noted with evident relish the "immense palaces, which, with the gilded gables of their roofs, once rivalled the magnificence of ancient Rome". Although time has had an inevitably corrosive effect on the remains since Giraldus' time, the excavated bath house and preserved amphitheatre still retain a powerful sense of ancient history.

At the back of the *Bull Inn* car park are the Roman **fortress baths** (April–Oct daily 9.30am–5.15pm; Nov–March Mon–Sat 9.30am–5pm, Sun noon–4pm; £2, £3.30 joint ticket with Legionary Museum; CADW). The bathing houses, cold hall, drain (in which teeth, buttons and food remnants were found) and communal pool area are remarkably intact and beautifully presented, with highly imaginative uses of audiovisual equipment, sound commentary and models. A few steps along the High Street, a Victorian Neoclassical portico is the sole survivor of the original **Legionary Museum** (April–Oct Mon–Sat 10am–6pm, Sun 2–6pm; Nov–March Mon–Sat 10am–4.30pm, Sun 2–4.30pm; £2.10, £3.30 joint ticket with baths), now housed in the modern building behind. There are hundreds of artefacts dug from the remains of Isca and a smaller fortress at nearby Burrium (Usk). These include intricately carved gemstones, lamps, tools, dental equipment, belt buckles, soldiers' amulets, dice, game counters and personal hygiene items such as tweezers and nail cleaners. The museum's new **Capricorn Centre**, although aimed squarely at school parties, is interesting for the re-created Roman barracks where you can try on a typical soldier's armour plating.

Opposite the Legionary Museum, Fosse Lane leads down to the hugely atmospheric Roman **amphitheatre** (unrestricted access), the only one of its kind preserved in Britain. Hidden under a grassy mound called King Arthur's Round Table until excavation work brought it to light in the 1920s, the amphitheatre was built around 80 AD, the same time as the Colosseum in Rome; legions of up to six thousand would take seats to watch the gory combat of gladiators, animal baiting or military exercises. The amphitheatre is backed by grassy stepped walls, on which the members of the legion would sit, tightly packed in, to watch activities in the middle. Over the road, alongside the school playing fields, are the scant foundations of the legion's **barracks**.

The belief that Caerleon was the seat of King Arthur's court is a long-standing one. Lord Tennyson came here to research the rumours, and today, you can do no better than wander around the sublime **Ffwrrwm Centre** (most shops daily 9.30am–5.30pm), off the High Street, and talk to the various traders there who subscribe passionately to the belief. Whatever, the Ffwrrwm is a very special place: stunning courtyard sculptures draw their inspiration from ancient Celtic and Arthurian lore, surrounded by some great craft and New Age shops and a wonderful café-cum-bistro. Near the entrance to the complex, you can even clasp the gold horns of a Welsh fertility bull, an act that is supposed to lend you untold powers of procreation.

Practicalities

Caerleon's **tourist office** (daily: April–Oct 10am–6pm, Nov–March 10am–4.30pm; ☎01633/422656, *www.caerleon.co.uk*) lies next to the legionary museum on High Street. A far wider range of information can be found in the various outlets in the Ffwrrwm Centre (see overleaf), notably in the gateside antique shop and the delightful Celtic Spirit shop.

Staying in Caerleon is a more amenable option than nearby Newport. There's central, shared-bathroom B&B at *Pendragon*, 18 Cross St (☎01633/430871; ②), and the fractionally pricier *Great House* on Isca Road (☎01633/420216; ②). If you want a private bathroom, you've a choice of surprisingly good rooms at the Caerleon campus of the *Gwent College of Higher Education* (late June to mid-Sept; ☎01633/430088; ②), fifteen minutes' west along High Street (beyond the Legionary Museum), and the plush *Priory Hotel* (☎01633/421241; ⑤) opposite the baths on Main Street.

By far the best place to **eat** is the *Oriel* bistro (☎01633/430238) in the Ffwrrwm courtyard, with outdoor seating in summer and a roaring fire in winter. It's normally a daytime venue, but will open in the evenings for group bookings if called in advance. Alternatively, the *Olde Bull Inn* on the High Street is good for food, drink and live entertainment, and you can follow in the footsteps of Lord Tennyson by eating and drinking at the *Hanbury Arms*, at the bottom of the High Street above the river.

The Valleys

No other part of Wales is as instantly recognizable as **the Valleys**, a generic name for the string of settlements packed into the narrow cracks in the mountainous terrain to the north of Newport, Cardiff and Swansea. Coming through Monmouthshire, the change from rolling countryside to sharp contours and a post-industrial landscape is almost instantaneous, though the greenery evident today is a far cry from the slag heaps and soot-encrusted buildings of thirty or more years ago.

Each of the valleys depended almost solely on coal mining, and though it's more or less defunct today, the industry has left its mark on the staunchly working-class towns, where row upon row of brightly painted terraced housing, tipped along the slopes at some incredible angles, are broken only by austere chapels, the occasional remaining pithead or the miners' old institutes and drinking clubs.

This is not traditional tourist country, and yet is without doubt one of the most interesting and distinctive corners of Wales. Some of the former mines have re-opened as gutsy and hard-hitting museums, with **Big Pit** at Blaenafon and the **Rhondda Heritage Park** at Trehafod being the most absorbing. Other civic museums, at **Pontypool**, **Pontypridd** and **Merthyr Tydfil**, have grown up over decades, chronicling the lives (and, all too frequently, the deaths) of miners and their families. A few older sites, such as vast **Caerphilly Castle** and the sixteenth-century manor house of **Llancaiach Fawr**, have been attracting visitors for hundreds of years. But it is beyond the mainstream sights that the visitor can gain a more rounded impression of valley life, whether in the Utopian workers' village at **Butetown**, the roundhouses at **Nantyglo**, fortified against an anticipated workers' uprising, the iron gravestones of **Blaenafon**, the dignified memorials found in almost every community to those who died underground or, in the heartrending case of **Aberfan**, when a loose slag tip buried a primary school, and nearly 150 people, in 1966. South Wales, perhaps more than any other part of Britain, demonstrates the true cost of being the world's first industrialized nation.

Now much cleaned up, the Valleys combine unique sociological and human interest with staggering beauty in the sheer hills that rise behind each community. As a result of the formidable terrain, each valley was almost entirely isolated. Canals, roads and train lines competed for space along the valley floor, petering out as the contours

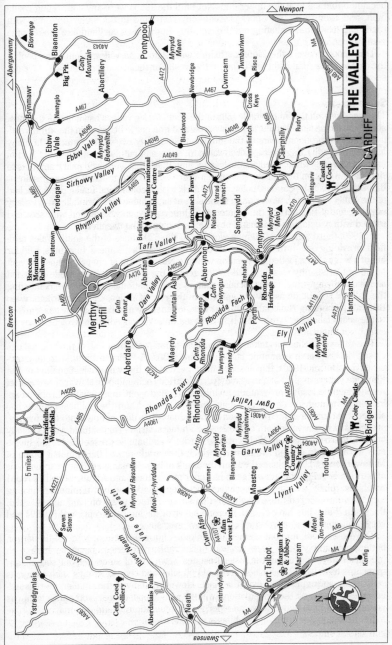

THE VALLEYS

became untameable at the upper end. Not until the 1920s were any connecting roads built, and even today, transport is frequently restricted to the valley bottoms, with roads and train lines radiating out through the south Wales coalfield like spokes on a giant wheel.

This section covers the Monmouthshire and Glamorgan valleys from Pontypool in the east to Cwm Afan and Port Talbot in the west. For the account of the Vale of Neath, see p.120.

Some history

The land beneath the inhospitable hills of the south Wales valleys had some of the most abundant and accessible natural seams of coal and iron ore to be found in the world, readily milked in the boom years of the nineteenth and early twentieth centuries. In many instances, wealthy English capitalists came to Wales and ruthlessly stripped the land of its natural assets, while simultaneously exploiting those that were paid paltry amounts to risk life and limb in the mines. The mine owners were in a formidably strong position – thousands of Welsh peasants, bolstered by their Irish, Scottish and Italian peers, flocked to the Valleys in search of work and some sort of sustainable life. The Valleys – virtually unpopulated at the start of the nineteenth century – became blackened with soot and packed with people, pits and chapels by the beginning of the twentieth.

In 1920, there were 256,000 men working in the 620 mines of the south Wales coalfield, providing one-third of the world's coal resources. Vast Miners' Institutes, paid for out of a wages' levy, jostled for position with the Nonconformist chapels, whose fervent brand of Christianity was matched by the zeal of the region's politics, trade-union-led and avowedly left-wing. Great socialist orators rose to national prominence, cementing the Valleys' reputation as a world apart from the rest of Wales, let alone Britain. Even Britain's pioneering National Health Service, founded by a radical Labour government in the years following World War II, was based on a Valleys community scheme by locally born Aneurin Bevan.

The Valleys' decline has taken place in rapid bursts, with over half of the original pits closing in the harsh economic climate of the 1930s. A Welsh cabinet secretary proposed in the mid-1930s that losses could be cut by the wholesale flooding of the Rhondda valleys as part of a massive hydroelectricity scheme. World War II saw a brief respite in the closure programme, which continued even more swiftly in the years immediately after. As coal seams have been exhausted and the political climate has shifted, the number of men employed in the industry has dipped down into four figures, precipitated by the aftermath of the 1984–85 miners' strike. No coalfield was as solidly behind the strike as south Wales, whose workers and families responded wholeheartedly to the call to defend the industry which their trade union, the National Union of Mineworkers (NUM), claimed was on the brink of being decimated. The year-long war of attrition between the intransigent Thatcher government and Arthur Scargill's NUM was bitter, finally seeing the government victorious as the number of miners returning to work outnumbered those staying out on strike. Fifteen years on, and all but one of the south Wales pits have closed, the sole survivor having been reprieved in 1994 and very profitably run as a workers' co-operative ever since.

The Valleys without coal seemed unthinkable, but nonetheless, some of the larger, better-populated valleys have staged considerable recoveries: Japanese high tech industries have moved into industrial estates hewn out of smoothed-out slag heaps, museums have been established at the old pit sites and civic amenities such as sports centres are springing up all over the place. However, many of the smaller, more isolated valleys have seen their population dwindle, with shops, chapels and pubs closing as young people have fled to leave an older, ex-pit generation behind that may well prove to be the last major group of inhabitants in some towns.

Pontypool

The first identifiably Valleys town – although never a coal-mining centre – heading west is **PONTYPOOL** (Pontypŵl), on the Llwyd River that winds up from the Usk at Caerleon. A sprawling, hilly town, it's hardly likely to keep you busy for long, although it's worth finding time for a short stop at the **Valley Inheritance Museum** (Mon–Sat 10am–5pm, Sun 2–5pm; £1.20), housed in a Georgian stable block at the western entrance of Pontypool Park. The building was attached to the estate of a mansion belonging to the Hanbury family, local landowners and industrial pioneers, and the museum casts a wide net over the town's history and trades, all of which seems to have sprung from the one family. Founding father Richard Hanbury (1538–1608), the exhibition dryly notes, was a true entrepreneur, "but on occasion his enterprise led to prison sentences for fraud". The Hanburys established Pontypool's staple tinplate-making industry which led, in turn, to elaborate japanning and thence to ironworking. The museum makes a good starting point for a stiff but short hike up the side of the valley to a couple of products of Victorian whimsy (both May to early Sept Sat, Sun & bank holidays 2–5pm; free): the **Shell Grotto** (30min), with its interior completely plastered in molluscs; and the more traditional **Folly Tower** (20min further).

A rare surviving feature of Valleys towns can be found in Pontypool, in the shape of the steamy *Mario's Café* at the bottom of Broad Street. Italian emigrants flocked to south Wales in the nineteenth century, many shunning mining and opening quite grand chrome-plated coffee houses. As successive generations have abandoned the family business, cafés have closed all over the Valleys, but *Mario's* has remained.

Pontypool's **train station** is inconveniently situated over a mile to the east of the town centre, making **buses**, which stop by the handsome Victorian town hall, a far easier option.

Blaenafon and around

Road and river continue six miles north from Pontypool to the iron and coal town of **BLAENAFON**, at the source of the Llwyd River. With a lofty hillside position making it feel far less claustrophobic, Blaenafon has a very different feel to many valley towns, but its decline is testified by a shrinking population of little more than 5000, a quarter of its nineteenth-century size. The town's Victorian boom can be seen in its architecture, most notably the impressively florid **Working Men's Hall** that dominates the town centre, and where miners would pay a halfpenny a week for the use of the library and other recreational and educational facilities. The parish **church of St Peter** is a good example of what became known as Enginehouse Churches – an enginehouse being the sole type of building familiar to local masons. If it's open, wander in to see the tomb covers, pillars and even the font, all fashioned out of iron. Just downhill from the church the town's contracting nature has forced the post office and local hot bread shop to join forces under one roof.

Blaenafon's **tourist office** just off the Brynmawr Road (April–Oct Mon–Fri 9.30am–4.30pm, Sat 10am–5pm, Sun 10am–4.30pm; ☎01495/792615), shares a building with the town's **ironworks** (same hours and phone; £1.50; group tours all year, minimum £20; CADW). Though the works were founded in 1788, iron smelting in this area dates from the sixteenth century. Limestone, coal and iron ore – ingredients for successful iron smelting – were locally abundant, and during the early nineteenth century, the Blaenafon works grew to become one of the largest in Britain, finally closing in 1900. The remains of the site offer a thorough picture both of the process to produce iron and the workers' lifestyles that went with it. At the **museum**, housed in the Stack Square cottages (built for the foremen and craftsmen between 1789 and 1792), there are exhibitions on the history of iron- and steel-making in the Llwyd Valley. Unless you're on a pre-booked guided tour, you'll have to content yourself with staring from the viewing area at the awesome sight of the line of late Georgian blast furnaces and the adjoining water-balance lift, where water diverted from a stream was used to lift the iron from the site onto tramlines and thence to the canal.

Big Pit

Just as it is now possible to visit the scene of Blaenafon's iron industry, the town's defunct coal trade has also been smoothly transformed into a tourist attraction: **Big Pit** (March–Nov daily 9.30am–5pm, last underground tour 3.30pm; £5.75, surface tour only £2) lies three-quarters of a mile west of the town in wide, open countryside; a half-hourly shuttle bus runs from Blaenafon. The colliery closed exactly a century after its 1880 opening. Of all the mining museums in south Wales, Big Pit brings the visitor closest to the experience of a miner's work and life, as you descend 300ft, kitted out with lamp, helmet and very heavy battery pack, into the labyrinth of shafts and coal faces for a guided tour. The guides – most of whom are ex-miners – lead you through explanations and examples of the different types of coal mining, from the old stack-and-pillar operation, where miners would manually hack into the coal face before propping up the ceiling with a wooden beam, to more modern mechanically worked seams. Constant streams of rust-coloured water flow by, adding to the dank and chilly atmosphere that must have terrified the small children who were once paid twopence for a six-day week (of which one penny was taken out for the cost of their candles) pulling the coal wagons along the tracks. Back on the surface, the old pithead baths, blacksmiths, miners' canteen and winding engine house have all been preserved and filled with some fascinating displays about the local and south Wales mining industries, including a series of characteristically feisty testimonies from the miners made redundant here in 1980.

Out on the rolling moorland by the entrance of the pit, the old mine train line has been brought partly back into use and is now known as the **Pontypool and Blaenafon steam railway** (April–Sept Sun & bank holidays only 11am–4pm; £2), worth taking for the couple of hundred yards to the evocative *Whistle Inn*, once the main pub for the miners, but now dependent on tourists. The atmosphere is unashamedly nostalgic, with a vast collection of miners' tin lamps hanging from the ceiling.

The Sirhowy Valley and Ebbw Vale

West of Pontypool and Blaenafon, the settlements of the **Ebbw Vale** are hemmed in by some of the Valleys' best forest scenery. Particularly popular is the **Cwmcarn Forest Drive** (Easter–Aug daily 11am–7pm; Sept daily 11am–6pm; Oct Sat & Sun 11am–5pm; £2.50), reached from the main A467 in **CWMCARN** village, two miles north of workaday **RISCA** (Rhisga), where the Sirhowy and Ebbw valleys divide. The drive is a seven-mile circuit affording magnificent views over the old pit towns and the distant sparkle of the Severn estuary. Just before the start there's a café and **visitor centre** (April–Sept daily 10am–6pm; Oct–March daily 10am–5pm; ☎01495/272001) and a nice grassy **campsite** (☎01495/272001) where you can pitch a tent for £5. Along the route, near Car Park 7, is the Iron Age hillfort of **Twmbarlwm**. A small cairn on the summit suggests its earlier use as a Bronze Age burial ground and the site's defensive position was also exploited by Roman and Norman settlers.

The Ebbw valley divides into two just short of **ABERTILLERY**, which sits at the foot of the Ebbw Fach, the smaller of the two valleys. High above the divide, a mile to the east, is the twelfth-century hilltop church of **St Illtyd**, commanding superb views all round. There's little to keep you in Abertillery itself, although you might consider continuing through to the sprawling upland settlement of **NANTYGLO**, four miles north. Signposted on the western edge of the town are two remarkable fortified

roundhouses, built in the nineteenth century by the local ironmaster, Joseph Bailey, an English Anglican renowned for his harsh treatment of workers. Bailey was fearful enough of insurrection to build these mini-castles in 1816, complete with four-feet-thick walls and iron plate doors with musket holes.

From Risca, the Sirhowy River winds west past the village of **CWMFELINFACH** before turning north to run parallel with Ebbw Vale. The obligatory **country park**, on the forested slopes to the south of the village, offers some good walks and a **camping barn** (☎01495/270991); the main entrance lies off the big roundabout at the suburb of **Crosskeys**, where the valleys divide. Three miles north, the Sirhowy town of **BLACKWOOD** (Coed Duon) is home to one of the most splendid of the Valleys' many **Miners Institutes** (☎01495/227206), now the well-restored home of theatre, choirs and music, including (in this, the birthplace of the Manic Street Preachers) numerous rock and dance events.

Caerphilly and the Rhymney Valley

Travelling west, the next major settlement is **CAERPHILLY** (Caerffili), seven miles north of Cardiff and at the foot of the **Rhymney Valley**. The only feature of any interest in this flattened and colourless town is its **castle** (June–Sept daily 9.30am–6pm; April, May & Oct daily 9.30am–5pm; Nov–March Mon–Sat 9.30am–4pm, Sun 11am–4pm; £2.50; CADW), with an inner system of defences overlooking the outer ring, all looming out of its vast surrounding **moat**. The castle is striking for its sheer bulk and for being the first in Britain to be built concentrically. Occupying over thirty acres, the medieval fortress with its cock-eyed tower presents an awesome promise that's not entirely fulfilled inside. Built on the site of a Roman fort and an earlier Norman fortification, the castle was begun in 1268 by Gilbert de Clare, who wanted to protect the vulnerable coastal plains around Cardiff from the warring of Llywelyn the Last. Two years later, Llywelyn largely destroyed the castle, which was swiftly rebuilt, but for the next few hundred years, Caerphilly was little more than a decaying toy, given at whim by kings to their favourites – most notably by Edward II to his minion, and some say lover, Hugh le Despenser, in 1317. The Civil War necessitated the building of an armoury within the castle, which prompted Cromwell to seize it, drain the moat and blow up the towers. By the early twentieth century, Caerphilly Castle was in a sorry state, sitting amidst a growing industrial town that saw fit to build in the moat and the castle precincts. Houses and shops were demolished to allow the moat to be reflooded in 1958.

You enter the castle through a great **gatehouse** that punctuates the barbican wall by a lake, much restored and now housing an exhibition about the castle's history. A platform behind the barbican wall exhibits medieval war and siege engines, pointing ominously across the lake. From here, a bridge crosses the moat, part of the wider lake, to the outer wall of the castle itself, behind which sits the hulking inner ward. On the left is the southeastern tower, outleaning its rival in Pisa and with a great cleft in its walls where Cromwell's men are said to have attempted to blow it sky high. It now seems that Cromwell had less to do with the tilt than common old subsidence, but the story is too good to pass up. With the exception of the ruined northeastern tower, the other corner turrets have been blandly restored since the Civil War, with the northwestern tower housing a reasonably interesting exhibition designed to give a thorough overview of Welsh castles, their methods of construction and some speculative facts and figures about the day-to-day life of their medieval inhabitants. More interesting is the massive eastern gatehouse, which includes an impressive upper hall and oratory and, to its left, the wholly restored and reroofed **Great Hall**, largely built around 1317 by Hugh le Despenser.

Caerphilly is also, of course, known for its crumbly white **cheese**, which is made the traditional way at several dairies around town and sold in the shop below the **tourist**

office, opposite the castle entrance (daily: Jan–Easter 10am–4pm; Easter–Oct 10am–6pm; Nov & Dec 10am–5pm; ☎029/2088 0011, *www.caerphilly.gov.uk*). Both the castle and the tourist office are a five-minute stroll down Cardiff Road from the **bus** and **train stations**. **Accommodation** nearby includes the excellent self-catering rooms right by the castle at *The Courtyard*, Nantgarw Road (☎029/2086 6666; ③), and the three-hundred-year-old *The Cottage Guest House* (☎029/2086 9160, *thecottage@tesco.net*; ③) on the roundabout a mile north of the castle on the A468, a quality B&B with en-suite rooms. Caerphilly is hardly noted for its **eating**, but the *Courthouse* inn on Cardiff Road, overlooking the castle, serves a great-value ploughman's and assorted pub meals; and you shouldn't pass up the *Maenllwyd Inn* (☎029/2088 2372), outside the village of **Rudry** some three miles east of Caerphilly, which serves an astounding array of imaginative – if not always successful – meals and ales in very cosy surroundings. Reservations are recommended.

The Rhymney Valley

North of Caerphilly, the Rhymney Valley becomes increasingly industrialized as it steers past a seamless succession of small towns and rotting industry. There's little reason to stop until **NEW TREDEGAR**, twelve miles north of Caerphilly, where the **Elliot Colliery Winding House** (Easter–Oct Sat, Sun & bank holidays 2–5pm; £1), with its gleaming steam engine that once powered the colliery's high speed lifts is worth half an hour of your time.

At the very head of the valley, a mile beyond Rhymney town and just short of the A465 Heads of the Valleys road, is **BUTETOWN** (Drenewydd), a tiny settlement utterly different from any other in the area. Built as a model workers' estate in 1802–03 by the Marquess of Bute, a member of Wales' richest land- and resource-owning family, the town was originally conceived as the beginning of a whole new, airy workers' community. His idealism was unusual amongst the ironmasters and coal owners of the day and, sadly, only the central grid of houses was built. Two ironworkers' cottages in the main street have been converted into **Drenewydd museum** (Easter–Oct Sat, Sun & bank holiday Mon 2–5pm; £1; other times by appointment on ☎01685/843039), a small local affair detailing life for nineteenth-century employees, still arduous despite the uplifting surroundings.

A mile east of Butetown, the **Bryn Bach Country Park**, on the northern edge of the close-knit little town of **TREDEGAR**, has an attractive **campsite** by a small lake, with showers and visitor-centre-cum-café.

The Taff and Cynon valleys

Like the Rhymney, the River Taff also flows out into the Bristol Channel at Cardiff, after passing through a condensed 25 or so miles of industry and population that obscure the former **china works** at Nantgarw. The first town in the Taff vale is **Pontypridd**, one of the most cheerful in the Valleys, and where the Rhondda River (see p.88) hives off west. Continuing north, the river splits again at **Abercynon**, where the Cynon River flows in from Aberdare, site of Wales' only remaining deep mine. Just outside Abercynon is the enjoyable sixteenth-century **Llancaiach Fawr** manor house, while to the north, the Taff is packed into one of the tightest of all the Valleys, passing **Aberfan** five miles short of the imposing valley head town of **Merthyr Tydfil**.

Nantgarw

Barrelling north along the A470, you'd never suspect that the **China Works Museum** (Tues–Sun 10am–5pm; £1) lurks behind a copse of trees at **NANTGARW**. For less than five years in the 1810s, the pottery here produced some of the finest porcelain in the world, the few florid examples on display only serving to whet your appetite for the extensive collection in the National Museum in Cardiff. Master porcelain painter William Billingsley set up the works with high ambition using Valleys coal and Cornish clay, but the extremely difficult "soft paste porcelain" process resulted in just a ten percent firing success rate and the enterprise soon folded. Production at the site continued in a more workaday fashion with the manufacture of clay smoking pipes and field drains until it finally shut up shop in the 1920s. One of the firing kilns has now been rebuilt and the main building contains small displays on the process and the history of the site.

Pontypridd

PONTYPRIDD's quirky arched **bridge** of 1775 was once the largest single-span stone bridge in Europe. It was built by local amateur stonemason William Edwards, whose previous attempts had crumbled into the river below. His final effort stands to this day, its three holes either side designed to lessen the bridge's overall weight and allow gusty winds through.

On the other side of the river is **Ynysangharad Park**, where Sir W. Goscombe John's gooey double statue and tomb in honour of Pontypridd weaver Evan James and his son represents allegorical figures of music and poetry. In 1856, James composed the stirring *Mae Hen Wlad Fy Nhadau* (*Land of My Fathers*) that has become the Welsh national anthem.

By the bridge at the end of Taff Street, the **Pontypridd Historical and Cultural Centre** (Mon–Sat 10am–5pm; 25p) is housed in what was the town's chapel. Built in 1861, it has been lovingly restored, and boasts unusually ornate ceiling bosses, pillars, pulpit, stained-glass window and organ that all contribute to the reverential atmosphere. The centre's contents amount to what is one of the best museums in the Valleys – a real treasure trove of photographs, video, models and exhibits that succeed in painting a warm and human picture of the town and its outlying valleys. There are exhibitions of old Pontypridd in photographs and paintings, transport in the area, and records from the nearby Albion colliery, at which 290 men and boys died in an underground explosion in 1894. Pontypridd is the home town of crooner Tom Jones and opera star and actor Sir Geraint Evans, both celebrated amongst the exhibitions here.

Near the elegant and impressive train station, **John Hughes' Grogg Shop** on Broadway caricatures legions of rugby stars and Welsh celebrities in oddball sculpture, and a short walk past the pubs at the bottom of Taff Street brings you out parallel to Market Street and the chaotic bustle of the old-fashioned **market** which spills out into the surrounding streets and squares on Wednesday and Saturday, the main trading days. If you're here on Tuesday or Friday night, pop along to Tabor Hall in the Pwllgwaun suburb of Pontypridd to listen to the local **male voice choir**, which starts rehearsing at 7.30pm.

Pontypridd is one of the best bases in the Valleys, as it is well connected to bus, train and road networks. The **train station** is a ten-minute walk south of the old bridge on The Graig. The **tourist office** (Mon–Sat 10am–5pm; ☎01443/409512 or 402077) is in the Historical and Cultural Centre on Bridge Street. **Accommodation** is rather scarce: in town try the sedate *Millfield Hotel* in Mill Street (☎01443/480111; ②) or the *Morning Star* B&B on The Graig (☎01443/486594; ①), both near the station. If you want to stay right in the thick of the action, try the bustling *Market Tavern* on Market Street (☎01443/485331; ①). Generally, though, more appealing options lie three or four miles away close to Llancaiach Fawr Manor (see overleaf).

Food options are fairly basic, with a huddle of cheap takeaways and restaurants opposite the station and along Taff Street – one to note is *Prince's*, a busy mix of tearoom, restaurant and patisserie. There's also a hearty café in the Muni Arts Centre on Gelliwastad Road, above Taff Street. while the *Maltsters Arms*, by the bridge over the river, serves good meals and ales in a friendly atmosphere. For **drinking**, make for the musical *Globe*, behind the station up on Graig High Street; the lively *New Inn* on Market Street; or, just over the bridge from the Heritage Centre, the *Llanover Arms* on Bridge Street.

Llancaiach Fawr

The river divides at **Abercynon**, four miles up the Taff valley, with the Cynon River flowing in from Aberdare in the northwest. Abercynon is a stark, typical valley town of punishingly steep streets lined with blank, grey houses, fading out into a coniferous hillside. Two miles east of Abercynon, just north of the village of **NELSON**, is the six-teenth-century **Llancaiach Fawr Manor** (Tues–Fri 10am–5pm, Sat 10am–6pm, Sun noon–6pm; £4.50; ☎01443/412248), a Tudor house, built around 1530, that has been transformed into a living-history museum set in 1645, the time of the Civil War, with all of the guides dressed as house servants and speaking the language of seventeenth-century Britain. Although there is great opportunity for the whole experience to be night-marishly tacky, it is quite deftly done, with well-researched period authenticity and numerous fascinating anecdotes from the staff; visitors are even encouraged to try on the master of the household's armour. Special tours – candlelit, murder-mystery and seventeenth-century evenings – are also available. Regular buses from Pontypridd, Cardiff and Ystrad Mynach station pass the entrance.

If you want to **stay**, try the well kept and extremely friendly *Fairmead* guesthouse almost opposite the manor (☎01443/411174; ②); not too far away, there's the tradition-ally styled, floral *Llechwen Hall* (☎01443/742050, fax 742189; ④ including breakfast) which sits high on the hills to the south of Nelson, signposted off the A470 a couple of miles north of Pontypridd. *Llechwen* also serve inexpensive bar meals and moderately priced dinners.

The Welsh International Climbing Centre

Entire towns devastated by pit closures are commonplace hereabouts, but **BEDLINOG**, nine miles north of Pontypridd, has thumbed its nose at decline by open-ing the **Welsh International Climbing Centre**, Taff Bargoed Centre (daily 10am–10pm; ☎01443/710749). With what looks like acres of vertical and overhanging surfaces towering sixty feet from the floor of a purpose-built hanger, this is the largest indoor climbing wall in Europe. The **climbing wall** (£6.50 peak, £4.50 weekdays before 5pm) is mainly geared towards experienced climbers, but there are stacks of boulder-ing sections for simply mucking around on, and beginners are catered for with an all-day family introductory package (£35) that includes tuition and practice time. Exercise rooms and a sauna are available, there's a restaurant and bar open at weekends and evenings and even hostel beds in small, clean dorms. The centre is signposted off the A470 at Abercynon; the Belindog bus will get you here eventually from Cardiff, but if you call ahead, someone will pick you up from the train station at Edwardsville on the well-trafficked Cardiff to Merthyr line.

Aberfan

North of Abercynon, the Taff valley contains one sight that is hard to forget: the two neat lines of distant arches that mark the graves of the 144 people killed in October 1966 by an unsecured slag heap sliding down a hill and onto the Pantglas primary school in the village of **ABERFAN**. Thousands of people still make the pilgrimage to the village graveyard, to stand silent and bemused by the enormity of the disaster. The human cost – including 116 children who died huddled in panic at the beginning of their school day – is beyond comprehension. Amongst the gravestones that strive to rationalize the tragedy, one of the most humbling and beautiful valedictions is to a ten-year-old boy, who, it simply records, "loved light, freedom and animals". Official enquiries all told the sorry tale that this disaster was an almost inevitable eventuality, given the cavalier approach to safety so often displayed by the coal bosses. Gwynfor Evans, then the newly elected first Plaid Cymru MP in Westminster, spoke with well-founded bitterness when he said "let us suppose that such a monstrous mountain had been built above Hampstead or Eton, where the children of the men of power and wealth are at school . . .". That, of course, could never have happened.

Merthyr Tydfil

MERTHYR TYDFIL sits in a shallow bowl of hills at the top of the Taff valley, on the cusp of the industrial Valleys to the south and the grand, windy heights of the Brecon Beacons to the north. Though it's a robust and enjoyable town today, Merthyr's appeal lies in its fascinating, unique pedigree.

Merthyr's strategic site was first exploited by the Romans as an outpost of their base at Caerleon (see p.77). In 480 AD, Tydfil, Welsh princess and daughter of Brychan, Prince of Brychianog, was captured as she rode through the area, and murdered for her Christian beliefs. She became St Tydfil the Martyr, and her name was bestowed on the scattered population of the area.

In the seventeenth century, the village became a focal point for Dissenters and Radicals, movements which, through poverty and crass inequality, gained momentum in the eighteenth century as the town's four massive ironworks were founded to exploit locally abundant seams of iron ore and limestone. Merthyr became the largest iron-producing town in the world, as well as by far the most populous town in Wales: in 1831, the town had a population of 60,000, more than Cardiff, Swansea and Newport combined. Workers flocked from all over Britain and beyond, finding themselves crammed into squalid housing whilst the ironmasters built themselves great houses and palaces on the better side of town. Merthyr's radicalism bubbled furiously, breaking out into occasional riots and prompting the election of Britain's first socialist MP, Keir Hardie, in 1900. It was here that the first red flag was raised, when rioters in 1831 gathered around a standard dipped in the blood of a killed calf.

However, the town's precipitous development saw it peak and trough earlier than other places: of the four mighty ironworks, only one was still open at the end of World War I, and that closed in the 1930s. In 1939, a Royal Commission suggested that the town be abandoned and the inhabitants shifted to the coast. The plan was forgotten when war broke out.

The Town
The town centre is wedged in between the High Street and the River Taff, but the sights listed here are all around the Taff to the immediate northwest. The **Ynysfach Engine House** was once the powerhouse behind the mighty Cyfartha ironworks. It's now been opened up to the public – to arrange access, call the castle (see overleaf); you'll pay £1 to go in – with costumed mannequins portraying scenes from Merthyr's past as a centre of iron and steel making, and an entertaining video about the town's industrial history. The overall effect is gritty, with a special look at the social conditions in the urban chaos of the nineteenth century.

Half a mile further up the River Taff, tucked amongst modern houses just off Nant-y-Gwenith Street (the lower end of the Neath Road), is **Chapel Row**, a line of skilled ironworkers' cottages built in the 1820s. One of these holds composer **Joseph Parry's Birthplace** (March–Sept Thurs–Sun 2–4pm; Oct–March enquire in advance at the castle, see overleaf; 60p), though this mini-museum is most interesting as a social record of slightly better-than-average workers' domestic conditions of the nineteenth century. Parry's music, including the national favourite *Myfanwy*, is piped between rooms, and the upstairs section of the house is given over to a display of his life and music.

Back across the other side of the river, just beyond the Brecon Road, is a home in absolute contrast to Parry's humble and cramped birthplace: **Cyfartha Castle** (April–Sept daily 10am–5.30pm; Oct–March Mon–Fri 10am–4pm, Sat & Sun noon–4pm; £1.60), built in 1825 as an ostentatious mock-Gothic castle for William Crawshay II, boss of the town's original ironworks. It's set within an attractive, 160-acre park that slopes down to the river and once afforded Crawshay a permanent view over his iron empire. Cyfartha's current incarnation, though, is as a museum, and a great one at that: going through the well-re-created Valleys Italian café takes you down into the old wine cellars for a gutsy history of the town. Starting with tales of the martyr Tydfil, the Penydarren Roman fort and ruined Morlais Castle, the narrative soon leads into Merthyr's industrial and political heritage. Merthyr's place in working-class history is well examined, with an interesting set of panels and pamphlets on the 1831 riot. Other exhibits look at Aberfan, the 1984–85 miners' strike, pubs and the temperance movement as well as the beleaguered 1980s Sinclair C5 car, constructed here at the Hoover plant – "built by Hoover, driven by suckers" as the local phrase had it.

Upstairs, the castle's opulent main rooms, all chandeliers and acres of curtains, now house a superb collection of Welsh and international art. Welsh highlights include an uncharacteristically gentle study of *The Elf* by monumental sculptor Goscombe John, and works by local painters Penry Williams, Augustus John, Cedric Morris, Kyffin Williams and Alfred Jones, whose double portrait of Salome is quite mesmerizing. Works by other artists – Jack Yeats and Edward Burne-Jones among them – complement mementos from Crawshay's empire.

The surrounding park contains landscaped walks, a plant nursery, café, bowling green, tennis courts, a pitch-and-putt course and a stage set next to the main lake. You can rent a bike here, too.

Practicalities

The **train station** is on the east of the town centre, a minute's walk from the High Street. North from here is Glebeland Street and the **bus station**, where services depart for all parts of south and mid-Wales. The **tourist office**, 14a Glebeland St (Mon–Sat 9.30am–5.30pm; ☎01685/379884), is behind the bus station. Municipal **bike rental** (☎01685/371555) is available in the summer from Cyfartha Castle.

Accommodation is varied, including the unpretentious *Tregenna Hotel* in Park Terrace, next to Penydarren Park (☎01685/723627; ③); there are humbler surroundings at the *Hanover Guest House*, 31 Hanover St (☎01685/379303; ①), or the *Penylan*, 12 Courtland Terrace (☎01685/723179; ①). There's a **campsite** four miles north of town in the beautiful surroundings of *Grawen Farm*, Cwmtaf, near Cefn-Coed (☎01685/723740).

There are plenty of daytime **food** outlets in the main shopping area of the town centre, with a few cafés, Chinese and Indian restaurants open into the evening along the High Street. At the bottom of the High Street, the *Fountain Tearooms* is good for sandwiches and cappuccino, and the nearby *Crown Inn* has good bar food. You could also try the historic *Three Horseshoes Inn* on Dynevor Street, where up to three hundred Chartists once crammed into the small bar. Either of these will also prove amenable for a night's **drinking**, as will the downbeat *Belle Vue* and lively *Narrow Gauge Inn*, both on Glebeland Street.

The Rhondda

For many people, the twin valleys of the **Rhondda** – each sixteen miles long and never as much as a mile wide – are the essence of all that the region stands for. Others may disagree, but the Rhondda was certainly the heart of the massive south Wales coal industry, an industry that provided around one-third of the entire world's coal, and it's here that you'll find the region's quintessential heritage distilled into straggling hillside communities. Hollywood played its part in promoting the area, with the Oscar-winning weepie *How Green Was My Valley*, although the story was based on author Richard Llewellyn's early life in nearby Gilfach Goch, strictly speaking outside the valley.

In 1860, tentative mining explorations had taken place in Rhondda's quiet, fertile land, and the two valleys housed around 3000 people. By 1910, nearly 160,000 were squeezed into the available land, in ranks of houses grouped around sixty or so pit-heads. The Rhondda, more than any other of the Valleys, became a self-reliant, hard-drinking, chapel-going, deeply poor and terrifically spirited breeding ground for radical religion and firebrand politics. The Communist Party ran the town of Maerdy (nick-named "Little Moscow" by Fleet Street in the 1930s) for decades. The 1984–85 miners' strike saw solidarity in the Welsh pits on a greater scale than any other part of Britain. But the last pit in the Rhondda, the heart of the coal-mining industry, closed four days short of Christmas in 1990. Left behind is not some dispiriting ragbag of depressing towns, but a range of new attractions, cleaned-up hillsides and some of the friendliest pubs and working men's clubs to be found anywhere in Britain. Hillwalking, with astounding views over the tight little towns, is now serious business.

The Rhondda starts just outside **Pontypridd**, winding through the mountains along-side train line, road and river for a few miles to **TREHAFOD** and the colliery museum of the **Rhondda Heritage Park** (April–Sept daily 10am–6pm; Oct–March Tues–Sun 10am–6pm; last admission 4.30pm all year round; £5.50), formed by locals when the Lewis Merthyr pit closed in 1983. You can explore the engine winding houses, lamp room, fan house and a simulated "trip underground", with stunning visuals and sound effects, re-creating 1950s and late nineteenth-century life (and death) through the eyes of colliers. A chilling roll call of pit deaths and a final narration by Neil Kinnock about the human cost of mining – especially for the Valley women – are very moving. The Trehafod **train station** is just a five-minute walk from the Heritage Park.

The Rhondda's two valleys divide at the solid town of **PORTH** ("Gateway"), a mile beyond the museum. The Rhondda Fach (Small Rhondda) River twists its way north-wards through the smaller and frequently forgotten valley of the same name, passing endless archetypal Valleys towns like Ynyshir, Pontygwaith, Tylorstown, Ferndale and

MALE VOICE CHOIRS

Fiercely protective of its reputation as a land of song, the voice of Wales is most commonly heard amongst the ranks of **male voice choirs**. Although they can be found all over the country, it is in the southern, industrial heartland that they are loudest and strongest. The roots of the choirs lie in the Nonconformist religious traditions of the seventeenth and eighteenth centuries, when Methodism in particular swept the country, and singing was a free and potent way of cherishing the frequently persecuted faith. Throughout the breakneck industrialization of the nineteenth century in the Glamorgan valleys, choirs of coal miners came together to praise God in the fervently religious way that was typical of the packed, poor communities. Classic hymns like *Cwm Rhondda* and the Welsh national anthem, *Mae Hen Wlad Fy Nhadau* (*Land of My Fathers*), are synonymous with the choirs, whose full-blooded interpretation of them continues to render all other efforts insipid.

The collapse of coal mining in the twentieth century has left a few choirs perilously short of members, although most continue to practise with almost religious devotion, performing in Wales and abroad with regularity. Each small Valleys town has its own choir, most of whom happily allow visitors to sit in on rehearsals. The Wales Tourist Board issues a leaflet, available from tourist offices, which gives contact phone numbers for each choir's secretary. Contact them directly, and take the chance to hear one of the world's most distinctive choral traditions in full, roof-raising splendour.

Maerdy – row after row of tiny houses clinging grimly to sheer valley walls. **Rhondda Fawr (**Big Rhondda) stretches from the outskirts of Pontypridd to Blaenrhondda and is blessed with a train line, a decent road and most of the sights.

The first notable settlement is **TONYPANDY**, birthplace of Lord George Thomas, former honey-tongued Speaker of the House of Commons. Tonypandy is a mile short of **LLWYNYPIA**, wedged in by walkable forested hillsides. From here, a steep two-mile climb leads up to **Mynydd y Gelli**, where remains of an Iron Age hut settlement and a Bronze Age burial chamber and stone circle can be seen.

On the other side of the valley from Llwynypia, a sheer path climbs up to the notorious 1960s hilltop estate of **PENRHYS**, built as a lofty antidote to the wedged-in valley settlements all around. Unfortunately, the Sixties optimism rapidly disintegrated, leaving a sink estate exposed to the worst of the weather and beset by bad services and numerous social problems. On the hillside looking down into the Rhondda Fawr, you can see the grotty Catholic shrine and well of **St Mary** by the main road in Penrhys. The road, river and train line wind tortuously past an endless stream of towns to **TREORCHY** (Treorci), one of the most famous mining towns in Wales, largely due to the international status of its **Royal Male Voice Choir**, the oldest in Wales. Visitors are welcome to rehearsals, which take place each Sunday, Tuesday and Thursday; pre-arrange with Mr Morgan (☎01443/435852) at the Treorchi Primary School in Glynocli Road. Treorchy is also home of the splendid **Parc and Dare Hall** (☎01443/773112 or 775654). The Hall houses a theatre and an exhibition about Paul Robeson, "honorary Welshman" and black American spiritual singer and civil rights activist.

From Treorchy, the A4601 branches off the valley road and heads west up the mountainside, twisting its way around Mynydd Maendy and Mynydd Llangeinwyr. One of the most spectacular roads in Wales, it divides to head west down the Cwm Afan and south for the Cwm Ogwr Fawr. At the top of the Rhondda Fawr is **TREHERBERT**, its straggle of houses continuing up the valley at **BLAENCWM** and **BLAENRHONDDA**, two communities effectively bypassed since a new road was built in the 1930s by unemployed miners, connecting Treherbert to the forests and lakes of Hirwaun Common en route to Brecon (see p.205).

Spectacular **walks** abound in the Rhondda. A mildly difficult two-mile hike from Blaencwm, for instance, leads to the remarkable mound of **Penpych**, sitting sentinel over the Rhondda Fawr, while a diversion east at Ferndale passes the remains of a Roman marching camp, **Twyn-y-Briddallt**, and **Old Smokey**, a huge pile of colliery spoil with excellent views, before winding up at the isolated little village of **LLAN-WONNO**, home to remote glades, an ancient church and a good village pub. At the top of the valley, from the vast site of Maerdy colliery (the last Rhondda pit), a path edges along the infant river, past the rocky height of **Castell Nos**, an old border defence castle, and on up to the Lluest Wen reservoir.

Practicalities

A **train** line, punctuated with stops every mile or so, runs the entire length of the Rhondda Fawr, from Pontypridd to its terminus at Treherbert. **Buses** also cover the route, continuing up into the mountains and the Brecon Beacons. **Accommodation** in the twin valleys is sparse, but good options include the business-oriented *Heritage Park Hotel*, next to the Rhondda Heritage Park at Trehafod (☎01443/687057, fax 687060; ④), which has its own pool. Also close to Porth are *The Rickards* on Trebanoy Road (☎01443/688023; ①), and *Tegfan*, Celyn Isaf, Tonyrefail (☎01443/670831; ②), a couple of miles south of Porth. Although, for the most part, eating options in the Rhondda towns mean a range of chip shops, Chinese takeaways and pickled eggs in the pubs, some of the **pubs** and **working men's clubs** (which you'll generally need to be invited into, although there are many people more than happy to do this for you) serve food.

The Ogwr, Garw and Llynfi valleys

Running west from the Rhondda, these three valleys are less harsh in appearance than their neighbours: the contours are slightly softer, the open spaces wider and the towns smaller and lower key. The **Ogwr Valley** plunges south from the Rhondda Fawr's Treorchy village, through the sleepy settlements of **Nant-y-moel** and **Ogmore Vale**, before the main road forks at **Pont-yr-awel** for the branch road over to the Garw Valley. High between the two is the one-horse hamlet of **LLANGEINOR**, little more than a fine medieval church, circular village green, good country pub and the starting point for numerous paths radiating out over the upland moors.

The Ogwr Valley descends through orderly little townships en route into **BRID-GEND** (Pen-y-bont ar Ogwr), an ancient settlement that guards the entrance to the three valleys. Consequently, it was deemed important enough to house two Norman castles, either side of the river. The "old castle" survives only in the name of the suburb on the town-centre side of the river, while opposite, the scant remains of the "new castle", high on a wooded hill above the A4063 Maesteg road, are notable mainly for the surviving late-Norman decorated gateway. That aside, there's not much to occupy you in Bridgend, although it's a useful transport interchange, with a good selection of shops and a few handsome buildings. Just over a mile northeast of the town are the more substantial remains of **Coity Castle** (free access; CADW), built around the end of the twelfth century by one of the earliest Norman knights in the area, who, it is said, married the daughter offered to him by the local Welsh chieftain. A large outer ward encloses the original keep and some domestic buildings dating from the fourteenth to sixteenth centuries. Bridgend is also very handy for Porthcawl, Ewenny Priory and beyond, detailed in the Vale of Glamorgan section (pp.117–118).

The **Garw Valley** seems in a world of its own; it is one of the dead-end valleys that consists of a road, river and the disused bed of a railway crammed in on the valley floor, before they all peter out into the wooded hillsides. Most of the scars of its mining past have now been levelled and landscaped, leaving the valley surprisingly pretty and, as it's well off any tourist track, very rewarding for good walks and congenial company in the pubs and shops. Some hope to restore the railway line and run steam trains along the Garw, but for the moment road transport is the only option.

At the lower end of the valley, the **Bryngarw Country Park** (daily dawn–dusk; parking £1.50) is a pleasant diversion. Landscaped gardens, exceptional flower collections and mature woodlands are gathered around a **visitor centre** (April–Sept daily 10am–6pm; ☎01656/725155) and the restored Bryngarw House, which now houses a bistro and conference centre. The head of the valley is at **BLAENGARW**, where the old **Workmen's Hall** (details on ☎01656/871911) has metamorphosed into a remarkable new community space with a cinema, workshop, new technology and performance areas; even the hall's typically austere frontage has been transformed with stunning murals and mosaics. Situated at the butt-end of one of the most remote valleys in south Wales, Workmen's Hall is a remarkable symbol of Blaengarw's confidence in the future.

The **Llynfi Valley**, stretching up from Bridgend and Tondu along the A4063, is broad-bottomed and leafy, the main settlement being the downbeat town of **MAESTEG**, struggling to find replacements for its lost collieries. Although this is true of many towns in the Valleys, it is in these more westerly corners of the region that the economic pinch is being felt most keenly. There is understandable resentment here that the better-known valleys, particularly the Rhondda, Cynon and Taff, have soaked up so much of the area's publicity and available funds. Continuing through Maesteg, the main road links up with the A4107 at Cymer, for Cwm Afan.

The only **accommodation** in this area is at *Bryngarw House* (☎01656/729009, fax 729007; ④ including dinner) in the country park, although this is usually for pre-booked conferences, wedding parties and the like. A mile east, over the hill in the Llynfi valley, there's B&B at *Chestnut Ways* (☎01656/724665; ②) on the main A4063 in Coytrahên. If you're exploring the area, or want to catch something at the Blaengarw Workmen's Hall, telephone the hall for suggestions as to someone local who might offer B&B. Otherwise, there are numerous fine sites to pitch a **tent**.

Cwm Afan, Port Talbot and Margam

Although not as idyllic as its optimistic "Little Switzerland" tourist board tag would have it, **CWM AFAN**, winding its way between the top of the Llynfi valley and the coast at Port Talbot, is nonetheless a bucolic spot that warrants exploration, with all traces of industry long expunged. The valley's main attraction is the **Afan Forest Park**, 9000 acres of hilly forest land around an excellent **countryside centre** (April–Sept daily 10.30am–5pm; Oct–March Mon–Fri 10.30am–4pm Sat & Sun 10.30am–5pm; summer parking £1.20; ☎01639/850564), three miles west of dour little **CYMMER**. The centre houses the **South Wales Miners' Museum** (same times; £1), where an informal collection of mining memorabilia, looking at miners' home and working lives, religion and dangers, fills numerous glass cases. X-rays and lung segments show the horrific effects of silicosis and pneumoconiosis. On a more uplifting note, there's also an impressive longitudinal diagram of the south Wales coalfields in stained glass. The centre also organizes regular events and walks, has vary basic **camping** (£1 per person) and **rents bikes** (£11 a day) which are good enough for a waymarked, ten-mile circuit mostly on disused railway tracks, but are not up to the more precipitous routes through the forest.

The valley descends towards the sea, reaching the floor village of **PONTRHY-DYFEN** in a couple of miles. Actor Richard Burton was born in a house at the foot of one of the impressive viaducts that slice through the village. From here, roads either side of the river continue south to the industrial sprawl of **PORT TALBOT**, still dominated by its massive steelworks. It's a town in which you're unlikely to linger, though a few Victorian touches remain in the largely modern town centre, and the docks, including the impressive modern deep-water harbour with its mile-long breakwater, provide plenty of action. The suburb of **Aberavon** has a long and sandy, if fairly featureless, seafront lined with a few fun pubs and nightclubs as well as the ever-popular Afan Lido (☎01639/871444), site of big concerts and sports events, and the swish new AquaDome, a leisure pool with all the trimmings.

A couple of miles southeast of Port Talbot, on the other side of junction 38 of the M4, lies **MARGAM**, originally a Cistercian settlement and later the home of various industrial magnates. The first left turn after the motorway junction leads to the impressive **Abbey church**, the sole remaining Cistercian house of worship in Wales. The harmonious Italianate frontage is largely due to nineteenth-century restoration, although original twelfth-century features can be seen here and inside – the solid arcades are particularly notable. The neighbouring **Margam Stones Museum**, housing numerous important Roman, Celtic and medieval standing stones, is currently closed and plans for its future are uncertain.

Lying just the other side of the Abbey church and accessed by car along the next turnoff from the main road, **Margam Country Park** (attractions April–Sept daily 10.30am–5pm, park 10am–7pm, last entry 4pm; £3.50; Oct–March park only Wed–Sun 10am–5pm, last entry 3pm; £1) is centred around the nineteenth-century Gothic pile of **Margam Castle**. There's a lot to see and do within the grounds: walks go up to the ruined hilltop Capel Mair, around Mynydd-y-Castell Iron Age fort and through superb floral grounds dotted with some exciting contemporary sculpture by some big names like Barbara Hepworth and Elizabeth Frink. Tucked in by the Abbey church walls are the impressive remains of the original Cistercian abbey, most notable for the surprisingly intact vaulting of the twelve-sided chapter house, which survived the Dissolution of the Monasteries only to have its roof collapse under the weight of weed and plants in 1799. Nearby is Margam's showpiece **orangery**, a splendid Georgian outhouse, built in 1790 and 327ft long. Nestled in the same corner are a kids' "fairyland" play area and a great box-hedge maze. Waterfalls, sculpture and some splendid shrubbery fill the spaces around the ceremonial boardwalk, leading up to the castle. The mansion was gutted by fire in 1977, but you can still wander into the lobby and peer up the octagonal lantern tower and see a few models and photos. In the courtyard, there's a café, shop and unbelievably crass display of Crown Jewel replicas.

Practicalities

There is very little tourist **accommodation** in these parts – once again, those **camping** have it easiest with a dedicated site at the Afan Forest Park and numerous quiet unofficial spots. In Cymer village, *Brynteg House* (☎01639/851820; ①) is a decent small B&B and teashop. Better still, *Ty'n-y-Caeau* (☎01639/883897; ②) is a seventeenth-century vicarage-cum-guesthouse just off the main road in Margam village, on the other side of the motorway junction from Margam Park. There are numerous cheap and stodgy **cafés** in Port Talbot and Aberavon, or you can find food in the *St Oswald's* bar on Station Road in Port Talbot.

Cardiff

Official capital of Wales since only 1955, the buoyant city of **CARDIFF** (Caerdydd) has swiftly grown into its new status. The city's evolution has been hastened by a number of progressive developments, not least the new, sixty-member Welsh National Assembly which, together with massive regeneration around the Cardiff Bay waterfront and a fabulous new national sports stadium, are giving the city the feel of an international capital.

Many of the city's rivals – amongst them Machynlleth, seat of Glyndŵr's parliament, Swansea, a large, sprawling and unmistakably Welsh city, and even Ludlow, an English border town once the seat of the Council of the Marches – dismissed Cardiff as a young upstart. True, the civic charter incorporating Cardiff dates only from 1905 and, before the coal-exporting explosion during the nineteenth century, it was an insignificant fishing village. The "not very Welsh" charge is also frequently levelled at the city: in some ways, this is justified, since Cardiff is very anglicized compared with Swansea. You are much less likely to hear *Cymraeg* on Cardiff's streets, though the concentration of Welsh-speaking media folk in the city is beginning to change that. Besides, Cardiff's standard-bearers question the inherent snobbery in arguing that a young and vibrant city should *not* be the nation's capital? Cardiff is an exciting city that is still developing and, unlike Edinburgh or London, which rest on their wistful and long histories, Cardiff pushes on, as one of Europe's largest regeneration projects transforms the old dockland around Cardiff Bay into a vast freshwater marina bounded by the new National Assembly building, spruce waterfront towers, new museums and transport systems.

Some history

It is known that some of the Roman tribes from Isca settled in Cardiff, building a small civilian village alongside the military fort. The fort is thought to have been uninhabited from the Romans' departure until the Norman invasion, when William the Conqueror offered Welsh land to his knights if they could subdue the local tribes. In 1093, Robert FitzHamon built a simple fort on a moated hillock that still stands today in the grounds

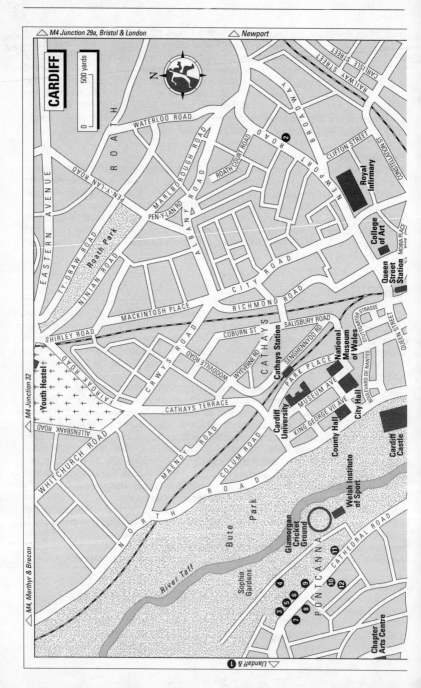

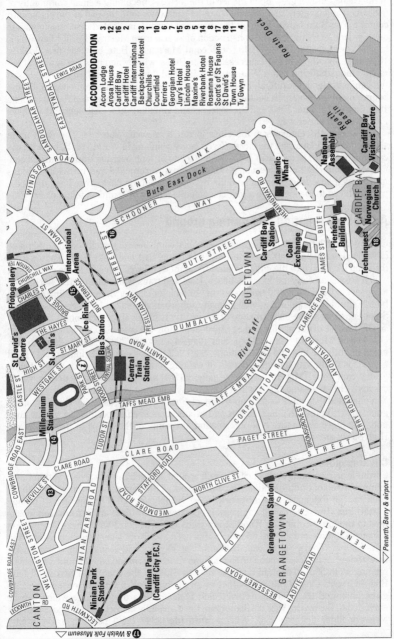

ACCOMMODATION

Acorn Lodge	3
Arosa House	12
Cardiff Bay	16
Cardiff Hotel	2
Cardiff International Backpackers' Hostel	13
Churchills	1
Courtfield	10
Ferriers	6
Georgian Hotel	7
Jury's Hotel	15
Lincoln House	9
Maxine's	5
Riverbank Hotel	14
Rosanna House	8
Scott's of St Fagans	17
St David's	18
Town House	11
Ty Gwyn	4

© Crown copyright

of the castle. A town grew up in the lee of the fortress, becoming a small community of fishermen and farmers that remained a quiet backwater until the end of the eighteenth century. The Bute family, lords of the manor of Cardiff, instigated new developments on their land, starting with the construction of a canal from Merthyr Tydfil (then Wales' largest town) to Cardiff in 1794. The second Marquis of Bute built the first dock in 1839, opening others in swift succession. The Butes, who owned massive swaths of the rapidly industrializing south Wales valleys, insisted that all coal and iron exports used the family docks in Cardiff, and it became one of the busiest ports in the world. By the beginning of the twentieth century, Cardiff's population had soared to 170,000 from its 1801 figure of around 1000, and the spacious and ambitious new civic centre in Cathays Park was well under way.

The twentieth century saw the city's fortunes rise and plummet. The dock trade slumped in the 1930s, and the city suffered heavy bombing in World War II, but with the creation of Cardiff as capital in 1955 – widely felt to be long overdue – optimism and confidence in the city have blossomed. Many large governmental and media institutions have moved here from London, and the development of the dock areas has provided a positive boost to the cityscape and lent a tangible feeling of optimism to the place.

Arrival, information and getting around

Cardiff–Wales international **airport** is ten miles southwest of the city on the other side of Barry. Hourly buses #X91 (Mon–Sat), #X5 (Mon–Sat) and #145 (Sun) operate from the main terminal into the city **bus station** on the southwestern side of the city centre, which serves all National Express buses, local and trans-Wales bus routes. Across the forecourt is Cardiff Central **train station**, for all inter-city services (including a speedy hourly shuttle to London), as well as many suburban and Valley Line services. **Queen Street station**, at the eastern edge of the centre, is for local services only.

The **tourist office** at 16 Wood St (April–Sept Mon–Sat 9am–6.30pm, Sun 10am–4pm; Oct–March Mon–Sat 9am–5.30pm, Sun 10am–4pm; ☎029/2022 7281), is immediately north of both the bus and train stations. Staff will book accommodation, provide good free maps of the city and give details of walking tours and jaunts such as the Guide Friday **bus tour** (May to early Nov daily; £6.50), an open-top double-decker which carves a circuit around the city and Cardiff Bay, allowing you to get on and off at will. You should also be able to pick up a copy of *Buzz!*, a free, occasionally ribald monthly guide to arts in the city; the free arts and events sheet *freetime* performs a similar function. For more alternative-type information, try some of the shops in the Castle and High Street arcades (see p.100).

City transport

Cardiff is an easy and compact city to walk around, as even the bay area is within thirty minutes' stroll of Central station. Once you're out of the centre, however, it's best to fall back on the extensive **bus network**, most reliably operated by the garish orange Cardiff Bus (Bws Caerdydd) company. It operates sales offices and information kiosks next to the tourist office on Wood Street (Mon & Fri 8am–5.30pm, Tues–Thurs & Sat 8.30am–5.30pm) and in the Marks & Spencer store on Queen Street (Mon–Wed 9am–5.30pm, Thurs–Sat 8.30am–5.30pm). The city is divided into four colour-coded **fare zones**, and prices depend on the number of zones crossed and the time you travel, ranging from 50p off-peak in a single zone to £1.30 in the rush hour across all four. Bought from a Cardiff Bus sales office or on the bus itself, a **City Rider** ticket (£2.50) gives unlimited travel around Cardiff and Penarth for a day, a range which can be extended to Barry, the Vale of Glamorgan, the Caerphilly district and Newport with the Network Rider ticket (£4.50). With a **multiride** ticket (£10) you can travel around

---

THE CARDIFF CARD

Valid for two days, a **Cardiff Card** (£12) offers substantial savings, giving free access to major sights in and around Cardiff, a free "Guide Friday" bus tour of the city and unlimited travel on all Cardiff Bus and Valley train services. You'll need to pack it in to get full value in the two days, but you could always buy two consecutive cards and still come out on top: get them from tourist offices and bus and train stations.

Affiliated sights include the grounds (but not tours) of Cardiff Castle, the National Museum & Gallery, Techniquest, the Museum of Welsh Life, Newport's Tredegar House, the Roman Legionary Museum at Caerleon, Caerphilly Castle, the Rhondda Heritage Park, Llancaiach Fawr Manor and assorted minor attractions.

Cardiff and Penarth for a week, though you might find the best deal of all is to purchase a **Cardiff Card** or two (see box, above).

The **last buses** leave the city centre at around 11.20pm, so if you're staying out of town, you'll have to rely on **taxis** late at night. These can be found in ranks at Central station, Duke Street by the castle and Queen Street station. Alternatively, reliable cab companies include Capital Cars (☎029/2077 7777) and Metro Cabs (☎029/2046 4646).

Accommodation

Cardiff's accommodation spans the full range, with major hotels concentrated in the city centre and a dense belt of guesthouses and hotels lining the genteel and leafy Cathedral Road, in the suburb of Pontcanna, a fifteen-minute walk from the city centre. There is little reason to try elsewhere, though there's a clutch of guesthouses fifteen minutes' walk northeast out of the city centre on Newport Road, and you might consider staying in the breezy resort of Penarth (see p.113), a ten-minute train hop around the bay.

Hotels

Cardiff Bay, Schooner Way, Atlantic Wharf, Cardiff Bay (☎029/2047 5000, fax 2048 1491). Grand Victorian building at the head of Bute Dock midway between downtown and Cardiff Bay. Very smart and comfortable, with a pool and gym. Weekend rates are less expensive. ⑦.

Cardiff Hotel, 138 Newport Rd, Roath (☎029/2049 1964). Informal and well-placed small hotel with a licensed bar and en-suite rooms. ①.

Churchills, Cardiff Rd, Llandaff (☎029/2056 2372, fax 2056 8347). Mock-Edwardian hotel in a quiet part of the city near the cathedral of Llandaff. ④.

Courtfield, 101 Cathedral Rd, Pontcanna (☎ & fax 029/2022 7701). Popular, comfortable and nicely furnished hotel with a largely gay clientele. ③.

Georgian, 179 Cathedral Rd, Pontcanna (☎ & fax 029/2023 2594). Good value in a comfortable small hotel with some fairly spacious, en-suite rooms. ②.

Jury's, Mary Ann St (☎029/2034 1441 fax 2022 3742). Large, plush modern and business hotel opposite the new International Arena. ⑦.

Lincoln House, 118 Cathedral Rd (☎029/2039 5558, fax 2023 0537). Elegant small hotel restored in a Victorian style: button-leather couches, heavy brocade and even a couple of four-poster beds. Rates include breakfast. ④.

St David's Hotel and Spa, Havannah St, Cardiff Bay (☎029/2045 4045, fax 2031 3075, *www. rfhotels.com/stdavids/index/html*). Right on the waterfront, Cardiff's flashest and most luxurious hotel is all clean lines and elegant, understated decor. Rooms have all the expected accoutrements (including superb views from the balconies), there's a spa on site and rates include breakfast. ⑦.

Scott's of St Fagans, Greenwood Lane, St Fagans (☎029/2056 5400, fax 2056 3400, *scottsofstfagans@ btinternet.com*). Four miles from Cardiff and a world away from most hotels in Wales, this old post office has been remodelled into a minimalist hotel with top quality, beautifully decorated rooms and an excellent restaurant on site – rates include breakfast. ③.

Town House, 70 Cathedral Rd, Pontcanna (☎029/2023 9399, fax 2022 3214, *www.travel~uk.net/thetownhouse*). Restored Victorian house with en-suite rooms, a comfortable lounge and better than average facilities. ③.

B&Bs and guesthouses

Acorn Lodge, 182 Cathedral Rd, Pontcanna (☎029/2022 1373). Pleasant, quiet and one of the cheapest B&Bs on this street, a 15min walk from the city centre. Some rooms are en suite. ①.

Arosa House, 24 Plasturton Gardens, Pontcanna (☎029/2039 5342). Very friendly and reasonably priced B&B in a quiet street just off Cathedral Rd. ①.

Ferriers, 130 Cathedral Rd, Pontcanna (☎ & fax 029/2038 3413). Not the cheapest, but one of the best-value B&Bs in Cardiff, welcoming and inexpensive with excellent service and some en-suite rooms. ②.

Maxine's, 150 Cathedral Rd, Pontcanna (☎029/2022 0288, fax 2034 4884). Yet another decent B&B with very low rates. ①.

Riverbank Hotel, 53–59 Despenser St (☎029/2037 8866, fax 2038 8741, *riverhotel@aol.com*). Comfortable hotel with en-suite rooms, immediately across the river from the Millennium Stadium and only five minutes walk from the centre of town. ③.

Rosanna House, 175 Cathedral Rd, Pontcanna (☎029/2022 9780). Very cheap, reflected, to some extent, in the decor of the place. Handy for the city and the river. ①.

Ty Gwyn, 7 Dyfrig St, off Cathedral Rd, Pontcanna (☎029/2023 9784). Close to the city centre and well placed for Pontcanna Fields and the River Taff. Friendly and quiet. ②.

Hostels and self-catering

Cardiff International Backpacker, 98 Neville St (☎029/2034 5577, fax 2023 0404). Reachable via half-hourly buses from Central station (#78, #80 or #82), this well-kept hostel has Internet access, pool table, on-site café and bar, and fairly cramped kitchen facilities but easy access to downtown restaurants. Bunks in single sex and mixed dorms (max 8) for £13 and some private rooms(①).

Cardiff YHA Hostel, 2 Wedal Rd, Roath Park (☎029/2046 2303, fax 2046 4571, *cardiff@yha.org.uk*). Large, purpose-built building just underneath the A48 Eastern Avenue flyover at the top of Roath Park, almost two miles from the city centre and reachable via buses #78, #80 or #82 from the central bus station. No curfew.

Cardiff University, Cathays (☎029/2087 4027, fax 2087 4990, *conference@cardiff.ac.uk*). Thousands of student rooms (many en-suite) available from June to September on a room-only, B&B or self-catering basis. A good and cheap option. ①.

The City

Cardiff's sights are clustered around fairly small, distinct districts. Compact and easily navigable on foot, the **commercial centre** is bounded by the River Taff – source of the nickname of generations of expatriate Welsh – on the western side. The Taff flows past the walls of Cardiff's extraordinary **castle**, an amalgam of Roman remains, Norman keep and Victorian fantasy. Nearby is the great new **Millennium Stadium**, home of Welsh rugby and the nation's soccer team. Near the southeast tip of the castle walls is Cardiff's main crossroads, where great Edwardian shopping boulevards Queen Street and High Street conceal a world of arcades, great stores and predictably bland malls. North of the castle are a series of white Edwardian buildings – the spacious **civic centre** around **Cathays Park**, home of the **National Museum**, **City Hall** and **Cardiff University**.

A mile south of the commercial centre is the area around **Cardiff Bay**, once the city's liveliest district and on the up again since the inception of the Cardiff Bay redevelopment project and the construction of the barrage to form a vast freshwater lake. The surrounding waterfront has been spruced up considerably, and will soon be the site of the brand new National Assembly building and a multipurpose arts complex, the Millennium Centre.

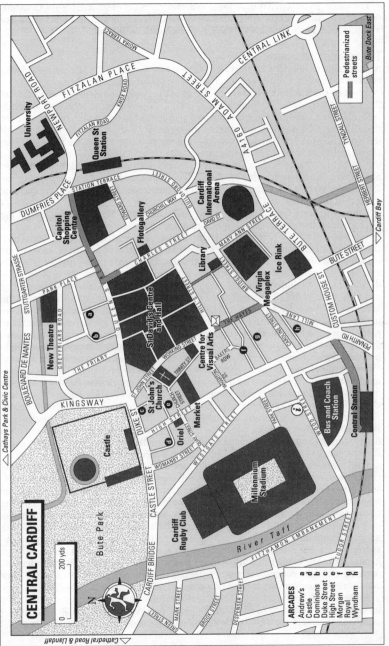

CENTRAL CARDIFF

N

0   200 yds

ARCADES
Andrew's   a
Castle   d
Dominions   b
Duke Street   c
High Street   e
Morgan   f
Royal   g
Wyndham   h

Pedestrianized streets

© Crown copyright

The other city area that is most likely to detain you is the elegant suburb of **Llandaff**, two miles northwest of the city centre above the banks of the Taff, and still feeling like a closely knit village built around the city's patchwork **cathedral**.

The commercial centre

A rough square bounded by the castle, Queen Street station, the International Arena and Central station, Cardiff's commercial centre makes a surprisingly compact city.

Between Central station and Castle Street is the prickly, retractable-roofed form of the steel **Millennium Stadium**, a sleek new 72,500-seat giant shoehorned so tightly onto its Taff-side site that the surrounding walkways had to be cantilevered out over the river. The location was once occupied by the legendary Cardiff Arms Park, and though the old terraces and the famous name have now gone, the turf is still the home of Welsh rugby, and when Wales have a home match – particularly against old enemy England – the stadium and surrounding streets are charged with good-natured, beery fervour. Sadly there was no such game for the stadium's inaugural set of matches during the 1999 Rugby World Cup, when Wales lost in the quarter-finals to Australia, the eventual winners of the tournament.

Running up from Central station to the castle walls is **St Mary's Street**, one of the city's grandest boulevards of ornate Victorian and Edwardian shop frontages. St Mary's Street leads north to become the **High Street**, where at no.18, you'll find **Oriel** (Mon–Sat 9am–5.30pm), Cardiff's best venue for international and Welsh modern art exhibitions (*Oriel* is Welsh for "gallery"). It's also the capital's prime stockist of Welsh-interest publications and is great for maps and travel paraphernalia. Off High Street is the elegant, c.1900 **indoor market**. Along both streets, Edwardian arcades, cleaned up and with some of the city centre's most interesting shops inside, lead off between the buildings. Of these, **High Street** and **Castle arcades**, at the top of High Street, are the most rewarding, packed with great club clothes shops, quirky gift places and a range of esoteric emporia from which you can pick up fliers for clubs and events. Further down the High Street towards Central station, the glorious Morgan Arcade and its near neighbour, the Royal Arcade, run east to the bottom of **The Hayes**, a pedestrianized street of disparate restaurants and some great pubs. A few yards to the south, The Hayes meets up at a junction of five streets by the belching towers of the **Brains brewery**, opposite the **Wales National Ice Rink**, home to one of Britain's top ice hockey teams, the Cardiff Devils. At the junction, Bridge Street runs away to the east and into the elegant Regency part of the city centre around David and Charles streets. At 31 Charles St is **Ffotogallery** (times variable), one of the country's foremost galleries for bold and often hard-hitting photographic exhibitions. Slicing off south from The Hayes, opposite the *Marriott* hotel, is atmospheric Mill Lane, Cardiff's **café quarter**.

The Hayes leads north to the beautifully sandblasted and colonnaded frontage of the Old Library, recently reopened as the superb **Centre for Visual Arts** (CVA: Tues & Wed 11am–6pm, Thurs–Sat 11am–9pm, Sun 11am–5pm; £3.50; *www.cva.org.uk*). This now ranks as Wales' largest gallery space – though there's no permanent collection, the centre has so far shown extremely high-quality works, from old masters to contemporary installations as well as touring exhibitions. No matter what else is on, you shouldn't miss **Fantasmic**, a hands-on gallery that's ostensibly to help kids interpret and appreciate art, but is a lot of fun for just about anyone. There's over a hundred things to push, pull, touch and listen to – sensory boxes, shadow puppets, colour theatre – all presenting artistic concepts at a simple level: Lego sets and interactive screens allow you to create your own art and the properties of different materials are explored.

At the Centre for Visual Arts, The Hayes divides around the fifteenth-century grey limestone parish **church of St John**. The most notable feature – the slender tower – is difficult to appreciate with the cluster of buildings around it, although the light and graceful interior is worth seeing, especially for the floridly pompous altar in the south aisle by prolific Victorian sculptor, Goscombe John. The right turn at the Old Library is **Working Street**, a very busy shopping area, especially around the entrances to the gargantuan **St David's Centre** and the **St David's Hall** complex, which, between them, have succeeded in obliterating a huge section of the old city centre, although St David's Hall serves as a much-needed concert and entertainment venue.

Queen Street is Cardiff's most impressive shopping thoroughfare, now pedestrianized with many of the fine nineteenth-century buildings spruced up, only to be covered over with the shop frontages so typical of a British shopping street. At its western end, a typically pugnacious statue of **Aneurin Bevan**, postwar Labour politician and classic Welsh firebrand, stands aloof from the bustle.

Cardiff Castle

The geographical and historical heart of the city is **Cardiff Castle** (daily: March–Oct 9.30am–5pm with tours every 20min; Nov–Feb 9.30am–3.30pm with 5 tours per day; £5 full tour, £3 shorter tour, £2.30 grounds only), an intriguing, appealing hotchpotch of remnants of the city's past. The fortress hides inside a vast walled yard, each side measuring well over 200 yards long and corresponding roughly to the outline of the original fort built by the Romans, Cardiff's first inhabitants. A few dozen yards of **Roman wall**, the sole reminder of their presence, has been unearthed to the immediate right of the entrance in the thirteenth-century Black Tower on Castle Street, and is now lit and labelled, along with some excellent three-dimensional murals depicting life in a Roman fort. Tucked into the southeastern corner wall beyond the Roman segment are the dry **regimental museums** of the Queen's Dragoon Guards and the Welsh Regiment, filled with a starchy collection of military memorabilia. From here, walkways lead along the **battlements**, offering some excellent views over the city and the gracious Portland-stone buildings of Cathays Park.

Occupying the northwestern corner of the castle grounds is a neat Norman motte crowned with the eleventh-century **keep**, with views down onto the turrets and towers of the **domestic buildings**, dating in part from the fourteenth and fifteenth centuries, but much extended in Tudor times, when residential needs began to overtake military safety in terms of priority. Ultimately, it was the third Marquis of Bute (1847–1900), one of the richest men on the globe, who lavished a fortune on upgrading his pile, commissioning architect and decorator William Burges (1827–81) to aid him. With their passion for the religious art and the symbolism of the Middle Ages, they systematically overhauled the buildings, adding a spire to the octagonal tower and erecting a clock tower; but it was inside that their imaginations ran free, and they radically transformed the crumbling interiors into palaces of vivid colour and intricate, high-camp design. These buildings can only be seen as part of the guided tour, making the extra fee well worthwhile.

The tour starts in the square-cornered **clock tower**, running through the **Winter Smoking Room** at the bottom, up to the **Bachelor's Bedroom** and bathroom and, above that, the **Summer Smoking Room**. All are decorated in rich patterns of gold, maroon and cobalt, with many of the images culled from medieval myths and beliefs. From here, the tour goes through the 1878 **Nursery**, with hand-painted tiles and silhouette lanterns depicting contemporary nursery rhymes, the 1881 **Arab Room**, decorated by imported craftsmen, and into the grand **Banqueting Hall**, which dates orginally from 1428, but was transformed by Bute and Burges with the installation of a riotously kitsch fireplace to commemorate Robert the Consul, Earl of Gloucester and late Norman lord of the castle. In all the rooms, fantastically rich trimmings complement the dizzily gaudy style so beloved of two nineteenth-century eccentrics, and it's worth remembering that, as one of over sixty residences owned by the Butes in Britain alone, Cardiff was only lived in for six weeks of the year.

The last point of note in Cardiff Castle can only be seen from outside the precincts. The **Animal Wall**, where stone creatures are frozen in impudent poses, was another tongue-in-cheek nineteenth-century creation, running all along the route of Castle Street west to the river bridge.

Cathays Park and the civic centre

On the north side of the city centre, only a hundred yards from the northeastern wall of the castle precinct, is the area known most commonly as **Cathays Park**. The park itself is really the large rectangle of greenery that forms the centrepiece for the impressive Edwardian buildings of the **civic centre**, but the term Cathays Park is generally used for the whole complex. Dating from the first couple of decades of the twentieth century, the gleaming white buildings arranged with pompous Edwardian precision speak volumes about Cardiff's self-assertion, even half a century before it was officially declared capital of Wales. The processional **Boulevard de Nantes**, named after Cardiff's twin city in Brittany, fronts the complex on the city-centre side.

Centrepiece of the complex is the magnificent, domed, dragon-topped **City Hall** (1905), an exercise in ostentatious civic self-glory that reaches a peak in the particularly showy first-floor Marble Hall: all Sienese marble columns and statues of Welsh heroes. Amongst the (all male) figures are twelfth-century chronicler Giraldus Cambrensis, thirteenth-century native prince of Wales, Llywelyn ap Gruffydd, fifteenth-century national insurgent and perpetual hero, Owain Glyndŵr, Welsh king Henry Tudor and tenth-century architect of Wales' progressive codified laws, Hywel Dda (Howell the Good). Overseeing them all is the figure of Dewi Sant himself – the national patron saint, St David.

The low-key **Law Courts** (1906), stand to the left of the City Hall, with the **National Museum and Gallery** (see below) balancing the view on the right-hand side. Behind them, two ruler-straight boulevards, evidently designed with ceremonial splendour in mind, run through the rest of the civic centre, arranged in symmetrical precision around **Alexandra Gardens** in the middle. At the very centre of the park is the colonnaded circular **National War Memorial** (1928), a popular and surprisingly quiet place to sit and contemplate the rush of civic and governmental duty all around. At the north end of the western boulevard, **King Edward VII Avenue**, is the **Temple of Peace** (1938), dedicated just before the outbreak of World War II to Welsh men and women the world over who were fighting for peace and relief of poverty. The eastern road, **Museum Avenue**, runs past an assortment of buildings belonging to Cardiff University. At the northern head of Cathays Park is the ugliest and most foreboding building of them all: the principal Cardiff departments of the **Welsh Office**.

National Museum and Gallery

The **National Museum and Gallery** (Tues–Sun & bank holiday Mon 10am–5pm; £4.50) is one of Britain's finest. Housed in a large, white, domed Portland-stone building that was constructed in sections from 1912 through to 1992, it manages to carry off the illusion of a singular *grand projet*. As a national museum, it attempts both to tell the story of Wales and reflect the nation's place in the wider, international sphere.

The most obvious crowd-pleaser, starting on the ground floor at the back of the entrance lobby, is the epic **Evolution of Wales** gallery, a natural history exhibition packed with high-tech gizmos and a staggering amount of information. It starts with a stirring large-screen video presentation, *Dyma Gymru* (This is Wales), pumped full of stunning aerial footage taken over mountains, waterfalls and other natural Welsh wonders. It then goes on to explain, through fossils, rocks and footage of volcanoes, earthquakes and the galaxies, the slow beginnings of life on earth. Dinosaurs and the early mammals get a good look in, a main attraction being a terrific *Tyrannosaurus rex* skull.

The environmental education continues in the adjacent **Natural History** galleries, with a magnificent collection of sparkling crystals, re-creations of assorted environments – mountain, wetland, seashore, dunes – and some great interactive technology and interpretive boards. It then heads upstairs with a display entitled "Man and the Environment", featuring numerous animals and their habitats, and culminates in the world's largest leatherback turtle, caught off Harlech in 1988 and condemned to spend the rest of eternity frozen in a curious diving position, half-smile still lingering. Displays looking at the effect of mankind on our changing environment complete the section.

The first floor also houses the excellent **archeology galleries**, whose treasures include intricate gold torques from the Bronze Age and the dazzling **Caergwrle Bowl**, a gold votive container in the shape of a boat that's more than 3000 years old. Leading off is an unusually interesting **coin** collection, with some good panels on the history of Welsh and British minting, and the **Tregwynt Treasure Trove**, an impressive cache of gold and silver coins dating back to the Civil War uncovered near Fishguard in 1996. At the back, there's an inspirational collection of 23 stones and 14 casts, spanning the earliest carved fragments (around the fifth century), through Celtic and early Christian standing stones to the more elaborate examples of the early medieval age.

THE ART COLLECTIONS

The Evolution of Wales and Natural History galleries occupy the entire western and central flank of the ground and first floors. The eastern side of the building is home to the **art galleries**. Galleries One to Ten examine Wales' artistic heritage, starting with a marble altar from the first century BC and taking in works from the medieval Renaissance, including some stunning pieces from the studios of Botticelli and El Greco. There's a strong collection from the **eighteenth-century** British and Italian schools, inevitably rich in the work of Wright, Gainsborough and Reynolds. This era was perhaps the heyday of Welsh art, and the three main protagonists – Richard Wilson, William E Parry and Thomas Jones – are well represented. Wilson's skill in capturing Wales' unique light can be seen to lustrous effect in his studies of castles at Caernarfon, Dolbadarn and Pembroke, as well as more emotionally intense pieces such as the beautiful *Pistyll Cain*. One of Wilson's protégés, William Hodges, also makes an appearance, most notably in his gentle evocation of *Llanthony Priory*.

Scattered throughout the first ten rooms is an intriguing, eclectic ragbag of British art of the last 150 years: Frank Brangwyn's teeming canvases, a typically rich and detailed collection of Pre-Raphaelites, and an astonishingly gaudy gold, silver and enamel table centrepiece given by the people of Wales to the Duke and Duchess of York (later King George V and Queen Mary) for their wedding in 1893. Welsh painters are well highlighted: you'll find cool, blanched portraits by Gwen John, and her brother Augustus' measured, intensely poetic depictions of *Dylan Thomas* and Newport "supertramp" *W.H. Davies*. There's also a superb, and growing, collection of **ceramics**, one of Wales' most prolific areas of applied art.

But the most exciting artworks are contained in Galleries Eleven through Fifteen, kicking off with a fabulous **sculpture** collection, including many by the celebrated one-man Welsh Victorian statue industry, Goscombe John. Far better here than on the dreary municipal plinths they usually adorn, his male studies verge on the homoerotic and his female forms are exquisite.

Mesmerizing pieces by Rodin pepper the building, particularly in Gallery Twelve, where a copy of *The Kiss* and his original *Eve* (with the downcast figure in contrast to the life-affirming lovers) share space with the watery landscapes of Boudin, Renoir's coquettish *The Parisienne*, and numerous works by Manet, including the intricately observed *Effect of Snow at Petit Montrouge*.

Gallery Thirteen houses what is arguably the museum's strongest suit, its collection of **Impressionists**, the bequest of two local wealthy sisters, Margaret and Gwendoline

Davies. The sisters' favourite was Cézanne, whose work features alongside artists such as Sisley (including his view of Penarth), Carnière, Degas and Pissarro. Van Gogh's stunning *Rain at Anvers* – angry slashes of rain run right across the otherwise harmonious canvas – was painted just weeks before his suicide. Gallery Fourteen includes Postimpressionists, Futurists and Surrealists such as Magritte, Sickert, Sylvia Gosse, Harold Gilman's colourful London scenes and studies by Edward Morland Lewis, including a bold depiction of *The Strand, Laugharne*. Finally, Gallery Fifteen houses a hearty collection of British **abstractionism**, with a strong Welsh bent. Highlights include some stunning and wild pieces by Welsh supremo Ceri Richards, Evan Walters' piercing 1936 portrait of a *Welsh Miner*, Josef Herman's rousing *Miners Singing* and Kyffin Williams' brooding Welsh skies and jagged landscapes. Some sculpted pieces, including some fine works by Henry Moore, among them *Upright Motif*, and Barbara Hepworth's haunting *Oval Sculpture*, complete the room.

Cardiff Bay

Although you can get there by train (every 20min from Queen St station) and bus (#7 or #8 from outside Central station), it's only a thirty-minute walk south of the centre to the **Cardiff Bay** area. The stroll is set to become even more pleasant once Bute Street – the ruler-straight connecting road running through tatty Butetown – is transformed into a swish ceremonial boulevard, though like much else hereabouts, there is considerable uncertainty over when (and if) the plan will come to fruition. Nonetheless, Cardiff Bay – the spicier tag of **Tiger Bay** (immortalized by locally born chanteuse Shirley Bassey) being rarely used these days – is on the up, and nothing is being allowed to get in the way of its rapid gentrification.

Comprised of two distinct parts – the firmly multiracial, Taff-side suburbs of **Butetown** and **Grangetown** and the all-new **Millennium Waterfront** – the Cardiff Bay area is going through immense and rapid change. New roads and roundabouts are being cut through rusted wasteland, riotous Victorian and Edwardian frontages have been swabbed clean, and soulless new buildings – with a clutch of honourably spirited exceptions – are spreading like advanced fungus. Cardiff Bay has become one of the world's biggest regeneration projects, aiming to transform the seedy (but quite appealing) dereliction of the old docks into a designer heaven. However, no one wants Cardiff Bay to become a white elephant, an outcome that looks increasingly unlikely with the decision to site the new Welsh Assembly building right in its heart. For now, Butetown and the docks are among the most fascinating parts of Cardiff, where ostentatious Victorian shipping company headquarters rub shoulders with spruced-up dockers' housing, and sleek restaurants lurk in the shadow of glittering postmodern company headquarters.

Central to the whole project is the kilometre-long **Cardiff Bay Barrage**, built right across the Ely and Taff estuaries, transforming a vast mudflat into a freshwater lake and creating eight miles of useful waterfront. Its creation didn't come without controversy. In short, one of Britain's most important habitats for wading birds was sacrificed on the altar of redevelopment, with proponents championing a vast new marina and a new waterfront opera house to support their cause – though infighting has so far scuppered any concrete evidence of the latter (see box opposite).

To find out about what's going on, visit the startling **Cardiff Bay Visitor Centre**, Harbour Drive (May–Sept Mon–Fri 9am–7.30pm, Sat & Sun 10am–7.30pm; Oct–April Mon–Fri 9am–5pm, Sat & Sun 10.30am–5pm; free), a giant tubular eye peering out over the bay that's a thinly disguised PR job for the more controversial developments taking place hereabouts. Despite that, it's well worth a look, if only for the scale model of the entire docks area, illuminated to show different infrastructure developments at the touch of a button. Adjacent is a park dotted with some great pieces of public art and sculpture, a striking red **lightship** used as a Christian café, and the gleaming white, stumpy-spired **Norwegian church** (daily 10am–4pm), an old seamen's chapel in which Roald Dahl was christened, that has now been converted into a excellent café (see p.107) and exhibition space.

Harbour Drive curls around to an empty lot where the new **National Assembly for Wales** building is set to be built by sometime in 2001. Plans talk of a slate, steel and glass structure with Assembly members visible from outside as they go about their business. The current Assembly building, the red-brick Crickhowell House, will be used as office space, as will the adjacent and magnificent, but currently empty, **Pierhead Building**, which has beckoned ships into Cardiff port since its construction in 1896. A typically rich Victorian neo-Gothic terracotta pile, it was built for the Bute Dock Company and perfectly embodies the wealth and optimism of the Bute family and their docks.

Behind the National Assembly site and the Pierhead Building is another empty lot which, by the end of 2001, should be occupied by the **Millennium Centre**, a multi-use arts centre that is the spiritual successor to the doomed opera house. Nearby, the sweeping wavy roofline and vast glass-brick wall of the **Atlantic Wharf** make a striking impression for what is essentially a big box filled with a twelve-screen multiplex, bowling alley and a few restaurants.

Further west around the waterfront, the metal-and-glass-crowned **Techniquest**, on Stuart Street (Mon–Fri 9.30am–4.30pm, Sat & Sun 10.30am–5pm; £4.50), is by far the largest and most impressive "hands-on" science museum in the UK, packed full of exhibits, experiments and numerous chances to play like a five-year-old. It also includes a planetarium (£1) and science theatre.

Back from the waterfront are some interesting places to wander. James Street, behind Techniquest, is the main commercial focus, while the cleaned-up old buildings around Mount Stuart Square are impressive, particularly the mammoth **Exchange**

CARDIFF BAY OPERA HOUSE

Planned and serenaded as the showpiece for the Cardiff Bay development, a national **Opera House** was hoped to do for Cardiff what Sydney's had done for that city. With the outstanding international success of the Welsh National Opera, a suitably monumental permanent home was seen as the final seal on Wales' choral and operatic reputation.

In the late 1980s, an international architecture competition was won by radical Iraqi architect, Zaha Hadid with a startling design known as the "crystal necklace", a square of thrusting, angular glass containing a central courtyard. From here, things went downhill. Initially enthusiastic, the distinctly illiberal Welsh press became increasingly hostile towards the unconventional Ms Hadid and succeeded in stirring up considerable public antipathy towards both the design and, ultimately, the entire concept of an opera house. Rumblings about elitism and lack of consultation began to surface, fuelled by the leader writers of the *Western Mail* and *South Wales Echo*. The notoriously conservative London architecture and media establishments also weighed in, sneering at Cardiff's brash presumption and Hadid's lack of credentials (she was previously known only for a striking-looking but malfunctioning fire station in Germany).

Hadid's 1995 reworking of the design failed to staunch the flow of criticism, and in the face of mounting hysteria, the formerly enthusiastic Millennium Commission – awash with money from the UK National Lottery – got cold feet and pulled funding.

Hopes to have something built in the year 2000 have now disappeared, though there seems to be general enthusiasm for current plans to erect a multipurpose arts and cultural complex, the **Millennium Centre**, designed more conventionally and with a wider remit than just opera. The fact that Hadid's opera house would have fulfilled many such functions anyway seems to support the contention that it was never an argument about the elitism of opera; rather a small-minded, reactionary response that has damaged Wales' reputation considerably in the international cultural sphere.

Building. Built in the 1880s as Britain's central Coal Exchange, the building saw the world's first £1 million deal struck in 1911 and is now used as a conference and exhibition centre. A few yards away, on the corner of West Bute Street, the old church of St Stephen has been converted into a superb new performance space, **The Point** (see p.110).

From Bute Park to Llandaff

Between Cardiff Castle and the River Taff lies **Bute Park**, once the private estate of the castle, and now containing an **arboretum**, superb flowerbeds, the foundation remains of an old priory and some pleasant walks along the Taff banks. The main road crosses over the river at Cardiff Bridge, with a right turn leading up into the coolly formal **Sophia Gardens**. A quarter of a mile along the river is the multipurpose **Welsh Institute of Sport**, the national sports centre. Beyond this is the home of Wales' sole first-class cricket team, Glamorgan, and the less formal open spaces of **Pontcanna Fields**, which lead along the Taff for a couple of miles to the suburb of Llandaff.

A small, quiet ecclesiastical village, **Llandaff** is two miles northwest of the city centre along Cathedral Road. The church that has now grown up into the city's **cathedral** is believed to have been founded in the sixth century by St Teilo, but was rebuilt in Norman style from 1120 and well into the thirteenth century. From the late fourteenth century, the cathedral fell into an advanced state of disrepair, hurried along by the adverse attention of Cromwell's soldiers during the Civil War. In the early eighteenth century, one of the twin towers and the nave roof collapsed. Restoration only began in earnest in the early 1840s, and Pre-Raphaelite artists such as Edward Burne-Jones, Dante Gabriel Rossetti and the stained-glass firm of William Morris were commissioned for colourful new windows and decorative panels. Llandaff is evidently not a lucky cathedral, however, for in January 1941, a German landmine destroyed whole sections of it. Faithful and painstaking restoration was finally completed in 1960.

The fusion of different styles and ages is evident from outside, especially in the mismatched western towers. The northwest tower is by Jasper Tudor, a largely fifteenth-century work with modern embellishments, whilst the adjoining tower and spire were rebuilt from nineteenth-century designs. Inside, Jacob Epstein's overwhelming *Christ in Majesty* sculpture, a concrete parabola topped with a circular organ case on which sits a soaring Christ figure, was the only entirely new feature added in the postwar reconstruction, and dominates the nave today. At the west end of the north aisle, the **St Illtyd Chapel** features Rossetti's cloying triptych *The Seed of David*, whose figures – David the shepherd boy, David the King and the Virgin Mary – are modelled on Rossetti's Pre-Raphaelite friends. Along a little further, in the south presbytery, is the tenth-century Celtic cross that is the cathedral's only pre-Norman survivor.

At the far end of the cathedral is the elegantly vaulted and beautifully painted **Lady Chapel**, notable for its gaudy fifteenth-century reredos on the back wall that contains, surrounded by golden twigs and blackthorn in each niche, bronze panels with named flowers (in Welsh) in honour of Our Lady. Over two dozen flowers take their Welsh names from the Virgin Mary.

Eating

The city's long-standing internationalism, particularly its Italian influence, has paid handsome dividends in its range of **restaurants**. Most places are within easy walking distance of the city centre, with a particular concentration in the "Café Quarter" around Mill Lane. There are also good options in the cheaper corners of Cathays and Roath (particularly the curry houses along Crwys, Albany and City roads), a stone's throw from the centre beyond the university. Some of the action has now moved a mile west to suburban Canton, and to Cardiff Bay; the latter boasts an incongruous mix of old dockers' haunts and expensive showpiece bars and restaurants. Note that we've only listed telephone numbers for places where a reservation is recommended.

For bargain-priced **takeaways** in the city centre, your best bet is Caroline Street, between St Mary Street and the bottom of The Hayes. St Mary Street, especially the lower end towards the station, is the home of numerous reliable pizza and pasta chains.

City centre

Bwyty Hayes Island, The Hayes. In the thick of things outside the new Centre for Visual Arts, this popular, inexpensive outdoor snack bar is a great place to while away half an hour on a pleasant day.

Café Latte, 48 Charles St. Licensed café and bar with a sunny garden out back and good for tucking into hearty breakfasts, club sandwiches and pastries.

Celtic Cauldron, Castle Arcade. Inexpensive, friendly daytime café dedicated to bringing a range of simple Welsh food – soups, stews, laver bread, cakes – to an appreciative public.

Giovanni's, The Hayes (☎029/2022 0077). One of Cardiff's most popular Italian restaurants, the moderately priced *Giovanni's* is lively and enormously friendly, with a wide menu of old favourites and some unusual house specialities. Closed Sun.

Jags, 4 Church St. Eat-in and take-out sandwich bar serving good filled baguettes: try roasted peppers and cream cheese or chicken tikka with mint yogurt dressing. Good espresso too.

Juboraj II, 10 Mill Lane (☎029/2037 7668). One of Cardiff's best south Asian restaurants and still moderately priced – the place to go if you want quality Indian artworks and raga music with your thali.

Las Iguanas, 8 Mill Lane (☎029/2022 6373). Lively and enjoyable Mexican restaurant in the heart of the café quarter, with fair-priced portions of well-cooked classics.

Louis Restaurant, 32 St Mary St. Charming old-fashioned tea rooms with a clientele of genteel old ladies and bargain-hungry students. Food is basic, cheap, lavish in quantity and superb in quality. Last orders 7.45pm Mon–Sat; closed Sun.

Metropolis, 60 Charles St (☎029/2034 4300). Slick modern restaurant and bar that's all floorboards, chrome and smart sofas. Expect anything from salmon fishcakes with tomato coulis to calves livers and mash on the reasonably priced menu.

Minsky's, Cathedral Walk, off Charles St. Café-showbar tucked behind Debenhams – a bit heavy on the loud music but reliable for good-value snacks and meals.

Noble House, 9–10 St David's House, Wood St (☎029/2038 8317). A great, reasonably priced Chinese restaurant, with an excellent range of Peking and Szechuan dishes.

Porto's, St Mary's St (☎029/2022 0060). Authentic Portuguese restaurant in a dark wood-beamed room, serving massive portions of traditional favourites from endless variations on dried cod to the Madeiran speciality, *espetada*: skewers of tender chargrilled meat or fish doused with garlic butter.

Servini's, 3 Wyndham Arcade, off Mill Lane. Tasty sandwiches and salads to take away or eat in.

Tang's, 15–23 Westgate St (☎029/2022 7771). Quite pricey, but the best all-round Chinese restaurant in the city centre, whose owners have a long pedigree in Cardiff cuisine.

Cardiff Bay

Norwegian Church Café, Harbour Drive. Cosy spot for Norwegian open sandwiches, salads, scrumptious cakes and good coffee.

Tides, *St David's Hotel* (☎029/2045 4045). Elegant, expensive modern dining with wonderful Cardiff Bay views and imaginative, superbly prepared dishes: try seared scallops with a sweet chilli dressing and Brecon venison with glazed apples and juniper sauce.

Woods Brasserie, Stuart St (☎029/2049 2400). One of Cardiff's most stylish and pricey establishments where you'll definitely need to book in advance to sample delicacies such as foie gras parfait, sea bass with egg tagliatelli, or the delicious tiger prawns. Lunches are a good bet if you're watching your budget.

Out from the centre

Armless Dragon, 97 Wyvern Rd, Cathays (☎029/2038 2357). Unusual and enjoyable place, with a good range of Welsh dishes amongst a wider bill of fresh fish, game and some decent vegetarian choices, all moderate to expensive in price. Closed Sun.

Blas ar Gymru, 48 Crwys Rd, Cathays (☎029/2038 2132). With a name meaning "taste of Wales", this comfortable restaurant boasts a highly imaginative, moderately priced menu made up of delicious traditional recipes from every corner of Wales. Leave room for the selection of Welsh cheeses. Closed Sun.

Cibo, 83 Pontcanna St, off Cathedral Rd (☎029/2223 2226). Serving ciabatta sandwiches, pasta, pizza and a blackboard of daily specials and desserts, this small, inexpensive and welcoming trattoria provides a slice of Italy in Cardiff. Simple food, well cooked and presented, and served without fuss. No credit cards.

Greenhouse, 38 Woodville Rd (☎029/2023 5731). Modern, licensed vegetarian restaurant serving the likes of wild mushroom soup with amontillado sherry and tasty vegetable tarts. Closed Sun & Mon.

Le Gallois, Romilly Crescent, Canton (☎029/2034 1264). Sophisticated and fashionable restaurant on a busy suburban road and serving delicious (and expensive) French cuisine to discerning punters.

Pizzeria Villagio, 73 Merthyr Rd, Whitchurch (☎029/2052 2483). Simple and authentic family-run trattoria, two miles northwest of the city centre, with a solid selection of cheap pizza, pasta and Italian main dishes.

Saverio, 110–112 Caerphilly Rd, Heath (☎029/2062 3344). Busy, friendly, traditional Italian trattoria two miles the north of the city centre.

Scott's of St Fagans (see p.97). Classy, suitably expensive Pacific Rim and Modern British cuisine served up in a airy conservatory close to the Rural Life museum (see p.112). Menu highlights include pan-fried monkfish with an avocado mousse, or for Sunday brunch, salmon on an artichoke and red onion salad. Closed Sun evening and all day Mon & Tues.

Drinking

Cardiff's pub life has expanded exponentially over recent years, with chic cosmopolitan bars beginning to displace some of the more traditional Edwardian palaces of etched smoky glass and deep-red wood. Don't forget Cardiff's own beer, Brains, whose Bitter is pale and refreshing and whose Dark is a deep mild that should not be missed on a visit to its home city.

Chapter, Market Rd, Canton (☎029/2030 4400). A couple of smart bars in the arts complex with a good choice of real ale and whisky.

Flyhalf & Firkin, Westgate St. Opposite the Millennium Stadium, and always popular, especially on international match days.

Golden Cross, 283 Hayes Bridge Rd. Laid-back restored Victorian pub, rich in atmosphere and with some beautiful tiled pictures of yesteryear Cardiff; a great bet for an unhurried pint.

Hogshead Bar at the Owain Glyndŵr, St John St. Shiny, modern bar right in the heart of the city with a good selection of well-kept real ales.

Model Inn, 14–15 Quay St. The main pre-club watering hole for the beautiful youth with resident DJs playing house and garage.

Mulligan's, corner of St Mary's and Caroline streets. Packed Irish pub with regular live music sessions.

Old Arcade, Church St. Small, old-fashioned arcade bar next to the market, opening its lounge bar on busy nights only. Popular with rugby fans for its game memorabilia.

Po Na Na, St Mary St. Not quite a pub nor a music venue but something in between with North African souk decor and platters from garage and jazz to rare groove. Open until 2am, but you'll need to be early to get in. Closed Sun.

Prince of Wales, St Mary St. Huge, new and frenetic pub that's part of the JD Wetherspoon chain and hauls them in for some of the cheapest pints of Brains in town.

Nightlife

Top-flight **concert venues** such as St David's Hall and the Cardiff International Arena have brought internationally acclaimed orchestras and performers to the city, although these sterile environments are no match for the sweatier gigs and traditional rock found in some of Cardiff's earthier pubs and clubs. The burgeoning Welsh rock scene, both English- and Welsh-language, breaks out regularly in the capital, as does a club and dance scene that is verging on serious trendiness. As club nights change frequently, it's a good idea to call ahead and find out what's going on; numbers are listed below.

Venues and clubs

Club Metropolitan, Bakers Row (☎029/2022 2615). Slightly scruffy venue for some of the best Indie/alternative dance nights in town, with plenty of students drawn by the drink promotions.

Clwb Ifor Bach, 11 Womanby St (☎029/2023 2199). Sweaty and massively fun live music and dance club on three floors with nightly gigs, sessions or DJs, including Seventies and funk nights. Widely regarded as the city's greatest supporter and purveyor of Welsh-language acts.

Dog and Duck, 23 Womanby St (☎029/2022 4754). Late-night, beer-swilling music club with a broad playlist and a predominantly student clientele.

The Emporium, 8–10 High St (☎029/2066 4577). Reliable and perennially fashionable dance club, popular for techno, garage and drum 'n' bass from a succession of guest DJs.

Evolution, Atlantic Wharf. (☎ 029/2046 4444). Cardiff's biggest and flashiest club, stationed firmly in the mainstream.

The Forum, 43–45 Queen St (☎029/2022 7717). Humungous club, with a packed party atmosphere and a range of mainstream and Ibizan-style house and trance. Licensed until 4am, with occasional all-nighters.

Hip'po Club, 3–7 Penarth Rd (☎029/2034 1463). Fairly laid-back dance club without dress restrictions, but with a late licence and a garden. Cool tunes from resident DJs.

Royal Oak, 200 Broadway, Newport Rd (☎029/2047 3984). Odd live-music pub, with something of a fetish for boxing memorabilia – there's even an old boxing ring.

Sam's Bar, 63 St Mary St (☎029/2034 5189). Lively mixed bar-cum-club, with everything from live heavy metal, drag and comedy shows and pumping house DJs. Good for the happy hour (Mon–Thurs 5–7pm), when you can hang outside and check the pulse of the café quarter.

Time Flies (☎029/2022 2915). Held at ever-changing venues, this legendary monthly dance event is Cardiff's biggest night out, with big-name DJs drawing in punters from miles around.

University Union, Park Place (☎029/2039 6421). Big-name live bands and assorted dance nights in this impressive club complex, open to non-students.

The lesbian and gay scene

Although the scene in the city is far from massive, it has grown in both size and confidence over the last few years. One notable new feature is the Mardi Gras lesbian and gay festival, which first took place in 1999 and seems destined to become an annual event. Held in the castle grounds, the festival centres on live acts and stalls; for more information, call the Friend number (see below) or the Cardiff Community Safety Partnership (Mon–Fri 10am–5pm; ☎029/2087 2632). The best sources for current information and advice are **Friend**, an information line for gay men (Tues–Sat 8–10pm; ☎029/2034 0101), and **Lesbian Line** (Tues 8–10pm; ☎029/2037 4051). It doesn't take too much effort to discover what's going on, as practically all of the venues are on Charles Street, just off Queen Street in the city centre – there are also the beginnings of a scene around Mill Lane and Bute Terrace: try the *Golden Cross* (listed under "Drinking", opposite). All venues are for men and women.

Club X, 39 Charles St (☎029/2040 0876). Stylish and popular gay club, open until at least 2am Wed–Sat.

Exit Bar, 48 Charles St. Opposite *Club X*, this late-opening (until midnight) disco bar, with loud music and frantic atmosphere, is the venue of choice for pre-club drinks.

King's Cross, Hayes Bridge Rd/Caroline St. Large and long-established gay pub, with few frills but a friendly atmosphere.

Wow, Bute Terrace. Smart, lively and exceeding popular pub and club with animal print sofas, spiky rubber seats and lavishly mirrored toilets that's the newest on the scene. Kick off the night at *Atlantica*, next door, which has similarly imaginative decor and a dance floor.

Theatre, cinema and live music

Theatre in Cardiff encompasses everything from the radical and alternative at The Point and Chapter to big, blowzy productions at the New Theatre, current home of the Welsh National Opera (*www.wno.org.uk*). Classical **music** is best heard at St David's Hall, although the Cardiff International Arena has siphoned off some of the more prestigious shows. If you're after some traditional Welsh song, check out the twice-weekly rehearsals (Wed & Fri 7.30–9.30pm) of the **Cardiff Male Voice Choir**, which take place at Cowbridge Road Methodist Church in Canton (☎029/2059 4497). Members of the public are welcome, but you should phone first.

Theatre

Bute Theatre, Welsh College of Music and Drama, North Rd (☎029/2037 2175). Student, amateur and travelling productions.

Chapter Arts Centre, Market Rd, Canton (box office ☎029/2030 4400, *www.chapter.org*). Multi-functional arts complex that's home to fine British and touring theatre and dance companies.

New Theatre, Park Place (☎029/2087 8889). Splendid Edwardian city centre theatre that plays host to big London shows.

The Point, West Bute St, Cardiff Bay (☎029/2049 9979). This performance space converted from an old church is good for experimental theatre, music and dance, as well as more mainstream events.

Sherman Theatre, Senghennydd Rd, Cathays (☎029/2023 0451). An excellent two-auditorium repertory theatre hosting a mixed bag of new and translated classic Welsh-language pieces, stand-up comedy, children's entertainment, drama, music and dance. Many plays on Welsh themes in both English and Welsh.

Cinema

Capitol Odeon, Capitol Shopping Centre, Queen St (☎01426/915487).

Chapter Arts Centre, Market Rd, Canton (see above). Cardiff's main art-house and alternative film centre, with four screens.

Odeon, 55 Queen St (☎0870/505 0007).

UCI, Atlantic Wharf (☎0990/888990).

Classical and rock music venues

Cardiff International Arena, Mary Ann St (☎029/2022 4488). Large and imposing venue rising high over the city centre's southern streets and playing host to classical concerts, opera and major rock and pop gigs.

St David's Hall, The Hayes (☎029/2087 8444). Part of the massive St David's shopping centre, this large and glamorous venue is possibly the most architecturally exciting building in town. Home to visiting orchestras and musicians from jazz to opera, it's frequently used by the excellent BBC National Orchestra of Wales as well as major rock gigs.

University Concert Hall, Corbett Rd, Cathays Park (☎029/2087 4816). Home of public concerts by university and local orchestras, jazz groups and easy-listening ensembles.

Welsh National Opera – see New Theatre, above.

Listings

Airlines Cardiff Air Travel for general information (☎01446/711777); Manx Airlines (☎029/2034 2797).

Airport Cardiff International, out at Rhoose, near Barry (☎01446/711111).

Banks and exchange All major banks have branches along High St or Queen St. In addition there's American Express at 3 Queen St (Mon–Fri 9am–5.30pm, Sat 10am–1pm; ☎029/2066 5843), and Thomas Cook at 16 Queen St (Mon–Fri 9.30am–5pm, Sat 10am–1pm; ☎029/2022 4886); both Ames and Thomas Cook will cash currency and traveller's cheques.

Bike rental The Waterfront Bike Hire (☎029/2048 4110; £7 half-day, £9 a day) rent decent machines from their stand in Britannia Park right by the Cardiff Bay Visitor Centre. On the other side of the river footbridge from Radyr station (two stops north beyond Cathays on the Valleys line), try Taff Trail Cycle Hire, Forest Farm Country Park, Whitchurch (Easter–Oct daily 10am–6pm; ☎029/2075 1235).

Books Dillons at 1–2 St David's Link, The Hayes; Lear's at 37 St Mary St; Waterstone's, 2a The Hayes and in the Cardiff Students' Union in Senghennydd Rd, Cathays.

Bus enquiries Cardiff Bus (☎029/2039 6521); National Express (☎029/2034 4751).

Car rental Avis, 14–22 Tudor St (☎029/2034 2111); Enterprise, 45 Penarth Rd (☎029/2038 9222); Hertz, 9 Central Square (☎029/2022 4548).

Dentist For emergency dental work, try the Riverside Health Centre, Wellington St, Canton (☎029/2037 1221).

Football Cardiff City FC, Ninian Park, Sloper Rd (☎029/2039 8636).

Hospital The University of Wales Hospital is in Heath, two miles north of the city centre (☎029/2074 7747).

Internet access The *Cardiff Cybercafé*, 1st floor, 9 Duke St (Mon–Fri 11am–7pm, Sat 10am–6pm; ☎029/2023 5757) is all cyber and no café, but has fast machines at £2.50 a half hour.

Laundries Drift Inn, 104 Salisbury Rd, Cathays Park; GP, 244 Cowbridge Rd, Canton; Launderama, 60 Lower Cathedral Rd.

Newspapers and magazines The Cardiff-based daily *South Wales Echo* is a fairly uninspiring read, although it does have some good listings, especially for films in the city. For a wider overview of arts and events, pick up the free monthly *Buzz!*, available from the tourist office, and cafés and bars around town.

Pharmacy Boots, 5 Wood St (Mon–Sat 8am–8pm, Sun 6–7pm; ☎029/2023 4043).

Police Cardiff Central Police Station, King Edward VII Ave, Cathays Park (☎029/2022 2111).

Post office The Hayes (Mon–Fri 9am–5.30pm, Sat 9am–12.30pm).

Rugby International games at the Millennium Stadium (aka Cardiff Arms Park; ☎029/2023 2661) and club matches next door on the smaller Arms Park pitch (☎029/2038 3546).

Swimming pools and spas Welsh Institute of Sport, Sophia Gardens (☎029/2030 0500). The swanky *St David's Hotel* (see p.97) offers the full hydrotherapy works, and you get glorious views of the Bay as you ease through the marine hydro pool, work out in the gym or pool and submit yourself to all manner of restorative and beauty treatments. Non-resident day packages range from £40 to £100, including lunch.

Travel agencies USIT in the YHA shop, 13 Castle St (☎029/2022 0744); John Cory Travel, Park Place (☎029/2037 1878); Welsh Travel Centre, 240 Whitchurch Rd, Cathays (☎029/2062 1479).

Around Cardiff

On the edge of the Cardiff suburbs, the thirteenth-century fairy-tale fortress of **Castell Coch** stands on a hillside in woods. West of the city, the massively popular **Museum of Welsh Life** tells the country's history with bricks and mortar, with a sundry collection of buildings salvaged from all over Wales. The museum lies in the grounds of the rambling Elizabethan country house of **St Fagans Castle**, restored over the centuries by its various owners. Neither of these sights are on rail lines, though frequent buses provide access to both.

Castell Coch

Four miles north of Llandaff is the plain village of **TONGWYNLAIS**, above which the coned turrets of **Castell Coch** (June–Sept daily 9.30am–6pm; April, May & Oct daily 9.30am–5pm; Nov–March Mon–Sat 9.30am–4pm, Sun 11am–4pm; £2.50, headset tour 50p; CADW) rise mysteriously out of the steep wooded hillside. A ruined thirteenth-century fortress, Castell Coch was rebuilt and transformed into a fantasy castle in the late 1870s by William Burges for the third Marquess of Bute. With its working portcullis and drawbridge, Castell Coch is the ultimate wealthy man's medieval fantasy, isolated on an almost Alpine hillside, yet only a few hundred yards from the motorway and Cardiff suburbs. Many similarities with Cardiff Castle can be seen here, notably the outrageously lavish decor, culled from religious and moral fables, that dazzles in each room. Lady Bute's bedroom, at the top of one of the three towers, comes complete with a fabulously painted double dome, around which are 28 panels depicting frolicking monkeys, some of which were considered lascivious for their day. However, the castle was hardly ever lived in and sees more life today, especially in the tearooms situated in the valet's room. Bus #136 from Central station turns round at the castle gates, or the #26 drops in Tongwynlais, from where it's a ten-minute climb.

The Museum of Welsh Life and St Fagans Castle

Separated from Cardiff by only a sliver of greenery, the village of **ST FAGANS** (Sain Ffagan), four miles west of the city centre, has a rural feel that is only partially disturbed by the busloads of tourists that regularly roll in to visit the **Museum of Welsh Life** (daily: May–Aug 10am–6pm; Sept–April 10am–5pm; £5.50). A branch of the excellent National Museum and Gallery, it's constructed around **St Fagans Castle**, a country house built in 1580 on the site of a ruined Norman castle and furnished in early nineteenth-century style, complete with heavy oak furniture and gloomy portraits. The mansion's formal gardens and eighteenth-century fishponds have also been restored to something akin to their original design.

A collection of period buildings from all corners of Wales have been carefully dismantled and rebuilt on this site since the museum's inception in 1946. The most impressive element is the fifty-acre **outdoor collection**, particularly the diminutive whitewashed 1777 **Pen-Rhiw Chapel** from Dyfed, the pristine and evocative Victorian **St Mary's Board School** from Lampeter and the ordered mini-fortress of a 1772 **Tollhouse** that once guarded the southern approach to Aberystwyth. Many of the domestic structures are farmhouses of different ages and styles – compare, for example, the grandeur of the seventeenth-century red-painted **Kennixton Farmhouse** from the Gower or the homely Edwardian comforts of **Llwyn-yr-Eos Farm** with the threadbare simplicity of the Gwynedd farmworkers' **Llainfadyn Cottage**.

The best demonstration of how life changed over the years for a section of the Welsh population comes in the superlative **Rhyd-y-car** ironworkers' cottages from Merthyr Tydfil. Built originally around 1800, each of the six houses, with their accompanying strip of garden, has been furnished in the style of a different era – stretching from 1805 to 1985. Even the frontages and roofs are true to their age, offering a wade through working-class Welsh life over the past two centuries. Next door are the Victorian **Gwalia Stores** from the mining community of Ogmore Vale, whose smell of polished mahogany is as evocative as the starchy-aproned assistants and jars of boiled sweets on sale. A large and interesting variety of workplaces, including a stinking **tannery**, a **pottery**, three **mills**, a **bakehouse** and a **smithy**, most of which house people demonstrating the original methods, make up a large number of the remaining buildings. Hourly bus #32 (and the irregular #C1) leaves Central station for the village.

The Vale of Glamorgan

The bowl of land at the very bottom of Wales is known as the **Vale of Glamorgan**, a rich, pastoral land of gentle countryside shelving down to a cliff-ridden coastline, punctuated by long, sandy beaches. The Vale does not feature on many visitors' itineraries, as most speed through from Cardiff to Swansea, the Gower and the west. This is a shame, though, for the quiet and pretty towns, together with the sheer profusion of excellent beaches and tumbledown castles, warrant a good couple of days' exploration. Brash seaside resorts at **Porthcawl** in the west and **Barry** to the east contrast with the far more refined, breezy atmosphere of **Penarth**, a prim seaside town clinging to the coat-tails of Cardiff. In between lie yawning wide bays and spectacular ruins, linked by bracing coastal walks. At the western tip of the Vale coast is **Kenfig**, a vast, grass-spotted desert of coastal dunes and nature reserves.

Inland, the lower parts of the Vale are a curious mix of urban reminders such as Wales' major **airport** at Rhoose and occasional looming factories, set against rolling green pastureland sprinkled with charming, if scarcely thrilling, market towns like **Cowbridge**, **Llantrisant** and **Llantwit Major**.

Its proximity to Cardiff makes the Vale easy to explore using **public transport**. The main-line train route through the Vale has a stop at Bridgend, a useful interchange for bus services to the coast and some of the larger inland settlements, although buses from Cardiff reach most places. Barry and Penarth, almost suburbs of Cardiff, are easily reached by bus and train.

Penarth and around

Considering itself a cut above the boisterous capital of Cardiff and the downbeat resort of Barry, **PENARTH** is a quietly enjoyable town wedged between the two. The Cardiff Bay developments over on the other side of the Ely estuary are lending benefits to the town, and new roads are drawing Penarth ever more inexorably into the big city's net, despite the actions of locals to ensure the independence of this half plush suburb, half seaside resort. In any event, Penarth is an easy, enjoyable day out from Cardiff, and a reasonable place to stay, made all the more appealing by the prospect of being able to walk across the barrage to the Cardiff Bay area less than a mile away.

The Town

Penarth is the end of the train line from Cardiff, receiving half-hourly shuttle trains that ply their way from here, through the capital, and out into the valleys. From the train station, a path on the right leads up to Stanwell Road, which continues into the clean-cut Edwardian shopping streets of the town centre.

The red-brick **Turner House Art Gallery** (opening times variable; £1; 029/2070 8870) is on the Plymouth Road, and houses temporary exhibitions, usually brought out from the National Museum's vast collection.

The Dingle path runs down the left-hand side of the Turner House, leading into the showy civic **Alexandra Park**, from whose oceans of flowerbeds, benches full of elderly inhabitants and bandstand it's easy to glean Penarth's genteel character. This picture only intensifies on continuing down the hill onto the charmingly fusty **Esplanade**, with the amusement arcade in the green bubble of a hall on the pier, which also houses the seasonal tourist office and a few fish-and-chip stands. The overall effect, even in the garishly painted wrought-iron seafront, is sedately pleasing.

It seems thoroughly in keeping with the spirit of Penarth that you can spend the day **cruising** the local coastline aboard the *Waverley*, a genuine seagoing paddle steamer that makes sporadic visits to Penarth Pier throughout the summer (though it's sometimes replaced by the more conventionally propelled but no less gracious *Balmora*). A schedule is published well in advance, covering day-trips ranging from cruises around Flat Holm to longer journeys up the Severn Estuary or across the Bristol Channel to ports on the north Devon coast (£10–20). Tickets allowing overnight stays are available, and there are also less expensive sailings from Porthcawl and Swansea. To book a trip, call ☎01446/720656.

Flat Holm and Lavernock Point

Two miles due south of Penarth is **Lavernock Point**, jutting out into the Bristol Channel, a forlorn setting for campsites and pubs, but notable as the place in which conversation was first heard by means of radio waves. This – as a plaque on the wall of the dismal Victorian chapel notes – took place on May 11, 1897, when Guglielmo Marconi sent the immortal words "Are you ready?" over to his assistant George Kemp on the island of **Flat Holm**, three miles out in the Bristol Channel. From Penarth or Lavernock, it is easy to see that Flat Holm (Welsh) and its near neighbour, Steep Holm (English) live up to their names, with Steep Holm jutting proudly out of the water like a great whale and Flat Holm, by contrast, looking like a large dirty plate crowned with a lighthouse that's tipping gently into the waves.

Flat Holm has been used as a Viking anchorage, a cholera hospital and a lookout point. Today it's an interesting and beautifully remote nature reserve, the nest of thousands of gulls and shelducks. **Boats** operated by the Flat Holm Project, Old Police Station, Harbour Road, Barry (☎01446/747661; £8), depart most weekends in summer from Barry Harbour and should be booked well in advance. Most are day-trips giving four hours on the island (including a history, flora and fauna tour), though it's occasionally possible to stay overnight in a small **hostel** mostly reserved for education groups.

Lavernock Point is a fifteen-minute walk from the bus stop on the B4267. Half-hourly bus #P4 operates from Cardiff and Penarth, dropping just near the mildly diverting **Comeston Medieval Village**, which, if you can catch it when it isn't too busy, makes for an agreeable half hour.

Practicalities

Penarth's **tourist office** kiosk (Easter–Sept daily 10am–5.30pm; ☎029/2070 8849) is at the head of the pier on the Esplanade. For those wishing to see Cardiff without the bustle of city life, staying in Penarth is a good option – **accommodation** ranges from the well-placed *Croeso* guesthouse at 13 Plymouth Rd near the station (☎029/2070 9167; ①), and the *Alandale*, just down the road at no. 17 (☎029/2070 9226; ①), to the frillier but magnificent surrounds of the Victorian *Raisdale House Hotel* on Raisdale Road, off the Plymouth Road (☎029/2070 7317, fax 2035 0310; ③). The dingy *Lavernock Point Holiday Estate* on Fort Road (☎029/2070 7310) has tent pitches and cabins generally let by the week. For a day in the lap of luxury, *Avalon* on Beach Road (☎029/2053 1131) is a great, if pricey, leisure, health and beauty centre where you can use the sauna, sunbeds, Turkish bath, spa pool and indoor swimming pool.

Along Penarth Esplanade are a number of pricey **restaurants**. Cheapest for hearty English and Italian snacks is *Rabaiotti's*. Pizza and pasta are available at *Villa Napoli* in the *Glendale Hotel*, 10 Plymouth Rd, or there's the *Prince of India* (closed Sun) at 13 Ludlow Lane, tucked behind the main shops on Windsor Road. For **pubs**, try the enjoyably scruffy and youngish *Railway*, behind the station on Plymouth Road.

Barry and around

Six miles southwest of Penarth, **BARRY** (Barri) is the quintessential Welsh resort of old, whose speciality of loud, chip-swallowing, beer-swilling seaside fun is a million miles from the effete coastal charms of Penarth, or any of the small villages further along the Vale coast. However, until the 1880s, when it was developed as a rival port to the Bute family's Cardiff, Barry was a small fishing village, and line upon line of neat, genteel avenues – many with cheap B&Bs – still run down to the town's quieter, stonier beach at **The Knap**; here, you'll find a 1920s open air **lido pool**, currently in a sad state of disrepair.

Most of the resort's activity centres on **Barry Island** (Ynys y Barri), a stump of land that sticks out from the town along Harbour Road, a riotous sprawl of funfairs and chip shops, interspersed with a laser centre and crazy-golf green. It's all pinned out along a cheerfully pristine prom where kids can still take pony and trap rides for a few pennies. Bang opposite is the **Pleasure Park** (erratic but generally daily: July & Aug 1–10pm; Easter–June & Sept 6–10pm), a shabby collection of rides, arcades and fairground attractions. Until recently, there were more rides at a former holiday camp nearby, but the beachside site is currently being redeveloped, with a hotel, multiplex and restaurants all expected.

The Barry Island sprawl stretches out behind barbed-wire fences along one headland that frames the eastern end of the main beach, sandy **Whitmore Bay**. Running behind the sands is a promenade, much-smartened but still awash with fun pubs, cheap cafés and bleeping, flashing amusement arcades.

Dyffryn Gardens and Llanerch Vineyard

The A4226 heads north from Barry, past the child-oriented **Welsh Hawking Centre** (daily 10.30am–5pm; £3), where a resident population of over 250 birds of prey can be seen and held. Off to the right, lanes descend to the hamlet of **DYFFRYN** and the magnificent **Dyffryn Gardens** (April–Oct daily 10am–8pm; March Sat & Sun 10.30am–4.30pm; £3), set around the Victorian home of a local merchant. Seldom busy, the gardens offer everything from formal lilyponds and billiard table-smooth lawns to joyous bursts of floral colour and the russets, golds and greens of an arboretum. By the lane junction just south of the gardens, you'll find the **St Lythan Long Cairn**, over four thousand years old. It's nowhere near as impressive, however, as its near neighbour, the **Tinkinswood Long Cairn**, a huge, capstoned burial chamber, around 4500 years old. Legend has it that anyone who sleeps beneath the fifty-ton monolith for a night will either die, go raving mad or become a poet: a threat commonly ascribed to other megalithic sites in Wales, such as Cadair Idris (see p.299). You'll find it on the other side of the Dyffryn Gardens entrance, just beside the wooded lane between Dyffryn and **St Nicholas**, a village on the A48 just two miles from Cardiff's Culverhouse Cross roundabout.

Among rolling hills four miles northwest of St Nicholas and one mile south of junction 34 of the M4 you'll find **Llanerch Vineyard** (March–Dec daily 10am–5pm; £3), served infrequently by the #32 bus from Cardiff. This is Wales' most successful winery, producing around 20,000 bottles of white and rosé Cariad wine each year, most of it sold within Wales. The entry fee includes a self-guided tour among the vines and a patch of ancient woodland and, of course, a taste of the finished product.

Practicalities

Frequent trains from Cardiff rattle through Barry Docks and Barry stations before terminating at Barry Island, just steps from the **tourist office** (April–Sept daily 10am–6pm; ☎01446/747171). **Accommodation** in Barry town is plentiful enough, although most places are cheap guesthouses away from the waterfront. Those worth trying include the chintzy *Knights Hotel*, 59 Colcot Rd (☎01446/747496; ①), and the cheerful *Haylings Guest House*, near the beaches and Barry Island at 1 Romilly Rd (☎01446/748614; ①). Out of town, there's very comfortable en-suite B&B at *Llanerch Vineyard* (☎01443/225877, fax 225546, *llanerch@cariadwines.demon.co.uk*; ③), and a similar affair two miles southwest at *Cartreglas Farm* (☎01446/772368, fax 775553; ②), just north of the village of St Donats. Off the A4226 north of Barry, a mile and a half short of the junction with the A48, *Whitton Rosser Farm* (☎01446/781427) has **hostel** accommodation that's mainly geared towards groups.

The Vale coast

West of Barry, the **coast of the Vale** of Glamorgan alternates between craggy cliffs and wide, white-sand beaches. Considering its location between Wales' two great cities, it's surprisingly quiet – you can easily lose all signs of civilization along some of the excellent cliff and beach walks. Until **Kenfig**, you aren't even aware of the industrialized nature of the area, as most of the old-fashioned little towns and seashore villages seem to have escaped the effects of development – a few garish caravan parks notwithstanding.

Llantwit Major

On first impressions, **LLANTWIT MAJOR** (Llanilltud Fawr) is mundane, with modern housing estates and rows of ugly shops only reluctantly revealing the tiny kernel of winding streets at its heart. This is where, in around 500 AD, the scholarly St Illtud educated a succession of young men at his monastery, giving the town the chance to claim the title of Britain's earliest centre of learning. Amongst Illtud's pupils were St David himself and St Patrick, who was abducted from the monastery by Irish pirates to become their patron saint.

Buses drop passengers behind the modern shopping precinct, from where it's a short walk down East Street into the town centre. A miniature **town hall** sits just before the main town square, built in the fifteenth century as the replacement of one destroyed by Owain Glyndŵr; it now serves as council offices. From here, Burial Lane winds its way past the triangular pub-lined village square and down to the front of the magnificent **parish church**, sheltering in a hollow next to the trickle of the Col Huw River.

The first thing that strikes you about the church is its size: it is, in fact, two churches joined at the tower. The older west church, nearer the stream, dates from around 1100; aisles were added in the twelfth and thirteenth centuries to transform it into the nave of a new church. The west church is notable for the collection of decorative Celtic crosses and stones arranged haphazardly inside. Prize amongst these is the exquisitely carved eighth-century boulder at the back of the church, on which the letters ILT and half of a U (remains of ILTUD) can still be made out. A guidebook (£2) about the church and its history is available inside.

At the junction at the top of Burial Lane, Colhugh Street descends for a little over a mile along the scrubby valley of the Col Huw River to the partially sandy **beach**, starting point for some wonderful walks along the caves and inlets of the stratified cliffs and back into the rolling countryside. The best route to take is the path that runs west along the clifftops for two miles to **St Donat's Bay**, dominated by a mock-Gothic castle, dating back to the fourteenth century, that was bought and restored by US tycoon Randolph Hearst in the 1930s, and is now an international college and multipurpose **arts centre** (information ☎01446/792151, box office 794848) easily at the forefront of Welsh efforts to internationalize local culture. As well as theatre, film, dance, exhibitions and community outreach, the centre hosts the excellent **Wales International Storytelling Festival** (Sept) and the **Vale of Glamorgan Festival** (Sept). Halfway along the route, a path dips down to the beach at **Tresilian Bay**, from where you can return to Col Huw cove along the beach.

Llantwit Major is blessed with good pubs and recreational facilities, making it pleasant enough to **stay**. Try the quiet *West House Country Hotel* (☎01446/792406, fax 796147, *www.westhouse.u-net.com*; ④), between the parish church and the castle ruins; for B&B, there's the friendly *Curriers* in the main square (☎01446/793506; ①). Rose Dew Farm on Ham Lane South has the *Acorn* **campsite** (☎01446/794024) where a few tents fight for space amongst the caravans.

For **food**, there are cheap takeaways along East Street and its continuation, Boverton Road, or, in the old town centre, try the daytime *Truffles* café in Church Street, where you should leave plenty of room for the sublime home-made chocolates. Most of the town centre **pubs** do food at lunchtime and in the evening. Of them all, the *Old White Hart* on the Square is best for a meal and has a nice enough atmosphere, although the nearby *Tudor Tavern* is more of an earthy drinking hole.

Southerndown and Ogmore

West of Llantwit Major, the coast ducks and dives past remote cliffs and sandy beaches, punctuated by small streams trickling in from the lush farmland behind. **SOUTHERN-DOWN** is a diffuse holiday village of touristy pubs and one excellent restaurant – *Frolics* on Beach Road (☎01656/880127; closed Sun & Mon), with a creative, wholesome and fairly expensive menu dictated entirely by seasonal specialities – reservations are advisable during the summer. However, the real reason for coming here is **Dunraven Bay**, a beautiful, wide beach backed by jagged cliffs of perfectly defined layers of limestone and shale. In the busy car park by Dunraven Beach is the **Heritage Coast Centre** (☎01656/880157), a small information point about walks and drives along this splendid section of the south Wales coastline. Dunraven is at the western end of a magnificent five-mile **coastal walk**, dipping down into tiny, wooded valleys and up across wide stretches of cliff and sand.

The village of **OGMORE** (Ogwr) is a straggling, windswept sort of place, but lies close to the remains of **Ogmore Castle**, situated about a mile north along the coast from Southerndown. Stunningly situated at the very bottom of a flat valley that is sided by tree-clad hillsides which reveal the peaks of sand dunes behind, the castle dates from the Norman Conquest in around 1100, but its solid central stone keep, in which a few original windows are still intact, was added later in the twelfth century.

Ewenny Priory

The village of **EWENNY**, two miles further up the B4524, is interesting mainly for the towering remains of Benedictine **Ewenny Priory**, tucked away down leafy lanes three-quarters of a mile to the east. Founded in 1141, the priory's formidable, fortress-like walls were intended to protect against the hostile Welsh, who saw the Benedictines as little more than lapdogs of the Norman invaders. The walls, strengthened continuously throughout the thirteenth century, are still very much intact today, broken only by the two huge gateways in which the portcullis holes can still be seen. The priory was dissolved during the Dissolution of the Monasteries, shortly after which a private house was built in the precincts, and it is not possible to visit.

The priory **church**, on the other side of the mansion, is squat and powerful, brooding over the ecclesiastical remains scattered around it. It is divided into two sections by a plain early medieval rood screen. On the western side (nearest to the rest of the priory) is the nave, whose damp, cold interior includes some splendid Norman windows. This nave served as the parish church, as opposed to the eastern chancel, which housed the monastic chapel.

Merthyr Mawr

On the banks of the Ogmore River two miles west of Ewenny, the small village of **MERTHYR MAWR** seems a rural haven of unexpected beauty. A narrow lane steers around into the village of neat thatched and whitewashed cottages, continuing along a wooded glen to its end on the edge of the great dune desert of Merthyr Mawr, stretching over to the distant sea. By the car park is the gaunt ruin of **Candleston**, a fifteenth-century fortified manor house that was abandoned in the nineteenth century as the shifting sands came too close.

Porthcawl

With the usual selection of tatty bungalows and tawdry caravan parks, **PORTHCAWL** is one of Wales' most enduring family resorts. But after resting on its laurels for a few years, the town has finally pulled its socks up, managing to retain its populist air while shrugging off the worst excesses of promenade tackiness. The seafront has been spruced up with new paving, a liberal lick of paint and even the introduction of a smart little "road train" running along the prom. Once you've exhausted the fun of the fair, though, there's little to do other than striking out on enervating walks along the coast or swimming from the sandy beach.

Half-hourly **buses** connect Bridgend with Porthcawl, depositing travellers at the top of the pedestrianized John Street in the town centre. A two-minute walk straight down John Street leads to the Old Police Station, housing the **tourist office** (mid-April to mid-Sept Mon–Sat 9.30am–5pm, also Sun in July & Aug; ☎01656/786639), where you can pick up a fairly useful free town guide, as well as a local history **museum** (sporadic but often daily 2–5pm; 50p). John Street continues down to the Esplanade, a typical line of Victorian and Edwardian hotels along a rocky beach, and where you'll find the domed **Grand Pavilion**, home to assorted seaside entertainment shows, pantomimes and a cinema. East, the Esplanade runs to a lifeboat station at the harbour before veering north alongside the coast as Eastern Promenade, the home of Porthcawl's solid seaside attractions: the **Coney Beach amusement park** behind whelk stalls and candy floss shops that look out over the donkey rides on Sandy Bay, and two vast caravan parks perched over this cove and neighbouring Trecco Bay. On the northwest side of town, a twenty-minute walk from the centre, is the far quieter and more beautiful **Rest Bay**, noted locally as a swimming beach. During the summer, several ageing passenger cruisers offer occasional day-trips (around £15) out into the Bristol Channel and across to the Devon coast: call the tourist office for details.

Accommodation in Porthcawl is plentiful, cheap and concentrated around Mary Street, Gordon Road and Esplanade Avenue: right in the centre are the *Minerva Hotel*, 52 Esplanade Ave (☎01656/782428; ①), which has en-suite rooms; the welcoming *Rosedale Guesthouse*, 48 Esplanade Ave (☎01656/785356; ①); and the cheapest of the lot, *Rossett Guesthouse*, 1 Esplanade Ave (☎ & fax 01656/771664; ①). For something a little more upmarket, try the *Atlantic Hotel* on West Drive (☎01656/785011, fax 771877; ⑤), an establishment in the grand resort tradition recently refurbished to a high standard – rates include breakfast. **Campers** can stay about fifteen minutes' walk north of town at *Brodawell* (☎01656/783231), a simple field site.

There are dozens of places to **eat** in the hotels, pubs and cafés strewn around the town centre: *Enrico's*, 37 The Esplanade (☎01656/78556) turns out respectable pizza, pasta and an extensive range of main courses; *Tribal Coconut*, 27 The Esplanade (☎01656/785304), plunders menus from around the world; and *Pietro's*, a new addition between the two restaurants, serves up fine cakes, coffee and Sidoli ice cream. Of the many **pubs**, the *Royal Oak*, 128 John St, has decent beer and generous food.

Kenfig

The cliffs and beaches north of Porthcawl stop at the one-time fishing port of **KENFIG** (Cynffig), two miles along the coast, where a thriving community founded in the Bronze Age was finally overwhelmed by the shifting sand dunes in the sixteenth century – they have obliterated whole swaths of land, burying houses and the church in its path; the only surviving remains of the town are the miserable stumps of the **castle**. Today, the dunes of Kenfig Burrows have been stabilized by marram grass plantations, and the whole site is open as a **nature reserve** (summer daily 10am–5pm; winter Sat & Sun 2–5pm), with a small display about local wildlife and advice for those who want to go walking or bird-watching at the hide by the freshwater **Kenfig Pool**. Apart from the inevitable gulls, frequent visitors here are oystercatchers, ringed plovers and redshanks. Most remarkable is the reserve's backdrop: first the smoking stacks of the Port Talbot steelworks and second, the great, hazy curve of Swansea Bay stretching for dozens of miles to the Gower. Don't miss the historic *Prince of Wales* pub over the road from the nature reserve, the main survivor of the old port.

The inland Vale

Although not as startlingly scenic as the coast, the Vale of Glamorgan's rural land is speckled with some interesting towns, villages and ruined castles, connected by small, high-hedged lanes. **Llantrisant**, a hilltop market town just off the M4, sits astride the border of mountainous valley and rural vale, while **Cowbridge**, seven miles south, nestles firmly in a green patchwork of countryside, quietly secure in its status as the unofficial capital of the Vale.

Llantrisant

LLANTRISANT perches dramatically between two peaks that rise suddenly out of the flattened valley of the rivers Ely and Clun, ten miles west of Cardiff. It was once encircled by fortifications to exploit its natural position as a watching post over the Vale of Glamorgan, and retains its stump of a castle, next to the church.

The town centre is focused on the **Bull Ring**, where there's a suitably wild-eyed statue (donated by the Cremation Society) of **Dr William Price** (1800–93), dressed in his favoured druid's outfit of moons, stars and a fox fur on his head. Dr Price subscribed to some precocious beliefs – vegetarianism, nudity, republicanism, the unhealthiness of socks, anti-smoking, free love and the potential environmental disasters from mass industrialization. He is best remembered for cremating his dead infant son, Iesu Grist (Welsh for "Jesus Christ"), in a makeshift service on Llantrisant Common in January 1884, burning the small body in an oil drum. He was arrested and, in a sensational trial at Cardiff, acquitted, after which cremation was made legal in the UK.

Overlooking the Bull Ring is the **Model House Craft and Design Centre** (Tues–Sun 10am–5pm; free), which serves as one of the region's best centres for exhibitions, workshops and conventions. It also houses a shop where local crafts are sold, the excellent *Workhouse* café (this was once the town workhouse) and a permanent display on the work of the **Royal Mint**, moved here from London in 1967. All British coins are now minted at Llantrisant, and the small display runs through some of the historical background including examples of coins from the eighteenth and nineteenth centuries and some of the heavy old machinery that once had to be employed.

Cowbridge

The A48 now bypasses **COWBRIDGE** (Y Bont Faen) – and you might want to do the same – although the smugly prosperous town boasts an interesting range of architectural styles and numerous good pubs and restaurants. Cowbridge's Norman street pattern, focusing on the main thoroughfare, is still evident, stretching for almost a mile in a virtual straight line. On the south side of the High Street, Church Street leads under the narrow gatehouse that is the sole remainder of the town's fourteenth-century walls. One-third of a mile further east along the High Street, *Basil's Brasserie* (✆01446/773738; closed Sun) is a good place to eat – it's wise to reserve a table in the summer months.

A little more than a mile out of town, down a quiet lane fringed with high hedges, there is a tiny lay-by opposite the Regency finery of Howe Mill. A path opposite leads along the bank of the River Thaw for quarter of a mile to the gauntly impressive ruins of **Beaupre Castle**, largely an Elizabethan manor house. Built by the local noble family, the Bassetts, Beaupre is a huge shell of ruined Italianate doorways and vast mullioned windows in the middle of a quiet Glamorgan field.

The Vale of Neath

The **Vale of Neath** likes to think of itself as a world apart from the Valleys, looking more towards Cymric Swansea than anglicized Cardiff. **Neath**, focal point of the Vale, is a curious town with antiquities from the Roman, Norman and medieval periods, all set in grim industrial surroundings that somehow make them all the more remarkable. The River Neath flows in from the northeast, past **Aberdulais**, with its impressive, industrial waterfalls, harnessed to generate hydroelectric power. The falls are on the Dulais River, which heads north to the **Cefn Coed Colliery Museum**. The valleys to the east of the Vale of Neath are dealt with in the Valleys section (see pp.78–93).

Neath

The town of **NEATH** (Castell-Nedd) has overcome its past as a centre of copper smelt-ing to become a spacious, pleasantly ordinary place that is much overshadowed by near neighbour Swansea. The tumbledown **castle** ruins (closed to the public) sit unhappily in a corner of the Safeway car park, and not far away in the Gwyn Hall on Orchard Street, you'll find the borough **museum** (Tues–Sat 10am–4pm; free), a mildly interest-ing ramble through Neath's history over the past six thousand years, housed in the splendid surroundings of the Old Mechanics' Institution. Just outside of town on the A465 are the remains of **Neath Abbey** (free access; CADW). The ghostly, dark silhouette of the abbey, founded in the early twelfth century, is wedged in amongst an industrial estate and oily canal. In the sixteenth century, a chunk of the building was converted into a mansion, which later metamorphosed into a copper-smelting works.

Aberdulais and around

Two miles further up the River Neath (accessible by hourly bus from Station Square in Neath) is the village of **ABERDULAIS**, where the River Dulais tumbles over the scoops and platforms of the **Aberdulais Falls** (March Sat & Sun 11am–4pm; April–Oct Mon–Fri 10am–5pm, Sat & Sun 11am–6pm; £2.80; NT). The natural power of the site was first harnessed in 1584 for a copper works that developed into a corn mill, iron-works and a tin-plating unit during the nineteenth century. One hundred and sixty mil-lion litres of deep-green water course over the rocks every day, gouging out bowls of rock and pouring over precarious lips jutting out over the spume below. Some of it is still harnessed, via a mini-hydro station installed during the site's restoration in 1991, and by Europe's largest generating water wheel, built in the original wheel pit. It's all wonderfully interpreted throughout the site, notably in the **turbine room**, where you can see turbine feed water rushing by, inches away, through a glass panel. Nearby, in the old stable block, there are replicas of some of the many paintings of the falls, a venue beloved of eighteenth- and nineteenth-century landscapists, including Turner.

Traffic hurtles by on the A465 dual carriage outside, disturbing the tranquillity of the **canal basin**, directly opposite the Falls. It's quite an interesting spot; there's the dis-used canal fed by a curious low-slung aqueduct over the wide River Dulais, and the four-mile towpath walk up to the basin at **Resolven** is beautiful, as the man-made waterway crisscrosses the route of the river at the bottom of the Vale of Neath. The path starts just behind the *Railway Tavern* pub.

The main A465 heads up the Vale from Aberdulais, with the A4109 branching off north to the **Cefn Coed Colliery Museum** (daily: April–Sept 10.30am–6pm; Oct–March 10.30am–4pm; £3), three miles away. Although not as impressive as the

Rhondda Heritage Park or Big Pit, Cefn Coed includes a huge working winding engine and some well-presented exhibitions about the site, once the deepest anthracite mine in the world. There are also some glorious signposted walks from the museum up into the surrounding wooded hills.

Swansea

Over forty years ago, local boy Dylan Thomas called **SWANSEA** (Abertawe) an "ugly, lovely town", and no one has described Swansea so neatly or accurately since. Large, sprawling and boisterous, Swansea is the second city of Wales, with great aspirations to be the first. It's far more of a Welsh town than Cardiff, and you'll hear *yr iaith*, the Welsh language, spoken daily on its streets.

Thomas' scathing but affectionate epithet rings true at every turn. A jumble of tower blocks and factory units dot the sloping horizons, gathered around the concrete city centre, massively rebuilt after devastating bomb attacks in World War II. But multifarious charms show themselves on closer inspection: some intact old corners of the city centre, the spacious and graceful suburb of Uplands, a wide seafront overlooking the huge sweep of Swansea Bay, and a bold marina development around the old docks. Spread throughout are some of the best-funded **museums** in Wales. Another great bonus is the city's position on the fringe of the ever-popular Gower, with the seaside resorts of **Mumbles** and **Oystermouth** (for both, see p.130), now little more than salty suburbs.

Some history

The city's Welsh name, Abertawe, refers to the settlement at the mouth of the River Tawe, a grimy ditch that is slowly being teased back to life after centuries of use as a sewer for Swansea's metal trades. The English name is believed to have been prompted from Viking sources, suggesting that a pre-Norman settlement existed in the area. The first reliable origins of Swansea came in 1099, when a Norman castle was built here as an outpost of William the Conqueror's empire. A small settlement grew near the coalfields and the sea, developing into a mining and shipbuilding centre that, by 1700, was the largest coal port in Wales.

Copper smelting became the area's dominant industry in the eighteenth century, soon attracting other metal trades to pack out the lower Tawe valley, which grew into a five-mile stretch of rusting, stagnant land and water that has only recently begun to be relandscaped. Drawn by the town's flourishing metal trades, a swiftly growing port and the arrival of the Swansea Canal, thousands of emigrants moved to the city from all over Ireland and Britain; by the nineteenth century, the town was one of the world's most prolific metal-bashing centres.

Smelting was already on the wane by the beginning of the twentieth century, although Swansea's port continued to flourish. Britain's first oil refinery was opened on the edge of the city in 1918, with dock developments growing in its wake. Civic zeal, demonstrated best in the graceful 1930s Guildhall dominating the west of the city, was reawakened after the establishment of an important branch of the University of Wales here in 1920, but World War II had a devastating effect on Swansea, with thirty thousand bombs raining down in three nights in 1941. The rebuilding of the centre has left a series of soulless concrete streets and underpasses weaving between shopping centres, although now, with a population of around 200,000, Swansea is undergoing something of a renaissance. With a resurgent music and club scene, the sparkling new National Literature Centre, Tŷ Llên, and some spirited redesigns of streets and squares in the city centre, Swansea is bouncing back.

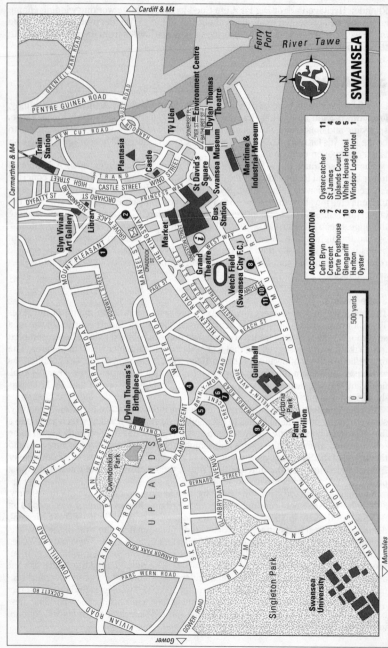

△ Cardiff & M4

River Tawe

Ferry Port

SWANSEA

N

△ Carmarthen & M4

PENTRE GUINEA ROAD

BRENFELL PARK ROAD

BRUS ROAD

NEW CUT ROAD

Train Station

HIGH STREET

ALEXANDRA RD

ORCHARD ST

DYFATTY ST

STRAND

CASTLE STREET

Plantasia

Castle

WIND STREET

Tŷ Llên

SOMERSET PL

PIER ST

BATHURST ST

Environment Centre

Dylan Thomas Theatre

St David's Square

Swansea Museum

Maritime & Industrial Museum

PRINCESS WAY

Library

Glyn Vivian Art Gallery

GROVE PLACE

THE KINGSWAY

MANSEL ST

CRADDOCK ST

MOUNT PLEASANT

CROMWELL STREET

Market

Grand Theatre

ⓘ

WEST WAY

Bus Station

Vetch Field (Swansea City F.C.)

NELSON STREET

PAGE ST

SINGLETON STREET

WESTERN STREET

ARGYLE ST

ST HELEN'S ROAD

BEACH ST

OYSTERMOUTH ROAD

TERRACE ROAD

Dylan Thomas's Birthplace

WALTER ROAD

BRYN-Y-MOR ROAD

CWMDONKIN DR

EATON CRESCENT

KING EDWARDS ROAD

ST HELEN'S AVENUE

Guildhall

Victoria Park

Patti Pavilion

Cwmdonkin Park

UPLANDS CRESCENT

UPLANDS

BERNARD STREET

GLANBRYDAN AVENUE

FINAN CRESCENT

PANT-Y-CELYN ROAD

NIXON DR

CWMDONKIN TERRACE

DYFED AVENUE

GLANMOR ROAD

SKETTY ROAD

GLAMOR PARK ROAD

PARC WERN ROAD

TOWNHILL ROAD

VIVIAN ROAD

COCKETT RD

GOWER ROAD

BRYN MILL LANE

BRYN ROAD

MUMBLES ROAD

Singleton Park

Swansea University

▽ Gower

▷ Mumbles

500 yards

0

ACCOMMODATION

Cefn Bryn	3	Oystercatcher	11
Crescent	7	St James	4
Forte Posthouse	2	Uplands Court	6
Glengariff	10	White House Hotel	5
Harlton	9	Windsor Lodge Hotel	1
Oyster	8		

Arrival, information and getting around

Swansea is the main interchange station for services out to the west of Wales and for the slow line across the middle of the country to Shrewsbury in Shropshire. The **train station** is at the top end of the High Street, a ten-minute walk from the bus station, from where local and national services fan out to all corners of south Wales and beyond. The **bus station**, complete with a highly efficient information office, is sandwiched between the Quadrant shopping centre and the Grand Theatre. On the northern side of the bus station you'll find the municipal **tourist office** (Mon–Sat 9.30am–5.30pm; ☎01792/468321, *www.swansea.gov.uk*), where you can pick up the comprehensive bi-monthly magazine *What's On Outlook*.

As most of the sights are within walking distance of each other, **getting around** Swansea is easy. Popular suburbs near the University, such as Uplands and Sketty, are a bracing half-hour walk from the centre, although SWT buses cover the suburbs thoroughly, and run out into Mumbles and the Gower.

Accommodation

As a lively city on the edge of some of Wales' most popular and inspirational coast and rural scenery, Swansea makes a logical base. Transport is good out into the surrounding areas, and **beds** in the city are less expensive than those in the more picturesque Gower. Dozens of dirt-cheap hotels and B&Bs line the seafront Oystermouth Road, pitched at those catching the Swansea–Cork ferry, and for a few pounds apiece more you can stay in the more salubrious surroundings of leafy Uplands. There are no hostels in Swansea, and only one city-edge **campsite** – *Ynysforgan Farm*, yards from junction 45 of the M4 in Morriston (☎01792/775587) – but you're better off heading for the Gower.

Cefn Bryn, 6 Uplands Crescent, Uplands (☎01792/466687). Cheery enough family-run hotel in Swansea's most elegant suburb. ②.

Crescent, 132 Eaton Crescent, Uplands (☎ & fax 01792/466814). Large, pleasant, well-converted Edwardian guesthouse. All rooms have showers, and half have superb views over the city and the bay. ②.

Forte Posthouse, Kingsway (☎01792/651074). City centre business hotel with all the facilities you'd expect, including a pool, gym and assorted restaurants. ④.

Glengariff, 372 Oystermouth Rd (☎ & fax 01792/458137). Pleasant, if fairly basic, seafront hotel, but with satellite TV in the rooms. ③.

Harlton, 89 King Edward Rd, Brynmill (☎ & fax 01792/466938). Budget guesthouse that's a little yellow around the edges but perfectly adequate and very cheap. ①.

Oyster, 262 Oystermouth Rd (☎01792/654345). Small, friendly hotel with some en-suite rooms, and serving great local cuisine. ①.

Oystercatcher, 386 Oystermouth Rd (☎01792/456574). Cheap and cheerful place with a slightly wider range of facilities than many others in this price band. ②.

St James, 76b Walter Rd, Uplands (☎01792/649984). Small, welcoming hotel in an airy Victorian house. ②.

Uplands Court, 134 Eaton Crescent, Uplands (☎01792/473046). Enjoyable guesthouse in a gracious Victorian villa that's situated in a pleasant area. ①.

White House Hotel, 4 Nyanza Terrace, Uplands (☎01792/473856, fax 455300, *www.thewhitehouse hotel.co.uk*). Extremely well-kept guesthouse with excellent rates for its well appointed rooms; all have satellite TV, and you pay a little more for a private bathroom. Extensive breakfasts are included in the rates, and you can get a good three-course evening meal for £10. Internet access is available. ①.

Windsor Lodge Hotel, Mount Pleasant (☎01792/642158, fax 648996). Like a country hotel in the city, this two-century-old house has nicely decorated en-suite rooms, elegant but comfortable lounges and an evenings-only restaurant serving British and French cuisine. ④.

The City

Swansea's train station faces out onto the morose **High Street**, which heads south into Castle Street and past the remains of the **castle**. The most obvious landmark of the ruins are the semicircular arcades, built into the wall between 1330 and 1332 by Bishop Gower to replace a Norman predecessor. The castle enjoys a new, improved setting against the recently overhauled **Castle Square**, a pleasant amphitheatre of steps surrounding a fountain. The ragbag of architecture around it, however, is still postwar Swansea at its most unadventurous – particularly the dull 1950s block entirely given over to *McDonald's*. If you're a Dylan Thomas fan, or just keen on books, it is worth popping down Wind Street (pronounced as in "whined") to Salubrious Passage for the **Dylan Thomas Bookshop**, filled to the rafters with material on the great man.

A block behind the High Street, the retail park on the Strand includes the great pyramidal glasshouse of **Plantasia** (Tues–Sun & bank holiday Mon 10am–5pm; £2.20), a sweaty world of wondrous tropical plants inhabited by a kind of mini-zoo of tamarin monkeys, butterflies and numerous insects, an aquarium and a thirteen-foot Burmese python.

Alexandra Road forks right off the High Street immediately south of the station, leading down to the **Glynn Vivian Art Gallery** (Tues–Sun 10.30am–5.30pm; free), on the corner of Clifton Hill, a road so steep that the pavement gives way to steps every few yards. This delightful Edwardian gallery houses an inspiring collection of Welsh art including works by Gwen John, her brother Augustus, whose mesmerizing portrait of *Caitlin Thomas*, Dylan's wife, is a real highlight, and Kyffin Williams; the grimy mining portraits of Josef Herman; and a whole room of the huge, frantic canvases of Ceri Richards, Wales' most respected twentieth-century painter. In the early nineteenth century, Swansea was a noted centre of fine porcelain production, of which the gallery houses a large collection, together with pieces of contemporary works from Nantgarw, near Cardiff. Look out too for the frequently changing temporary exhibitions, which are of a consistently high standard.

Belle View Way, off Alexandra Road just south of the gallery, leads to the ugly traffic island that acts as a focus for Swansea's shopping districts, with Orchard Street (a pedestrian link to the High Street), The Kingsway and Princess Way all converging on the same gloomy spot. The main shopping streets lie to the southwest, bounded by The Kingsway and Princess Way. Sheltering underneath the Quadrant Centre, the curving-roofed **market** makes a lively sight, with plenty of bustle, colourful stalls and the smells of flowers, fresh baking and food. On sale are local delicacies such as laver bread, a delicious savoury made from seaweed, as well as cockles trawled from the nearby Loughor estuary, typical Welsh cakes, fish and cheeses.

The Maritime Quarter

The spit of land between Oystermouth Road, the sea and the Tawe estuary has been christened the Maritime Quarter – tourist-board-speak for tarted-up old docks – with a centrepiece of a vast marina surrounded by legions of modern flats. To the north, a small grid of nineteenth-century streets is home to a couple of worthwhile sights.

Entering the area from the east, the main road bridge over the Tawe is guarded by a World War II ack-ack gun that stands as a memorial to the Luftwaffe decimation suffered by Swansea. The city's old South Dock, now cleaned and spruced up, features the **Swansea Museum** (Tues–Sun 10.30am–5.30pm; free), or more properly the Royal Institution of South Wales, on Victoria Road. Wales' oldest public museum was founded in 1835, and much of it is still enticingly old-fashioned, although recent revamping has glitzed up many of the displays. The biggest draw is a wizened Egyptian mummy, but there's plenty of archeological finds, local porcelain and pottery in ancient glass cases, and a marble bust of Gower son, Edward Evans, who perished with Scott in Antarctica in 1912. A small grid of nineteenth-century streets around the museum has been thoughtfully gentrified, and now houses some enjoyable cafés, pubs and restaurants.

Tucked behind the museum in Somerset Place is the new **Tŷ Llên** (Tues–Sun 10.30am–4.30pm; free), the National Literature Centre for Wales. Opened on St David's Day 1995 as part of Swansea's UK City of Literature celebrations – and properly named the Dylan Thomas Centre – it boasts a theatre space, two galleries, a restaurant, book-shops and craft shops. Tŷ Llên is an impressive enough structure, combining the heavily spruced-up nineteenth-century Guildhall with a honeyed modern extension, but it would have been even more striking had the original design – a sweeping glass creation by Wil Alsop, winner of the high-profile competition launched around the proposal – not been scrapped in an unfortunate precursor to the wrangles with Cardiff's planned Opera House (see p.105). Inside, there's a permanent extensive display on Dylan Thomas, including a mock-up of the shed in which he wrote (see Laugharne, p.151) where a fascinating video on his life and work plays continuously.

A hundred yards or so west, behind the *Evening Post* building, the city's **Environment Centre** (daily 10am–4pm; free) is housed in the old telephone exchange on Pier Street. As well as a resource centre for all things green and peaceful, there are regularly changing exhibitions inside.

From here, Burrows Place leads down to the marina and the superb **Maritime and Industrial Museum** (Tues–Sun 10.30am–5.30pm; free). Taking Swansea's seaside position as its starting point, the museum presents a lively history of the city, with a particularly compulsive section on the history of the heavily industrialized Lower Swansea valley. The many vehicles include an old tram that once rattled along the seafront to Mumbles and a rare example of Gilbern cars, Wales' principal contribution to the motor industry which produced all of 800 sporty numbers between 1966 and 1973. Don't miss the working **woollen mill**, where rows of black machinery, greasy with the wool's lanolin, are operated by staff who gradually turn raw fleece into blankets. The museum's tramshed annexe houses a lively history of the Mumbles railway, built in 1804 as the world's first passenger-carrying railway and closed in 1960, with numerous fact-filled wall displays and a great video showing scratchy footage of the big red locomotives in action. The collection is set to change during the first three years of the new millennium, as a large maritime collection formerly in Cardiff is fused with existing displays to form the Wales Waterfront Museum.

The Maritime Museum faces out onto a flotilla of yachts bobbing in the marina. Close by stands John Doubleday's statue of Dylan Thomas, dubbed "A Portrait of the Artist as Someone Else", due to its remarkable lack of resemblance to the poet. Just behind the statue, on Gloucester Place, is the mural-splattered warehouse that has now become the **Dylan Thomas Theatre**, which intersperses productions of his work with visiting and local companies' offerings. Slap opposite is the **Swansea Arts Workshop** (daily 11am–5pm; free) in a beautifully converted old chapel. Changing exhibits complement a small shop selling quality local crafts.

West Swansea

West of the city centre, St Helen's Road dips down to the seafront near the tall white tower of the **Guildhall** and Walter Road, staying inland until the airy suburb of **Uplands**. The Guildhall, a typically soaring example of 1930s civic architecture, contains **Brangwyn Hall** (☎01792/301301 for access), a frequent venue for some excellent classical concerts that takes its name from one Sir Frank Brangwyn, who painted the eighteen enormous British Empire Panels lining the hall. Immediately behind the Guildhall, down by the coast road, the most prominent feature of **Victoria Park** is the **Patti Pavilion**, a poorly maintained but once graceful green-roofed hall with glass sides, a gift from opera singer Adelina Patti, brought here from her home at Craig-y-nos in the Brecon Beacons (see p.204). The pavilion – used for concerts, variety shows, gigs and even raves – was rebuilt with the help of the BBC TV show *Challenge Anneka*. Unfortunately, planning permission had not been sought and a predictable rumpus ensued before retrospective permission was granted.

Three-quarters of a mile further along the coast road, the drab, postwar buildings of **Swansea University** afford a commanding view over the bay stretching to Mumbles Head. Within the complex is the eclectic **Taliesin Arts Centre**, Swansea's most imaginative performance space, together with the **Ceri Richards Gallery** (Mon–Fri 10.30am–5pm, Sat noon–6pm; free), specializing in touring exhibitions, frequently by contemporary Welsh and Celtic artists. A new addition to the building is the **Egypt Centre** (Tues–Sat 10am–4pm; free), Wales' pre-eminent Egyptology exhibit. The collection is split in two: The House of Death, with all the expected funerary paraphernalia; and The House of Life, covering more of the daily grind beside the Nile, though even here most of the artefacts come from tombs. The approach here is essentially educational – you could spend hours genning up on Nefertiti or just take a quick look at the display of amulets or the mysterious truncated pyramid placed as an offering in the tomb of one of the New Kingdom's more colourful characters, Paneb.

At Blackpill, a mile or so further west and midway between Swansea city and Mumbles, are the **Clyne Gardens** (unrestricted access), the fifty-acre grounds of the Vivian family's old estate. There are some lovely walks through rhododendron glades, bog gardens, woods, meadows and past a few follies, and the gardens are particularly spectacular each May when the azaleas are in bloom.

Hourly buses leave the Quadrant depot to trundle along Walter Road in the direction of Uplands, which is otherwise a half-hour walk from the city centre. North of the main road, leafy avenues rise up the slopes past the sharp terraces of **Cwmdonkin Park**, at the centre of which is a memorial to Dylan Thomas inscribed with lines from *Fern Hill*, one of his best-known poems. From the park, the views over huddles of houses down to the curving shoreline are breathtaking. On the eastern side of Cwmdonkin Park is Cwmdonkin Drive (reached from the main road via The Grove), a sharply rising set of solid Victorian semis, notable only for the blue plaque that marks no. 5 as Thomas' birthplace.

Eating, drinking and nightlife

Swansea's metamorphosis from a sturdily working-class, industrial city into a would-be tourist centre continues unabated, and is manifest in its pubs, restaurants and entertainment centres. Many of the grittier, older establishments survive, but increasing numbers are being steadily gentrified, particularly along Wind Street where a handful of fashionable places have recently sprung up. This leaves a fairly stark choice between grotty, if more interesting, places and some rather sterile newer developments. As a major Welsh town, the city is well placed for **nightlife**, with most passing performing artists obliged to make a stop here. Clubwise, Swansea divides into brasher youthful places along The Kingsway, while a slightly older crowd frequent establishments along Wind Street.

Restaurants and cafés

Bengal Brasserie, 67 Walter Rd, Uplands (☎01792/643747). Best of the many Indian restaurants in Swansea and well worth the ten-minute walk from the city centre.

Bizzie Lizzie's, 55 Walter Rd (☎01792/473379). Though it's unprepossessing from the outside, it's well worth venturing into this relaxed and informal cellar-bar bistro for the good range of cheapish Welsh, international and vegetarian dishes.

Casa Reba, 8 Craddock St, off The Kingsway (☎01792/643526). Spanish eatery with a reasonable lunch menu and a more extensive and expensive evening selection.

Eleo's Brasserie, 33 The Kingsway (☎01792/648609). Gloriously tacky mock olde-worlde bistro, with pub classics and pasta dishes in large quantities at reasonable rates. An associated daytime café and patisserie is next door.

Govinda's, 2 Humphrey St (☎01792/455438). Vegetarian restaurant in the Hare Krishna tradition, selling very cheap, if somewhat insipid, meals and freshly pressed juices.

Hanson's, Pilot House Wharf (☎01792/466200). Low-key restaurant on the far side of the marina at the end of Bathurst Street serving tasty and well-presented dishes such as chicken with Mediterranean vegetables in a red pepper sauce or salmon in lemon butter. Closed Sun evening.

Hwyrnos, Green Dragon Lane, off Wind St (☎01792/641437). Fixed moderately priced Welsh evening menu plus harp-twanging entertainment in an extremely convivial, bordering on boozy, atmosphere. It's mainly aimed at groups, but if you call ahead they'll try to match you up with another party.

Monkey Café, 13 Castle St. Groovy, inexpensive, mosaic-floored café with a relaxed atmosphere. Great for whiling away an hour over coffee or tucking into sandwiches, cakes and a selection of Mexican and Italian dishes, many vegetarian.

New Capriccio, 89 St Helen's Rd (☎01792/648804). Popular Italian restaurant with bargain lunch menu. Closed Sun evening and Mon.

Ribcage Brasserie, 18 Anchor Court, Victoria Quay, Swansea Marina (☎01792/648555). Lively, inexpensive eatery popular with a young, pre-club set, and serving steaks, burgers, Tex-Mex, salads and the like.

Steak by Night, 10 Craddock St, off The Kingsway (☎01792/466810). Late-opening, standard-priced and lively steakhouse, with a dependable menu.

219 High St (☎01792/459050). Swansea's finest modern restaurant; the highlights of the suitably pricey menu include goat's cheese and vegetable terrine with herb and pesto vinaigrette or chargrilled tuna with bitter leaf salad. Puddings, such as rhubarb creme *brûlée* are sublime. Closed Sun & Mon.

Tŷ Llên, Somerset Place (☎01792/463980). Refined but relaxed dining in the National Literature Centre, with a good range of reasonably priced local specialities.

Bars, pubs and clubs

Adam and Eve, 205 High St. Traditional pub that's well known for the excellence of its beer. A great atmosphere and varied clientele.

Bush Inn, High St. Only worth mentioning in warning: don't be deceived by the charmingly olde-worlde exterior – inside, it's a loud, video-filled nightmare.

Celtic Pride, 49 Uplands Crescent, Uplands (☎01792/645301). Good local pub with almost nightly live music, including jam sessions and Welsh music.

Code, 15 The Kingsway (☎01792/476520). At the heart of Swansea's cheesier clubland, with mainstream house music midweek and more demanding hip-hop or drum 'n' bass at weekends.

Duke of York, Princess Way. Swansea's best venue for jazz and blues music, as its *Ellington's* club (small fee payable) hosts nightly gigs.

Escape Club, Northampton Lane, off The Kingsway (☎01792/652854). Enormous, purpose-built dance venue that pulls the big name DJs for a dizzying array of club nights.

No Sign Bar, 56 Wind St. A narrow frontage leads into a long, warm pub interior that's a frequent starting point for nights out along this street. The etymology of the name is explained in depth in the window.

Palace, 156 High St (☎01792/457977). Two-room club that vies with *Escape* for the most hardcore tunes.

Po Na Na, 22 Wind St (☎01792/465187). New but thriving club with Moroccan "Souk" decor and a music policy centred around garage and hip-hop. Small cover on Saturday and any other night they have a DJ; call ahead to check what's on. Closed Sun.

Queen's Hotel, Gloucester Place, near the marina. Large old hotel and pub firmly in the Swansea seafaring tradition, with good snack lunches and Sunday roasts and bags of gritty atmosphere.

Theatre, cinema and classical music

Brangwyn Hall, The Guildhall, South Rd (☎01792/635489). Vastly impressive music hall in the Art Deco civic centre that hosts regular concerts by the BBC National Orchestra of Wales and others.

Dylan Thomas Centre, Gloucester Place, by the marina (☎01792/463980). Reruns of Thomas' classics, intertwined with other modern works.

Grand Theatre, Singleton St (☎01792/475715). One of Britain's best provincial theatres, with a wide-ranging diet of visiting high culture, comedy, farce and music.

Patti Pavilion, Victoria Park (☎01792/477710). Restored former opera hut of chanteuse Adelina Patti, now home to numerous musical and theatrical performances.

Taliesin Arts Centre, Swansea University (☎01792/296883). Welsh, English and international visiting theatre, music and film, including offbeat and alternative fare.

UCI Cinema, The Strand (☎01792/645005). Ten-screen multiplex.

Listings

Bike rental Schmoo's Cycles on Lower Oxford St (☎01792/470698; closed Sun) rent bikes and will deliver and pick up within ten miles.

Books Try the Dylan Thomas Bookshop on Salubrious Passage; the Uplands Bookshop at 27 Uplands Crescent; or Waterstone's on Oxford St.

Bus enquiries The SWT office is in the Quadrant Centre bus station, Plymouth St (Mon–Fri 8.30am–5.30pm, Sat 8.30am–5pm); for telephone enquiries call ☎01792/475511 (Mon–Sat 8.30am–6pm, Sun 10am–6pm).

Car rental Enterprise (☎01792/480484) have the best value rentals, will deliver and pick up, and often have excellent value weekend specials.

Ferries Swansea–Cork Ferries (☎01792/456116) leave roughly once a day for Cork in Ireland from the dock around a mile east of the town centre. The crossing takes about ten hours and generally leaves at 9pm.

Festivals The annual Swansea Festival of Music and the Arts takes place around October, and the city's Beer Festival occupies the Patti Pavilion in mid-April; details of both from the tourist office.

Hospital Singleton Hospital, Sketty Park Lane, Singleton, West Swansea (☎01792/205666).

Internet access Swansea Central Library, Alexandra Rd, opposite the Glyn Vivian Art Gallery has Internet access (Mon–Sat 9.30am–5pm) for £1.50 a half-hour.

Laundries Brynmill Launderette, 121 Rhyddings Terrace, Brynmill; Lendart, 71 Uplands Crescent, Uplands.

Pharmacies Kingsway Pharmacy, 39 The Kingsway (Mon–Sat 10am–6pm).

Police The main station is near the train station on Orchard St (☎01792/456999).

Post office 35 The Kingsway (☎01792/655759).

Rugby Swansea Rugby Club, one of Wales' premier sides, play at St Helen's Park in Uplands (☎01792/648654).

Soccer Swansea City FC at the Vetch Field (☎01792/474114).

Surfing Information and equipment for water sports and other outdoor activities is available from the High Adventure shop, 6 Wind St (☎01792/648712).

Gower

A fifteen-mile peninsula of undulating limestone, **GOWER** (Gŵyr) points down into the Bristol Channel to the west of Swansea. The area is fringed by sweeping yellow bays and precipitous cliffs, caves and blowholes to the south, and wide, flat marshes and cockle beds to the north. Brackened heaths with prehistoric remains and tiny villages lie between, with castle ruins and curious churches spread evenly around. Out of season, the winding Gower lanes afford opportunities for exploration; but in the height of the summer, they are congested with caravans shuffling from one overpriced car park to another.

Gower can be said to start in Swansea's western suburbs, along the coast of Swansea Bay that curves round to a point in the pleasantly old-fashioned resort of **Mumbles** and Mumbles Head, which marks the boundary between the sandy excesses of Swansea Bay and the rocky inlets that dip and tuck along the serrated coastline of southern Gower. This southern coast is punctuated by sites exploited for their defensive capacity, best seen in the eerie isolation of the sandbound **Pennard Castle**, high above **Three**

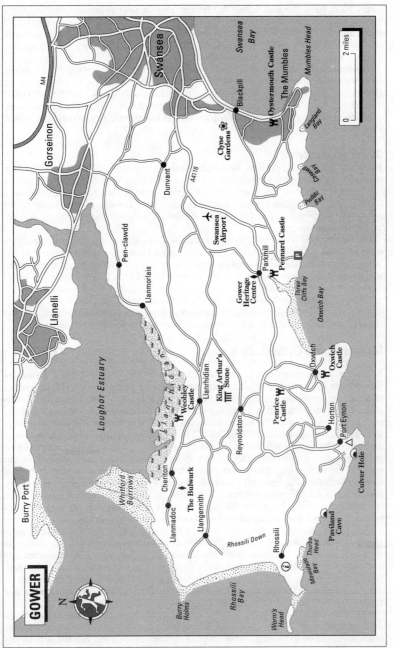

Cliffs Bay. West, the wide sands of **Oxwich Bay** sit next to inland reedy marshes, beyond which is the glorious village of **Port Eynon**, home to an excellent youth hostel and a beautiful beach. West of Port Eynon, the coast becomes a wild, frilly series of inlets and cliffs, topped by a five-mile path that stretches all the way to the peninsula's glorious westernmost point, **Worms Head**.

Rhossili Bay, a spectacular four-mile yawn of sand backed by the village of Rhossili, occupies the entire western end of Gower from Worms Head to the islet of **Burry Holms**, and provides some the best surfing opportunities in Wales. The northern coast merges into the tidal flats of the estuary, running past the salted marsh of **Llanrhidian**, overlooked by the gaunt ruins of **Weobley Castle**, and on to the famous cockle beds at **Pen-clawdd**.

Gower practicalities

There are no train services on Gower, but with its proximity to urban Swansea **bus** transport is reasonably comprehensive. Daily services run from Swansea to Mumbles every ten minutes; from Swansea to Pennard every hour; and from Swansea to Rhossili, Oxwich and Port Eynon every couple of hours. There are also regular buses to the northwestern corner around Llanrhidian, Weobley Castle and Llangennith, again originating in Swansea.

Driving around Gower in peak season can be frustratingly slow and parking chronically expensive. Cycling, together with walking, are ideal ways to tour the area, as the peninsula's attractions are all within a short distance of each other and, in many cases, well off-road. The only **bike rental** on Gower is from Clyne Valley Cycles in Walters Row, Dunvant (☎01792/208889; you can also pick up a machine in Swansea (see p.128).

It's worth bearing in mind that **accommodation** is limited on Gower, and generally in very short supply throughout the summer. Even when you find something, the chances are the bathroom won't be en suite unless you're paying a sizeable amount.

Mumbles and Oystermouth

At the far westernmost end of Swansea Bay and on the cusp of Gower, **Mumbles** (Mwmbwls) is a lively and enjoyable alternative base to Swansea, and its diverse range of seaside entertainment, fine restaurants and the legendary Mumbles Mile of pubs make it even more attractive. Derived from the French *mamelles*, or "breasts" (a reference to the twin islets off the end of Mumbles Head), Mumbles is now used to refer to the entire loose sprawl of **OYSTERMOUTH** (Ystumllwynarth) – a term used pretty much interchangeably with Mumbles. Here, the seafront is an unbroken curve of budget hotels, breezy pubs and cafés leading down to the old-fashioned pier and funfair towards the rocky plug of Mumbles Head. Behind the promenade, a busy warren of streets climb the hills, lined with souvenir shops, department stores and a glut of fine restaurants – Mumbles is deservedly renowned for its cuisine. Around the headland, reached either by the longer barren coast road or a short walk over the hill, is the district of **Langland Bay**, with a sandy beach quite popular with surfers.

The hilltop above the town is crowned by the ruins of **Oystermouth Castle** (April–Oct daily 11am–5.30pm; £1). Founded as a Norman watchtower, the castle was strengthened by the Normans to withstand Welsh attacks before being converted into a residence during the fourteenth century. Today you can see the remains of a late thirteenth-century keep next to a more ornate three-storey ruin incorporating an impressive banqueting hall and state rooms. The surrounding parkland affords spectacular views over the Mumbles headland, Swansea and its sweeping bay.

The scores of pubs along the seafront constitute the **Mumbles Mile**, one of Wales' most notorious pub crawls. The focus was traditionally *The Mermaid*, which was much favoured by the young Dylan Thomas. It burnt down a few years ago; probably for the best, as it had become packed full of Dylan Thomas kitsch and memorabilia and witlessly renamed *Dylan's Tavern*. These days, places worth a lingering stop include *The Antelope*, the *Oystercatcher* and the *White Rose* – all enjoyable, if somewhat commercialized.

Practicalities

The small **tourist office** (daily: June–Aug 9.30am–5.30pm; April, May, Sept & Oct 10am–4pm; (☎017792/361302) is in a Portakabin on the seafront, near the foot of Newton Road. Staff can advise on **accommodation** around Gower as well as in Mumbles. Good choices here include: *Henfaes Guesthouse*, 4 Rotherslade Rd (☎01792/366003; closed Nov–March; ①), which has been recently refurbished and has good beach access; the shorefront *Tides Reach*, 388 Mumbles Rd (☎01792/404877; ②), an elegant Victorian town house with en-suite rooms; the tastefully furnished and very welcoming *Alexandra House*, 366 Mumbles Rd (☎01792/406406, fax 405605; ②); or the sumptuous *Osborne Hotel* (☎01792/366274, fax 363100; ⑥), high on a clifftop in Rotherslade Road, Langland Bay. Above Langland Bay, on Langland Court Road, is the mock-Tudor *Langland Court Hotel* (☎01792/361545, fax 362302; ⑤) and, up the road in Higher Lane, the delightful *Hillcrest House Hotel* (☎01792/363700; ④), which serves exceptionally good food. The only **hostel** at this end of Gower is at *Clyne Farm Centre*, Westport Avenue (☎01792/403333), which has six-bunk rooms, bargain campsites and serves breakfasts as big as you like. It's located just off the A4118 in Blackpill, roughly midway between Mumbles and Swansea, and you can arrange for someone to come and pick you up if you arrive by bus, train or ferry.

There are several good **places to eat** – not for nothing is Mumbles twinned with Kinsale, Ireland's culinary capital. Highlights include the inexpensive *Coffee Denn*, 34 Newton Rd, which is good for coffee, sandwiches and light lunches, but especially notable for cakes, pastries, handmade chocolates and imaginative ice-cream sundaes. The moderately priced *Seafront 604*, 604 Mumbles Rd, does a reasonable line in Mexican and Latin American meals, but for something special, head for *Patricks*, 636 Mumbles Rd (☎01792/360199; closed Sun evening), a fairly formal and expensive restaurant serving delicious dishes such as baked pawpaw with Indonesian spiced risotto or guinea fowl with wild mushrooms.

If you need to do some washing, try Baywash (☎01792/403423) on Mumbles Road opposite the *West Cross Inn*.

The south and west Gower coasts

From Mumbles Head, the limestone crags of the **southern Gower coast** twist and delve the fifteen miles or so to Worms Head, at the bottom of Rhossili Bay. Many of the sandy bays that rupture the cliffs are easily accessible by car, so they tend to be crowded in peak season.

From Mumbles Head to Three Cliffs Bay

The first few miles of the southern Gower coast are highly developed, with stern hotels and beach huts backing some fine sands. Best locally is **Langland Bay**, a good gash of sand between two headlands, the beach is very popular with surfers, partly because it is only a mile or so from the middle of Mumbles. The narrow, golden-sanded **Caswell Bay** comes next, but it's best to crack on around the stunning cliff path to the tiny and remote old smugglers' haunt of **Brandy Cove**, or pebbly **Pwlldu Bay**, which is owned by the National Trust and backed by a wooded ravine that offers many stunning walks. Brandy Cove and Pwlldu Bay are inaccessible by car; park in Bishopston village and walk the last mile or so.

Three miles along, huge **Three Cliffs Bay** is one of Gower's finest beaches, a silent valley fringed by dunes and the eerie ruins of **Pennard Castle**. Although justifiably popular, its relative inaccessibility ensures that it's never too packed. The best approach is from the car park at **Southgate**, from where you hike a mile or so west along cliff tops inhabited by semi-wild ponies to Three Cliffs Bay, where you turn inland and follow the boundary of the golf course to the castle. Otherwise, you can try one of the paths that fan out along the tufty valley of the Pennard Pill from **PARKMILL**, a tourist honeypot on the main A4118. Here, the twee charms of the **Gower Heritage Centre** (daily 10am–6pm; £2.60) are best suited to folk needing to entertain kids; there's a working Welsh flour mill and the chance to have a go at throwing a clay pot or feeding bread to assorted waterfowl.

A mile north of Parkmill (reachable via the lane that heads past the Heritage Centre) is the Neolithic (3000–1900 BC) burial chamber known, in honour of the thirteenth-century lords of Oystermouth Castle, as **Parc le Breos**. Although over-restored and not intrinsically fascinating, the roofless chamber is impressive, if only because of its age and sheer size – seventy feet long and divided into four separate chambers. In 1869, the skeletons of two dozen people were found inside. Just beyond the chamber and to the right, a deep fissure in a limestone outcrop marks the position of the dank and musty **Cathole Rock Cave**, in which flint tools, dating back over 12,000 years have been found.

The best local **B&B** is almost a mile up a lane beside the Heritage Centre: one of the original Gower manor houses, the grand and welcoming *Parc-le-Breos House* (☎01792/371636, fax 371287; ②) also rents bikes (£8 per day), and leads full-day horseback sightseeing trips for £18. Alternatively, there's the well-equipped *Winston Hotel* at 11 Church Lane in Bishopston village (☎01792/232074, fax 234352; ③), which has an indoor pool, sauna and a restaurant but somehow misses the beat at every opportunity. **Campers** should make for *North Hills Farm* (April–Oct; ☎01792/371218), overlooking Three Cliffs Bay between Parkmill and Penmaen.

Oxwich

One of the most curious landscapes in Gower is the reedy **nature reserve** around **Oxwich Burrows**, a flatland of salt and freshwater marshes reached via the lane that forks left off the A4118 at the ruined gatehouse of the privately owned **Penrice Castle**. The marshes are dotted with pools and bounded by ancient woodland and, down by the coast, sweeping dunes. Close by on the coast, the scattered village of **OXWICH** is grouped next to the gaping sands of Oxwich Bay. The sands and sea around here regularly receive awards – including the coveted EU blue flag – for their quality, and this is certainly one of Gower's most popular resorts. One way to sample the waters between May and mid-September is with Gower Windsurfing (☎01797/701318), who will take you out for around £10 an hour and offer tuition for beginners and experts.

The squat church of St Illtud sits alone, away from the village, at the top of the beach. A quieter beach can be found just over a mile away at **Slade Sands**, reached along the lane that climbs from the Oxwich crossroads past the ruins of a Tudor manor, known as **Oxwich Castle** (May–Sept daily 10am–5pm; £2; CADW). It's a fine example of Tudor gentrification, as Sir Rice Mansel (member of a powerful Welsh dynasty) upgraded his ancestral home into what we see today between 1520 and 1538. His son Edward added the multiwindowed eastern range, a pile of rooms together with a highly fashionable long gallery that fell into ruin shortly afterwards.

The popularity of Oxwich is evident in its plentiful **accommodation**: B&Bs include *Little Haven* (☎01792/390940; ①; closed Dec), *Surfsound Guesthouse* (☎ & fax 01792/390822; ②) and *Woodside* (☎01792/390791; ②; closed Nov–Feb), all on the main street and all with en-suite rooms. Nearby, the staid *Oxwich Bay Hotel* (☎01792/390329, fax 391254; ④) enjoys splendid isolation by the sands near the parish church. The *Oxwich Camping Park* on the Penrice road over a mile back from the beach (April–Sept; ☎01792/390777), has a swimming pool and laundry on site.

Street Festival, Cardiff Bay

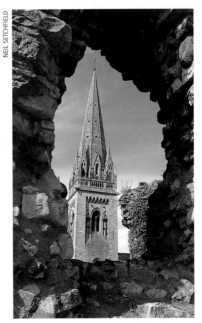

Millennium Stadium, Cardiff

Llandaff Cathedral, Cardiff

The Steel Wave, Newport

Aberfan Memorial

Green Bridge of Wales, Pembrokeshire

Three Cliffs Bay, Gower

Strumble Head, Pembrokeshire

Hay-on-Wye, Powys

Carreg Cennan

Craig-y-Fan and Tor-y-Foel, Brecon Beacons

Horton and Port Eynon

The rocky cliffs from Oxwich Point fade into wide stony bays towards the quiet village of **HORTON**, with a decent beach, and brasher **PORT EYNON**, busy and touristy by comparison, with a clutch of chip shops and the laid-back *Ship Inn*. The villages' sands and dunes are sheltered by a prominent headland, easily reached by a series of paths that wind their way along the shore from the car park, past the Victorian lifeboat station, now the youth hostel, and above the bleak ruins of the old shoreline salt house and oyster pools. The headland, owned by the National Trust, is a wild and windy spot, where tufted grass gives way to sharp limestone crags. A natural cave at the tip can be seen from above, a great dome-shaped chasm that plummets into the hillside. Around the headland to the west is the more ordered and accessible **Culver Hole**, built into the cliffs. A man-made cave, it may originally have been a stronghold for the long-gone Port Eynon castle, and has served its time subsequently as a smugglers' retreat, dovecote and armoury.

The lichen-spattered limestone headland casts good views over the curve of Port Eynon Bay and the cliffs round to Rhossili, five miles west. This **coastal path** is the most spectacular walk on Gower, veering along crags above thundering waves for five miles. The only real beach along this stretch is the secluded **Mewslade Bay**, just short of Rhossili and accessible by the path from Pitton. Along the coast walk, about midway between the two villages, is **Paviland Cave**, the site of an astonishing find in 1823: the skeleton of a Stone Age hunter, dated to at least 19,000 years old. At **Thurba Head**, on the eastern side of Mewslade Bay, there are a few scant remains of an Iron Age hillfort sited magnificently a few hundred feet above the waves.

Port Eynon hogs the accommodation limelight. Its YHA **hostel** (☎ & fax 01792/390706; ①; closed Nov–March) is particularly good; a welcoming former lifeboat station necessarily well sited right by the beach, and with a warden who is passionately knowledgeable about the area. Otherwise, there's the *Culver House Hotel* (☎01792/390755; ②), the simple but appealing *Highfield* (☎01792/390357; ①), four hundred yards from the water on the main road, or **camping** at *Carreglwyd Park* (☎01792/390795) and *Bank Farm*, off the A4118 towards Horton (☎01792/390228).

Rhossili, Worms Head and Llangennith

The village of **RHOSSILI** (Rhosili), at the western end of the Gower, is a centre for walkers and beach loungers alike. Dylan Thomas described the terrain to the west of the village as "rubbery, gull-limed grass, the sheep-pilled stones, the pieces of bones and feathers", and you can tread in his footsteps to **Worms Head**, an isolated string of rocks with the spectacular appearance of a basking Welsh dragon, accessible for only five hours at low tide. At the head of the road, near the village, is a well-stocked, helpful **National Trust information centre** (April–Oct daily 10.30am–5.30pm; Nov–Dec Sat & Sun 11am–4pm; ☎01792/390707). It posts the tide times outside for those heading for Worms Head, and holds details of local companies renting surfing and hanggliding equipment.

Below the village, a great curve of white sand stretches away into the distance, a dazzling coastline vast enough to absorb the crowds, especially if you are prepared to head a little way north along it towards **Burry Holms**, an islet three miles distant that is cut off at high tide. The northern end of the beach can also be reached along the small lane from Reynoldston, in the middle of the peninsula, to **LLANGENNITH**, on the other side of the towering sandstone **Rhossili Down**, rising up to 633ft. In the village, PJ's Surfshop (☎01792/386669) has a wide range of **rental surfboards** (£7 per day), wetsuits (£7 per day) and boogie boards (£5 per day); staff also update the 24hr "Surfline" (60p per minute at all times). A mile away at the Hillend campsite (see overleaf), the Welsh Surfing Federation's Surf School (☎01792/386426) runs half-day (£18) and full-day (£28) **surfing courses**.

There are some great B&Bs in Rhossili village, including: *Hampstead* (☎ & fax 01792/390545; ②) almost half a mile back from the beach but with superb views from the large rooms, some of which are en-suite; and the very friendly *Meadow View*, a mile from the beach (☎01792/390518, fax 390522; ①) with small but nicely furnished rooms. There's a **campsite** a further half-mile from the beach at *Pitton Cross Park* (☎01792/390593), on the B4247. At a pinch you could eat at the *Worms Head Hotel* in the middle of the village, but anyone with transport is better making for the *King Arthur Hotel* in Reynoldston (see below).

Accommodation in Llangennith is comfortable and convenient at *The Post Office* (☎ & fax 01792/386201, *jan@llangennithpo.demon.co.uk*), right in the centre of the village, or at *Hillend* (☎01792/386204), a caravan and campsite at the end of the southern lane from Llangennith, behind the dunes that bump down to the glorious beach.

Mid and north Gower

The great sweep of land that rises to the north of the main Gower road does not attract anything like the number of visitors that the south and west do, solely due to the lack of comparable coastline: the northern fringe of the Gower is a flattened series of marshes and mudflats merging indistinguishably with the sands of the Loughor estuary. Wading birds, gulls and bedded cockles can all be found amongst the flats, dunes and inlets burrowing into the land from the estuary.

Gower's central plateau is often ignored, with much of the countryside nothing more than a pleasant patchwork of pastoral farmland. The great ridge, Cefn Bryn, stretched across the centre of the peninsula, is savage and impressive, its wiry peat and grass dotted with hardy sheep, ancient stone cairns and holy wells. The best views over the peninsula are from the road brushing over its roof.

Reynoldston and King Arthur's Stone

The **Cefn Bryn** ridge of sandstone stretches out across the middle of Gower, climbing over five hundred feet to give some astounding views to both coasts of the peninsula. It is most easily explored from the quiet village of **REYNOLDSTON**, grouped around a sheep-filled village green. The village's pub, the *King Arthur Hotel* (☎01792/390775; ③), which has comfortable en-suite rooms, hosts live folk and rock music nights and dishes up the best meals at this end of the peninsula. Alternatively, stay a mile northwest of Reynoldston at the luxurious *Fairyhill* (☎01792/390139, fax 391358; ⑦), a gorgeous country-house hotel, with a superb restaurant open to guests and non-guests alike.

From Reynoldston, a dramatic road rises up the slope of Cefn Bryn before skating across its summit in a perfect, straight line. There are several tracks leading off from the road, which provide clear views to both Gower coasts, but you might be best off stopping at the small car park about a mile east of Reynoldston; from here, a path across the boggy moor leads to **King Arthur's Stone**, a massive and isolated burial chamber capstone dating from at least 4000 BC and weighing over 25 tons.

From Llanrhidian to Llanmadoc

The small and unremarkable village of **LLANRHIDIAN** sits above the great marsh of the same name, a largely inaccessible goo of mud and water virtually indistinguishable from the sands of the Loughor estuary. Views from the village pub, the *Welcome to Town*, are superb. An unclassified road weaves west for two miles towards **Weobley Castle** (April–Oct Mon–Sat 9.30am–6.30pm, Sun 2–6.30pm; Nov–March Mon–Sat 9.30am–4pm, Sun 2–4pm; £2; CADW). Gaunt against the backdrop of the marsh and the estuary, the castle was built as a fortified manor in the latter part of the thirteenth century.

KING ARTHUR'S STONE

Gower, more than any other concentrated landscape in Wales, is littered with dolmens, standing stones and other prehistoric remains. The most celebrated of them all – indeed, the most well known in Wales – is **King Arthur's Stone**, just north of the lane that climbs out of Reynoldston across Gower's central ridge.

Anything up to 6000 years old, the dolmen – a thrusting capstone resting on six supporting stones – is mentioned, often as *Maen Ceti*, in documents dating back a thousand years. It is said to be a thirsty stone, occasionally making a nocturnal flit to Port Eynon for a drink in the sea. Alternatively, the reputation possibly arises from its alleged position over an underground stream – certainly there are many surfacing around it.

From King Arthur's Stone, a line leads across the road to the Lady's Well, a spring deemed holy and now enclosed in a hut, and through to Penmaen's ruined chapel and Neolithic burial chamber, some three miles southeast. The line passes numerous stones and mysterious remains and is a well-worn route, charged with a special energy, that features in some curious photographs with streaks and dots in hitherto clear skies.

The lane continues two miles west to the village of **Cheriton**, with its charming thirteenth-century church, and then on to **LLANMADOC**, where you can park and venture onto the land spit of **Whitford Burrows**, a soft patch of dunes now open as a nature reserve. Paths lead from Llanmadoc village up the steep hump of **Llanmadoc Hill** to the south. **The Bulwark**, a lonely and windy hillfort, can be seen at the eastern end of Llanmadoc Hill's summit ridge.

B&Bs along Llanmadoc's main road include the seventeenth-century *Britannia Inn* (☎ and fax 01792/386624; ③), where you can get a decent pint of real ale, and the *Tallizmand Guesthouse* (☎01792/386373; ②), which has en-suite rooms and accepts dogs. Better still, drive some seven miles east to the wonderful *Aberlogin Fawr*, New Road, Wernffrwd, Llanmorlais (☎01792/850041; ③), one of the most luxurious B&Bs in these parts.

travel details

Unless otherwise stated, frequencies for trains and buses are for Monday to Saturday services. Sunday averages 1–3 services though the main routes are more frequent and some routes have no Sunday service at all.

Trains

Cardiff to: Abergavenny (hourly; 40min); Barry Island (every 20–30min; 30min); Bridgend (every 30min; 20min); Bristol (every 30min; 50min); Caerphilly (every 20min; 20min); Carmarthen (5 daily; 1hr 30min); Chepstow (hourly; 30min); Crewe (hourly; 2hr 40min); Fishguard Harbour (1–2 daily; 2hr 20min); Haverfordwest (5 daily; 2hr 40min); Llanelli (17 daily; 1hr 10min); Llwynypia (every 30min; 50min); London (hourly; 2hr); Maesteg (hourly; 50min); Manchester (hourly; 3hr 10min); Merthyr Tydfil (hourly; 1hr); Neath (hourly;

40min); Newport (every 15–30min; 10min); Penarth (every 20min; 10min); Pontypool (hourly; 30min); Pontypridd (every 15min; 30min); Swansea (hourly; 50min); Tenby (4 daily; 2hr 30min); Trehafod (every 30min; 30min); Ystrad Rhondda (every 30min; 50min).

Newport to: Abergavenny (hourly; 30min); Bristol (every 30min; 40min); Caldicot (hourly; 10min); Cardiff (every 15–30min; 10min); Chepstow (hourly; 20min); Hereford (hourly; 50min); London (hourly; 1hr 50min); Pontypool (hourly; 20min); Swansea (hourly; 1hr 20min).

Swansea to: Cardiff (hourly; 50min); Carmarthen (hourly; 50min); Ferryside (12 daily; 40min); Fishguard Harbour (1–2 daily; 1hr 30min); Haverfordwest (7 daily; 1hr 30min); Kidwelly (12 daily; 30min); Knighton (4 daily; 3hr 10min); Llandeilo (4 daily; 1hr); Llandovery (4 daily; 1hr 20min);

Llandrindod Wells (4 daily; 2hr 20min); Llanelli (hourly; 20min); Llanwrtyd Wells (4 daily; 1hr 50min); London (2 daily; 3hr); Milford Haven (7 daily; 2hr); Narberth (every 2hr; 1hr 20min); Newport (hourly; 1hr 20min); Pembroke (6 daily; 2hr); Tenby (7 daily; 1hr 40min); Whitland (7 daily; 1hr 10min).

Buses

Bridgend to: Blaengarw (hourly; 35min); Cardiff (hourly; 50min); Cowbridge (every 30min; 20min); Cymer (hourly; 1hr); Kenfig (hourly; 40min); Llantrisant (hourly; 50min); Llantwit Major (hourly; 40min); Margam Park (hourly; 20min); Swansea (hourly; 50min).

Cardiff to: Abergavenny (hourly; 1hr 20min); Aberystwyth (2 daily; 4hr); Bangor (1 daily; 8hr); Barry Island (hourly; 50min); Birmingham (5 daily; 2hr 30min); Blaenafon (hourly; 1hr 40min); Brecon (1 daily; 1hr 20min); Bristol (10 daily; 1hr 10min); Caernarfon (1 daily; 7hr 40min); Caerphilly (every 30min; 40min); Cardiff–Wales Airport (hourly; 30min); Chepstow (hourly; 1hr 20min); Cowbridge (every 30min; 30min); Heathrow Airport (8 daily; 2hr 50min); Holyhead (1 daily; 8hr 50min); Lampeter (2 daily; 3hr 10min); Llantwit Major (hourly; 1hr); London (6 daily; 3hr 10min); Machynlleth (1 daily; 5hr 30min); Merthyr Tydfil (every 30min; 45min); Nelson (hourly; 35min); Newport (every 30min; 30min); Penarth (every 30min; 30min); Pontypridd (hourly; 20min); Senghenydd (hourly; 50min); Swansea (every 30min; 1hr); Welshpool (1 daily; 4hr 30min).

Chepstow to: Bristol (hourly; 1hr); Caerwent (hourly; 30min); Cardiff (hourly; 1hr 20min); Monmouth (16 daily; 50min); Newport (hourly; 50min); Penhow (hourly; 40min); Tintern (8 daily; 20min); Trellech (8 daily; 30min); Usk (6 daily; 45min).

Merthyr Tydfil to: Abergavenny (hourly; 1hr 30min); Brecon (10 daily; 40min); Cardiff (every 30min; 45min); Swansea (hourly; 1hr).

Monmouth to: Abergavenny (6 daily; 40min); Chepstow (16 daily; 50min); Newport (8 daily; 1hr); Raglan (8 daily; 20min); Ross-on-Wye (7 daily; 40min); Tintern (8 daily; 30min); Trellech (8 daily; 20min); Usk (8 daily; 30min).

Neath to: Aberdulais (hourly; 15min); Cymer (hourly; 35min); Pontrhydyfen (hourly; 25min).

Newport to: Abergavenny (hourly; 1hr 10min); Abertillery (every 30min; 1hr); Birmingham (5 daily; 2hr); Blaenafon (every 30min; 1hr 10min); Brecon (every 2hr; 2hr); Bristol (10 daily; 50min); Caerphilly (every 30min; 40min); Caerwent (hourly; 40min); Cardiff (every 20min; 40min); Chepstow (hourly; 50min); London (5 daily; 2hr 50min); Monmouth (8 daily; 1hr); Pontypool (every 30min; 45min); Raglan (8 daily; 45min); Usk (8 daily; 30min).

Swansea to: Aberdulais (hourly; 45min); Aberystwyth (2 daily; 3hr); Brecon (2–3 daily; 1hr 30min); Bristol (10 daily; 2hr 30min); Cardiff (every 30min; 1hr); Dan-yr-ogof (4 daily; 1hr); Llangennith (3 daily; 1hr 20min); Merthyr Tydfil (hourly; 1hr); Mumbles (every 10min; 15min); Neath (every 30min; 30min); Oxwich (6 daily; 40min); Pennard (hourly; 30min); Port Eynon (7 daily; 50min); Rhossili (Mon–Sat 10 daily, none on Sun; 1hr).

CHAPTER TWO

SOUTHWEST WALES

The most westerly outpost of Wales, the counties of Carmarthenshire and, in particular, Pembrokeshire, attract thousands of visitors each year. The principal draw is the fabulous scenery: bucolic and magical inland, where Carmarthenshire follows the Tywi Valley into the heart of the country, and glorious along the coast: sweeping and flat around Carmarthen Bay and rocky, indented and spectacular around the Pembrokeshire Coast National Park and its 186-mile path.

The last remnants of industrial south Wales peter out at **Llanelli**, before the undistinguished county town of **Carmarthen**. Of all the routes that converge on the town, the most glorious is the winding road along the Tywi Valley, past ruined hilltop forts and the **National Botanic Garden of Wales** on the way to **Llandeilo** and Wales' most impressively positioned castle at **Carreg Cennen**, high up on a dizzy plug of Black Mountain rock. Burrowing further inland, the sparsely populated countryside of remote hills and tiny valleys is broken only by endearing small market towns such as **Llandovery**, and the gloomy ruins of **Talley Abbey** and the Roman gold mines at **Dolaucothi**.

The wide sands of southern Carmarthenshire, just beyond Dylan Thomas' adopted home town of **Laugharne**, merge into the popular south Pembrokeshire bucket-and-spade seaside resorts of **Tenby** and **Saundersfoot**. Tenby sits at the entrance to the south Pembrokeshire peninsula, divided from the rest of the county by the Milford Haven and Daugleddau estuary, which brings its tidal waters deep into the heart of the pastoral county. The peninsula's turbulent, rocky coast is ruptured by some remote historical sites, including the Norman baronial castle at **Manorbier** and **St Govan's chapel**, a minute place of worship wedged into the rocks of a sea cliff near Bosherston. At the top of the peninsula is the old county town of **Pembroke**, dominated by its fearsome castle, across the Milford Haven estuary from small seaside villages and tiny islands along the rugged curve of **St Bride's Bay**, inland of which is the market town and transport interchange of **Haverfordwest**, dull but seemingly difficult to avoid. St Bride's Bay's rutted coastline is one of the most glorious parts of the coastal walk, leading north to brush past the impeccable city of **St David's**, where the exquisite cathedral shelters from the town in its own protective hollow. St David's, founded by Wales' patron saint in the sixth century, is a magnet for visitors; aside from its own charms, there are opportunities locally for spectacular coast and hill walks, hair-raising dinghy crossings to local islands and numerous other outdoor activities.

ACCOMMODATION PRICE CODES

Throughout this guide, hotel and B&B accommodation is priced on a scale of ① to ⑨, the number indicating the **lowest price** you could expect to pay per night in that establishment for a **double room in high season**. The prices indicated by the codes are as follows:

① under £40	④ £60–70	⑦ £110–150
② £40–50	⑤ £70–90	⑧ £150–200
③ £50–60	⑥ £90–110	⑨ over £200

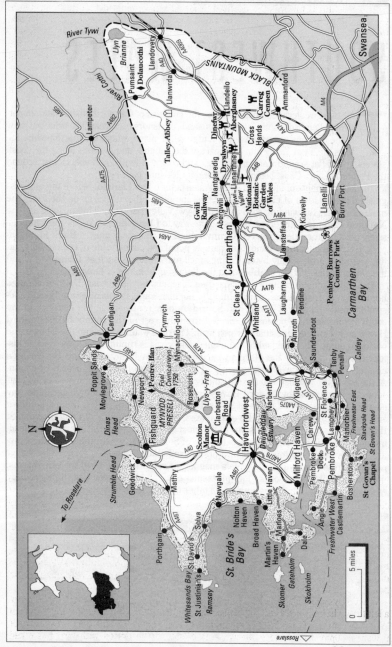

© Crown copyright

The coast turns towards the north at St David's, becoming the southern stretch of Cardigan Bay. Sixteen miles away by road, and well over thirty by rugged nips and tucks of the coastal walk, is the pretty port of **Fishguard**, terminus for ferries to Rosslare in Ireland. The northernmost section of the Coast Path, from Fishguard to the outskirts of Cardigan and past the delightful little town of **Newport**, is the most dramatic and remote. To the south and southeast are the eerie **Mynydd Preseli**, relic-spattered mountains overlooking windswept plateaux of heathland and isolated villages – none more remote than along the leafy **Cwm Gwaun**, a lovely and much-bypassed valley cutting through the hills.

Getting around

Despite the remoteness of much of southwestern Wales, public transport is surprisingly efficient and comprehensive. Direct **train** services connect Cardiff and Swansea with Llanelli, Carmarthen, Tenby, Haverfordwest, Milford Haven and Fishguard, while the Heart of Wales line shuffles out of Swansea and Llanelli to Llandeilo and Llandovery before delving into Powys. Connecting bus services out to the smaller towns and villages are regular and dependable, especially to the more popular destinations of Laugharne, Saundersfoot, Broad Haven and Dale on St Bride's Bay, and St David's.

Bus services are more thorough in peak tourist season, when most coastal villages have a fairly regular operation. Carmarthen and Haverfordwest are the principal bus terminuses, with services radiating out from Tenby, Pembroke and Fishguard. Only in the deserted lanes of northern and eastern Pembrokeshire does bus travel become difficult, although it's excellent walking and cycling country, and there are ample places to rent **bikes** throughout the area. Off the mainland, most of the islands are connected by regular (seasonal) **boat** services, although few of these allow for overnight stops.

From Llanelli to Carmarthen

Reached from Swansea on a new road and rail bridge over the muddy River Loughor (Afon Llwchwr), **LLANELLI** marks the informal border between anglicized southeast Wales and the *bro*, Welsh Wales, where the native language is part of everyday conversation. Once known as Tinopolis after its major industry, Llanelli is now famed for the sprawling Felinfoel and Buckley breweries, and for the Scarlets, one of the country's most famous and successful **rugby teams**. In 1972, they managed to beat the New Zealand All Blacks, a slender victory over which there is still much crowing. The Scarlets play at Stradey Park, out on the A484 to Burry Port, where the goalposts are topped with red tin saucepans as a reminder of the town's origins. To book tickets for games, call ☎01554/774060. If neither rugby nor beer appeal, there's little to keep you here. It's a good half-mile walk through monotonous streets from the train station to the town centre, much rebuilt in recent years but with little to distinguish it from any other comparably sized settlement. Half a mile north of the centre, off the A476 Felinfoel Road, the graceful upland houses of the metal masters surround the pleasant glades of **Parc Howard**, with superb views down to the sea. The park centres on the Victorian home of Sir Stafford Howard, tinplate merchant and Llanelli's first mayor. The house now serves as the town **museum** (Mon–Fri 11am–1pm & 2–4pm, Sat & Sun 2–4pm; free), a diverting enough collection of civic artefacts, old photos and paintings of the district, a load of Llanelli pottery and a few surprises, such as a nightdress and chemise belonging to Queen Victoria.

In truth, you can visit the best thing about Llanelli before you even get to the town: a left turn when the road and rail bridge enters Carmarthenshire leads to the excellent Wildfowl and Wetland Centre (daily: Easter–Sept 9.30am–5pm; Oct–Easter 9.30am–4.30pm; £4.25), an extensive area of salt marsh dotted with bird hides and landscaped walkways. It has recently undergone considerable expansion with uneconomic farmland adapted to the needs of wildfowl, with "natural" ponds created around existing mature hedgerows, and even owl nesting sites fashioned from old sewer pipes. Important populations of lapwing, redshank, and overwintering pintail, widgeon and teal are already drawing legions of bird-watchers, but the centre caters just as well to kids and the curious, mainly through the imaginative Discovery Centre – it's easy to lose most of a day here.

The most notable **accommodation** in Llanelli is the *Hotel Miramar* at 158 Station Rd (☎01554/754726, fax 772454; ①) – the speciality Portuguese restaurant here is excellent. The *Awel y Môr* guesthouse at 86 Queen Victoria Rd (☎ & fax 01554/755357; ①) is also good. For **food**, there are a few cheap Indian and Chinese restaurants on Station Road, and good, boozy **pubs** around: try Murray Street for a variety, including the cheery *Queen Victoria*.

Burry Port and Pembrey

Four miles west, along the sands of the Loughor estuary, is the undistinguished town of **BURRY PORT** (Porth Tywyn). Five minutes' walk south of the train station, the harbour is a pleasant surprise, as – a few theme pubs notwithstanding – the town shows no sign of any nautical connection. It was here that Amelia Earhart, the first woman to fly the Atlantic, landed after a journey of nearly 21 hours in June 1928 – there's a memorial stone by the harbour.

The village of **PEMBREY**, a mile west along the A484, is virtually indistinguishable from Burry Port. To the east of the settlement, the flat expanse of **Pembrey Burrows** forms an area of alternating wetland and dunes, now featuring a family-oriented **country park** (daily dawn–dusk; £1 per car except July & Aug 9am–4.30pm £4 per car, April–June & Sept £3 per car) with an adventure playground, miniature train, pony trekking, nature trails, bike rental and a short **dry ski slope** (May–Sept daily 10am–6pm; Oct–April Mon–Fri 2–10pm, Sat & Sun 10am–6pm; ☎01554/824443). The country park leads down to the seven-mile **Cefn Sidan** sands, a gentle slope of beautiful beach curving around the end of the Burrows. At the northern end of the Burrows, an old airfield has been recently converted into the **Welsh Motor Sports Centre** (☎01554/891042), a rally school and venue for Formula Three racing and numerous motorcycling and driving events.

Kidwelly

The next stop (request only) along the train line from Llanelli is **KIDWELLY** (Cydweli), a sleepy little town dominated by an imposing **castle** (June–Sept daily 9.30am–6pm; April, May & Oct daily 9.30am–5pm; Nov–March Mon–Sat 9.30am–4pm, Sun 11am–4pm; £2.20; CADW), on a steep knoll over the River Gwendraeth. The castle – and an accompanying priory that has since been demolished – were established around 1106 by the Bishop of Salisbury as a satellite of Sherborne Abbey in Dorset. Kidwelly's strategic position, overlooking vast tracts of coast, was the main reason for its construction. On entering through the massive fourteenth-century gatehouse, you can still see portcullis slats and murder holes, through which noxious substances could be tipped onto unwelcome visitors. The **gatehouse** forms the centrepiece of the impressively intact semicircular outer ward walls, which can be climbed for some great views over the grassy courtyard and rectangular inner ward above the river. This is the oldest surviving part of the castle, dating from around 1275, with the upper storeys added in the fourteenth century by warlord Edward I's nephew. Views from the musty solar and hall, packed into the easternmost wall of the inner ward, show the castle's defensive position at its best, with the river directly below. Although the whole castle is long since roofless, the remains are some of the most intact of any medieval Welsh castle that has not been extensively restored. As well as climbing the walls of the outer ward, stairs in the inner ward also lead into the upstairs rooms, largely domestic quarters.

A fourteenth-century town **gate**, just above the medieval bridge of the same age, shields the castle approach from the main through road. More entertaining, the small-scale **Industrial Museum** up Priory Street (Easter & June–Aug Mon–Fri 10am–5pm, Sat & Sun 2–5pm; free) is housed in an old tinplate works on the northwest edge of the town. Many of the works' old features have been preserved, including the rolling mills where long lines of tin were rolled and spun into wafer-thin slices.

On the other side of the train station from the town is the old **quay**, cleaned up and restored into an appealingly remote and forlorn picnic area and nature reserve. From here, there are views of wading birds skimming over the nearby mudflats and old saltings of the Gwendraeth estuary, once an important port for the medieval town.

In Kidwelly, there's decent pub **accommodation** at the *Old Malthouse* by the castle (☎01554/891091; ③), and superb en-suite B&B at *Penlan Isaf* (☎01554/890084, fax 891191; ①), a dairy farm overlooking the town. For something grander, try *Gwenllian Court* (☎01554/890217, fax 890844; ⑤), a country hotel with plenty of amenities. You can **camp** at *Tanylan Farm* (☎ & fax 01267/267306), which perches alongside the estuary between Kidwelly and Ferryside. Good **food** and **drink** are available at the cosy *Boot and Shoe*, 2 Castle St.

St Ishmael and Ferryside

As the train leaves Kidwelly and hugs the side of the River Tywi's estuary, the views out across the water are magnificent. You'll pass by a tiny chapel at **ST ISHMAEL**, built to serve a medieval village that was completely destroyed in a storm three hundred years ago, and is now buried deep beneath the flats; another storm in 1896 briefly revealed the remains of houses. A mile further on, **FERRYSIDE** (Glanyfferi) is a tranquil village that grew as a day-trip destination for Valley miners. Although the train station still remains (request stop only), Ferryside is far quieter today, its narrow streets facing Llansteffan Castle across the calm waters and circling sea birds. A yacht club, fishing centre and sandy beach make up the village facilities, together with a handful of pubs and restaurants. **Accommodation** can be found at *Beach Cottage* on Foreshore (☎01267/267507; ①), and there's good **food** and **drink** at the *White Lion Hotel* in the main square, and at the inexpensive, daytime *Ferry Cabin* restaurant, which does wonderfully fresh sea trout – known around these parts as *sewin*.

Carmarthen

The ancient and unquestioned capital of its region, **CARMARTHEN** (Caerfyrddin) does not entirely live up to the promise of its status. Although it's a useful transport interchange and lively market town, with some excellent shops and sixty pubs for 15,000 inhabitants, there's an undeniably down-at-heel and cheerless atmosphere which doesn't encourage you to stay for long – fortunately, with so many beautiful and interesting places nearby, there's little need to. It's the first major town in west Wales, where the native language is heard at all times, and was once – in the early eighteenth century – the largest town in all of Wales on the strength of its position at the tidal limit of the River Tywi.

Founded as a Roman fort, Carmarthen's most popular moment of mythological history dates from the Dark Ages and the supposed birth of the wizard Merlin just outside the town – Myrddin, in Welsh, gives Carmarthen its name. In the late eleventh century, the Normans began a castle near the remains of a Roman fort, extending its walls to

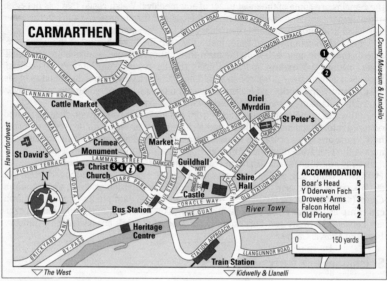

© Crown copyright

encompass a growing village. In 1313, Carmarthen was granted its first charter by Edward I, helping the town to flourish as an important wool centre, and the town was taken by Owain Glyndŵr in the early years of the fifteenth century. An eisteddfod was founded in the mid-fifteenth century, and is still used as the basis for today's National Eisteddfod. The importance of the town grew, attracting trade and new commerce, industrial works, a key port and a position as a seat of local government, a status still held by Carmarthen as the county town of Carmarthenshire.

Arrival, information and accommodation

Trains between Swansea and Pembrokeshire stop at the **train station**, which lies over the Carmarthen bridge on the south side of the River Tywi. All **buses** terminate at the bus station on Blue Street, north of the river, and many connect with the arrival and departure of trains. The town's **tourist office** is on Lammas Street, close to the Crimea Monument (daily: Easter–Oct 9.30am–5.30pm; Nov–Easter 10am–4.30pm; ☎01267/231557, *www.carmarthenshire.gov.uk*), although more esoteric information on the alternative scene can be found in Aardvark Wholefoods in Mansel Street or, for Welsh-language events, Siop y Pentan in the market square. For **bike rental**, go to Ar Dy Feic ("On Yer Bike") south of the river on Llangunnor Road (☎01267/221182).

There's lots of **accommodation** in town, especially on Lammas Street, where you'll find the *Boar's Head* (☎01267/222789, fax 222289, *kaw@boars-head-hotel.demon.co.uk*; ②), one of the town's grandest old coaching inns, the rather anodyne *Falcon Hotel* (☎01267/237152, fax 221277; ③), and the low-key *Drovers' Arms* (☎01267/237646; ②). B&B is best at *Y Dderwen Fach*, 98 Priory St (☎01267/234193; ①), and the *Old Priory* guesthouse, 20 Priory St (☎01267/237471; ①), both out along the main road to Lampeter and Llandeilo. If you're looking for something a little more remote, then you shouldn't pass up *Tŷ Mawr* (☎01267/202332, fax 202437; ⑤), an oak-beamed country-house hotel in the entirely unspoilt village of **Brechfa**, some twelve miles northeast of Carmarthen.

The Town

Approaching from the train station, the stern facade of the early twentieth-century **County Hall** shields the rambling streets of the town centre, and largely swallows up the uninspiring remains of Edward I's **castle** off **Nott Square**. The most picturesque eighteenth- and nineteenth-century part of town lies spread out at the base of the castle, around King Street and Nott Square, the town's main shopping hub.

Lying just off Nott Square is the town's handsome eighteenth-century **Guildhall**, from which Darkgate leads on to Lammas Street, a wide Georgian thoroughfare flanked by coaching inns, some interesting local shops and branches of all the main banks. Mansel Street leads north off Lammas Street to the indoor **market**, a great centre for local produce, secondhand books, antiques and endearingly useless tat, as well as hosting several cheap cafés. On the main market days – Wednesday, Saturday and, to a lesser extent, Friday – stalls spill outside into a slate-grey modern square.

From Nott Square, King Street heads northeast towards the sturdy tower of **St Peter's church**, architecturally undistinguished but well placed amongst the trees and surrounding town houses. Inside, Carmarthen's status as one of the most important Roman towns in Wales is evident from the altar in the western porch. Opposite is the Victorian School of Art that has now metamorphosed into the excellent **Oriel Myrddin** (Mon–Sat 10.30am–4.45pm; free), a craft centre and art gallery that shows the work of local artists. Half a mile further east, just off Priory Street, lie the insubstantial remains of a **Roman amphitheatre**, excavated in the late 1960s. In contrast with the atmospheric bowl at Caerleon, Carmarthen's remnants, surrounded by modern housing, are no more than a few grass humps.

Hidden away down by the river is the small **Heritage Centre** (Wed–Sat 11am–4pm; free) where the town's history is condensed into a series of cameos concentrating on Carmarthen's role as a commercial port.

Eating, drinking and entertainment

You can get great daytime **snacks** at the old-fashioned *Morris Tea Rooms*, almost opposite the Lyric Theatre on King Street, at the vegetarian café in the Waverley Stores health food shop, 23 Lammas St, and at *Caban y Dderwen*, 11 Market St, which has a few Welsh specialities. For evening meals, the best bet is the smartish but inexpensive *Hamilton's Brasserie & Wine Bar*, 11–12 Queen St (☎01267/235631), or, right next door, *The Queens*, a friendly, oak-panelled pub. The best-value pub food can be found at the *Boar's Head* on Lammas Street, and there's a huge range of unremarkable pizzas on offer at *MP's Pizzeria*, just off Nott Square at 20b Bridge St, which opens until just after pub closing hours. For a pricier treat, there's the superb *Quayside Brasserie* on the Towi quay (☎01267/223000), great for fresh local meat, fish and seafood, and especially popular at lunchtime.

Some of the town's many **pubs** get a little raucous at times, though the unpretentious *Drovers' Arms* on Lammas Street is more sedate and has some superb beers. There's often **live music** at the *Boar's Head* on Lammas Street or in the Civic Hall at the Nott Square end of King Street, and at the end of June and beginning of July, there's the **Carmarthen Festival**, a varied stew of music, art, poetry and dance – call the tourist office for details.

The Tywi Valley

The **River Tywi** curves and darts its way east from Carmarthen through some of the most magical scenery in south Wales. It's not hard to see why the Merlin legend has taken such a hold in these parts – the landscape does seem infused with a kind of eerie splendour. The thirty-mile trip from Carmarthen to **Llandovery** is punctuated by gentle, impossibly green hills topped with ruined castles, notably the wonderful **Carreg Cennen** near Llandeilo. Along the way, a couple of budding gardens have sprung up in the last couple of years: one completely new in the form of the **National Botanic Garden of Wales**; the other a faithful reconstruction of the original walled gardens around the long-abandonned house of **Aberglasney**.

The year-round tourist office in Carmarthen (see p.142) has a great deal of **information** about the Tywi Valley and surrounding area. There's a smaller office in the Crescent Road car park at **Llandeilo** (Easter & May–Sept Mon–Sat 10am–5pm; ☎01558/824226). A regular **bus** service runs from Carmarthen to Llandeilo, with the majority of the buses using the A40 via Nantgaredig and Pontargothi; several services turn off on to the B4300 at Nantgaredig, heading for Llanarthne and the Botanic Gardens.

Abergwili and around

The severe grey Bishop's Palace at **ABERGWILI** was the seat of the Bishop of St David's between 1542 and 1974, and now houses the **Carmarthen County Museum** (Mon–Sat 10am–4.30pm; free), a spirited amble through the history of the area. This surprisingly interesting exhibition covers the history of Welsh translations of the New Testament and Book of Common Prayer – both translated for the first time here in 1567. Local pottery, archeological finds, wooden dressers and a lively history of local castles are presented in well-annotated displays. The upstairs section looks at crime and policing, geology, education, the local coracle industry and the origins of Wales' first eisteddfod in Carmarthen in 1450.

A mile east of Abergwili, the main A40 road passes the sharp slopes of **Merlin's Hill** (Bryn Myrddin), reputedly the sleeping place of the great wizard. Close by, the *Whitemill Inn* in the quiet roadside hamlet of **Whitemill** (Felinwen) has very good-value pub food. In the hamlet of **NANTGAREDIG**, just over three miles from Abergwili, there's little apart from the welcoming *Four Seasons Hotel* (☎01267/290238, fax 290808; ③), complete with restaurant, swimming pool and leisure club. Nearby **PONTARGOTHI** has the slightly touristy *Cresselly Arms* and the chintzier, but more locally frequented *Cothi Hotel* (☎01267/290251, fax 290156; ③).

Llanarthne and around

The village of **LLANARTHNE**, a mile south of the main A40, is home to the National Botanic Garden of Wales (see opposite), and two superb pubs: the *Golden Grove Arms* (☎01558/668551; ②), which serves up hearty food and has extremely comfortable accommodation, and the delightfully wacky *Paxton Inn*, home of live jazz and innumerable guest beers.

High above the village, accessible by a steep twenty-minute walk or a more leisurely drive around the lanes, is **Paxton's Folly**, a castellated tower providing an exhilarating viewpoint over the rural patchwork below. Sir William Paxton, a London banker, built the folly after trying to bribe the electors of Carmarthen to make him MP with one of the most expensive campaigns in history, and the promise to pay for a bridge over the Tywi at Dryslwyn if successful. When the electors rejected him, he refused to build the bridge and constructed his folly overlooking the proposed site.

Four miles east of Llanarthne is the luscious estate of the **Gelli Aur Country Park** (daily dawn–dusk; parking £1), built around an 1824 baronial mansion, Gelli Aur, which translates as "Golden Grove". Around the house are some elegantly coiffured gardens, a deer park, nature trails and an impressive arboretum.

Despite William Paxton's petulance, there is now a bridge over the Tywi from below the tower over to **DRYSLWYN** and its forlorn **castle** (no set hours), straddling the top of a mound next to the river. Dryslwyn was built by Rhys ap Rhys Gryg, one of the Welsh princes of Deheubarth, in the thirteenth century, overlooking an important crossing point of the river. He had originally sided with Edward I before turning against him, incurring the king's wrath and an 11,000-strong army to besiege him in the castle in 1287. The collapsed stone walls surround a desolate inner courtyard, currently being restored as part of the castle's renaissance. Although the remains of the castle are barely worth the climb, the views are delightful.

The National Botanic Garden of Wales

One mile south of Llanarthne stands the brand new National Botanic Garden of Wales (daily: June–Aug 10am–7pm, March–May, Sept & Oct 10am–5.30pm, Nov–Feb 10am–4.30pm; £6.50; *www.gardenofwales.gov.uk*), on the 500-acre remains of William Paxton's once-immense estate. Rather than the expected grand country house – which burnt down in 1931 – the gardens centre on a vast Norman Foster-designed glasshouse that looks like a giant contact lens lost in the grass of the Tywi Valley. A Mediterranean climate is maintained inside and planting reflects the wonderful (and threatened) bio-diversity in regions around the world sharing similar weather conditions: the Cape region of South Africa, southwestern Australia, Chile, California and the Mediterranean itself are all represented in separate zones. It's early days yet – the gardens open fully in May 2000 – but in the absence of mature specimens, staff have taken the imaginative and effective approach of replicating the process of regeneration after a lightning-fire has swept through. Nonetheless, you can already wander through a small olive grove and see an abundance of species, many quite varied.

Outside, the **Temperate Woods of the World** section parallels the glasshouse displays with a series of one-acre plots, each dedicated to regions that share the Tywi Valley's wet but mild climate. Here, southwest China, the South Island of New Zealand, the American Pacific Northwest and highland Cameroon are so faithfully represented that it's easy to imagine you've left Wales altogether. Elsewhere, moorland environments get a similar treatment, and in between here and temperate woods sections, you can wander around an unusual double-walled garden designed to extend the season for ripe fruit, visit several educational facilities, and stroll the **Broadwalk**, an attractive path with a small stream meandering down the centre that finishes in an ammonite-shaped fountain.

Sustainability is a key issue here, and it's heartening to see rainwater caught and used for irrigation, glasshouses heated by burning wood coppiced on the grounds and human waste transformed into clean water by means of a series of reed beds. The theme runs through to a large section of the surrounding land which is being turned over to **organic farming**, using Welsh breeds of cattle and sheep which eventually end up on a plate in the visitors' restaurant. In keeping with this sustainable approach, you can get a thirty percent entry fee reduction if you arrive without a car. At the moment, that means by foot or bike, but there are plans for bus links.

Aberglasney and Dinefwr Castle

The Tywi Valley winds four miles east from Llantharne to Aberglasney (April–Oct daily 9.30am–6pm; £4; *www.aberglasney.org*), half a mile south of the A40 near Broad Oak, a large manor house partly dating back to the fifteenth century. Locals had always known about the decaying and abandoned house, and it had even been given Listed Building status, but it was only in 1994, when the grand eight-columned portico came up for sale at Christie's for £13,000, that the authorities sat up and took notice. The portico was withdrawn from the sale and reattached to the house as part of the major restoration undertaken by the Aberglasney Trust, although the stabilised shell of the building is destined to play second fiddle to its all-but unique set of **gardens**. Once massively overgrown, this series of mostly sixteenth- to eighteenth-century walled gardens have already regained much of their original formal splendour, and archeological work continues to uncover more about the history of the site. Planting has begun to reproduce the kitchen garden and what is thought to be the only secular cloister garden in Britain. A walkway leads around the top of the cloister giving access to a set of six Victorian aviaries, and great views over the Jacobean Pool garden and the mature woodlands beyond. The highlight, though, is the yew tunnel, five yews planted in line around 300 years ago and trained over to root on the far side. It's somewhat unkempt at the moment, but over the next decade, the tunnel should, like the rest of the garden, begin to look as it was once intended.

The strategic importance of the Tywi Valley is underlined by the presence of the tumbledown ruins of **Dinefwr Old Castle**, (unrestricted access) reached through the extensive Dinefwr Park, which forms a spectacular isolated spot on a wooded bluff over the river a couple of miles east of Aberglasney. The castle was built in the twelfth century by Lord Rhys, who had successfully united the warring Welsh princes against the Normans. The strategic site had been used for a previous castle, built as a royal fortress in the ninth century and used by Hywel Dda, "Hywel the Good", king of Deheubarth and codifier of Welsh laws (see p.154).

By 1523, the Dinefwr Old Castle had become ill-suited to the needs of Lord Rhys's descendants, who aspired to something a little more luxurious. It was abandoned and is now a dramatic shell across the park from the "new" castle, now named **Newton House** (April–Oct Mon & Thurs–Sun 11am–5pm; £2.80, park only £2; NT). Built in 1660 half a mile north of the old castle, Newton House was added to over the ensuing centuries and given a new limestone facade in the 1860s. The National Trust is currently restoring the house, and visitors are allowed to see increasing numbers of the gracious period rooms. Lined by Rhys (or Rice) family portraits, the library sits pretty beneath a remodelled seventeenth-century plaster ceiling. More of Lord Dinefwr's paintings are on display in the drawing room, including a bizarre portrait of canal builder and industrialist Thomas Keymer dressed as a Chinaman. You can also climb a splendid stairwell to a viewing platform that was added when buttresses were needed to prop the house up in the nineteenth century. The spectacular parkland surrounding the house (open all year; free) was landscaped mainly in the 1770s by George Rhys, whose work was much admired and slightly enhanced by Capability Brown following a visit in 1775. It now contains rare white cattle, fallow deer and a woodland nature reserve.

Llandeilo and Carreg Cennen Castle

A mile east of the Dinefwr castles, the main street – Rhosmaen Street – of the handsome small market town of **LLANDEILO** climbs up from the Tywi bridge, behind which are the tourist office (see p.144) and the train station. Although there is little in the way of actual sights in the town, Llandeilo is brilliantly situated in a bowl of hills amidst the Tywi Valley and on the edge of the magnificent uplands of the Black Mountain (see p.202). It's a quiet, rustic little place, whose few streets cluster around the main thoroughfare and the unusual raised graveyard (split by the main road) of the parish **church of St Teilo**.

Among several places to stay in Llandeilo are: *Tŷ Teilo*, a cosy B&B at 41 Alan Rd (☎01558/822437; ①), and the *Cawdor Arms* on Rhosmaen Street (☎01558/823500, fax 822399, *www.cawdor-arms.co.uk*; ④). This is one of Wales' best old coaching inns, especially appealing for the evening meals which, though expensive (£21 for three courses), are beautifully presented, served with aplomb and are wonderful value for money. If that's too pricey, try *Y Capel Bach* bistro (☎01558/822199) a couple of doors down, or, by day, the inexpensive *Fanny's*, by the churchyard at 3 King St. Llandeilo is positively stuffed with pubs: the supposedly haunted *Three Tuns Inn* on Carmarthen Street (between King and Rhosmaen streets) is good for live music, the imposing *Castle Hotel*, opposite *Y Capel Bach* on Rhosmaen Street, brews its own Watkins beer, serves decent food and lays on entertainment, while for plain old beer and pub food, head down the road to old coaching inn, the *White Horse*.

Pick up information on alternative local happenings at the excellent Friends of the Earth-run Green House shop, opposite the HSBC bank on Rhosmaen Street.

Carreg Cennen Castle and around

Isolated in the rural hinterland four miles southeast of Llandeilo is the most magnificently sited castle in the whole of Wales: **Carreg Cennen Castle** (daily: April to late Oct 9.30am–7.30pm; late Oct to March 9.30am–4.30pm; £2.50; CADW), just beyond the tiny hamlet of Trapp. It was first constructed on its fearsome rocky outcrop in 1248, although Sir Urien, one of King Arthur's knights, is said to have built his fortress here first. Built primarily as a Welsh stronghold, Carreg Cennen fell to the English in 1277 during Edward I's initial invasion of Wales. The castle lasted as an inhabited fortress until 1462, when it was partially destroyed by the Earl of Pembroke, William Herbert, who believed it to be the base of a group of lawless rebels.

The most astounding aspect of the castle is its commanding position, three hundred feet above a sheer drop down into the green valley of the small Cennen River. The car park and the child-oriented **rare breeds farm**, with rare species of cows, sheep and goats, are at the bottom of a long path that climbs sharply up, opening out quite astounding views towards the uncompromising purple lines of the Black Mountain, standing in utter contrast to the velvet greenery of the Tywi and Cennen valleys. The castle seems impenetrable, its crumbling walls merging with the limestone on which it defiantly sits. The highlights of a visit are the views down the sheer drop into the river valley and the long descent down into a watery, pitch-black cave that is said to have served as a well. Torches are essential (50p rental from the excellent tearoom near the car park), although it is worth continuing as far as possible and then turning them off to experience absolute darkness. The tearoom near the car park has a superb selection of home-cooked Welsh dishes, and you'll find B&B in nearby **TRAPP** at *Tŷ Isaf* (☎01558/822002; ②), in a farmhouse and its outlying cottages. The village also boasts a good pub, and the superb **Trapp Arts & Crafts Centre** (March–Christmas Tues–Sun 10.30am–6pm), the region's best showcase for local artisans, where imaginative temporary exhibitions complement the main business of selling.

The A40 and train line trail one another to the northeast of Llandeilo, through a pastoral landscape, in which biblical reminders, testimony of the Welsh fervour in the Christian faith, can be seen in the hamlets of **BETHLEHEM**, where the friendly village shop and tearoom will keep your Christmas cards ready to be franked with the blessed postmark, and nondescript **SALEM**, either side of the main road. **LLANGADOG**, halfway between Llandeilo and Llandovery, is a pretty little town under the glowering bluff of the Black Mountain. Three miles southwest of the town is **Garn Goch**, a massive Iron Age hillfort spread over fifteen acres, as impressive for its bleak position of isolation as for the remaining earthworks and stone rampart. On the main A40, just after the Llangadog turning, there's a decent **campsite** at *Abermarlais Park* (☎01550/777868 or 777797).

Llandovery and around

Twelve miles northeast of Llandeilo, the town of **LLANDOVERY** (Llanymddyfri) boasts architecture and a layout that have changed little for centuries. Like so many other mid-Wales settlements, an influx of New Agers since the 1960s has had a discernible effect on the town: there's an independent theatre, and alternative-type bookshops and wholefood stores abound. Alongside this more alternative flavour, Llandovery is still a major centre for cattle markets, which take place every other Tuesday. Around the town, there are good excursions out into breathtaking country-side to the Dolaucothi Gold Mine and Talley Abbey to the west, Rhandirmwyn and Llyn Brianne to the north and the Black Mountain to the southeast (this last covered in "Central Wales", pp.202–203).

Arrival and accommodation

Llandovery is a natural base for exploring the Tywi Valley, being well connected by bus and train, and containing several good pubs, guesthouses and eating places. The **train station** sits on the main A40 just before it becomes Broad Street, and **buses** leave from Broad Street and the Market Square. The joint **tourist office** and Brecon Beacons National Park visitor centre (Easter–Sept daily 10am–5.30pm, Oct–Easter Mon–Sat 10am–4pm, Sun 2–4pm; ☎01550/720693), is in the new heritage centre on Kings Road, the continuation of Broad Street, and comes well stocked with leaflets on local walks and natural history. Local guides and books are stocked in the Old Printing Office, near the war memorial on Broad Street. Information on alternative events can be found at the Iechyd Da health-food shop in Broad Street.

You'll find Llandovery's most ostentatious **accommodation** at the colonnaded *Castle Hotel* on Broad Street (☎01550/720343, fax 720673; ⑤), where the nineteenth-century travelling writer George Borrow lodged for a night. A better bet lies across the square at *The Drovers*, 9 Market Square (☎01550/721115; ①), an eighteenth-century town-house full of antique furniture and with a guests' bar. Less central B&Bs include: *Mrs Billingham's*, Pencerrig New Road (☎01550/721259; ①); *Llwyncelyn* (☎01550/720566; ①), which serves evening meals and can be found on the way out of town towards Llandeilo; the superb, Gothic-styled en-suite rooms at *Cwm Rhuddan Mansion* (☎01550/721414; ②), a mile west on the A4069; and, a mile further out on the same road, *Cwm Gwyn Farm*, Llangadog Road (☎01550/720410; ①). The nearest **campsite**, a mile east of Llandovery off the A40, is the *Erwlon* (☎01550/720332).

The Town

On the south side of the main Broad Street, a grassy mound holds the scant remains of the town's **castle**. There are good views from the ruins over the shallow waters of the Bran River, which splits from the Tywi a mile short of the town, and the huddled grey buildings that make up Llandovery itself.

Broad Street has been the main through route for years, as can be seen from the solid early nineteenth-century town houses and earlier inns that line it; the road widens up towards the cobbled, rectangular Market Square, crowned by a clock tower. This thoroughfare has changed little since George Borrow visited the town in 1854 as part of his grand tour of Wales, remembering it as the "pleasantest little town in which I have halted in the course of my wanderings". Above the tourist office, the community-run **Llandovery Heritage Centre** (Easter–Sept daily 10am–5.30pm, Oct–Easter Mon–Sat 10am–4pm, Sun 2–4pm; donation appreciated) is a great example of its kind. As well as the everyday artefacts of local people, there are some excellent depictions of local legends such as the Lady of the Lake from Llyn y Fan Fach and hero bandit Twm Sion Cati, the "Welsh Robin Hood". Other displays look at the drovers and their Black Ox bank (which became a part of the present-day Lloyds TSB bank), the Heart of Wales railway, hymn-writer William Williams and seventeenth-century vicar Rhys Prichard, author of *Canwyll y Cymry* ("The Welshmen's Candle").

Stone Street heads north from the Market Square, past some slightly tattier pubs and up to the **Llandovery Theatre**, a shadow of its former self but worth a brief visit for an update on events in the area.

Eating and drinking

The best places to **eat** in Llandovery are the numerous pubs; try the *White Swan* in the High Street or the *Castle Hotel* on Broad Street, which offers delicious. moderately-priced lunchtime and evening food. The town also has a number of daytime cafés and tearooms, mainly around the Market Square. Out of Llandovery, the *Royal Oak Inn* in Rhandirmwyn (see overleaf), is well worth the trip for its imaginative menu of nicely-cooked classics.

For **drinking**, the eccentric and bizarrely old-fashioned *Red Lion*, a red, collonaded house nestled in an easy-to-miss corner at 2 Market Square, can't be beaten. If you can't find it, or if – as frequently happens – the landlord has chosen to close early, try the nearby *King's Head*, or, round the corner, the young and sporty *Greyhound* (*Y Milgi*) in Stone Street.

The Dolaucothi Gold Mine, Talley Abbey and Brechfa Forest

The countryside to the west of Llandovery is blissfully quiet, with just a handful of main roads and lanes that rarely contain traffic of any volume. The principal route off the A40 between Llandeilo and Llandovery, the A482 heads towards the straggling village of **PUMSAINT** (Five Saints), whose etymology is explained in the stone seen near the entrance of the **Dolaucothi Gold Mine**, half a mile off the main road (late May to mid-Sept daily 10am–5pm; site £2.60, underground tour £3.60; NT): the indentations in the rock are said to be the marks left by five sleeping saints, who rested here one night.

Pumsaint is the only place in Britain where the Romans definitely mined gold, laying complicated and astoundingly advanced systems to extract the precious metal from the rock; the remains of Roman workings – a few water channels and an open cast mine – can still be seen from the self-guided walk around the site. The Romans left in 140 AD, and the mine lay abandoned until 1888, when the promise of gold opened it once more; further probes unearthed gold, but not enough to justify costs, and the mines closed once again. Today, the underground tour goes deep into the mine workings and usually allows visitors, equipped with the mine's panning dishes, to prospect for gold themselves.

A mile to the north of Pumsaint, a characteristically straight road heads north above the valley of the Twrch River. This is a segment of **Sarn Helen** (Sarn y Lleng), a trans-Wales Roman road built between forts at Caernarfon and Carmarthen, often crossing some of the country's bleakest terrain. Its whimsical name may be a corruption of the Welsh, meaning Causeway of the Legion, although it is more popularly held to refer to Helen, the Welsh wife of a Roman chieftain in Britain.

Southwest of Pumsaint is the village of **TALLEY** and the landmark crumbling tower of its twelfth-century **abbey**, sited spectacularly alongside the reeds and lily pads of two gloomily dark lakes. Established in the late 1100s, Talley was Wales' only Premonstratensian abbey, lasting as such only into the next century. Adjoining the distinctly unimpressive ruins is the serene **church of St Michael**, intact from its foundation in 1773 and still including its original box pews.

Just north of Talley, the B4310 winds west from **Llansawel** to plunge into the valley of the Afon Cothi, surrounded by the towering conifers of the **Brechfa Forest**, one of the best spots for guaranteed solitude in Wales and the starting point for many good walks. You can pitch a **tent** by the forest streams or at a good serviced site at the *Red Dragon Inn* (☎01558/685527) in Rhydcymerau, on the B4337, deep in the forest's northern fringe. Otherwise, the best base is the unspoilt village of **BRECHFA**, with the superb, oak-beamed *Tŷ Mawr* country hotel (☎01267/202332, fax 202437; ⑤), the *Glasfryn* B&B (☎01267/202306; ②), and a great pub, the *Forest Arms*. Other local **accommodation** includes the *Brunant Arms* (☎01558/650483; ①) in **Caio**, a mile east of the gold mine, a characterful pub which also offers mouthwatering food, loads of board games and regular debates. If money's not too tight, *Glanrannell Park Hotel* (☎01558/685230; ⑨), just south of Pumsaint in **Crugybar**, is a fine place: acres of grounds, an informal, jolly atmosphere and knowledgeable local hosts.

Towards Llyn Brianne

The land to the north of Llandovery – mostly near the northern banks of the River Tywi – is equally remote, and even more spectacular, with walks following the river valley and fanning out over the hills. The old lead-mining hamlet of **RHANDIRMWYN**, above the winding river and with some of the best views hereabouts, is a good base, reached by daily postbuses from Llandovery. Here, you'll find the popular *Royal Oak Inn* (☎01550/760201; ②), which offers great food, drink and B&B **accommodation**; just below the village, there's also a riverside **campsite** (☎01550/760257); you register with the warden at Hafod-y-Pant farm, three-quarters of a mile away by track, on the lane that winds up the slopes from Cynghordy train station and under the spectacular 102-foot-high viaduct that curves its way over the little valley of the Afon Brân. Midway between the viaduct and Hafod-y-Pant, there's the delightful farmhouse B&B *Llanerchindda* (☎01550/750274; ②), the base for many a Cambrian Way walker (see p.411).

The lane that clings to the Tywi's right bank continues north from Rhandirmwyn, through wooded glades and past gnarled shoulders of mountain, with the glittering river always in view. Three miles beyond Rhandirmwyn, there's a car park at the Ystradffin chapel for the RSPB's **Dinas Nature Reserve**, deep within which is the reputed hideout cave of Twm Sion Cati (see p.148). You're discouraged from seeking out the bandit's cave – slightly up the hill from the riverside path and still waymarked by arrows on posts – lest you disturb the red kites, woodpeckers, nuthatches, redstarts and pipits, but even so, this is a delightful spot: wooden walkways traverse the ancient woodland, a burst of flowers, butterflies, water and twisted trees. Once through, you can walk along the banks of the fast-flowing Tywi up to its confluence with the River Doethie.

A mile beyond Dinas, lanes widen for the traffic that bustles towards **Llyn Brianne**, at whose southern end are a car park and visitor facilities. Considering the reservoir was only built in the 1970s (to supply Swansea), it has folded well into the contours of the land and there are some good shoreline walks. Despite the increase in industry and visitors, it's still a remarkably peaceful area. Walks around the lake and beyond link up to isolated youth hostels and camping sites along the Abergwesyn Pass (see p.227).

Southern Carmarthenshire

Frequently overlooked in the stampede towards the resorts of Pembrokeshire, southern Carmarthenshire is a quiet part of the world, with few of the problems of mass tourism suffered by more popular parts of Wales. The coastline is broken by the triple estuary of the Tywi, Taf and Gwendreath rivers, forking off at right angles to each other; between the Tywi and Taf is a knotted landscape of hills and tiny, winding lanes. One decent road, the B4312, penetrates this slip of land, petering out at Llansteffan, a village cowering below the hilltop ruins of its castle.

On the other side of the Taf estuary, the village of **Laugharne** is the area's sole big tourist attraction, on the strength of its position as a place of pilgrimage for Dylan Thomas devotees. A curious and insular village, Laugharne was the last home of the Thomases, whose boathouse has been turned into a loving museum to the writer, and whose regular drinking hole is as much a part of the pilgrimage as the house. Laugharne's recently reopened castle is a further incentive to visit.

Beyond Laugharne, the coast is formed by a seemingly endless sweep of sand, once a venue for an assortment of land speed record attempts orchestrated from the seasonally busy resort of **Pendine**. Back on the A40, **Whitland** is an architecturally unremarkable town, but historically significant as the site of the first parliament in Wales.

Regular trains connect Carmarthen with Whitland and the west, and buses fill in the gaps, with a service from Carmarthen and St Clears to Laugharne and Pendine. Another service also leaves Carmarthen for Llansteffan.

Llansteffan

The impressive ruins of a **castle** (free entry) loom above the seemingly forgotten village of **LLANSTEFFAN** (sometimes anglicized to "Llanstephan"), on the opposite bank of the Tywi estuary from Ferryside (see p.141). It's a ten-minute walk up from the tawdry beachside car park to the solid castle gatehouse, the most interesting survivor of this Norman ruin, which was built between the eleventh and thirteenth centuries by the Anglo-Norman de Camille family, attracting the occasional wrath of the Welsh as a result.

The entrance used today is not the original gatehouse, which was converted into living quarters in the fourteenth century: its bricked-up entrance is obvious from outside. In both gatehouses, however, the portcullis and murder holes can still be seen. A couple of other towers, in considerably more advanced states of dereliction, punctuate the crumbling walls that surround the D-shaped grassy courtyard in the middle. From the top of the towers, it's easy to appreciate the importance of this site as a defensive position, with far-reaching views in all directions. It's no surprise that, before the present castle, there was an Iron Age promontory fort here, known to have been occupied from 600 BC.

From the castle, descend the path down towards Wharley Point, past *Parc Glas*, formerly a milk-and-rum tavern, and continue down the lane towards the beach. The door in the wall on the right conceals **St Anthony's Well**, with its supposed powers of healing for lovesickness.

Informal **tourist information** for the Llansteffan area is available at the friendly post office (☎01267/241487) in the village of **LLANGAIN**, halfway between Carmarthen and Llansteffan. There's **accommodation** in Llangain at *Brynderwyn* (☎01267/241403; ①), on Old School Road opposite the post office, and substantial, tasty pub meals down the street at *Tafarn Pantydderwen*. **B&B** in and around town is available at *Brig y Don* on The Green (☎01267/241349; ①), and, two miles short of the village from Carmarthen and with superb views over the estuary, at *Pantyrarthro Manor* (☎01267/241226; ①). There's also a **campsite** at *Church House Farm* in Llangain (☎01267/241274). A couple of miles beyond Llansteffan, overlooking Laugharne and the Taf estuary, there's very good **bunkhouse** accommodation at *The Holt* on Mwche Farm (☎01267/241782).

The best sources of reliable budget **food** are the *Sticks Inn* on Main Street, and the *Wern Inn* in Llangynog, five miles north of Llansteffan.

Laugharne

When quiet, the village of **LAUGHARNE** (Talacharn), on the other side of the Taf estuary from Llansteffan, is a delightful spot, with a ragged castle looming over the reeds and tidal flats and narrow lanes snuggling in behind. Catch it in high season, though, and you're immediately aware that Laugharne is increasingly taken over by the legend of Dylan Thomas, the nearest thing Wales has to a national poet. Wherever you go you'll meet people who knew him; some genuine, others gently milking the memory.

At the end of an excruciatingly narrow lane (not suitable for cars) beside the estuary, you'll stumble across the **Dylan Thomas Boathouse** (daily: Easter & May–Oct 10am–5.30pm; Nov–Easter 10.30am–3.30pm; £2.75), the simple home of Thomas, his wife Caitlin and their three children from 1949 until he died from "a massive insult to the brain" (spurred by numerous whiskies) on a lecture tour in New York four years later. It's an enchanting museum with a feeling of inspirational peace above the ever-changing water and light of the estuary and its "heron-priested shore". The upstairs is given over to video on Thomas's life and a selection of local artists' views of the estuary and the village – none so rewarding as the one from the windows. Downstairs, the family's living room has been preserved intact, with the rich tones of the man himself reading his work via a period wireless set. Numerous artefacts are encased or on display, and contemporary newspaper reports of his demise show how he was, while alive, a fairly minor literary figure: the *Daily Mirror* manages a small obituary on page five, while even the *Carmarthen Journal* relegates the story to second place behind the tale of a missing local farmer. A small tea room and outdoor terrace give views over the water and a welcome chance for refreshment. Back along the narrow lane, you can peer into the blue garage where Thomas wrote: a gas stove, curling photographs of literary heroes, pen collection and numerous scrunched-up balls of paper on the cheap desk suggest quite effectively that he is about to return at any minute. The poet and Caitlin, who died in 1994, are buried together in the graveyard of the parish church in the village centre, marked by a simple white cross.

Laugharne is probably the closest to the fictional Llareggub, Thomas' town of darkly rich characters in *Under Milk Wood* – an honour, it is claimed, that is shared with New Quay in Cardiganshire. Whichever village he really meant, Laugharne has numerous Thomas connections and plays them with curiously disgruntled aplomb – none more so than the great alcoholic's old boozing hole, **Brown's Hotel** on the main street, where, in the nicotine-crusted front bar, Dylan's cast-iron table still sits in a window alcove overlooked by low-key memorabilia. You're left in no doubt, though, that this is foremost a pub, not a shrine.

The main street courses down to the ornate ruins of **Laugharne Castle** (May–Sept daily 10am–5pm; £2; CADW). Built in the twelfth and thirteenth centuries, most of the original buildings were obliterated in Tudor times when Sir John Perrot transformed it into a splendid gentleman's mansion. The mix of medieval might and Tudor finery is an intriguing one, especially in the impressive Inner Ward, dominated by two original towers, one of which you can climb for some good interpretive displays and, from the domed roof, sublime views over the huddled town. Like so many Welsh castles, Laugharne, built as an Anglo-Norman lookout over the sea, was taken by the Welsh princes Llywelyn the Great (in 1215) and Llywelyn the Last (in 1257), who also captured the then lord of the manor, Guy de Brian IV. The "castle brown as owls" (Dylan Thomas) has a connection with another famous Welsh writer, Richard Hughes, who lodged in the adjoining Castle House between 1934 and 1942. His *Danger* (1924), about a disaster in a Welsh mine, was the world's first radio drama, although Hughes remains best known for his novel, *A High Wind in Jamaica*. There's a small exhibition on him in the shore-facing gazebo in the castle's delightful gardens, landscaped to original Victorian specifications.

Opposite the castle entrance is the tiny toytown **Town Hall**, topped by a white-washed Italianate bell tower, which once served as a single-cell prison.

Practicalities

Laugharne has surprisingly little **accommodation**: try the *Runnymede* guesthouse on Clifton Street (☎01994/427367; ①), the main road as you come in from St Clears. Clifton Street becomes King Street as it continues into the village centre, passing grand, pink *Castle House* (☎ & fax 01994/427616, *www.laugharne.co.uk*; ③), with gorgeous estuary views from the grounds and from some of the large en-suite rooms. Beyond the central square, Market Street becomes Gosport Street and passes, at no. 20, the very welcoming *Swan Cottage* (☎01994/427409; ②), which has just one en-suite room. By the *New Three Mariners* pub in the centre of town, Newbridge Road heads down to *The Cors* (☎01994/427219; ④), a small but gracious country house that doubles up as a classy restaurant (closed Mon–Wed, reservations essential). A little out of town, you can do no better than the delightful B&B of *Brunant Farm* (☎ & fax 01994/240421; ②), high on the hills two miles southeast of Whitland and offering excellent, moderately-priced dinners. The nearest **campsite** is *Ants Hill* (☎ & fax 01994/427293; a few hundred yards north of Laugharne.

For **eating**, the choice is a little wider. Close to the town hall, the *Studio Tavern & Portreeve's Restaurant* (☎01994/427476) serves up moderately priced meals extending to mackerel pâté and cider-baked lamb; while the *Stable Door* (☎01994/427777; closed Mon & Tues), immediately behind, offers meals such as salmon fishcakes or Hungarian pork and mushrooms – reservations are advised for both places during the

---

DYLAN THOMAS

Dylan Thomas (1914–53) was the quintessential Celt – fiery, verbose, richly talented and habitually drunk. Born into a snugly middle-class family in Swansea's Uplands district (see p.126), Dylan's first glimmers of literary greatness came when he was posted, as a young reporter, on the *South Wales Evening Post* in Swansea, from which some of his most popular tales in *Portrait of the Artist as a Young Dog* were inspired. Thomas' wordy enthusiasm is well demonstrated in a passage describing his gulping down a pint of beer, waiting for the senior reporter to join him for a pub crawl: "I liked the taste of beer, its live, white lather, its brass-bright depths, the sudden world through the wet brown walls of the glass, the tilted rush to the lips and the slow swallowing down to the lapping belly, the salt on the tongue, the foam at the corners."

Rejecting the coarse provincialism of Swansea and Welsh life, Thomas arrived in London as a broke 20-year-old in 1934, weeks before the appearance of his first volume of poetry, which was published as the first prize in a *Sunday Referee* competition. Another volume followed shortly afterwards, cementing the engaging young Welshman's reputation in the British literary establishment. He married in 1937, and the newlyweds returned to Wales, settling in the hushed, provincial backwater of Laugharne. Short stories – crackling with rich and melancholy humour – tumbled out as swiftly as poems, further widening his base of admirers, although they remained numerically small until well after his death and, like so many other writers, Thomas has only gained star status posthumously. Despite his evident streak of hedonism and his long days in Laugharne's *Brown's Hotel*, Thomas was a surprisingly self-disciplined writer, honing his work into some of the most instantly recognizable poetry written in the twentieth century, mastering both lyrical ballads of astounding simplicity and rhythmic metre, as well as more turgid, difficult poetry of numerous dense layers. Perhaps better than anyone, he writes in an identifiably Celtic, rhythmic wallow in the language. Although Thomas knew little Welsh – he was educated in the time when the native language was stridently discouraged – his English usage is definitively Welsh in its cadence and bold use of words.

Thomas, especially in public, liked to adopt the persona of what he perceived to be an archetypal stage Welshman: sonorous tones, loquacious, romantic and inclined towards a stiff tipple. Playing this role was particularly popular in the United States, where he journeyed on lucrative lecture tours. It was on one of these, in 1953, that he died, poisoned by a massive whisky overdose. Just one month earlier, he had put the finishing touches to what many regard as his masterpiece: *Under Milk Wood*, the "play for voices". Describing the dreams, thoughts and lives of a straggling Welsh seaside community over a 24-hour span, the play has never dipped out of fashion and has lured Wales' greatest stars, including Richard Burton and Anthony Hopkins, into the role of chief narrator. The small town of Llareggub (mis-spelt Llaregyb by the po-faced BBC, who couldn't sanction the usage of the expression "bugger all" backwards) is loosely based on Laugharne, New Quay in Cardiganshire, and a vast dose of Thomas' own imagination.

summer. *Brown's Hotel* (see p.152) serves large, stodgy meals until 8.30pm, guaranteed to fill anyone. Down on the square, there's more limited fare at the *Under Milk Wood Inn*, and perfectly good fish and chips to sit in or take away. The best **drinking** hole in Laugharne is the effortlessly cheery *New Three Mariners*.

Pendine and Whitland

Follow the road five miles southwest from Laugharne, and you'll reach the tatty seaside resort of **PENDINE** (Pentywyn), home to a mass of caravan parks, souvenir shops, cheap cafés and vast tracts of out-of-bounds military land. The crowning glory here is the six-mile-long stretch of sand that sweeps away to the east which, for a frenetic few years in the mid-1920s, was the scene of a series of attempts at the world land speed record. In 1927, Malcolm Campbell reached 174.88mph here, a mark former record holder and Welsh rival J.G. Parry-Thomas thought he could better. A month later, his 27-litre, aircraft-engined and chain-driven *Babs* hurtled along the beach only to explode: Parry-Thomas died gruesomely when he was decapitated by the chain. *Babs* was recovered but then buried in the sand for a respectful 42 years, until it was dug up in 1969 and restored. Each July and August *Babs* is on display at the seafront **Speed Museum** (April–Sept daily 10am–5pm; free), which otherwise has mildly interesting panels on those heady times and a few motorcycles also used in record attempts. The headquarters for the land speed attempts was the *Beach Hotel*, which still displays photographs and mementos of the glory days. True to its history, you can even drive on Pendine Sands, although in summer it'll cost you £1.50 for the privilege, and the maximum speed limit is 10mph – boy racers beware.

From Pendine, the A4066 leads back through Laugharne; you can also wind north through narrow lanes to the A40, the route to the historically significant **WHITLAND** (Y Hendy Gwyn), a small town dominated by a hulking dairy complex. It was here – in 930 AD – that Hywel Dda (Hywel the Good), king of Deheubarth, called together representatives from all the other Welsh kingdoms to the first all-Wales assembly, designed to pull together disparate bands of legislation in order to codify common laws for the whole of Wales. There, the representatives set up an elaborate and exhaustive code of egalitarian laws for their kingdoms, including the right of bastard children to be equal to legitimate siblings, the ending of marriage by common consent, the equal division of land between man and wife upon separation, and the equal division of land amongst all children upon the death of the parents. Many of these customs survived until the Tudors conquered Wales, and Welsh people today still hold great pride in the fairness and lack of oppression in a once independent Wales. The tales of Hywel Dda are told at a **commemorative centre** (Easter–Sept Mon–Sat 10am–5.30pm; free), where his laws are inscribed (in Welsh) on stone tablets around the walls. It's located two minutes from the train station on St Mary Street.

Tenby and around

On a natural promontory of great strategic importance, the beguilingly old-fashioned **TENBY** (Dinbych-y-Pysgod) is everything a seaside resort should be, wedged between two sweeping beaches fronting an island-studded seascape. Narrow streets duck and wind downhill from the medieval centre to the harbour, past miniature gardens fashioned to catch the afternoon sun. Steps pitching down the steeper slopes provide magical viewpoints to the dockside arches which still house fishmongers selling the morning's catch, while rows of brightly painted houses and hotels are strung out along the clifftops. Simply walking around the streets and along the beaches at low tide is a delight, but Tenby is best visited during quiet times such as May or late

---

"LITTLE ENGLAND BEYOND WALES"

Ever since the Normans stormed their way through Wales, securing their positions with powerful castles in strategic places, Pembrokeshire has been effectively divided. But the origin of the colonized southern section of the county goes back even further, to the days when Viking raiders came in by sea and snatched the best land – the sandy southern coast and the fertile pasture of the Daugleddau estuary. The Normans only continued an already established practice, intermingling with the existing Vikings (to produce a very English racial mix) and keeping the Celtic Britons (ie the Welsh) to the northern part of the county.

Today, the racial divide of the past is still evident. **"Little England Beyond Wales"** is the name given to an area that falls south of what has become known as the **Landsker Line**, an easily traceable invisible boundary through the heart of Pembrokeshire. Along the line, you'll find some sixteen castles or castle tumps (such as Roche, Haverfordwest, Llawhaden and Narberth). Either side, village names are demonstrably Welsh or incongruously anglicized. This strange history dictates much: the south of the county has developed mass appeal to English migrants and tourists, whilst the north tends to attract fellow Celts and other Europeans. Politically, the Tenby and Pembroke area has inclined towards the most Unionist of UK parties, the Conservatives (who hold very little sway in the rest of Wales), whilst the north dallies between the old Liberal tradition and modern Welsh nationalism in the shape of Plaid Cymru. The bottom line to this is that south Pembrokeshire can be something of a po-faced disappointment, while the northern part of the county is wilder, more rugged and far less predictable – a truly Welsh experience.

September – in busy months, you'll be fighting for space with hordes of fellow holidaymakers.

Tenby's pedigree is long. First mentioned in a ninth-century bardic poem, the town grew under the twelfth-century Normans, who erected a castle on the headland in their attempt to colonize south Pembrokeshire and create a "Little England beyond Wales" – an appellation by which the area is still known today (see box, above). Three times in the twelfth and thirteenth centuries, the town was ransacked by the Welsh; the last time, in 1260, by Prince Llywelyn himself. In response, the castle was refortified and the stout town walls that remain largely intact were built. Tenby prospered as a major port for a wide variety of foodstuffs and fine goods between the fourteenth and sixteenth centuries, but decline followed. Relief came with the arrival of the train line in the mid-nineteenth century, and the town rapidly became a fashionable resort. Now firmly middle-market, Tenby gives off an extremely conservative air, and the lines of neat, prosperous hotels and expensive shops standing haughtily along the seafront cater to a large population of retirees. That said, there's plenty of entertainment here, and a huge number of pubs and restaurants to attract visitors of any age.

Tenby is also one of the major stopping-off points along the **Pembrokeshire Coast Path** (see p.162), and if you're walking the route, Tenby provides a welcome burst of glitter and excitement amidst mile upon mile of undulating cliff scenery. The **national park** boundary skirts around the edge of the town, and further along the coast are the two picturesque sandy stop-offs of **Amroth** and **Saundersfoot**. A couple of miles offshore from Tenby, the old monastic ruins of **Caldey Island** make for a pleasant day-trip.

Arrival, information and accommodation

The train station is at the western end of the town centre, at the bottom of Warren Street. Some buses stop at South Parade, at the top of Trafalgar Road, although most (including National Express coaches) call at the bus shelter on Upper Park Road.

The tourist office faces the North Beach on The Croft (daily: mid-July to Aug 10am–9pm; Easter to mid-July & Sept 10am–6pm; Oct 10am–5.30pm; Nov–March Mon–Sat 10am–4pm; ☎01834/842402). It has details of day tours by bus to St David's and the west Pembrokeshire coast (£5; see pp.175 & 180) that cannot be done on public transport. A nice way to explore Tenby is to join one of Marion Davies' ninety-minute **guided town walks** (June–Sept daily; Oct–May Mon–Sat; £3; reservations recommended ☎01834/845841), which leave from the *Lifeboat Tavern* in Tudor Square at 8pm and spend an hour and a half exploring the towns past and the people who inhabited it.

Alongside its curious collection of hippie ephemera and painfully twee gifts, Equinox on St Julian Street has a wall of posters detailing local gigs and festivals.

Accommodation

As a major resort, there are dozens of hotels and guesthouses in Tenby, all pressed from pretty much the same mould. Prices are a little higher than elsewhere in west Wales, and in high summer the place is still full to bursting point. Nonetheless, decent and reasonable **accommodation** is not hard to find, but if you don't find anything suitable in town, you could consider staying in the less crowded confines of nearby coastal villages such as Saundersfoot (see p.161) or Penally (see p.163). There are caravan sites all around Tenby: most take **tents**, especially those around the village of New Hedges around a mile and a half north on the A478. In the peak summer season you'll also find tap-in-a-field sites which spring up for a couple of months.

HOTELS AND GUESTHOUSES

Ashby House, 24 Victoria St (☎01834/842867). A comfortable, low-key hotel next to the Esplanade and the South Beach. ②.

Atlantic, The Esplanade (☎ & fax 01834/842881, *www.smoothhound.co.uk/hotels/atlant1.html*). The best – and priciest – of the hotels along the South Beach, with a high standard of rooms, a couple of good restaurants and even a small indoor pool. The seafront rooms are considerably larger and more expensive. Rates include breakfast. ⑤.

Boulston Cottage, 29 Trafalgar Rd (☎01834/843289). Consistently among the cheapest B&Bs in Tenby, always spotless and run by a wonderful Spanish woman. ①.

Castle View, 15 The Norton (☎01834/842666). Well located, staring out over Castle Hill and the harbour, this is a friendly hotel with en-suite rooms. ②.

Coach Guesthouse, 11 Deer Park (☎01834/842210). Cheery, welcoming hotel near the train station. ①.

Fourcroft, The Croft, North Beach (☎01834/842886, fax 842888, *www.walledtowns.com/4croft*). The only remaining hotel on the northern esplanade, a cheerful family place with jacuzzi, sauna and small outdoor pool. ⑤.

Glenthorne Guest House, 9 Deer Park (☎01834/842300). Large guesthouse, well reputed and excellent value. ①.

Lyndale Guest House, Warren St (☎01834/842836). Welcoming, small B&B near the train station, happy to cater for vegetarians. ①.

Tenby House, Tudor Square (☎01834/842000). Pleasantly old-fashioned but recently refurbished town centre pub-hotel with well-appointed en-suite rooms above the bar – expect some noise at weekends. ⑤.

HOSTELS AND CAMPSITES

Manorbier YHA hostel, Skrinkle Haven, near Manorbier (☎01834/871803, fax 871101). Bright, modern grey and yellow corrugated-iron clad YHA hostel overlooking the cliffs four miles west of Tenby and near the Manorbier bus route from town. Tent spaces available. Closed Nov to mid-Feb.

Meadow Farm, Northcliff (☎01834/844829). This small and semi-official site on the northern fringes of town is a great alternative to the family fun park-style places. Closed Oct–March.

Pentlepoir YHA hostel, Old School, Pentlepoir (☎01834/812333). A low-price YHA hostel in a converted school right on the A478 near Saundersfoot station and connected to Tenby by the #350 bus. Closed early Oct–March.

Well Park, off the A478 at New Hedges (☎01834/842179). High class caravan and camping site a mile north of town with reasonable rates considering the facilities. Closed Nov–March.

The Town

Tenby is shaped like a triangle, with two sides formed by the coast meeting at Castle Hill. The third side is formed by the remaining town **walls**, which are reached from the train station after a ten-minute walk straight up Warren Street. South Parade runs alongside the massive twenty-foot-high wall, first built in the late thirteenth century and massively strengthened in 1457 by Jasper Tudor, Earl of Pembroke and uncle of the future king, Henry VII. Further refortification came in the 1580s, when Tenby was considered to be in the frontline against a possible attack by the Spanish Armada. In the middle of the remaining stretch, the only town gate still standing is **Five Arches**, a semicircular barbican that combined practical day-to-day usage as an entrance for the town's citizens and peacetime visitors with hidden lookouts and angles acute enough to surprise invaders. The wall continues south to the Esplanade, with a long line of snooty hotels facing out over the smarter and far less commercialized South Beach.

The centrepiece and most notable landmark of the town centre is the 152-foot spire of the largely fifteenth-century **St Mary's church**, between St George's Street and Tudor Square. A pleasantly light interior shows the elaborate ceiling bosses in the chancel to good effect, and fifteenth-century tombs of local barons demonstrate

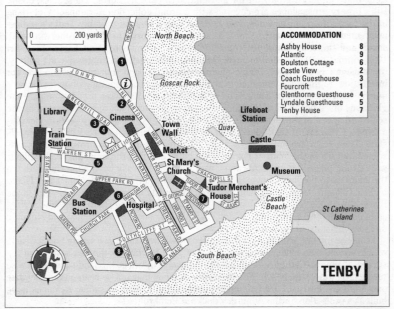

© Crown copyright

Tenby's important mercantile tradition. On the western side of St Mary's runs Frog Street, home of numerous craft shops and an indoor **arcade market**, containing craft stalls and gift shops.

Wedged between the town walls and the two bays, the **old town** makes a thoroughly enjoyable place to wander, with many interesting and unusual shops tucked away down small alleyways and steps. Many of the original medieval lanes are still intact in the immediate area around the parish church. Due east, on the other side of the church, **Quay Hill** runs parallel, a narrow set of steps and cobbles tumbling down past some of the town's oldest houses to the top of the harbour. Wedged in a corner of Quay Hill is the **Tudor Merchant's House** (April–Sept Mon, Tues & Thurs–Sat 10am–5pm, Sun 1–5pm; Oct Mon, Tues, Thurs & Fri 10am–3pm, Sun noon–3pm; £1.80; NT), built in the late fifteenth century for a wealthy local merchant at the time when Tenby was second only to Bristol as an important west coast port. The rambling house is on three floors, packed with period furniture from the sixteenth century (with later additions), although more notable are the examples of the local penchant for tapering Flemish-style chimneypieces. The walls are adorned with three surviving Tudor religious frescoes.

Crackwell and Bridge streets run down to the picturesque **harbour**, which can look idyllic if it's not too crowded. Sheltered by the curving headland and fringed by handsome pastel-shaded Georgian and Victorian town houses, it's a great place to stroll around on a warm evening. During the day, it's the scene of considerable activity as the departure point for numerous excursion boats, the most popular being the short trip over to Caldey Island (see opposite). Above the harbour is the headland and **Castle Hill**, where paths and flowerbeds have been planted around the sparse ruins of the Norman **castle**. A surviving gatehouse is the most impressive remain, although fragments of walls, an archway and windswept tower are scattered around a site that's impressive only for the all-round views that it affords. These days, Castle Hill's breezy grass slopes are covered with a proud collection of rampant Victoriana in the form of ornate benches, vast beds of bright flowers (notably Tenby's indigenous small daffodil in springtime), a pompous memorial to Prince Albert, a bandstand, and the town **museum** (Easter–Oct daily 10am–6pm; Nov–Easter Mon–Fri 10am–5pm; £1.80), founded in 1878. Doubling as a small but impressive art gallery, the museum is typical of Tenby: slightly ponderous and municipally minded, but interesting. Right at the entrance is an eye-catching contemporary photo of Tenby's north beach after the *Sea Empress* oil spill of February 1996 (see p.177). Compare the glutinous black beach with its golden present and it's hard not to be impressed by the scale and speed of the cleanup. In the museum proper, the geology section includes a five-foot mammoth tusk found near Milford Haven, ancient axes and a woman's skull dated from around 1300 BC. The local history gallery is entertainingly presented, but it's in the Wilfred Harrison art collection that the museum really shines, with strong pieces by Augustus and Gwen John, and locally born Nina Hamnett. On the stairs up to the floor above, there are some mesmerizing studies of Caldey Island by Eric Gill and David Jones, who hail from the artists' commune at Capel-y-ffin in the Black Mountains (see p.220). Upstairs, there's an interesting room of pristine stuffed animals, including a terrifying golden eagle, and a collection of lifeboat and shipping memorabilia.

From the top of Castle Hill, there are great views over the more sedate South Beach, which becomes so extensive at low tide that it all but chases the sea away from the shores of tiny St Catherine's Island (no access), cut off at high tide but otherwise reached by way of the beach. The remains of the fort that can be seen on the islet date only from 1869, when Lord Palmerston constructed a chain of similar defences to be built as a protection for the Admiralty docks at Pembroke.

Caldey Island

Looming large over Tenby's seascape is **Caldey Island** (Ynys Pyr), a couple of miles offshore due south of the Esplanade. Celtic monks first settled here in the sixth century, perhaps establishing an offshoot of St Illtud's monastery at Llantwit Major (see p.116). The exact duration of this Celtic settlement is unclear, although the ninth-century Latin inscription on the island's sixth-century Ogham stone would indicate that the community was still thriving then. Nothing is then known of the island until 1113, when English king Henry I gave it to Norman nobleman, Robert Fitzmartin, who in turn gave it to his mother. In 1136, it was given to the Benedictine monks of St Dogmael's at Cardigan, who founded their priory here. Upon the Dissolution of the Monasteries in 1536, the Benedictine monks left the island and a fanciful succession of owners bought and sold it on a whim, until it was, once again, sold to a Benedictine monastic order in 1906 and subsequently to an order of Reformed Cistercians. The island has been a monastic home almost constantly ever since.

Boats leave Tenby Harbour every fifteen minutes in season (mid-May to mid-Sept Mon–Fri 9.45am–4pm; mid-July to early Sept also Sat 1–4pm; Easter to mid-May & mid-Sept to early Oct occasional sailings; ☎01834/842402; £6) for the twenty-minute journey to the island. Tickets (not tied to any specific sailing) are sold at the kiosk in Castle Square, directly above the harbour. On landing at Caldey's jetty, a short walk leads through the woods to the island's main settlement.

The village itself is the main hub of Caldey life. As well as a tiny post office and popular tearoom, there's a **perfume shop** selling the herbal fragrances distilled by the monks from Caldey's abundant flora. The narrow road going to the left leads down to the heavily restored **chapel of St David**, whose most impressive feature is the round-arched Norman door. Opposite is the gathering point for daily (men-only) tours of the garish twentieth-century **monastery**, a white, turreted heap that resembles a Disney castle. In July and August tours take place every couple of hours.

A lane leads south from the village to the old **priory**, abandoned at the Dissolution and restored at the beginning of the twentieth century. Centrepiece of the complex is the remarkable twelfth-century **St Illtud's church**, marked out by its curiously blunt (and leaning) steeple. This houses one of the most significant pre-Norman finds in Wales, the sandstone **Ogham Cross**, carved with an inscription from the sixth century and added to, in Latin, during the ninth – it was found under the stained-glass window on the south side of the nave. The church's rough flooring is largely comprised of pebbles from the island's beaches. The lane continues south from the site, climbing up to the gleaming white island **lighthouse**, built in 1828. Views from here are memorable.

Eating and drinking

There are dozens of **cafés** and **restaurants** around the town – in high season, the beachfronts (especially the North Beach) are packed in by cheap places that shut up shop during the winter. Many of the restaurants in the narrow town centre streets are tourist traps, overpriced and less than memorable – once again, pub food is often far better value.

Restaurants and cafés

Bay Tree, Tudor Square. Smartish, moderately priced wood-floored bistro with a slightly more imaginative selection of meat and vegetarian dishes than in most places nearby.

Fecci and Sons, Upper Frog St. Genuine Italian snackery and ice-cream parlour, with over sixty speciality ice-creams.

La Cave, Upper Frog St (☎01834/843038). Relaxed and impressive restaurant and wine bar, with moderately priced, well-cooked local specialities.

Pam Pam, Tudor Square. Just about the best of the avowedly "family" restaurants, serving good-value portions of everyone's favourite dishes.

Quay Room, Quay Hill. Dark and cosy café and bar that's a world away from the chips'n'vinegar atmosphere outside, and is the best place in town for decent espresso. Located downstairs from (and associated with) the *Plantaganet*.

Plantaganet, Quay Hill (☎01834/842350). Cosy, expensive and thoroughly enjoyable restaurant serving local specialities, tucked next to the Tudor Merchant's House. Apparently, it's the oldest house in Tenby – you can see a thirteenth-century Flemish chimney en route to the loo.

Pubs

Coach and Horses, Upper Frog St. Animated, wood-beamed bar popular with a young crowd who appreciate the good beer and reasonable bar snacks.

Five Arches Tavern, St George's St. Upmarket and rather snooty, but pleasant enough, and with good food.

Lamb, High St. Reasonably priced bar food makes up for the slightly pricey drinks in this convivial, mixed-age pub.

Lifeboat Tavern, Tudor Square. Popular and enjoyable young people's pub.

Normandie Hotel, Upper Frog St. Old-fashioned pub, which suffers from being too bright and loud, though it does have live music at weekends. Good food available at all times.

Tenby House, Tudor Square. Another young favourite, which borders on the rowdy of a weekend evening. Good for live music.

Three Mariners, St George's St. Home of good beer and regular live music.

Listings

Bike rental Try Bro Bikes (☎01843/844766) by the roundabout at the bottom of Greenhill Rd, or, less conveniently, Broadmoor Garage in Kilgetty (☎01834/813266), four miles north of town.

Car rental Five Arches Garage, South Parade (☎01834/842244).

Cinema For mainstream movies right in town, try the Royal Playhouse on White Lion St (☎01834/844809).

Exchange The main banks are on Tudor Square and have currency-changing facilities.

Festivals The fairly highbrow Tenby Arts Festival (☎01834/842974 or 842291), in mid-Sept, has a rowdy and lively Fringe.

Hospital Trafalgar Rd (☎01834/842040).

Internet access Free access is available at the library on Greenhill Rd (Mon–Fri 9.30am–1pm & 2–5pm, Sat 9.30am–12.30pm), and for a small fee at The Cyber Centre on Nelson's Walk off Upper Frog St (☎01834/844700).

Laundry Try Washeteria, Lower Frog St, or Broadwell Hayes, near the viaduct.

Leisure centre Marsh Rd (☎01834/843574), including a swimming pool.

Pharmacies Boots, High St; Craven, White Lion St.

Police Warren St (☎01834/842303).

Post office Warren St.

Taxis Local Taxis (☎01834/844603).

Amroth and Saundersfoot

AMROTH marks the easterly end of the 186-mile **Pembrokeshire Coast Path**, which winds and darts its way around every cove and cliff in the county, right the way around to St Dogmael's, just outside Cardigan (see p.267). It's a pleasant village, without being especially exciting: the beach is good, with south-facing sands ensuring maximum sunshine. For those starting or finishing the path at Amroth, a bed for the night might be a welcome necessity: the best places in the village are the *Ashdale* (☎01834/813853; ①) and *Beach Haven* (☎01834/813310; ①), which has some en-suite rooms. The *New Inn* is right next to the beach and is an enjoyable place to eat and drink, if generally packed come the summer. From the centre of Amroth, a signposted walk (The Knights' Way), or a drive around the steep lanes, leads up to the **Colby Woodland Garden** (April–Oct daily 10am–5pm; £2.80; NT), about a mile, as the crow flies, above the village. The estate, wedged deep into a wooded valley, was, until the nineteenth century, mined extensively for anthracite and iron ore. It's very pleasant, if hardly spectacular: highlights include the sloping walled garden (11am–5pm) and, in May and June, the explosion of colour in the rhododendron bushes. There's also a local art and craft gallery containing some fine pieces amongst the landscapes and flower prints.

The coast between Amroth and Tenby is one long line of caravan parks, broken only by the picturesque harbour of **SAUNDERSFOOT**, built originally for the export of local anthracite and coal. The town has been attracting visitors for centuries, and is a lively, good-natured place; now all the industry has folded, the harbour and the wide yawn of sand are used purely for recreational purposes. The main focus of activity is the large **harbour** area, where there is a predictable clutch of cafés, tawdry shops, boisterously fun pubs and even the opportunity to try out waterskiing with Jones & Teague (☎01834/813429), on the far end of the harbour wall.

Saundersfoot's **train station** is located a mile northwest up The Ridgeway from the harbourside **tourist office** (Easter–Oct Mon–Sat 10am–1pm & 2–5.30pm; plus mid-July to Aug Sun, same hours; ☎01834/813672). If you want to **stay** in the village, try *Cliff House* (☎01834/813931; ②), right in the centre on Wogan Terrace, or *The Valley*, on Valley Road towards the train station around half a mile from the harbour. A mile and a half north of Saundersfoot towards Amroth, the thoroughly enjoyable *Wiseman's Bridge Inn* (☎01834/813236; ①), is a beachside pub with B&B facilities and gloriously isolated **camping**; the best proper campsite, though, is a mile south of Saundersfoot and just short of Monkstone Point at *Trevayne Farm* (April–Aug; ☎01834/813402), from where there are excellent views over Saundersfoot and the great arc of sand that sweeps round to Amroth and Pendine. There's a **YHA hostel** in the Old School at Pentlepoir (☎01834/812333; closed mid-Oct to March), on the A478 near Saundersfoot station.

Saundersfoot has plenty of **places to eat**: the best bets are the charming *Old Chemist Inn* on The Strand and, around the main harbour square, the *Royal Oak* on Wogan Terrace. In Pentlepoir village, just the other side of Saundersfoot station, you can occasionally hear live music at the *Fountainhead* pub.

South Pembrokeshire coast

The southern zigzag of coast that darts west from Tenby is a strange mix of caravan parks and Ministry of Defence shooting ranges above some spectacularly beautiful bays and gull-covered cliffs. From Tenby, the A4139 passes through **Penally**, little more than an extended suburb of the town, before delving down past the **Lydstep Haven** beach. A road dips south here, past **Skrinkle Haven** and into the winding streets of **Manorbier**, where the ghostly castle sits above a small bay. Three miles inland from here is the quintessentially pretty village of **St Florence**, its narrow lanes crowned by a profusion of Flemish chimneys.

The coast nips and tucks in past some excellent, and comparatively quiet beaches, passing the tourist magnet of **Freshwater East** before rising up to some impressive cliffs en route to the beautiful **Barafundle Bay** and the National Trust's **Stackpole Head**. Behind Stackpole, and the neighbouring **Broad Haven** beach, is the picturesque village of **Bosherston** and its lily lakes. Travelling west, the first of the area's many MOD artillery ranges lies between Bosherston and the coast, and you have to cross it in order to see the remarkable and ancient **St Govan's chapel**, squeezed into a rock cleft above the crashing waves.

On foot, you can get closer to the best of the scenery by way of a four-mile section of the Pembrokeshire Coast Path, walking west and brushing along the top of some of Wales' most dramatic cliffside scenery, including the **Stack Rocks** and limestone arch that mark the last point of access on this part of the coast. All around and to the west are **artillery ranges**, forcing the Coast Path inland in order to avoid snipers. The next point of access on the coast is the west-facing **Freshwater West**, a wide beach popular

THE PEMBROKESHIRE NATIONAL PARK AND COAST PATH

Of the ten national parks in England and Wales, the **Pembrokeshire Coast National Park** (*www.pembrokeshirecoast.org.uk*) is the only one that is predominantly sea-based, hugging the rippled coast around the entire southwestern section of Wales. Established in 1952, the park is not one easily identifiable mass, rather a series of occasionally unconnected patches of coast and inland scenery. Starting at its southeastern corner, the first segment clings to the coast from Amroth through to the Milford Haven waterway, an area of sweeping limestone cliffs and some fabulous beaches. The second (and by far the quietest) part courses around the inland pastoral landscape of the Daugleddau estuary, which plunges deep into the rural heart of Pembrokeshire southeast of Haverfordwest. Superb for scenic cliff walking, the third section is around the beaches and resorts of St Bride's Bay, where the sea scoops a great chunk out of Wales' westernmost land. In the north of the county, the boundary of the park runs far inland to encompass the Mynydd Preseli, a barren but invigoratingly beautiful range of hills dotted with ancient relics.

Crawling around almost every wriggle of the coast, the **Pembrokeshire Coast Path** winds 186 miles from Amroth in the south, to its northernmost point at St Dogmael's near Cardigan. For the vast majority of the time, the path clings precariously to clifftop routes, overlooking rocks popular with sunbathing seals, craggy offshore islands, unexpected gashes of sand and shrieking clouds of sea birds. Only on the southwestern end of the Castlemartin peninsula, where the coast is given over to army training camps and rifle ranges, does the path veer inland for any major length; it also ducks briefly inland along the Milford Haven estuary, where the close proximity of a couple of belching great oil refineries and the huge expanse of hill-backed water provide one of the route's many surprises.

The most popular and ruggedly inspiring segments of the Coast Path are around St David's Head and the Marloes peninsula, either side of St Bride's Bay, the stretch from the castle at Manorbier to the tiny cliff chapel at Bosherston along the southern coast and, generally quieter, the undulating contours, massive cliffs, bays and old ports along the northern coast, either side of Fishguard. These offer miles of windswept walking amongst great flashes of gorse, heather and seasonal plants, as well as the opportunity to study thousands of sea birds at close quarter. Basking seals are frequent visitors to some of the more inaccessible beaches, particularly around the time when pups are born in the autumn. This is reckoned to be a major cause of the occasional accidents along the route, as people try to gain better views of the creatures and consequently tip over the edge.

Of all the **seasons**, spring is perhaps the finest for walking: the crowds are yet to arrive and the clifftop flora is at its most vivid. There are numerous publications available about the Coast Path, of which the best is Brian John's *National Trail Guide* (£11), which includes 1:25,000 section maps of the route. The national park publishes a handy *Coast Path Accommodation* guide (£2), detailing B&Bs and campsites the entire length of the route, available from tourist and national park offices and bookshops. It also publishes the excellent free newspaper, *Coast to Coast*, which contains exhaustive listings of special walks, boat trips and other events, and which you can pick up from the various national park offices listed throughout this chapter. A further path has been created around the haunting Daugleddau estuaries, inland from the Milford Haven. For details of both the national park and the Coast Path, contact the Information Officer at the Pembrokeshire Coast National Park Authority, Winch Lane, Haverfordwest, Pembrokeshire SA61 1PY (☎01437/764591 ext 5135).

with surfers, reached across windy grass dunes and heathland. The peninsula tapers out to the west, a long finger of rugged coastline pointing out towards the main part of the county. The westernmost village is **Angle**, sitting on the edge of its bay and facing out across the Milford Haven towards the grim reminders of industrialization in the shape of a vast oil refinery.

Penally, Manorbier and St Florence

Just over a mile down the A4139 from Tenby, the dormitory village of **PENALLY** is unremarkable save for the vast beach, a wide and sunny sprawl of sand that runs right up to become Tenby's South Beach a mile further up. The coastal path hugs the clifftop from the viewpoint at Giltar Point, just below Penally, reaching the glorious privately owned beach at the 54-acre headland of **Lydstep Haven** after two miles; it's a beautiful spot, with limestone caverns to explore in the craggy Lydstep Point, and worth the nominal entrance fee. Although some of the caverns here are only accessible at low tide, the Smuggler's Cave is safe at all times.

A mile further west is the cove of **Skrinkle Haven**, reached via steep steps from the car park at the end of the little lane off the Manorbier road. Above the beach is the excellent Manorbier **YHA hostel** (see Tenby, p.156), where you can also **camp**. There's another campsite at *Whitewell Caravan Park* (☎01834/871569), sandwiched between the main road and train line just west of the town. Of the pubs, the lively *Cross Inn*, near Penally station, is best.

Manorbier

The next part of the Coast Path heads inland to avoid the artillery range that occupies the beautiful outcrop of Old Castle Head, then leads straight into the quaint village of **MANORBIER**, pronounced "Manner-beer" (Maenorbŷr), birthplace in 1146 of Giraldus Cambrensis, Gerald of Wales (see p.355), who described the castle here as "excellently well defended by turrets and bulwarks, and . . . situated on the summit of a hill extending on the western side towards the sea". Founded in the early twelfth century as an impressive baronial residence, the castle (Easter–Sept daily 10.30am–5.30pm; £2) sits above the village and its beach on a hill of wild gorse. The Norman walls are in a very decent state of repair, surrounding an inner grass courtyard in which the extensive remains of the castle's chapel and state rooms jostle for position with the nineteenth-century domestic residence, whose TV aerial strikes a note of contemporary discord. Views from the ramparts are wonderful, taking in the corrugated coastline, bushy dunes, deep-green fields and smoking chimneys of the tinted village houses. In the walls and buildings are a warren of dark passageways to explore, occasionally opening out into little cells populated by lacklustre wax figures, purporting to illustrate the castle's history. Needless to say, prime position goes to a waxwork of Gerald himself.

The lane below the castle leads past the curious, elongated tower of the parish church down to Manorbier's shell-shaped **cove**, a sandy break in the red-sandstone cliffs. For a more secluded bathe, follow the path on the left of the beach (as you face the sea) up over the headland known as the Priest's Nose, past the Neolithic cromlech (burial chamber) known as the **King's Quoit**, with its lopsided capstone, and round for just over half a mile to the steep steps down to often-deserted **Precipe Beach**. At high tide, the beach is entirely flooded, so check times carefully.

In Manorbier, you'll find **accommodation** at the smart, comfortable and non-smoking *Old Vicarage* (☎01834/871452; ②), and there's a **campsite** at *Park Farm* (☎01834/871273) on the northern side of the village, just off the B4585 towards Manorbier station, but still within staggering distance of the *Castle Inn* in Manorbier.

Swanlake Bay and Freshwater East

Past Manorbier, the lanes and Coast Path wriggle ever westwards, with the path skirting across the top of the beautifully remote, and always quiet, **Swanlake Bay**, a mile from Manorbier; car drivers will find it almost impossible to find a place to park, although just off the small lane from Manorbier to Hodgeston, the farmers at East Moor Farm and *West Moor Farm* (☎01834/871204; ②), where you are also able to **camp**, usually allow a few people to park and walk the remaining distance. Swanlake is a far better option than the next beach along, close to the garish village of **FRESH-WATER EAST**, whose magnificent sheltered beach is spoiled by the profusion of hideous sprawling holiday developments that back on to it.

St Florence

Three miles north of Manorbier is the delightful little village of **ST FLORENCE**, whose whitewashed stone cottages, many with their original medieval Flemish chimney stacks, sit huddled around the tiny lanes. The Ritec stream, along whose banks there is a beautiful walk which takes you east of the village, was once an inlet, and St Florence an important port during the Middle Ages before the stream retreated. If you want to **stay** here, the country-house atmosphere of *Elm Grove* (☎01834/871255; ③) comes at a very reasonable price. *Elm Grove* also serves meals, and the village pubs are excellent: the wonderful *New Inn* is the first amongst equals in this village of good boozers.

Stackpole Quay to Angle

One of the best starting points for walks along the breathtaking clifftops is the rocky little harbour at **Stackpole Quay** (NT), reached via the small lane from Freshwater East through East Trewent. This is one of the smallest harbours you'll find anywhere along the Pembrokeshire coast, with barely enough room for two boats in between slabs of stratified limestone. With the added bonus of the *Boathouse Tearooms*, it's a gorgeous spot, and just a taster for the scenic wonders further west as the Coast Path meanders through the National Trust's Stackpole Estate. A half-mile walk brings you to **Barafundle Bay**, which is inaccessible by car and ranks as one of the finest beaches in Pembrokeshire, with clear water and a soft beach fringed by wooded cliffs. South of the beach is a spectacular stretch of the Coast Path leading to **Stackpole Head**, a tufted plateau on craggy arches jutting into the sea.

The path continues around the coast, through the dunes of **Stackpole Warren**, to **BROAD HAVEN** – the next spot on the coast accessible by car – where a pleasant small beach overlooks several rocky islets now managed by the National Trust. Basing yourself here gives good access inland to the nearby **Bosherston Lily Ponds**, three reed-fringed fingers of water artificially created in the late eighteenth century for coarse fishing, but now beautifully landscaped. The westernmost lake is the prettiest, especially in late spring and early summer when the lilies that form a carpet across its surface are in full bloom. You can still fish here, obtaining a permit (£5 a day) from *Ye Olde Worlde Café*, a couple of hundred yards away in the village of **BOSHERSTON**. From here it's a mile to the coast, reached across the MOD training grounds peppered with warning signs and barriers across the road that are only opened "when there is no tank or helicopter firing" – which, in practice, is most of the time. For further information consult National Park information offices or the knowledgeable staff at the Bosherston post office. Persevere down the lane through the series of unwelcoming gates and you'll reach a spot overlooking the cliffs where **St Govan's chapel** is wedged: it's a remarkable tiny, grey chapel, known to be at least eight hundred years old (and possibly as much as fourteen hundred). Legend has it that Saint Govan chose this spot to be buried when a gang of hoodlums attacked him on the clifftop and the cliffs opened up and folded gently around him, protecting him from certain death. The steps descend straight into the sandy-floored chapel, now devoid of any furnishings, save for the simple stone altar. At its side, steps lead into a small cell hewn from the rock, containing the fissure that is reputed to have sheltered Saint Govan. Steps continue down to the spume of the sea hurtling at the rocks. Here, you get a magnificent close-up of the precarious crags, caves and arches, deep turquoise water, rigidly straight rock strata and limestone worn and washed by the sea. Good-value **accommodation** is found at the enjoyable *St Govan's Inn* in Bosherston village (☎01646/661311; ①), which caters mostly to rock climbers and serves mountains of inexpensive food.

All the land to the west of St Govan's chapel is dominated by the dugouts and abandoned shells and army tanks, and, apart from the narrow strip of clifftop land on which the Coast Path runs, is entirely out of bounds. The path skirts along the top of the cliffs to the west for four miles, past a striking cleft in the rocks known as **Huntsman's Leap** and two isolated beaches at **Bullslaughter** and **Flimston Bay** to the **Stack Rocks**. Alternatively, a lane – with restricted opening times – runs down to the Stacks from the outskirts of the village of Merrion on the B4319, passing the mournful little chapel at **FLIMSTON** village, a hamlet forcibly abandoned to the army.

The Stack Rocks jut out of the sea here like a series of tall, lichen-spattered stepping stones. A hundred yards further west (and as far as you're allowed to go) is a graceful, curving limestone arch rising out of a wave-flattened platform of rock, known as the **Green Bridge of Wales**. On a quiet day, the only company you will have are the shrieking gulls, guillemots and kittiwakes swooping to their perches on the limestone ledges. The land to the west, appropriated by the military, contains some of the most spectacular coastal scenery in the county, as well as some superb dunes and important ancient remains. **Climbers** eager to see the caves of Linney Down and the stacks and caves of the southern coast should apply in writing to The Commandant, RAC Castlemartin, Merrion, Pembroke SA71 5EB. Permits to enter the 5884-acre "Range West" are issued between mid-August and January only, and you must specify the cliffs you want to climb.

Castlemartin, Freshwater West and Angle

Forced to turn inland here, the Coast Path continues back up the lane to Merrion and follows the B4319 through the village of **CASTLEMARTIN** – whose church houses an organ once owned by Mendelssohn. Here you can **stay** at peaceful *Chapel Farm* (☎ & fax 01646/661312, *chapelfarm@aol.com*; ②). The Coast Path follows the B4319 a couple of miles to **Freshwater West**, a west-facing beach resort that's excellent for surfing, although the currents can be too strong for swimming. The desolation of the wind-battered dunes behind the beach make for interesting walking.

The B4319 meets the B4320 from Pembroke near the **Devil's Quoit**, a Neolithic burial chamber topped by an impressive capstone. The road continues west into the last finger of the peninsula, reaching the remote village of **ANGLE** at the western end of a wide curve of mud known as **Angle Bay**. Angle consists of one long street, bounded by old, coloured cottages and some impressive pubs. **West Angle Bay**, a secluded spot a mile to the west of the main village, is better for swimming, and overlooks another of the Lord Palmerston protective forts on **Thorn Island**. The fort was, until recently, the secluded *Thorn Island Hotel* for which guests were picked up by boat from the beach, though it has now been sold and its future is uncertain. There is currently no accommodation with a roof in Angle, though you can camp at *Castle Farm* (☎01646/641220) just behind the village church. For **eating** and **drinking**, try the convivial *Hibernia Inn*, right in the village centre; alternatively, take a ten-minute walk east along the shore to

THE PEMBROKESHIRE ENERGY INDUSTRIES

On both sides of the magnificent Milford Haven waterway, the most prominent features on the landscape belong to the refineries that fringe the waters. Storage tankers, observation towers and security fences litter the Coast Path here, the most blighted stretch being the five miles between the west side of the Pembroke River estuary and Angle Bay.

As well as occasional disasters such as the dreadful *Sea Empress* episode (see p.177), the presence of so much polluting and potentially hazardous industry in this rural corner of Wales has many ramifications. A few years ago, a huge fire at the Texaco refinery on the south side of the Haven prompted many residents of Rhoscrowther and Pwllcrochan to leave the area, and forced eviction of these villages occasionally surfaces as an option, hardly helping the remaining residents' confidence.

However, matters are improving. One of the three refineries has closed down and the two that remain have cleaned up their act considerably, while the neighbouring Pembroke power station is being dismantled after a major public campaign in the late 1990s forced its closure. Though designed as an oil-burning power station, the plant's owners, National Power, decided it would be more economic to convert it to burn orimulsion, a controversial fuel which even they admitted has a "kill factor" some 442 times greater than ordinary crude oil. Orimulsion had been burned elsewhere, notably at the now-closed Richborough station in Kent, England, where local crops suffered drastically, land was poisoned and car paint blistered – pure coincidence according to the owners. The company threatened to close Pembroke power station altogether, unless consent was given for its conversion, and consequently gained the support of some local trade unions and councillors, for whom the jobs and prosperity were paramount. Fortunately, though, public pressure won out in the end. Orimulsion stayed away and, as promised, the plant has now closed, heralding an unequivocal victory for the environment and the health of local people.

the delightful and decidedly rustic *Point House* inn, whose fire is said to have burned continuously for over three hundred years until the mid-1990s, when the decision was made to light it only in winter.

Pembroke and around

The old county town of **PEMBROKE** (Penfro) and its fearsome **castle** sit on the southern side of the Pembroke River, a continuation of the massive Milford Haven waterway that was described by Nelson as the greatest natural harbour in the world. The slightly over-restored castle is nonetheless an essential sight, dominated by its vast 75-foot Norman keep. But aside from the harbour and the town's wonderful **Museum of the Home**, Pembroke is surprisingly dull, with one long main street of attractive Georgian and Victorian houses, some intact stretches of medieval town wall and little else to catch the eye.

The town grew up solely to serve the castle, the mightiest link in the chain of Norman strongholds built across southern Wales. Drawn out along a hilltop ridge, the walled town flourished as a port for Pembrokeshire goods to be exported from the main quay, situated alongside the waters below the imposing walls of the castle, to all parts of Britain, as well as Ireland, France and Spain.

Cromwell attacked the town in 1648 in the midst of the English Civil War. By this stage, the castle was partially derelict and it was only the strength of the recently repaired town walls that enabled the citizens to withstand the worst of the onslaught. They were beaten, however, by a 48-day siege and by the Parliamentarian troops seizing the water supply, after which Cromwell ordered the continued demolition of the castle and walls.

Pembroke then developed as a centre of leather making, weaving, dyeing and tailoring, never really regaining its former importance. In the twentieth century, the small town was on a serious slope of decline, its port long since overtaken by neighbouring sites. One fortunate result of this is that Pembroke is mercifully free of postwar development in the centre, although the fringes around the main street are largely modern and bland.

Around the town are several noteworthy sights, the most interesting being the ruined Bishop's Palace in **Lamphey**, a country residence for the bishops of St David's in the thirteenth century, and a couple of miles further on, the attractive town of **Carew**, with its Celtic cross and castle. **Pembroke Dock**, three miles north of Pembroke, grew up in a grid pattern during the nineteenth century to serve its parent town as a naval dockyard.

The Town

A tidal mass of mud, the **Pembroke River** flows in from the Daugleddau to frame the northern side of Pembroke town centre. Running parallel to the southern bank is the long **Main Street**, which stretches from the train station (as Station Road) in the east to the mighty lines of the castle.

Opposite the castle walls at 7 Westgate Hill (the continuation north of Main Street) is the delightfully eccentric **Museum of the Home** (May–Sept Mon–Thurs 11am–5pm; £1.20), an all-encompassing name for the thousands of objects packed into this steep town house. It's a collection of utterly ordinary items from the eighteenth to the twentieth centuries, loosely gathered into themes – the dairy, toiletries, personal and smoking accessories, kitchen equipment, bedroom accessories and children's games. The enthusiasm of the owners, who show people around with illuminating conversation and great interest, makes the sensation somewhat akin to being let loose in a small stately home.

From the museum and the castle gates, Main Street widens out past multicoloured shop frontages of eighteenth- and nineteenth-century construction, dipping down for over half a mile towards the towered **St Michael's church**, heavily, and unsympathetically, restored by the Victorians. Blackhorse Walk turns north, running down to the Mill Pond and the most impressive remnants of the thirteenth-century town **walls** running between the demolished East Gate and Barnard's Tower, a medieval towered house attached to the walls.

The castle

Pembroke's history is inextricably bound up with that of the **castle** (daily: April–Sept 9.30am–6pm; March & Oct 10am–5pm; Nov–Feb 10.30am–4.30pm; £3), founded as the strongest link in the chain of fortresses built by the Normans across south Wales to tame and subjugate the people. In the early years following the Norman invasion, the people of Deheubarth (west Wales) avoided the conquest, thanks to a tacit agreement between Rhys ap Tewdwr and the Norman victors. Upon his death in 1093, however, Norman lord Roger de Montgomery didn't hesitate for a moment in charging into the area and capturing it by force from the surprised natives. Pembroke's powerful bulk, protected by a hill on its southern side and water on the other three, proved impregnable to the Welsh, who attempted to besiege it. But to no avail; it has never been under the control of the Welsh. The earldom of Pembroke, created in 1138, was passed down to the Marshals, or local landowners awarded an earldom, who almost entirely rebuilt the castle between 1189 and 1245, and over the ensuing three centuries enforced the feudal rule of "Little England Beyond Wales" (see p.155), a primitive (but successful) way of ensuring Welsh subservience to the English in the farthest-flung corner of the country, by establishing firm English military rule from the chain of powerful castles built in a string across Pembrokeshire. In 1452, Henry VI granted the title and castle to

Jasper Tudor, whose nephew Harri (or Henry) was born here and became king, as the Lancastrian heir to the throne, after defeating Yorkist Richard III at Bosworth Field in 1485. During the Civil War, Pembroke was a Parliamentarian stronghold until the town's military governor suddenly switched allegiance to the King. Cromwell's troops sacked the castle after besieging it for 48 days.

Despite Cromwell's incessant battering and centuries of subsequent neglect, the sheer, bloody-minded bulk of Pembroke still inspires awe, even if it is largely due to extensive restoration over the last century. Entering through the soaring gatehouse brings you into the large, grassy courtyard, around which the battlements are broken up by great hulking towers. These marked the positions where the town walls formerly attached themselves to the fortress.

At the back of the courtyard is the inner ward, grouped around the castle's most eye-catching feature: the vast, round Norman **keep**, 75ft high, with walls 18ft thick and crowned by a dome. The intact towers and battlements contain many heavily restored communal rooms, now empty of furniture (and to a large extent, atmosphere too), although the walkways and dark-roofed passages that connect them give ample chance to chase around spiral stairways into great oak-beamed halls. Some of the rooms, mainly in the gatehouse, are used to house some excellent displays on the history of the castle and the Tudor empire.

In the keep, the view of the dank, dripping interior is quite disorientating, as the tower seems to taper upwards. Even better is the eerie view into the yawning innards from the top, which can be reached via steps in the massive walls. The tower was probably built at the beginning of the thirteenth century by William Marshal. One clue to its age comes in the two contrasting windows in its side – one round-headed and Norman, the other pointed and Perpendicular – suggesting that the construction spanned the transitional period between the two architectural ages.

Alongside the keep is a cluster of domestic buildings, largely ruined and unrestored, and seeming insignificant in comparison with the magnitude of the rest of the castle. Apart from a dungeon tower – complete with grille to peer through into the gloomy cell below – there's a Norman Hall, where the period arch has been disappointingly over-restored and reinforced. Adjacent is the Oriel or Northern Hall, a Tudor re-creation of an earlier antechamber. A set of steps at the side of the Northern Hall leads down and down into a huge natural cavern, dank and slimy, way below the castle, where light is beamed in through a barred hole in the wall that looks out over the waterside path.

Practicalities

Pembroke's **train station** is on the easternmost side of the town centre on Station Road. From there, head left out of Station Drive, over the roundabout and down the Main Street into the town centre. The **tourist office** is on Commons Road (Easter–Oct daily 10am–5.30pm; Nov Tues, Thurs & Sat 10am–4pm; ☎01646/622388), parallel to Main Street, and can provide a useful free town guide and a fair bit of information on the Pembrokeshire National Park and Coast Path.

If you decide to **stay**, don't bypass *Beech House B&B*, 78 Main St (☎ & fax 01646/683746; ①), one of Pembroke's oldest residences. Though it only has shared bathrooms, for comfort and hospitality, *Beech House* easily outdoes places charging twice as much; one room has a four-poster bed. If it's full, try the slightly pricier *Merton Place House*, a few doors up at 3 East Back (☎01646/684795; ①), which has a pleasant walled garden at the back. Pricier places in town aren't great shakes, and you might be better off staying in Lamphey (see opposite), a couple of miles to the east.

Food is easy to find in Pembroke: try *The Pantry*, at 4 Main St near the castle, for stodgy and cheap daytime and early evening snacks, or the nicely-cooked bar food at the *King's Arms Hotel* at 13 Main St. Further along at no. 63, *The Left Bank*

(☎01646/622333) is about as un-Pembroke as could be, all stripped-wood floors bold colours, and a well thought out French cuisine that wins the plaudits of discerning locals. The prix fixé menu goes for £20 if you eat two course, £24 for a full three-courser. The best of the dozens of **pubs** is the *Old Cross Saws* at 109 Main St, although it's hard to beat a summer evening at the *Waterman's Arms*, over the bridge on Northgate Street, where you can while away the hours on a veranda overlooking the Mill Pond. The *Castle Inn* at 17 Main St is the weekend drinking hole of choice for the town's youth before they troop across the road to the *Mississippi Showboat* nightclub.

Pembroke Dock

Workaday **PEMBROKE DOCK** (Doc Penfro) is principally of interest for the ferries to Rosslare in Ireland, which leave from the port some three miles north of its parental city. The town sprang up almost instantaneously in the nineteenth century as a result of a local argument that developed when Milford Haven refused to provide a home for a naval dockyard. Constructed according to a rigid grid plan and with some handsome Victorian buildings flanking the wide streets, Pembroke Dock's fortunes have fluctuated severely between recession and boom, but today, thanks to the oil refineries and the development of a deep-water dock, the town is on a firmer footing than it has been for decades.

Pembroke Dock's **train station** leads out on to Water Street, from where Pier Road heads right down the hill to Hobbs Point, from where there's a spectacular panorama over the boats and smoking stacks of the Daugleddau River. Down on the harbourside, off Front Street, a rickety bridge leads to the **Gun Tower** (April–Oct Mon–Sat 10am–5pm; free), a converted Victorian military defence post that was originally one of numerous fortifications built to guard the Milford Haven waterway. It now houses a few moderately diverting exhibits on its own history, and a small **tourist office** (☎01646/622246; same hours as the Gun Tower). Immediately west is the imposing dockyard, sheltering behind high walls and containing the **ferry terminal** for the twice-daily Irish Ferries (☎0990/134252) service to Rosslare in Ireland; boats currently depart at 3.15am and 3pm, and the journey takes four hours. The terminal contains another **tourist office** (Easter–Oct daily 11am–3.30pm; ☎01646/622753).

Though Pembroke itself makes a better base, there is decent accommodation here at the friendly, good-value *White Hart* pub (☎01646/681687; ①), 100 yards from the ferry terminal, while the *Welshman's Arms* on London Road has excellent food. The pricier continental *La Brasseria* is nearby on Laws Street (☎01646/686966).

Lamphey

The humdrum village of **LAMPHEY** (Llandyfai), two miles east of Pembroke, is best known for the ruined **Bishop's Palace** (daily 10am–5pm; £2; CADW) which stands off a quiet lane to the north of the settlement. Dating from at least the thirteenth century and abandoned at the Reformation in the mid-sixteenth century, the palace was built as a country retreat for the bishops of St David's, though it was in use as Crown apartments for a few decades afterwards. Stout walls surround the scattered ruins, with many of the palace buildings having long been lost under the grassy banks. Most impressive are the remains of the Great Hall at the entire eastern end of the complex, with fourteenth-century Bishop Gower's hallmark arcaded parapets on its top, similar to those that he built in the Bishop's Palace of St David's (see p.183). Lit only by narrow slits, the gloomy hall beneath the Great Hall has the feeling of a crypt.

Lamphey is a pleasant place in which to linger: it's on the train line to Pembroke, and there's a good range of **accommodation**: try the *Court Hotel* (☎01646/672273, fax 672480, *thecourthotel.lamphey@btinternet.com*; ⑤), a white Georgian mansion opposite the Bishop's Palace ruins – it's a bit over the top, but it does have an indoor pool and assorted ways to pamper yourself. *Lamphey Hall Hotel* (☎01646/672394; ③) by the church is more modest, and half a mile to the east along The Ridgeway, you can sleep cheaply at the *Barn at the Back of Beyond* (☎ & fax 01646/672047, *barnatbeyond@dial. pipex.com*) a farmhouse **hostel** with four-bunk rooms, self-catering facilities, and evening meals for groups if prearranged: bring a sleeping bag. You can eat very well at the moderately-priced *Dial Inn* on The Ridgeway (☎01646/672426), a pub-cum-country restaurant with a wide choice of mostly traditional dishes, all nicely cooked, prettily presented and a little overpriced.

Carew

The tiny village of **CAREW** (Caeriw), four miles east of Pembroke by the Carew River, is a pretty place that can become unbearably packed in high season. Just south of the river crossing, by the main road, is the village's **Celtic cross**, erected as a memorial to Maredydd, ruler of Deheubarth, who died in 1035. The graceful, remarkably intact taper of the shaft is covered in fine tracery of ancient Welsh designs.

Beyond the cross, an Elizabethan walled garden houses the ticket office for **Carew Castle** and **Mill** (Easter–Oct daily 10am–5pm; £1.80 castle only, £2.65 castle & mill). A hybrid of Elizabethan fancy and earlier defensive necessity, the castle is reached across a field. Explanatory models illustrate the development of the site, which is an excellent example of the organic nature by which castles grew, from the Norman tower believed to be the original gatehouse, through the thirteenth-century front battlements, to the newer Tudor gatehouse and the Elizabethan mansion grafted onto them all. A few hundred yards west of the castle is the **Carew French Mill**, last used in 1937 and the only extant mill powered by the shifting tides in Wales. The impressive eighteenth-century exterior belies the pedestrian exhibitions and self-guided audiovisual displays of the milling process at different stages.

Mid-Pembrokeshire

The central slab of Pembrokeshire is generally either ignored or actively avoided by visitors intent on reaching the more obvious coastal pleasures to the south and west. Certainly the waterfront petrochemical plants along this stretch are a far cry from the limestone cliffs and wheeling seabirds elsewhere, and none of the towns are especially exciting, but the villages dotting the arms of the **Daugleddau estuary** are delightful and almost entirely unspoilt.

Pembroke Dock lies on the southern banks of the magnificent Daugleddau river estuary, the continuation of one of the world's greatest natural harbours, the **Milford Haven**. This spawned an eponymous Quaker community on the northern bank, which now seems, rather sadly, to be searching for a new post-industrial identity by ploughing vast sums into the development of some dubious tourist features. Seven miles to the north, the chief town of the region, **Haverfordwest**, makes an important market and transport centre that, despite some handsome architecture, remains rather soulless. A few miles northeast of here, **Scolton Manor** houses the county museum.

The A40 arrives in Haverfordwest from the east, brushing through an unspectacular but effortlessly pleasant rural landscape on the way. Just south of the road, five miles from town, **Picton Castle** sits above the wide, tidal waters of the Daugleddau, a river estuary flooding the valleys of inland Pembrokeshire and providing a surprisingly maritime feel amidst such impressively rolling countryside. Dotted around the muddy estuary are creaky little villages and some fine walks and pubs. The main road roars on, bypassing the stout little town of **Narberth**, the self-appointed capital of the **Landsker**

borderlands – a revived name for the imaginary, but effectively real, line that divides the anglicized corner of south Pembrokeshire from its Welsh-speaking neighbour (see p.155). Near the town are some big-time tourist attractions, among them the mighty **Oakwood** theme park, home to Europe's largest wooden roller coaster.

A branch train line leaves the main Fishguard route at Whitland, calling at Narberth en route to Pembroke and Pembroke Dock. The train line divides again at Clarbeston Road, with the Milford Haven-bound branch calling at Haverfordwest. A reasonable bus service throughout the area has most routes starting at either Pembroke or Haverfordwest.

Milford Haven

One of the most impressive sights in this part of Wales is the view from the 1970s **Cleddau Bridge** (car toll 75p), which curves out of Pembroke Dock over to **NEY-LAND** on the opposite bank. Pedestrians can also cross it: the views over the jutting headlands are magical, the masts of boats far below and the full skies reflected in the clear water. Even the refineries look attractive from this far up. Even better, try to synchronize your journey over the bridge with a decent sunset, when the glowing sun dips perfectly into the estuary mouth. If you need to while away an hour or two before (or after) sunset, pop down to the *Old Ferry Inn*, immediately below the bridge, for high standard but relatively inexpensive meals and real ales.

The waterway below – the Milford Haven — has long been an important harbour, and was even recognized by William Shakespeare:

> *...how far it is*
> *To this same blessed Milford; and, by the way,*
> *Tell me how Wales was made so happy as*
> *To inherit such a haven.*

(Imogen in *Cymbeline*, Act III, scene 2)

Taking its name from the waterway, the town of **MILFORD HAVEN** (Aberdaugleddau), four miles west of Neyland, was founded in the late eighteenth century by a group of early American settlers from Nantucket who were imported as whalers. The grid pattern they imposed – principally three streets rising sharply parallel to the waterway – survives today amid new civic and religious buildings. Despite a magnificent site and interesting heritage, Milford Haven hasn't got much going for it. The town has seen hard times of late, with the dead-beat town centre receiving little of the development money pumped into the horribly sterile dockside "marina". The waterside is impressive, though, with tugs and steamers ploughing up the glittering waters of the Haven which stretch out below the pleasant public gardens.

Hamilton Terrace skirts around the waterside to the tarted-up **docks**, home of an assortment of museums – the child-oriented **Kaleidoscope discovery centre** (April to mid-Sept Mon–Fri 10am–6pm, Sat & Sun 10am–5pm; £4.30), a tawdry **Dockside Gallery**, some dull cafés and restaurants and the genuinely interesting town **museum** (Easter–Oct Tues–Sun 11am–5pm; £1.20), housed in an eighteenth-century warehouse originally designed to store whale oil. Exhibits include photographs and mementos from the fishing trade, an explanation of the modern oil industry, details of the Quaker beginnings of the town and some fascinating archive material of Milford Haven in wartime.

On the western side of the docks and estuary, **Fort Hubberston** is the most explorable of Pembrokeshire's nineteenth-century Palmerston defence forts. Built between 1860 and 1865, the barracks were home to some 250 men in the late nineteenth century, and, although rickety and somewhat vandalized, the building is an eerie and interesting place to poke around. Nearby is the ruined octagonal dome of the **Hakin Observatory**, the sole remaining relic of town founder Charles Francis Greville's dream to build a "mathematical college".

Practicalities

Milford Haven **train station** is located under the Hakin road bridge, next to the docks. The only reasons to stray from the docks area and into the town proper are to visit the **tourist office** at 94 Charles St (April–Sept Mon–Sat 10am–5pm; ☎01646/690866), or west Wales' only professional **theatre**, the Torch (☎01646/695267), on St Peter's Road, at the end of Charles Street.

Accommodation is handiest a few yards from the docks towards Hakin, at the well-kept and bargain-priced *Cleddau Villa B&B*, 21 St Anne's Rd (☎01646/690313; ①), though *Belhaven House Hotel*, 29 Hamilton Terrace (☎01646/695983; ②), is also good with en-suite rooms for a few pounds more. There's a **campsite** at *Sandy Haven*, near Herbrandston, two miles west of town (☎01646/693180). For **food**, try the inexpensive *Sewin Restaurant* down by the docks.

Haverfordwest and around

Lying seven miles northeast of Milford Haven in the valley of the Western Cleddau, the ancient settlement of **HAVERFORDWEST** (Hwlffordd) grew up around the Gilbert de Clare castle which dominates the skyline to this day. The town prospered as a port and trading centre in the seventeenth and eighteenth centuries, and its command of local trade ensured that Haverfordwest deposed Pembroke as the county town of Pembrokeshire. Despite its natural advantages, a slew of rich architecture from its glory days and some recent jazzing up along the river, Haverfordwest is scarcely a place to linger.

The diminutive Castle Square forms the heart of the town. From here, a small alleyway to the right of Woolworths ascends to the castle, which fails to live up to the expectations created by views of it from down below: all there is to see is a dingy shell of the thirteenth-century inner ward. Next to the castle, in the imposing governors' house, is the town museum (Easter–Oct Mon–Sat 10am–4pm; £1), a motley collection of minor art pieces and some fairly interesting local history. Back down below, the Riverside Shopping Centre follows the river from Castle Square up to the Old Bridge, next to the bus terminus and tourist office; adjoining the centre is a small indoor market (Mon–Sat). The more architecturally appealing parts of Haverfordwest lie up the handsome High Street, rising from the River Cleddau. The commanding St Mary's Church, founded in the thirteenth century, stands on the corner of Market Street opposite the preserved remains of a Georgian town-house vault.

Practicalities

The **train** station is a ten-minute walk east of the town centre, while **buses** come and go from the depot at the end of the Old Bridge, near the **tourist office** (May–Sept Mon–Sat 10am–5.30pm; Oct–April Mon–Sat 10am–4pm; ☎01437/763110). Next to the tourist office, the Holiday Information Centre, at 2 Riverside Quay, houses a booking agency for the excellent self-catering Coastal Cottages of Pembrokeshire scheme (☎01437/765765, fax 767738) and a bureau for the many outdoor pursuits under the Activity Wales banner (☎01437/766888). There's also a helpful **Pembrokeshire National Park office** at 40 High St, staffed by extremely knowledgeable volunteers: this is the place to come for detailed information on flora, fauna and even rock climbing in the park. Information of the alternative ilk is available from the Pembrokeshire Primrose Company and Celtic Gift Shop at 24 Market St and Swales Music Centre by St Mary's church.

For low-cost **accommodation**, try *College Guest House*, 93 Hill St (☎01437/763710; ①), or the *Villa House*, St Thomas Green (☎01437/762977; ①). There are slightly pricier rooms at the solidly Georgian *Castle Hotel* in Castle Square (☎01437/769322; ③), and the *Hotel Mariners* on Mariners Square (☎01437/763353, fax 764258; ⑤) is the swishest place in town. There's a **campsite** two miles northwest on the A487, at the *Rising Sun Inn* in Pelcomb Bridge (☎01437/765171). For lunchtime **food**, grab a freshly filled baguette from *Samuel's*, on the pedestrian Bridge Street, or duck into *Morillo's*, opposite *Samuel's*, a strange but successful combination of sit-in chippy and Italian café that serves the best coffee and ice cream in town. Evening meals are best at the inexpensive *George's* pub on Market Street (closed Sun), where the trout in orange and almond sauce is superb.

Picton Castle and Scolton Manor

The main A40 heads east out of Haverfordwest past the train station. After two or three miles, signs point south towards **Picton Castle** (April–Sept Tues–Fri & Sun 10.30am–5pm; £4), a graceless building, something of a hybrid of architectural styles from the fourteenth to the eighteenth centuries, but sited in glorious **grounds** (April–Oct Tues–Sun 10.30am–5pm; £2.75) with views over the Eastern Cleddau and its valleys.

Four miles northeast of Haverfordwest, along the B4329, **Scolton Manor** (April–Oct Tues–Sun & bank holidays 10.30am–5.30pm; £1) is a modest stately mansion, dating from 1840, which forms the nucleus of the Pembrokeshire County Museum. It's a good place to appreciate the lifestyle of a rich Victorian family: the rooms of gilt, brocade and fine furnishings in total contrast with the perfunctory cellar, larder and laundry below. There's a fine collection of prints and maps detailing some of the lost Picturesque estates of Wales, a Carriage House filled with traps, a steam engine on a short strip of track and a wealth of illuminating local artefacts. There's a good **café** on site and a surrounding **country park** (daily: April–Oct 9am–6pm; Nov–March 9am–4.30pm; parking £1) with a visitor centre that emphasises environmental awareness.

Narberth and the Landsker Borderlands

In contrast to Milford Haven and Haverfordwest, the area now known as the **Landsker Borderlands** forms a quiet, charming part of mid-Pembrokeshire, broken by some beautiful villages that are still well off the beaten tourist track. *Landsker* is an Anglo-Saxon word meaning "frontier", and is used in this sense as a definition of the division between Cymric north Pembrokeshire and the anglicized south (see p.155). The division is ancient, going back to the Norman colonization of the south of the county, but despite its archaic tenor, the name is a comparatively recent sobriquet – first mentioned in this context in the 1930s.

The "capital" of the borderlands is **NARBERTH** (Arberth), a pleasing little town on the train line to Tenby, just off the main A40. According to The Mabinogion, a collection of ancient Celtic folk tales and legends, the town was the court of Pwyll, and its ruined **castle** was probably the old home of the Welsh princes. At the far eastern end of the town is the **train station**, at the top of Station Road. This runs down to St James Street and connects with the market square and the bottom of the town's neat High Street. Dividing the High Street is the curious, spiky **town hall**, built in the 1830s to mask the municipal water tank underneath. It is currently unoccupied, though there are murmurs that some form of Landsker visitor centre may reopen on the site. At the top end of the High Street, **Queen's Hall** (☎01834/861212) is one of the best emerging venues in Pembrokeshire, hosting world music concerts, trance and techno raves, theatre, art exhibitions and more.

One hundred yards down the hill on the market square, the **Wilson Museum** (Mon–Fri 10.30am–4.30pm, also Easter–Sept Sat 10.30am–12.30pm; £1) contains a collection of disparate artefacts mostly donated by local people; the net result is a beguiling slice of Narberth life over the past couple of centuries, with themes such as local transport, religion and education soon forgotten in the pursuit of yet more trivia. Look out especially for the 1887 "geared facile" a rare type of penny-farthing still with its original hard rubber tyres, and a bottle collection from the spirit merchants who once owned the building and now operate from premises up the street. Next door, the **Step Studios** is a new gallery that stages workshops as well as art exhibitions.

Blackpool Mill and Oakwood

Narberth lies to the east of the most impressive scenery around the Daugleddau estuary. The tidal reach of the Eastern Cleddau River goes as far as **Blackpool Mill** (daily: April–June 10.30am–5pm; July & Aug 10am–6pm; Sept 11am–5pm; Oct 11am–5pm; £2.50), four miles west of Narberth. An elegant four-storey stone block, the mill was built in 1813 to grind wheat using water power, although this source was replaced at the beginning of the twentieth century by turbines. Much of the machinery has been restored and can be seen throughout the building, alongside replica workshops filled with bland wax models. Below the mill, a series of "caverns" (actually just the man-made basement) have also been filled with models, this time replica brown bears, hyenas and a huge Welsh dragon in a fanciful attempt to depict life in prehistoric Wales.

The A4075 heads south from Blackpool Mill, past two big local attractions. First is the **Oakwood** theme park (April–June & Sept–Oct daily 10am–5pm; July & Aug daily 10am–11pm; £11), Wales' largest such site and a good day out. The star attractions are *Megaphobia*, Europe's largest wooden roller coaster, and the stomach churning *Vertigo* ride (the latter an additional £10 per ride), but there's also tobogganing, water rapid rides, boating, go-karting, a Wild West town and numerous smaller rides. Immediately south, **CC2000** theme park (daily 10am–11pm; free entry, then various prices) is firmly family-oriented, with garish "fun" restaurants amidst sundry attractions, most celebrated of which is the *Crystal Maze*, a series of interactive challenges along the same lines as the television programme that it's named after.

On the banks of the Eastern Cleddau

Fanning out to the west of Blackpool Mill are the quiet lanes that wind down towards the muddy banks of the Cleddau estuary. It's a charming landscape of small, inconsequential settlements and, along the eastern bank at least, great walking. The waymarked **Landsker Borderlands Trail** runs the entire length of the Eastern Cleddau, starting from Blackpool Mill, and soon reaching the lonesome hamlet of **LANDSHIPPING**, whose desolate **quay**, a mile south, was once a busy ferry point and coal port. Here, the two Cleddau (*dau gleddau*, or "two swords") rivers meet, with the main estuary plunging southwards through wooded hillsides. Pretty **LAWRENNY** village, four miles south, is dominated by the four-storey tower of the magnificent twelfth-century **St Caradoc's church**. A track alongside the church winds up to the site of Lawrenny's old castle, now a picnic area with tremendous views over the confluence of the Cresswell and Carew rivers at **Lawrenny Quay**, about half a mile from the village. This is one end of the best short walks along the estuary – a water's-edge stroll past ancient oak woodlands with views of the almost Toytown **Benton Castle** (privately owned) on the other bank.

The path hugs the northern bank of the Cresswell for two miles before reaching tiny **CRESSWELL QUAY** (Cei Cresswell), home to the waterfront *Cresselly Arms*, one of the finest pubs in west Wales, where beer comes in frothing jugs but food is conspicuously absent. You can stay just yards away at Cresswell House (see opposite). A mile west of Cresswell Quay, the old limestone quarrying village of **WEST WILLIAMSTON** is the gateway to **Williamston Park** (free access), a National Trust/Dyfed Wildlife Trust nature reserve jutting out into the folds of the rivers Cresswell and Carew.

North of Narberth, the most spectacular scenery is along the rich, non-tidal valley of the Eastern Cleddau, especially in the idyllic and steep village of **LLAWHADEN**, whose ghostly **castle** (free access, collect key from post office if locked) sits on a bluff above the river. Once a residence of the Bishop of St David's, the castle's remains reflect its later role more as a luxurious home than as a defensive fort. Most impressive is the decorative, square, fourteenth-century gatehouse, dating from the castle's major transformation into a bishop's palace.

Practicalities

Accommodation in Narberth is limited, though there are a handful of occasional B&Bs along Station Road, Spring Gardens, St James Street and into the Market Square. B&B rooms are on offer above the *Welsh Kitchen* restaurant on the market square (☎01834/869199; ①), and at comfortable *Plas Hyfryd* (☎01834/869006, fax 869008, *david.jones30@virgin.net*; ③) a country house hotel on Moorfield Road at the top end of town. There are a couple of nearby **camping** options: *Noble Court* (☎01834/861191), half a mile north on the B4313, and, on the northeastern fringe of town, *Dingle Farm* on Jessie Road (☎01834/860482).

The hamlet of **ROBESTON WATHEN**, just over a mile northwest of Narberth, has a couple of reliable guesthouse pickings, both on the A40: *Highland Grange Farm* (☎01834/860952; ②), which serves meals and has a license; and the simpler *Canton House* (☎01834/860620; ①) with shared bathrooms. Elsewhere in the area, *Knowles Farm*, a mile north of Lawrenny village (☎01834/891221, fax 891344, *owenlp@globalnet.co.uk*; ②), is a great farmhouse B&B that's conveniently close to the start of some wonderful walks. The brand new **Lawrenny YHA hostel** (☎01646/651270; ①; closed Nov–March) is housed in a refurbished Victorian school in the village: an infrequent postbus runs to Lawrenny from Narberth. In Cresswell Quay, *Creswell House* (☎01646/651435; ②) is appealingly situated by the estuary and is a short stumble from the wonderful Cresselly Arms. **Bike rental** in the area is available from the Blackpool Mill and at Cross Inn Stores (☎01834/813266) at Broadmoor near Kilgetty, five miles south of Narberth.

In Narberth, there's good **food** at *Café Olé* in the Queen's Hall arts venue (see p.173); across the road and under the same managemnt is the *Deli & Patisserie*, ideal for picnic supplies. Pub **food** is best at the *Coach and Horses* at the top of the High Street, or the *Angel Inn* further down by the town hall. **Drinking** is easy, with a multitude of good pubs: try the youthful *Eagle Inn*, behind the Wilson Museum at the bottom of Water Street, or the memorabilia-bedecked *Kirkland Arms* on St James Street; the *Cresselly Arms* (see opposite) is always convivial.

St Bride's Bay

The most westerly point of Wales – and the very furthest you can get from England – is one of the country's most enchanting areas. The coast around **St Bride's Bay** is broken into rocky outcrops, islands and broad, sweeping beaches curving around between two headlands that sit like giant crab pincers facing out into the warm Gulf Stream amidst the crashing Atlantic. The southernmost headland winds around every conceivable angle, offering calm, east-facing sands at **Dale**, sunny expanses of south-facing beach at **Marloes** and wilder west-facing sands at **Musselwick**. Between the latter two, the peninsula descends to its dramatic end at the **Deer Park**, just beyond **Martin's Haven**, where boats for the offshore islands of **Skomer**, **Skokholm** and **Grassholm** depart.

The middle scoop of the bay combines the typical ruggedness with a little more in the way of golden sands, backed by teeming, popular holiday villages such as **Little Haven**, **Broad Haven** and **Newgale**. From here, the spectacularly lacerated coast veers to the left and the **St David's peninsula**, along stunning cliffs interrupted only by occasional gashes of sand. Just north of **St Non's Bay**, the tiny cathedral city of **St David's**, founded in the sixth century by Wales' patron saint, is a justified highlight. Rooks and crows circle above the impressive ruins of the huge **Bishop's Palace**, sitting beneath the delicate bulk of the **cathedral**, the most impressive in Wales. The St David's peninsula, more windswept and elemental than any other part of Pembrokeshire, tapers out just west of the city at the popular **Whitesands Bay** and the hamlet of **St Justinian's**, staring out over the crags of **Ramsey Island**.

Bus transport to most corners of the peninsula radiates out from Haverfordwest: a twice-weekly service to Dale and Marloes, a daily service to Broad and Little Haven and an hourly service to Newgale, Solva and St David's.

Dale, Marloes and the offshore islands

The tiny village of **DALE**, fourteen miles west of Haverfordwest, huddles behind a shingle beach and at the head of a huge bite out of the coast. Blighted by views of oil refineries, Dale is not an especially attractive village, but its sheltered, east-facing shore makes the town an extremely popular – and often unbearably crowded – yachting and water-sports centre. Most of the water-bound activity is focused around the beachside shack of West Wales Wind, Surf and Sailing (☎01646/636642), which offers lessons (£30–50 per half-day) at various levels in all manner of aquatic shenanigans: mainly windsurfing, surfing, sailing and kayaking. With adequate proficiency you can rent equipment: a basic windsurfing rig will set you back £20 per day, a more high-tech ensemble goes for £25 per day, and a kayak costs £18. Cheaper still, you can hire a boogie board (£6) and make the five-minute hike over the hill to the pounding surf at West Dale (see opposite), though you should be wary of underwater rocks and strong currents if you decide to take to the brine here.

A SHORT CIRCULAR WALK AROUND ST ANN'S HEAD

Note: The OS Outdoor Leisure 1:25,000 map #36 (South Pembrokeshire) is recommended for this walk.

The start and finish point is the free National Trust car park on the site of the old radar centre at **Kete** (SM 803042), just over a mile down the lane from Dale village. From the car park, turn left onto the lane and take the path that forks sharply right after a few yards. This path follows the edge of a couple of fields, before joining the Coast Path proper at a stile. Turn left (south), passing the scant bumps of an old Iron Age fort on **Little Castle Point**, where the path veers east, meandering past Vomit Point. Views west are spellbinding, especially over the rocky humps of islands out in the bay. Before long, the buildings of St Ann's Head loom into view and the path briefly joins the lane that terminates at the lighthouse. To the right is a viewpoint, worth a short diversion, over Cobbler's Hole, a spectacularly folded and fissured set of cliffs.

The path runs alongside the lane as it approaches the lighthouse, but doubles back on itself just before reaching it. You are now heading north again, past old walled cottage allotments and down some steps, built in 1800 to ease the arrival of materials for the new lighthouse that was being built at the time. Mill Bay looms into view on the right, and the path skirts around the top of the mainly shingle beach, nipping up and down before settling into another pleasant stretch as it heads towards the mighty modern beacons erected to warn of problems in the Haven. Just beyond is the old Palmerston fort at West Blockhouse Point, now a Landmark Trust holiday property. A few hundred yards later, the main path splits into three. Left leads up to a farm track and, ultimately, back to the car park at Kete, whilst right descends gently to the safe, sandy beach of **Watwick Bay**, one of the most pleasant – and crowd-free – anywhere on the Pembrokeshire coast.

THE SEA EMPRESS OIL SPILL

Pembrokeshire hit the world headlines in February 1996 when the fully-laden *Sea Empress* oil tanker, bound for Milford Haven, hit the rocks off St Ann's Head. The ensuing crisis was handled badly from the start, with local residents evacuated, kept ill-informed and fed conflicting news stories. But Pembrokeshire's all-important tourist industry was under serious threat, and the county council, the National Park authority and the Wales Tourist Board quickly moved into damage-limitation mode.

A full nine days after the initial spill, a salvage operation finally cranked into life. By this time, prevailing southerly and easterly winds had caused the black slick to spread along the south Pembrokeshire coast, reaching even the beaches of Carmarthenshire and the Gower. Tens of thousands of sea birds died, beaches were smothered and much of Pembrokeshire's unique coastal flora was damaged. The cleanup, however, has been remarkable. Although the long-term effects of the detergent sprayed on the sea will take years to assess, its efficacy cannot be doubted. By the summer of 1996, all of the beaches and cliffs had been exhaustively scrubbed and the sea had returned to its usual sparkling turquoise.

Beyond the ecological tale, the *Sea Empress* disaster has heightened local sensibilities. Schoolchildren have worked on projects about the spill, exhibitions have been drawn together and local residents formed new campaigning organizations, groups and links.

The calm waters of Dale are deceptive, and as you head south towards **St Ann's Head**, one of the most invigoratingly desolate places in the county, the wind speed whips up, with waves and tides to match. Blasted by some of the highest winds in Britain (gale force on an average of 32 days per year), buffeted by extraordinarily strong tide-races and virtually frost-free throughout the winter, the coastline here offers invigorating, spectacular walking, despite being the site of the 1996 *Sea Empress* wreck (see box above). Thankfully, all visible reminders of the spill have now vanished. The Coast Path sticks tight to the undulating coastline, passing tiny bays en route to the St Ann's lighthouse. Tucked in the eastern lee of St Ann's Head is **Mill Bay**, where Henry VII landed in 1485, marching the breadth of his native Wales and gathering a loyal army to face Richard III at Bosworth Field.

The windsurfing folk at the beachside water-sports shop offer B&B **accommodation** on the Dale waterfront (①) – breakfast is taken at *Planet Dale*, a good-value, summer-only greasy spoon café usually full of board riders. It's also open in the evenings, and there's live music most weekends. The *Post House Hotel* (☎01646/636201; ②), in the middle of the village just behind the real-ale *Griffin Inn*, has en-suite rooms and optional evening meals; and, for a touch of luxury, there's *Allenbrook* (☎01646/636254, fax 636954; ②; closed Dec), a charming country house close to the beach. If you want something in the country nearby, try the farmhouse B&B at *Skerryback* (☎01646/636598, fax 636595; ②), a couple of miles to the east on the coast path at Sandy Haven.

Marloes and around

The coast turns and heads north from St Ann's Head, reaching the sandstone-backed West Dale Bay, less than a mile from Dale on the opposite side of the peninsula. Warnings are usually given about the unpredictability of the currents and hidden rocks in the sea here, and you may find the broad sands of **MARLOES**, a mile to the north of West Dale, a safer place to swim and big enough to remain relatively uncrowded. A great sandy curve dissected by rocky spills, Marloes Sands is best known for its stunning cliffs of grey, gold and purple folds of rock, alternate layers of grey shale and old red sandstone. The most impressive way to appreciate the difference is by seeing the Three Chimneys, two-thirds of the way along the sands. These three vertical lines of hard Silurian sandstone and mudstone were formed horizontally and forced up by ancient earth movements. There was a fourth "chimney" which crumbled in a severe storm in 1954. The beach is crowned at its western end by Gateholm Island, accessible at mid-tide and below (no set hours; free). It's a site of great importance: pottery, pieces of jewellery and over 130 Iron Age hut circles have been found here, and it's thought to have been an ancient monastic community. Today, Gateholm is powerfully atmospheric and a great place to camp. The easiest access to the island is from the YHA hostel (see below), a hundred yards before which is a large National Trust car park.

A rough track leads from the north of the car park to meet the lane to **MARTIN'S HAVEN**, a cluster of houses and a car park on a slim neck of the peninsula that faces out to Skomer island. If you're walking, the mile-long Coast Path walk from the Gateholm end of Marloes Sands is wonderful, with easy access to a couple of tiny, deserted coves. Inexplicably bypassed by the Coast Path is the sublime headland of **Deer Park** (which incidentally has no deer, and probably never did), the very far tip of this peninsula, reached by a small gateway in the wall just beyond the car park. Paths radiate out all over the headland, all with stunning views over the offshore islands and the entire yawn of St Bride's Bay: if you can catch a decent sunset here, you'll see none better. There's a small Dyfed Wildlife Trust information point at Martin's Haven, the principal departure point for **boats** to the offshore islands of Skomer, Skokholm and Grassholm (see below).

North of the Deer Park, the Coast Path continues less than half a mile from the village of Marloes round to **Musselwick Sands**, a beautiful and unspoilt beach which can be dangerous at high tide. Further north along the peninsula is the narrow **St Bride's Haven** beach, at the end of the lane that peters out by the tiny chapel of St Bride, whose cemetery is on the way to a tiny but beautiful inlet, well sheltered from the winds and with a small beach. There are some good rockpools around the beach.

Marloes is tolerably well off for **accommodation**, with the excellent *Foxdale Guesthouse*, opposite the church in Glebe Lane (☎01646/636243; ①), and the en-suite *Lobster Pot* (☎01646/636233; ③), nearby in the centre of the village above Marloes' only real restaurant, the *Lobster Pot*, which, unsurprisingly, serves up a good range of seafood. You can pitch a **tent** up the street at the field-and-toilets *Greenacre* site behind *Foxdale Guesthouse*, and at *Runwayskiln* (☎01646/636257) close to the **Marloes Sands YHA hostel** (☎01646/636667; closed Nov–March); the latter consists of a series of converted farm buildings overlooking the northern end of Marloes Sands. *West Hook Farm* (☎01646/636424) near Martin's Haven also has camping.

Skomer, Skokholm and Grassholm

Skomer (boats April–Oct Tues–Sun 10am, 11am & noon; £12) is a 722-acre flat-topped island that dominates the near horizon of Martin's Haven. It has the finest **sea bird** colonies in northern Europe, the remains of hundreds of ancient hut circles, a stone circle, collapsed defensive ramparts and settlement systems and a Bronze Age standing stone known as Harold's Stone, located near the narrow neck where the boats land. Of all the sea birds on Skomer, perhaps the most noted are the 200,000-plus Manx shearwaters, but there are also puffins, gulls, guillemots, storm petrels, cormorants, shags and kittiwakes. Land birds include buzzards, skylarks, jackdaws, chough, owls and peregrines. If you head to the north of Skomer, facing out over the Garland Stone, there's a good chance of seeing basking grey seals, especially in the autumn. In spring and early summer, wild flowers carpet the island. You can also see the island by way of non-landing, round-Skomer cruises (April–Oct Tues–Thurs & Sun at 1pm; £6); summertime evening cruises can also be booked through the National Park (Tues & Fri 7pm; £6; ☎01437/720392).

Two miles south of Skomer is the 240-acre island of **Skokholm** (boats June–Aug Mon 10am; £15.50; booking essential on ☎01437/765462), whose warm red-sandstone cliffs are a sharp contrast to Skomer's grey severity. Britain's first bird observatory was founded here in the 1930s, and the island is still rich in birdlife. The boat trip includes a guided tour conducted by the island's warden.

Each Monday, Thursday and Friday, boats also head six miles west of Skomer to the tiny islet of **Grassholm** (boats June–Sept: landing trip Mon 10am & Fri noon, guided trip Thurs 5pm; £20; ☎01646/601636), a rough, two-hour journey if the weather's not good. From the mainland, Grassholm looks like a small icing-covered cake: the "icing" is, in fact, a swarming mass of 70,000 gannets, one of the largest colonies in the northern hemisphere, that covers well over half the island.

All of the boat trips are operated on the *Dale Princess* (*www.dale-sailing.co.uk*). No booking is required for Skomer and Grassholm trips, although this can be done, if desired, at National Park information centres. **Accommodation** is also available on Skomer (self-catering) and Skokholm (fully catered): contact the Dyfed Wildlife Trust (☎01437/765462).

Little Haven and around

Altogether flatter and more easily walked, the coast north of **LITTLE HAVEN** is, in places, disappointingly blighted by tacky seaside developments. Little Haven village is the exception – a picturesque old fishing village and coal port that descends in steep streets to a sheltered stony beach, extremely popular with divers and swimmers in summer. At low tide, walks along the shore towards Broad Haven are superb: you can explore caves and rockpools or just enjoy the full westerly skies. **Accommodation** is best at *Whitegates* (☎01437/781552, fax 781386; ①) overlooking the village on the road to Broad Haven, or a mile above the village at *Bower Farm* (☎01437/781554; ②), a very friendly B&B. The nearest **camping** is at *Howelston Farm* (☎01437/781253), up the hill south of Little Haven. The most noteworthy places to **eat** are *The Nest Bistro* (☎01437/781728; no credit cards), right in the centre of Little Haven, where you can get locally caught fresh fish dishes for around £12, and the redoubtable *Swan Inn* (Wed–Sat) by the harbour, with bar snacks available all day and an excellent and expensive restaurant specializing in local seafood. For a cheaper bite, cross the harbour and sample the great meals at the *Castle Inn*.

Quite different from Little Haven are the garish charms of neighbouring **BROAD HAVEN**, a mass of fun pubs and caravan parks above a wide, popular beach fringed by some remarkably fissured and shattered cliffs. Broad Haven also boasts the immediate area's widest selection of **accommodation** – try the en-suite rooms at *Ringstone* on Haroldstone Hill, half a mile north of town (☎01437/781051, fax 781050; ②); *Anchor Guesthouse*), opposite the beach on Enfield Road (☎01437/781051, fax 781050; ②); or the modern and spacious **YHA hostel** (☎01437/781688, fax 781100, *broadhaven@ yha.org.uk*; closed Nov to mid-Feb), almost on the seafront at the north end of the village. There's also **camping** at the tacky *Broad Haven Holiday Park* (☎01437/781277). Haven Sports on Marine Road (☎01437/781354), just behind the *Galleon Inn*, rents out windsurfing equipment (tuition available) and mountain bikes.

The Coast Path cuts inland from here, occasionally coinciding with a stray country lane that opens out sublime views through the wind-flattened gorse and trees. Worth seeking out a couple of miles north is the quieter sandy beach at **DRUIDSTON HAVEN**, hemmed in by steep cliffs and reached along small paths at the bottom of the sharply sloping lane from Broad Haven. Easiest access to this delightful beach is from *Druidston Hotel* (☎ & fax 01437/781221; ③), a popular, easy-going place with a cellar bar that spills out onto the clifftops. Self-catering cottages on site, including an old circular croquet pavilion, are also available to rent. Just before the hotel, a lane heads inland for a few hundred yards to the tiny hamlet of **DRUIDSTON**, where you can **camp** at *Shortlands* (☎01437/781234).

Nolton Haven and Solva

A mile along the coast, **NOLTON HAVEN** is little more than a picturesque cluster of houses and caravans around a sheltered shingle cove. Part of the tracks of a long defunct tramway that brought coal down to the jetty from the nearby Trefrane colliery can be seen here. **Accommodation** in the village includes the harbourfront *Mariner's Inn* (☎01437/710469; ②), which serves excellent, if pricey dinners, and *Nolton Haven Farm* (☎01437/710263; ①), which has some en-suite rooms. For camping, there's *Longlands* (☎01437/710234), a third of a mile short of the village on the Druidston side. Just inland is the village of **Nolton**, where *Celtic Corner* (☎01437/710254) at North Nolton Farm in the centre of the village stages nights of raucous harp-twanging, boozing, local delicacy devouring and even a bit of dancing (May–Sept Wed).

A cliff path and small lane climb out of Nolton Haven, descending half an hour's walk from the village to the southern end of the vast, west-facing **Newgale Sands**, popular with families and surfers alike. The southern end of the beach, away from the main Haverfordwest–St David's road and the tawdry little village of **NEWGALE**, is a better bet for seclusion. Brandy Brook, disgorging onto the beach just beyond Newgale's *Duke of Edinburgh* pub, marks the boundary of "Little England Beyond Wales" (see box p.155) and the extent of Norman colonization of Pembrokeshire. Two miles inland from the beach, the **Penycwm YHA hostel** (☎01437/721940, fax 720959, *penycwmhostel@whitehouse.prestel.co.uk*; ①), has several double en-suite rooms – meals are available if booked in advance.

The coast turns west beyond Newgale, rising abruptly to spectacular, riveted cliffs that help to create a wilder, somehow more Celtic landscape than that of southern Pembrokeshire. The Coast Path from Newgale to **SOLVA** (Solfach), three miles west, is marvellous, with easy clifftop walking, magnificent views over the rippled coast and, and, in the lee of the Dinas Fach headland, a secluded sandy beach at **Porthmynawyd**. Solva itself is a pleasant, if heavily touristed, village sitting at the top of an inlet that runs down to the sea by the **Gwadn beach**. Above the beach, the **Gribin Headland** stands wedged between the valleys of the Solva and Gribin rivers – as well as the superb views, it's worth climbing for the impressive Iron Age earthwork on its summit.

In Solva, it's better to **stay** at the head of the inlet in the picturesque Lower Village, where you'll find the en-suite *Caleb's Cottage* (☎01437/721737; ①) on the main road just a couple of doors from the *Ship Inn*; almost opposite is the homely *Old Printing House* (☎01437/721603; ①). In the upper village and about half a mile towards St David's on St Bride's View is the lovely *Pendinas* (☎01437/721283; ①), with shared bathrooms and great sea views. The nearest **campsite** is a fifteen-minute walk above Upper Solva at *Llanungarfach Caravan Park* (☎01437/721202). In the centre of the village, *The Old Pharmacy* (☎01437/720005; no credit cards) serves excellent **meals** with imaginative use of local seafood and meats, as well as a good selection of vegetarian options. The *Cambrian Hotel* is dependable enough for a **drink**.

St David's

ST DAVID'S (Tyddewi) is one of the most enchanting and evocative spots in Britain. This miniature city clusters around its purple- and gold-flecked cathedral at the very western point of Wales on a windswept, treeless peninsula of awesome ruggedness. The country's spiritual and ecclesiastical centre, St David's is totally independent of Canterbury, and the granting of official city status in 1995 has only reinforced its importance.

Traditionally founded by the Welsh patron saint himself in 550 AD, the see of St David's has drawn pilgrims for a millennium and a half – William the Conqueror included – and by 1120, Pope Calixtus II decreed that two journeys to St David's amounted to the spiritual equivalent of one pilgrimage to Rome. The surrounding city – in reality, never much more than a large village – grew up in the shadow cast by the cathedral, and St David's today still relies on the imported wealth of newcomers to the area, attracted by its savage beauty. With numerous historical sites, outdoor pursuit centres, good cafés, superb walks, bathing and climbing, St David's and its peninsula are an absolute must if you want to experience Wales at its wildest.

Arrival, information and activities

As it enters St David's, the main road from Haverfordwest (here called High Street) passes the attractive new **tourist office** (Easter–Oct daily 9.30am–5.30pm; Nov–Easter Mon–Sat 10am–4pm; ☎01437/720392, *www.stdavids.co.uk*), and continues for two hundred yards down High Street to the **bus terminus** in New Street.

Local **boat companies** organize trips to the outlying islands (detailed on p.185), and schedules are available from their offices in St David's. In addition to their roster of boat excursions, Ramsey Island Cruises (April–Oct; ☎0800/854367 or 01437/721911, *www.ramseyisland.co.uk*) offer **bike rental** (£10 per day) and run guided minibus trips that include the St David's Discovery Tour (2hr; £7.50), which covers local history, myths and legends, and the tour of north Pembrokeshire (3hr; £10). The booking office is beside the *Low Pressure Café*, just behind TYF No Limits at 1 High St (☎0800/132588, fax 01437/721611, *www.tyf.com*); the latter rents surfboards, boogie boards, kayaks and surf skis for £10–15 per day (you are responsible for transporting equipment from the shop to the sea and back), and run a full calendar of rock climbing, surfing and kayaking courses and breaks. The most immediately appealing activity on a short visit is **coasteering**, an exhilarating multi-sport combination of scrambling over rocks, jumping off cliffs and swimming across the narrow bays of St David's Peninsula. It is geared for just about anyone (even non-swimmers), operates throughout the year and, like all their other activities, costs £45 for a full day and £35 for half a day. Multi-day sessions can also be arranged.

Accommodation

There are numerous places to **stay** on the St David's Peninsula, with prices fairly high in season at the larger hotels, but coming down dramatically for the rest of the year. Campsites abound in and around the city.

HOTELS AND GUESTHOUSES

Alandale, 43 Nun St (☎01437/720404). Small, friendly and central guesthouse with some en-suite rooms, and healthy breakfasts included in the rates. ②.

Old Cross, Cross Square (☎01437/720387, fax 720394, *oldcross@stdavids.co.uk*). Comfortable and creaky but modernized hotel with decent-sized en-suite rooms and a good restaurant. Closed Xmas–Feb. ⑤.

Pen Albro, 18 Goat St (☎01437/721865). About the cheapest B&B in town, right next to the *Farmers Arms* nightspot. ①.

Ramsey House, Lower Moor (☎ & fax 01437/720321). Excellent small hotel on the road to Porth Clais, with superb Welsh evening meals included in the rates. ⑤.

St Non's, Goat St (☎01437/720239). Rambling old-fashioned country hotel near the River Alun. ⑤.

Twy-y-Felin, High St (☎0800/132588, fax 01437/721611). Built around a converted windmill, this B&B is mostly given over to residential courses run by TYF No Limits (see above), but is open to all. Rooms are comfortable, there's a lively bar on site and camping in the grounds. ②.

The Waterings, High St by the tourist office (☎01437/720876). Luxurious en-suite rooms and suites in a former marine research establishment which retains the maritime theme. Pitch and putt on the lawn. ③.

Whitesands Bay, Whitesands (☎01437/720403). Family-oriented beach hotel above the very popular strip of sand with en-suite rooms and an outdoor pool. ⑤.

Y Glennydd, 51 Nun St (☎01437/720576). Town-centre B&B in a converted Victorian house with some en-suite rooms. ①.

HOSTELS AND CAMPSITES

Caerfai Farm, Caerfai Bay (☎01437/720548). The best campsite around, based in an organic dairy farm 15 minutes' walk from the city. Closed Oct–April.

Glan-y-mor, Caerfai Rd (☎01437/721788). The nearest campsite to town, with a restaurant on site and offering scuba diving instruction.

Llaethdy YHA hostel, Llaethdy (☎01437/720345, fax 721831). Large and popular hostel in a former farmhouse and outbuildings, two miles northwest of St David's near Whitesands Bay. Closed Nov–March.

Lleithyr Farm, Whitesands Bay (☎01437/720245). Campsite and caravan park just off the B4583, half a mile short of Whitesands Bay.

Pencarnon Farm, off St Justinian's Rd (☎01437/720324). Basic, though still one of the best campsites in the area, fantastically set above a virtually private beach.

Rhosson Ganol, St Justinian's (☎01437/720361). Popular year-round campsite, handy for the boats out to Ramsey Island.

The Town

As it enters St David's, the main road from Haverfordwest becomes High Street and courses down to Cross Square, a triangular centrepiece around a **Celtic cross**. High Street continues under the thirteenth-century **Tower Gate**, which forms the entrance to the serene **Cathedral Close**, backed by a windswept landscape of distant farms and knobbly rocks scattered aound a heathland almost devoid of trees.

The cathedral lies down to the right, hidden in a hollow by the River Alun. This apparent modesty is explained by reasons of defence: a towering cathedral, visible from the sea on all sides, would have been far too vulnerable. On the other side of the babbling Alun lie the ruins of the Bishop's Palace. From the Cross Square, New Street heads north past the enjoyable **Oceanarium** (daily April–Sept 10am–6pm; Oct–March 10.30am–4pm; £3; *www.sealife.demon.co.uk*), complete with a shark tank overlooked by a viewing gallery.

There are numerous small commercial **art galleries** and craft outlets throughout St David's: a few are dreadful, but most reflect the quality of the many artists attracted to this unique corner of Wales. Worth singling out is the excellent St David's Studio Gallery at 28 High St, good both for crafty giftware and the prints and paintings of its exuberant owner, Stan Rosenthal.

The cathedral

The gold-and-purple 125-foot stone tower of the **cathedral** (£2 donation requested; *www.stdavidscathedral.org.uk*) is approached down the Thirty-Nine Articles – steps named after Thomas Cranmer's key tenets of Anglicanism – that run from beyond the powerfully solid **Tower Gate**, the last remaining of four medieval originals. The tower has clocks on only three sides (the people of the northern part of the parish couldn't raise enough money for one to be constructed facing them), and is topped by pert golden pinnacles that seem to glow a different colour from the rest of the building. You enter the cathedral through a porch in the south side of the low twelfth-century nave, although the line of the former higher roof can be clearly seen outside of the tower. The most striking feature of the nave is the intricate latticed oak **roof**, built to hide sixteenth-century emergency restoration work undertaken when the nave was in danger of collapse. The nave floor still has a discernible slope and the support buttresses inserted in the northern aisle of the nave look incongruously new and temporary.

At the crossing, an elaborate **rood screen** was constructed under the orders of fourteenth-century Bishop Gower, who envisaged it as his own tomb. Behind the rood screen and the organ, the choir sits directly under the magnificently bold and bright lantern ceiling of the tower, another addition by Gower. The round-headed arch over the organ was built in Norman times, contrasting with the other three underpinning the tower, which are pointed and date from the rebuilding work that took place in the

1220s. At the back of the right-hand choir stalls is a unique **monarch's stall**, complete with royal crest, for, unlike any other British cathedral, the Queen is an automatic member of the St David's cathedral Chapter. A sign – "Reserved for the Sovereign", as if she might just pop in unannounced – underlines the point. The misericords under the choir seats display some ribald medieval humour; there's one of a chaotic wild boar hunt and another of someone being seasick. Behind the left-hand choir stalls, the **north transept** contains the tomb of St Caradoc, with two pierced quatrefoils, in which it is believed people would insert diseased limbs in the hope of a cure. Off the north transept, steps from St Thomas' chapel lead up to the **Chapter Library** (July & Aug Mon–Fri 2–4pm; Sept–June Mon only; £1), which includes the Royal Charter of June 1995 that granted St David's city status.

Separating the choir and the presbytery is a finely traced, rare **parclose screen**. The back wall of the **presbytery** was once the eastern extremity of the cathedral, as can be seen from the two lines of windows. The upper row has been left intact, while the lower three were blocked up and filled with delicate gold mosaics in the nineteenth century, surrounded by over-fussy stonework. The colourful fifteenth-century roof, a deceptively simple repeating medieval pattern, was extensively restored by Gilbert Scott in the mid-nineteenth century. At the back of the presbytery, around the altar, the **sanctuary** has a few fragmented fifteenth-century tiles still in place. On the south side is a beautifully carved sedilla, a seat for the priest and deacon celebrating Mass. To its right are thirteenth-century tombs of two bishops, Iorwerth (1215–31) and Anselm de la Grace (1231–47), and on the other side of the sanctuary is the disappointingly plain thirteenth-century tomb of St David, largely destroyed in the Reformation.

Behind the filled-in lancets at the back of the presbytery altar is the Perpendicular **Bishop Vaughan's chapel**, crafted out of a soft honeyed stone, with an exquisite fan tracery roof built between 1508 and 1522. Bishop Vaughan's statue occupies the niche to the left of the altar. To the right is an effigy of Giraldus Cambrensis, Gerald of Wales, his mitre placed not on his head, but at his feet – a reminder that he never attained the status of bishop for which he was evidently desperate. Opposite, facing west, a peephole looks into the presbytery. Around the opening, the four crosses may well predate the Norman church. The bottom cross is largely obscured by a casket that reputedly contains some of the intermingled bones of St David and his friend, St Justinian. Behind the chapel is the ambulatory, off which the simple **Lady Chapel** (with some sentimental Edwardian stained glass) leads. Either side of the Lady Chapel are tombs in wall niches: the one on the left was originally believed to have been for Bishop Beck (1280–96), the builder of St David's Bishop's Palace, but now houses Bishop Owen (1897–1926), whose devoted service to the Church in Wales and the Welsh nation is symbolized by the roaring dragon above him.

The Bishop's Palace

From the cathedral, a path leads over the tiny, clear River Alun to the splendid **Bishops' Palace** (June–Sept daily 9.30am–6pm; April, May & Oct daily 9am–5pm; Nov–March Mon–Sat 9.30am–4pm, Sun 11am–4pm; £2; CADW), built by bishops Beck and Gower around the beginning of the fourteenth century. The huge central quadrangle is fringed by a neat jigsaw of ruined buildings in extraordinarily rich colours: the distinctive green, red, purple and grey tints of volcanic rock, sandstone and many other types of stone. The **arched parapets** that run along the top of most of the walls were a favourite feature of Gower, who did more than any of his predecessors or successors to transform the palace into an architectural and political powerhouse. Two ruined but still impressive halls – the **Bishops' Hall** and the enormous **Great Hall**, with its glorious rose window – lie off the main quadrangle, above and around a myriad of rooms adorned by some eerily eroded corbels. Underneath the Great Hall are dank vaults containing an interesting exhibition about the palace and the indulgent lifestyles of its occupants. The destruction of the palace is largely due to Bishop Barlow (1536–48), who supposedly stripped the buildings of their lead roofs to provide dowries for his five daughters' marriages to bishops.

Eating, drinking and entertainment

With only one pub to its name, St David's can hardly be said to rock. Entertainment is otherwise limited to the annual **classical music festival** held at the end of May in the cathedral, and regular **craft fairs** in the Cathedral Hall; the tourist office has details. There are, however, several reasonable places to eat.

Cartref, Cross Square (☎01437/720422). Enjoyable, moderately priced restaurant with a menu of well-cooked local dishes served in large portions. Open March–Dec.

Farmers Arms, Goat St. The city's only pub. Young, lively, very friendly and especially enjoyable on the terrace overlooking the cathedral on a summer's evening.

Foster's Bistro, 51 Nun St (☎01437/720576). Small and highly regarded restaurant with a menu of reasonably priced local dishes and international favourites. Open April–Oct.

Low Pressure Café, 1 High St. Great inexpensive snackery that's also a good place in which to hang out and meet the travelling and outdoor crowd for which St David's has become something of a magnet.

Morgan's Brasserie, 20 Nun St (☎01437/720508). A charming, moderate to expensive restaurant specializing in locally caught fresh fish and serving delicious desserts.

St David's Peninsula

Surrounded on three sides by inlets, coves and rocky stacks, St David's is an easy base for some excellent walking around the headland of the same name. A mile south and accessed along the signposted lane from the main Haverfordwest road just near the school, popular **Caerfai Bay** provides a sandy gash in the purple-sandstone cliffs, rock from which was used in the construction of the cathedral. To the immediate west is the craggy indentation of **St Non's Bay**, reached from St David's down the tiny rhododendron-flooded lane, signposted to the *Warpool Court Hotel*, that leads off Goat Street. Saint Non reputedly gave birth to Saint David at this spot during a tumultuous storm around 500 AD, when a spring opened up between Non's feet, and despite the crashing thunder all around, an eerily calm light filtered down onto the scene.

St Non's received pilgrims for centuries, resulting in the foundation of a tiny chapel in the pre-Norman age, whose successor's thirteenth-century ruins now lie in a field to the right of the car park, beyond the sadly dingy well and coy shrine where the nation's patron saint is said to have been born. The 1934 **chapel**, built in front of the austere 1929 **Retreat House** (details of stays and religious courses from Father Angelo on ☎01437/720224), was constructed in simple Pembrokeshire style from the rocks of ruined houses, which, in turn, had been built from the stone of ancient, abandoned churches.

The road from St David's to St Non's branches at the *St Non's Hotel*, where Catherine Street becomes a winding lane that leads a mile down the tiny valley of the River Alun to its mouth at **PORTH CLAIS**. Supposedly the place at which Saint David was baptized, Porth Clais was the city's main harbour, the spruced-up remains of which can still be seen at the bottom of the turquoise river creek. Today, commercial traffic has long gone, replaced by a boaties' haven.

Running due west out of St David's, Goat Street ducks past the ruins of the Bishop's Palace and over the rocky plateau for two miles to the harbour at **ST JUSTINIAN'S**, little more than a ruined chapel, lifeboat station and ticket hut for the frequent **boats** over to **Ramsey Island**. Less than two miles long, this dual-humped plateau has been under the extremely able stewardship of the RSPB since 1992 and is quite enchanting. Birds of prey circle the skies above the island, whose feathered population is better known for the tens of thousands of sea birds that noisily crowd the sheer cliffs on the island's western side. On the beaches, seals laze sloppily below the deer paths beaten

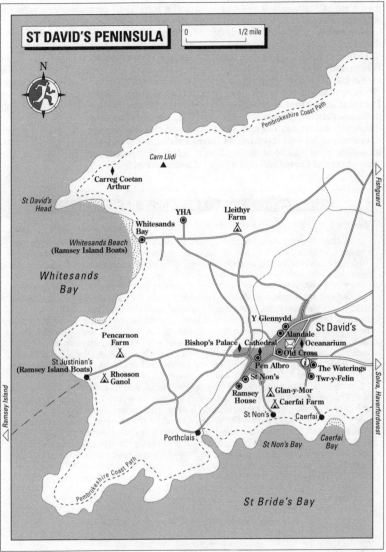

ST DAVID'S PENINSULA

0   1/2 mile

N

Pembrokeshire Coast Path

Carn Llidi ▲

Carreg Coetan Arthur

St David's Head

YHA ◉

Lleithyr Farm ⋏

Whitesands Bay ◉

Whitesands Beach (Ramsey Island Boats) ◉

Whitesands Bay

◁ *Fishguard*

Pencarnon Farm ⋏

Y Glennydd ◉◉ Alandale

St David's

Bishop's Palace ◢ Cathedral ◉

◉ Oceanarium

St Justinian's (Ramsey Island Boats) ●

Old Cross ◉

Pen Albro ◉

◁ *Solva, Haverfordwest*

Rhosson Ganol ⋏

i ◉● The Waterings

St Non's ◉

Twr-y-Felin ◉

◁ *Ramsey Island*

Ramsey House ◉

◉ Glan-y-Mor

⋏ Caerfai Farm

St Non's ●

Caerfai ●

Porthclais ●

St Non's Bay

Caerfai Bay

Pembrokeshire Coast Path

St Bride's Bay

out by a herd of red deer. Two companies run boats – weather permitting – around Ramsey, but only Thousand Islands Expeditions, on the square in St David's (April–Oct; ☎0800/163621 or 01437/721686) can land you on the island for up to five hours (£10): in season, trips run daily except Tuesday. During the springtime nesting season, you see more from boats which circle the island but don't land: Ramsey Island Cruises, beside the *Low Pressure Café* in St David's (see opposite) run daily round-the-island trips from St Justinian's (£10 for an hour and a half). Both companies also offer an assortment of day-trips that dart into caves to seek out seals, sea birds and porpoises. Look out too for trips out to Grassholm and a thunder through the Bitches, a tidally-produced rapid between the mainland and Ramsey – an absolute soaking is guaranteed.

Thousand Island Expeditions operate a Ramsey circumnavigation (1.5hr; £10) from **Whitesands Bay** (Porth Mawr), two miles to the north and reached from St David's via the B4583 off the Fishguard road. Campsites and cafés line the popular Whitesands Bay shore, and as the beach faces west, surfing is good. The spectacularly beautiful **Porthmelgan**, a narrow slip of cove reached by a fifteen-minute walk northwest along the Coast Path from Whitesands car park, is far less crowded, largely on account of the dangerous swimming. The thin spit of rock and cliff that juts out into the ocean less than a mile to the west comprises **St David's Head**, site of an Iron Age coastal fortress, its outline most visible in spring. Rising behind Whitesands and Porthmelgan, the gnarled crag of **Carn Llidi** tops a pastoral patchwork of fields.

A CIRCULAR WALK AROUND ST DAVID'S HEAD

Note: OS 1:25,000 Outdoor Leisure map #35 (North Pembrokeshire) is advised for this walk.

The tapering finger of rock that tumbles down from the slopes of Carn Llidi, a little over a mile north of St David's is one of the most mysterious and magical places in Wales. Evidence of ancient civilization is everywhere, and numerous mystics and seers have pinpointed the area as a focus of the earth's natural energies.

Starting from the Whitesands Bay car park, double back on yourself up the lane to St David's. Go past the twin semi-detached houses and take the left track opposite the caravan park. Where the lane forks, take the right turning, signposted to Upper Porthmawr. Take the track between the two farmhouses and continue climbing, following the right track at the National Trust sign. Ascend to the rocky top of Carn Llidi (595ft) on the obvious track, passing two cromlechs – capped burial stones – on the lower slope. At the top, you get mesmerizing views over the whole of St Bride's Bay, the patchwork of the Dewisland peninsula, the cathedral, the rocky outcrops of Ramsey, Skomer and Grassholm, the dips of the coast north up to Strumble Head, Whitesands Bay and miles of glittering sea.

Retrace your steps down the hill, past the cromlechs, and take the first obvious right path. This leads swiftly down to a hedge-backed green lane; turn right and keep walking as it curves gently round. On reaching the kissing gate, turn right into the peaceful little valley below the craggy carns. The slope on the right has been excavated to reveal the extensive remains of an Iron Age field and settlement system, although this will be hard to see if the bracken is high. Take the first left path before the valley reeds and cross the peaty brook and bridleway, continuing up to meet a green road and then the main Coast Path. Turning left towards the headland brings you along and above some superb cliffs, speckled with wild flowers and squawking sea birds. After a few hundred yards, above the path to the left, you should spot Carreg Coetan Arthur (Arthur's Quoit), a 6000-year-old capstoned burial chamber. The path strikes on towards the end of the headland. Shortly, a line of broken wall indicates the first line of defence of Clawdd-y-Milwyr (The Warrior's Dyke), an Iron Age fort that occupied the very tip of this promontory. Although the Coast Path now ducks down to the other shore, you can continue over the dyke and see the three lines of defensive ditches crossing the headland.

Turning south, walk along the clifftop with the sandy cove of Porthmelgan down below. The path bumps gently down to the beach, a pleasant alternative to the crowds and ice creams of Whitesands. At mid-tide and lower, there are even some great caves to poke around in. From here, the Coast Path climbs back to Whitesands Bay. Just before reaching the car park, a memorial stone records the fact that there once stood a St Patrick's chapel here, built between the sixth and tenth centuries. St Patrick, a Welshman who became the patron saint of Ireland, is said to have sailed from here for Ireland in the late fourth century AD.

From St David's to Fishguard

The north-facing coast that forms the very southern tip of Cardigan Bay is noticeably less commercialized and far more Welsh than the touristy coasts of south and mid-Pembrokeshire. From the crags and cairns above St David's Head, the Coast Path perches precariously on the cliffs, where only the thousands of sea birds have access. The first point of contact with the sea for humans is the black-sand beach at **Abereiddi**, half a mile short of the quieter sands of **Traeth Llyfn**.

Although the major income from this part of west Pembrokeshire is now tourism, the stumpy remains of old mines, quarries and ports at Abereiddi and **Porthgain** bear witness to the slate and granite industries that once employed hundreds. Industry dies down towards **Trefin** and up to the more remote beaches and inlets that punctuate the coast as it climbs up to the splendid knuckle of **Strumble Head**. To the east is **Carregwastad Point**, the site of the last invasion of Britain in 1797. The event is also remembered in **Fishguard**, where local soldiers tricked the invading French into unconditional surrender at the *Royal Oak Inn* in Upper Fishguard's neat little centre. Immediately either side of the upper town lie **Goodwick**, where ferries leave for Ireland, and cutely picturesque **Lower Fishguard**, most famous as the set for the glitzy 1971 movie version of *Under Milk Wood*, with the immortal coupling of Richard Burton and Elizabeth Taylor.

Abereiddi to Abercastell

A quiet lane leaves St David's and runs parallel to the coast across the rocky Pembrokeshire plateau, where the few trees have been blasted into spooky shapes by the relentless gusts off the Irish Sea. A small lane turns left five miles from St David's and tumbles down into the bleak hamlet of **ABEREIDDI**, at the head of its stony, black-sand beach. You can find tiny fossilized animals in the shale of the beach, which can become extremely crowded in midsummer. Above the beach are remains of workers' huts, industrial units and a tramway that once climbed over the hill to Porthgain, all part of the village slate quarry that closed in 1904. The old quarry itself was blasted for safety reasons, producing an inland lagoon where the seawater, combined with the minerals, has turned a violent shade of bright blue, but is unfortunately not suitable for swimming in. Near Abereiddi is the homely and welcoming *Cwmwdig Water Guesthouse* (☎01348/831434; ②), tucked between the two lanes from Llanrhian and Croes-goch.

Following the Coast Path past the Blue Lagoon brings you down to **Traeth Llyfn**, about half a mile away; car drivers can take the track through Barry Island Farm halfway down the lane between Llanrihan and Porthgain. Traeth Llyfn is sandier and more peaceful than the beach at Abereiddi, although heed the warnings that currents are deceptively strong and can be perilous for mediocre swimmers.

The lane parallel to the coast passes the hamlet of Cwmwdig Water and leads to tiny **LLANRIHAN**, from where a left-hand turn descends over a mile or so to the rambling village green of **PORTHGAIN**, a fascinating old port that grew up around its slate works, the stumpy remains of which, together with an old brickworks, lime kiln and eerie ruins of workers' cottages, are huddled around the tiny quay. It also has the best pub in the county: the marvellous *Sloop Inn*, an eighteenth-century stone house with excellent beer, good food and numerous wall-mounted photographs of the old port in its sepia heyday. For pricier fare, the *Harbour Lights* (☎01348/831549), across the village green, has a far-flung reputation for well-cooked local seafood and vegetables.

Two miles further east, where the lane makes its sole intersection with the coast, is **Aber Draw** (also known as Aber Felin), a small and rugged beach just short of the village of **TREFIN** (Trevine). The natural rock chair by the village water pump used to be employed as the seat of a mock-mayor, elected annually from amongst the villagers.

Trefin is well blessed with **B&Bs**: there's *Cranog House* on Ffordd Abercastell (☎01348/831392; ①); and the superb *Old Court House* (☎01348/837095; ②), which also offers hearty vegetarian meals, pick-ups from Haverfordwest or Fishguard and all-in walking holiday packages. There's a **YHA hostel** in the old school on Ffordd-y-Avon (☎ & fax 01834/831414; closed Nov–March). The *Ship Inn* is a good bet for **food**.

The coastal lane continues east to **ABERCASTELL**, past the 4500-year-old **Carreg Samson** cromlech (burial chamber), topped by a sixteen-foot capstone, at Longhouse. The vast capstone and its precarious supporting stones make for an awesome sight as you approach from Longhouse, framed as it is by lush hills, rocky inlets and the sea. If you're walking, continue past the cromlech and down to the coast path into Abercastell, where the harbour, once used for the export of limestone and coal and just above a muddy beach, is now an attractive and popular spot. From Abercastell, one of the most scenic parts of the Coast Path zigzags east along the wild, vertiginous cliffs to the point at **Trwyn Llwynog**, about two miles away.

Mathry to Carregwastad Point

Deserted lanes and a beautiful stretch of Coast Path meander around the coast from Abercastle to the secluded bay at **Aber Mawr**, two miles directly north of the inland village of **MATHRY** (Mathri), where the ancient *Farmers Arms* does excellent food and drink. Bang opposite the pub, **Jim Harries Woodturners** (workshop Mon–Fri 10am–12.30pm & 1.30–5pm; shop Mon–Fri 9.30am–6pm, Sat & Sun 10am–4pm) gives you the chance to see local craftsfolk at work and buy the finished products. It's pricey and aimed squarely at passing coach parties, but there are some decent affordable bits to be found. In the wooded valley above Aber Mawr, the *New Mill* (☎01348/891637; ①) at Tregwynt, three miles north of Mathry near St Nicholas, is popular with Coast Path walkers. **Bike rental** is available from Preseli Mountain Bikes (☎01348/837709), at the village of Parcynole Fach on the road between Mathry and St Nicholas.

Two miles east of the village of Mathry is **CASTLEMORRIS** (Casmorys), to the north of which **Llangloffan Farm** (May–Sept Mon–Sat 10am–12.30pm; April & Oct Mon, Wed, Thurs & Sat 10am–12.30pm) provides demonstrations of its home-spun cheesemaking process. A mile and a half further north, the **Felin Tregwynt Woollen Mill** (free entry) is an old whitewashed stone building where you can see wool being spun and processed and mooch around the inevitable gift shop. There are some interesting modern sculptures in the grounds.

The headland – known as **Pen Caer** – that rises to the north, peaking at **STRUMBLE HEAD**, is delightful: tiny hedge-backed lanes bump around between rocky cairns, fields of wild flowers and sudden glimpses of the shimmering sea. This is the closest the Welsh mainland gets to Ireland, and from its lofty heights you can usually see ferries zipping across the waters en route to and from Fishguard.

The Coast Path running up the west side of Pen Caer is remote and spectacular, affording a full panorama of views. Between the sandy stretch of Aber Mawr and the craggy Strumble Head, the only semi-accessible beaches are **Aber Bach**, immediately north of Aber Mawr, and the west-facing gash of **Pwllcochran**, a mile further north. There's a superbly sited clifftop **YHA hostel** (☎ & fax 01348/891233; closed Nov–March) with a couple of private double rooms (①) above the strands of **PWLL DERI**, nearly two miles further north. **Camping** is also allowed here. Looming large on the inland side of the hostel are the three crags of **Garn Fawr** (699ft), most easily reached from the car park at their eastern edge, on the lane up to Strumble Head. Garn Fawr is easy to climb and well worth the effort: there are some impressive remains of ditches, ramparts and hut circles from its days as an early Iron Age fort, and, on a good day, you can see as far as the Wicklow Mountains of Ireland and the Llŷn peninsula and Snowdon in north Wales. Even if visibility doesn't allow such sights, the views over the headland and coast are quite gorgeous.

THE SAINTS AND STONES TRAIL

Leaflets available from all local tourist offices describe this excellent **car or bike** trail, which leads around some of northern Pembrokeshire's most remote and atmospheric little **churches**. In each one, you'll find good information, a leaflet on the church and occasionally even a kettle and a tin of biscuits. The saints to whom the churches are dedicated are generally some of the lesser-known Celtic heroes; stones date from around the fifth century. Many of the sites predate Christianity as important places of worship, some as far back as the Bronze Age. You can follow the trail without deviation (a steepled church icon on a brown sign indicates the route) or dip into parts of it as you head around the lanes of north Pembrokeshire.

Strumble Head, a mile or two due north of Garn Fawr, is reached either by the rugged coast path – with astounding views over the two-mile long "wall" of cliffs to the south – or the far more gentle perambulation of a floral country lane. The last farm before the headland is *Fferm Tresinwen* (☎01348/891621), a good place to **camp** for great walks along the promontories and coves of this enchanting stretch of coast. At the headland, the 1908 **lighthouse** is perched atop **Ynys Meicel**, connected to the mainland by a foreboding metal footbridge. It's a peaceful, invigorating spot: great for sea bird spotting and idly watching jet vapour trails in the sky (this is one of the principal routes into London's Heathrow Airport).

Between Strumble Head and the coat-tails of Fishguard, the riveted coast is best known for an historical quirk. This is the site of the last attempted invasion of Britain, by a rabble of Franco-Irish soldiers in 1797 (see below for more detail on this). After having landed at **Carregwastad Point** (where the event is marked by a headstone), the disorganized army made its base at **Trehowel Farm**, midway between Strumble Head and the quiet little hamlet of **LLANWNDA**. Trehowel was stocked up with food and drink for an imminent family wedding, and a recent shipwreck had meant that most local farms were full of contraband liquor. The would-be conquerors set to the victuals with gusto, swiftly becoming too drunk to threaten an acquiescent dormouse. The soldiers' sole moment of action came when they attacked the idyllic little **church of St Gwyndaf** in Llanwnda and stole some of the silver plate within. Although there are no mementos of the church's most bizarre episode, it's well worth a visit for its charming setting, ancient history that winds back beyond the eighth century and collection of pre-Norman carved stones, embedded in its walls. The mile-long path from Llanwnda to Carregwastad Point is a fabulous walk, as it coasts gently down fields and across the top of a craggy cwm. Go over the stile and along the path on the other side of the track from the church entrance.

Fishguard

The coast road runs around the bay, along the Parrog beach and past the 900-yard East Breakwater, before climbing sharply up Gas Works Hill to **FISHGUARD** (Abergwaun), occupying its own lofty headland. Though it's an enjoyable place in its own right, with good sea views from the easy coastal walks around town, Fishguard is often seen only as a brief stopping-off place to the ferries and speedy catamarans which leave regularly for Rosslare in Ireland from the suburb of **Goodwick** (Wdig).

Approaching from the south, you pass the Goodwick foreshore where the tourist office and a cybercafé share the foyer of **Ocean Lab** (daily 11am–5pm; £2), a child-oriented imaginary journey into prehistoric waters. From there, the A487 becomes West Street, which meets up with the High Street and Main Street by the town hall and Market Square; it's along these three streets that most of the town's shops, banks, pubs and restaurants lie. Near the town hall is the **Royal Oak Inn**, the scene of the Franco-Irish surrender in 1797 (also see above). The hapless forces arrived to negotiate a ceasefire, which was turned by the assembled British into an unconditional surrender. Mementos of the event can be seen in the pub. Part of the invaders' low morale – apart from the drunken farces in which they'd become embroiled – is said to have been sparked off by the sight of a hundred local women marching towards them. The troops mistook their stovepipe hats and red flannel dresses for the outfit of a British Infantry troop and instantly capitulated. Even if that is not true, it is an undisputed fact that 47-year-old cobbler Jemima Nicholas, the "Welsh Heroine", single-handedly captured fourteen French soldiers. Her grave can be seen next to the uninspiring Victorian **parish church**, St Mary's, behind the pub. Across the street, the church hall is home to the **Fishguard Tapestry** (April–Oct Mon–Sat 10am–5pm, Sun 2–5pm, Nov–March Mon–Sat 11am–4pm, Sun 2–4pm; £1.50), a local version of the Bayeaux Tapestry embroidered to celebrate the bicentennial of the Franco-Irish surrender. Look especially for a grim, Amazonian Jemima surrounded by a dozen dejected-looking French soldiers.

Main Street winds northeast before plummeting down around the coast towards **Lower Fishguard** (Cwm), a cluster of old-fashioned holiday cottages around a muddy, thriving pleasure-boat port – a total contrast to the vast operation on the other side of the town at Goodwick, where the ferries leave for Ireland. Views from Lower Fishguard over the town headland and to the port breakwater are superb.

Practicalities

Buses stop by the town hall in the central Market Square, right outside Fishguard's **tourist office** (June–Aug daily 10am–5.30pm; April & May, Sept & Oct daily 10am–5pm; Nov–March Mon–Sat 10am–4pm; ☎01348/873484); which is just steps away from Seaways bookshop on West Street, a source of Wales-oriented books together with information on Ireland. There's a subsidiary tourist office in the foyer of the Ocean Lab in Goodwick (same times as main office; ☎01348/872037); half a mile west from here along Quay Road is the terminus for **ferries** and fast-cats to Ireland; the 4–6 daily services are fully listed on p.6. The **train station** is next to the ferry terminal on Quay Road. Stopping right outside the terminal, buses usually meet ferries (though seldom the fast-cats), and a **taxi** (☎01348/874491) into town will cost around £3.

Accommodation is plentiful and cheap, with most places well used to visitors coming and going at odd times for the ferries. Next to the port on Quay Road is the faded but still elegant *Fishguard Bay Hotel* (☎01348/873571; ④). Three minutes drive away, on Tref-Wrgi Road, you'll find comfortable en-suite rooms at *Glanmoy Lodge* (☎01348/874333, fax 875050; ②); and up in Fishguard proper, just a minute's walk from the tourist office, there's the dorm beds at *Hamilton Backpackers Lodge*, 21–23 Hamilton St (☎01348/874797). Also central and easy to find, *Three Main Street* (☎01348/874275; ③) has an expensive and excellent restaurant. Five miles up the coast and halfway to Newport, the *Fron Isaf Farmhouse* (☎01348/811339; ①; closed Nov–March) is a quiet place with sea and mountain views. The clifftop *Pwll Deri* YHA **hostel** is just four miles south (see p.188), and the nearest **camping** is at *Tregroes Touring Park* (☎01348/872316), a mile southwest of Fishguard just off the A40.

Fishguard is equally well served for places to **eat** and **drink**. In the main town, there's a superb and expensive restaurant in the *Manor House Hotel* on Main Street. Cheaper snacks are available in the daytime from the splendid *Annie Francis Caffi Pobydd*, on the roundabout by the town hall, which becomes an evening seafood restaurant for six weeks each July and August. Pub food is plentiful and reliable: try the nautically themed *Bennett's Navy Tavern* on the High Street or the upmarket, historical *Royal Oak*. For plain old drinking, try the earthy and beery *Fishguard Arms* on Main Street or the staunchly traditional *Cambrian Arms* on Hamilton Street. Tuesday is folk night at the *Royal Oak* – participants are especially welcome. Down in Lower Fishguard, the eccentric *Ship Inn* is unmissable, with lots of interesting clutter all over the walls and ceiling.

Mynydd Preseli

In a county celebrated for some of the most magnificent coastal scenery in Britain, Pembrokeshire's interior is frequently overlooked. The **Mynydd Preseli** (Preseli Hills) occupy a triangle of land in the north of the county, flecked with prehistoric remains and roughly bounded by the coast in the north, the B4313 to the west and the A478 to the east. After miles of sea bird-swirling coastline, the rickety walled lanes and gloomy bare hills come as a refreshing change.

From Fishguard, the Gwaun River wriggles southeast through its cwm, Europe's oldest glacial vale. It's a surprising slash of lush greenery through the barren, stone- and sheep-spattered hills, the tiny villages and remote churches seemingly untouched by the modern age. Indeed, residents of the Cwm Gwaun retain an attachment to the pre-1752 Julian calendar, celebrating New Year in the middle of January.

The main A487 coast road is the only major **bus** route hereabouts, cruising from Fishguard to Cardigan through the delightful small town of **Newport**, a fine and friendly base for the area. Just south of the town is the Preseli's most impressive and historic peak, **Carn Ingli**. Further south, the brooding mountains shelter innumerable standing stones, stone circles, hillforts, cairns and earthworks. Ancient sites – whether in the reconstructed Iron Age settlement at **Castell Henllys** or the bucolic church at **Nevern**, complete with 1500-year-old inscribed stones and a "bleeding" yew tree – are the mainstay of a visit to this powerful corner of Wales. As a further incentive, it's all conveniently close to the final (or first) stretch of the Pembrokeshire Coast Path. The cognoscenti's favourite part of the path is that between Newport and St Dogmael's, blessed with awesome solitude, abundant natural life and stunning cliff formations.

Newport, Nevern and the coast

The A487 skims all too quickly through **NEWPORT** (Trefdraeth), an ancient and proud little town with a good deal to be proud about. Set on a gentle slope that courses down to the estuary of the Afon Nyfer, Newport still elects a mayor annually, a legacy of its days as the capital of the Norman Marcher Lordship of Cemmaes. One visible manifestation of this heritage is the annual custom, in August, of the "Beating of the Bounds", when the Mayor and the Lord Marcher beat out the town's boundaries on horseback. Newport is a quietly enjoyable place today, with great shops, superb accommodation, food and drink, welcoming inhabitants and a selection of fine coastal and hill walks on the doorstep.

The Town and Carn Ingli

From the main thoroughfare, Long Street and Lower St Mary Street head down to the tidal banks of the Afon Nyfer. A path hugs the southern shore of the estuary, over which squawking sea birds circle and skim the water's edge. Turn east (or take the Parrog Road if you're driving) for a gentle stroll along to the **Parrog**, Newport's nearest beach, mostly shingle but complete with sandy stretches at low tide. The best nearby beach is the vast dune-backed **Traethmawr**, on the other side of the estuary, reached over the town bridge down Feidr Pen-y-Bont. Just short of the bridge, on the town side, **Carreg Coetan Arthur**, a well-preserved capped burial chamber, can be seen behind the newish holiday bungalows. The footpath that runs along the river either side of the bridge is marked as the Pilgrims' Way; follow it eastwards for a delightful riverbank stroll to Nevern (see overleaf), a couple of miles away. Back on Lower St Mary Street, the old town school has metamorphosed into a spanking new youth hostel (see p.193) and the **West Wales Eco Centre** (Mon–Fri 9.30am–4.30pm, and often longer in summer; free), a venue for exhibitions, advice and resources on various aspects of sustainable living.

South of the main street, a number of pretty thoroughfares rise up to the town's intriguing **castle** (private), a modern residence fashioned out of the medieval ruins. The other obvious landmark is the three-storeyed tower of the massive **St Mary's church**, an ancient site that was heavily "restored" by the Victorians. Fortunately, the church's original Norman font escaped the worst of their efforts. Follow Mill Lane, on the western flank of the castle, or Church Street, from the front of St Mary's, for the relatively easy two-hour ascent of **Carn Ingli** (Hill of Angels), once the core of an active volcano. The peak was inhabited perhaps as recently as Roman times – certainly, the stone embankments of the Iron Age hillfort and the nearby Bronze Age hut circles prove that this was some sizeable community before that. The hill's name comes from the belief that St Brynach lived here in quiet contemplation, with the angels as his companions.

The coast

Either side of Newport, the Coast Path runs through some sublime scenery. To the west of town, the trail edges around the nodule of Dinas Head (also known as Dinas Island), en route to Fishguard. Two miles west of the Parrog beach, the most popular Dinas beach is the northeast-facing stretch at **CWM-YR-EGLWYS**, where the scant seafront ruins of the twelfth-century **St Brynach's church** are all that survived a huge storm on the night of October 25, 1859, when the rest of the church and some 114 ships at sea were wrecked.

The walk around Dinas Head offers splendid views over the huge cliffs, inhabited by thousands of nesting sea birds between May and mid-July. On the other side of the "island", three-quarters of a mile west of Cwm-yr-Eglwys via the path through Cwm Dewi, or two and a half miles around the Coast Path and the headland, is the grey-sand beach of **Pwllgwaelod**, accessible by car off the A487 through the dour village of Brynhenllan. Sadly, the *Sailors' Safety Inn*, where a light was kept burning to help the ships' navigation, closed after 401 years in 1994. It is now being converted into B&B accommodation. Next door, the *Old Sailors* tearoom and restaurant is open throughout the summer season.

The segment of Coast Path to the east of Newport, running to the fringes of Cardigan at St Dogmael's, is perhaps the wildest stretch of the whole path. The only part accessible by car is at the spectacularly folded cliffs of **Ceibwr Bay**, eight miles from Newport near the pretty pastel village of **MOYLEGROVE** (Trewyddel). Any section along here is comparatively hard going: the path plummets and climbs along the ridged coast, passing rocky outcrops, blowholes, caves, natural arches, ancient defensive sites and thousands of sea birds.

Nevern, Pentre Ifan and Castell Henllys

Only a little more than a mile by road to the east of Newport, but about double that along the pleasant riverside walk, the straggling village of **NEVERN** (Nanhyfer) is darkly atmospheric, with a couple of intriguing sights. The ruined and overgrown **castle**, a thirteenth-century replacement of a Norman construction on the site of an earlier Welsh fortress, sits high above the village on a bluff. Below, the brooding bulk of the **church of St Brynach**, founded in the sixth century and with an intact Norman tower, has numerous features of interest. The churchyard is roofed by ancient yews, giving it a dank, dark presence. Note the second tree on the right, the famous **"bleeding yew"**, so called for the brown-red sap that oozes mysteriously from its bark. Legend has it that it will continue to bleed until a Welsh lord of the manor is reinstated in the village castle – unlikely in the foreseeable future, given its tumbledown state. Also outside the church, just by the main doorway, is the stunning **Great Cross**, an inscribed tenth-century Celtic masterpiece standing some 13ft high. St Brynach's interior is no less interesting. If you stand at the back, you can easily divine how the chancel has been built slightly out of alignment with the nave, supposedly to represent Christ's inclined head on the cross. In the windowsills of the south transept, there are two ancient inscribed stones: one, the **Maglocunus Stone**, with Latin and Ogham inscriptions from about the fifth century AD, and the other, the **Cross Stone**, marked with a very early Celtic cross.

Lanes to the south of Nevern lead to the well-signposted cromlech at **Pentre Ifan**. This vast burial stone, with its sixteen-foot arrowhead topstone precariously balanced on large stone legs, dates back over four thousand years. The views from here are superb, situated as it is on the cusp of the stark, eerie Mynydd Preseli with the pastoral rolls of the countryside to the east. A couple of miles east of Nevern, signposted off the A487, the Iron Age hillfort of **Castell Henllys** (Easter–Oct daily 10am–5pm; £3) is undergoing archeological excavation that is turning up more and more of its past. Some re-created huts, complete with thatch, have been built on their prehistoric foundations and, throughout the summer, there are ample chances to try ancient skills, from basket weaving to rare animal husbandry. Sculpture trails through the woods and river valley bring to life the tales of The Mabinogion.

Practicalities

Newport is without doubt the best base in north Pembrokeshire. The cheerful national park **tourist office** (April–Sept Mon–Sat 10am–5.30pm; ☎01239/820912, *www.newport-pembs.co.uk*) is on Long Street, as is the **post office**, outside of which are boards full of local information. The wholefood shop, Bwydydd Cyflawn, on East Street has news of less mainstream events. **Bike rental** is available in town from the *Llysmeddyg* guesthouse on East Street (see below).

There's plenty of **accommodation** in town. Tucked in behind the Eco Centre on Lower St Mary Street, the Newport **YHA hostel** (☎ & fax 01239/820080; closed Nov–March) is a classy conversion of the old school. A mile south of town on Ffordd Cilgwyn, at the bottom of the slopes of Carn Ingli, *Brithdir Mawr* (☎01239/820164) is a great independently-run bunkhouse. The *Golden Lion* pub (☎01239/820321, fax 820686; ①), on East Street, offers cheap B&B rooms, as does *Llysmeddyg* guesthouse, also on the main street (☎01239/820008; ①). There are slightly pricier rooms at *Hafan Deg*, off Long Street (☎01239/820301; ②), and en-suite rooms at *Trewarren* (☎01239/820455; ②), over the river half a mile to the north, overlooking the estuary and with great views: follow Feidr Pen-y-Bont from town. If your budget is a bit bigger, don't miss the superb *Cnapan Country House* on East Street (☎01239/820575, fax 820878; ③; closed Jan & Feb). The nearest **campsite** is the *Morawelon* (☎01239/820565), just west of town at the Parrog, with pleasant gardens and its own café. **Food** and **drink** is also plentiful: unbeatable are the exquisite meals, made from fresh local and even wild produce, at the *Cnapan Country House* (see above). Otherwise, there are solid pub classics, including a good veggie menu, at the *Royal Oak* on Bridge Street, good Indian meals, with Kashmiri specialities, at the *Llwyngwair Arms* on East Street and great daytime snacks from the *Fronlas Café* and the *Fountain House Foods* deli on Market Street.

Cwm Gwaun and the inland hills

The valley of the burbling Afon Gwaun is one of the great surprises of Pembrokeshire. Surrounded as it is by bleak shoulders of bare mountain, the steep, wooded sides and lush vegetation of Europe's oldest glacial vale come as a complete contrast. Even if the locals weren't reputed to live by the pre-1752 Julian calendar, there would still be something otherworldly and timeless about Cwm Gwaun.

The B4313 leaves the skirts of Fishguard, heading southeast into the valley. At the first tiny settlement of **LLANYCHAER**, cross the river and head up the extremely steep lane to reach the **church** and "**cursing**" **well** of the lost settlement of **Llanllawer**, a few hundred yards further on. The well had a pre-Christian reputation for offering curses and ill omens if you left a bent pin, although most pilgrims sought miraculous cures, particularly for eye conditions. The lane running east opposite the well and church leads to seven large standing stones – the longest megalithic alignment in Wales – in **Parc y Merw** (the Field of the Dead), just short of Trellwyn Farm. Back on the main road, nearly a mile beyond Llanychaer, a lane branches off the B4313 to the left, soon crossing the river near a picnic site from where there are some good walks up into the old oak forests that line the valley. Two miles on, you reach the scattered settlement of **PONTFAEN**, complete with its time-warped pub, the *Dyffryn Arms* (see p.195). If you double back on yourself at the pub, following the lane that crosses the river and rises up a sharp hill, you soon reach Pontfaen's exquisitely restored **church**, dedicated, as are so many round here, to St Brynach. The circular graveyard indicates that this was a pre-Christian site of worship before the church was traditionally founded by the wandering Breton saint in 540 AD. In the graveyard, there are two impressive stone crosses, dating from between the sixth and ninth centuries. By the mid-nine-teenth century, the church was in ruins and it took the initiative and wealth of the Arden family, who moved to the adjoining Pontfaen House in the 1860s, to restore it. The intricate interior is notable for its squint, enabling all the congregation, including those in the "cheap" seats, to see what was going on, and a delicious early twentieth-century copy of a Fra Angelico *Madonna* painting.

Back on the lane that follows the Afon Gwaun, a further two miles brings you to the quite delightful **Gerddi Penlan-Uchaf** (Easter–Nov daily 9am–dusk; £1.75), a set of hillside gardens cut through by a stream with wonderful views over the valley. Their speciality lies in the thousands of miniature flowering and alpine plants, together with some impressive dwarf conifers.

It is further south and east that the brooding nature of the Mynydd Preseli makes itself most apparent. This is bleak, invigorating countryside, the wild, open hills scattered with the relics of ancient civilizations, and, more often than not, the remains of dead sheep which have succumbed to the harsh weather conditions. On the southern slopes, near the village of **MYNACHLOG-DDU**, you'll see the characteristic Preseli blue stone, which was used to construct Stonehenge, some 140 miles away, between 2000 and 1500 BC. The main range of the Preselis lies just north of the village, crossed by an ancient trackway, in use for at least 3500 years, known as the **Golden Road**. This is best reached from the Croesfihangel tumulus, on a minor lane a mile southwest of the village of Crymych, or, at the other end, at Bwlch-Gwynt, a mile south of Tafarn-y-Bwlch on the B4329. The track connects many of the Preselis' cairns and ancient sites, such as **Beddarthur**, an eerie stone circle that is supposed to be the great king's burial place, **Foeldrygarn** ("the Hill of Three Cairns"), with its hugely impressive Iron Age ramparts and hut circles, and **Carn Menyn**, probably the quarry from which the majority of the Stonehenge boulders were mined.

Quarrying the stones of Preseli has gone on for thousands of years, and more modern examples can be seen near the weird little village of **ROSEBUSH**, just off the B4313 to the west of Mynachlog-Ddu. The bizarre nineteenth-century Klondike atmosphere of the place – complete with corrugated iron shacks – is partially explained by the fact that it was built quickly as a would-be resort by the Victorians on the arrival of the railway. Follow the path due north out of the village past the old slate quarries, mined into the twentieth century, through the coniferous blandness of Pantmaenog Forest and up onto the Golden Road. An alternative route, on the eastern edge of the forest, leads to the highest point of the mountain range (and, indeed, of Pembrokeshire), at **Foel Cwmcerwyn** (1760ft). This was the site of a legendary battle between King Arthur and his followers and the giant boar, Twrch Trwyth, as detailed in The Mabinogion. Topped by a Bronze Age cairn, the rounded hill sits above **Craig y Cwm**, the last glacial valley (c. 8000 BC) in the area.

From the Tafarn Newydd crossroads near Rosebush, the B4329 continues south towards Haverfordwest, with a right turn after about two miles signposted for Llys-y-Frân, a 187-acre reservoir and attendant country park. The modern visitor centre contains a fairly decent restaurant, *Merlin's Pantry* (booking essential on ☎01437/532694 or 532273), a useful shop and a **bike rental** outlet (☎01437/532694; March–Oct).

Practicalities

Before you start into the hills, it makes sense to buy the National Park's *Walking in the Preseli Hills* (£2.45; available from the region's tourist offices). **Bike rental** is available either in Newport or in Llys-y-Frân (see above). **Accommodation** in the area is limited: on the far side of the Cwm Gwaun from the Gerddi Penlan-Uchaf is the supremely relaxing *Tregynon Country Farmhouse Hotel* (☎01239/820531, fax 820808, *tregynon@uk-holidays.co.uk*; ④), overlooking the valley and offering the highest standards of comfort and cuisine. **Camping** is easy enough – there's loads of good common land watered by trickling springs, or, if you need your home comforts, the *Gwaun Vale Touring Park* (☎01348/874698) is on the Fishguard side of Llanychaer, and is usually relatively wind-free even when the coast path is getting battered.

For even more remote stays, *Yethen-Isaf* (☎01437/532256; ②) is a cheerful farmhouse B&B just over a mile west of Mynachlog-Ddu and handy for walks along and around the Golden Road. Rosebush makes for a good base – the *Old Post Office* (☎01437/532205; ②) is a great B&B and restaurant, particularly noted for its vegetarian specialities, and there's always the corrugated-iron *Tafarn Sinc* (*Zinc Tavern*) in which to while away an evening. Alternatively, just up the road at the B4313/B4329 crossroads, the *Tafarn Newydd* (*New Inn*) hosts frequent folk and other music sessions, and serves excellent food. There's also a campsite and B&B, the *Rosebush Caravan & Camping Park* (March–Oct; ☎01437/532206; ①) in the village. Pubs in the area worth checking out are *Tate's* at Tafarn Newydd, and the *Bridge End Inn* at Llanychaer; all serve food. Pure **drinking**, however, is best done at the rustic, remote *Dyffryn Arms* at Pontfaen, where you can enjoy good company in an old-fashioned living room.

travel details

Unless otherwise stated, frequencies for trains and buses are for Monday to Saturday services; Sunday averages 1–3 services, though the main routes are more frequent and some routes have no Sunday service at all.

Trains

Carmarthen to: Cardiff (5 daily; 1hr 30min); Ferryside (12 daily; 10min); Fishguard Harbour (1–2 daily; 1hr); Haverfordwest (9 daily; 40min); Kidwelly (12 daily; 20min); Llanelli (hourly; 30min); London (2 daily; 4hr); Milford Haven (7 daily; 1hr); Narberth (7 daily; 30min); Pembroke (8 daily; 1hr 10min); Swansea (hourly; 50min); Tenby (8 daily; 40min); Whitland (7 daily; 20min).

Fishguard Harbour to: Cardiff (1–2 daily; 2hr 20min); Swansea (1–2 daily; 1hr 30min).

Haverfordwest to: Cardiff (5 daily; 2hr 40min); Carmarthen (9 daily; 40min); Milford Haven (11 daily; 20min); Swansea (7 daily; 1hr 30min).

Llanelli to: Cardiff (17 daily; 1hr 10min); Carmarthen (hourly; 30min); Llandeilo (4 daily; 40min); Llandovery (4 daily; 1hr); Llandrindod Wells (4 daily; 1hr 50min); Llanwrtyd Wells (4 daily; 1hr 30min); Pembrey & Burry Port (hourly; 5min); Shrewsbury (4 daily; 3hr 30min); Swansea (hourly; 20min).

Milford Haven to: Carmarthen (7 daily; 1hr); Haverfordwest (11 daily; 20min); Swansea (7 daily; 2hr).

Pembroke to: Lamphey (7 daily; 3min); Manorbier (7 daily; 10min); Pembroke Dock (7 daily; 10min); Swansea (6 daily; 2hr); Tenby (7 daily; 20min); Whitland (7 daily; 50min).

Tenby to: Cardiff (4 daily; 2hr 30min); Carmarthen (8 daily; 40min); Lamphey (8 daily; 20min); Narberth (8 daily; 20min); Pembroke (7 daily; 20min); Pembroke Dock (7 daily; 30min); Penally (7 daily; 2min); Saundersfoot (8 daily; 10min); Swansea (7 daily; 1hr 40min); Whitland (8 daily; 30min).

Whitland to: Cardiff (4 daily; 2hr); Carmarthen (7 daily; 20min); Haverfordwest (12 daily; 20min); Milford Haven (10 daily; 40min); Narberth (8 daily; 10min); Pembroke (7 daily; 50min); Swansea (7 daily; 1hr 10min); Tenby (8 daily; 30min).

Buses

Carmarthen to: Aberaeron (6 daily; 1hr 40min); Aberystwyth (2 daily; 2hr 35min); Cardigan (hourly & 2 journeys Sun; 1hr 30min); Cenarth (hourly & 2 journeys Sun; 1hr 5min); Drefach Felindre (hourly & 2 journeys Sun; 50min); Haverfordwest (5 daily; 1hr); Kidwelly (hourly; 25min); Lampeter (6 daily; 1hr 10min); Laugharne (hourly; 30min); Llanarthne (5 daily; 30min); Llandeilo (15 daily; 40min); Llandovery (8 daily; 1hr 15min); Llansteffan (6 daily; 20min); Narberth (3 daily; 40min); Newcastle Emlyn (hourly & 2 journeys Sun; 1hr); Pembrey (5 daily; 30min); Pendine (hourly; 45min); Saundersfoot (2 daily; 45min); Swansea (hourly; 1hr 30min); Tenby (2 daily; 1hr); Trelech (6 daily; 45min).

Fishguard to: Cardigan (hourly; 50min); Haverfordwest (hourly; 40min); Newport, Pembrokeshire (hourly; 20min); St David's (7 daily; 50min); Trefin (7 daily; 30min).

Haverfordwest to: Broad Haven (2–5 daily; 20min); Cardigan (hourly; 1hr 20min); Carmarthen (5 daily; 1hr); Dale (2 daily Tues & Fri; 40min); Fishguard (hourly; 40min); Manorbier (hourly; 1hr 10min); Milford Haven (half-hourly; 20min); Narberth (5 daily; 20min); Newgale (hourly; 20min); Newport, Pembrokeshire (hourly; 1hr

10min); Pembroke (hourly; 50min); St David's (hourly; 40min); Solva (hourly; 30min); Tenby (hourly; 1hr 20min).

Llandeilo to: Carmarthen (15 daily; 40min); Llanarthne (5 daily; 30min); Llandovery (9 daily; 45min); Talley (Tues & Fri 1 daily; 20min).

Llandovery to: Brecon (Mon–Sat 5 daily, none on Sun; 40min).

Milford Haven to: Broad Haven (2 daily; 30min); Dale (2 daily; 30min); Marloes (2 daily; 40min); Pembroke (hourly; 40min); St David's (2 daily; 2hr).

Newport, Pembrokeshire to: Fishguard (hourly; 20min); Haverfordwest (hourly; 1hr 10min).

Pembroke to: Bosherston (2 daily Mon–Fri; 1hr); Castlemartin (2 daily; 30min); Freshwater East (2 daily Mon–Fri; 10min); Haverfordwest (hourly; 50min); Manorbier (hourly; 20min); Milford Haven (hourly; 40min); Pembroke Dock (numerous; 10min); Stackpole (2 daily Mon–Fri; 50min); Tenby (hourly; 40min).

Pembroke Dock to: Carew (3–4 daily; 10min); Pembroke (numerous; 10min).

St David's to: Broad Haven (2 daily; 40min); Fishguard (7 daily; 50min); Haverfordwest (hourly; 40min); Milford Haven (2 daily; 2hr); Solva (2 daily; 10min).

Tenby to: Amroth (7 daily; 40min); Carmarthen (2 daily; 1hr); Haverfordwest (hourly; 1hr 20min); Manorbier (hourly; 20min); Narberth (10 daily; 50min); Pembroke (hourly; 40min); Pendine (7 daily; 45min); Saundersfoot (every 30min; 10min).

Ferries and fast ferries

Fishguard to: Rosslare, Ireland (4–6 daily; 1hr 40min on a fast ferry, otherwise 3hr 30min).

Pembroke Dock to: Rosslare (2 daily; 4hr).

CHAPTER THREE

CENTRAL WALES

The great tranche of central Wales is often viewed as little more than a corridor by which to reach the coast. Nothing could be further from the truth, however: though its secrets have barely been uncovered, the area boasts some of Wales' most enjoyable towns and striking scenery.

The vast county of **Powys** takes up a full quarter of Wales, its southern end dominated by the **Brecon Beacons National Park**, stretching from the moody heights of the Black Mountain in the west, through the gentler Beacons themselves, and east to the English border beyond the confusingly named Black Mountains. The main centres within the Beacons are **Abergavenny**, in the far southeast, and the small city of **Brecon**, a curious mix of traditional market town, army garrison and often very pretty tourist centre.

The bleaker part of the Beacons lies to the west, around the raw peaks of the **Black Mountain** and **Fforest Fawr**. A few roads cut through the glowering countryside, connecting popular attractions such as the immense **Dan-yr-ogof caves**, opera prima donna Adelina Patti's gilded home and theatre at nearby **Craig-y-nos** and the quite stunning caves and waterfalls around the walking centre of **Ystradfellte**. Walkers are equally well catered for in settlements like **Crickhowell** and **Talgarth**, small towns set in quiet river valleys.

At the northern corner of the National Park, the border town of **Hay-on-Wye** draws in thousands to see the town's dozens of bookshops, housed in warehouses, the old castle and outdoor yards. West of Hay, the peaks of the **Mynydd Eppynt** now form a vast training ground for the British army, on the other side of which lie the old spa towns of Radnorshire – earthy **Llanwrtyd Wells**, moribund **Llangammarch Wells**, the gritty centre of **Builth Wells** and twee **Llandrindod Wells**. Crossed by spectacular mountain roads such as the **Abergwesyn Pass** from Llanwrtyd, the countryside to the north is barely populated and supremely beautiful – quiet, occasionally harsh country dotted with ancient churches and introspective villages, from the border towns of **Presteigne** and **Knighton**, home of the flourishing **Offa's Dyke path** industry, to inland centres like **Rhayader**, the nearest centre of population for the grandiose reservoirs of the **Elan Valley**.

Montgomeryshire is the northern portion of Powys, similarly underpopulated and as remote as its two southern siblings. In common with most of mid-Wales, country

---

ACCOMMODATION PRICE CODES

Throughout this guide, hotel and B&B accommodation is priced on a scale of ① to ⑨, the number indicating the **lowest price** you could expect to pay per night in that establishment for a **double room in high season**. The prices indicated by the codes are as follows:

① under £40	④ £60–70	⑦ £110–150
② £40–50	⑤ £70–90	⑧ £150–200
③ £50–60	⑥ £90–110	⑨ over £200

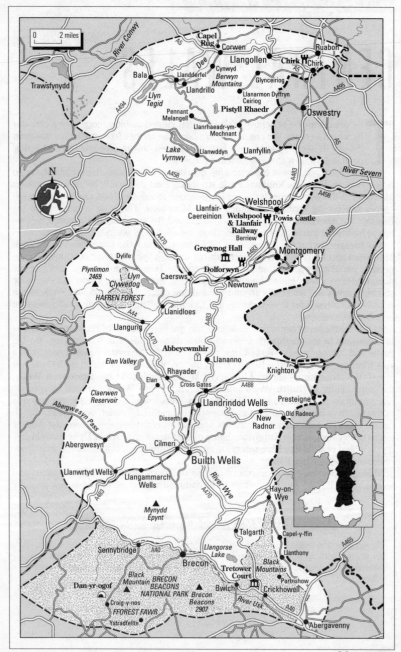

© Crown copyright

towns such as the beautiful **Llanidloes** have a healthy stock of old hippies amongst the population, resulting in a greater-than-expected presence of health-food shops, healing groups and arts activity. To the west, the inhospitable mountain of **Plynlimon** is flecked with boggy heathland and gloomy reservoirs, beyond which the popular and hearty town of Machynlleth is stranded out on a limb of Powys (see p.292). The eastern side of Montgomeryshire is home to the anglicized old county town, **Montgomery**, between the robust town of **Welshpool**, on the English border, and the downbeat centre of **Newtown**, worth visiting only for devotees of early socialist **Robert Owen**, who was born in the town. The northern segment of the county is even quieter, with regional centres like **Llanfyllin** and **Llanrhaeadr-ym-mochnant** that are little more than villages, leaving the few crowds seen around here to cluster along the banks of **Lake Vyrnwy**, a flooded-valley reservoir which has harmoniously moulded itself into the landscape around it.

Immediately north of Powys is the mountainous strip of land stretching up the **Dee Valley**, an area that combines northern ruggedness (it's a well-defined route into Snowdonia) with the smoother border countryside of Powys and the Marches. Though **Chirk Castle** is the only extant Marcher fortress of note, it remains a potent reminder of the centuries after the Norman conquest of England, when powerful barons fought the Welsh princes for control of these fertile lands. The Dee Valley remained more firmly Welsh than the Marches, and three hundred years after the arrival of the Normans, the area was the site of the first big revolt against them. From his base near **Corwen**, Wales' greatest hero, Owain Glyndŵr, attacked the property of a nearby English landowner, sparking a fourteen-year campaign which, at its height, saw Glyndŵr ruling most of Wales by means of Parliaments held at points along the Cambrian coast (see p.445). Little remains in the valley to commemorate the era, and most people drive through oblivious of its heritage. **Llangollen** is the valley's main draw, with an international eisteddfod folk music festival each July and a broad selection of ruins, rides and rambles to tempt visitors throughout the rest of the year.

Getting around

Road transport in central Wales is fairly easy, with the swift A40 and A438 running from the English border to Carmarthen, Brecon and the west. Further north, the A44 heads into Radnorshire from Leominster in Herefordshire. The A458 heads off the north Wales-bound A5 at Shrewsbury down to Welshpool and Montgomeryshire. Stay on the main A5 for access to Llangollen and the Dee Valley. This makes getting to the mountains easy, but tends to force **cyclists** onto quieter roads such as the B4401 through the Vale of Edeyrnion, and the narrow lanes at the head of Glyn Ceiriog.

Public transport takes more forward planning. **Train** services are restricted to a stop at Chirk on the Chester–Shrewsbury line, the Heart of Wales line from Shropshire to Swansea via Knighton, Llandrindod Wells, Llanwrtyd Wells and smaller stops in between and the Shrewsbury–Machynlleth route through Welshpool and Newtown. Larger centres such as Brecon, Llanidloes, Rhayader, Builth Wells, Hay-on-Wye and Llangollen have no stations. For them, and for the rest of this huge area, sporadic **bus** services (including school and post services) provide the only access. Staples of the mid-Wales bus scene include the two-hourly #94 from Wrexham, through Llangollen, Corwen, Bala and on to Dolgellau on the Cambrian coast, and the three-times-daily #47, which runs up the spine of southern Powys from Brecon through Builth to Llandrindod Wells, where it meets connections for Newtown, Welshpool and the north. Nearby towns such as Wrexham, Abergavenny, Machynlleth and, over the border, Oswestry, provide useful intersection points. Available from libraries, tourist offices and main post offices, the most useful overview of all these services is the free *Wales Bus, Rail and Tourist Map & Guide*, which details operators and their different services.

BRECON BEACONS NATIONAL PARK

With the lowest profile of Wales' three national parks, the **Brecon Beacons** are the destination of thousands of urban walkers from the industrial areas of south Wales and the West Midlands of England. Rounded, spongy hills of grass and rock tumble and climb around river valleys that lie between sandstone and limestone uplands peppered with glass-like lakes and villages that seem to have been hewn from one rock. Known for their vivid quality of light, the hills of the Beacons disappear and re-emerge from hazy blankets of cloud, with shafts of sun sharpening lush green fields out of a dullened patchwork.

Covering 520 square miles, the National Park straddles southern Powys and northern Monmouthshire from west to east. The most remote parts are to the west, where the vast, open terrain of **Fforest Fawr** and the **Black Mountain** form miles of tufted moorland and bleak, often dangerous peaks, tumbling down to the porous limestone country in the southwestern section, a rocky terrain of rivers, deep caves and spluttering waterfalls, especially attractive around the village of **Ystradfellte** and in the chasms of the **Dan-yr-ogof caves**. To the northwest lie the lonely Black Mountains, separated from the Beacons themselves by the Monmouthshire and Brecon Canal, which forges a passage along the Usk Valley. Built around the beginning of the nineteenth century to support coal mining, iron ore and limestone quarrying, the canal is a marvellous feat of engineering, successfully steering a 25-mile lock-free stretch (the longest in Britain) through some of the most mountainous terrain in Wales. Spreading back from the canal's banks are the region's main residential areas as well as the majority of its hotels and guesthouses, so it's quite likely that this is where you'll end up staying: towns such as the sturdy county seat of **Brecon**, or the overgrown village of **Crickhowell**, with its beautiful double castle at nearby **Tretower**, set amid almost impossibly green hills, all make agreeable bases. Nestled under the Black Mountains, **Abergavenny** makes an ideal base for exploring these brooding peaks, as well as the Beacons themselves and even the eastern Valleys around Blaenafon and Pontypool (see p.81 for both). Lying underneath the northern bluff of the Black Mountains is the pleasant border town of **Hay-on-Wye**, at the point where the mountains dissolve into the softer contours of Radnorshire.

Getting around and accommodation

Getting around the largely rural territory of the Brecon Beacons National Park can be difficult. Abergavenny is the only town with a **train** station, though Merthyr Tydfil (see p.87), on the southern flank of the park, is well connected by rail to Cardiff. **Buses** are a much better bet, with relatively frequent services (4–6 a day is common) along the major routes; a smattering of services only run on certain days. The main routes are from Brecon to Abergavenny and on to Newport, Brecon to Merthyr via Libanus, and Swansea to Brecon via the Dan-yr-ogof showcaves; detailed listings of services in the area are contained in the free *Explore the Brecon Beacons* leaflet, available from tourist offices and bus companies.

The relatively compact nature of the region, the profusion of narrow lanes and the many opportunities to get off road make this a great place to **travel by bike**: there are rental outlets in Brecon and Abergavenny (see p.210 & 215).

Though the best of the Brecon Beacons' **accommodation** is listed in this guide, there are plenty more low-budget options, most listed in two booklets available from area tourist offices. *Camping on Farms* (35p) lists around thirty low-cost sites scattered throughout the park, while the accurately named *Bunkhouse Accommodation in and around the Brecon Beacons* (free) covers over a dozen bunkhouses – most cost under £10 a night. If you're interested in self-catering accommodation, contact Brecon Beacon

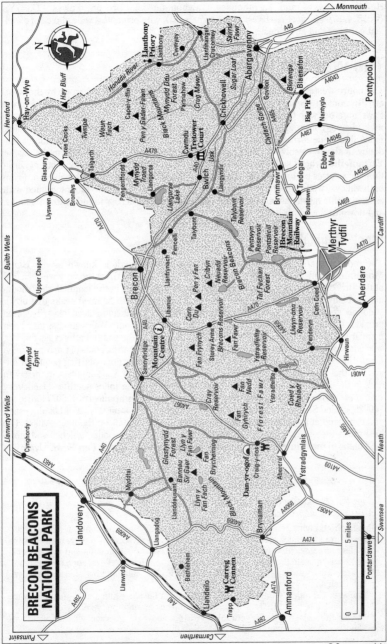

BRECON BEACONS NATIONAL PARK

© Crown copyright

Holiday Cottages and Farmhouses, Talybont-on-Usk, Brecon, Powys LD3 7YS (☎01874/676446, fax 676416, *www.wiz.to/beacons*), who promote a wide choice of excellent cottages and farmhouses in the area.

The western Beacons

The entire western half of the Brecon Beacons National Park is taken up by the western Beacons, a region comprising the bleak uplands of Black Mountain and Fforest Fawr, together with the sparsely populated valleys in between. It is in the valleys where most visitors congregate, chiefly at the **Dan-yr-ogof** showcaves, where some of Wales' finest limestone formations are given the son et lumière treatment. Limestone's tendency to slowly dissolve is more powerfully demonstrated over the hills to the east at **Ystradfellte**, where sink holes swallow the River Mellte only to spew it out again in time for a series of three waterfalls, one so undercut that you can walk behind it. From both valleys, wondrously lonely walks thread their way up to the moors imbued with ancient Celtic mysticism and offering tremendous views across to the central Beacons, and down to the south Wales Valleys.

Black Mountain

The most westerly expanse of upland in the national park is known as the **Black Mountain** (Mynydd Ddu), rising between the A4069 and A4067, at the very western end of the Brecon Beacons National Park. Despite being named in the singular, the "mountain" actually covers an unpopulated range of barren, smooth-humped peaks that break suddenly at rocky escarpments towering over quiet streams and glacial lakes. The area provides the most challenging and exhilarating walking in south Wales and has long been popular with trippers from the Valleys, just a few miles to the south. Paths cross the wet, wild landscape from Dan-yr-ogof in the east, and from the soaring ruins of Carreg Cennen Castle, just short of Llandeilo in the west (see p.147). Other good starting points for forays into the open Black Mountain uplands are Tyhwnt, near Ystradgynlais, in the south and, in the north, the hamlet of **LLANDDEUSANT**, seven miles south of Llandovery (see p.147), also home to a charming **YHA hostel** and **campsite** (☎01550/740619, fax 740225; closed Sept–March) in the former village pub. Two miles west of Llanddeusant, you can camp at the pleasant *Pont Aber Inn* (☎01550/740202) on the main A4069. The best walks (see box, below) from Llanddeusant runs along wooded gulches and moorland bluffs to the twin glacial lakes of **Llyn y Fan Fach** and **Llyn y Fan Fawr**. Llyn y Fan

A WALK AROUND LLANDDEUSANT

Note: the OS Outdoor Leisure 1:25,000 map #12 (Brecon Beacons – Western & Central Area) map is recommended for this walk

Passing both Llyn y Fan Fach and Llyn y Fan Fawr, this bleak and lonely ten-mile circular walk from Llanddeusant weaves through classic glacial scenery: valleys slashed with tumbling streams cut between purple hills, while occasional mounds and moraines of rock debris indicate the force of the ice pushing through the valleys. Such heaps sometimes grew to a size large enough to form a natural dam, building up a lake, such as Llyn y Fan Fach, in its wake.

The walk (10 miles; 4–5hr; 1400ft ascent) starts in Llanddeusant and climbs steeply to Llyn y Fan Fach, from where a precarious path leads around the top of the escarpment, following the ridge to **Fan Brycheiniog** (2630ft), above the glassy black waters of Llyn y Fan Fawr. A remote path heads from here to the cross-moor road, two miles away.

Fach features in one of Wales' most oft-told myths of a beautiful maiden, together with her herd of magic cattle, who rose from the lake to marry a local farmer. The maiden's father had sanctioned the union only on the condition that if the farmer struck his daughter three times, she would return to the lake. Such occasions inadvertently occurred, the final blow being either when he slammed a gate and hit her or when he shook her at a funeral for laughing. The maiden silently left the man and, with her cattle, disappeared beneath the lake's icy waters once more.

The Fforest Fawr

Covering a vast expanse of hilly landscape between the Black Mountain and the central Beacons southwest of Brecon, **Fforest Fawr** (Great Forest) seems something of a misnomer for an area of largely unforested sandstone hills dropping down to a porous limestone belt in the south. The "forest" tag refers more to the old definition of a forest as land used as a hunting ground.

The hills rise up to the south of the A40 west of Brecon, with the A4067 Sennybridge–Ystradgynlais road piercing the western side of the range and the A470 Brecon–Merthyr road defining the Fforest's eastern limit. Between the two, a wonderful, twisting mountain road rises up out of the fertile valley of the Senni River three miles south of Sennybridge, straining up to cross the bleak plateau towards the top of Fforest Fawr and descending into the limestone crags around the hamlet of **YSTRAD-FELLTE**, little more than a handful of houses, a church and a pub, the *New Inn*. It is, however, a phenomenally popular centre for walking, as a result of the dazzling countryside on its doorstep. Lush, deep ravines – a total contrast to the barren mountains immediately to the north – carve their way through the limestone ridge south of the village, with great pavements of bone-white rock littering fields next to cradling potholes, disappearing rivers and crashing waterfalls. As a classic limestone landscape, the Ystradfellte district is recognized as one of the most impressive in the British Isles.

A mile south of Ystradfellte, the River Mellte tumbles into the dark and icy mouth of the **Porth-yr-ogof** (White Horse Cave), emerging into daylight a few hundred yards further south. It's a mighty sight, as the clear water tumbles into a gaping hole overhung by a great shelf of limestone. A signposted path heads south from the Porth-yr-ogof car park and into the green gorge of the River Mellte. Continue for little more than a mile to the first of its three great waterfalls, **Sgwd Clun-Gwyn** (White Meadow Fall), where the river crashes 50ft over two huge, angular steps of rock before hurtling down course for a few hundred yards to the other two falls, the graceful **Sgwd Isaf Clun-Gwyn** (Lower White Meadow Fall), and, a little further on, the mighty **Sgwd y Pannwr** (Fall of the Fuller).

The path continues through the foliage to the confluence of the rivers Mellte and Hepste, half a mile further on. A quarter of a mile along the Hepste is the most impressive, and most popular, of the area's falls, the **Sgwd yr Eira** (Fall of Snow), where the rock below the main tumble has eroded back six feet, allowing people to walk directly behind a dramatic twenty-foot curtain of water – particularly dazzling in afternoon or evening light. There's a shorter signposted path to Sgwd yr Eira from just above Sgwd Isaf Clun-Gwyn, and an even shorter direct two-mile walk from the village of **Penderyn**, off the A4059 three miles north of Hirwaun, reached by regular buses from Aberdare.

In Ystradfellte, you'll find the popular *New Inn*, which serves basic meals, and, half a mile to the south and just a short walk from Porth-yr-ogof, a cosy **YHA hostel** (☎ & fax 01639/720301; open April to mid-Sept and winter weekends). Just up the lane from Ystradfellte, you can **camp** at *Penllwyn-Einon Farm Bungalow* (☎01639/720542), or in numerous informal spots in the woods.

Dan-yr-ogof showcaves and Craig-y-nos

Six miles of upland forest and squelchy moor lie between Ystradfellte and the **Dan-yr-ogof showcaves** (April–Oct daily 10am–4pm; Nov–March phone for details; ☎01639/730801 or 730284, *www.dan-yr-ogof-showcaves.co.uk*; £6.95), off the A4067 to the west. Only discovered in 1912, they claim to form the largest system of subterranean caverns in northern Europe, and although relentless marketing has turned them into something of an overdone theme park the extent and size of the caverns is truly awe-inspiring.

There are no guided tours here: you simply follow the concrete path and listen to some rather simplistic commentary from unseen speakers. The path first leads you into the **Dan-yr-ogof** cave, the longest showcave in Britain and a bewildering subterranean warren of caverns framed by stalactites and frothy limestone deposits spewing, frozen, over the crags and walls. Back outside, you pass a downbeat re-created Iron Age "village", and through a hideous park of fibreglass dinosaurs to get to the **Cathedral Cave**, a much broader affair winding through a succession of spookily lit caverns where water cascades relentlessly down the walls and crusts of thin stalactites, looking like spun pasta squeezed through the rock, hang above. In the final cave, a 150-foot-long, 70-foot-high cathedral, light and sound come together in the shape of a swelling classical soundtrack and dancing light show that's impressive despite its inherent tawdriness. Reachable via a precarious path behind the dinosaur park, **Bone Cave**, the third and final cavern, was known to be inhabited by prehistoric tribes – in honour of this, a fenced-off assortment of dressed-up mannequins that make Bronze Age woman look like a reject from Miss Selfridge are complemented by another son et lumière show.

Unless you want to get an early start on the caves, or are using them as a base for walking, there's little here to make you stay, though you can **camp** at the site (£4 per person), and, in a less commercialized manner, up the track behind the *Tafarn-y-Garreg* pub at *Maes-yr-eglwys Farm* (☎01639/730849). A few yards down a side road opposite the caves, the *Gwyn Arms* serves decent pub meals.

A quarter of a mile south of the cave complex is the spiky shape of the nineteenth-century **Craig-y-nos Castle**, a grand folly built in 1842 and fancifully extended from 1878, when it was bought by Adelina Patti, the celebrated Italo-American opera singer. In her forty years of residence, she turned the place into a Disneyesque castle, even adding a gaudy, scaled-down version of the Drury Lane opera house for performances. After years of careless development, and dashed hopes of reopening the place as a country opera house – a sort of Welsh Glyndebourne – the future of the house is uncertain, though groups can go on a tour of the restored theatre if booked in advance (☎01639/730205). Some 44 acres of the grounds have been turned over to the Brecon Beacons National Park and operate as **Craig-y-nos Country Park** (unrestricted entry). The car park and visitor centre is the starting point for signposted and leafleted walks around a landscaped site along the banks of the young River Tawe.

The central Beacons

Far more popular for walking and pony trekking than the wet and wild Black Mountain and Fforest Fawr and easily accessible from Brecon, just six miles to the north, the **central Brecon Beacons** – after which the whole national park is named – are grouped around the two highest peaks in south Wales, Pen y Fan and Corn Du. Although neither peak reaches 3000ft, the terrain is unmistakably, and dramatically, mountainous: classic old red-sandstone country with sweeping peaks rising up out of glacial scoops of land.

The highest peak in the Beacons, **Pen y Fan** (2907ft), together with **Corn Du** (2863ft), half a mile to the west, represent the most popular ascents in the park. The most direct route up is the well-trampled red-mud path that starts from Pont ar Daf, half a mile south of Storey Arms on the A470 midway between Brecon and Merthyr Tydfil. The ascent is a comparatively easy five-mile round trip gradually climbing up the southern flank of the two peaks. A longer and generally quieter route (see box, below) leads up to the two peaks from the "Gap" route, the pre-nineteenth-century (and possibly Roman) main road that winds its way north from the Neuadd reservoirs, through the only natural break in the sandstone ridge of the central Beacons to the bottom of the lane that eventually joins the main street in the Brecon suburb of Llanfaes as Bailihelig Road. Although the old road is no longer accessible for cars, car parks at either end open out onto the track for an eight-mile round-trip ascent up Pen y Fan and Corn Du from the east.

Brecon

BRECON (Aberhonddu) stands at the northern edge of the Beacons, its proliferation of well-proportioned Georgian buildings bearing testimony to its past importance. It is now a fairly workaday place, principally attractive for the its proximity to the best upland sections of the national park. Many walkers base themselves here and explore the well-waymarked hills to the south of the town, in particular **Pen y Fan** (see above) the highest, most challenging peak in south Wales. Brecon is also a good base for the more sedentary, with an appealing jumble of architecture and a good social scene.

A CIRCULAR WALK AROUND CORN DU AND PEN Y FAN

Note: The OS Outdoor Leisure 1:25,000 map #12 (Brecon Beacons West & Central) is recommended for this walk.

Few walkers visiting the Brecon Beacons for the first time can resist an ascent of the two highest peaks: Corn Du and Pen y Fan. Most take one of the shorter routes from the A470 south of Brecon, but connoisseurs prefer this longer and infinitely more rewarding **circular route** (8 miles; 4–5hr) which describes a circuit around a ridge-top horseshoe of the Beacons.

The hike starts at the car park by the late Victorian Neuadd reservoirs. Go through the gate and head down left through a gully and up onto the top of the grassy dam of the lower, smaller reservoir. Go to the end, through the muddy gap and up the hill in front, keeping the partly cleared plantation forest on your left-hand side. Keep to the fairly well-defined track and, when the forest ends, continue up the sharp gradient ahead, keeping the little stream gully on your left. This is the toughest, steepest and often boggiest part of the walk, but before too long you're up on the top of a windy ridge, commanding wide views over the reservoirs, the Beacons and way beyond. Head right along a well-defined path along the ridge top. The slope to the right becomes gradually sharper and more cliff-like as you continue over tiny streams that course down to the valley below. When the ridge on which you're walking narrows to a thin spit, views to the left down the completely uninhabited Cwm Crew are delightful. Corn Du and Pen y Fan are now looming in the foreground – follow the obvious path that strikes up the sandstone ridge to the first summit. Note how eroded the main path from the A470 is when you meet it just short of the peak.

Follow the obvious route from the summit of Corn Du down to a shallow saddle and up again to the peak of Pen y Fan, the highest point in south Wales. From both, the views over the mountains and valleys to Brecon are awesome. You can continue beyond Pen y Fan up to the next summit, Cribyn, and then descend to the Gap, where the wall of hills is breached by a track that may have been a Roman through route. Alternatively, without missing too much, you can take a right by the stream in the valley between Pen y Fan and Cribyn, following the rough track around the base of Cribyn to meet the Gap track. Turn right and continue along above the Neuadd reservoirs, turning right at the stream gulch to return to the car park.

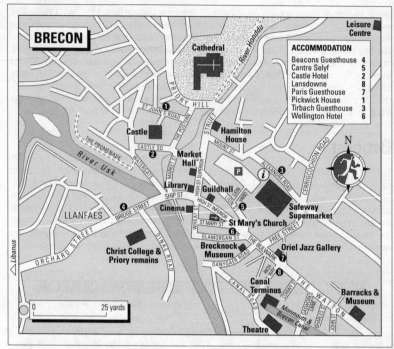

BRECON

Leisure
Centre

Cathedral

ACCOMMODATION

Beacons Guesthouse	4
Cantre Selyf	5
Castle Hotel	2
Lansdowne	8
Paris Guesthouse	7
Pickwick House	1
Tirbach Guesthouse	3
Wellington Hotel	6

Castle

Hamilton
House

Market
Hall

Library

Guildhall

Cinema

Safeway
Supermarket

LLANFAES

St Mary's Church

Christ College &
Priory remains

Brecknock
Museum

Oriel Jazz Gallery

Canal
Terminus

Barracks &
Museum

0   25 yards

Theatre

© Crown copyright

A Roman fort was built near here, but the town only started to grow with the building of a Norman castle and Benedictine monastery, founded in 1093 on the banks of the Honddu River, which gives the town its Welsh name. To the dual strands of military and ecclesiastical importance was added the status of regional market centre and cloth weaving town. In the seventeenth-century Civil War, the townsfolk unequivocally demonstrated their neutrality between the forces of Parliament and the Crown by demolishing most of the castle and large sections of the town walls, dissipating the appeal for either side of seizing their town.

Information

The **tourist office** (daily: Easter–Oct 10am–6pm; Nov–Easter 9am–4.45pm; ☎01874/622485) and **Brecon Beacons National Park office** (Easter–Oct daily 9.30am–5.30pm; ☎01874/623156, *www.breconbeacons.org*) share the same building in the Lion Yard car park off Lion Street, next to the new Safeway supermarket. You can also get general Brecon information from the town's Web site: *www.brecon.co.uk/*. The tourist office holds details of local bus services, which leave from the central Bulwark for Swansea, Abergavenny and Hay-on-Wye. For details of the town's annual **jazz festival**, held over a long weekend in mid-August, call ☎01874/625557, and to get the lowdown on gigs and other local events, look in the window of F.H. Jones newsagents in The Bulwark or on the boards in the Market Hall foyer on High Street Superior. There is free **Internet access** at the town library on Ship Street (Mon–Fri 9.30am–5pm, Sat 9.30am–1pm).

Accommodation

Brecon is a compact town with ample **accommodation** to suit all pockets, though a couple of places around the £50 mark are especially good. The suburb of Llanfaes, across the river from the main town, has plenty of smaller hotels and B&Bs on its main street, but be warned, though, that rooms in Brecon can be tricky to come by during the jazz festival.

Hotels and guesthouses

Beacons Guest House, 16 Bridge St, Llanfaes (☎ & fax 01874/623339, *www.beacons.brecon.co.uk*). Rambling converted town house in an excellent position. Good, cheap evening meals also available. ②.

Cantre Selyf, 5 Lion St (☎01874/622904, fax 622315, *www.imaginet.co.uk/cantreselyf*). Large and imposing seventeenth-century town house, all creaking floors and moulded plaster ceilings, but sensitively modernized with private bathrooms and firm cast-iron beds. Delicious breakfasts, and evening meals on request. ③.

Castle Hotel, Castle Square (☎01874/624611, fax 623737, *hotel@breconcastle.co.uk*). Large and sumptuous hotel built into the castle ruins, overlooking the Usk. All rooms are en suite and with satellite TV, while larger rooms with a decent view are more expensive. ③.

Lansdowne Hotel, 39 The Watton (☎01874/623321, fax 610438). Classy town-centre hotel in a handsome Georgian corner house with a restaurant on site. ②.

Llanfaes Guest House, Llanfaes (☎01874/611115, *www.tybesta.demon.co.uk*). Exclusively lesbian and gay retreat in a pleasant Georgian town house. Phone for details. ①.

Nant Ddu Lodge Hotel, Cwn Taf (☎01685/379111, fax 377088, *www.nant-ddu-lodge.co.uk*). High-standard hotel and restaurant in a Georgian building with an unparalleled location at the foot of the Beacons, ten miles south of Brecon on the A470 and closer to Merthyr Tydfil, but firmly within the national park. ⑤.

Paris Guest House, 28 The Watton (☎01874/624205). Smart Georgian house converted into a low-key and friendly, if chintzy, town-centre B&B. ①.

Pickwick House, St John's Rd (☎01874/624322, fax 624700, *isobel@pickwick.prestel.co.uk*). Warm and welcoming town-house B&B near the cathedral, with comfortable en-suite rooms and excellent evening meals (£15 for 3 courses, coffee and home-made petit fours) which, like the breakfasts, are freshly cooked and predominantly organic (and vegetarian if required). ③.

Tirbach Guest House, 13 Alexandra Rd (☎01874/624551). Small and pleasant budget B&B up behind Safeway, with shared bathrooms and an accommodating host. ①.

Wellington Hotel, The Bulwark (☎01874/625225, fax 610459). Imposing old coaching inn that dominates the town's main square. ④.

Hostels, bunkhouses and campsites

Brynich Caravan and Camping Park, Brynich (☎ & fax 01874/623325). Award-winning, well-equipped site a mile east of town, just off the A470, overlooking the town and the river.

Cwmgwdi Farm, two miles from central Brecon (☎01874/622034). Very basic – and quiet – campers' field, on the leftmost lane from Llanfaes' Ffrwdgrech Road.

The Held Bunkhouse, Cantref (☎ & fax 01874/624646). Basic but comfortable and warm hostel accommodation a mile south of Brecon's western suburb of Llanfaes (take the Bailhelig Road). Bring sleeping bag.

Llwyn-y-Celyn YHA hostel, Libanus, seven miles southwest of Brecon (☎01874/624261, fax 625916). Isolated farmhouse hostel, just off the A470 and main bus route to Merthyr. Camping permitted. Closed Dec to mid-Feb.

Ty'n-y-Caeau YHA hostel, Groesfford, just over two miles east of Brecon (☎01874/665270, fax 665278). The nearest YHA hostel to Brecon, reached via the path (Slwch Lane) from Cerrigcochion Road in town or a mile from bus stops at either Cefn Brynich lock (Brecon–Abergavenny buses) or Troedyrharn Farm (Brecon–Hereford buses). Some private rooms (①). Closed Dec–Feb.

Upper Cantref Farm Bunkhouses, Cantref Pony Trekking Centre, near Llanfrynach (☎01874/665223). Overlooking the Cynrig River, three miles southeast of Brecon. Dormitory-style accommodation with kitchen and showers. Also takes campers, who can pitch tents in the grounds.

The Town

Buses decant their passengers in at the western end of **The Bulwark** where it fattens out to become Brecon's imposing central square, flanked by the solid-red sixteenth-century tower of the otherwise unremarkable **St Mary's church**, an assortment of old-fashioned shop frontages and the elegant Georgian portico of the **Wellington Hotel**.

At the junction of The Bulwark and Glamorgan Street is the neo-Grecian frontage of the **Brecknock Museum** (Mon–Fri 10am–5pm, Sat 10am–1pm & 2–5pm; April–Sept also Sun noon–5pm; £1), where a display of local trades includes a re-created smithy and a collection of agricultural implements unique to the area. More interesting are the walk-through history of Wales and a nineteenth-century assize court, last used in 1971 and preserved in all its ponderous splendour, overseen by the high judge's throne as if judgements came from God himself. You can hear pronouncements of a sort via a somewhat unconvincing re-creation of a court hearing conducted in Welsh and English. Elsewhere, there's a finely carved four-poster, a gleaming balance and weights used in the local produce market, inscribed stones dating back to the fifth century and a selection of painstakingly carved Welsh love spoons that were betrothal gifts for courting Welsh lovers, some of them over four hundred years old.

Running east, The Bulwark becomes **The Watton** outside the **Oriel Jazz gallery** (daily 1–4pm; free), which capitalizes on Brecon's astonishingly successful annual jazz festival. The gallery presents a fascinating romp through the archives of twentieth-century music, from the rhythms of West Africa, through New Orleans, Chicago and New York to Europe, with rare video footage of some of the jazz greats. Further along The Watton, the foreboding frontage of the South Wales Borderers' **barracks** glares across the street to its **museum** (April–Sept daily 9am–5pm; Oct–March Mon–Fri 9am–5pm; £2), packed with mementos from the regiment's three-hundred-year existence. Amongst the gung ho bravado, most noticeable are the tales of the 1879 Zulu War when 140 Welsh soldiers defended against an attack by 4000 Zulu warriors. From The Watton, a series of small streets run down to the northern terminus of the **Monmouth and Brecon Canal**, where afternoon cruises aboard the *Dragonfly* (☎0831/685222; £5) ease their way out of town for an enjoyably relaxed two-hour cruise. The Theatr Brycheiniog **arts and entertainment centre** (☎01874/611622) rises above the canal basin and stages pretty much any production that can be lured here, many of which are very good.

North and west of The Bulwark are a cluttered grid of streets, packed with Georgian and Victorian buildings. The High Street Inferior is the main route northwest, passing the **Sarah Siddons** pub, converted from the 1755 birthplace of the great actress. High Street Inferior swiftly comes to a car-congested crossroads. Straight ahead, Ship Street descends down to the **River Usk**, a bridge crossing the Usk next to the point where the smaller Honddu River flows in from the north. Over the Usk, the southern suburb of **Llanfaes** is best known for its Dominican **friary**, whose ruined thirteenth-century church is now the centrepiece of **Christ College** school, on the immediate western side of the Usk.

From the town centre crossroads, High Street Superior goes north, past the long **Market Hall**, home of a twice-weekly produce market (Tues & Fri) and, on the third Saturday of each month, an excellent **craft market**. The road becomes The Struet, and passes **Hamilton House and Garden** at #13 (Mon–Fri 10am for a 1hr guided tour; £2.50; ☎01874/610200), a unique attempt to restore a timber merchant's Regency town-house as accurately as possible. Inside the house, every surface has been sampled and tested to ensure materials and colours are as authentic as possible, an ethic continued outside where flowers – lavender, asters, roses, and various species unfamiliar to modern gardeners – have been selected according to pollen analysis and shaped into a garden in the Ornamental Picturesque style. Work won't be completed until 2002 at the earliest, but it already gives an insight into life here in the 1830s, and seeing the restoration in progress is a bonus in itself.

Off to the left, over the rushing waters of the Honddu, Priory Hill climbs up to the stark grey buildings of the monastery settlement, centred on the **cathedral**, or Priory Church of St John the Baptist. The building's dumpy external appearance belies its lofty interior, graced with a few Norman features intact from the eleventh-century priory that was built here on the site of a probable earlier Celtic church. The hulking Norman font sits at the western end of the nave, near the entrance, from where the south aisle runs down to the most interesting of the many family memorials, the **Games monument** (1555), made up from three oak beds and depicting an unknown woman whose hands remain intact in prayer, but whose arms and nose have been unceremoniously hacked off. The fine vaulting in the elegant choir is the nineteenth-century work of prolific restorationist Gilbert Scott, who worked on St Asaph and St David's cathedrals, and designed St Pancras Station in London. There's a mildly interesting, **heritage centre** (Easter–Sept Mon–Sat 10.30am–4.30pm, Sun 2–4pm; free) in a converted sixteenth-century tithe barn in the cathedral close. Among the gilded vestments lies the unusual Cresset Stone, a large boulder indented with thirty scoops in which to place torches.

Between the cathedral and the River Usk, the few remains of the town's **castle** are moulded into the walls of the *Castle Hotel*. The end result is a powerful, if bizarre, amalgam that looks its best from along **The Promenade** by the River Usk, reached from the town-centre side of the river bridge. In high summer, motor and rowing boats can be rented along the river bank.

Eating and drinking

Despite its status as an important regional centre, Brecon is only tolerably well served for **food**. There are dozens of daytime cafés, and no shortage of belly-filling fare in the evening, but finding something really worthwhile isn't easy without leaving town. As a lively and cosmopolitan town, there's broad scope for **drinking** in Brecon, although some of the pubs in the near vicinity of the barracks are definitely worth avoiding.

Restaurants and cafés

Beacons Guest House, 16 Bridge St, Llanfaes. Open to non-residents for excellent, inexpensive lunches, teas and dinners, many inspired by traditional Welsh recipes.

Castle Hotel, Castle Square. Worth investigating for the good-value fixed dinner menu in this enjoyable restaurant, contained in the town's smartest hotel.

Fancy-A-Fayre, Market Hall Arcade. Perfect for filling your picnic basket with delicious cakes, quiches and pastries.

George Hotel, George St. Town pub with a conservatory restaurant serving hearty portions of well-prepared dishes, such as chicken and mushroom pie or lamb and apricot casserole, at around the £6 mark.

Seland Newydd, Pwllgloyw, four miles north on the B4520 (☎01874/690282). Peaceful country pub offering the best meals around Brecon, served either outside (lunch only) or in the elegant wood-beamed interior. Chicken on a bed of bubble and squeak might be followed by pan-fried sole with a prawn mousseline and lemon and raspberry syllabub.

Waterfront Bistro, Canal Basin. Airy waterside café and bistro that's open daily for substantial lunches or just a coffee, and for pre-theatre dinner whenever there's a show on. Mains £10–12.

Watergate Fish Bar, Ship St. Brightly lit traditional chip shop almost on the bridge itself, with a few tables.

Pubs

Boars Head, Ship St. Two very different bars: the front is basic and the best place to meet locals, whereas the back bar is loud and resembles a youth club.

Bull's Head, The Struet. Small and cheery locals' pub, with views over the Honddu River and towards the cathedral. Good-value food and occasional live music.

Gremlin Hotel, The Watton. Ancient pub with an informal atmosphere and great selection of bar snacks and larger meals (not served on Sun and Mon evenings).

Old Cognac, High Street Inferior. No-nonsense town pub, offering cholesterol-packed lunchtime food.

Sarah Siddons, High Street Inferior. Named after the famous actress, born here when the pub was known as the *Shoulder of Mutton*. A replica of Gainsborough's aloof portrait of her now forms the pub sign. A busy place, popular with off-duty soldiers.

Wellington Hotel, The Bulwark. Surprisingly unstuffy hotel bar, a frequent venue for live music, especially jazz.

Activities and entertainment

Just off the A470 (turn off at Libanus), six miles southwest of the town, the **Brecon Beacons Mountain Centre** (daily March–June & Sept–Oct 9.30am–5pm; July & August 9.30am–6pm; Nov–Feb 10.30am–4.30pm; ☎01874/623366) sits on a windy ridge amongst gorse heathland and overlooks some of the most inspiring scenery in the Beacons. As well as an excellent café, there are interesting displays on the flora, fauna, geology and history of the area, together with a well-stocked shop of maps, books and guides. Intentional lack of waymarking make these necessary for the walks that fan away from the centre around the lofty heath, and across the river valley to the more challenging peaks of Corn Du and Pen y Fan (see p.205). Buses leave Brecon for Merthyr, with a stop at Libanus school, from where it is a one-mile uphill walk along the lane next to the church up to the centre.

Four miles southeast of town, between the villages of Llanfrynach and Pencelli, the **Water Folk Canal Centre** has a small museum (Easter–Oct daily except Fri 10am–5.30pm; £1.50) stuffed with canal art and memorabilia and which, more excitingly, also runs horse-drawn barge trips (Easter–July, Sept & Oct Wed, Sat & Sun noon & 3pm; August daily noon & 3pm; £3.50).

Brecon is well served for sports and recreational facilities: the old-fashioned Coliseum **cinema** is on Wheat Street (☎01874/622501), near the central crossroads, and there's an indoor **swimming pool** and impressive new leisure centre a mile northeast of the centre on the Cerrigcochion Road at Penlan (☎01874/623677). Brecon has several **bike rental** outlets: handiest to town is Brecon Cycle Centre, 9 Ship St (☎01874/622651) who offer quality machines for £15 a day; Ben's Bike Hire in Pencelli, five miles southeast of Brecon (☎01874/665635), are a little cheaper

---

THE TAFF TRAIL

The whole of the Brecon Beacons National Park lends itself nicely to cycling, but to give your exploration some structure, consider riding a section of the **Taff Trail**. This 55-mile route from Brecon to Cardiff Bay passes through a wonderful cross-section of south Welsh scenery: the Usk Valley, the Brecon Beacons uplands, former coal mining Taff Valley and urban parkland. Most of the route – which is open to hikers and bikers – is on forest trails, designated pathways and country lanes and is seldom steep, though you can always ease the burden by stopping off at pubs and restaurants along the way. These are marked on the free *Taff Trail* fold-out map, available from tourist offices and park information centres, which also shows the location of train stations and the occasional trail-side campsite.

Perhaps the best way to tackle the whole trail is to start in Brecon (where there is bike rental), ride to Cardiff – downhill almost all the way – then catch a train back to Merthyr Tydfil and ride the fifteen miles back over the hills to Brecon. Keen riders could do this in a day, though you might prefer to break the journey in Pontypridd or Cardiff.

The Usk Valley

The wide, fertile Usk Valley runs southeast from Brecon running parallel to the Monmouth and Brecon Canal and effectively dividing the Brecon Beacons proper from the Black Mountains to the northeast. The A40 provides the access through the region, connecting Brecon with Tretower, Crickhowell and Abergavenny, and providing a backbone for dozens of minor lanes which twist south over the Brecon Beacons or north into the bucolic headwaters of some of the Usk's tributaries. As the valley is home to the vast majority of the national park's residents, and consequently contains the greatest concentration of facilities for visitors, you'll probably find yourself spending a fair bit of time here.

While Brecon gives the most direct access to the park's highest peaks, you may find that the Usk Valley offers better walking bases. **Talybont-on-Usk** isn't much of a place, but is well set for access to the eastern Beacons (see box, overleaf). The village of **Llangorse** is mainly notable for the ropes course that provides a good wet-day diversion; Talgarth is the closest town to the northern Black Mountains; and the fourteenth-century manor house at **Tretower** certainly warrants a couple of hours.

For an extended stay you'll probably be better off in either Crickhowell or Abergavenny. There's not a whole lot to actually do in either place, but both are well served with hotels, restaurants and pubs, and access to the Black Mountains to the north is unparalleled.

Talybont and around

Tidy little **TALYBONT-ON-USK**, six miles southeast of Brecon, is top-heavy with bridges, a testament to its transport history. A disused rail bridge cuts across the main street, an aqueduct carries a canal over the Caerfanell River, and a classic example of an old Dutch-style drawbridge takes a small lane over the canal. This lane heads south from the Talybont, through the hamlet of **Aber**, to the 323-acre **reservoir**, built to supply water to Newport, and crowded in by steep, conifer-forested hillsides. The lane continues up onto the rocky hillsides, past the waterfalls on the Nant Bwrefwr and beyond to the isolated and hauntingly beautiful **Neuadd reservoirs** in the north, a good starting point for walks to the summits of Pen y Fan and Corn Du along the old "Gap" road (see box, p.205), or, to the south, the busier and more popular **Pentwyn** and **Pontsticill** (aka Taf Fechan) **reservoirs**. Car parks, snack bars and signposted forest walks form the bulk of most people's experience of these latter two reservoirs, although two eastbound paths at either end of the Pontsticill reservoir enable escape from this in favour of a fairly steep climb up the rocky slopes for wonderful views over the lakes. Below Pontsticill, the tiny **Brecon Mountain Railway** (April–Oct mostly daily; ☎01685/722988) shuttles passengers along a two-mile section of track on the eastern bank of the reservoir and down to the hamlet of **Pant**, just north of urban Merthyr Tydfil (see p.87).

Regular Brecon–Crickhowell **buses** stop at Talybont. Amongst the village **pubs**, the *White Hart* is enjoyably basic and the *Star* (☎01874/676635; ②) more inspired in its choice of food, jazz and theme nights, range of beers and good **B&B**. For a little more, you're better served at the *Usk Inn* (☎01874/676251, fax 676392, *mtatusk@aol.com*; ④), a village pub transformed into country inn with very good rooms and food. Aber, a little over a mile south of Talybont, has very good B&B at *Abercynafon Lodge* (☎01874/676342; ③), and a further mile up the road you can **camp** at the north end of Talybont Reservoir (☎01874/676307 or 676605).

A CIRCULAR WALK AROUND THE EASTERN BEACONS

Note: The OS Outdoor Leisure 1:25,000 map #13 (Brecon Beacons Eastern Area) is recommended for this walk.

Starting at the Blaen-y-glyn car park (SO 064169), on the lane between Talybont and Pontsticill/Merthyr, cross the road and take the track opposite that threads down to the right and passes rapids and falls along the River Caerfanell. Continue for about 600 yards, over a concrete bridge, and take the left path at the fork. This heads uphill, with the plantation forest to your left (and a good comparison with the natural woodland across the valley to the right). Continue into the forest and take the left fork where the path splits into three. After about 300 yards, you come to a clearing, where you take a sharp left over the stream and continue past the picnic tables, fording another stream and taking a sharp right uphill to a fence and stile. Turn right along the forest track, then left at the Torpantau car park entrance, and head up the steep bank for about a third of a mile – the views over the valley of Glyn Collwn are superb here. At the corner of the forest, bear slightly right, away from the stream. It's a hard climb up to the ridge of Craig y Fan Ddu, straight ahead, but well worth it for some stunning vistas. The path swings left, shortly approaching the lip of the slopes to the right. Keep the ridge immediately to your right, cross the stream, and continue across the boggy moorland, still climbing gently. After about a mile, there's a short descent to Bwlch y Ddwyallt, where five paths converge.

Take the first right path, and, after 100 yards or so, strike left, crossing below a peat bog. Cross a stream and head towards the bottom of the rocky edge ahead. A monument, lying between two heaps of twisted metal, marks the spot of a wartime RAF plane crash. Climb up the slope to the top of the ridge, and then walk along its rim in a southeasterly direction, keeping the quarried cliffs to your right. After half a mile, you'll reach a spur of land with steep slopes on either side. Head straight on, down the steep grassy slope in front, across a patch of moor and then right, following a fence, down into the valley. Cross the stile and turn left along the river path, past some little waterfalls. At the footbridge, you can either cross the river and return by the original path, or continue on this bank, past numerous falls and pools. Either way, the road and car park are reached in about 700 yards.

Llangorse and around

North of Talybont, the B4560 threads its way four miles through rolling countryside to the pristine village of **LLANGORSE** (Llangors), sheltering in the western lee of the Black Mountains. The settlement is a mile northeast of the reed-shored **Llangorse Lake** (Llyn Syfaddan) which was noted for its miraculous properties (blood-red water, groaning sounds and mythical lost city) in medieval times, but is a rather more pedestrian affair today. A popular outdoor recreational centre, the lake hosts rowing, canoeing, fishing, windsurfing and yachting, as well as mountain-bike and caravan rental and the *Lakeside* campsite (☎01874/658226). Most of the activity around here (particularly if you've got kids to entertain) takes place a mile south of the village at Gilfach farm, site of the **Llangorse Rope Centre** (daily 10am–10pm; ☎01874/658272, fax 658280), an imaginative joint indoor climbing wall and ropes confidence course geared towards youth groups but open to all. Experienced climbers (£3.75 plus £1 membership) can rent gear cheaply, and there are activity sessions (£7 for 1hr; £10 for 2hr) introducing you to climbing and abseiling. The farm is also home to a **riding centre** that offers off-road trekking for beginners (£8 for 1hr), riding for the somewhat skilled (£15 for 2hr) and hacking for the experienced (£19 for 2hr).

The rope centre has an inexpensive **bunkhouse**; preference is generally given to groups using the centre, but it's worth asking, particularly during the school holidays. A mile up the road in Llangorse itself, there's top-quality **B&B** at *Pen-y-Bryn House*

(☎01874/658606, fax 658280; ②). The best food is at the excellent, moderately-priced *CXVII Castle Inn*, while the friendly *Red Lion* (☎01874/658238; ②), on the corner of the lane leading down to the lake, offers superb food and decent B&B.

Five miles north of Llangorse, **TALGARTH** is a spirited and friendly village built around its unusual town hall and the brooding bulk of **St Gwendoline's church** tower, constructed in the fourteenth century but harking back to Talgarth's position as a defence centre against the Norman invasion. The *Tower Hotel* on The Square (☎ & fax 01874/711253; ③) is the town's main centre for eating, drinking and **B&B**. There's also a cheerful independent hostel, *Joe's Lodge* (☎01874/711845) on the Hay Road. The *Bridge End Inn*, over the bridge from the *Tower Hotel*, is good for live music and a cheerful atmosphere, while the superb, centrally located *Book Shop Café* is good for snacking while perusing travel literature and maps.

Between Talgarth and the neighbouring village of **BRONLLYS** is **Bronllys Castle**, of which only a large twelfth-century cylindrical tower remains – climb to the top for stunning views up the Llynfi River valley and beyond to the light-washed peaks of the Black Mountains. There are some great places to **eat** and **sleep** around here: just north of Bronllys, the *Honey Café*, open daily until 10pm, has been around since 1935 and has newsy notice boards. Heading up the A470 brings you to the relaxing, fifteenth-century *Griffin Inn* (☎01874/754241, fax 754592, *www.griffin-inn.co.uk*; ⑤), serving delicious local dishes. In Llyswen, *Llangoed Hall* (☎01874/754525, fax 754545, *www.llangoedhall.com/llangoed*; ⑨) is a luxurious mansion once owned by Laura Ashley's husband, while just outside the village of Erwood and near A470, *Trericket Mill* (☎01982/560312; ①) offers good B&B, bunkhouse accommodation and camping.

Tretower

Twelve miles south of Talgarth, the solid round tower of the **castle and court** (daily: March 10am–4pm; April, May & Oct 10am–5pm; June–Sept daily 10am–6pm; £2.20; CADW) at **TRETOWER** (Tre-tŵr) was built to guard the valley pass, and still rises out of the valley floor, dominating the view from both the A40 and A479 mountain road. The bleak, round thirteenth-century tower replaced an earlier Norman fortification, and in the late fourteenth century a comparatively luxurious manor house was built a couple of hundred yards away over a sheep-filled field, gradually being expanded more over the ensuing years. In the summer, Shakespeare and more contemporary plays are acted out in the inspirational surroundings of the court (call ☎01874/730279 for details), with its family rooms and ostentatious, beam-ceilinged Great Hall facing in on the central cobbled courtyard and square sandstone gatehouse. With restoration work still underway, exposed plaster and beams give a good insight into late medieval building methods. An open-air gallery and wall walk enable you to view the site on the upper level, while an enjoyable, self-guided headset tour takes you around the site. If you're here on a Friday in June or July, join the free guided tour of the medieval garden, which begins at 2.15pm.

Six miles north of Tretower, the hamlet of **PENGENFFORDD** is a good base for walks in the Black Mountains, including up to the vast nearby Iron Age hillfort of **Castell Dinas**, whose 2500-year-old ditches and grass ramparts sit 1500ft up in a magnificent position under an outlying crop of the mountain range, commanding views far down the valley of the Rhiangoll river. The site's combined practicality for shelter, defence and settlement were used again when a medieval castle was built to complement Tretower at the other end of the valley, but a few isolated bits of rubble are all that remain. The *Castle Inn* sits at the base of Castell Dinas on the main road in Pengenffordd (☎01874/711353; ②) is a popular base for walkers, offering camping, B&B, bunkhouse accommodation, food and drink. *Upper Trewalkin Farm* (☎ & fax

01874/711349; ②), up in the lanes between Pengenffordd and Talgarth, is a brilliant farmhouse B&B with en-suite rooms, and staggering views over Castell Dinas and the Black Mountains.

Crickhowell

One of the liveliest bases in the Black Mountains, **CRICKHOWELL** (Crucywel), on the northern shore of the wide and shallow Usk, has a grand seventeenth-century **bridge** with thirteen arches visible from the eastern end and only twelve from the west, spawning many a local myth. Bridge Street rises from the river and up to the uninspiring mound of the ruined **castle** and the wide **High Street**. New Road runs parallel to Bridge Street from the river, passing the steeple of the town's fourteenth-century **church of St Edmund**. There really isn't that much to see in the town, but its spectacular northern backdrop is **Table Mountain** (1481ft), whose brown cone presides over the rolling green fields below. The best access is along the path that goes off by the electricity substation past The Wern off Llanbedr Road, at the summit are remains of the 2500-year-old hillfort (*crug*) of Hywel, from which the town, tumbling down the slopes below into the Usk Valley, takes its name. An alternative, and far shorter, route to Table Mountain starts from the delightful village of **LLANBEDR**, some two miles north of Crickhowell, and heads up alongside the stream behind the *Perth-y-pia* bunkhouse (see below). The views are amongst the best in the area. Many walkers follow the route to the north from Table Mountain, climbing two miles up to the plateau-topped limestone hump of **Pen Cerrig-calch** (2302ft).

Practicalities

Crickhowell has many facilities in quite a compact space. The enthusiastic **tourist office** (April–Oct daily 9am–1pm & 2–5pm; ☎01837/812105, *www.crickhowell.co.uk*) is in Beaufort Chambers on Beaufort Street. **Accommodation** is abundant, with a grandiose coaching inn, the *Bear Hotel*, on Beaufort Street (☎01873/810408, fax 811696; ④); and the cheerfully relaxed *Dragon* on the High Street (☎01873/810362, fax 811868; ②). For B&B, try the budget *Greenhill Villas* on Beaufort Street (☎01873/811177; ①) or the rooms with en-suite bathrooms at *Tŷ Gwyn* (☎01873/811625; ②) an impressive stone gatehouse on Brecon Road, just beyond Porth Mawr. For something a little more plush, base yourself at *Tŷ Croeso* (☎ & fax 01873/810573, *tycroeso@ty-croeso-hotel.freeserve.co.uk*; ③), a welcoming small hotel and restaurant in Dardy, close to the canal around a mile west of Crickhowell.

There's also the town-centre *Riverside Park* **campsite** on New Road (☎01873/810397). A mile north of town, just beyond the turning for Llanbedr, is the superb *Perth-y-pia* (☎01873/810050; ③), an elevated outdoor centre offering excellent B&B and hostel accommodation as well as home-cooked evening meals; there's also camping just opposite at *Tŷ-mawr* (☎01873/810164). Across the river from Llanbedr, *Gellirhydd Farm* (☎01873/810466; ①) offers great B&B and the chance to learn all kinds of woodcraft.

There's no shortage of places to **eat** and **drink** in and around Crickhowell. If dining to the strains of Cliff Richard whilst surrounded by floor-to-ceiling Cliff photos and memorabilia sounds like your cup of tea, head for the *Queen Coffee Tavern* on Standard Street, just off High Street, for straightforward breakfasts, burgers and sandwiches at low prices; otherwise, try the more soberly decorated *Cheese Press* on the High Street. Evening food is almost universally available in the town's pubs: the *Bear Hotel* (see above) wins legions of awards for its heavenly, pricier-than-average bar and restaurant food; the local delicacies on offer in the *White Hart* on Brecon Road are cheaper, and there's the similar but staid *Six Bells* on New Road. Hearty, if pricey, Welsh cuisine is available at *Tŷ Croeso* (see opposite). Down by the town bridge, the *Bridge End* pub, part of which is an old tollhouse, is a very fine bet for excellent food, including some impressive vegetarian selections.

The Crickhowell Adventure Gear shop, next to the market cross at 1 High St sells all of the predictable caving and walking paraphernalia, while Mountain and Water (☎01873/831825) offer canoeing, kayaking, climbing, orienteering and mountain activities.

Abergavenny

Although only a couple of miles and a few hills away from the iron and coal towns of the northern valleys, **ABERGAVENNY** (Y Fenni) owes its origins to the weaving trades and markets, giving it an entirely different feel. Despite Neolithic finds and the certainty that a small Roman outpost was situated here, the first main settlement in the town was around the Norman castle, which was built by the English king Henry I's local appointee, Hameline de Ballon, with the express aim of securing enough power to evict local Welsh tribes from the area, an important through route into Wales. Hostility to the Welsh reached its peak at Christmas 1175, when William de Braose, then lord of the town, invited Gwent chieftains to the castle, only to murder them all. The town grew, shaken badly by the Black Death (1341–51) and a routing by Owain Glyndŵr in 1404, but continued to prosper, thanks largely to the weaving and tanning trades that developed from the sixteenth century. The industries of Abergavenny prospered alongside its flourishing market, still the focal point for a wide area, drawing many people up from the valleys every Tuesday. In World War II, Hitler's deputy, Rudolf Hess, was kept in the town's mental asylum as a prisoner after his plane crash-landed in Scotland in 1941. He was allowed a weekly walk in the nearby hills, growing, it is said, to love the Welsh countryside. This combination of urban amenities and the vastly rewarding upland scenery on its doorstep is Abergavenny's main attraction today, making the town an excellent base for forays into the central and eastern sections of the Brecon Beacons.

Arrival and information

Abergavenny is well connected to the national rail network, with fast and frequent trains from Cardiff, Newport and Hereford stopping at its **train station**, on Station Road, half a mile southeast of the centre along the A4042. Buses depart in all directions from Swan Meadows **bus station**, right in the heart of things on Cross Street and adjacent to a joint **tourist office** (daily: April–Oct 9.30am–6pm; Nov–March 10am–4.30pm; ☎01873/857588, *www.abergavenny.co.uk*) and **Brecon Beacons national park office** (Easter–Sept daily 9.30am–5.30pm; ☎01873/853254, *www.breconbeacon.org*). The latter is especially good for maps, planned walking routes and leaflets on local wildlife, flora and fauna. Bob Hemmings in Abergavenny **rents bikes** for around £15 a day (call to arrange delivery on ☎01873/856563), as do Pedalabikeaway (☎01873/830219) which is located out of town but deliver. **Narrowboats** for exploring the Monmouthshire and Brecon Canal can be rented from the British Waterways office at nearby Govilon (☎01873/830328). **Concerts** and **theatre** take place in the spiky Victorian town hall on Cross Street (☎01873/852721) and the Melvill Theatre, Pen-y-pound (☎01873/853167).

Accommodation

On the whole, accommodation around Abergavenny is good and abundant, and extends beyond those listed overleaf to several moderate B&Bs on the Monmouth Road, between the town centre and the station, and the Brecon Road, on the western side of town. The nearest place to pitch a **tent** is *Pyscodlyn Farm Caravan and Camping Site* (☎01873/853271), two miles west of town off the A40.

Aenon House, 34 Pen-y-pound (☎01873/858708). About the cheapest B&B in town, this former Baptist teaching college is surrounded by appealing gardens. ③.

Allt Yr Ynys, Walterstone (☎01873/890307, fax 890593, *allthotel@compuserve.com*). Some nine miles northeast of Abergavenny and actually in England, this top-of-the-line country house hotel in a sixteenth-century manor still sports moulded ceilings and oak panelling, but has tastefully modernised rooms, an indoor pool, an award-winning restaurant and even clay pigeon shooting. ⑤.

Guest House, 2 Oxford St (☎01873/854823). Friendly town-centre B&B adjoining the popular local *Mansel Restaurant*; rooms have shared bathrooms. ③.

King's Arms, Neville St (☎01873/855074). Surprisingly cheap and well-appointed town-centre pub between Castle and High streets; most rooms have private bathrooms. ②.

Maes Glas, Raglan Terrace, Monmouth Rd (☎ & fax 01873/854494). Great B&B with shared bathrooms, close to the town's train station. ①.

Middle Ninfa Farm Bunkhouse, Llanfoist (☎01873/854662). Difficult-to-find self-catering accommodation located halfway up a mountain three miles south of Brecon. Bring sleeping bags, towels and food, and call for directions. ①.

Park Guest House, 36 Hereford Rd (☎01873/853715). Plush B&B in a beautiful Georgian town house near the station and town centre. Exceptionally good value. ①.

Pentre House, Brecon Rd (☎01873/853435). Roomy, friendly Georgian country house at the turning for Sugar Loaf mountain. Lovely gardens, wonderful breakfasts and a very welcoming atmosphere. Shared bathrooms. ①.

Pen-y-clawdd Court, Llanfihangel Crucorney (☎01873/890719, fax 890848). Exquisite and unusual Tudor manor house where great lengths have been taken to preserve the tenor: there's no electricity in the dining room (breakfasts are eaten by candlelight), and there's underfloor heating rather than radiators. En-suite rooms are all highly individual, and as if that weren't enough, they're growing a 3000-yew maze outside. ⑤.

Smithy's Bunkhouse, Lower House Farm, Pantygelli (☎01873/853432). Self-catering dormitory accommodation under the slopes of the Sugar Loaf a couple of miles north of town. It is only five minutes walk to a real ale pub, but you'll need to bring food and sleeping bags.

The Town

From the train station, Monmouth Road rises gently into the town centre, becoming Cross Street and, finally, High Street. Off to the right are Monk Street and, next to the blue-turreted Victorian Gothic town hall, Market Street, which runs down past the sites of the frenetic Tuesday (livestock) and Friday (produce) markets.

Any street heading left off Cross or High streets leads to Castle Street, where the dark, fragmented remains of Abergavenny's medieval **castle** moulder. The castle's keep was entirely remodelled in the nineteenth century, and left to sit in the middle of the shabby ruins like an incongruously ugly Lego model. The castle's only real saving features are its serene position near the River Usk, at the bottom of the bowl of surrounding hills, and its mildly interesting **town museum** (March–Oct Mon–Sat 11am–1pm & 2–5pm, Sun 2–5pm; Nov–Feb Mon–Sat 11am–1pm & 2–4pm; £1). Displays cover the town's history, using photographs and billboards, and re-created interiors including a saddlery, a sanitized Border farmhouse kitchen of 1890 and Basil Jones' grocery shop, once on Main Street. After the death of Jones' son in 1989, the contents of the shop were transported to the museum lock, stock and biscuit barrel. Some of it was recent, but much of it dated from the 1930s and 1940s – WWII vegetable tins and decorations marked for the coronation of Edward VIII that never happened – and some dating back to the nineteenth century. You can get a good idea of how it might have looked *in situ* by visiting the outdated Saddler's stationers, on Main Street just uphill from the imposing *Angel Hotel* – even buying a newspaper here takes three times as long as normal.

Abergavenny's parish **church of St Mary**, on Monk Street, contains some superb effigies and tombs that span the entire medieval period. Originally built as the chapel of a small twelfth-century Benedictine priory, the existing building goes back only as far as the fourteenth century, although some of the monuments within predate the building itself. There are effigies of members of the de Braose family, along with the tomb and figure of Sir William ap Thomas, founder of Raglan Castle, and Dr David Lewis (died 1584), the first Principal of Jesus College, Oxford. Look too for the **Jesse Tree**, a recumbent, twice-lifesize statue of King David's father, which would once have formed part of an altarpiece tracing the family lineage from Jesse to Jesus. The Jesse Window at Llanrhaeadr in the Vale of Clywd (see p.387) tells the same tale.

Eating and drinking

There are places to **eat** everywhere in Abergavenny – from the legion of takeaways in Cross Street, Market Street and along the Brecon Road, to excellent lunchtime and evening food in virtually all of the town's pubs.

Great George, Cross St. Young and lively pub, especially appealing for the weekend discos and Sunday evening live music.

Great Western, Station Rd. Nostalgia-soaked railway pub next to the station, with inexpensive, dependable food.

Greco, Cross St. A huge place, great for piles of cheap cholesterol. Open until 7.30pm daily.

Greyhound Vaults, Market St. Great for a wide range of tasty, moderately priced Welsh and English specialities, including the best vegetarian dishes in town.

Hen and Chickens, Flannel St, off High St. Staunchly traditional pub, with the best beer in town and a separate dining room for food.

Somerset Arms, Victoria St, by the junction of Merthyr Rd. Soothingly old-fashioned locals' pub with cheap, hearty food and excellent real ale.

Sue's Coffee House, Flannel St. Good for daytime snacks of the sandwiches, soups and salads variety.

Swan, behind the tourist office on Cross St. Endearingly shabby town-centre hotel pub, with a good bar menu.

Trading Post, 14 Neville St. Coffee house and bistro that's at the sophisticated end of Abergavenny eating; great for reading the paper over a cappuccino or tucking into £6–10 mains ranging from tortillas and chicken to tortellini and pizza.

Walnut Tree Inn, on the B4521 at Llanddewi Sgyrrid, two miles north of town (☎01873/852797). Legendary foodies' paradise, drawing diners from all over Britain. It's exorbitantly expensive (especially in the evening), but the food, from the owner's native Italy, is astounding. Closed Sun & Mon.

The Black Mountains

The northeasternmost section of the Brecon Beacons National Park is known as the **Black Mountains**, not to be confused with its singular namesake forty miles west. Far quieter than the central belt of the Brecon Beacons, the Black Mountains combine some of the awesome remoteness of Fforest Fawr with the dry terrain and excellent walking of the central Beacons. The wide valley of the River Usk – home to Tretower, Crickhowell and Abergavenny – divides the Beacons heartland from the Black Mountains, whose sandstone range rises to better defined individual peaks than can be found in the western end of the national park. The only exception to the unremitting sandstone is an isolated outcrop of limestone, long divorced from the southern belt, that peaks due north of Crickhowell at Pen Cerrig-calch.

Unlike the Black Mountain or Fforest Fawr to the west of the park, the Black Mountains have the feeling of a landscape only partly tamed by human habitation. Tiny villages, isolated churches and delightful lanes are folded into the undulating green landscape. Close to hand there is immediate access from the town to the three south-ernmost lumps of the Black Mountains, **Blorenge**, **Sugar Loaf** and **The Skirrid** – really only a taster for the remote beauty further north.

The most popular and rewarding areas to walk are in the east of the mountains, along the lane past Llanthony Priory and along the southern band of peaks, easily reached from Abergavenny and Crickhowell, notably Pen Cerrig-calch (see p.214), Table Mountain (see p.214) and the Sugar Loaf. The mass of rippling hills in the centre and to the north are less easy to reach, although a couple of good paths cross the contours.

Blorenge, Sugar Loaf and The Skirrid

From the grounds of Abergavenny Castle, the surrounding skyline is dominated by three southern outposts of the Black Mountains that climb out of the river plain. To the southwest is **Blorenge** (1834ft), a corruption of "Blue Ridge", accessible from the road that strikes off the B4246 a mile short of Blaenafon. The open road climbs the shale- and sheep-covered slopes to the car parks near the radio masts. An easy walk from here leads across boggy heathland to a long cairn at the summit, from which there are some glorious views south over the old mining region and north over the Usk valley, Abergavenny and the Black Mountains. When the winds comply, you'll frequently see **hang gliders and paragliders** perfecting their art from the summit, a piece of land recently bought from the National Coal Board by the south Wales chapter of their gov-erning body. There is a steeper ascent of the Blorenge from **Llanfoist**, a mile southwest of Abergavenny, which cuts past the church and under the canal before zigzagging up the mountain.

The broad and smooth cone of **Sugar Loaf** (1955ft) commands the Black Mountains foothills to the northwest of Abergavenny. Falling away from its summit are paths that scour the windswept slopes before descending to tiny villages in the valleys of the Usk, the Grwyne Fawr and the Grwyne Fechan. The easiest ascent is from the south, taking the right fork of Pentre Lane off the A40, half a mile west of Abergavenny, and follow-ing the road that climbs Mynydd Llanwenarth. A longer, but fairly easy climb goes from the Rholben or Deri Spurs, to the immediate east of Mynydd Llanwenarth; on the north side of the mountain, from the Fforest Coal Pit down by the Grwyne Fawr, the most glo-rious ascent is also the longest.

At 1595ft, **The Skirrid** (Ysgyryd Fawr) is the most eye-catching mountain in the area. Shooting up from the Gavenny valley, three miles northeast of Abergavenny, the hill almost seems man-made in its neatness: the gentle green fields climb about halfway, stopping suddenly in favour of purple scrub and bracken. The best path, although it is still a steep ascent, leads from the lay-by on the B4521 just short of the *Walnut Tree Inn* in Abergavenny (see overleaf). The almighty chasm that splits the peak is said to have been caused by the force of God's will on the death of Christ, a the-ory that has drawn Saint Michael and legions of ensuing pilgrims to this bleak, inhos-pitable but breathtaking spot. At the summit, a few leaning boulders are the sole remains of a forbidden chapel built by persecuted Catholics.

The Vale of Ewyas

In total contrast to the urban blights in the north valleys just a few miles away, the northern finger of Monmouthshire and the extreme eastern boundary of the Brecon Beacons National Park, stretching along the English border, is one of the most enchanting and reclusive regions in Wales. The main A465 Hereford road leads north out of Abergavenny, passing the surreal mound of The Skirrid on the right-hand side.

Six miles out of town, the road bypasses the village of **Llanfihangel Crucorney**, where a lane diverges off to weave through the Vale of Ewyas along the bank of the Honddu River, past the remote village of **Cwmyoy** with its wonky, subsided church, and on to the crumbling old religious institutions of **Llanthony Priory** and **Capel-y-ffin**. Parallel to the Honddu, a couple of miles and some impressive mountains to the west, is the **Grwyne Fawr**, a sparkling river that flows through the heart of some of Wales' most peaceful and gentle countryside, a patchwork of lush fields moulded along improbably shaped hills. Folded amongst the contours is one of the country's most perfect small churches at **Partrishow**. There is no useful bus service in this area.

Llanfihangel Crucorney, Partrishow and Cwmyoy

Better geared up to suck in the tourists than anywhere else in these parts, the village of **LLANFIHANGEL CRUCORNEY** (Llanfihangel Crucornau, the Holy Place of Michael at the Corner of the Rock) is named in honour of the tales of St Michael and The Skirrid (see opposite). On the main village street, quietened by the new bypass, are the odd fifteenth-century **church**, whose tower is divided from the nave by an abandoned roofless section, and the **Skirrid Inn**, which makes bold claims to be the "oldest pub in Wales", a fact singularly difficult to prove.

From the village, the main road through the valley heads north into the beautiful Vale of Ewyas, along the banks of the Honddu River. After a mile, a lane heads west towards the enchanting valley of the **Grwyne Fawr**, lost deep in the middle of quiet hills. The road is well worth following, if only for the discovery of the hamlet of **PARTRISHOW**, where a bubbling tributary of the Grwyne Fawr trickles past the delightful **church** and **well** of St Issui. First founded in the eleventh century, the tiny church was remodelled in the thirteenth and fourteenth centuries, with major restoration work needed in 1908 to prevent it collapsing. The finest interior feature is the lacy fifteenth-century rood screen, carved out of solid Irish oak and adorned with crude symbols of good and evil, most notably in the corner, where an evil dragon consumes a vine, a symbol of hope and well-being – the rest of the whitewashed church breathes simplicity by comparison. Of special note are the wall texts painted over the apocalyptic picture of a skeleton and scythe. Before the Reformation, such images were widely used with the intent of teaching an illiterate population about the scriptures; however, King James I ordered that such "Popish devices" should be whitewashed over and repainted with scripture texts. Here, the ghostly grim reaper is once again seeping through the whitewash. Encased in glass by the pulpit is a rare example of a 1620 Bible in Welsh.

Back on the main, the A465 winds its way on the valley's western side, past the fork at the *Queen's Head* pub (☎01873/890241; ④), excellent for B&B and pony trekking, and a bargain place to **camp**. It's well worth taking the little lane that peels off the main road here, as it dips down over the river and into the village of **CWMYOY**, where all eyes are drawn to the amazing spectacle of the **parish church of St Martin**, whose age and history are shrouded in uncertainty, and which has subsided substantially due to geological twists in the underlying rock. Nothing squares up: the tower leans at a severe angle from the bulging body of the church and the view inside from the back of the nave towards the sloping altar, askew roof and straining windows is unforgettable.

Llanthony

Four miles further into the Vale of Ewyas, the hamlet of **LLANTHONY** is nothing more than a small cluster of houses, an inn and a few outlying farms around the wide-open ruins of **Llanthony Priory** – a grander setting, and certainly a quieter one, than

Tintern Abbey (see p.65). Though on a far more modest scale than Tintern, Llanthony has the edge in many respects. Whereas Tintern has grown into a mini-industry, supporting garish restaurants and shops around the ruins, Llanthony remains much as it has been for 800 years, retaining a real sense of spirituality and peace against a superior backdrop of river and mountain. Its origins are swaddled in myth and hearsay, but the priory is believed to have been founded on the site of a ruined chapel around 1100 by Norman knight William de Lacy, who, it is said, was so captivated by the spiritual beauty of the site that he renounced worldly living and founded a hermitage, attracting like-minded recluses and forming Wales' first Augustine priory. The church and outbuildings still standing today were constructed in the latter half of the twelfth century. Roving episcopal envoy Giraldus Cambrensis visited the emerging priory church in 1188, noting that "here the monks, sitting in their cloisters, enjoying the fresh air, when they happen to look up at the horizon behold the tops of mountains, as it were touching the heavens". Now that this same church, with its row of wide, pointed transitional arches and squat tower, is roofless, the heavens (and the sheep-speckled Black Mountains) are even nearer. A track behind the ruins winds up to the Offa's Dyke Path (see p.236), straddling the England–Wales border on its lofty, windy ridge.

Fashioned out of part of the tumbledown priory, the *Abbey Hotel* here (☎01873/890487, fax 890844; ②) was built in the eighteenth century as a hunting lodge and has a cellar bar with arches constructed in the twelfth century. It's usually closed on winter weekdays, and you'll be required to book in for both nights on summer weekends. A hundred yards along the road from the priory is the thick-set *Half Moon Inn* (☎01873/890611; ①), home of superb beer, good-value food and comfy beds.

Capel-y-ffin and the Gospel Pass

From Llanthony, the road climbs slowly alongside the narrowing Honddu River before coasting gently along by ruined farmhouses for four miles to the isolated hamlet of **CAPEL-Y-FFIN**, just yards over the Monmouthshire border in Powys. Locked in the middle of sheer hills, Capel-y-ffin has a strangely devotional feel, due principally to the fact that the village is made up of little more than two chapels and a curious ruined monastery. The minute, whitewashed eighteenth-century chapel on the main road has an apt text inscribed into one of its windows: "I will lift up mine eyes unto the hills from whence cometh my help" – at Capel-y-ffin, you can barely help doing anything else. A lane forks off by the phone box, leading up to the ruins of the privately owned (and confusingly named) **Llanthony Monastery**, founded in 1870 by the Reverend Joseph Lyne. The religious order failed to survive his death in 1908, but the place later became a self-sufficient outpost of the art world when, in 1924, it was bought by English sculptor, typeface designer and mild eccentric Eric Gill, whose commune, a motley collection of artists and their families, drew much of their creative inspiration from the tiny valley of Nant y Bwch, threaded by a stream that runs by the lane, which can be followed all the way to its source underneath the commanding heights of **Rhiw Wen**.

From Llanthony Monastery, the road narrows as it weaves a tortuous route up into the **Gospel Pass** and onto the glorious roof of the Black Mountains (see p.217). A howling, windy moor by **Hay Bluff**, five miles up from Capel-y-ffin, affords vast views and terrific walking over spongy hills, punctuated by bleak crags and the distant view of tiny villages. The road drops just as suddenly as it climbed, descending five miles into Hay-on-Wye.

Facilities are scarce around here; *The Grange* (☎01873/890215; ②) is a comfortable B&B with extensive grounds (including a portion of Offa's Dyke) in which you can pitch a tent. Capel-y-Ffin **YHA hostel** (☎01873/890650; closed Dec & Jan, Nov & Feb weekends only), which also has **camping**, lies a mile up the valley from the hamlet itself.

Hay-on-Wye

The sleepy border town of **HAY-ON-WYE** (Y Gelli), at the northern tip of the Brecon Beacons, is known to most people for one thing – books. Hay saw its first secondhand bookshop open in 1961 and has since become a bibliophile's paradise, with just about every spare inch given over to the trade, including the old cinema, houses, shops and even the ramshackle stone castle. There are now over thirty bookshops here – the largest containing around half a million tomes – alongside an increasing number of antique shops and galleries. Unfortunately, there has been a certain amount of cashing in on the town's popularity, and while you can almost always find what you want, you'll probably have to pay more than you'd expect.

As a border town full of non-local folk, Hay has little indigenous feel, although its setting amongst soft mountains, together with its creaky little streets, maintain a sense of unhurried charm. It's a fascinating place to visit, bursting alive in the summer with riverside parties, travelling fairs and a vast shifting population. In the last week of May, all fashionable London literary life decamps to Hay for the **Hay Festival of Literature** (☎01497/821217), held in venues around the town. The atmosphere at this time is superb, although accommodation gets booked up well in advance. At any time of the year, the beauty of the countryside surrounding Hay makes staying in the town a sensible option. South of the town, one of the most awesome mountain roads in south Wales climbs up into the Black Mountains and under the glorious viewpoint at Hay

© Crown copyright

Bluff before descending into the Gospel Pass and Vale of Ewyas. This is wonderful walking country, although the little ribbon of road laid seemingly casually across the springy moor can get horribly congested in high summer.

Arrival and information

Buses from Brecon and Hereford stop by the Oxford Road car park, next to the **tourist office** (daily: Easter–Oct 10am–1pm & 2–5pm; Nov–Easter 11am–1pm & 2–4pm; ☎01497/820144, *www.hay-on-wye.co.uk*), which is housed in a grim craft centre and publishes an invaluable **free booklet** detailing the towns bookshops, galleries, restaurants and bars. Staff can also advise on and book local accommodation, which gets booked up long in advance for the festival. **Bike** (and **canoe**) **rental** is available from Paddles & Pedals, yards away at 15 Castle St (☎01497/820604).

Accommodation

Belmont House, Belmont Rd (☎ & fax 01497/820718). Classy Georgian guesthouse on the continuation of Broad Street with spacious rooms. ③.

Brookfield House, Brook St (☎01497/820518). Small, friendly B&B in a sixteenth-century listed building off Lion Street. ①.

Cwm Dulais House, Heol-y-Dwr (☎01497/820179). Cheerful B&B on the back road behind Lion Street. ①.

Old Black Lion, Lion St (☎01497/820841). Excellent accommodation in a captivating thirteenth-century inn, which favours candlelight in the evenings. ③.

Old Post Office, Llanigon, two miles south of Hay (☎01497/820008, *www.hay-on-wye.co.uk/oldpost*). A wonderful vegetarian, non-smoking seventeenth-century B&B which is well placed for local walks, including the Offa's Dyke Path (see p.236). ①.

Radnors End campsite (☎01497/820780 or 820233). A 5min walk from town, across the Wye bridge and on the road to Clyro, this is a beautiful setting overlooking Hay, with showers and washing machine on site.

Seven Stars, Broad St (☎01497/820886, fax 821488). Popular town pub near the clock tower, with a good range of bedrooms. ①.

Swan Hotel, Church St (☎01497/821188, fax 821424). The town's most formal hotel, with high-standard if somewhat sanitized rooms and classy dining. ⑤.

The Town

If you don't like books, you'll probably want to avoid Hay, as the written word is the chief concern of this small market town. The best bookshop to start sampling the wares is up the track towards the castle that starts opposite the tourist office, where you'll find Richard Booth's **Hay Castle Bookshop**, with racks of overspill books under canopied covers outside, together with honesty boxes for payment. The shop itself specializes in an unlikely mix of photography, transport, humour and American Indians, along with bindings sold by the shelf-foot (anything from £8 to £200 per foot) which are popular with interior designers and theme pub developers. You can also find many a tract containing the thoughts of King Richard and even a recording of *The King of Hay's Greatest Hits*, which includes an address by Booth. Here – or from the tourist office – you can pick up the invaluable, *Hay-on-Wye Booksellers & Printsellers* leaflet (free), detailing all of the town's literary concerns. Just beyond the Castle Bookshop is the **castle** itself, a fire-damaged Jacobean mansion built into the walls of a thirteenth-century fortress, and owned – like just about everything in Hay – by Richard Booth. The ruling monarch lives in part of the castle, affected by fires in 1939 and 1978, and is soon to open his Throne Room, a kind of devotional museum complete with "Royal" balcony.

Richard Booth, whose family originates in the area, opened the first of his Hay-on-Wye **secondhand bookshops** in 1961. Since then, he has built an astonishing empire and attracted other booksellers to the town, turning it into the greatest market of used books in the world. There are now over thirty such shops in the minuscule town, the largest of which – Booth's own flagship – contains around half a million volumes.

Whereas so many mid-Welsh and border towns have seen populations ebb away over the past fifty years, Hay is booming on the strength of its bibliophilic connections. Booth views this transformation of a hitherto ordinary little market town as a prototype for reviving an agrarian economy, depending on local initiatives and unusual specialisms instead of handouts from vast statutory or multinational corporations. He is unequivocal in his condemnation of bulky government organizations such as the Wales Tourist Board and the Development Board for Rural Wales, which, he asserts, have done little to stem the flow of jobs and people out of the region but which have succeeded instead in lining the pockets of a chosen few. This healthy distaste for hefty bureaucracy, coupled with Hay's geographical location slap on the Wales–England border and Booth's own self-promotional skills, led him to declare Hay independent of the UK in 1977, with himself, naturally, as king. He appoints his own ministers and offers "official" government scrolls, passports and car stickers to bewitched visitors. Although such a proclamation of UDI carries no weight officially, most of the people of Hay seem to have rallied behind King Richard and are delighted with the publicity – and visitors – that the town's continuing high profile attracts.

King Richard continues to take his self-appointed role seriously, pumping out a series of tracts and pamphlets on subjects dear to his heart, from the predictable rallying cries against supermarket developments to criticism of the town's high-profile annual literary festival, founded on the basis of Hay's bibliophilic reputation. Amongst the egotism and occasional self-righteousness, Booth hits many targets accurately, and his criticism of the homogenization and consequent decline of rural communities due to crass actions by government and big business is a theme to which many have subsequently been drawn. Booth's ideas and the events surrounding the 1977 delaration are laid out in his hard-bound autobiography *My Kingdom of Books* (Y Lolfa); you can also consult his Web site at *www.richardbooth.demon.co.uk*.

Walking from the tourist office to the bottom of Oxford Road and turning left into Castle Street, you'll come immediately to the **Hay Cinema Bookshop**, housed in the old town cinema and particularly good for new remaindered editions at low prices. Most of the town's bookish activity takes place in the other direction along Castle Street, where **H.R. Grant and Son** at no. 6 and **Castle Street Books** at no. 23 are the best in town for contemporary and historical guides and maps, the former selling works pertaining to nineteenth-century diarist Reverend Francis Kilvert and his winsome journals (see below). Beyond the open-sided, colonnaded **Buttermarket** at the top end of Castle Street, **Richard Booth's Bookshop**, 44 Lion St, is the largest shop in Hay, a huge, draughty warehouse of almost unlimited browsing potential. Lion Street dips down to Broad Street at the clock tower near **Y Gelli Auctions** (☎01497/821179), with regular sales of books, maps and prints. Further along tree-lined Broad Street is **West House Books**, best for Celtic and women's works.

Around Hay

From Broad Street, Bridge Street passes over the River Wye and climbs the hill towards **CLYRO**, little more than a mile away. Sheltering behind the busy A438, the village is home to a couple of small commercial art galleries trading on the strength of Clyro's connections with nineteenth-century wandering parson Francis Kilvert. Although he was vicar of Clyro for only seven years (1865–72), the village, its idyllic surroundings and its precisely recorded inhabitants featured prominently in his published diaries, drawing a steady trickle of pilgrims to see the place ever since.

The A438 heads south, through the one-horse hamlet of **LLOWES**, whose dowdy church of St Meilig houses a superb three-ton seventh-century Celtic cross. A mile further, a lane to the right climbs to **MAESYRONNEN**, where the low-roofed barn chapel, built in 1696, is the oldest surviving Nonconformist worship house in Wales. If it's locked, and you want to see the whitewashed interior with its old benches and stacked wooden pulpit, get the key from the Old Post Office in Ffynnon Gynydd, a mile up the lane.

Eating, drinking and entertainment

As a centre for walking, as well as the ubiquitous book trade, Hay is very well served for **food and drink** outlets. There are some good restaurants, and the pubs span the entire spectrum, from rustic bars little changed in decades to foodie haunts and cheerful places where you'll often find **live music**.

Blue Boar, Castle St. Tasteful wood-panelled bar on the corner with Oxford Road. Excellent beer and reasonable summer food.

Granary, Broad St. Unpretentious, moderately priced café and bistro, with a wide range of excellent vegetarian and meat-based meals, many made from local produce. Save space for wonderful desserts, ice cream and good espresso.

Kilverts, Bull Ring at the corner of Market St and Bell Bank (☎01497/821042). Warm and friendly locals' pub, with an imaginative, moderate to expensive menu which might extend to crab and prawn terrine or chargrilled sirloin with brandy and mushroom sauce. In summer, there's live Celtic, world and other music outdoors in the marquee most Thursdays and occasional weekends.

Old Black Lion, Lion St (☎01497/820841). Beautiful, olde-worlde pub that avoids any hint of kitsch. Superb, award-winning meals in the bar, or more robust fare in the pricier restaurant.

Pinnochio's, 2 Broad St (☎01497/821166). Relaxed, popular and reasonably priced Italian restaurant, with a delightfully convivial atmosphere on a warm summer's evening.

Swan Hotel, Church St. Good downstairs bar, popular for its pool tables and games machines. Bar snacks are hearty and good value, and more substantial meals are served at the formal and expensive *Cygnet* restaurant.

Three Cocks Hotel, Three Cocks, five miles southwest of Hay on the A438 (☎01497/847215). A stuffy hotel with an expensive and enjoyable tasty Belgian restaurant on its ground floor.

Three Tuns, Broad St. Time-warped pub with a dusty, flagstoned bar filled with disorganized mounds of memorabilia. Go easy on the lethal local draught cider.

THE POWYS HEARTLAND

Aside from the new industrial county boroughs, the only Welsh county with no coastline is **Powys**, which hugs the English border along its eastern side, the Welsh landscape occasionally penetrated by fingers of rural Shropshire and Herefordshire. Though the name of Powys harks back to a fifth-century Welsh kingdom, it was the local government reorganization in 1974 that created the current county boundaries, which extend from the fringes of the Glamorgan valleys through the sparsely populated lakelands of Radnorshire and up to the open expanses of the Berwyn Mountains. The southern reaches fall within the bounds of the Brecon Beacons National Park, but the true heartland – the particularly old counties of Radnorshire and Montgomeryshire – lie to the north. This is mostly quiet country, filled with small market towns where the introduction of an out-of-town superstore is the biggest thing to happen for decades. Between the towns, the contours of the impossibly green, sheep-flecked farmland are shaped by the glassy lakes and lively rivers that run down from the open moorland of the Cambrian Mountains, which form the county's spine.

Over the years, the quality and pace of life in Powys has proved irresistible to successive waves of hippies and "alternative" lifestylers who have progressively integrated with originally inward-looking farming communities to form an unexpectedly cohesive whole. It is this as much as the landscape and the detritus of ten centuries of Anglo-Welsh conflict that make the Powys heartland so appealing.

Towards the south of the county, four distinctly individual communities jointly form the **Wells towns**, each formed around a reputedly health-giving spring. Rain falling on the Welsh hills is put to more direct use in the **Elan Valley**, where four reservoirs form the focus of countryside noted for its abundance of red kites. To the east, close to the English border, **Presteigne** warrants an afternoon for its museum set up in the former judge's lodgings, while **Knighton** makes more of its position midway along the ancient defence of Offa's Dyke, drawing hikers and the merely curious. The archetypal small towns of Llanidloes and Montgomery do little to prepare you for **Newtown**, a former textile centre once at the heart of the socialist movement. This being Wales, there are a few castles dotting the landscape, the most alluring being the enormous **Powys Castle** in Welshpool, and **Chirk Castle**, which has guarded the entrance to the bucolic **Glyn Ceiriog** for the best part of eight hundred years.

The Wells towns

Straddling the old border of Brecknockshire and Radnorshire, around fifteen miles north of Brecon, mid-Wales' four spa towns are strung out along the Heart of Wales rail line and the main A483. Up until the eighteenth century, all were obscure villages, but then came the great craze for spas, and anywhere with a decent supply of apparently healing water joined in on the act. Royalty and nobility spearheaded the fashion, with spas such as Llandrindod gaining a reputation for licentiousness and a general air of lawless reverie. Come the arrival of the railways, the four Welsh spas became the domain of everyone, although each had its own clientele and appealed to different social groups. Locked in mountainous countryside at the foot of the eerily bleak **Mynydd Eppynt** range, the westernmost spa of **Llanwrtyd Wells** was a popular haunt of the Welsh middle classes in the nineteenth century. From the town, the River Irfon winds up into the mountains towards the hamlet of **Abergwesyn**, from which a narrow road climbs up, before dropping down into Tregaron (see p.277). Four miles east along the river, the waters of tiny, nondescript **Llangammarch Wells** contain barium chloride, a popular Victorian remedy for rheumatism and heart problems.

East of here, the larger town of **Builth Wells** is best known nowadays as the home of the huge Royal Welsh Showground, while the pretty, if somewhat twee and anglicized **Llandrindod Wells**, is the only one of the four in which the spa is in a decent state of repair. There are some excellent and fairly gentle walks around Llandrindod, as well as some beautiful, isolated churches – notably, at **Cefnllys** and **Disserth**.

Llanwrtyd Wells and around

Of the four spa towns, **LLANWRTYD WELLS**, around twenty miles northwest of Brecon, is the most appealing. It's friendlier, livelier, more Welsh, more unspoiled and in more beautiful surroundings than the other three. This was the spa to which the Welsh – farmers of Dyfed alongside the Nonconformist middle classes from Glamorgan – came to great eisteddfodau in the valley of the Irfon. The town shows obvious signs of its Victorian heyday, especially in the tall nineteenth-century town houses that line the streets.

Main Street runs through the centre of town, crossing the turbulent Irfon River just below the main square. On the opposite side of Main Street, a lane winds for half a mile along the river to the *Dolecoed Hotel*, built near the original sulphurous spring. Although the distinctive aroma had been noted in the area for centuries, it was truly "discovered" in 1732 by the local priest, Theophilus Evans, who drank from an evil-smelling spring after seeing a rudely healthy frog pop out of it. The spring, named **Ffynon Droellwyd** (Stinking Well), wells up in a dome-shaped extension in the fields behind the dilapidated red-and-white spa buildings.

The *Neuadd Arms* pub in the main square is the base for a wide range of bizarre and entertaining annual events, including a Saturnalian shindig in mid-January, a Man versus Horse race, a Drovers' Walk (both June), a town festival on the first weekend in August, walking expeditions, a snorkelling competition in a local bog (end of August), a beer festival in November and a New Year's Eve torchlight procession through the town.

Practicalities

Llanwrtyd's **tourist office** is in Tŷ Barcud on the main square (June–Aug daily 10am–5.30pm; Sept–May Mon–Sat 10am–4pm; ☎01591/610666, *llanwrtyd-wells.powys.org.uk*); it has all the usual facilities and also doubles as a **red kite centre**, with lots of information on this distinctive bird of prey. **Accommodation** – which should be booked well in advance when there are festivals on – includes the boisterous *Neuadd Arms* in the main square (☎01591/610236; ③), which also rents out **bikes**; the solidly Victorian *Belle Vue Hotel* a few yards away (☎01591/610237; ①); *Haulwen B&B*, Main Street (☎01591/610449; ①), and the cheaper *Oakfield House* on Dol-y-coed Road (☎01591/610605; ①). The *Stonecroft Inn* in Dolecoed Road (☎01591/610332) is a superb pub with great food and regular live folk, R&B and rock music as well as bunks in a small, self-catering **hostel** annexe. There's another independent hostel three miles southeast of town at *Caban Cwmffynnon* (☎01591/610638), just beyond the hamlet of **Cefn-gorwydd**, which is also the base of Dinefwr Treks, from where you can book biking, bird-watching and pony trekking trips. The moderate *Drovers' Rest* **restaurant** (☎01591/610246), by the river bridge, serves wholesome, traditional Welsh dishes and snacks. Right in the centre of town, the *Belle Vue* also provides cheap, hearty food, as does the *Neuadd Arms*.

Mynydd Eppynt and Llangammarch Wells

The gorgeous scenery around the town of Llanwrtyd Wells is one of its biggest attractions, and nowhere is this more evident than in the country to the south, where the remote **Crychan Forest** and the doleful mountains of the **Mynydd Eppynt** make up the northern outcrops of the Brecon Beacons and are most dramatically viewed from along the roads that snake across the moors from the towns of Garth and Builth. The bulk of the Eppynt has been appropriated by the British Army, as evidenced by the many red flags flying stiffly, signs warning you not to stop or touch anything and, saddest of all, the spooky **Drovers' Arms**, midway between Garth and Upper Chapel on the B4519, once a welcome respite for those droving cattle across the mountains and now a boarded-up wreck. Thankfully, another old drovers' inn, the gas-lit *Griffin* (☎01982/552778), on the B4520 between Upper Chapel and Builth, is thriving.

The B4519 descends dramatically from the Eppynt above a beautifully isolated valley, the **Cwm Graig Ddu**, from where the views over miles of soft farmland and rippling hills are overwhelming. At the bottom of the hill, a lane forks left, soon to join the River Irfon as it winds to **LLANGAMMARCH WELLS**, four miles east of Llanwrtyd. A mile before the village is the exquisite black-and-white-timbered **Lake Country House** (☎01591/620202, fax 620457, *www.ndirect.co.uk/~lakehotel*; ⑦), the home of the now-defunct barium well that attracted Lloyd George and foreign heads of governments searching for cures, and probably the best reason to come here. The village is excellent for fishing, but singularly dull otherwise.

Abergwesyn and the Pass

Although the drovers' roads and inns across the Mynydd Eppynt are now forbidden territory, the most spectacular of the drovers' routes is thankfully still open. The lane from Llanwrtyd meets up with another road from Beulah at the riverside hamlet of **ABERG-WESYN**, five miles north of Llanwrtyd. From here, a quite magnificent winding thread of a road – the **Abergwesyn Pass** – climbs up alongside the dwindling river, leaving it at the perilous **Devil's Staircase** and pushing up through dense conifer forests to wide, sparse valleys bereft of any sign of human habitation, framed by craggy peaks, bubbling waterfalls and blotches of gorse and heather. At the little bridge over the tiny Tywi River, a track heads south past an isolated, gas-lit **YHA hostel** (☎01974/298680; closed late Sept to April) at **DOLGOCH**. On the other side of the river, a new road channels past the thick forest on to Llyn Brianne (see p.150), a couple of miles further on. This is as remote a walking holiday as can be had in Wales – paths lead from Dolgoch, through the forests and hillsides to the tiny chapel at **SOAR-Y-MYNYDD** and beyond, over the mountains to the next YHA hostel, *Tŷ'n-y-cornel* (☎01550/740225; closed late Sept to late March), five strenuous miles from Dolgoch.

From Dolgoch, the Abergwesyn Pass continues over the massive, wide terrain, before dropping down along the rounded valley of the Berwyn River and into Tregaron (see p.277). Although the entire Llanwrtyd–Tregaron route is less than twenty miles in length, it takes a good hour to negotiate the twisting, narrow road safely. The old drovers, driving their cattle to Shrewsbury or Hereford, would have taken a good day or two over the same stretch.

Builth Wells and around

Very much the spa of the Welsh working classes, **BUILTH WELLS** (Llanfair ym Muallt) still caters to local people. An earthy agricultural town that has little to detain you, it's a useful centre for transport, cheap accommodation and entertainment, and can make a reasonable base for exploring the area around.

The most pleasant area in Builth is the verdant stretch along the Wye, below the architecturally undistinguished High Street, where you'll find the multipurpose **Wyeside Arts Centre** (☎01982/552555), converted out of the town's Victorian Assembly Rooms right by the Wye bridge. On the other side of the river, Builth's major modern source of prosperity, the **Royal Welsh Showground** (☎01982/553683), hosts numerous agricultural events, together with monthly flea markets and occasional specialized collectors' fairs. The massive **Royal Welsh Show**, a giant coming-together of all matters agricultural, takes place in mid-July.

Practicalities

Builth Road **train station** is nearly three miles north of the town and inaccessible by public transport. **Buses** depart from the car park alongside the river bridge, in which the **tourist office** (Easter–Sept daily 10am–6pm; Oct–Easter Mon–Sat 9am–12.30pm & 1.30–4.45pm; ☎01982/553307) is to be found. **Bike rental** is from Builth Wells Cycles at Fairleigh on Smithfield Road (☎01982/552923).

Accommodation comes cheap: try the *Lion Hotel* (☎01982/553670; ②), near the bridge on Broad Street, which has fairly ordinary rooms and budget dorms; the reliable *Owls* B&B (☎01982/552518; ②) on High Street is equally good value. For **food**, there are numerous cheap daytime cafés, and pubs such as the *Lion Hotel* and the *White Horse*, the liveliest pub in town with regular live music and quizzes.

Cilmeri

In the centre of **CILMERI**, an unassuming village that straggles along the main A483 road and rail line between Builth and Llanwrtyd, the *Prince Llywelyn* pub seems incongruously placed as a reminder of Welsh martyrdom in a fairly anglicized corner of eastern Wales. A hundred yards further up the main road towards Llanwrtyd, all becomes clear when you catch sight of a large, pointed granite boulder on a small hillock, said to be the spot at which, in December 1282, Llywelyn ap Gruffydd (the Last), was killed by English troops as he was escaping from the abortive Battle of Builth, four miles away. On realizing who they had killed, it is said that the English soldiers hacked off Llywelyn's head, whereupon it was dispatched to London and paraded victoriously through the city's streets. The English tablet by the monument calls Llywelyn "our prince". Its Welsh equivalent, tellingly, describes him as *ein llyw olaf* – "our last leader". Semantics aside, you are unlikely ever to see the monument without someone's fresh flowers adorning it.

Llandrindod Wells and around

If anything can sum a town up so succinctly, it is the shiny new plaque at **LLANDRINDOD WELLS** (Llandrindod) train station, commemorating the 1990 "Revictorianisation of Llandrindod railway station". The town has not been slow to follow suit, peddling itself as Wales' most upmarket Victorian inland resort as if the very life of the place depended upon it.

It was the railway that made Llandrindod, arriving in 1864 and bringing carriages full of well-to-do Victorians to the fledgling spa. Llandrindod blossomed, new hotels were built, neat parks were laid out and the town came to rival many of the more fashionable spas and resorts over the border. Even now, after faintly gloomy Builth, Llandrindod, with its overall feeling of space, can seem like a breath of fresh air. Its fine nineteenth-century buildings have been swabbed and sandblasted, ornate cast-iron verandas restored, and the spa brought back to some kind of life. There is plenty of accommodation in the town, a good range of things to do and the surrounding countryside – like all of mid-Wales – offers an endless variety of excellent walks.

Arrival, information and getting around

Buses arrive outside the **train station**, in the heart of town between the High Street and Station Crescent. Follow Station Crescent to the right, then turn right onto Temple Street to reach the **tourist office** (April–Sept Mon–Fri 9.30am–5.30pm, Sat & Sun 9.30am–5pm; Oct–March daily 10am–1pm & 2–5pm; ☎01597/822600), which holds details of the different local bus companies, their routes and times, and will also book accommodation. For a wider view of festivals and gigs in the area, consult the posters in the *Herb Garden* veggie restaurant (see p.230) or, on Middleton Street (which connects Station Crescent and Spa Road), Van's Good Food Shop, sheltering behind a brilliant-red frontage reminiscent of a gaudy Victorian traction engine. The town's largest annual event is, no surprise, August's **Victorian Festival**, which culminates in a firework extravaganza over the town lake. The longer-established annual town **eisteddfod** takes place in early October. **Market day** is Friday. **Bike rental** costs £15 a day from the Greenstiles (☎01597/824594) in the Automobile Palace right by the cycle exhibition (see opposite).

Accommodation

As rural mid-Wales' major tourist centre for the past 130 years, Llandrindod is well served for hotels, B&Bs, restaurants and cafés, even if its strait-laced past is reflected in the notable lack of pubs.

Disserth Farm, Disserth, three miles southwest of Llandrindod (☎01597/860277). Campsite in a beautiful riverside setting, next to the lovely village church.

Drovers Arms, Howey, almost two miles southwest of town (☎01597/822508, fax 822711, *www.drovers.co.uk*). Superb inn, with fine beer, food and accommodation. ②.

Greylands, High St (☎01597/822253). Tall Victorian red-brick house in the town centre, near the station and all amenities. ①.

Griffin Lodge Hotel, Temple St (☎01597/822432). Cheerful hotel in a sturdy Victorian house with some en-suite rooms. ①.

Guidfa House, Crossgates (☎01597/851241, fax 851875, *guidfa@globalnet.co.uk*). Very comfortable Georgian guesthouse almost three miles north of Llandrindod on the A483, with mostly en-suite rooms and great meals made from local produce. ②.

Kincoed Hotel, Temple St (☎01597/822656). Well-appointed old town-centre hotel, opposite Kwik Save supermarket. ①.

Metropole Hotel, Temple St (☎01597/822881, fax 824828). Large and faded but still elegant old spa hotel, the centrepiece of the town, with an excellent indoor swimming pool and a refined dining room that's open to non-residents. ⑤.

Rhydithon, Dyffryn Rd (☎01597/822624). One of the smartest and friendliest guesthouses in town, just off the High Street. ①.

The Town

Llandrindod's Victorian opulence is still very much in evidence in the town's grandiose public buildings, especially the lavishly restored **spa pump room** inside the pleasant **Rock Park**, with its trickling streams and well-manicured glens. European Union regulations only sanction the use of one of Llandrindod's spa taps in the café inside: a tiny (but more than ample) glass costs 10p, or you can step outside for a free gulp from the chalybeate fountain outside. A walk from the pavilion leads to "Lovers' Leap", a re-created bit of Victorian nonsense that's just a fake cliff with mediocre views over the river. The architecture around the park entrance is Llandrindod at its most confidently Victorian, with large, elaborately carved terracotta frontages and expansive gabling. From here, the **High Street** runs to the town centre, containing good record, antique, book and junk shops.

Behind the tourist office on Temple Street, you'll find the small **Radnorshire museum** (Tues–Thurs 10am–1pm & 2–5pm, Fri 10am–1pm & 2–4.30pm, Sat & Sun 10am–5pm; £1), where the exhibition is largely dedicated to excavated remains from the Roman fort at Castellcollen, a mile northwest of Llandrindod; kitsch Victoriana – including a small group of dolls – makes up the bulk of the rest. A new **red kite gallery** has been fitted out, with some stunning photos of airborne majesty and an video following a red kite's life cycle. Next to the museum is a glutinous **grotto**, a nineteenth-century whimsy built by a local doctor. West of Temple Street is Spa Road, from which a left turn leads down to the **Grand Pavilion**, home of tea dances and other genteel pursuits.

A town of water-taking and bridge tournaments seems a incongruous place for Britain's **National Cycle Exhibition** (daily 10am–4pm; £2.50), unobtrusively located in the so-called Automobile Palace at the corner of Temple Street and Spa Road. Most items in the nostalgic collection of over 250 bikes are original, though the oldest style is a reproduction Hobbyhorse from 1818. From there, pretty much the whole spectrum is covered: boneshakers, Ordinaries (aka penny-farthings), an eight-foot-high "Eiffel Tower" advertising bike from 1899, trikes, tandems and styles that look way too uncomfortable to ever have been a success.

Cefnllys

One of the most popular walks from Llandrindod heads east from the town along Cefnllys Road and through some beautiful wooded pockets to the banks of the River Ithon at **CEFNLLYS**, just under two miles away. A car park by the river leads on to

Shaky Bridge, whose name dates from when just two planks of wood connected the two banks – a more solid structure is in evidence today. On the other side of the Ithon, the castle mound rises to the right and you'll see the dumpy witch's-hat spire of the thirteenth-century **St Michael's church** ahead. In Victorian times, the rector removed the church roof to persuade the few remaining parishioners to travel into up-and-coming Llandrindod instead for worship. There was an outcry and a collection, and the roof was restored just two years later; photographs in the church show this strange period in its history. Back on the Llandrindod side of the river, **Bailey Einon Wood** is a designated nature reserve running three-quarters of a mile along the river, with some enchanting walks through its open glades.

Disserth

The other outlying former parish of Llandrindod is **DISSERTH**, lying a couple of miles to the south of the town, off the A483 at Howey, where the **church of St Cewydd** lies beside the Ithon in one of its most pastoral stretches. Resembling a fat medieval barn with a squat stone tower attached, the church escaped the restorative zeal of the Victorians, and its seventeenth-century wooden box pews were left intact, many with family names still discernible. The 1687 triple-decker pulpit, looking more like an auctioneer's lectern, also survives from pre-Victorian days.

Where the lane to Disserth heads west off the A483 at Howey, another lane also climbs up into the **Carneddau Hills**. About two miles after leaving the main road, a number of paths leave the lane and delve south into the rocky terrain, where glacial features such as moraines and abandoned blocks of stone litter the landscape.

Eating and drinking

Aspidistra, Station Crescent. Decent daytime café serving cheap and wholesome sandwiches snacks and meals.

Dillraj, Emporium Buildings, Temple St. Extremely classy but not overpriced Indian restaurant, opposite the tourist office.

Drovers Arms, Howey, almost two miles southwest of town (see overleaf). Real ale pub serving excellent, inexpensive traditional Welsh dishes as well as English and vegetarian fare; desserts are delicious.

Franky's, Temple St. Garish cellar bar-cum-bistro, compensated for by the good range of reasonable pizzas.

Herb Garden, Spa Rd. Earthy, inexpensive vegetarian eatery offering good, wholesome meals and snacks, together with occasional culinary theme evenings.

Llanerch Inn, Llanerch Lane. Central Llandrindod's only pub, and an excellent one. It's a cosy sixteenth-century inn that predates most of the surrounding town, with lots of pub games and a solid menu of good-value, well-cooked classics.

North and East Radnorshire

Before the reorganization of British counties in 1974, Radnorshire was the most sparsely populated county in England and Wales, and it's still a remote area, especially to the north and east. In the northwest, **Rhayader** is the only settlement of any real size, and, although fairly plain to look at, it's an excellent base, with some friendly pubs. Most people stay here in order to explore the wild, spartan countryside to the west of the town, a hilly patchwork of waterfalls, bogland, bare peaks and the four interlocking reservoirs of the **Elan Valley**, built at the beginning of the twentieth century and displaying a grandiose Edwardian solidity.

The countryside to the northeast of Rhayader is slightly tamer, with lanes and bridlepaths delving in and around the woods and farms, occasionally brushing through minute settlements like the village of **Abbeycwmhir**, named for the deserted Cistercian abbey that sits below in the dank, eerie valley of the Clywedog Brook. From here, the hills roll eastwards towards the English border and some of the most intact parts of **Offa's Dyke**, the eighth-century King of Mercia's border with the Welsh princes. The handsome town of **Knighton**, perched right on the border, is at the centre of the 177-mile path that runs along the dyke and is well geared-up for walkers and cyclists, with good accommodation and cheery pubs and cafés. Seven miles south and inches from England, the dignified little town of **Presteigne** contains a few reminders of its former importance as a county capital. The River Lugg flows through Presteigne from the Radnorshire hills, passing the isolated church at **Pilleth**, where Owain Glyndŵr captured Sir Edmund Mortimer, agent of the English king, in 1402.

Rhayader and around

RHAYADER (Rhaeder Gwy, literally "waterfall on the Wye"), ten miles west of Llandrindod Wells, has boomed during the twentieth century as mid-Radnorshire's principal base for exploring the spectacular hills and reservoirs of the Elan Valley. Although the waterfall invoked by the town's name virtually disappeared when the town bridge was built in 1780, the Wye still frames the town centre, running in a loop around the western and southern sides. Rhayader was a centre of the mid-nineteenth-century **"Rebecca Riots"**, when local farmers disguised themselves in women's clothing in order to tear down tollgates that were prohibitively expensive for itinerant and local workers.

Rhayader's handsome four main streets – named North, South, East and West – meet at a small clock tower in the centre of town. Fifty yards up East Street from the clock tower, there's a tiny **folk museum** (Easter–May Sat 10am–noon & 2–5pm; June to mid-July Fri 2–5pm, Sat 10am–noon & 2–5pm; mid-July to Sept Mon, Wed & Fri 2–5pm, Sat 10am–noon; free), good for its examination of the construction of local reservoirs in the Elan Valley, as well as an enjoyably haphazard clutter of agricultural and industrial artefacts from the area. Three miles north of town, just off the A470, is the lovely **Gilfach Farm nature reserve** (unrestricted access; free), showpiece of the Radnorshire Wildlife Trust. Within the 418 acres are meadows, oak forest, moorland and river habitats supporting a huge variety of wildlife and flora. The restored longhouse barn has now been kitted out as a **visitor and exhibition centre** (April–Sept Fri–Mon 10am–5pm; £1.50), showing live video footage from ten birds' nests around the reserve. To watch kites **feeding**, head to **Gigrin Farm** (£2.50), off South Road (the A470 from Builth) on the outskirts of town, where they are lured daily at 3pm (2pm in winter).

Practicalities

Buses stop in the main Dark Lane car park, opposite the **tourist office** (April–Oct daily 9.30am–12.30pm & 1.30–5.30pm; Nov–March Mon–Tues & Thurs–Sat 10am–4pm; ☎01597/810591, *www.rhayader.co.uk*), which shares its building with a leisure centre. Rhayader has always been well serviced for visitors, and eighteenth-century coaching inns still line the main streets. More modern **accommodation** includes the enjoyable *Elan Valley Hotel*, two miles west of Rhyader (see p.233), the en-suite *Bryncoed* B&B on Dark Lane (☎01597/811082; ①), opposite the tourist office, the *Elan Hotel* on West Street (☎01597/810373; ②), or *The Mount* on East Street (☎01597/810585; ①), a friendly B&B and the base for Clive Powell Mountain Bikes, from where you can rent **bikes** or arrange to join an organized cycling trip around the tracks of mid-Wales – there's also a shop outlet (☎01597/811343) opposite the *The Mount*. Almost two miles northeast of town, off the Abbeycwmhir Road, is *Beili Neuadd* (☎01597/810211; ②), a very relaxing farmhouse B&B. There's a **campsite** at *Wyeside* (☎01597/810183), a few hundred yards north of town off the A44, and a **laundry** on East Street.

During the day, *Carole's Old Swan* tearooms, at the junction of West and South streets, is the place to go for simple **food**. Evening meals are good at the moderate *Brynafon* restaurant (☎01597/810735), half a mile south on the road to Builth Wells, or the *Elan Valley Hotel* (see opposite). Despite having a population of less than two thousand, there are twelve **pubs** in Rhayader, most offering reasonable pub food. Try the old-fashioned *Cornhill Inn* on West Street, or, over Bridge Street in the small hamlet of **LLANSANTFFRAED CWMDEUDDWR**, usually shortened to Cwmdeuddwr, the tiny, ancient *Triangle*, whose toilets are on the other side of the street, and where darts players must stand in a special floor hole for fear of spearing the roof. More upmarket, the *Brynoafon* restaurant (☎01597/810735), half a mile south on the road to Builth Wells, is good for evening meals.

Elan Valley

Until the last decade of the nineteenth century, the untamed countryside west of Rhayader received few visitors, although the poet Shelley did holiday here: his honeymoon retreat at Nantgwlyllt was amongst the couple of dozen buildings submerged by the waters of the **Elan Valley** reservoirs, a nine-mile-long string of four lakes created between 1892 and 1903 to supply water to the rapidly growing industrial city of Birmingham, 75 miles away; in the 1950s, a supplementary reservoir at Claerwen, to the immediate west, was opened (see opposite). Although the lakes enhance an already beautiful and idyllic part of the world, the colonialist way in which Welsh valleys, villages and farmsteads were seized and flooded to provide water for England is something the tourist boards prefer to gloss over. The natural resentment against this has perhaps been best expressed by poet R.S. Thomas in his soulful elegy, *Reservoirs*:

> *There are places in Wales I don't go:*
> *Reservoirs that are the subconscious*
> *Of a people, troubled far down*
> *With gravestones, chapels, villages even;*
> *The serenity of their expression*
> *Revolts me, it is a pose*
> *For strangers, a watercolour's appeal*
> *To the mass, instead of the poem's*
> *Harsher conditions. There are the hills,*
> *Too; gardens gone under the scum*
> *Of the forests; and the smashed faces*
> *Of the farms with the stone trickle*
> *Of their tears down the hills' side.*

The "watercolour's appeal" of the Elan Valley is, nonetheless, extremely strong, not only for the landscape but the profusion of rare plants and birds in the area. **Red kites** are especially cherished – in the 1930s, when numbers were down to just a couple of breeding pairs, the Elan Valley looked set to enter the history books as their last outpost in Britain. Loss of habitat, along with nest robbing by collectors and poisoning at the hands of farmers were largely to blame, but conservation work undertaken by a few dedicated individuals saved the day. Since then, the kites have staged an impressive recovery (now numbering over five hundred individuals) and have become so common here they've started repopulating the rest of the country.

From Rhayader, the B4518 heads southwest four miles and just bypasses **ELAN** village, a curious collection of stone houses built in 1909 to replace the reservoir constructors' village that had grown up on the site. Just below the dam of the first reservoir, **Caban Coch**, the **Elan Valley visitor centre** (mid-March to Oct daily 10am–6pm;

☎01597/810898), incorporates a tourist office and a permanent exhibition that's sensitive to the English Victorian imperialism that built the reservoirs, stressing just how grim conditions were in nineteenth-century Birmingham, how rich the wildlife and flora around the lakes are and even how some of the water is now drunk in Wales. Frequent guided **walks** and even **Land Rover safaris** head off from the centre. The only place to **stay** here is the *Elan Valley Hotel* (☎ & fax 01597/810448, *www.rhayader. co.uk/elan*; ③), an imposing neo-Colonial pile on the Rhayader side of Elan village, which attracts a youngish clientele with its fine food (inexpensive bar meals and moderately priced formalish dining), drink and regular programme of music, literary and storytelling weekends and parties.

From the visitor centre, a road tucks in along the bank of Caban Coch to the **Garreg Ddu** viaduct, where a road winds along the bank for four spectacular miles to the vast, rather chilling 1952 dam on **Claerwen Reservoir**. More remote and less popular than the Elan lakes, Claerwen is a good base for the more determined walker; you can follow a path from the far end of the dam and walk the harsh but beautiful eight miles or so across the mountains and past smaller, natural lakes to the abbey of Strata Florida (see p.279). Alternatively, the path that skirts around the northern shore of Claerwen leads across to the lonely **Teifi Pools** (see p.279), glacial lakes from which the Teifi River springs.

Back at the Garreg Ddu viaduct, a more popular road continues north along the long, glassy finger of **Garreg Ddu** reservoir, before doubling back on itself just below the awesome **Pen-y-garreg** dam and reservoir; if the dam is overflowing, the vast wall of foaming water is mesmerizing. At the top of Pen-y-garreg lake, it's possible to drive over the final, or more properly the first, dam on the system, at **Craig Goch**. This is the most-photographed of all the dams, thanks to its gracious curve, elegant Edwardian arches and neat little green cupola. The lake beyond it is fed by the Elan River, which the road crosses just short of a junction. A bleak, invigorating moorland pass heads west from here to drop into the eerie moonscape of Cwmystwyth (see p.289), while the eastbound road funnels into a beautiful valley back to Rhayader. On the way back, fork off the Elan Valley Road in Rhayader onto the smaller Aberystwyth Road.

The only **bus** route hereabouts is the #103 postbus from Llandrindod and Rhayader (Mon–Fri), which runs as far as the Elan Valley visitor centre. The two services allow you to spend around three hours in and around the visitor centre.

Abbeycwmhir

ABBEYCWMHIR (Abaty Cwm Hir) seven miles northeast of Rhayader, takes its name from the abbey whose sombre ruins lie behind the village. Cistercian monks founded the abbey in 1146, planning one of the largest churches in Britain, whose 242-foot nave has only ever been exceeded in length by the cathedrals of Durham, York and Winchester. Destruction by Henry III's troops in 1231 scuppered plans to continue the building, however. The sparse ruins of what they did build – a rocky outline of the floorplan – lie in a conifer-carpeted valley alongside a gloomy green lake, lending weight, if only by atmosphere, to the site's melancholic associations. Llywelyn ap Gruffydd's body, after his head had been carted off to London, was rumoured to have been brought here from Cilmeri in 1282, and a new granite slab, carved with a Celtic sword, lies on the altar to commemorate this last native prince of Wales. It should look incongruous, but somehow it only adds to the eerie presence of the ruins and the village.

Presteigne and around

The architecture of tiny, old-fashioned **PRESTEIGNE** (Llanandras), twenty miles east of Llandrindod Wells, reeks of its former status as county town, but its contemporary feel has more to do with the sizeable community of rat-race refugees who first descended on the town in the 1960s and have continued to arrive ever since. There's a relaxed pace to the place, perfect for mooching around the centre – Broad, High and Hereford streets – dipping into some enjoyably musty secondhand book and antique shops in between the quality craft shops and laid-back cafés.

Presteigne lies snugly between the B4362 town bypass and the River Lugg, the border with England, which flows under the seventeenth-century bridge at the bottom of the handsome Broad Street. Just before the bridge, the solid parish **church of St Andrew** contains Saxon and Norman fragments, as well as a sixteenth-century Flemish tapestry. To the left of the main churchyard entrance are twin gravestones that give an insight into early nineteenth-century morals: the original stone commemorates one Mary Morgan, who in 1805 gave birth to a "bastard" child that her father persuaded her to murder; he then sat on the jury that condemned her to death. A sanctimonious inscription records that she was "unenlightened by the sacred truths of Christianity" and "became the victim of sin and shame and was condemned to an ignominious death". Opposite is a later stone erected in repentance by the townsfolk, inscribed "He that is without sin among you, let him first cast a stone at her".

Mary Morgan's trial would have taken place up the street at the **Judge's Lodging** (daily: May–Oct 10am–6pm; Nov–April 10am–4pm; £3.50), a beautifully interpreted trawl through the rooms where circuit judges stayed while presiding over the local assizes. The building spent long years as the district museum, and folk had forgotten that many of the original furnishings had been stashed in the attic, a boon when the decision was made to restore the place to its 1868 grandeur. You now follow an audio tour, being "introduced" to characters along the way but with the freedom to stop and inspect the furnishings and even lounge on the sofas. Nothing is roped off or hidden behind screens, and it feels more like visiting a private home than a museum. The oil lamps that light the upper floors and the gas-flame lighting in the servants' quarters provide a whiff of authenticity. You finally emerge in the courtroom, where an alleged thief that you've "met" in the cells is being tried. Other rooms contain leftovers from the district museum and a section devoted to explaining George Borrow's claim that Presteigne is "Neither in Wales nor in England but simply in Radnorshire".

From the museum, Broad Street heads up to the main crossroads, with the High Street forking west and Hereford Street to the east. On the corner of Hereford and Broad streets the nineteenth-century Italianate Assembly Rooms also house the town's library. High Street contains the town's most impressive building, though, the Jacobean **Radnorshire Arms**, built as a private home for John Bradshaw, a signatory on the death warrant of Charles I, and converted into an inn in 1792.

Practicalities

Buses from Knighton, Kington and Leominster stop outside the *Radnorshire Arms* or at the coach park on the bypass. The Judge's Lodging also contains the **tourist office** (same hours; ☎01544/260650) where you can get details of local **accommodation**, which ranges from period luxury at the classy *Radnorshire Arms* (☎01544/267406, fax 260418, *hotel@radnorshire.fsbusiness.co.uk*; ⑤) to the no-nonsense *Farmers Inn* (☎01544/267389; ②) – both are on Hereford Street. You can **camp** cheaply at *Gumma Farm* (☎01547/560243), two miles west on the road to Discoed, or there's a fuller site, including caravans, at *Rockbridge Park* (☎01547/560300), half a mile nearer town on the banks of the River Lugg.

Presteigne has become a centre for folk and traditional music with excellent **festivals** in July and over the August bank holiday (details from the tourist office): the former organized by the excellent free music paper *Broad Sheep*, available from venues around town.

The *Farmer's Inn* on Hereford Street is the town's liveliest pub, and serves decent **food**, though for something a little more formal, make for the *Radnorshire Arms* with a moderately priced restaurant and a heavy wood-beamed bar. Alternatively, the cafés on the High Street are worth investigating, as is the enjoyably laid-back *Hat Shop* restaurant and bar at no.7, and the old-fashioned *Barley Mow* on Hereford Street.

Old and New Radnor

Just off the A44 six miles southwest of Presteigne and looking like it's been hewn straight from the hillside, **OLD RADNOR** was once the home of King Harold, killed at the Battle of Hastings by William the Conqueror's troops. The site of his castle is down the lane running southeast from the large, very English-looking **church**, overlooking a wooded vale. Inside the church, a massive eighth-century font on four stone feet is the most remarkable legacy. Opposite, the rambling, fifteenth-century *Harp Inn* (☎01544/350655; ②) has been magnificently restored from its earlier use as a farm cottage.

NEW RADNOR, just over two miles to the west, was built as a small Norman settlement and then planned, in the thirteenth century, to be expanded into a major city and capital of Radnorshire. The project faltered, confirming Wales' antipathy towards large settlements in favour of the more common feature of scattered farmsteads. Today, you enter the village from the A44 to the southeast, past a Victorian steeple erected to honour local dignitary Sir George Cornewall Lewis. This is the only feature of the village that seems to suggest any kind of metropolitan status, as the couple of streets are deathly quiet with just the *Radnor Arms* on Broad Street to liven things up.

North of New Radnor, the deep-clefted valleys and wooded hillsides of **Radnor Forest** offer some of the region's best walking. The most popular route is along the driveable track that forks north off the A44 just over a mile west of New Radnor, leading into a thick forest and to the rushing cascade of the **Water-break-its-neck** waterfall, at its foaming best in winter.

Knighton

KNIGHTON (Tref-y-clawdd, "the town on the dyke"), six miles north of Presteign, straddles King Offa's eighth-century border as well as the modern Wales–England divide, and has come into its own as the most obvious centre for those walking the **Offa's Dyke Path**. Located almost exactly halfway along the route, Knighton, although without many specific sights, is a lively, attractive place that easily warrants a stopoff.

So close is Knighton to the border that the town's **train station** and its accompanying hotel are actually in England. From here, Station Road crosses the River Teme into Wales and climbs a couple of hundred yards into the town, joining the pretty Broad Street at Brookside Square. Further up the hill is the town's Victorian, alpine-looking clock tower, where Broad Street becomes West Street and the steep High Street soars off up to the left, past rickety Tudor buildings and up to the mound of the old **castle**. In West Street, the excellent **Offa's Dyke Centre** (Easter–Oct daily 9am–5.30pm; Nov–Easter Mon–Fri 9am–5pm; ☎01547/528753, *www.offa.demon.co.uk/offa*) also houses the **tourist office** (same hours; ☎01547/529424). Looming high above Knighton, a mile off the A4113, the **Powys County Observatory** (July & Aug tours 2pm daily except Wed; Sept–June Sun & bank holidays only; £3; ☎01547/520247) has a planetarium, camera obscura and solar telescope, and runs tours, evening groups and courses – phone for details.

Accommodation is plentiful and geared towards the backpacking market. There's the basic but cheerful *Red Lion* on West Street (☎01547/528231; ①); the *Fleece House* B&B, Market Street (☎01547/520168; ②), with some en-suite rooms; and the bargain *Offa's Dyke House*, 4 High St (☎01547/528634; ①) which serves evening meals and offers **camping**. There's another low-cost tent field at *Panpwnton Farm* (☎01547/528597), over the river and half a mile up the lane that forks left at the station. Classier rooms, and delicious, imaginative meals, are available a mile east along the A4113 at *Milebrook House Hotel* (☎01547/528632, fax 520509, *hotel@milebrook.kc3ltd.co.uk*; ⑤), where you can also cast a fly into the River Teme.

OFFA'S DYKE

George Borrow, in his classic book *Wild Wales* (see p.480), notes that once "it was customary for the English to cut off the ears of every Welshman who was found to the east of the dyke, and for the Welsh to hang every Englishman whom they found to the west of it". Certainly, **Offa's Dyke** has provided a potent symbol of Welsh–English antipathy ever since it was created in the eighth century as a demarcation line by King Offa of Mercia, ruler of the whole of central England. It appears that the dyke was an attempt to thwart Welsh expansionism.

Up to twenty feet high and sixty feet wide, the earthwork made use of natural boundaries such as rivers in its run north to south, and is best seen in the sections near Knighton in Radnorshire and Montgomery. Today's England–Wales border crosses the dyke many times, although the basic boundary has changed little since Offa's day. The glorious **long-distance footpath**, opened in 1971, runs from Prestatyn on the north Clwyd coast for 177 miles to Sedbury Cliffs, just outside Chepstow in Gwent, and is one of the most rewarding walks in Britain – neither too popular to be unpleasantly crowded, nor too similar in its landscapes. The path is maintained by the Offa's Dyke Association, whose headquarters are in the Offa's Dyke Centre in Knighton (see overeleaf).

For **eating and drinking**, it's hard to beat the comfortable *Horse and Jockey* at the town end of Station Road, which has a vast menu for lunch and early evening, serves huge, tasty pizzas until 11pm and packs in live music and discos as well. The *Red Lion* has large, inexpensive portions of basic pub food, and for breakfast, try *Ginger's*, a greasy spoon café on Church Street.

You might also find folk and jazz in the *Plough Hotel* on Market Street. The local **bike rental** firm, Wheely Wonderful (☎01568/770755), is over the border in Shropshire at Petchfield Farm, Elton, near Ludlow; they will deliver to Knighton if you're without a car.

Montgomeryshire

The northern part of Powys is made up of the old county of **Montgomeryshire** (Maldwyn), an area of enormously varying landscapes and few inhabitants. The best base for the spartan and mountainous southwest of the county is the solid little town of **Llanidloes**, a base for ageing hippies less than ten miles north of Rhayader on the River Severn (Afon Hafren), which arrives in the town after winding through the dense **Hafren Forest** on the bleak slopes of **Plynlimon**.

From Llanidloes, one of Wales' most dramatic roads rises past the chilly shores of the **Llyn Clywedog** reservoir, squeezed into sharp hillsides, and up through the remote hamlets of **Staylittle** and **Dylife**. This stark, uplifting scenery contrasts with the gentler, greener contours that characterize the east of the county, where the muted old county town of **Montgomery**, with its fine Georgian architecture, perches above the border and Offa's Dyke. The Severn runs a few miles to the west, near the impeccable village of **Berriew**, home of the bizarre **Andrew Logan Museum of Sculpture** and below the dank hilltop remains of **Dolforwyn Castle**. Further south, the Severn runs in a muddy channel through drab **Newtown**, good only as a transport interchange and for followers of **Robert Owen**, the pioneer socialist.

In the north of the county, **Welshpool** forms the only major settlement, packed in above the wide flood plain of the Severn. An excellent local museum, the impossibly cute toy rail line that runs to **Llanfair Caereinion**, good pubs and reasonable hotels make the town a fair stop for a day or two. On the southern side of Welshpool is Montgomeryshire's one unmissable sight, the sumptuous **Powis Castle** and its exquisite terraced gardens. The very north of the county is pastoral, deserted and beautiful. The few visitors that there are throng **Lake Vyrnwy** and make their way down the dead-end lane to the **Pistyll Rhaeadr** waterfall, leaving the leafy lanes and villages like **Llanfyllin** and **Llanrhaeadr-ym-mochnant** intact for those searching for peace, cheerful pubs and good walking.

Llanidloes and around

Thriving when so many other small market towns seem in danger of atrophying, the secret of success for **LLANIDLOES** seems to be in its adaptability, from rural village to weaving town and, latterly, a centre for artists, craftsfolk and assorted alternative lifestylers. One of mid-Wales' prettiest and most welcoming towns, Llanidloes' four main streets meet at the black-and-white **market hall**, built on timber stilts in 1600, allowing the market – now long since moved – to take place on the cobbles underneath. Running parallel along the length of the market hall are China Street and Long Bridge Street, the latter good for interesting little shops such as the very browsable Nature Gallery art store. Off Long Bridge Street to the left is Church Street, which opens out into a yard surrounding the dumpy parish **church of St Idloes**, whose impressive fifteenth-century hammerbeam roof is said to have been poached from Abbey Cwmhir.

Going west from the market hall is Short Bridge Street, a line of fine architecture that runs down to the River Severn, past two imposing nineteenth-century chapels – one Zionist, one Baptist – staring across the road at each other. Heading the other way from the market hall is Great Oak Street, the town's most important and attractive thoroughfare. At the bottom of the street is the **town hall**, originally built as a temperance hotel to challenge the boozy **Trewythen Arms** opposite. A plaque on the hotel commemorates Llanidloes as an unlikely seeming place of industrial and political unrest, when, in April 1839, Chartists stormed the hotel, dragging out and beating up special constables who had been dispatched to the town in a futile attempt to suppress the political fervour of the local flannel weavers. The town's wonderfully eclectic **museum** (Easter–Sept daily 11am–1pm & 2–5pm; Oct–Easter closed Sun & Mon; free) forms part of the tourist office complex in the town hall. The diverting collection of old local prints and mementos, including pictures of boomtown Dylife (see p.239), pale beside the stuffed two-headed lamb, born locally in 1914. Also housed in the museum is a **red kite centre**, with live transmission from nests in the Hafren Forest. Great Oak Street is also home to a branch of **Laura Ashley**'s empire, whose mission to wrap the world in floral fabric started just up the road in **Carno**.

Practicalities

Llanidloes is a good base, with friendly pubs and restaurants and plenty of places to stay. China Street curves down to the car park from where all **bus** services operate. The **tourist office** (Mon–Sat 10am–5pm; ☎01686/412605) is in the town hall, close to the market hall on Long Bridge Street. For news of alternative events – like the **Fancy Dress Night**, on the first Friday of July, when the pubs open late, the streets are cordoned off and virtually the whole town gets kitted out – pick up the free monthly community paper, the *Llani Gazette*, or visit the excellent Resource Centre on Great Oak Street. At the bottom of the road is the area's best **bookshop**, Great Oak, with loads of Celtic and Welsh-interest stuff and a barn full of good new and secondhand fiction.

Accommodation spans the delightful *Red Lion Hotel* (☎01686/412270; ②) and the more modest *Unicorn* (☎01686/413167, fax 413516; ①), both on Long Bridge Street. China Street houses the chintzy *Mount Inn* (☎01686/412247; ②), and the handsome *Severn View* B&B (☎01686/412207; ①). You can **camp** around fifteen minutes walk north of town at *Dol-llys Farm* (☎01686/412694), which is cheap and allows campfires down by the infant Severn.

Among the many options for **food**, there's wholesome, mostly vegetarian fare in the laid-back *Great Oak Café* on Great Oak Street, the cheap and hearty *Traveller's Rest* on Long Bridge Street or, for a bit of a treat, the summer-only *Orchard House* on China Street (☎01686/413606; ③) which also has en-suite B&B rooms. Most of the **pubs** here serve food – the inexpensive *Unicorn* hotel (see overleaf) and the moderate *Lloyds*, on Cambrian Place are the best bets. The most laid-back of the lot is the *Crown and Anchor*, towards the top of Long Bridge Street. Award-winning food is also available at the cheerful *Blue Bell Inn*, four miles down the A470 in the village of **LLANGURIG**.

Llyn Clywedog, Plynlimon, Dylife and Staylittle

Four miles northwest of Llanidloes, the beautiful **Llyn Clywedog reservoir** was built as recently as the 1960s and has settled well into the folds of the Clywedog Valley. At its southern end, the modern concrete dam is Britain's tallest (237ft), towering menacingly over the remnants of the **Bryntail lead mine**, through which a signposted path runs. The roads along the southern shores of Clywedog wind around into the dense plantation of **Hafren Forest**, the only real sign of life and vegetation on the bleak, sodden slopes of **Plynlimon** (Pumlumon Fawr). There's a car park at **RHYD-Y-BEN-WCH**, in the heart of the forest, from where **walking paths** fan out, the most popular being a six-mile round trip following the infant River Severn up through the trees, past a waterfall and out to its source, a saturated peat bog in some of the harshest terrain in Wales. For more detail of walks and mountain bike routes in the district, pick up the *Guide to the Forest and River Walks: Hafren* leaflet (50p) from tourist offices.

Plynlimon is bleak and difficult walking if you venture beyond the fairly well-trodden path to the Severn's source. Water oozes everywhere in this misty wilderness, with four other rivers – the Wye included – rising on its tufted slopes. The rivers Hengwm, Llechwedd-mawr and Rheidol have been dammed on Plynlimon's western side to form the desolate, black-watered reservoir of **Nant-y-Moch**, reached by road via Ponterwyd (see p.287). There is little sympathetic landscaping here, the lake looking nothing more than the flooded valley that it is.

The hamlet of **STAYLITTLE** (Penfforddlas) – whose English name comes from a village blacksmith who was so quick at shoeing horses his smithy became known as Stay-a-little – is above the Clywedog River at the northern end of Llyn Clywedog. Just north of the village, the mountain road to Machynlleth forks left, running past the

---

GLYNDŴR'S WAY

A fairly new long-distance footpath, **Glyndŵr's Way** weaves its 123 miles through Montgomeryshire and northern Radnorshire countryside well reputed for the solitude that it offers. Running from Knighton in the south, the path climbs up into the remote hills to the northwest before turning south four miles south of Newtown. From here, the path plunges through the pastoral hills and past only occasional settlements towards Abbey Cwmhir, where it again turns and heads north towards Llanidloes and Llyn Clywedog, passing the 103 lofty turbines of the Penrhyddlan and Llidiartywaun Windfarm, the largest in Europe. From Llyn Clywedog, the path heads across the mine-scarred mountains around Dylife and down into Machynlleth. It then ducks back inland, along the A489 for a few miles before dipping down into the hills, up over the A470 and across its bleakest stretch: the wet and wild upland moor south of the A458. Through the Dyfnant Forest, Glyndŵr's Way zigzags down to the shores of Lake Vyrnwy, eastwards along the River Vyrnwy and over its last few miles to Welshpool.

Well signposted all the way, Glyndŵr's Way is far quieter than Offa's Dyke path, both in the number of settlements en route and the number of people attempting it. Varied scenery includes barren bog, exhilarating uplands, reservoirs, undulating farmland and sections of river-valley walking.

plunging ravine of the Twymyn River to the north. Old mine workings herald the approach to **DYLIFE**, or "Place of Floods", a lead-mining community of around two thousand people in the mid-nineteenth century, with a reputation as a lawless, licentious gambling pit. The mine closed in 1896, and the population has since dwindled to around just twenty, although this increases when walkers and devotees of good beer and food flock to the old *Star Inn* during the warmer months. Good walks from Dylife include up to Pen-y-crogben, the mine-clad slope that rises to the south of the village, and west to **GLASLYN**, or "blue lake", and the reedy shores of **Bugeilyn**. The superb **Glyndŵr's Way** footpath (see box, opposite) crosses this patch on its way to Machynlleth. A popular viewpoint on the road two miles west of Dylife has been furnished with a cheery memorial to broadcaster and author **Wynford Vaughan-Thomas** (1908–87), whose outstretched slate hand points out to the dozens of rippling peaks and verdant valleys.

Newtown and around

Despite its name, **NEWTOWN** (Y Drenewydd), thirteen miles northeast of Llanidloes, was founded in the tenth century around a small castle, growing steadily until its population explosion in the nineteenth century as a centre for weaving and textiles. As in so many other places, the town's traditional industry has all but disappeared, and it hasn't really found anything to replace it. Although the centre of town is bland enough not to cause offence, it's not a terribly stimulating place and hardly one in which to linger – although you might find yourself making transport connections here, and there is an excellent theatre, the **Hafren** (☎01686/625007), and a strong music scene.

Of Newtown's sights, the High Street is home to the original base of the **W.H. Smith** chain of newsagents, now housing a small and reasonably interesting **museum** (Mon–Sat 9.30am–5.30pm; free) about the company and its growth since it was established in 1792. A block west, the car park where you'll find the bus depot and tourist office is also home to **Oriel 31** (Mon–Sat 10am–5pm; free), a great gallery of imaginative temporary exhibitions, classes and occasional live music, poetry readings and storytelling. On Severn Street, opposite the nineteenth-century red terracotta **clock tower**, is the house in which early socialist **Robert Owen** was born in 1771, now open as a **Memorial Museum** (Mon–Fri 9.30am–noon & 2–3.30pm, Sat 9.30–11.30am; free) that explains this remarkable man's life (see box overleaf). The museum's visitors' book indicates just how much of a shrine the place has become, with a roll call of socialist politicians and trade unionists scrawling their thanks for Owen's work in its pages. Displays include Owen's own notebooks and ledgers, contemporary paintings of his communities in America and New Lanark, and newspaper records of establishment disdain for his work.

Over the river at 5–7 Commercial St, the **Textile Museum** sits above six cramped old weavers' cottages (free). Exhibits show the dramatic ebbs and flows of the town's staple trade, from the flannel and handloom factories of the 1790s, through the social unrest and industrial decline of the 1830s and 1840s (Wales' first Chartist demonstration took place here in 1838), the revival of trade thanks to Pryce Pryce-Jones' world-first mail order service and its subsequent dwindling to nothing by 1935. Pryce-Jones' **Royal Welsh Warehouse** – an industrial cathedral that dominates the eastern approach to the town centre – is now a deadbeat shopping centre.

Five miles north of Newtown, the mock-Tudor **Gregynog Hall** was the home from 1920 of Gwendoline and Margaret Davies, aesthete sisters who inherited a vast fortune from their port-building father and spent much of it on a world-class art collection, most of which now resides in Cardiff's National Museum of Wales (see p.102). Gregynog became the headquarters for their artistic revival, including the establishment of a world-famous small press, which is up and running once more. It's now an extramural

ROBERT OWEN

Born in Montgomeryshire in the late eighteenth century, **Robert Owen** (1771–1858) left Wales to enter the Manchester cotton trade at the age of eighteen and swiftly rose to the position of mill manager. His business acumen was matched by a strong streak of philanthropy towards his subordinates. Fundamentally, he believed in social equality between the classes and was firmly against the concept of competition between individuals. Poverty, he believed, could be eradicated by co-operative methods. Owen recognized the potential of building a model workers' community around the New Lanark mills in Scotland and joined the operation in 1798, swiftly setting up the world's first infant school, an Institution for the Formation of Character and a model welfare state for its people.

Owen's ideas on co-operative living prompted him to build up the model community of New Harmony in Indiana, USA, which he had established between 1824 and 1828, before handing the still struggling project over to his sons. Before long, and without the wisdom of its founder, the idealistic tenets of New Harmony collapsed under the weight of greed, ambition and too many vested interests. Undeterred, Owen, by now back in Britain, was encouraging the formation of the early trade unions and co-operative societies, as well as leading action against the 1834 deportation of the **Tolpuddle Martyrs**, a group of Dorset farm labourers who withdrew their labour in their call for a wage increase. Owen's later years were dogged by controversy, as he lost the support of the few sympathetic sections of the British establishment in his persistent criticism of organized religion. He gained many followers, however, whose generic name gradually changed from Owenites to socialists – the first usage of the term. Owen returned to Newtown in his later years, and died there in 1858.

outpost of the University of Wales, offering public courses in Welsh language and culture and hosting an annual music **festival** in late June: the hall is not generally open to the public, though you can wander through the grounds at any time.

Two miles north of town, on the A483 to Welshpool, there's a great **quad-biking** centre at Severn Valley Quad Trekking, Broniarth Farm (☎01686/625560).

Practicalities

Newtown's **train station** is on the southern edge of the town centre, and a path heads straight up past the ugly Victorian parish church of St David and up Back Lane to the **bus station** and **tourist office** (Easter–Sept daily 10am–5.30pm; Oct–Easter Mon–Sat 9.30am–5pm; ☎01686/625580). For information on gigs and festivals – such as the superb **Mid Wales May Festival** (☎01686/621975), a weekend of music, poetry, storytelling and street theatre – check out the Ian Snow craft and clothing shop at 1 The Cross.

If you have to **stay** in Newtown, your best bets are the *Plas Canol* guesthouse, between the station and the town centre on New Road (☎01686/625598; ①), and *Yesterdays* (☎01686/622644; ①), behind the clock tower in Severn Square, which also offers super Welsh speciality dishes. Out of town, you can't go wrong with *Lower Ffrydd* (☎ & fax 01686/688269; ②), a sixteenth-century antique-filled house with an acre of grounds, oak-beamed en-suite rooms and excellent freshly cooked meals.

The cosy sixteenth-century *Bank Cottage* on The Bank (closed Sun), is the place to go for sandwiches, daily blackboard specials and some wonderful desserts, while the mock-Jacobean *Pheasant Inn* on Market Street is equally good for tasty **lunches** and real ales. *Caruso's*, 30 Shortbridge St (☎01686/623444) serves decent pizza in tricolore surroundings and will also deliver locally. You won't be stuck for **pubs** – there are loads, even if most are eminently avoidable. The *Lion Inn*, near the clock tower, is good for live music, late drinking and discos, while Commercial Street's *Bell Hotel* and Severn Street's *Sportsman* host regular live folk, R&B and blues.

Dolforwyn Castle

The A483 continues northeast from Newtown, affording occasional glimpses of the River Severn and in almost constant proximity to the reed-filled **Montgomery Canal**. Three miles from Montgomery, there's a small left turn leading up to the *Dolforwyn Hotel* and the gaunt remains of unsignposted **Dolforwyn Castle**. Described by Jan Morris as "the saddest of all the Welsh castles", this was the very last fortress to be built by a native Welsh prince on his own soil – Llywelyn ap Gruffydd in 1273 – as a direct snub to the English king, Edward I, who had expressly forbidden the project. Llywelyn built his fortress and started to construct a small adjoining town as a Welsh fiefdom to rival the heavily anglicized Welshpool, just up the valley. Dolforwyn only survived for four years in Welsh hands before being overwhelmed after a nine-day siege by the English, and the castle was left slowly to rot. In the past twenty years, the remains have been excavated, and significant portions of the fragile old castle have emerged on the wind-blown hilltop, with its astounding views over the Severn valley, four hundred feet below. The small left turning after the hotel leads down to the entrance to Yew Tree Cottage, otherwise identified by a rusty corrugated-iron shack and twin gates. The track leading up is a public path that winds its way up to the lonely ruins. The path circles around the castle and heads north, coming to a stile after a hundred yards or so. Crossing this, and heading diagonally across the field towards the track and another stile, the path brushes past the fragmentary earthwork remains of Llywelyn's lost market town.

Montgomery and around

Eight miles northeast of Newtown, the tiny town of **MONTGOMERY** (Trefaldwyn) is Montgomeryshire at its most anglicized. It lies at the base of a dilapidated **castle** on the Welsh side of Offa's Dyke and the present-day border. The castle was started in 1233 by the English king, Henry III, and today's remains are not on their own worth the steep climb up the lane at the back of the town hall, although the view over the lofty church tower, handsome Georgian streets and the vast green bowl of hills around the town is wonderful. The impressively symmetrical main thoroughfare – well-named Broad Street – swoops up to the perfect little red-brick **town hall**, crowned by a pert clock tower. Facing the town hall, Arthur Street goes down to the right and the **Old Bell Museum** (April–July & Sept Wed–Fri & Sun 1.30–5pm, Sat 10.30am–5pm; Aug Sun–Fri 1.30–5pm, Sat 10.30am–5pm; £1), an unusually enjoyable local history collection of artefacts from excavations, scale models of local castles, an old workhouse exhibition and mementos from Montgomery civic life.

At the other end of Broad Street, the rebuilt tower of Montgomery's parish **church of St Nicholas** dominates the snug proportions of the buildings around it. Largely thirteenth-century, the highlights of its spacious interior include the 1600 canopied tomb of local landowner, Sir Richard Herbert, and his wife, Magdalen. They lie in prayer on top, with their eight (apparently angelic) children (including Elizabethan poet George Herbert) in beatific kneeling positions behind them. Under the couple lurks a shrouded cadaver. The two medieval effigies on the floor at the end of the tomb are of uncertain origin, although the farther one is thought to be of Sir Edmund Mortimer ("revolted Mortimer", as Shakespeare had him), son-in-law of Owain Glyndŵr, brother-in-law of Hotspur and once Constable of Montgomery Castle. Equally impressive are the elaborately carved fifteenth-century double screen and accompanying loft, believed to have been built from sections removed from a priory over the border in Cherbury.

Montgomery is near one of the best preserved sections of **Offa's Dyke**, which the long-distance footpath shadows either side of the B4386 a mile east of the town. Ditches almost twenty feet high give one of the best indications of the dyke's original look and, to the south of the main road, the England–Wales border still exactly splices the dyke, twelve hundred years after it was built. If you want to **stay** here, the rambling *Dragon Hotel* (☎01686/668359, fax 668287, *dragon_michaels@compuserve.com*; ⑤), by the town hall, has an indoor pool and is dependable, if rather pompous. Better options are *Bronwylfa* (☎01686/668630; ①), a beautiful white Georgian town house on Broad Street, or *Little Brompton Farm* (☎ & fax 01686/668371; ②), two miles south of town and handy for the Offa's Dyke path. For **food** and **drink**, head for *The Checkers* pub, opposite *Bronwylfa* on Broad Street, livelier and younger than the *Dragon*.

Berriew

Three miles northwest of Montgomery, the neat village of **BERRIEW** (Aberrhiw) is more redolent of the black-and-white settlements over the English border than anywhere in Wales, its Tudor houses grouped prettily around a small church, the shallow waters of the Rhiw River and the posh half-timbered *Lion Hotel* (☎01686/640452; ⑤), which serves excellent home-cooked meals.

Just over the river bridge, the **Andrew Logan Museum of Sculpture** (April and Nov–Dec Sun 2–6pm; May–June and Sept–Oct Sat & Sun 2–6pm; July–Aug Wed–Sun 2–6pm; £2) makes for an incongruous attraction in such a setting, with a good selection of the notable British modern sculptor's work. Andrew Logan is the man who in the 1970s inaugurated the great drag-and-grunge ball known as the Alternative Miss World Contest, launchpad of the formidable Divine's career, from which astounding costumes and memorabilia form a large chunk of the exhibits at the museum. There's also Logan's oversized horticultural sculpture, including giant lilies encrusted with shattered mirrors and vast metal irises that rise to scrape the roof, as well as his smaller-scale jewellery and model Goddesses that only add to the sublime camp of the exhibition.

Welshpool

Three miles from the English border and just five miles north of Berriew, eastern Montgomeryshire's chief town of **WELSHPOOL** (Y Trallwng) was formerly known as just Pool, its prefix added in 1835 to distinguish it from the English seaside town of Poole in Dorset. It's not a particularly Welsh place, lying in the anglicized valley of the River Severn (Afon Hafren) and with a history that depended largely upon the patronage of English landlords and kings. The town's bypass has cleared its streets of excessive traffic, and left a number of well-proportioned roads crowned with some Tudor and many good Georgian and Victorian buildings. But it's for sumptuous **Powis Castle**, one of the greatest Welsh fortresses, that Welshpool is on most people's agenda.

Arrival, information and accommodation

The pompous neo-Gothic turrets of the old Victorian **train station** (its modern replacement is directly behind) sit at the top of Severn Street, which leads down into the town centre, formed by the intersection of Severn, Berriew, Broad and Church streets. The **tourist office** (daily 9.30am–5.30pm; ☎01938/552043, *weltic@powys.gov.uk*), is fifty yards up Church Street in the Vicarage Gardens car park.

There is plenty of **accommodation** in town, though in the centre, the only place with en-suite rooms is the *Royal Oak* (☎01938/552217; ⑤), a traditional coaching inn at the main crossroads. Dozens of **B&Bs** line Salop Road; of them all, *Montgomery House* (☎01938/552693; ①) is the surest bet. Other places include *Severn Farm* on Leighton Road (☎01938/553098; ①), just beyond the industrial estate to the east of the station, which will also let you pitch a **tent**, and two superb farmhouse B&Bs just north of town: *Gungrog House* (☎01938/553381, fax 556224; ②), in Rhallt, and a little further towards the village of Guilsfield (Cegidfa), the beautiful *Lower Trelydan Farm* (☎01938/553105; ②).

The Town

Arriving at Welshpool's modern **train station** gives a false sense of what to expect from the town, which is much more attractive than the modern mess around the rail lines would lead you to believe. Two hundred yards along Severn Street, a humpback bridge over the much-restored **Montgomery Canal** hides the canal **wharf**, from where Montgomery Canal Cruises dispatch gaudily painted narrowboats that will chug you up the navigable section for a couple of hours (☎01938/553271; £3.50). Groups of up to twelve people can rent a self-drive narrowboat for a full day for £75. There's also an old wharfside warehouse here that has been carefully restored as the **Powysland Museum** (Mon, Tues, Thurs & Fri 11am–1pm & 2–5pm, Sat & Sun 2–5pm; also May–Sept Sat & Sun 10am–1pm; £1), an impressively wide collection looking at the history of the local area. Of particular interest is the display about the impact of the Black Death in these parts (half the town's population died), and Roman remains from the now obliterated local Cistercian abbey of Strata Marcella.

Right at the centre of town are the crossroads, where the Georgian **Royal Oak Hotel** acts as a firm reminder of the junction's importance on the old coaching route. Broad Street is the most architecturally interesting of the streets leading off from here, with the ponderous Victorian town hall and its dominating clock tower overlooking some fine Tudor and Jacobean town houses. On New Street, behind the NatWest bank, you can wander around an early eighteenth-century circular **cockpit** (bank hours; free). Broad Street changes name five times as it rises up the hill towards the tiny Raven Square terminus station of the **Welshpool & Llanfair Railway**, half a mile beyond the town hall. The eight-mile narrow-gauge line (April & May Sat & Sun; June–Sept roughly daily; £7.50 return; ☎01938/810441) was open to passengers for less than thirty years, closing in 1931 – these days, scaled-down engines once more chuff along the appropriately modest valleys of the Sylfaen Brook and Banwy neu Einion River to the almost eerily quiet village of **LLANFAIR CAEREINION**, a good daytime base for walks and pub food at the *Goat Hotel*. The **post office**, opposite the church, stocks free leaflets of some good local circular walks.

Eating and drinking

Welshpool's four main streets are home to most of the town's **eating** and **drinking** establishments. The best restaurant in town is the moderately priced *Tyler's Brasserie* on the High Street (☎01938/555006; closed Wed & Sun, and Mon & Tues lunchtimes), which does great stuffed baguettes, hot Cajun chicken salad and espresso. The *Shilam Tandoori* at 13 Berriew St, and *The Corn Store* on Church Street (☎01938/554614) are also good. Cheap and filling breakfasts, lunches and teas are served in the *Buttery*, opposite the town hall on the High Street. Many of the town's **pubs** do lunchtime food, with some, notably the *Talbot* in the High Street, serving excellent evening meals as well. Other good pubs for evening entertainment include the small, dark *Mermaid* on the High Street and the *Powys Arms* up Salop Road, with live music, quizzes and karaoke.

Powis Castle

In a land of ruined castles, the sheer scale and beauty of **Powis Castle** (April–June, Sept & Oct Wed–Sun 1–5pm; July–Aug Tues–Sun 1–5pm; £7.50, or £5 gardens and museum only; NT), a mile from Welshpool up Park Lane, is the real reason for coming to the town. On the site of an earlier Norman fort, the castle was started in the reign of Edward I by the Gwenwynwyn family; to qualify for the site and the barony of De la Pole, they had to renounce all claims to Welsh princedom. In 1587, Sir Edward Herbert bought the castle and began to transform it into the Elizabethan palace we see today.

Inside, the **Clive Museum** – named after Edward Clive, son of Clive of India, who married into the family in 1784 – forms a lively account of the British in India, through diaries, notes, letters, paintings, tapestries, weapons and jewels, although it is the sumptuous period rooms that impress most, from the vast and kitsch frescoes by Lanscroon above the balustraded staircase to the mahogany bed, brass and enamel toilets and decorative wall hangings of the state bedroom. The elegant Long Gallery has a rich sixteenth-century plasterwork ceiling overlooking winsome busts and marble statuettes of the four elements, placed in between the glowering family portraits.

Designed by Welsh architect William Winde, the **gardens** are spectacular. Dropping down from the castle in four huge stepped terraces, the design has barely changed since the seventeenth century, with a charmingly precise orangery and topiary that looks as if it is shaved daily. Summertime outdoor concerts, frequently with firework finales, take place in the gardens.

Llanfyllin and around

The hills and plains of northern Montgomeryshire conceal a maze of deserted lanes and farm outposts along the contours that swell up towards the north and the foothills of Denbighshire's Berwyn Mountains. The only real settlement of any size is **LLAN-FYLLIN**, a peaceful but friendly hillside town, ten miles northwest of Welshpool in the valley of the River Cain. The High Street is a busy centre of bright pubs, cafés, shops and a weekly Thursday market. Narrow Street forks off from here, climbing to the restored **well of St Myllin**, who has reputedly looked after inhabitants of his town since the sixth century by curing the ailment of any Llanfyllin citizen. From here, views over the town, its unusual plain red-brick church (few churches were built in eighteenth-century Wales) and the looming Berwyn Mountains, are delightful.

Llanfyllin is short on places to **stay**, with only an ancient and somewhat overpriced coaching inn, the *Cain Valley* Hotel, on the High Street (☎01691/648366, fax 648307; ④). On the whole, you're better off in Llanrhaeadr-ym-mochnant (see below), around Lake Vyrnwy (see opposite), or some five miles southwest at the tranquil, ivy-draped seventeenth-century *Cyfie Farm* (☎ & fax 01691/648451; ③), in a beautiful garden setting just south of the tiny village of Llanfihangel-yng-Ngwynfa. There's a fine **restaurant** on the Llanfyllin High Street in the shape of *Seeds* (☎01691/648604), with a three-course set dinner menu including good vegetarian options for £20. Alternatively, there's cheap eating at *Eagles* café on the High Street, or good pub food in the bar of the *Cain Valley* (see above), far less snooty than the posh restaurant. The *New Inn* is the earthiest of the High Street's pubs.

Though services are somewhat sketchy, you can explore the region by **bus**, via the very infrequent G1 service to Llanfyllin and Llanrhaeadr-ym-mochnant from Welshpool, and the equally scarce #445 from Oswestry to Llandwyn at Lake Vyrnwy.

The Tanat and Rhaeadr valleys

Parallel to the valley of the River Cain, three or four miles to the north, are the luscious valleys of the Afon Tanat and its tributary, the Rhaeadr. A sparsely populated, little-changed backwater, this is a beguiling area set against the looming Berwyn Mountains.

For a place so near the English border, **LLANRHAEADR-YM-MOCHNANT** is surprisingly Welsh. Six miles north of Llanfyllin, this small, low-roofed village is best remembered as the serving parish of Bishop William Morgan, who translated the Bible into Welsh in 1588 (see p.391), an act which ensured the survival of the old tongue. The village has three great **pubs** – the *Three Tuns*, *Hand Inn* and *Wynnstay Arms*, and excellent value **B&Bs**: on the central square, rooms at *Powys House* (☎01691/780201; ①) have shared bathrooms; alternatively, try the plusher *Llys Morgan* (☎01691/780345; ③), on the road towards Pistyll Rhaeadr. If you're interested in trying out a **bicycle** (with a view to buying, of course), nip along to The Tandem Shop (☎01691/780050) on Market Street, Britain's only specialist in tandems and bikes specifically designed for women.

Llanrhaeadr lies at the foot of the wild walking country of the southern Berwyn Mountains. A lane from the village courses northwest for four miles alongside the Rhaeadr River, through an increasingly rocky valley, before coming to an abrupt halt at **Pistyll Rhaeadr**, supposedly Wales' highest waterfall at 150ft. The river tumbles down the crags in two stages, flowing under a natural stone arch that has been christened the Fairy Bridge. When it's quiet, tame chaffinches swoop and settle all around this enchanting spot, although the charms are a little hard to appreciate amid the crowds on a warm summer Sunday. Right by the car park, the summer-only *Tan-y-Pistyll* licensed café and B&B (☎01691/780392; ②) is nothing special, but its location is superb the owners also run a good **campsite** in the back field.

The B4396 runs east from Llanrhaeadr, along the Tanat Valley and through the village of **LLANGEDWYN**. A mile or so after the village, few visitors make it up one of the left turns leading to **SYCARTH**, only a mile from the English border, but one of the most Welsh of all shrines: a grass mound marks the site of Owain Glyndŵr's ancestral court, reputedly a palace of nine grand halls. Bard Iolo Goch immortalized this Welsh Shangri-la as a place of "no want, no hunger, no shame/ No-one is ever thirsty at Sycarth".

Just to the east of Sycarth, the English–Welsh border tightly encircles the 740-foot limestone crag of **Llanymynech Rocks** (now a nature reserve), before cutting down to run right through the middle of the village of **LLANYMYNECH**. Indeed, the divide runs slap through the village's *Lion Hotel* – not so long ago, thanks to the now dead Welsh ban on licensing on the Sabbath, half the pub had to remain "dry" on Sunday, while the other (English) half downed beer with gusto. Just over the road, the *Bradford Arms* does superb bar and restaurant food.

The B4391 hugs the river as far as the soporific little **LLANGYNOG**, where it heads north into the Berwyn Mountains and Denbighshire. Cowering under the rocky screes of Craig Rhiwarth, the village is a low-key walkers' base. The lane by the bridgeside fish-and-chip shop leads to a stunning four-mile hike over the top of Y Clogydd and down to the elfin charms of Pistyll Rhaeadr (see above). Less strenuously, you can walk (or drive) two miles further up the Tanat Valley to the hamlet of **PENNANT MELANGELL**, sitting low in a quiet valley of sheer sides and sparkling brooks, the site of one of Wales' most enduring myths. Legend has it that the eighth-century saint Melangell was praying in the valley when a hare being chased by a hunt pack led by Prince Brochwel took refuge in her skirts. The hounds drew to a sudden stop before her and fled howling. The prince drew his horn to his lips to call them, only to find himself unable to remove it. The prince was so moved by Melangell's gentle humanity that he granted her the valley, in which she built a religious community. The idyllic little **church** (daily: May–Oct 10am–6pm; Nov–April 10am–4pm) that sits here today dates from the eighth century, although the site was one of worship and spiritual significance way before. Inside, a twelfth-century shrine (the oldest known in Britain) and supposed effigy of St Melangell lie beneath an exquisite barrel roof. Melangell's grave is in the semicircular *cell y bedd* at the back of the church. Intact Norman features include a window in the main church, the south door porch and the font. By the Norman doorway at the back, a locally discovered whale bone is mounted on the wall.

Lake Vyrnwy

A monument to the self-aggrandizement of the Victorian age, the four-mile-long **Lake Vyrnwy** (Llyn Efyrnwy) combines its functional role as a water supply for Liverpool with a touch of architectural genius in the shape of the huge nineteenth-century dam at its southern end and the Disneyesque turreted straining tower which edges out into the icy waters. It's a magnificent spot, and a popular centre for walking and bird-watching. A commemorative stone at the eastern end of the dam arrogantly celebrates "taking and impounding the waters of the Rivers Vyrnwy, Marchnant and Cowny", which flooded a village of four hundred inhabitants in the process.

Constructed during the 1880s, Vyrnwy was the first of the massive reservoirs of mid-Wales. The village of Llanwddyn was flattened – it can still be seen when drought drops the level of the lake – and rebuilt at the eastern end, its people receiving compensation of just £5 for the loss of their homes. The story is told, somewhat apologetically, in the **Vyrnwy Visitor Centre** (daily 10.30am–5.30pm; Jan–March Sat & Sun only; free), which is located in modern **LLANWYDDYN** on the western side of the dam and combines with an **RSPB Visitor Centre** (same hours). RSPB staff here are in charge of a small hide across the road, where you can sit and watch forest birds (and cheeky squirrels) attacking the feeders outside the windows. A few yards down the road, there's a **tourist office** (Easter–Oct daily 10am–5pm; Nov–Easter Fri–Mon 10am–4pm; ☎01691/870346) and *Mandy's Tea Shop* (☎01691/870377), from where you can **rent bikes** for £2 per hour. The *Bethania Adventure Centre* (☎01691/870615), in the boathouse near the dam, also rents bikes, offers **river rafting** and **sailing** trips, and doles out leaflets detailing modest walks through the woods around Llanwyddyn.

Lake Vyrnwy's immediate surroundings boast some of the best accommodation in the region, notably the grand *Lake Vyrnwy Hotel* (☎01691/870692, fax 870257, *www.lakevyrnwy.co.uk*; ⑦), overlooking the waters above the southeastern shore. It's a mite pricey, but dinners are worthwhile, B&B deals are a few pounds more than the room rate, and the full afternoon tea, served in a chintzy lounge overlooking the lake, is perfect for if you just want to have a look around. Close by, *Ty Uchaf* (☎01691/870286; ②) offers B&B and good tearooms; and a couple of miles east of modern **Llanwddyn** on the B4393, there's a farmhouse B&B with shared bathrooms not far away at *Tynymaes* (☎01691/870216; ①).

THE DEE VALLEY

Northern Powys peters out on the stark slopes of the Berwyn Mountains, on the other side of which lies the charming valley of the wide, meandering **River Dee**.

Along with the smaller towns of Bala and Corwen, **Llangollen** grew up partly as a market centre, but also served the needs of cattle drovers who used the passage carved by the river through the hills as the easiest route from the fattening grounds of northwest Wales to the markets in England. Long before rail and road transport pushed the dwindling numbers of drovers out of business at the end of the nineteenth century, they had already been joined by early tourists. Most made straight for Llangollen, where the ruins of both a Welsh castle and a Cistercian abbey lent a gaunt Romantic charm to a dramatic gorge naturally blessed with surging rapids. The arrival of the train in the middle of the nineteenth century made Llangollen a firm favourite with tourists from the mill towns of northwest England, but also opened up **Corwen** and **Bala**, market towns making the best of the new opportunities for income. The train line closed in the 1960s and Corwen slipped back into its former role, but Bala has become one of Wales' top water-sports venues, a centre for windsurfing and white-water kayaking. Between the two, the **Vale of Edeyrnion** slumbers at the foot of the fine walking country of the Berwyn range. Between Llangollen and the English border, the Dee is joined by one of its major tributaries, the River Ceiriog, which flows, parallel to and south of the Dee, down the peaceful valley of **Glyn Ceiriog** to the Marcher fortress of **Chirk Castle**.

Chirk and Glyn Ceiriog

Like the Berwyn foothills over the county border in Montgomeryshire, **Glyn Ceiriog** and its surrounds are blissfully quiet and starkly beautiful. Tiny lanes wind up from Llanrhaeadr-ym-Mochnant and the Tanat Valley to a tranquil stretch that's occasionally

– and very optimistically – promoted as the "Little Switzerland of Wales". However, other than Chirk Castle at the entrance to the valley, there are no compelling sights to draw you here, but the area makes a perfect getaway from the rigours of touring Wales.

Chirk and Chirk Castle

The Normans founded **CHIRK** (Y Waun) almost a thousand years ago, their motte remaining as a small tree-covered mound at the southern end of this pleasant enough village with long views up the valley to the Berwyn hills. Chirk's minor architectural features are laboriously explained on the *Chirk Town Trail* leaflet (available free from tourist offices in the region), but you're better off with its companion, the *Chirk Bridges Trail*, which details the circular route (2 miles; 1hr; negligible ascent) around Thomas Telford's towering 1801 aqueduct, built to carry the Llangollen Canal seventy feet above the river. The route is sporadically indicated by a red hand, the principal element on the local lairds' coat of arms and the source of all the "Hand" hotels which dot the region.

For the last 400 years, the Myddleton family have occupied the massive drum-towered **Chirk Castle** (April–Sept Wed–Sun noon–5pm, Oct Sat & Sun noon–5pm; £4.80; NT), squatting ominously on a rise half a mile to the west of Chirk. Roger Mortimer began the construction of this Marcher fortress at the behest of Edward I during the thirteenth century, and it eventually fell to the Myddletons. The approach to the castle is guarded by a magnificent Baroque **gatescreen**, the finest work done by the Davies brothers of Bersham, who wrought it between 1712 and 1719. The ebullient floral designs are capped by the Myddleton coat of arms, with a pair of wolves reproduced atop the cage-like gateposts (perhaps a memorial to one of the last wolves in Wales, said to have kept watch over the moat in the 1680s). From the gates, a mile-and-a-half-long avenue of oak leads up to the castle, an austere-looking place softened only by its mullioned windows. The original plan was probably to mimic Beaumaris Castle (see p.422), started just a couple of months earlier, but Chirk lacks Beaumaris's purity and symmetry. The east and west walls are both incomplete, stopping at the half-round towers midway along the planned length, and the towers have been cut down to wall level, probably after the Civil War when taller towers would have been vulnerable to mortar attack. Internal modifications have been no less extensive, leaving a legacy of sumptuous rooms reflecting sixteenth- to nineteenth-century tastes, many returned to their former states after some Victorian meddling by Pugin in the 1840s.

After touring the house, you should try to leave an hour spare to explore the beautiful ornamental gardens (opening an hour earlier than the castle and closing an hour later) or to trace the section of Offa's Dyke that runs across the front of the house, though it was flattened in 1758 for use as a cart track.

Glyn Ceiriog

Chirk Castle guards the entrance to the Glyn Ceiriog valley, for centuries an important route into the heart of Wales and over the Berwyns into Snowdonia. These days it is the minor B4500 which runs beside the river for five miles through the hamlet of Pontfadog to the slightly larger Glyn Ceiriog, then on a further four miles to **LLAN-ARMON DYFFRYN CEIRIOG** (usually referred to as Llanarmon DC), an appealing small village consisting of nothing but a church, a post office and some excellent accommodation catering to walkers. From February to November, the mountain-leader owners of *Gwynfa* (see overleaf) run Hillwalk Wales, offering guided hillwalks for people of all abilities (£10 per day; ☎01691/600287) and a series of residential weekend courses. From Llanarmon DC, you can link up with the walk on the Berwyns described on p.258 by taking the road heading northwest opposite the church. After five miles, you reach the memorial stone mentioned.

Practicalities

Trains on the Shrewsbury to Wrexham main line stop at Chirk's train station, midway along the half-mile-long Station Avenue. **Buses** stop in the centre of Chirk and infrequently penetrate the Glyn Ceiriog valley as far as Llanarmon DC. The many high-quality country **inns** in the region are an attraction in themselves, and all serve good **food**.

Ddol-Hir, Glyn Ceiriog (☎01691/718681). Small riverside caravan and campsite on the B4500 a mile west of Chirk.

Golden Pheasant Hotel, Llwynmawr (☎01691/718281, fax 718479). Traditional eighteenth-century rod-and-gun country hotel, with pleasant rooms. Food is served in both the formal restaurant and the wood-beamed bar. ⑤.

Gwynfa, Llanarmon DC, 200 yards along the Llanrhaeadr road (☎01691/600287). Attractive, comfortable non-smoking B&B, the home base for Hillwalk Wales (see overleaf). Vegetarian breakfasts and four-course evening meals for £10. Closed Dec & Jan. ①.

Hand Hotel, Church St, Chirk (☎01691/773472, fax 772479). Sixteenth-century coaching inn with fully fixtured, modernized rooms. Substantial breakfast included, and full dinners served in the restaurant. The warren of small bars all serve real ales. ⑤.

Hand Hotel, Llanarmon DC (☎01691/600666, fax 600262). Converted sixteenth-century farmhouse with a wood-beamed bar. Try to get one of the older, more atmospheric but less well-appointed rooms rather than those in the modern extension. ⑤.

The Lodge, Halton (☎01691/774424). Spacious, tastefully decorated rooms in a secluded Georgian mansion a mile north of Chirk, just off the A5. ②.

Tŷ Issa Farm, Pontfadog (☎ & fax 01691/718909). Predominantly vegetarian and non-smoking B&B in a seventeenth-century farmhouse with free fishing on site and even accommodation for horses. ②.

West Arms, Llanarmon DC (☎01691/600665, fax 600622, *gowestarms@aol.com*). Ancient farmhouse-turned-inn with a gorgeous inglenook fireplace and some characterful rooms. Morning tea and a hearty breakfast, plus sumptuous dinners and affordable bar meals. ⑤.

The Woolpack Inn, Pandy, a mile west of Glyn Ceiriog (☎ & fax 01691/718382). Gently modernized old mill with decent rooms, a restaurant and a bar lined with real-ale pumps. ③.

Llangollen and around

Seven miles northwest of Chirk and clasped tightly in the narrow Dee Valley between the shoulders of the Berwyn and Eglwyseg mountains, **LLANGOLLEN** is the embodiment of a Welsh town in both setting and character. Along the valley's floor, the waters of the River Dee (Afon Dyfrdwy) cut a wide arc around the base of **Dinas Brân**, a conical tor surmounted by the ruins of a native Welsh castle. At the apex of the bend, the Dee licks the angled buttresses of Llangollen's weighty Gothic bridge, which has spanned the river since the fourteenth century. On its south bank, half a dozen streets, their houses harmoniously straggling up the rugged hillsides, are labelled in both Welsh and English, and form the core of the scattered settlement flung out across the low hills.

As the only river crossing point for miles, Llangollen was an important town long before the early Romantics arrived at the end of the eighteenth century, when they were cut off from their European Grand Tours by the Napoleonic Wars. Turner came to paint the swollen river and the Cistercian ruin of **Valle Crucis**, a couple of miles up the valley; John Ruskin found the town "entirely lovely in its gentle wildness"; and writer George Borrow made Llangollen his base for the early part of his 1854 tour detailed in *Wild Wales* (see Books, p.480). The rich and famous came not only for the scenery, but to visit the celebrated **Ladies of Llangollen**, an eccentric pair of lesbians who became the toast of society from their house, **Plas Newydd**. But by this stage, some of the town's rural charm had been eaten up by the works of one of the century's

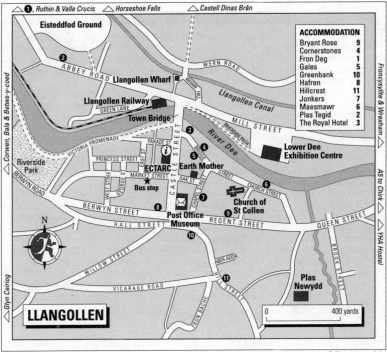

△ **❶**, *Ruthin & Valle Crucis*   △ *Horseshoe Falls*   △ *Castell Dinas Brân*

Eisteddfod Ground

❷ ABBEY ROAD

WERN ROAD

Llangollen Wharf ▪

WHARF HILL

Llangollen Canal

Llangollen Railway

GREEN LANE

MILL STREET

Town Bridge

VICTORIA PROMENADE

River Dee

RIVERSIDE PATH

❸

PARADE ST

❹

BRIDGE STREET

BERWYN ROAD

Riverside Park

PRINCESS STREET

EAST ST

❺

Earth Mother

Lower Dee Exhibition Centre

WEST STREET

GEORGE S

ECTARC

MARKET STREET

★ **Bus stop**

OAK ST

CHAPEL STREET

❻

CHURCH STREET

Church of St Collen

BERWYN STREET

❽

❼

HALL STREET

Post Office

Museum

❾

REGENT STREET

QUEEN STREET

BROOK STREET

❿

WILLOW STREET

ABER-ADDA

N

VICARAGE ROAD

HILL STREET

FRON FÂCH

⓫

Plas Newydd

LLANGOLLEN

0   400 yards

△ Corwen, Bala & Betws-y-coed
△ Glyn Ceiriog
Froncysyllte & Wrexham ▷
A5 to Chirk ▷
YHA Hostel ▷

ACCOMMODATION	
Bryant Rose	9
Cornerstones	4
Fron Deg	1
Gales	5
Greenbank	10
Hafren	8
Hillcrest	11
Jonkers	7
Maesmawr	6
Plas Tegid	2
The Royal Hotel	3

finest engineers, Thomas Telford (see box, overleaf), who squeezed both his **London–Holyhead trunk road** and the **Llangollen Canal** alongside the river. Canal trips run east to his majestic nineteen-span **Pontcysyllte Aqueduct** over the Dee, while steam-hauled trains now ply the reconstructed track west beyond the head of the canal at the Horseshoe Falls. If none of this is energetic enough, try the panoramic day-long walk along the limestone escarpment to the north of town (see box, p.253).

Llangollen's functional-looking streets can seem little different from those of any other Welsh town, but its rural environs are home to a wealth of historical sites, making the town a very popular base throughout the summer, particularly in early July when Llangollen struggles to cope with the thousands of visitors to Wales' celebration of worldwide folk music, the **International Music Eisteddfod** (see box p.252).

Arrival, information and getting around

Buses are the only form of public transport to reach Llangollen, with local services (and the daily Wrexham–London National Express coach) stopping on Market Street. The nearest **train station** is five miles away at Ruabon, and passed by frequent buses on the Llangollen–Wrexham run. With your own vehicle, the most spectacular way to approach Llangollen is over the 1350-foot Horseshoe Pass (A542) from Ruthin.

The **tourist office** (Easter–Oct daily 10am–6pm; Nov–Easter 9.30am–5pm; ☎01978/860828, *www.llangollen.org.uk*) is on Castle Street, fifty yards south of the

THOMAS TELFORD (1767–1834)

The English poet Robert Southey dubbed **Thomas Telford** the "Colossus of Roads" in recognition of his pre-eminence as the greatest road builder of his day, if not the greatest ever. Throughout the early years of the nineteenth century, he managed some of the most ambitious and far-reaching engineering projects yet attempted, and there was seldom a public work on which his opinion wasn't sought.

Born in Scotland, he was apprenticed to a stonemason in London where he taught himself engineering architecture, eventually earning himself a position working for the Ellesmere Canal Company, who were planning a canal to link the Severn, Dee and Mersey rivers. His reputation was forged on the **Pontcysyllte Aqueduct**, part of the **Llangollen Canal** which, though one of his earliest major projects, was recognized as innovative even before he had completed it. Though lured away to build the Caledonian Canal in Scotland and St Katherine's Docks in London, he continued to work in Wales, reaching the apotheosis of his road-building career by pushing the **London–Holyhead Turnpike** through Snowdonia.

After the 1800 Act of Union between Britain and Ireland, a good road was needed to hasten mail and to transport the new Irish MPs to and from parliament in London. What is now the A5 was wedged into the same valley as Telford's Llangollen Canal, then driven right through Snowdonia with its gradient never exceeding 1:20. The combination of its near-level route and the high quality of its well-drained surface cut hours off the journey time, but the Dublin ferries left from Holyhead on the island of Anglesey separated from the mainland by the Menai Strait. Telford's solution and his greatest achievement was the 580-foot-long **Menai Suspension Bridge**, strung 100ft above the strait to allow tall ships to pass under. Though the idea wasn't completely novel, the scale and the balance of grace and function won the plaudits of engineers and admiring visitors from around the world.

bridge and less than a hundred yards from the bus stop on Market Street. Alternative information is available at the Earth Mother New Age shop on Oak Street, and you can access the Internet nearby at The Gallery Computer World, 22 Chapel St (☎01978/869384; £3 per half hour).

Buses in the immediate locality are fairly infrequent, so you might as well resign yourself to **getting around** on foot – no great hardship as Valle Crucis, the most distant sight, is only a mile and a half along the towpath. **Bike rental** is available from the YHA hostel (see opposite) for £12 per day.

Accommodation

Finding **rooms** in Llangollen can be a chore in the middle of summer, especially during the Eisteddfod, though this is alleviated by people letting out one or two bedrooms in the peak period. The tourist office can book you into these as well as the ordinary guesthouses that are dotted all over the valley, though many of the cheaper ones are on Hill Street heading up towards Plas Newydd.

Hotels and guesthouses

Bodidris Hall, seven miles north of Llangollen on the A5104 (☎01978/790434, fax 790335). Secluded luxury in a largely Tudor building in nine acres of grounds, with log fires, oak beams and an award-winning restaurant. ⑥.

Bryant Rose, 31 Regent St (☎01978/860389). Low-cost, central B&B with large, airy rooms, some en suite. ①.

Bryn Howel, Trevor, two miles east off the A539 (☎01978/860331, fax 860119, *hotel@brynhowel.demon.co.uk*). One of Llangollen's better hotels, though the assiduous courting of the conference set strips it of some of its charm. Beautiful grounds and good facilities including sauna, solarium, free trout fishing and a top-class restaurant. Two-night deals are cheaper. ⑦.

Cornerstones, 15 Bridge St (☎01978/861569). Deluxe B&B with just two en-suite rooms, one heavy with oak beams, the other overlooking the river below. ①.

Fron Deg, Abbey Rd (☎ & fax 01978/860126). Overlooking the canal almost a mile from town beyond the Eisteddfod site, this very classy en-suite B&B is made more appealing by a wonderfully welcoming host. ②.

Gales, 18 Bridge St (☎01978/860089, fax 861313). Very comfortable and central guesthouse above the restaurant of the same name, with en-suite rooms and frilly decor. ③.

Greenbank Guesthouse, Victoria Square (☎01978/861835). Newly opened guesthouse with clean, bright simply furnished rooms that are some of the cheapest in town; all have TV and en-suite bathrooms. ①.

Hafren, Berwyn St (☎01978/860939). Good non-smoking B&B along the A5 to Corwen at the bottom of this price category with shared bathroom and no single supplement. ①.

Hillcrest, Hill St (☎ & fax 01978/860208). Appealing licensed guesthouse up towards Plas Newydd with en-suite rooms and meals available. ①.

Jonkers, 9 Chapel St (☎01978/861158). A couple of compact, low-beamed rooms in an ancient house with uneven floors and narrow stairways all tucked under the eaves of a great restaurant. One room has a four-poster, and both share the bathroom. ①.

Maesmawr, Church St (☎01978/860477). Central, budget guesthouse with off-street parking and (a rarity at the bottom end) some rooms dedicated to smokers. ①.

The Old Vicarage, Bryn Howell Lane, three miles east of Llangollen (☎ & fax 01978/823018). Very comfortable and spacious country guesthouse surrounded by beautiful grounds running down to the Dee. Take the A5 east, turn left at the *Aqueduct Inn*, then left after the bridge. ②.

Plas Tegid, Abbey Rd (☎01978/861013). Spacious and new B&B close to the Eisteddfod site, with great breakfasts and almost no supplement for singles. ①.

The Royal Hotel, Bridge St (☎01978/860202, fax 861824). Well-kept traditional nineteenth-century hotel by the bridge in town. ⑤.

Hostels and campsites

Canoe Inn, Mile End Mill, Berwyn Rd (☎01978/869043). Clean, basic accommodation in three- or four-bed dorms for £7 (£8 en suite) overlooking the canoe slalom site a mile west of town, and with simple café on site. ①.

Eirianfa, Berwyn Rd (☎01978/860919). Fully equipped riverside holiday park almost a mile west of the town on the A5.

Llangollen YHA hostel, Tyndwr Rd (☎01978/860330, fax 861709, *llangollen@yha.org.uk*). High-standard hostel with some private rooms (①) in a Victorian manor that's also one of the YHA's principal activity centres (see "Activities", p.256). It's a mile and a half east of town – go along the A5 towards Shrewsbury, turn right up Birch Hill, then right again. Open all day.

Wern Isaf Farm (☎01978/860632). Simple farmhouse campsite just under a mile up Wern Road. Turn right over the canal on Wharf Hill.

The Town

Few visitors can resist admiring the view up the valley from the parapet of the **town bridge** which, though widened and strengthened over the years, has spanned the river since the fourteenth century. Below it, the Dee pours through the fingers of shale which make up the unimaginatively dubbed "Town Falls" rapids, an occasional venue for canoe slaloms.

The bridge runs onto Castle Street, which heads due south past the tourist office to the **European Centre for Traditional and Regional Cultures**, or ECTARC (May–Sept Mon–Fri 10am–5pm, Sat & Sun 10am–6pm; Oct–April Mon–Sat 9am–5pm, Sun 10am–4pm; free). Primarily a centre for folk studies, ECTARC also presents six-monthly displays drawing on each of the fifteen EU countries in turn. Bibliophiles should cross the road to *Maxim's* café, above which there's a cavernous secondhand

THE LLANGOLLEN INTERNATIONAL MUSIC EISTEDDFOD

Llangollen is heaving in summer, but never more so than during the second week of July, when for six days the town explodes into a frenzy of music, dance and poetry. The **International Music Eisteddfod** comes billed as "the world's greatest folk festival" but unlike the National Eisteddfod (see Basics, p.46), which is a purely Welsh affair, the Llangollen event draws amateur performers from thirty countries, all competing for prizes in their chosen disciplines. Throughout the week, impromptu dances and choral performances burst into being anywhere that a group of people can congregate, often blocking traffic. Competitive performances are concentrated in the main venue, the **Royal International Pavilion**, on the north bank just west of the Gothic bridge, but performers occasionally present their works at other sites around the town, Plas Newydd and Valle Crucis included. When the day's competition is over, headlining stars often pack out the pavilion: Luciano Pavarotti and his 200-strong entourage fronted up in 1995 on the fortieth anniversary of his first performance here.

The festival has been held in its present form since 1947, when it was started more or less on a whim by one Harold Tudor to soothe the social wounds of World War II. Forty choirs from fourteen countries performed at the first (entirely choral) event, and it expanded, drawing praise quickly from Dylan Thomas, who declared that "the town sang and danced, as though it were right". Today over 12,000 international musicians, singers, dancers and choristers descend on this town of 3000 people, further swamped by up to 150,000 visitors. While the whole setup can seem oppressive, there is an irresistible *joie de vivre* as brightly costumed dancers walk the streets and fill the fish-and-chip shops.

Unless you are going specifically for the Eisteddfod, the week beginning the second Tuesday of July is a good time to stay away. Accommodation should be booked (most easily through the tourist office) several months in advance, though **tickets** (☎01978/861501, fax 861300, *tickets@lime.uk.com*) for all but the headlining shows can be obtained much closer the time, often on the day itself. All-day access to the site, with no guarantee of a seat, costs as little as £5 a day.

bookshop. Further along Castle Street, the small, basement **Post Office Museum** (daily 9am–5.30pm; £1) offers a bitty but moderately diverting display of letter writing and delivery paraphernalia. Some exquisite nineteenth-century nibs, inkstands and seals stand out from the ancient mail delivery bags and massed ranks of first-day covers.

Llangollen takes its name from the **Church of St Collen** on Church Street, off Castle Street (May–Sept daily 1.30–6.20pm; free). Dedicated to a sixth-century saint, the church features a fine fifteenth-century oak hammerbeam roof, said to have come from Valle Crucis (see p.255). The graveyard is of equal interest for the triangular, railed-off monument to Mary Carryll erected by her mistresses, the Ladies of Llangollen (see below), who are also buried with her in the churchyard and commemorated on the other two sides of her pillar.

Plas Newydd

Standing in twelve acres of formal gardens, half a mile up Hill Street from the southern end of Castle Street, the two-storeyed mock-Tudor **Plas Newydd**, Butler Hill (April–Oct daily 10am–5pm; £2.50) was, for almost fifty years, home to the celebrated **Ladies of Llangollen**. Lady Eleanor Butler and Sarah Ponsonby were a lesbian couple from Anglo-Irish aristocratic backgrounds, who tried to elope together at the end of the eighteenth century. After two botched attempts dressed in men's clothes, they were grudgingly allowed to leave in 1778 with an annual allowance of £280, enough to settle in Llangollen, where they became the country's most celebrated lesbians – though apparently they were affronted by the suggestion that their relationship was anything other than chaste. Regency society was captivated by their "model friendship" in what Simone de Beauvoir called "a peaceful Eden on the edge of the world". Despite their desire for a "life of sweet and delicious retirement", they didn't seem to mind the constant stream of gentry who called on them. They found the Duke of Wellington a "charming young man, hansom, fashioned tall and elegant" and commemorated his visit in typically self-absorbed manner by engraving "E.B & S.P. 1814" over the mantelpiece in the Oak Room. Walter Scott was also well received, though he found them "a couple of hazy or crazy old sailors" in manner, and like "two respectable superannuated clergymen" in their mode of dress. Thomas de Quincey humoured the ladies, if only to bend their favour towards his friend Wordsworth, who had displeased them by referring to their house as "a low roofed cot" in an inelegant poem he had composed in the grounds. Gifts of sculpted wood panelling form the basis of the riotous friezes of gloomy woodwork that weigh on your every step around the modest black-and-white-timbered house, and most of the rooms have been left almost empty, so as not to hide the panelling. This does make Plas Newydd appear a little sterile, with only one upper room being devoted to a few of the ladies' possessions and printed boards covering their life stories.

The north bank of the Dee

Wherever you are in Llangollen, the hills echo to the shrill cry of steam engines easing along the **Llangollen Railway** (April–Oct 3–8 services most days; call ahead at other times; ☎01978/860979; £7 return). Shoehorned into the north side of the valley, it runs west from Llangollen's time-warped station past Glyndyfrdwy, near the Horseshoe Falls, as far as Carrog, six miles up the valley: eventually it will go as far as Corwen. Operating along a restored section of the disused Ruabon–Barmouth line, belching

---

A WALK FROM LLANGOLLEN

Note: This walk is difficult to follow without the OS Landranger #117 map.

Climbing up to Dinas Brân, you get a fair idea of what is in store on Llangollen's **Precipice Walk** (14 miles; 7hr; 1800ft ascent), which traces the crest of the wonderful limestone escarpment formed by Trevor and Eglwyseg rocks. One of the most dramatic sections of the Offa's Dyke Path – though not the dyke itself – follows the base of these cliffs, but the tops make a far better walk, offering superb views down into the Vale of Llangollen and across the Berwyn Range to the south. Since the eastern half of what is effectively a circuit around Ruabon Mountain is the least interesting part, the walk is described anticlockwise so the best can be experienced when you're freshest. Although it is certainly a long walk, the worst of the climbing is quickly over and fine weather makes it a superb outing.

Start the walk on a narrow tarmac path over the canal from Llangollen Wharf signposted up towards the ruins of Castell Dinas Brân. From the castle the route ahead unfolds, down the north flank towards the tarmacked road which runs below the escarpment forming part of the Offa's Dyke Path. Turn right at the road and head east along it for three miles, always taking any left turns and keeping the open land of Ruabon Mountain on your left. Half a mile past Hafod Farm turn left to Bryn-Adda following a "Public Footpath" sign. The route then heads roughly north over dense heather to the forestry plantation at Newtown Mountain and on to the road near Mountain Lodge. Just past the entrance to the lodge, turn west up towards the top of the moor and the head of the valley known as World's End. Follow the southern perimeter of a plantation and pick up the path, which then follows the escarpment south back to Llangollen. The easiest way back is to continue past Dinas Brân to the end of Trevor Rocks, then follow the road down to town.

steam engines creep along the river bank, hauling ancient carriages which sport the liveries of their erstwhile owners. The railway recently gained some notoriety by offering steam train funerals, the body or ashes being loaded on a train equipped for a mobile wake. Local opposition – founded on fears that rail fanatics would have their ashes thrown in the fire box to be distributed over the valley – has scuppered plans for the time being. The occasional driver-experience courses, letting you behind the controls of a steam loco (£120 for 2hr) are proving less controversial. You can dine on the train, too (see p.256).

A short riverside walk from the station leads to **Lower Dee Exhibition Centre** on Mill Street (daily 10am–5pm; combined ticket valid all day £9, *www.dapol.co.uk*), an ugly light-industrial building converted to house a couple of wildly divergent museums. Fanfare is reserved for the **Doctor Who Museum** (individually £5.50), one man's mission to preserve the fantasy of this enduring British sci-fi TV drama. If you grew up with the programme you'll love it, but don't expect any chilling encounters: the only-just-animated Hall of Monsters serves only to confirm how shabby and low-tech the Daleks, Silurians, Axons and Sea Monsters were, the original costumes seemingly slapped together from lampshades and bubble-wrap. Train buffs will be drawn to the other half of the centre and the **Model Railway World** (£4.50), where demonstrations of die-casting and model-building give way to an extensive collection of large layouts – some of them token-operated – in every imaginable scale. Entry to either museum gives you the opportunity to watch model-making in progress in the parent Dapol toy factory.

Unless the weather is atrocious, you might prefer to wander across the road to **Llangollen Wharf**, starting point for trips along the Llangollen Canal. Until the coming of the railway in 1865, the waterway was the only means to carry slates from the quarries on the Horseshoe Pass. Designed as a water supply for the Shropshire Union Canal, the Llangollen canal was one of Britain's finest feats of canal engineering: from the artificial **Horseshoe Falls**, a crescent-shaped weir built in 1806 to feed water into the canal, its architect, Thomas Telford, managed to avoid using locks for the first fourteen miles. He did this by building the thousand-foot-long **Pontcysyllte Aqueduct** 126ft above the river, at **Froncysyllte**, four miles east, employing long cast-iron troughs supported by stone piers – a bold move for its time. Diesel-driven licensed narrowboats run from Llangollen Wharf, Wharf Hill (May & Sept Sat & Sun noon; June–Aug daily noon; £6), a two-hour one-way trip returning by road. Alternatively, you can drive to Froncysyllte on the A542 – or walk the towpath – and take a forty-minute narrowboat ride with *The Ribbon Plate* (April–Sept daily except Mon 11am & 3pm; July & Aug hourly; £1.25) across the aqueduct and back, turning a blind eye to the nearby chemical plant. More committed narrowboaters can rent one for the day from Trevor Wharf Services in Froncysyllte (☎01978/821749; £55–70), or for longer periods from Peter Jones at Five Star (☎01691/690322).

Castell Dinas Brân

It's the view both ways along the valley which justifies a 45-minute slog up to **Castell Dinas Brân** (Crow's Fortress Castle), perched on a hill 800ft above the town, and reached by a signposted path from Llangollen Wharf. The lure certainly isn't the few sad vaulted stumps which stand in poor testament to what was once the district's largest and most important Welsh fortress. Built by the ruler of northern Powys, Prince Madog ap Gruffydd Maelor, in the 1230s, the castle rose on the site of an earlier Iron Age fort. Edward I soon took it as part of his first campaign against Llywelyn ap Gruffydd (see p.444), and the castle was left to decay, John Leland, Henry VIII's antiquarian, finding it "all in ruin" in 1540.

Although not much to look at, it's a great place to be when the sun is setting, imagining George Borrow sitting up there translating seventeenth-century bard Roger Cyffyn:

Gone, gone are thy gates, Dinas Brân on the height!
Thy warders are blood-crows and ravens, I trow;
Now no-one will wend from the field of the fight
To the fortress on high, save the raven and the crow.

The Eisteddfod site, Valle Crucis Abbey and Eliseg's Pillar

Walking west from the town bridge, the Eisteddfod site soon hoves into view, heralded by the architecturally controversial but nonetheless impressive **Royal International Pavilion**. The 6000-seat white plastic structure was designed to evoke the shape of the traditional marquee formerly erected on the site each year, but looks more like some giant armoured reptile dropped from a great height into the green valley. Outside the Eisteddfod season, the auditorium acts as a concert venue and sports hall, the foyer operates as a **gallery** (Mon–Fri 10am–4pm; free) with reputable changing exhibitions of international fine art and north Welsh crafts, and side rooms host workshops ranging from alternative medicines to Chinese brush painting.

Following the A542 or the canal towpath a mile west, you pass Llangollen's **Motor Museum** (April–Oct Tues–Sun 10am–5pm; Nov–March Wed–Sun 11am–4pm; £2), a shed full of lovingly restored not-so-vintage cars and vans supplemented by a small **canal exhibition**, which admirably explains the construction of the Llangollen Canal in the context of Britain's canal building mania at the end of the eighteenth century.

Half a mile beyond, the gaunt remains of **Valle Crucis Abbey** (April–Sept daily 10am–5pm, £2; Oct–March unrestricted access; CADW), stand in Glyn y Groes, the "Valley of the Cross". In 1201, Madog ap Gruffydd Maelor of Dinas Brân chose this majestic pastoral setting for one of the last Cistercian foundations in Wales, as well as the first Gothic abbey in Britain. Despite a devastating fire in its first century, and a complement of far-from-pious monks, it survived until the Dissolution in 1535. The church fell into disrepair, after which the monastic buildings, in particular the monks' dormitory, were employed as farm buildings. Later, Turner painted the abbey, imaginatively shifting Dinas Brân a couple of miles west onto the hill behind.

Though less impressive than Tintern Abbey (see p.65), Valle Crucis does greet you with its best side, the largely intact west wall of the church pierced by the frame of a rose window. At the opposite end, the equally complete east wall guards a row of six graves, one of which is said to contain Owain Glyndŵr's resident bard, Iolo Goch. There are displays on monastic life upstairs, reached by a detour through the mostly ruined cloister and past the weighty vaulting of the chapterhouse.

The cross that gives the valley its name is the eight-foot-tall **Eliseg's Pillar** (unrestricted access; CADW), four hundred yards north by the A542. Erected to a Prince of Powys in the ninth century by his great-grandson, it originally stood 25 feet high but was smashed during the Civil War in the 1640s. The stump remains, but you can now only see half of the full 31 lines glorifying the lineage of the Princes of Powys, which Celtic scholar Edward Llwyd translated from the remaining pieces in 1696.

Eating, drinking and entertainment

Though not extensive by city standards, Llangollen boasts a fairly good selection of **restaurants** and no shortage of daytime **cafés** around town. Picnic ingredients are best bought at the Bailey's food emporium on Castle Street, next to the tourist office.

Outside Eisteddfod week, there's not a great deal of **nightlife**, but local bands (and even international Welsh acts such as Catatonia) do play from time to time, and it's always worth checking if there is anything going on at the Eisteddfod site or at ECTARC.

Restaurants and cafés

Berwyn Belle (☎01978/860583). Enjoy an expensive four-course dinner on the Llangollen Railway (see p.253) as it inches its way to Carrog and back. Runs Sat 7.30pm and Sun 1pm roughly May–Sept & Dec.

Cedar Tree Restaurant at the *Bryn Howel Hotel*, Trevor (☎01978/860331). Formal, expensive award-winning restaurant with great views of Dinas Brân across the lawns.

Gales Wine Bar, 18 Bridge St (☎01978/860089). Old church pews and one of the most extensive cellars around make this a great place for an evening of wine glugging, with decent, moderately priced bistro-style food to soak it all up and great home-made ice cream.

The Gallery, 15 Chapel St (☎01978/860076). Friendly restaurant serving a good range of medium-priced pizza and pasta dishes.

Jonkers, 9 Chapel St (see p.251). About the best of the town restaurants, serving quality, moderately priced bistro meals made with fresh, seasonal and mostly Welsh ingredients in a non-smoking environment with outside seating in summer. Closed Sun & Mon.

The Woolpack Restaurant, 13 Church St (☎01978/860300). Opposite *Gales* and in direct competition with it, though tending towards greater formality and slightly higher prices.

Pubs and entertainment

Bull Hotel, Castle St. Lively and central town pub (with a beer garden) that's the main gathering place for Llangollen's youth.

D Bar, *The Royal Hotel*, 1 Bridge St. Very youthful and lively, especially at weekends.

Hand Hotel, 26 Bridge St. Straightforward local pub where you can listen to the male voice choir in full song at 7.30pm on Mon & Fri.

Jenny Jones, Abbey Rd (☎01978/860653). Good pub with mixed clientele most nights, live country-and-western music on Wed and jazz on Thurs.

Jonkers (see above). Good restaurant which turns into a tiny and typically packed venue which hosts top class folk evenings every second Wednesday (Feb–June & Sept–Nov only) charging up to £10; book early.

Prince of Wales, Berwyn St. The place to be on Wednesday night for local rock, when it can be a bit of a zoo.

Royal International Pavilion, Abbey Rd (☎01978/860111). Year-round venue for anything from choral and classical concerts to pull-out-the-stops rock gigs.

Wynnstay Arms, 20 Bridge St. A child-friendly bar divided into several smaller rooms, with good beer.

Activities

The climb up to Dinas Brân and the Precipice Walk (see box) both make for excellent walks with magical valley views, but require considerably more effort than the gentle riverside walk along Victoria Promenade past the Town Falls. If the sight of all this white water gives you a taste for something more active, head a mile upstream to JJ Canoeing & Rafting at Mile End Mill on Berwyn Road (☎01978/860763), which offers modest **rafting trips** (£12 an hour) on the bouncy but less-than-menacing waters of the Dee. Skilled kayakers can use the slalom course all day for £5, and they offer a range of rock climbing, abseiling and multi-activity packages.

Llangollen's YHA hostel (see p.251) operates as an **activity centre**, offering plenty of short, introductory sessions in kayaking, caving, rock climbing, mountain biking and sailing. Two-day residential courses cost £70–90, with the week-long "Wet and Wild" extravaganza of canoeing, sailing, gorge walking and windsurfing priced at £225.

Corwen and around

In the early fifteenth century, Welsh rebel Owain Glyndŵr set out from **CORWEN**, eight miles west of Llangollen, to wrest back all Wales from the English barons (see p.445). There is precious little to commemorate this fact, only the shape of a dagger incised into a grey-stone lintel of the south porch of the thirteenth-century **church of St Mael and St Julien**, known as **Glyndŵr's Sword**. The Welsh hero, local landowner and scourge of Henry IV is said to have cast the "sword" in anger at the townspeople from atop the hill behind. It actually predates him by half a millennium, but you can still keep his prowess in mind as you follow a path leading up between dry-stone walls from the road to the right of the post office up to the **viewpoint**. Before doing that, take a look around the near-circular churchyard with its well-preserved Celtic cross and gravestone with indentations for penitents' knees. Inside the church, there is a fine Norman font.

In Glyndŵr's time and probably before, Corwen was an important cattle drovers' town. The two main routes out of north Wales – one from Anglesey and the Llŷn, the other from Ardudwy and Harlech – met here for the final push to the English markets. The arrival of the train killed off the cattle trade but not the town itself, which for a century became an important junction of the Barmouth and Rhyl train lines. Now a quiet market town, it does have a couple of sights nearby, including two fine ancient churches (see below). Glyndŵr aficionados will probably be interested in the thirty-foot-high truncated cone of **Owain Glyndŵr's Mount**, on the south bank of the Dee just over three miles east on the road to Llangollen, where he is supposed to have stood on lookout for his enemies. He may well have done so, but the earthworks are more likely to be a Norman motte-and-bailey castle.

Corwen's charms don't justify stopping overnight, although the *Corwen Court*, London Road (closed Dec–Feb; ☎01490/412854; ①), is a **B&B** with a difference: converted from a police station and courthouse, the cells are now single rooms, and the doubles are converted from the sergeant's family's quarters. If that doesn't suit, *Bron-y-Graig* (☎ & fax 01490/413007; ②) is only a few yards east along the A5, and offers authentically renovated Victorian rooms in a house built for the Sheriff of Denbigh. The welcoming *Powys House Estate* at Bonwm, a mile east on the A5 (☎01490/412367; ②), has its own outdoor swimming pool and tennis court; Mrs Jones, Tyn Llidiart, Carrog Road (☎01490/412729; ①) offers non-smoking rooms and the most outstanding breakfasts this side of anywhere.

Buses on the Llangollen–Bala route stop in the centre of Corwen.

Capel Rûg and Eglwys Llangar

Taking its name from the Welsh word for heather, **Capel Rûg** (May to late Sept Tues–Sat 10am–2pm & 3–5pm; £2; CADW), a mile west of Corwen on the A494, is one of Wales' best examples of an unmolested seventeenth-century church. Along with the Gwydir Uchaf Chapel, near Llanrwst (see p.326), it gives a charming insight into worship three hundred years ago, when Mass was a private clerical devotion, with the congregation kept behind rood screens.

Rûg didn't entirely escape, but much here is as it was built in 1637 by the former privateer and collaborator on William Morgan's Welsh Bible (see p.391), William Salusbury. The plain exterior design gives no hint of the richly decorated interior: wooden angels support a roof patterned with stars and amoebic swirls, and a painting of a skeleton said to represent the transient nature of life and the inevitability of death. Informative displays in the ticket office give more details of the building's use.

Your ticket to Capel Rûg also entitles you to an escorted visit from there to another little-changed church, **Eglwys Llangar** (normally locked, phone Capel Rûg

☎01490/412025 for tour times, usually 2pm), a mile to the south off the B4401, which dates back to the fourteenth century or earlier. Parish boundary changes in 1853 made this church redundant, saving its extensive fifteenth-century wall paintings and seventeenth-century figure of death from obliteration. The interior woodwork is wonderful, from the beamed roof and minstrels gallery down to the eighteenth-century box pews.

The Vale of Edeyrnion

Unless you're in a hurry to get from Corwen to Bala, take the quiet B4401 along the Dee through the peaceful villages of the Vale of Edeyrnion – Cynwyd, Llandrillo and Llandderfel – and past a couple of the best country hotels in the area; buses on the Llangollen–Bala route go right through the valley. None of the villages is particularly interesting, but any can act as a base for hikes on the largely undiscovered Berwyn Range to the east (see box below), where you can walk all day without seeing a soul.

The first village, two miles south of Corwen, is **CYNWYD**, home to a **YHA hostel**, *The Old Mill* (April–Sept; ☎ & fax 01490/412814), which has some private rooms (①); the budget *Pen-y-Bont Fawr* B&B(☎01490/412663; ①), in a converted barn behind the *Prince of Wales* pub, and a further half-mile south, *Hendwr Caravan Park* (April–Oct; ☎01490/440210), just one of several **campsites** which dot the river flats through the valley.

A WALK ON THE BERWYNS FROM CYNWYD OR LLANDDERFEL

Note: The OS 1:50,000 Landranger #125 map is recommended for this walk.

Henry II's 1165 expeditionary force encamped on the Berwyn Hills, until forced to flee back to England from the Welsh weather and the guerrilla tactics of Owain Gwynedd. Legend has it that the king beat his retreat along the ancient high-moor trackway, thereafter known as Ffordd Saeson (Englishman's Road). Whether he did or not, the path makes for a good route up onto these lonesome rocky heather-clad outcrops. The **walk** (10 miles; 5–6hr; 2500ft ascent) follows part of Ffordd Saeson starting from Cynwyd beside *Y Llew Glas* (The Blue Lion) pub, passing the YHA hostel up through a forest to the deep heather moorland pass of **Bwlch Cynwyd** (1700ft). An alternative to this direct route forks right a hundred yards after the YHA hostel and leads past a waterfall and serene lake, before rejoining the main path. From Bwlch Cynwyd, the circular route leads south, but if the skies are clear, the lone summit of **Moel Fferna** (2067ft), a mile or so to the north, makes a rewarding detour. South from Bwlch Cynwyd, follow the path beside the fence for a couple of miles across desolate, somewhat featureless land to the summit of **Pen Bwlch Llandrillo Top** (2037ft), then drop down the other side to an ancient drovers' road. Known locally as the Maid's Path, it was once the harvest-time route for girls heading east from Llandrillo, sometimes as far as Llanarmon Dyffryn Ceiriog, five miles from here (see p.247). If you don't have your own transport, try walking over the Berwyns from the Vale of Edeyrnion into Glyn Ceiriog: it is the closest you'll get to experiencing what the drover's life must have been like.

Near where you meet the drovers' road, a much later traveller is commemorated by a stone to "A Wayfarer 1877–1956, a lover of Wales". In the days before knobbly tyres and gas mono-shock suspension systems, one W M Robinson rode up here by bicycle, unwittingly laying the groundwork for scores of mountain bikers now following his lead along the bridleways. A metal box nearby contains a book to record your visit.

The cairned summit of **Cadair Bronwen** (2575ft), a mile and a half south of the memorial, is the only place in Wales where you can pick cloudberries (sharp-tasting orange blackberries); otherwise head east for Glyn Ceiriog or west for the Vale of Edeyrnion. After half a mile on the westerly path, a sign points to Llandrillo, while an unsigned path forks right to Cynwyd.

The Berwyns are equally accessible from **LLANDRILLO** where, after a day in the hills, you can lay your head at *Y Llwyn Guesthouse* (☎01490/440455; ①), which is a lot nicer than it looks from outside; alternatively, luxuriate in the elegant Georgian surroundings of *Tyddyn Llan Country House*, on the B4401 towards Bala (☎01490/440264; ⑤) and eat in its highly rated, expensive restaurant. For sheer grandeur, and the opportunity to stay in a house once frequented by Queen Victoria, you can't beat the hand-painted and intricately carved nineteenth-century interiors of *Palé Hall*, three miles south of Llandderfel (☎01678/530285, fax 530220, *palehall@fsb-dial.co.uk*; ⑥), located in peacock-inhabited grounds beside a trout stream available for guests' use. Superb and expensive three-course meals are also served to non-residents: tartlet of goats cheese and leeks and breast of wood-pigeon are typical dishes.

If your budget won't stretch to these kind of prices, continue along the B4401 past **LLANDDERFEL** to *Melin Meloch*, just two miles short of Bala (March–Nov; ☎01678/520101; ②), a B&B partly built from a converted thirteenth-century water mill beside the Dee which provides moderately priced communal meals by arrangement.

Bala

Easily reached either via the A494 from Corwen or over a spectacular mountain pass from Montgomeryshire's Lake Vyrnwy, the little town of **BALA** (Y Bala), at the northern end of Wales' largest natural lake, **Llyn Tegid** (Bala Lake), is a major water-sports centre with a modest sideline in remote walks on little-visited hills. If neither of these are of interest, there's little point in stopping here. The four-mile-long body of water is perfect for **windsurfing** in particular, with buffeting winds whipping up the valley formed by the Bala geological fault line, which slices thirty miles northeast from the coast, up the Talyllyn Valley, and between the Aran and Arenig mountains that flank the lake.

Bala's second lake, **Llyn Celyn**, five miles west of town, isn't that much smaller than Llyn Tegid, but is very much an artificial affair created to supply Liverpool, in England, with its drinking water. A modern chapel on the shore commemorates the valley-bottom village of Capel Celyn (flooded to create the reservoir) and its former inhabitants.

The Town

The narrow town sits slightly back from the lake edge, perhaps to avoid the catastrophe which, according to two legends, drowned the old town which stood where the lake now is. One tells of someone forgetting to put the lid on the well which, during the night, overflowed covering the valley and town. A more entertaining story records the fate of the quasi-legendary prince Tegid Foel, who was warned by a voice that, because of his cruelty to his people, "Vengeance will come". On the birth of his son, he held a banquet at which a hired harpist heard a voice saying "Vengeance has come". A bird led him away onto a hill where he slept, waking to find the town submerged beneath the lake which took the prince's name.

Bala has a role in Welsh history which far outweighs its current status. The district was of only minor importance before the eighteenth century, the Romans having built a fort at the southern end of the lake (not open to the public), and the Normans having erected a motte. This is now tree-covered and is known as **Tomen-y-Bala**, on Heol y Domen off the northern end of the High Street (keys from the council offices, 22–24 High St) which gives a panoramic view over the town. But it was **wool** – and socks in particular – that brought the town its fame. Until the Industrial Revolution killed the trade, most local men and women were involved in knitting, even clothing George III, who wore Bala stockings for his rheumatism. During this period, the people of Bala became noted for their piousness and followed the preachings of Nonconformist

THOMAS CHARLES AND MICHAEL D JONES

During the seventeenth and eighteenth centuries, the religious needs of the Welsh were being poorly met by the established Church. None of the bishops were Welsh, few were resident, and most regarded their positions as stepping stones to higher appointments. The preachings of the newly emerging Nonconformists – Quakers, Baptists and, later, Calvinist and Wesleyan Methodists – were therefore welcomed by the people. Congregations swelled from the middle of the eighteenth century, but conversion didn't get into full swing until the effects of itinerant religious teachers improved literacy and the strident sermons of native Welsh-speakers fired their enthusiasm. There were already over twice as many chapels as Anglican churches when the chief protagonist of Methodism in Wales, **Thomas Charles**, gave the movement a massive boost through the founding of the British and Foreign Bible Society, a group committed to distributing local-language Bibles worldwide.

He had already reprinted Bishop Morgan's 1588 original Welsh translation (see p.391), but was down to his last copy when 16-year-old Mary Jones (see p.299), the daughter of a poor weaver from the other side of Cadair Idris, arrived on his doorstep. She had saved money for six years to buy a Bible from Thomas Charles and, in 1800, walked the 25 miles to Bala, barefoot some of the way, prompting Charles to found the society.

Despite the rise in Nonconformism, many of the more pious converts sought greater freedom to worship as they pleased, in a land where they felt free; something denied them in Wales by the oppression of both the English Church and State. The reformist preacher **Michael D Jones** came to Bala enlisting recruits for his model colony outside Wales, and accordingly, he helped them found Y Wladfa, "The Colony", a Welsh enclave in Chubut Valley, Patagonia: in 1865 he transported 153 Welsh settlers, mostly from Bala, to Argentina, to set up a radical colony where Nonconformism and the Welsh language kept a tight rein. This was the start of a 3000-strong community (and the world's first society to give women the vote), which grew until 1912, when immigration stopped and linguistic assimilation accelerated. Jones stayed in Wales, setting up the Bala-Bangor Theological College and leading campaigns for Welsh causes, and many now regard him as "the father of modern Welsh nationalism".

ministers Thomas Charles and Michael D Jones (see box above). Charles is buried a mile south in the churchyard at Llanycil; his statue stands outside the Presbyterian church on Tegid Street, and a plaque locates his former home at 68 High St, in what is now a Barclays bank. A nearby plaque records Mary Jones' walk (see box above).

The only other thing to do around town is ride the **Bala Lake Railway** (April–Sept; ☎01678/540666; £6.50 return, £3.80 single), which starts half a mile south of Bala on the other side of the lake and runs for four miles along the route of the former Ruabon–Barmouth standard-gauge line, which closed in 1963. It's one of Wales' least interesting narrow-gauge runs, but you can ride the renovated north Wales slate quarry trains down the far side of the lake to Llanuwchllyn, and the *Eagles Inn* (see opposite), ten minutes walk away.

Practicalities

The best approach to Bala is the A4212 from south of Blaenau Ffestiniog over the wild uplands between the twin peaks of Arenig Fawr and Arenig Fach. Unfortunately, this can't be done by public transport as Bala's only **bus** is the #94, which runs from Wrexham and Llangollen through the Vale of Edeyrnion (see p.258) to Dolgellau and Barmouth, stopping on High Street. The **tourist office** on Pensarn Road (April–Oct daily 10am–6pm; ☎01678/521021, *bala.tic@gwynedd.gov.uk*), is half a mile south along High Street in the same building as the Penllyn Leisure Centre.

Accommodation

Bala and its immediate vicinity have plenty of places to **stay**, but you can also make the most of the surrounding countryside by staying in the Vale of Edeyrnion (see p.258), northeast of the town.

HOTELS AND GUESTHOUSES

Abercelyn, half a mile south of Bala on the A494 (☎01678/521109, fax 520556, *www.celtrail.com*). A fine country house in an eighteenth-century former rectory with lake views. ②.

Fron Feuno Hall (☎01678/521115, fax 521151). Gracious country house with a vast lounge overlooking Llyn Tegid, and comfortable, spacious rooms. Lots of thoughtful little touches make it all the more appealing, and you can get delicious evening meals by arrangement. Closed Dec & Jan. ⑤.

Traian, 95 Tegid St (☎01678/520059). Good-value, very welcoming central guesthouse with shared bathrooms. ①.

HOSTELS AND CAMPSITES

The Coach House, Tomen Y Castell on the A494, a mile and a half north of Bala (☎01678/520738, *balabunk@aol.com*). Superior self-catering bunkhouse with small dorms (£7.50) and communal lounge and cooking areas. Very reasonable meals are available on request and duvets can be rented (£1) if you haven't brought a sleeping bag.

Glanllyn, four miles south of Bala on the A494 (☎01678/540227). Family campsite across the lake, with water-sports gear for rent. Closed Nov–April.

Pen-y-Bont, on the B4402 Llandrillo road (☎01678/520549, fax 520006, *www.ukparks.com*). The nearest campsite, by the outlet of the lake. Closed Nov–March.

Tyn Cornel (☎ & fax 01678/520759) four miles west along the A4212. Simple riverside campsite geared towards paddlers from the nearby Tryweryn slalom site. Closed Nov–Feb.

Eating and drinking

Guests at the local country guesthouses and B&Bs can't go wrong with the meals offered in-house, but Bala still has its fair share of decent **restaurants** and **pubs**.

Eagles Inn, Llanuwchllyn. Cosy local ten minutes' walk from the Lake Railway station, which serves excellent bar meals and is handy for the local male voice choir rehearsals which take place in the village hall at 7.30pm on Thursdays.

The Old School, 2 High St (☎01678/521269). This cavernous and grandly decorated old school hall serves good-value no-nonsense fare such as a £6 all-day breakfast.

Plas Coch High St (☎01678/520309). Well-cooked, nicely presented and moderately priced à la carte dinners in this traditional hotel.

Plas-yn-Dre, 29 High St (☎01678/521256). Friendly licensed restaurant popular with locals for the broad choice and the Welsh lamb speciality.

The Ship, 30 High St. The best of the town's straightforward drinking pubs.

White Lion, High St. Ancient coaching inn and the best place to drink in town, a favourite with both locals and rosy-cheeked hill-walkers huddled around the inglenook fireplace. Decent bar meals, too.

Water sports

Slalom kayak fans can make for the National White Water Centre at **Canolfan Tryweryn** (☎01678/521083, *www.welsh-canoeing.org.uk*), below the Arenig mountains, four miles west up the A4212. When water is released – typically around 200 days a year – it crashes down a mile and a half through the slalom site where frequent competitions take place on summer weekends. When the site is free, the centre organizes the only thrilling **white-water rafting** trips in Wales (£10 for a 20min single run, or £150–200 for a group of up to seven for 2hr). Proficient **kayakers** can also take to the water (£5 per day for canoeing association members, £10 others). Gear rental is available.

Down on the shores of Llyn Tegid by the tourist office, Bala Adventure and Watersports Centre (☎ & fax 01678/521059) runs courses in windsurfing, open-water kayaking and sailing. They're mostly aimed at groups but you can get individual instruction for around £38 a day. Once you're proficient you can take to the water, although on top of rental fees (starting at £10 for two hours in a kayak) you have to pay to get on the lake – £3 for sailing and £2.50 for canoeing or fishing.

travel details

Unless otherwise stated, frequencies for trains and buses are for Monday to Saturday services, Sunday averages 1–3 services, though the main routes are more frequent and some routes have no Sunday service at all.

Trains

Abergavenny to: Cardiff (hourly; 40min); Hereford (hourly; 20min); Newport (hourly; 30min); Pontypool (hourly; 10min).

Knighton to: Llandrindod Wells (4 daily; 40min); Llanwrtyd Wells (4 daily; 1hr 10min); Shrewsbury (4 daily; 1hr); Swansea (4 daily; 3hr 10min).

Llandrindod Wells to: Knighton (4 daily; 40min); Llanwrtyd Wells (4 daily; 30min); Shrewsbury (4 daily; 1hr 40min); Swansea (4 daily; 2hr 20min).

Welshpool to: Aberystwyth (6 daily; 1hr 30min); Birmingham (6 daily; 1hr 30min); Machynlleth (6 daily; 1hr); Newtown (6 daily; 20min); Pwllheli (4 daily; 3hr); Shrewsbury (6 daily; 20min).

Buses

Abergavenny to: Brecon (7 daily Mon–Sat; 1hr); Cardiff (hourly; 1hr 20min); Clydach (hourly; 30min); Crickhowell (7 daily Mon–Sat; 20min); Llanfihangel Crucorney (6 daily; 15min); Merthyr Tydfil (hourly; 1hr 30min); Monmouth (6 daily; 40min); Newport (hourly; 1hr 10min); Pontypool (hourly; 25min); Raglan (6 daily; 20min).

Bala to: Corwen (8 daily; 30min); Dolgellau (9 daily; 40min); Llandrillo (8 daily; 20min); Llangollen (8 daily; 1hr).

Brecon to: Aberdulais (2–3 daily; 1hr 30min); Abergavenny (7 daily Mon–Sat; 1hr); Builth Wells (1–3 daily Mon–Sat; 40min); Cardiff (1 daily; 1hr 20min); Craig-y-nos/Dan-yr-ogof (2–3 daily; 30min); Crickhowell (7 daily Mon–Sat; 25min); Hay-on-Wye (6 daily; 50min); Hereford (6 daily;

1hr 45min); Libanus (9 daily; 10min); Llandrindod Wells (1–3 daily Mon–Sat; 1hr); Merthyr Tydfil (10 daily; 40min); Newport (5 daily; 1hr 50min); Pontypool (6 daily; 1hr 20min); Sennybridge (2–3 daily; 20min); Swansea (2–3 daily; 1hr 30min); Talgarth (6 daily; 30min); Talybont (7 daily Mon–Sat; 20min).

Builth Wells to: Llandrindod Wells (5 daily Mon–Sat; 20min); Rhayader (3 daily Mon–Sat; 30min).

Chirk to: Llangollen (7 daily; 20min); Oswestry (hourly; 30min); Wrexham (hourly; 40min).

Corwen to: Bala (8 daily; 30min); Denbigh (5 daily; 1hr); Llangollen (8 daily; 20min); Ruthin (5 daily; 30min).

Hay-on-Wye to: Brecon (6 daily; 50min); Hereford (5 daily; 1hr).

Knighton to: Ludlow (3 daily; 1hr 10min); Presteigne (5 daily; 30min).

Llandrindod Wells to: Abbeycwmhir (1 postbus daily Mon–Fri; 2hr); Aberystwyth (1 daily; 1hr 40min); Brecon (1–3 daily Mon–Sat; 1hr); Builth Wells (hourly; 20min); Disserth (2 daily; 15min); Elan Village (1 postbus daily Mon–Fri; 40min); Hay-on-Wye (1 daily Wed & Sat; 1hr); New Radnor (1 daily Fri & Sat; 30min); Newtown (3 daily; 1hr 10min); Rhayader (3 daily; 30min).

Llanfyllin to: Llanwddyn for Lake Vyrnwy (3–4 daily Mon–Sat; 30min); Oswestry (3–4 daily Mon–Sat; 45min); Welshpool (1 daily Mon–Sat; 40min).

Llangollen to: Bala (8 daily; 1hr); Chirk (7 daily; 20min); Corwen (8 daily; 20min); Wrexham (at least hourly; 30min).

Llanidloes to: Aberystwyth (1 daily; 1hr); Dylife (2 postbuses daily; 30min); Newtown (9 daily; 30min); Ponterwyd (1 daily; 40min); Shrewsbury (4 daily; 2hr); Welshpool (5 daily; 1hr 10min).

Llanwrtyd Wells to: Abergwesyn (1 daily post-bus; 20min); Builth Wells (2 daily; 50min).

Oswestry (Shropshire) to: Chirk (hourly; 30min); Llanfyllin (3–4 daily; 50min); Welshpool (5 daily; 1hr); Wrexham (hourly; 1hr).

Shrewsbury (Shropshire) to: Llanidloes (4 daily; 2hr); Welshpool (7 daily; 50min).

Welshpool to: Berriew (6 daily Mon–Sat; 20min); Llanidloes (5 daily; 1hr 10min); Llanfyllin (1 daily Mon–Sat; 40min); Llanymynech (5 daily; 30min); Montgomery (school bus; 25min); Newtown (7 daily; 40min); Oswestry (5 daily; 1hr); Shrewsbury (7 daily; 50min).

CHAPTER FOUR

THE CAMBRIAN COAST

ardigan Bay (Bae Ceredigion) takes a huge bite out of the west Wales coast, leaving behind the Pembrokeshire peninsula in the south and the Llŷn peninsula in the north. Between them lies the Cambrian coast, a loosely defined mountain-backed strip periodically split by tumbling rivers, which stretches up from Cardigan to Harlech and the shores of Tremadog Bay.

Before the railway and improved roads were built during the nineteenth century, the awkward barrier of the Cambrian Mountains served to isolate this stretch of coast from the rest of Wales, with only narrow passes and cattle-droving routes pushing through the rugged terrain to get to the markets in England. Today, large sand-fringed sections are peppered with low-key coastal resorts, peopled in the summer by families from the English Midlands. The presence of English-dominated resorts and the influx of rat-race refugees to this staunchly nationalistic part of the country has, in the past, fuelled local antipathy. Protests against the dilution of local culture and language have simmered down considerably in recent years, especially in the wake of Plaid Cymru's successes in local authorities and the Welsh national assembly ballots as well as UK-wide general elections. Nowadays, nationalist protests focus more on the wider issues of independence or Welsh emancipation – the Queen, for example, had to cut short a visit (for the first – and, so far, only – time in her reign) to Aberystwyth in 1997 due to the scale of the demonstration that greeted her. Centre stage in the demo was a local drag queen, anointing her "subjects" in stack heels and massive wig. Humour and theatre are an essential part of the new protest movement, and any foreign settlers who can subscribe to that, and who bother to learn the Welsh language, are easily integrated.

The Cambrian coast starts where the rugged seashore of Pembrokeshire ends, continuing in much the same vein of great cliffs, isolated beaches and swirling sea birds, punctuated with *sarnow*, stony offshore reefs largely exposed at low tide. North of the spirited town of **Cardigan**, the coast breaks at some popular seaside resorts – the best being **Llangranog** and **New Quay** – before the tiny and ordered Georgian harbour town of **Aberaeron**, recently designated the headquarters of the county of Ceredigion.

A bucolic **inland** alternative to the coastal resorts follows the **River Teifi**, which meets the sea at Cardigan and meanders through lush meadows past a clutch of small towns, prominent among them the stalwart market centre of **Newcastle Emlyn**, the lively university town of **Lampeter** and the charmingly old-fashioned community of **Tregaron**.

ACCOMMODATION PRICE CODES

Throughout this guide, hotel and B&B accommodation is priced on a scale of ① to ⑨, the number indicating the **lowest price** you could expect to pay per night in that establishment for a **double room in high season**. The prices indicated by the codes are as follows:

① under £40	④ £60–70	⑦ £110–150
② £40–50	⑤ £70–90	⑧ £150–200
③ £50–60	⑥ £90–110	⑨ over £200

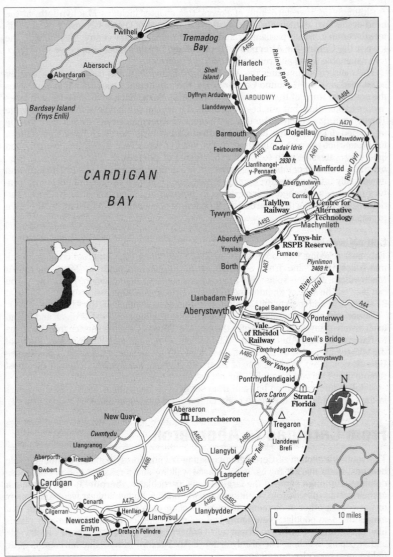

© Crown copyright

The coastal and inland routes connect at the robust and cosmopolitan "capital" of mid-Wales, **Aberystwyth**, built on the estuary of the **Rheidol**, a fast-falling river with dramatic ravines that make for great walking country. A narrow-gauge railway, an attraction in itself, climbs out of Aberystwyth to the popular tourist honeypot of **Devil's Bridge**, where three bridges, one on top of the other, span a turbulent chasm of waterfalls.

Although on a western limb of Powys, this chapter includes **Machynlleth**, at the head of the Dyfi estuary and a magical place, the seat of Owain Glyndŵr's putative fifteenth-century Welsh parliament and still a thriving market centre. Just outside the town is the **Centre for Alternative Technology**, Britain's most impressive showpiece for sustainable living and renewable energy resources.

The main road continues due north from Machynlleth, but trains and the smaller coast road skirt west around **Cadair Idris**, the monumental mountain that dominates the southern third of the **Snowdonia National Park**. Each of its crag-fringed faces invites exploration, but it is best approached from the south where the narrow-gauge Talyllyn rail line reaches the tiny settlement of **Abergynolwyn**, a great base for the unhurried delights of the **Dysynni Valley**. Cadair Idris' northern flank slopes down to the market town of **Dolgellau**, at the head of the scenic Mawddach estuary and linked by waterside path to the likeable resort of **Barmouth**. The coastal strip then broadens out with complex dune systems protecting the approaches to **Harlech** and its virtually intact castle, the southernmost link in Edward I's chain of thirteenth-century fortresses, perched high on its rocky promontory. Views from the fractured battlements sweep north towards the mountains of Snowdonia and west to the Llŷn peninsula.

Getting around

The most relaxing way to get fairly swiftly to and along the Cambrian coast is on the mid-Wales **train** line from Shrewsbury in England through to Machynlleth. At Machynlleth, the line splits: one branch runs south to Aberystwyth, from where you can pick up the Vale of Rheidol line to Devil's Bridge; the other swings north, calling at 25 stations in under sixty miles before terminating at Pwllheli on the Llŷn (see p.357).

Buses run almost parallel to the trains, also extending south to Cardigan and inland to all towns of any size. There's also the express Trawns Cambria service from Swansea to Bangor through Aberystwyth, Machynlleth, Dolgellau and Porthmadog. Many of the villages bypassed by the regular services rely on a skeletal network of **postbuses** (see Basics, p.31) working out of Aberystwyth and Machynlleth, though the most remote aren't served by public transport at all.

Detailed information on bus and train services as far south as Machynlleth appears in the Gwynedd and Ceredigion regional transport guides, available at tourist offices.

From Cardigan to Aberaeron

The southern section of Ceredigion coastline is enormously popular, combining safe beaches, lively market towns, great coastal walking and a resident pod of bottlenose dolphins. Although some of the larger towns, particularly **Aberporth**, have lost much of their scenic splendour to relentless waves of holiday homes and caravan parks, many of the coast's other settlements manage to cling onto some of the salty charm that makes them so popular: **New Quay** is a delightful hillside town, while smaller places like **Llangranog**, **Penbryn**, **Mwnt** and **Gwbert** neatly juxtapose superb countryside and sweeping beaches. The primly ordered **Aberaeron**, with its fine harbour, is quite unlike anywhere else on the coast.

Just inland, at the mouth of the Teifi, is the old county town of **Cardigan**, scarcely thrilling but pretty, cheerful and with an excellent range of pubs, accommodation and entertainment, as well as a sizeable travelling and New Age community.

The main A487 road runs parallel to the coast, meeting the sea at Aberaeron, and forms the basis of the regular #550 bus service linking the larger seaside villages and towns along this stretch.

Cardigan and around

An ancient borough and port until the Teifi estuary silted up in the nineteenth century, **CARDIGAN** (Aberteifi) was founded around its castle by the Norman lord Roger de Montgomery in 1093. The town is at the lowest bridging point of the Teifi estuary, rising up on the river's northern bank from its medieval bridge, its graceful simplicity making it the town's most attractive feature. Today, it's an appealing place in which to linger, its busy main street a jigsaw of historical architecture and its alleyways full of absorbing little shops and cafés. On the south side of the river, away from the town centre, an old granary houses the **Cardigan Heritage Centre** (*Canolfan Hanes Aberteifi*) (Mar–Oct daily 10am–5pm; £2). It's free to go into the first section, a coffee shop and exhibition about the rise and fall of the port of Cardigan, including shipping history and memories of the emigration boats that left the port bound for Canada and the USA. The entrance fee covers the excellent second section, which takes many diverting looks at nuggets of Cardigan's long history, including extremely well-researched and clearly explained tales of women who have featured prominently in the area during the last thousand years. There's usually a temporary exhibition or two to finish off the tour.

Across the river towards the town centre, the out-of-bounds castle mound, shored up by gross concrete buttresses, sits bulging at the town end of the medieval bridge. Sweeping up a hill around the site, Bridge Street becomes the picturesque High Street – leading off from here are several pavement-less thoroughfares, crammed with Georgian and Victorian buildings. High Street snakes past a good range of pubs and shops to the angular, turreted oddity of the **Guildhall**, with metal Welsh flags skewered adamantly to its grey frontage. Through the Guildhall courtyard is the town's **covered market**, a typically eclectic mix of fresh food and some good-quality craft and second-hand stalls. A couple of hundred yards up High Street (now called Pendre) from the Guildhall, Bath House Road dips down to the left and to the redoubtable **Theatr Mwldan**, whose imaginative programme of art, theatre, cinema and music, together with a decent daytime café and the tourist office, make it an essential stop.

Priory Street leads down the hill from the Guildhall, past the council offices and on to Finch Square, with the bus terminus and some cheery pubs and cafés. Spend some time hereabouts and you'll come to wonder why "Cardis" – residents of Cardiganshire, the former name of Ceredigion – are the traditional butts of Welsh jokes, always portrayed as being slightly dense and unimaginative. The spirited little town of Cardigan, and its entrepreneurially laid-back population, are as good a riposte as any to such negative stereotypes.

A mile out of town along the Teifi River is the large **Welsh Wildlife Centre** (daily 10am–5pm; £2.50), encompassing several important habitats – reedbeds, meadows, marshes and untouched oak woodland – for otters, badgers, butterflies and birds, including Wales' largest resident group of Cetti's Warblers. An uncomfortable combination of viewing hides and adventure playgrounds, the place seems torn between entertaining families and interesting enthusiasts, a lack of direction exemplified by an architecturally striking but inappropriate curved-glass **visitor centre** (closed Nov–March; ☎01239/621600).

Practicalities

The helpful **tourist office** (Easter–Sept daily 10am–6pm; Oct–Easter Mon–Sat 10am–5pm; ☎01239/613230, *cardigan@ceredigion.gov.uk*) is in the foyer of Theatr Mwldan on Bath House Road, although details of the many local green festivals and meetings are usually posted on the bulletin boards at the *Hungry Tummy* wholefood café, upstairs in the entrance hall of the market.

There's plenty of **accommodation**, with numerous B&Bs along the Gwbert Road, off North Road: *Brynhyfryd* (☎01239/612861; ①), at the town end, and *Maes-a-Môr* (☎01239/614929; ①), just up in Park Place, are the best. On the High Street, the old-fashioned *Black Lion* (*Llew Du*) pub (☎01239/612532; ②) has pleasant rooms and serves good meals. With your own transport, try the fifteenth-century *Rosehill Farm* in Llangoedmor, a mile and a half east of town (closed Nov–Feb; ☎01239/612019; ②), which boasts a gorgeous riverside setting and excellent evening meals. Cardigan is just beyond the northern end of the Pembrokeshire Coast Path (see p.162), which terminates four miles from town on the other side of the Teifi estuary at Poppit Sands, the site of the nearest YHA **hostel** (☎01239/612936; March–Oct only; ①). In July and August, the #407 and #409 buses stop right outside the hostel; at other times, they stop two miles short of it at St Dogmaels. **Camping** is allowed in the hostel grounds. Slightly nearer to Cardigan is the *Brongwyn Mawr Farm* caravan park (☎01239/613644), which also takes tents. It's just north of the village of Penparc, which is two miles north of Cardigan on the A487.

For **eating** and **drinking**, the café at Theatr Mwldan, open in the daytime, serves cheap vegetarian dishes and local specialities. More substantially, *Jackets*, 58 North Rd (☎01239/615206), serves pizzas, potatoes, kebabs and pies and runs a free delivery service. The licensed *Homely Kitchen* café on Pendre (☎01239/621863) serves good budget meals, and the *Rose of India* on Priory Street (☎01239/614891) dishes up reasonable curries. The *Red Lion* (*Y Llew Coch*), at the bottom of The Pwllhai near Finch Square, is the town's liveliest **pub**, with a pool room and live rock music at weekends, while the *Eagle*, at the southern end of the town bridge, serves the best pub food. The large and friendly *Angel Hotel* on St Mary Street hosts weekend **discos**.

The southern Ceredigion coast

One of the most popular stretches of coastline in the whole country, the rippled cliffs, expansive beaches and hedged lanes of the Ceredigion coast attract thousands of visitors every year, many of them keen to appreciate the tranquil ten miles of protected **Heritage Coast** from Ynys Lochtyn, near Llangranog, to New Quay.

The Gwbert Road heads out of the neat Cardigan suburbs before descending to the estuary edge and the straggling seaside village of **GWBERT**, whose eighteen-hole golf course is the only reason for staying here – in which case, the soulless but smart *Gwbert Hotel* (☎01239/621241; ③) is your best bet. More likely, you might spend an hour at the **Cardigan Island Coastal Farm Park** (Mar–Oct daily 9.30am–7pm or dusk; £1.70), half a mile beyond the hotel, which boasts farmyard creatures both domestic and exotic and the chance to spot fur seals on a coastal walk overlooking **Cardigan Island**. It's also a glorious spot in which to take tea and home-made *bara brith*, overlooking the ruffled coast and its turquoise sea. A mile or so to the east, tiny lanes bump down to the delightfully isolated hamlet of **MWNT**, where the exquisite sandy beach and cliffs are under the custody of the National Trust (car park £1.60). Set in windswept solitude above the cliffs, the tiny, whitewashed church is the oldest in Ceredigion – its foundation dates back to the sixth century, although most of today's thick-set building dates from the thirteenth century. Mwnt's most notable hour came in 1155, when invading Flemings landed here, only to be soundly routed by the Welsh. The occasion, which became known as *Sul Coch y Mwnt*, the Bloody Sunday of Mwnt, has been periodically remembered through the whole skeletons and other human bones that have been unearthed en masse in the vicinity. There's some good **camping** at Mwnt, though come supplied, as there are no shops nearby. Further along the track from the church is *Tŷ Gwyn*, a fairly basic site. Alternatively, a walk up through the wooded ravine behind the church brings you to *Blaenwaun Farm* site (☎01239/810354), also reached on the back lane from Felinwynt.

Four miles further east, the most popular stopping-off point on this stretch of coast has to be **ABERPORTH**, an elderly resort built around two adjoining bays, neither of them particularly pretty. The town's holiday resort status has long since robbed it of charm, and though it's packed full of places to stay, you're far better off pushing on to the infinitely preferable hamlet of **TRESAITH**, a mile east. This rewarding spot has a compact beach and, just around the rocks, a sandy cove with its own natural after-sea shower – a waterfall crashing down from the River Saith above. There are **dinghy races** from the surf-friendly beach on summer Sundays, and at low tide you can walk around to the wide, sandy, National Trust beach at **PENBRYN**. Once the beach has exhausted you, don't miss a pint in the cosy *Ship Inn*.

Tresaith's best **accommodation** is the non-smoking hilltop *Bryn Berwyn* guest-house (☎01239/811126; ③), ten minutes' walk from the beach. A couple of miles inland, one of the county's most appealing farmhouse hotels can be found at *Penbontbren Farm* (☎01239/810248, fax 811129; ⑤), just north of the village of Glynarthen, which also houses a superb restaurant specialising in local dishes. Back in Tresaith, at the far end of the otherwise grim *Llety Caravan Park* (☎01239/810354), there's a wonderful tent-only campsite that sits right above the footpath bumping down the cliffs onto the beach. The vehicle entrance is half a mile up the hill out of Tresaith on the way to Aberporth.

Just along the coast, three miles northeast of Tresaith, **LLANGRANOG** is the most attractive village on the Ceredigion coast, wedged in between hills covered with bracken and gorse. The very narrow main streets wind their way to the tiny seafront, well geared up for tourists with a good range of cafés, B&Bs, pubs and sporting activities. The beach can become horribly congested in midsummer – a quieter alternative is to head over to **Cilborth Beach**, reachable along the coast at low tide or via a cliff path leading along the glorious National Trust headland toward **Ynys Lochtyn** and a couple of other remote strips of sand. In Llangranog, you can **stay** at the excellent 350-year-old *Ship Inn* (☎01239/654423; ②), or the earthier *Pentre Arms* (☎01239/654345; ①) which also has one very cheap single room (£12); both do good food. Between Penbryn and Llangranog is the *Maesglas* caravan park (☎01239/654268), which takes tents. Signs around Llangranog point to an unlikely-seeming local activity: **skiing**. There's a decent artificial slope a mile east of the village at the Urdd Centre (☎01239/654656), just off the B4321. This outward-bound centre, owned by the Welsh-language youth organization, opens its slope up to the public for both skiing and snow-boarding; lessons are also available.

From Llangranog, you can walk along the coast path towards New Quay Head, where seasonal flowers swath wind-blasted hillsides and cliffs that drop dramatically into clear seas. The cave-walled beach at **CWMTYDU** is glorious, approached along tiny lanes dropping in hairpin bends from above. Here you'll find Cwmtydu Trekking Centre (May–Oct daily; ☎01545/560494) which runs well-priced one- or two-hour hacks. Between Cwmtydu and the handsome village of **LLWYNDAFYDD** is a complex of self-catering cottages at *Neuadd Farm* (☎01545/560324). In Llwyndafydd itself, just down the lane, the popular *Crown Inn* (closed Sun evening in winter) is deservedly noted for its beers and range of food.

New Quay

Along with Laugharne in Carmarthenshire, **NEW QUAY** (Cei Newydd) lays claim to being the original Llareggub in Dylan Thomas' *Under Milk Wood* (see p.153). Certainly, it has the little tumbling streets, prim Victorian terraces, cobblestone harbour, pubs and dreamy isolation that Thomas so successfully evoked in his "play for voices", as well, perhaps, as the darkly eccentric characters he excelled in describing. Certainly, the poet's own experience in New Quay (he and his young family lived here during the last half of World War II) showed him the odder side of human nature.

Thomas's metropolitan ways and poetic demeanour did not go down too well in such a close-knit little town, particularly so with an ex-commando officer, fresh home from the war, with whom he had a row in the *Black Lion* pub. The soldier, convinced that his wife was in a *ménage à trois* with Thomas and his wife Caitlin, followed the writer home and shot at his rented bungalow, the *Majoda*, with a machine gun, while the family was inside. The officer was charged with attempted murder in June 1945, and acquitted. Dylan Thomas and family left the area soon afterwards. It's hard to imagine such skulduggery in the streets today, as New Quay maintains an unhurried charm lost in so many of the other Ceredigion resorts. While it's not the place to come for a full-on bucket-and-spade seaside holiday, summer weekend nights, fuelled by a huddle of pubs and a transient surfing population, can get boisterously good-natured at times. With a fulsome range of eating and drinking options, it does make a great holiday base, with beaches, coastal walks and the odd boat trip to fill the days. Outside the summer, it is *the* place to be on New Year's Eve, when virtually the whole town gets kitted out in fancy dress and spends most of the night locked in the pubs or dancing out in the streets.

New Quay's main road cuts through the upper, residential part of town, past Uplands Square, from where acutely inclined streets swoop down to a pretty **harbour**, formed by its sturdy stone quay, and with a small, curving **main beach**. Back from the sand, the higgledy-piggledy lines of multicoloured shops and houses comprise the **lower town**, the more traditionally seaside part of New Quay, full of cafés, pubs and beach shops. Right by the harbour and over the road from the tourist office, there's a small roomful of old photos and memorabilia from New Quay's past in the **Heritage Centre** (May–Sept Fri–Sun noon–4pm; free), under the *Tŷ Gwyn* restaurant. More interesting is the **Marine Wildlife Centre** (April–Oct daily 10am–5pm; donation requested), tucked away down the slipway above the main harbour beach, which contains some interesting exhibits on the dolphins, seabirds and seals that inhabit Cardigan Bay.

It's easy to escape the town's bustle, such as it is. The northern stretch of beach soon gives way to a rocky headland, **New Quay Head**, where an invigorating path steers along the top of the sheer drops to **Bird Rock**, aptly named for the sheer profusion of razorbills and guillemots nesting here, and beyond to Cwmtydu. A route plan is available from the tourist office (see opposite).

Practicalities

Buses to New Quay stop on Park Street, just around the corner from Uplands Square and close to some reasonably priced **B&Bs**. These include the *Elvor* on George Street (☎01545/560554; ①), *The Moorings* on Glanmor Terrace (☎01545/560375; ①) and the *Hotel Penwig* on South John Street (☎01545/560910; ②). Right by the harbour, the *Hungry Trout* (☎01545/560680; ②) has a few en-suite rooms alongside their restaurant. The most lavish option, above the beach towards Cei Bach, is the luxurious, if extremely chintzy, *Ffynnon Feddyg* guesthouse (☎01545/560222; ③). There's a quiet caravan and tent **campsite** a mile down the B4342 at *Wern Mill* (☎01545/580699), just outside the lacklustre village of **Gilfachreda**, although the nearest to town is the *Neuadd* (☎01545/560709), behind the *Penrhiwllan Inn* at the top of the hill on the main road (A486) to Synod Inn.

Hidden among New Quay's innumerable cheap **cafés** are places like the *Mariner's*, by the harbour wall, which has an espresso machine, a rarity in these parts. For restaurant food, the best bet is the *Hungry Trout* (☎01545/560680), by the harbour on South John Street, for locally caught fish dishes and an imaginative vegetarian selection. New in town is a swish Italian eaterie, the *Rivabella* (☎01545/561333) on Margaret Street; next door is the *Seahorse Inn*, easily the town's best **pub**, where you'll find good food, a friendly crowd and regular music too. The *Wellington*, on the seafront, is lively and popular, and also serves decent scoff.

DOLPHINS AND DANGER

One of only two pods in Britain, the Cambrian coast's **bottlenosed dolphins** are one of New Quay's major attractions, and can often be seen frolicking by the harbour wall, particularly when the tide is full and the weather calm. There are also several **boat trips** geared around potential sightings. The pleasure jaunts run by New Quay Boat Trips, based at *The Moorings* on Glanmor Terrace (Easter & late-May to Sept daily; ☎01545/560375; 20min £1, 1hr £2.50), are the cheapest, but chances of a sighting are better on the Wildlife Cruises trips (☎01545/560032 or 0378/932792; £6 for 2hr, £15 4hr, £30 8hr), which go further offshore and up along the heritage coast on data-gathering exercises. These have a ranger on board and are bookable from the Marine Wildlife Centre (see opposite).

Although this stretch of coast is comparatively clean, Cardigan Bay's sea creatures are in constant danger from PCBs, inadequately treated sewage, monofilament fishing nets and noise from jetskis and powerboats, as well as occasional disasters like the 1996 *Sea Empress* oil spill at Milford Haven (see p.177). To get some idea of the results, make an appointment to visit the **Bird and Wildlife Hospital** (☎01545/560462; donations), a couple of miles inland of New Quay at Cross Inn, half a mile down the lane opposite the *Penrhiwgaled Arms*. A voluntary organization working with oil-soaked birds and diseased and injured seals and dolphins, the hospital is run by a team of dedicated volunteers who are usually happy to answer questions and show you their work.

The **tourist office** is centrally located at the junction of Church Street and Wellington Place (April–June & Sept daily 10am–5pm; July & Aug daily 10am–6pm; ☎01545/560865, *newquay@ceredigion.gov.uk*). You can rent canoes, surfskis and windsurfers from New Quay Watersports down by the main beach, and go pony trekking at Plas-y-Wern Riding Stables (☎01545/580156), a couple of miles out of town on the B4532. Four-hour **fishing trips** (☎01545/560375; £10) leave several times a day from the beach, and the town's **yacht club** (☎01545/560516) welcomes visitors. Details of the numerous **dolphin-watching** boats trips are given in the box above.

Aberaeron and around

New Quay may share its name with a town in Cornwall, but **ABERAERON**, seven miles up the coast, has more of a Cornish air, its large, deep harbour encased by pastel-shaded Georgian houses built in one fell swoop during the early nineteenth century by the Reverend Alban Gwynne. After the 1807 Harbour Act paved the way for port development, Gywnne spent his wife's inheritance dredging the Aeron estuary as a new port for mid-Wales and constructing a formally planned town around it – reputedly from a design by John Nash.

Georgian planning is most evident around the central **Alban Square**, with graceful terraces of quoin-edged buildings and the odd pedimented porch, all writ small in keeping with the Ceredigion coast. From there, the grid of narrow streets stretches away to the sea at **Quay Parade**, the neat line of ordered, colourful houses on the seafront.

Sadly, despite its architectural beauty, Aberaeron is almost unique amongst the Ceredigion resorts for its unappealing **beach** – its north end all stones and rubbish, its south end only marginally better. Consequently, the most agreeable activity in Aberaeron is just to amble around the waterfront, taking in the child-oriented attractions. Right on the harbour in Cadwgan Place, the **Hive on the Quay** (late-May to mid-Sept daily 11am–1pm & 2–5pm; £1) combines an exhibition of bees and a twenty-minute video on the life of a honeybee with chances to sample honey-based products, including delicious ice cream; it also has a good restaurant (see overleaf). The moderately diverting **Sea Aquarium**, past several old fishermen's houses at 2 Quay Parade

(Easter–Oct daily 10am–5pm; £3.50), has a tide pool of local fish and a good shark video. Upstairs, there's also an enjoyable photographic exhibition on old Aberaeron. The Aquarium is also the place from which to book **jet boat** trips around the bay aboard the *Sea Leopard* (1hr for £10; 2hr £17; book on ☎01545/570142). Off the main road at the southern end of town, a cluster of ageing stone buildings hous **Clôs Pengarreg** (summer daily 10am–6pm; rest of year Mon–Fri 10am–4pm), a better than average collection of craft shops, together with a model village and mini railway.

Llanerchaeron

While you're in Aberaeron, head three miles east along the A482 and check out **Llanerchaeron** (house and gardens April–Oct Thurs–Sun 11am–5pm; £2; parkland all year dawn–dusk; free; NT). The partially renovated remains of a late-eighteenth-century Welsh country estate, Llanerchaeron is a remarkable example of a type of holding once common in these parts. The National Trust has embarked on a ten-year project to restore the Nash-designed main house and a range of domestic buildings, gradually opening them to the public. Taking place a couple of times a year, special open days are the best bet for interior tours; for details, call ☎01545/570200. Otherwise, you're restricted to the grounds, though these in themselves are a fascinating time capsule of horticultural history, with exquisite, rambling walled gardens, early greenhouses and hotbeds with underground heating styled on Roman hypocausts. Ultimately, the aim is to run Llanerchaeron as a typical Welsh estate, complete with cattle and sheep. A rare opportunity to see behind the scenes of a restoration, the most rewarding time to visit is at 2pm on Thursdays in July and August for one of the volunteer-run guided **tours** (90p) of the estate. The #202 bus from Aberaeron to Lampeter passes within a mile of the site, and Ceredigion's first **cycle path** connects Aberaeron with Llanerchaeron. Apart from a small hill in town, the route is flat, as it follows the old railway line. Access to the cycle path is off South Road in Aberaeron. As it's only three miles, it's also a decent walk, taking about an hour.

Practicalities

Buses stop on the A487, here known as Bridge Street, from where it's a five-minute walk along Market Street to the **tourist office** on Quay Parade (July & Aug daily 10am–6pm; Easter–June & Sept daily 10am–5pm; Oct–Easter Mon–Sat 10am–5pm; ☎01545/570602, *aberaeron@ceredigion.gov.uk*). There is a good supply of decent budget **accommodation** in and around Aberaeron, but little in the way of luxury. A good option is the very smart *Llys Aeron*, almost a mile inland on Lampeter Road (☎01545/570276; ②). Otherwise, try the *Hazeldene*, South Road (☎01545/570652; ②), a quality B&B in a former sea captain's house ten minutes' walk from the town centre, with a water bed in one of the rooms. There's also the tastefully decorated *Castle Hotel* on Market Street (☎01545/570205; ②), and the welcoming and attractive *Fairview*, overlooking the harbour at 3 Cadwgan Place (☎01545/571472; ②), while the cheapest in town is the down-to-earth *Monachty Arms* at 7 Market Street (☎01545/570389; ①). The closest **campsite** is the *Aeron Coast Caravan Park* (☎01545/570349), just north of town on the A487, next to the petrol station. A further walk, but a more charming option, is the clifftop *Wide Horizons* site (☎01545/570043), about a mile south of town off the A487 Cardigan road.

For **food**, try the moderate *Arosfa*, 8 Cadwgan Place (☎01545/570120), an evening and Sunday-lunch restaurant serving traditional and invented Welsh dishes along with mainstream offerings. The Hive on the Quay exhibition (☎01545/570445) has a good fish restaurant with some European regional dishes, *Crafters Bistro* (☎01545/571721) at the Clôs Pengarreg craft centre is a decent option, and the *Apple Pie*, at 35 Alban

Square, is a good bakery-cum-deli-cum-café. Best for **pub food** is the *Harbourmaster*, next to the tourist office, which does superb French and seafood cuisine, or for a very meaty menu, try the steak bar at the homely *Prince of Wales* pub on Queen Street. For straightforward **drinking**, there's the *Monachty Arms*, 7 Market St (☎01545/570389), with its harbourside beer garden, and the *Black Lion*, Alban Square, which has a good range of guest real ales and Irish music most Thursday nights. The *Feathers Royal Hotel*, on the far side of Alban Square from the harbour, is the town's grandest venue, and has occasional live music. Otherwise, regular **entertainment** is restricted to the free Hymns on the Quay, a sort of open-air church service sung outside the tourist office at 7.30pm on Sundays during the school summer holidays. A new – and highly successful – initiative is the annual **Seafood Festival**, held on a Sunday in mid-July with loads of free food and drink augmenting the street entertainment; contact the tourist office for details.

The tourist office has route plans for local walks – including the **cliff path** to Cei Bach with its ancient church (usually closed) – and a National Trust shop. For summer **horse riding**, contact Gilfach Holiday Village, in Llwyncelyn, two miles south along the A487 (☎01545/580288; £8 an hour). The nearest **bike hire** is from Cyclemart (☎01570/470079), just off the B4337 towards the village of Cilcennin, signposted from the A482 Lampeter road.

The Teifi Valley

The Teifi is one of Wales' most eulogized rivers – for its rich spawn of fresh fish, its otter population, its meandering rural charm and the coracles that were a regular feature from pre-Roman times – and flows through some gloriously green and undulating countryside to its estuary at Cardigan. Small towns have grown up along its course, each hubs of enterprise in their time – witness the numerous water-driven mills in the valley – but mostly bypassed by the Industrial Revolution, making them perfect draws for alternative-lifestyle types spilling over from the New Age heartland of Powys.

The river is tidal almost as far up as the massive ramparts of **Cilgerran Castle**, four miles below the falls at **Cenarth**. Upstream, it flows around three sides of another fortress at **Newcastle Emlyn**, and also takes in the proudly Cymric university town of **Lampeter**. Beyond here, the river passes through a different, harsher scenery for eleven miles to **Tregaron**, a town Welsh in its language, feel and flavour, and a good base for nearby **Llanddewi Brefi**, with some spectacular walks up into the Abergwesyn Pass (see p.227) and the reedy bogland of **Cors Caron**. The river's infancy can be seen in the austere town of **Pontrhydfendigaid**, famous for its annual eisteddfod, and the nearby ruins of **Strata Florida Abbey**, beyond which the river emerges from the dark and remote **Teifi Pools**.

Cilgerran

Just a couple of miles up the Teifi from Cardigan is the attractive village of **CILGERRAN**. Behind the wide main street are the massive ramparts of the **castle** (daily: April–Oct 9.30am–6.30pm; Nov–March 9.30am–4pm; £2; CADW), founded in 1100 at a commanding vantage point on a high wooded bluff above the river, then still navigable for seagoing ships. This is the legendary site of the 1109 abduction of Nest (the "Welsh Helen of Troy") by a lovestruck Prince Owain of Powys. Her husband, Gerald of Pembroke, escaped by slithering down a toilet waste chute through the castle walls.

The massive dual entry towers still dominate the castle, and the outer walls are some four feet thicker than those facing the inner courtyard. Walkways high on the battlements – not for vertigo sufferers – connect with the other towers. The outer ward, over which a modern path now runs from the entrance, is a good example of the evolution of the keepless castle throughout the thirteenth century. Any potential attackers would be waylaid instead by the still-evident ditch and the outer walls and gatehouse, of which only fragmentary remains can be seen. Another ditch and drawbridge pit protect the inner ward underneath the two entry towers. The views over the forested valley towards the pink-and-grey Georgian fantasy castle of **Coedmore**, on the opposite bank, and towards Cardigan, are inspiring. If the castle is closed, get the key from the adjoining Castle House.

A footpath runs down from the castle to the river's edge, flanked by display boards telling the story of the emigrants to America, for whom Cardigan was the last sight of home, and the history of the Teifi Valley industries, particularly quarrying, brick making and coracle fishing. Guided two-hour trips (£7.50; book on ☎01239/613961) through the wooded valley aboard Canadian **canoes** leave from the quay during the summer months. If you want to see coracles in action, the best bet is Cilgerran's fun annual **coracle races**, which take place in August – call for details on ☎01239/613635.

Cenarth

A tourist magnet since the nineteenth century and still chock-full of tearooms and gift shops, **CENARTH**, seven miles upstream from Cardigan, is a pleasant spot, but hardly merits the mass interest it receives. The secret is that the village's main asset, its **waterfalls**, are close to the main road, ideal for lazy visitors. The low but impressive cataracts are a result of the Teifi being split by rocks as it tumbles and churns its way over the craggy limestone. The path to the falls runs from opposite the *White Hart* pub and past the **National Coracle Centre** (Easter–Oct daily except Sat 10.30am–5.30pm; £2.50; other times by appointment ☎01239/710980), a small museum with intriguing displays of original coracles from all over the world, half of them from Wales. Many of the exhibits date from the last two centuries, their hazel and willow shells covered in treated calico, but there are several older, more traditional ones cloaked in ox hide. Your entry fee also entitles you to visit the restored seventeenth-century **flour mill** (same hours) by the falls' edge. The adjacent *Three Horseshoes* pub serves good beer and bar meals.

Newcastle Emlyn and around

An ancient farming and droving centre, **NEWCASTLE EMLYN** (Castell Newydd Emlyn) still retains a robustly agricultural feel, particularly on Fridays, the bellowing and busy market day. The swooping meander of the Teifi River made the site a natural defensive position, first built on by the Normans. The "new" **castle**, of which only a few stone stacks and an archway survive, replaced their fortress in the mid-thirteenth century. Although the ruins aren't impressive, the site, surrounded on three sides by the river flowing through a valley of grazing sheep and rugby fields, is gently uplifting and quintessentially Welsh. The castle is tucked away at the bottom of dead-end Castle Terrace, which peels off the main street by a squat little stone **town hall**, topped by a curiously phallic cupola. Unsurprisingly, Bridge Street (Heol yr Bont), heads down from here to the stone bridge over the Teifi. Next to the old coaching inn, the *Emlyn Arms*, is the Oriel Celtic Nations **gallery** of original prints and engravings, including many from around Wales.

Although there are few other sights in the town there are at least some great pubs and places to eat, and with its strong sense of community, unhurried charm and fabulous scenery, Newcastle Emlyn is a good base from which to explore the surrounding area.

Practicalities

Newcastle Emlyn's **tourist office** (Easter–Sept Mon–Sat 10am–5.30pm; ☎01239/711333) and the tiny Attic **theatre** are both located in the town hall on Bridge Street. Information on more esoteric local happenings can be best found at the shop housing both the Sathya clothes and crafts outlet and the Riverside Health Centre, on the far side of the river bridge from the town centre. Inexpensive, central B&B **accommodation** is available at the cheerful *Pelican Inn* on Sycamore Street (☎01239/710606; ①), which also does tasty all-day food, and the smarter *Emlyn Arms* (☎01239/710317; ③) on Bridge Street. Further out, the *Maes-y Derw Guest House* (☎01239/710860; ②), half a mile towards Cardigan on the A484, with spacious Edwardian rooms, a restaurant and private fishing, is charming, as is *Fedwen Guest House*, Waungilwen, Felindre (☎01559/371421; ①), three miles towards the Museum of the Welsh Woollen Industry (see below) and set in five acres of grounds.

The best place to **eat and drink** is the deservedly popular *Bunch of Grapes*, a stylish bar on Bridge Street, with guest real ales and live Celtic music most Mondays and Thursdays. You can get a good lunch and coffee at the licensed *Snapdragon* (closed Sun; ☎01239/710404), over the bridge down by the Teifi, while straightforward boozing is enjoyable at the *Ivy Bush*, a gnarled old Welsh local on Emlyn Square, or the *White Hart* on Sycamore Street.

Museum of the Welsh Woollen Industry, Teifi Valley Railway and Ffostrasol

The lower Teifi's prolific past as a weaving centre is best seen in the village of **DREFACH FELINDRE**, five miles southeast of Newcastle Emlyn. At the beginning of the twentieth century, this was at the heart of the Welsh wool trade, with 43 working mills in and around the village. Today, the National Museum's **Museum of the Welsh Woollen Industry** (April–Sept Mon–Sat 10am–5pm; Oct–March Mon–Fri 10am–5pm; 50p), housed in a vast Edwardian mill, does a fine job of evoking the days when a full workforce churned out flannel shirts for miners or khaki for World War I soldiers' uniforms. Displays of old photographs and mementos set the tone for the main exhibit, long rooms full of carding and twisting machines, Jacquard looms and machinery for processes you never imagined existed. Natural dyeing is treated in some depth, along with fleece-to-fabric demonstrations of various working methods. Currently under extensive redevelopment, the museum will go back to charging a few pounds entry once the work is complete in late 2001. The museum is at the hub of twenty miles of paths, packed into a two-mile radius, along which workers walked to the mills.

A mile to the north at **HENLLAN**, the volunteer-run **Teifi Valley Railway** (Easter–Oct & Christmas daily; ☎01559/371077; £5) operates seven daily steam- and diesel-hauled trains along a mile and a half of narrow-gauge track. Seven miles further on, at the junction of the B4571 and the A486, the hamlet of **FFOSTRASOL** only merits a visit during the first or second week in July, when it plays host to the annual Gûyl Werin y Cnapan (☎01239/810045 or 858955), one of the largest **Celtic folk festivals** held anywhere in the world.

Llandysul and Llanybydder

The pace slows down even further as the lanes reach **LLANDYSUL**, sitting pretty above the Teifi some eight miles east of Newcastle Emlyn. Two main streets run parallel through the village, the lower one brushing past the massive Early English-style **church of St Tysul**, looming large over some lush riverside meadows. Two centuries back, the church porch served as a goalpost in the annual match of *chwarae pel*, an anarchic and extremely rough, day-long football-like game that ran the length of the village. Inside the church, there's an inscribed altar stone, thought to date from the sixth century, in the Lady Chapel.

Most of Llandysul's shops and pubs are on the upper main street, which changes name four times in a couple of hundred yards and boasts all the elements of an archetypal Welsh market town: amazingly old-fashioned shops, beguiling floral displays and creaky old pubs jostling for position amongst a jumble of architectural styles from grand town houses to low-slung cottages. If you want to **stay** in Llandysul, try the *Porth Hotel* (☎01559/362202; ②) on Church Street (the lower road), a traditional old pub with pleasant rooms. A couple of miles east along the Teifi, on the lane to Capel Dewi, there's also a lovely independent hostel in an old stone barn at *Pen Rhiw* (☎01559/363200); beds cost £6 per night. Back in Llandysul, for no-nonsense **drinking**, try the *Cilgwyn Bach* pub on Bridge Street, the southernmost section of the upper main street.

While Llandysul's fortnightly livestock market (Tues) is a reminder of the area's strong agricultural pedigree, the biggest, smelliest reminder comes in the shape of the monthly **horse market** in the moribund village of **LLANYBYDDER** (sometimes anglicized to Llanybyther on old road signs), some ten miles east of Llandysul along the Teifi. Held on the last Thursday of every month, the market is one of the biggest in Britain, bringing buyers and sellers together from all over. Amongst the hubbub of spoken Welsh and English, together with the noise of neighing horses, there's little to remind you that you're in the twenty-first century. Llanybydder is a sluggish sort of place on non-market days, when you'd half expect to see tumbleweed scudding along the deserted streets. If the place does tempt you to stay, whether for the quiet or some decent walks into the bleak hills to the south, the only real option is the central *Black Lion* pub (☎01570/480212; ②).

Lampeter

Five miles further along the Teifi from Llanybydder, **LAMPETER** (Llanbedr Pont Steffan) is the home of what may well be the most remote university in Britain, and certainly one of the oldest. Made a constituent member of the University of Wales in 1971, the St David's University College, was Wales' first, founded in 1822 by the Bishop of St David's to aid Welsh students who couldn't afford to travel to England for a full education. With a healthy student population (albeit one comprised substantially of theologians, many of them involved in Islamic studies), together with large numbers of resident hippies, the small town, with a permanent population of less than 2000, is well geared up for young people and visitors. Furthermore, with so many ex-students still living in the area, the town boasts thriving music and arts scenes, much of which are easily accessible to visitors. All this youthful culture rubs shoulders with Lampeter's more traditional agricultural base, as the market town for a wide and fertile area of rolling hills and green valleys.

There's not a great deal to see in Lampeter, and what you are able to visit is fairly low-key. **Harford Square** forms the hub of the town and is named after the local landowning family who were responsible for the construction of the early nineteenth-century **Falcondale Hall**, now an opulent hotel, on the northern approach to Lampeter. Around the corner from the square at 2 Bridge St, at the back of the Mulberry Bush health-food shop, is **Celtic Edge**, a showcase for the work of local artists.

The main buildings of the **University College** lie off College Street, and include C.B. Cockerell's original stuccoed quadrangle of buildings, dating from 1827 and modelled along the lines of an Oxbridge college. Tucked right underneath the main buildings, the motte of Lampeter's long-vanished **castle** forms an incongruous mound amidst such order. On the other side of Harford Square, the High Street is the most architecturally distinguished part of town, its eighteenth-century coaching inn, the *Black Lion*, dominating the streetscape; you can see its old stables and coach house through an archway. Go through the archway of the former town hall to reach the new municipal buildings by the

Walkers, Cwm Idwal, Gwynedd

Llyn Gwynant, Gwynedd, Snowdonia

Snowdonia, Gwynedd

Last drovers of Wales, Powys

Conwy castle and harbour, Conwy, Gwynedd

Wind turbine on moorland near Cerrigydrudion

Disused slate quarry, Penyrosedd, Gwynedd

Blaenau Ffestiniog, Gwynedd

STEVE BENBOW/THE PHOTOLIBRARY WALES

'Prisoner' Convention at Portmerion, Gwynedd

STEVE BENBOW/THE PHOTOLIBRARY WALES

The National Eisteddfod

STEVE PEAKE/THE PHOTOLIBRARY WALES

Chapel cat, Croesor, Gwynedd

DAVE NEWBOULD/THE PHOTOLIBRARY WALES

South Stack Lighthouse, Anglesey

Somerfield supermarket, which contain a minute civic **museum** (Mon–Thurs 9am–1pm & 1.45–4.30pm; free), mainly comprising curly old photographs of the town. You can also get to the museum from Harford Square by taking the alley by the Spar shop.

Practicalities

Lampeter makes a good base – it's a lively town, there are frequent gigs and theatre performances and enough pubs and cafés for any visitor. It's also in excellent **cycling** country, with the surrounding terrain gentle enough for inexperienced riders. There are no bike rental outlets in town, though you might be able to pick up a cheap second-hand cycle from Siop Peniffardding, next to Ralph's Bakery on College Street. There is a **tourist office** of sorts (Mon–Fri 9am–5pm; ☎01570/422426) in the new civic museum buildings (see above). It doesn't book **accommodation**, but rooms are easy to find: notice boards in the Mulberry Bush wholefood shop (see opposite) carry information about local B&Bs and longer lets. Alternatively, there's a good B&B, *Haulfan*, at 6 Station Terrace (☎01570/422718; ①), behind University College, and hotel accommodation in the recently refurbished *Black Lion* on High Street (☎01570/422172; ③). The best places to stay, though, lie slightly out of town: *Pantcelyn* (☎01570/434455; ①), a couple of miles west at Llanwnnen, has good rooms and will do evening meals, while the abundantly appointed, if slightly faded, *Falcondale Country House Hotel* (☎01570/422910; ⑤) is a Victorian mansion in fourteen acres of parkland, reached along a drive by the Murco garage on the A475 Newcastle Emlyn road, which picks up the top end of Lampeter's market. There's also a **campsite** five miles northeast at *Moorlands*, near Llangybi (☎01570/493543), and just off the B4343, running up the Teifi Valley towards Llanddewi Brefi, is one of the area's best farmhouse B&Bs at *Pentre Farm* (May–Oct; ☎01570/493313; ③), near Llanfair Clydogau, five miles from Lampeter.

There are plenty of decent places to **eat** and **drink** in town. Cheap and popular with students is the *Cottage Garden* restaurant (closed Sun), opposite the university on College Street, while well up the cholesterol scale, there's *Lloyds* on Bridge Street, an upmarket fish-and-chip shop and restaurant that opens until 9pm. Also on Bridge Street and fairly studenty is the friendly *King's Head* pub, with a wide-ranging menu and some very well-kept beer. Make sure you at least stick your head into *Conti's Café* on Harford Square – the food is cheap and none too spectacular, but the surroundings are wonderfully decayed, plastered with ageing accolades for the café's rich home-made ice cream. Serious foodies should head four miles out of town to *Seguendo di Stagioni* (☎01558/650671) in Harford. Local seasonal produce dictates the table d'hôte menu of this superb, justly expensive Italian restaurant, where beautiful preparation and exquisite flavours don't preclude hearty helpings. Also out of town, real-ale fiends will love the *Ram Inn*, a sixteenth-century drovers' inn, just over a mile to the south of Lampeter at the top of the hill in Cwmann. At the bottom of the hill, just over the river bridge from Lampeter, where the A485 meets the A482, the *Cwmann Tavern* is the best local bet for beery **live music** gigs and sessions. The Lampeter area is rich in festivals, groups and **womens' events** – check notice boards (see above) or arrive in time for September's Women in Tune Music Camp (☎01570/493356).

Tregaron and around

On the cusp of the lush Teifi Valley and the gloomy moors rising above it, the neat small town of **TREGARON**, ten miles northeast of Lampeter, has a tendency to enchant passing visitors. It feels almost untouched by the late twentieth century, and seems a bastion of the Welsh language and culture in an area that has suffered galloping anglicization over recent decades.

All roads to Tregaron lead into the spacious – and lately spruced-up – market square, hemmed in by solid eighteenth- and nineteenth-century buildings, of which the most impressive is the **Talbot Hotel**, a classically symmetrical old drovers' inn. The square and the inn were the very last points of civilization seen by drovers before heading out of town on the wild Abergwesyn Pass (see p.227), which rises above the Tregaron en route to Llanwrtyd Wells and beyond. The pristine **statue** in the centre of the square is of Tregaron-born Henry Richard (1812–88), the founder of the Peace Union, forerunner of the League of Nations and, subsequently, the United Nations. On the corner of the market square and Dewi Road is the Rhiannon craft design centre, a wonderful shop stocking jewellery in Celtic designs fashioned from Welsh gold and other materials, as well as goods made of slate and various Welsh-interest books. Overlooking the square is the squat bulk of the much-restored **St Caron church**, which sits in a large, circular churchyard – an indication that the religious settlement here predates Christianity.

A five-minute walk along Dewi Road (the route out to Llanddewi Brefi) brings you to Tregaron's new community-run **museum** and **red kite centre** (April–Sept daily 10.30am–4.30pm; Oct–March Sat & Sun noon–4pm; donation requested), housed in an old Victorian school. There's an eclectic mixture of local memorabilia, much inevitably drawn from the area's farming tradition. Other exhibits include a history of local education, with some great snippets from the nineteenth-century *Log Book of Tregaron National School*, when harvest times, market days and hiring fairs resulted in little or no attendance. The adjoining red kite centre includes an introductory video, with some lovely footage of the bird in flight and displays about the wildlife of the Cors Caron bog.

The river running through the middle of Tregaron is the Brennig, a babbling tributary of the Teifi which meanders through a wide, flat valley into the eerie wetland of **Cors Caron** (Tregaron Bog), two miles north. This national nature reserve of peat bog is one of the most prodigious wildlife areas in Wales, home to rare marsh grasses, black adders, buzzards and even the occasional red kite. There's a limited walkway along the disused rail line, but to really see the bog you'll need to follow the three-mile circuit along both the railway and the river; call the Countryside Council for Wales warden (☎01974/298480) to reserve the necessary permit; they can send it to you by post or arrange collection in Tregaron.

Practicalities

Buses arrive at the market square, by the Henry Richard statue. There's a small **tourist office** (Mon–Fri 9.30am–5pm; ☎01974/298144) in the council offices in Dewi Road, just off the main square, but it's manned irregularly. The choice of **accommodation** isn't wide: the *Talbot Hotel* on the square (☎01974/298208; ③) is much better for eating and drinking than sleeping, so you're better off a mile up the Aberystwyth road at *Neuaddlas* guesthouse (☎01974/298965; ①) or the *Lluest* on the Lampeter Road (☎01974/298936; ①). Three miles northeast is the remote Blaencaron **youth hostel** (April–Sept; ☎01974/298441; ①), perfectly positioned for walks on the towering moorland above a tiny stream, the Nant-y-groes Fawr. There's also a lovely riverside **campsite**, *Neuadd Brenig* (☎01974/298543), just out of town on the Abergwesyn mountain road.

There are a couple of **cafés** along the road to Aberystwyth, including the cheap and wholesome *Country Kitchen* by the river bridge. The *Cambrian Coffee Shop* (closed Sun and Mon), on Lampeter Road, is good for home-made snacks. Bar meals are served at the *Clwb Rygbi* on the Aberystwyth road and in the *Talbot Arms*. For plain **drinking**, hit *Y Llew Coch* (The Red Lion) by the river bridge, a young pub with a pool table and bar games.

Llanddewi Brefi

The Dewi Road from Tregaron runs south past a cottage hospital and along the Teifi to the tight little village of **LLANDDEWI BREFI**, where the present thirteenth-century **St David's church** is home to one of Wales' most persistent legends. According to local lore, a convocation of 118 Welsh churchmen met here in 519 AD and summoned Dewi Sant (Saint David). On appearing, Dewi began to speak to the men, but had trouble being heard, until the ground beneath him shuddered ominously and suddenly rose, giving him a natural platform from which he was able to continue speaking – the church sits on the mound to this day. Part of the church wall consists of two discernible stones inscribed with fragments of Latin script. These were originally part of a single memorial that dated from within a century of David's death – the first recorded mention of the Welsh patron saint – but they were broken up by an illiterate eighteenth- or nineteenth-century mason. There are also some interesting stones inside the church, one with Ogham inscriptions, while the graveyard has a cool and contemplative atmosphere, and contains a memorial to a local man rejoicing in the name of Ajax Ajax. Either of the village's two creaky pubs – the *Foelallt Arms* and the ancient *New Inn* – are great places to booze away an evening.

Pontrhydfendigaid, Strata Florida and the Teifi Pools

Six miles northeast of Tregaron, the last village on the Teifi is gloomy **PONTRHYD-FENDIGAID** ("Bridge near the ford of the Blessed Virgin"), a grey-stoned cluster remarkable only for its annual May eisteddfod in the enormous village pavilion, built to accommodate up to 3000 spectators. The infant Teifi flows in from the east, followed by a road that, after a mile, reaches the atmospheric ruins of the mighty **Strata Florida Abbey** (May–Sept daily 10am–5pm; £2; Oct–April unrestricted entry), bucolically located in the Ystrad Fflur, "the valley of the flowers". This Cistercian abbey was founded in 1164, swiftly growing into a centre for milling, farming and weaving, and becoming an important political centre for Wales. In 1238, a dying Llywelyn the Great, fearful that his work of unifying Wales under one ruler would disintegrate, summoned the lesser Welsh princes here to command them to pay homage to his son, Dafyd.

The church here was vast – larger than the cathedral at St David's and, although very little survived Henry VIII's dissolution of the monasteries, the huge, Norman west doorway gives some idea of its dimensions. Fragments of one-time side chapels include beautifully tiled medieval floors, and there's also a serene cemetery, but it's really the abbey's position that impresses most, in glorious rural solitude against wide open skies and fringed with a scoop of sheep-spattered hills. A twisting yew tree reputedly shades the spot where Dafydd ap Gwilym (see p.284), fourteenth-century bard and contemporary of Chaucer, is buried.

The narrow lane running due east from Strata Florida leads to Tyncwm, a farm with bridleways to the drenched grass and craggy outcrops around the **Teifi Pools**, a series of sombre lakes where the Teifi River rises. This is stern, but rewarding, walking country where you may be tempted to strike out over the rocky, squelchy moorland down to the Claerwen Reservoir (see p.233). More direct access to the pools can be had from the lane that forks off the B4343 in the village of **Ffair-Rhos**, a mile north of Pontrhydfendigaid. The *Teifi Inn*, at the junction with the B4343, is a wonderful pub, especially for its generous portions of superb food. If you want to stay in the area, *Lluest Fach* (☎01974/831486; ①) on Ystrad Meurig in Ffair-Rhos is a great, cheap option.

Aberystwyth

The liveliest seaside resort in Wales, and capital of the sparsely populated middle of the country, **ABERYSTWYTH** is an essential stop along the Ceredigion coast. With one of the most prestigious colleges of the University of Wales and the National Library both in the town, there are plenty of cultural and entertainment diversions here, as well as an array of Victorian and Edwardian seaside trappings. As a town firmly rooted in all aspects of Welsh culture, it's an enjoyable and relaxed place to gain a clear insight into the national psyche.

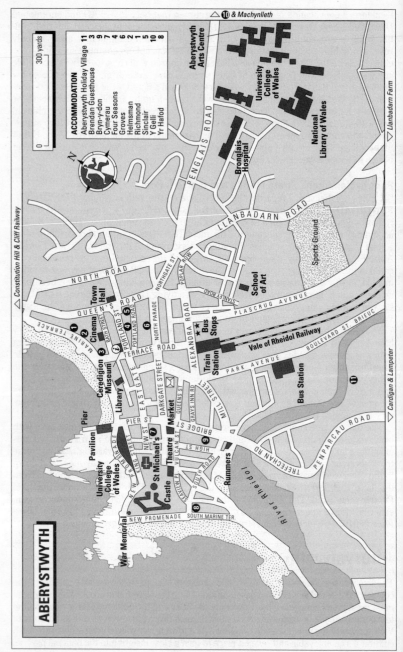

ABERYSTWYTH

ACCOMMODATION

Aberystwyth Holiday Village	11
Brendan Guesthouse	3
Bryn-y-don	9
Cymerau	7
Four Seasons	4
Groves	6
Helmsman	2
Richmond	1
Sinclair	5
Y Gelli	10
Yr Hafod	8

© Crown copyright

Historically, Aberystwyth has always been a little anti-establishment, and its anarchic soul shows through in many diverse ways. Pubs – and there are loads – stay open late, the political scene is distinctly green-tinged and radically Welsh, and the town has even gained the unlikely-seeming accolade of "the gay capital of Wales". In a country that still struggles to cope with an inherent conservatism, Aberystwyth is a salty blast of fresh air.

The precursor of Aberystwyth is the inland village of **Llanbadarn Fawr**, the seat of Wales' oldest bishopric between the sixth and eighth centuries. It grew around the thirteenth-century castle as Llanbadarn, minting its own coins and becoming a major headquarters for Owain Glyndŵr's revolutionaries in the Middle Ages. The *Cymdeithas yr Iaith* (Welsh Language Society) was founded in Aberystwyth 1963 and is still located in the town, and the National Library was begun here in 1907. It was no surprise that, after decades of Liberal domination, the Aberystwyth-dominated Ceredigion constituency finally plumped for a Plaid Cymru MP in the 1992 election, thus turning the whole west coast – from Anglesey to the bottom of Cardigan Bay – Plaid green on the political map.

As a seaside resort, Aberystwyth is hard to beat. Two long, gentle bays curve round between twin rocky heads: Constitution Hill to the north, and Pen Dinas to the south above the town harbour's marina, where both the Rheidol and Ystwyth rivers end their journeys through the valleys of Aberystwyth's hinterland (see p.286). The town rises up towards the east from the flat plains in between the two, peaking at Penglais, where the graceful Portland stone buildings of the National Library and the university gaze over the town.

Arrival and information

Aberystwyth's twin **train stations** (one for mainline trains and one for the Vale of Rheidol line) are adjacent to each other on Alexandra Road, a ten-minute walk from the seafront on the southeastern side of the town centre. **Local buses** stop outside the station, with **long-distance** ones using the depot further down the road by the entrance to the small park near Plascrug leisure centre. In addition, Aberystwyth acts as the hub of three **postbus** services which penetrate the town's hinterland. One service runs inland up the southern side of the Vale of Rheidol to Devil's Bridge, Cwmystwyth and towards the Elan Valley (see p.232); a second follows the Vale's northern side to Capel Bangor and Capel Dewi; and the third runs south into the villages of the Aeron Forest, Llangwyryfon and Blaenpennal. All leave from Chalybeate Street at the back entrance to the post office at around 7.30am and 2.30pm.

The busy **tourist office** (daily: July & Aug 9am–6pm; Sept–June 10am–5pm; ☎01970/612125, *aberystwyth@ceredigion.gov.uk*) is a ten-minute stroll from Alexandra Road, straight down Terrace Road towards the seafront: staff will help with accommodation and can sell you tickets for local events.

Accommodation

As in all major seaside towns, there are hundreds of **places to stay**, so beds are generally quite reasonable and easy to find. The tourist office will only give information on accommodation verified by the Wales Tourist Board, so, if desperate, or if the B&Bs offered are too pricey, there are a couple of reasonable places in the streets down towards the castle and others along South Marine Terrace.

Hotels and guesthouses
Brendan Guest House, 19 Marine Terrace (☎01970/612252). One of the better budget seafront B&Bs, with some en-suite rooms. ①.

Bryn-y-don, 36 Bridge St (☎01970/612011). Spirited and charming guesthouse with shared bathrooms, a hundred yards or so up from the train station. ①.

Conrah Country House Hotel, Chancery, Rhydgaled (☎01970/617941, fax 624546). Elegant Georgian house three miles south of town along the A487, with 22 acres of grounds, luxurious rooms, sauna and heated indoor pool. ⑥.

Cymerau, 8 New St (☎01970/617329). A decent and cheap option in the centre of town, with standard rooms and hearty breakfasts. ①.

Four Seasons, 50–54 Portland St (☎01970/612120, fax 627458). Comfortably decorated, upmarket Victorian town house behind the seafront, with an award-winning restaurant. ⑤.

Groves, North Parade (☎01970/617623, fax 627068). Welcoming town-centre hotel serving evening meals. All rooms have bathrooms. ④.

Helmsman, 43 Marine Terrace (☎ & fax 01970/624132). Tall seafront guesthouse in the middle of the curving Promenade. Book early for a sea view. ①.

Richmond, 44–45 Marine Terrace (☎01970/612201, fax 626706). Comfortable, family-run seafront hotel, with a full complement of en-suite rooms. ④.

Sinclair, 43 Portland St (☎ & fax 01970/615158). Small and beautifully modernized Victorian guesthouse benefiting from the intimacy of its size, and serving good evening meals. No smoking allowed. ②.

Y Gelli, at Plas Dolau, Lovesgrove (☎01970/617834). B&B in a modern Scandinavian-style house, part of the big Plas Dolau estate, three miles east of town, that is being restored by the owners. One room comes complete with its own sauna. ②.

Yr Hafod, 1 South Marine Terrace (☎01970/617579). Compact, cheerful and recently renovated B&B south of the castle, the best of the bunch on the seafront. ①.

Hostel, campsites and self-catering

Aberystwyth Holiday Apartments, 9 Northgate St (☎01970/612878). Self-contained, self-catering flats let by the week.

Aberystwyth Holiday Village, Penparcau Rd (☎01970/624211). Rather garish, family-oriented park, but handy nonetheless as it's the nearest campsite to the town centre, just over the Trefechan river bridge and up the hill.

Glan-y-mor Leisure Park, Clarach Bay (☎01970/828900). The best of the caravan parks in Clarach Bay, on the other side of Constitution Hill, to the north of Aberystwyth. It has caravans for rent and tent pitches.

Midfield, Southgate, Penparcau (☎01970/612542). Campsite just off the A4120 (A487) south of town. Free showers and games area.

Plas Dolau, Lovesgrove (☎01970/617834). Dorm accommodation in a characterful Victorian mansion just off the A44, three miles east of town. Cooking facilities available. Beds from £6–£12.

University of Wales, Penglais (☎01970/621960, fax 622899). Self-contained flats and B&B (£30) available during the student vacations and through the summer term on the university's Penglais site and also down by the seafront. Campus facilities include two sports halls and a heated swimming pool.

The Town

Constitution Hill (430ft) overshadows the northern end of the long Promenade, where it rises sharply away from the rocky beach. It's a favourite jaunt, crowned with a tatty jumble of amenities that include a café, picnic area, telescopes and an octagonal **camera obscura** (Easter–Oct daily 10am–5.30pm; free), a device popular in the pre-TV era and affording close-up and long-shot views over the town, the surrounding mountains and bays, plus a vista of the hordes of caravans to the north, looking like legions of tanks poised for battle. The existing structure was built in the 1980s on the ground plan of the original, but expanded to make it the largest of its type in the world. If you don't fancy the invigorating walk up, you can take the clanking 1896 **cliff railway** (Easter to mid-July & Sept–Oct daily 10am–6pm; mid-July to Aug daily 10am–9pm; £2 return) from the grand terminus building at the top of Queen's Road, behind the Promenade.

From the bottom of Constitution Hill, the **Promenade** – officially Marine Terrace – arcs away to the south, past ornate benches decorated with snakes, a continuous wall of hotels and guesthouses, a prim bandstand and a shingle beach. Terrace Road peels off to the left after a couple of hundred yards, almost immediately reaching the tourist office and the **Amgeuddfa Ceredigion** (Ceredigion Museum), atmospherically housed in the ornate Edwardian Coliseum music hall (Mon–Sat 10am–5pm; £1). Mementos of the building as a theatre and cinema give a sense of place to an otherwise disparate collection, on three floors, including cosy reconstructed cottages, dairies complete with all manner of separating and churning equipment, a nineteenth-century pharmacy, exhibits on the local geology and a surprisingly interesting look at the history of weights and measures.

Marine Terrace continues round to the spindly **pier**, beyond which a John Nash-designed turreted **villa** dominates the seafront. Dating from 1790, the villa was massively extended in the 1860s, as a hotel designed to soak up the anticipated masses arriving on the new rail line. The venture failed, though, and in 1872, it was sold to the fledgling university, whose property it remains. The Promenade cuts around the front of the building to a rocky headland, where the **castle** ruins (unrestricted access) stare blankly out to sea. Built by Edward I as part of his conquest of Wales, the thirteenth-century fortress is more notable for its breezy position than for the buildings themselves, of which the two outer gates are the most impressive remains. South of the castle is the quieter, sandy beach along South Marine Terrace, which peters out by the wide **harbour**, the mouth of the Rheidol and Ystwyth rivers.

A couple of blocks inland from the Promenade, you'll find the terminus of the **Vale of Rheidol Railway** (see p.286), next to the mainline train station on Alexandra Road. A hundred yards north of the station, Stanley Road forks off to the right, leading down to the splendid **School of Art** (Mon–Fri 10am–5.30pm; free) at Buarth Mawr. Originally bequeathed to the University by the Davies sisters of Gregynog Hall (see p.239), this impressive Edwardian building has been the home of the Art department since 1995. The public galleries on the ground floor house both touring exhibitions and those culled from the University's extensive permanent collection, with an emphasis on Welsh art.

North Parade meets up with Queen's Road at the bottom of Northgate Street; the latter winds east, becoming Penglais Road as it climbs the hill towards the university's main campus and the **National Library of Wales** (Mon–Fri 9.30am–6pm, Sat closes 5pm; free), an essential and enjoyable stop for anyone with an interest in matters Welsh. Housed in a massive white Edwardian building overlooking the town, the library's fine manuscripts include the oldest extant Welsh text, the twelfth-century *Black Book of Carmarthen*, and the earliest manuscript of The Mabinogion. Temporary exhibitions in the corridors and Gregynog Gallery are invariably excellent, as is the permanent **A Nation's Heritage** exhibition (Mon–Sat 10am–5pm; free), which provides a well-rounded introduction to the history of printing and the written word in Wales, with highlights such as the first Welsh Bible, printed in 1588, early maps of the country and the original 1856 score of national anthem *Mae Hen Wlad Fy Nhadau* and the first Welsh magazine from 1735. Some awesome landscape paintings – Turner's *Dolbadarn Castle* and Kyffin Williams' characteristically chunky *Farm, Llanfairynghornwy* amongst them – pepper the collection, alongside portraits by the likes of Richard Wilson and Augustus John. Tickets (☎01970/623816) need to be obtained in advance for entry into the **Reading Room**, which boasts an enormous range of texts, maps, photos and documents, including, as one of the UK's six copyright libraries, copies of every new book published in Britain.

While in the Penglais area, you might want to check out the ever-expanding **Aberystwyth Arts Centre**, a little further up the hill from the National Library in the middle of the University's main campus. Although it's something of a concrete hell-hole, a refurbishment programme is well underway and it's a pleasant place to while away an hour or two, looking at the various temporary art and ceramics exhibitions and craft shops, catching a movie or snacking in the cafeteria, which affords sublime views over the town and bay.

Llanbadarn Fawr

A mile inland from the main resort is **LLANBADARN FAWR**, the original settlement from which Aberystwyth grew. Barely distinct from Aberystwyth proper, it's a fairly humdrum knot of busy roads that would warrant little attention were it not for the stunning sight of the massive **St Padarn parish church**. Today's structure was completely rebuilt in the thirteenth century, but religious association with this spot far predates that. St Padarn, a Breton, established his monastic settlement here in the second half of the sixth century, decades before even St Augustine's mission to the English of 597 AD. The town's heyday was undoubtedly in its early years, as Giraldus Cambrensis noted that it was already in decline when he visited in 1188. Nonetheless, Llanbadarn continued to be one of the largest and wealthiest parishes in all Wales, covering some 240 square miles by the time of the dissolution of the monasteries in 1538.

There's plenty of interest in and around St Padarn: before stepping inside the church, note the astonishingly steep graveyard stacked vertiginously up the hillside behind. Inside, opposite the main door, hangs an enlargement of a page from *Rhygyfarch's Psalter* of 1079, one example of the beautifully decorated texts that the monks of Llanbadarn became well-known for. In the south transept, there's a fascinating exhibition on St Padarn's monastic foundation and the area's history which includes two beautiful tenth-century crosses, moved inside from the churchyard in 1916. The taller one, about eight feet high, is woven with exquisite Celtic tracery. Perhaps the most entertaining part of the exhibition deals with poet Dafydd ap Gwilym (*c.* 1320–70) and his upbringing in Llanbadarn parish. His poem *Merched Llanbadarn*, the Women of Llanbadarn, tells of his frustration at sitting in the church watching the beautiful parish girls, as this opening extract demonstrates:

Plygu rhag llid yr ydwyf,
Pla ar holl ferched y plwyf!
Am na chefais, drais drawsgoed,
Onaddun'yr un erioed,
Na morwyn fwyn ofynaig,
Na merch fach, na gwrach, na gwraig.

Passion doubles me over,
Plague take all the parish girls!
Because, frustrated trysting,
I've had not a single one.
No lovely, longed-for virgin,
Not a wench nor witch nor wife.

Eating, drinking and entertainment

Aberystwyth's cultural and gastronomic life is an ebullient, all-year-round affair, thriving on students in term time, visitors in the summer and a large esoterically inclined community thoughout the year. As well as a varied range of **pubs** and **restaurants**, the town is a good place to hear Welsh **music** and a lively centre for theatre and cinema.

For a slice of Edwardian gentility, take afternoon tea in any of the seafront hotels along the Promenade.

Restaurants and cafés

Bistro 33, 33 North Parade (☎01970/615332). Airy restaurant with a varied international menu concentrating on fresh and wholefood ingredients. Closed Sun.

Corners, cnr of Mill and Queen sts (☎01970/611024). Appealing bistro with no-nonsense lunches, good (if unadventurous) dinners and decent coffee. Closed Sun & Mon.

Gannets Bistro, 7 St James Square (☎01970/617164). Small restaurant that makes delicious and imaginative dishes from local farm and sea produce. Closed Tues.

Le Casablanca, 26 Eastgate St (☎01970/617024). Cheap and cheerful Mediterranean restaurant with a lively atmosphere and reasonable food. Bring your own alcohol.

Pipers, 26 Alexandra Rd (☎01970/624270). Unpretentious, moderately priced Italian restaurant also serving a broad range of British food.

Royal Pier Tandoori, The Pier (☎01970/624888). Swish, romantic but affordable end-of-pier restaurant, with views over the twinkling bay. Serves a good range of curries and bargain lunchtime specials for £5.

The Stop Inn, 12a Baker St (☎01970/625719). Tucked down an alleyway off Baker St, this inexpensive pasta joint makes some of Aberystwyth's best pizza.

Treehouse, 14 Baker St (☎01970/615791). Cheerful organic food shop and restaurant, good for daily specials.

Y Graig, 34 Pier St (☎01970/611606). Quirky wholefood café with a drinks licence, great atmosphere and eclectic clientele.

Yeskins, 49 North Parade (☎01970/615374). Daytime wholefood restaurant with a gallery. Everything is made to order so service tends to be a bit slow; you can bring your own booze to while away the wait.

Pubs

Bay Hotel, Marine Terrace. Student pub with regular discos, open until 1am.

Bear, below the *Marine Hotel*, Marine Terrace. Cellar bar on the seafront, usually packed with students and young people, particularly on Fri for live Welsh music.

Boar's Head, Queen's Rd. Friendly and lively gay-leaning pub, with regular discos on the small dance floor in the back bar.

Castle Hotel, South Rd. Harbourside pub built in the style of an ornate Victorian gin palace. Live local folk bands at weekends and a good bar menu with vegetarian specialities.

Flannery's, High St. Slightly ersatz Irish pub, but worth checking out nonetheless for regular live music.

Pier Hotel, Pier St. Endearing old town pub, its lounge entrance up a tiny side alley.

Rummers, Bridge St, by the River Rheidol bridge. Late-opening, popular pub and wine bar with outside seating by the river and live music Thurs–Sun.

Ship and Castle, cnr of Vulcan and High sts. Nautical-style bar, with a good range of beer, cider and food. Hosts regular Welsh and Irish folk music, best on Wed.

Weston Vaults, cnr of Thespian St and North Parade. Unpretentious and popular with students.

Y Cûps (*Coopers Arms*), Llanbadarn Rd. Firmly Welsh local, evident from the green, white and red exterior and an interior plastered with mementos of the world's minority nations. Fun and friendly, with regular Welsh folk and jazz nights and jam sessions.

Entertainment

Aberystwyth Arts Centre, the University, Penglais (☎01970/623232). The town's main venue for art-house cinema, touring theatre, classes, events and wide-ranging temporary exhibitions.

Commodore Cinema, Bath St (☎01970/612421). Screens mainstream current releases.

Theatr y Castell, St Michael's Place/Vulcan St (☎01970/624606). Venue for local amateur productions and a few touring companies.

Listings

Banks All major banks are along Great Darkgate Street and North Parade.

Bike rental Try On Your Bike in the Old Police Yard, Queen's Road (☎01970/626996), or Summit Cycles on North Parade (☎01970/626061).

Books Siop y Pethe, on North Parade, has a huge array of Welsh-interest books, magazines and music in both Welsh and English. There is also a good bookshop in the Aberystwyth Arts Centre, though Galloways, on Pier Street, has a wider range. Ystwyth Books, near the Market Hall on Princess Street, also sells maps and secondhand records.

Festivals The Aberystwyth Arts Centre (see overleaf) hosts Poetryfest in late June and Musicfest in late July (for more information on them both, call ☎01970/622889); the International Potters Festival also takes place here in early July; call ☎01970/622882 for more details. There's also a Festival of the Countryside in late June or early July, the town carnival at the end of July and some craft fairs at the Arts Centre towards Christmas.

Gay, Lesbian and Bisexual Line (Tues 6–8pm; ☎01970/615076).

Male Voice Choir Visitors are welcome to the rehearsals of the Cor Meibion group, held at the Tabernacle Chapel on Mill Street (Thurs 7.45–9.30pm; ☎01970/624494).

Post office 8 Great Darkgate St.

Sport Plascrug Leisure Centre (☎01970/624579), off the Llanbadarn Road, has two indoor pools, sauna, solarium, squash and tennis courts, indoor pitches and multigym. The University Sports Centre (☎01970/622280) is open to the public in the summer vacation.

Around Aberystwyth

Aberystwyth's sights run out long before it's time to hit the restaurants and nightlife, so there is every reason to go exploring beyond the town. Immediately inland is the **Vale of Rheidol**, a region of forested glades and remote villages, easily accessed by road or, more enjoyably, rail – the narrow-gauge steam train which serves the area is a draw in itself. Tourist attractions like **Devil's Bridge**, where the line terminates, are also obviously popular, although there are numerous other lesser-known beauty spots whose charms require only a little more imagination to discover.

The coast north of Aberystwyth also has its devotees, principally sunseekers drawn to the beach at **Borth** and the dunes close to the mouth of the Dyfi Estuary. Nature buffs will prefer to head further northeast to the RSPB's **Ynys-Hir Nature Reserve**, with its complex series of bird habitats.

The Vale of Rheidol

Inland from Aberystwyth, the Rheidol River winds its way up to a secluded, wooded valley, where occasional old industrial workings have moulded themselves into the contours, rising up past waterfalls and minute villages. It's a glorious route, and by far the best way to see this part of the world is on board one of the trains of the **Vale of Rheidol Railway** (April–Oct; ☎01970/625819; £10.50 return), a narrow-gauge steam train that wheezes its way along twelve miles of sheer rock faces, climbing six hundred feet in the process. It was built in 1902, ostensibly for the valley's lead mines but with a canny eye on its tourist potential. Today, the line is privately run, with between two and four trips offered daily.

If you'd rather drive, the easiest way is to take the A4120 along the south side of the valley direct to Devil's Bridge (see p.288) or the A44 along the north side; the two meet at Ponterwyd. The tiny hamlet of **CAPEL BANGOR**, five miles east of Aberystwyth along the A44, has little to recommend it other than the Rheidol Riding Centre

(☎01970/880863), from where you can book hacks for around £7 an hour; the 300-year-old *Tynllidiart Arms*, notable for its Belgian bottled beers and summertime draught cider; and the nearby **Cwm Rheidol Reservoir**, reached by a narrow riverside route off the main road. This is the final element in a small, showpiece hydroelectric scheme that starts high in the headwaters of the Rheidol River at the Nant-y-moch Reservoir. An **information centre** (April–Oct 10.30am–4.15pm; free), run by privatized electricity generator PowerGen, explains the scheme's significance, and a visit is essential to appreciate the free 45-minute tour of the **power station**, where you can see the impressive sluices and channels that funnel the water according to need, and the neighbouring **fish farm** (April–Oct daily 10.30am–4.30pm) a stone's throw up the road. Most gimmicky of all, but fun all the same, the reservoir dam and weir are floodlit nightly, from dusk until 11pm in the summer, 10pm in the winter.

Slight remains of old lead workings are evident on the banks of the reservoir, although the valley's mining legacy is better seen further along, as the road begins to narrow before finally disappearing into a wood as a mud track. From here, paths rise either side of the river to overlook the burned orange spoil, vividly coloured water and bright plants, fitted snugly into their green landscape. A sharp path on the south side of the river climbs up to Rhiwfron halt on the Rheidol railway (see opposite), and an even more punishing route from the northern bank scrambles up over the mines and into the sombre little village of **YSTUMTUEN**, a former lead-mining community whose school has been converted into a basic **YHA hostel** (April to early Sept; ☎01970/890693).

Llywernog Silver-Lead Mine and Ponterwyd

Travelling eastbound, the A44 winds up into **galena** country, tucked between the bleak moorland of Plynlimon (see p.238) and the rugged mountains to the south. The silver-rich lead ore was found throughout the region and scores of mines sprang up, each plugging away at the lode until waterlogging made the mines uneconomic. In the boom years, the latter half of the 1800s, the whole of northern Ceredigion was a mini-Klondike, attracting speculators and opportunists by the trainful. The remains – waste tips scarring hillsides and shafts pockmarking former sites – lie all around, most now hidden amongst the exotic evergreens of the Rheidol Forest. They can be visited on wonderful walks from the **Bwlch Nant-yr-Arian visitor centre** (Easter–Sept Mon–Fri & Sun 10am–5pm, Sat 12.30–5pm, closes 6pm July & Aug; free), perched above a magnificent valley scooped out of the wooded hillsides, seven miles east of Capel Bangor.

The soft contours of the forest make it difficult to imagine how stark the valley once looked. A truer picture unfolds a mile further east with the impressive barrenness around the **Llywernog Silver-Lead Mine** (July & Aug daily 10am–7pm; Easter–June & Sept–Oct Tues–Sun 10am–6pm; £4.50 including underground tour), which opened in the 1740s and closed in the early years of the twentieth century. Decay was well advanced when the place reopened in the early 1970s, but the site has expanded consistently over the years in a satisfyingly rough manner. A low-key mock-up of a working mine, housing an interesting museum, leads onto a collection of rusted machinery and the dank, dark mine itself, visitable on a great thirty-minute underground tour. Topside, you can pan for "fool's gold" or dowse for veins of galena.

The largest settlement to spring up around the mines was **PONTERWYD**, a mile from Llywernog on the banks of the Rheidol. There's nothing of interest here; indeed, one of the funniest sections in George Borrow's *Wild Wales* tells of his night in the inn at Ponterwyd – now the *George Borrow Hotel* – when the pompous Englishman met his match in a pugnacious landlord, who, even in 1854, was complaining about the numbers of unimaginative tourists ignoring his and other local villages and flocking instead to Devil's Bridge.

Devil's Bridge

Folk legend, idyllic beauty and travellers' lore combine at **DEVIL'S BRIDGE** (Pontarfynach), a tiny settlement twelve miles east of Aberystwyth – reached by road (A4120) or the Vale of Rheidol Railway – built largely for the growing visitor trade of the last few hundred years.

The main attraction is the Devil's Bridge itself, where three roads (the A4120, the B4343 and the B4574) converge and cross the churning River Mynach yards above its confluence with the Rheidol to form three bridges, one on top of the other. The road bridge in front of the striking, but distinctly antiquated, *Hafod Arms* hotel (☎01970/890232; ③) is the most modern of the three, dating from 1901. Immediately below it and wedged between the rock faces are the stone bridge from 1753, and, at the bottom, the original bridge, dating from the eleventh century and reputedly built by the monks of Strata Florida Abbey (see p.279). To see the bridges – and it is worth it, as they make a truly remarkable sight – you have to enter the turnstiles on either side of the modern road bridge. With your back to the hotel, the right-hand side (£1) is the shorter route, signposted to the Punch Bowl. Slippery steps lead down to the deep cleft in the rock, where the water pounds and hurtles through the gap crowned by the bridges. The Punch Bowl is the name given to a series of rock bowls scooped by the sheer power of the thundering river, which rushes through past bright-green mossy rocks and saturated lichen.

On the opposite side of the road is a ticket office (Easter–Oct daily 9.30am–5.30pm) – pay £2.20 or pass through turnstiles (£2) when closed – which opens out onto a path leading down into the valley and ultimately to the crashing **Mynach Falls**. The scenery here is magnificent: sharp, wooded slopes rising away from the frothing river, with distant mountain peaks surfacing on the horizon. A platform overlooks the series of falls, from where a set of steep steps takes you further down to a footbridge dramatically spanning the river at the bottom. From the platform, and from here, views over the confluence of the two rivers and towards the **Gyfarllwyd Falls** are awesome. Be warned, however, that Devil's Bridge has been a seriously popular day excursion for centuries, with no sign of its attraction waning. In order to escape some of the inevitable congestion, it is wisest to come here at the beginning or end of the day, or out of season.

THE PARSON'S BRIDGE WALK

Note: The OS Landranger #135 "Aberystwyth" map makes route finding a lot easier.

The circular **Parson's Bridge Walk** (6 miles; 3–4hr; 1000ft ascent) is one of the most popular and rewarding outings from Devil's Bridge, taking in a broad swath of the Rheidol scenery: mine workings, woods and waterfalls. Unfortunately, it does involve a little road walking, so get this over with first by taking the A4120 a mile and a half north of Devil's Bridge to a small church on the left. The path to the right of the church leads down to the Parson's Bridge, an unusual, modern glass-fibre structure thankfully replacing a predecessor which only just spanned the narrow fissure of churning water.

From here, the path climbs gently south across farmland, eventually meeting a narrow lane which winds into the former lead-mining village of **Ystumtuen**. Head south from the village past the YHA hostel to the end of the lane and take the track straight ahead, which drops down almost to river level through oak woods and reveals views across to the falls below Devil's Bridge. Swing west following the contour through recently felled forest to meet a lane that runs the length of the valley floor. Mine scars on the right and modest waterfalls to the left herald the narrow footbridge across the Rheidol. Cross this and turn sharp right to begin the stiff climb up to the railway, which you eventually cross close to Devil's Bridge.

The railway terminates at a tinpot brown-and-cream shack, just by Devil's Bridge **post office**, which has some worthwhile booklets on local walks. For **accommodation**, there's the *Hafod Arms* (see opposite) or *Ewbarfe Farmhouse* (☎01970/890251; ①), a mile north on the A4120, where you can also get a decent evening meal. Reasonably priced **camping** is offered at *Woodlands Caravan Park* (☎01970/890233) by the petrol station, just beyond the bridges.

The *Hafod Arms* serves **food**, as do a couple of simple cafés, but you're better off six miles west along the A4120 at the *Halfway Inn*, just beyond the spectacularly positioned village of **PISGAH**. Beers, ciders and hearty local dishes are complemented by Welsh folk choirs, live jazz and special events such as beer festivals or plays. If you're not driving or cycling, you could use the Vale of Rheidol narrow gauge railway and get off at Nantyronen halt, from where it's a steep half-mile trek up to the village.

The Vale of Ystwyth

The Ystwyth River runs pretty much parallel to the Rheidol, a couple of miles to the south. Four miles south of Devil's Bridge is the drab village of **PONTRHYDYGROES**, the former centre of local lead-mining activity. The B4574 climbs out of the village and past the delightful country estate of **Hafod**, once the seat of a great house belonging to the wealthy Johnes family. In the late eighteenth century, Thomas Johnes commissioned a mansion here in the Picturesque style; it was added to by John Nash, amongst others, and contained a library full of Welsh manuscripts, but was ravaged by a terrible fire in 1807. The sumptuous replacement house was demolished in 1962 as an unsafe ruin, and all that remains is the beautiful estate Johnes landscaped and forested two hundred years ago. The church, off the B4574, is the best place to embark on the waymarked **trails** that lead through the estate and down to the river. Johnes' larch forest, broken by trickling streams, monumental relics and planted glades, swoops down to the Ystwyth River, less than a mile from the church car park. A bridge spans the river, where paths fan out either way along its banks or up through the tiny valley of the Nant Gau.

Continuing east, a small road grinds up the hill into the bizarre moonscape surrounding **CWMYSTWYTH**, a small, semi-derelict village at the bottom of a valley of old lead mines, deserted in the late nineteenth century when the mines were exhausted. As the river shimmers past, the view is one of abandoned shafts, tumbledown cottages, twisted tramways and grey heaps of spoil littering spartan hillsides. The isolated road continues to climb the uninhabited slopes, before dropping down into the Elan Valley (see p.232) and its reservoirs.

North from Aberystwyth

The A487 runs north from Aberystwyth towards Machynlleth, slicing between the mountains to the east and the flat lands bordering the vast Dyfi Estuary. The seaward plain is one of the most surprising landscapes in Wales, at its heart a raised bog, **Cors Fochno**, visible from the main road but seen much better from the rail line or the coastal B4353. This short road, lined by towering sand dunes – by far the tallest things around – sneaks past **Borth**, a dreary but serviceable town stretching for nearly two miles along the seafront, to the national **nature reserve** at **Ynyslas**, the best place to explore the dunes themselves.

Inland, attractions worth heading off the A487 for include the roadside village of **Furnace** with its eighteenth-century iron foundry, now open as a museum, and **Ynys-hir**, an RSPB nature reserve with an impressive range of bird habitats.

Borth and Ynyslas can be reached from Aberystwyth on buses #511, #512, #520 and #524. The #514 to Machynlleth runs through Furnace and Ynys-hir.

Borth and Ynyslas

The drab resort of **BORTH**, five miles north of Aberystwyth off the B4353, is basically one long street, desolate in winter and heaving solid in the summer. As it was built solely for holiday-makers, the only occupants of its austere, washed-out Victorian houses are pubs, restaurants, tacky shops and B&Bs, interspersed with the odd caravan and campsite. The shallow **beach** is good for safe swimming, though, and if you've got kids you could take them to see the creatures at the **Animalarium** zoo half a mile off High Street near the train station (daily April–Sept 10am–6pm; Oct 11am–4.30pm; £2.75). **B&Bs** are plentiful – try the *Glanmor* (✆01970/871689; ③) on the High Street – or there's an Edwardian **youth hostel** (✆01970/871498, fax 871827) at the northern end of High Street, and the *Ynys Fergi* **campsite** on the road to the Animalarium. Borth's best **pub** is the superb *Friendship Inn*, in the middle of the main street. As well as an imaginative menu of home-cooked specialities, it also boasts a small art gallery and a lovely walled rose garden.

To the north, the flat landscape meets the formidable sand dunes that line the southern side of the Dyfi Estuary. The road follows the coast a couple of miles to **YNYSLAS**, entrance to the dramatic estuary-side **Ynyslas nature reserve** (£1 per car), most notable for its birdlife. In winter, wading and sea birds feed amongst the dunes and mudflats, while in summer, butterflies flit around vibrant sand plants growing in the grass. The views here are dramatic: for once, a Welsh vista almost uncluttered by mountains, panning over the sky, estuary and seascape, and across the river to the colourful huddle of Aberdyfi (see p.296). Staff at the Countryside Council for Wales **visitor centre** (Easter–Sept daily 10am–4pm; ✆01970/871640), the starting point for guided walks and tours that take place most summer weekends, can point you to the short circular dune walk or half a mile along the beach to the **fossilized forest**. At low tides, the sands near the water's edge are studded with the petrified stumps of a dozen or so 5000-year-old trees, a reminder that the coast was some twelve miles away when these trees were in their prime. A less prosaic explanation tells of a drowned land known as Cantre'r Gwaelod which was protected by sea walls and floodgates. Their keeper, Seithenyn, happened to get drunk the night of an almighty storm and the sea burst through, drowning a thousand people and their settlements.

Furnace and Ynys-hir

The Borth road rejoins the A487 a couple of miles south of the hamlet of **FURNACE** which, as its name suggests, grew principally as an industrial centre, firstly around silver refining and then iron smelting. Both activities centred around the **Dyfi Furnace** (unrestricted access), a barn-like building constructed to harness the power of the Einion River, with a water wheel driving the bellows.

The adjacent narrow lane follows the river through a forest and out into the idyllic **Cwm Einion**, known as "Artists' Valley" because of its popularity with nineteenth-century landscape painters. From the *Tŷ'n-y-cwm* tearoom a mile and a half east, footpaths head up into the deserted foothills of Plynlimon (see p.238), across the spongy moors and through conifer forests to the remote glacial lakes of **Llyn Conach** and **Llyn Dwfn**, three miles away.

Half a mile north of Furnace, a short lane runs seaward to *Ynys-hir Hall* hotel and restaurant (see p.294) and the RSPB's **Ynys-hir Nature Reserve** (daily: April–Oct 9am–dusk; Nov–March 10am–dusk; £2, free to members). The thousand-acre site, comprising five rich and distinct habitats, drips with diversity. Redstarts, pied-flycatchers and warblers flit about the ancient hanging oak woodland so typical of mid-Wales; cormorants flock to the estuarine salt marshes; red-breasted mersangers and elusive otters inhabit the freshwater streams and pools; remnant peat bogs are a riot of wild flowers in spring; and winter brings water rails to the reed beds to join the herons. The attractions are obvious to the birders who return time and again to the network of hides, but there's enough along the one- or two-hour designated trails to interest anyone.

Southern Cadair Idris and the Dyfi and Talyllyn valleys

The southern coastal reaches of Snowdonia National Park are almost entirely dominated by **Cadair Idris** (2930ft), a five-peaked massif standing defiant in its isolation. Tennyson claimed never to have seen "anything more awful than the great veil of rain drawn straight over Cader Idris", but catch it on a good day, and the views from the top – occasionally stretching as far as Ireland – are stunning. During the last Ice Age, the heads of glaciers scalloped out two huge cwms from Cadair Idris' distinctive dome, leaving thousand-foot cliffs dropping away on all sides to cool, clear lakes. The largest of these amphitheatres is Cwm Gadiar, the **Chair of Idris**, which takes its name from a giant warrior poet of Welsh legend, although some prefer the notion that Idris' Chair refers to a seat-like rock formation on the summit ridge, where anyone spending the night (specifically New Year's Eve, say some) will become a poet, go mad or die.

Cadair Idris' southern limits are lapped by the broad expanse of the Dyfi Estuary, which in turn bleeds into the grand scenery of the **Dyfi Valley**, "one of the greenest corners of Europe". Focal point for the valley is the genial town of **Machynlleth**, a candidate for the Welsh capital in the 1950s and site of Owain Glyndŵr's embryonic fifteenth-century Welsh parliament. The area is rife with the B&Bs and businesses of the

AROUND CADAIR IDRIS

© Crown copyright

New Agers who have flocked to this corner of Wales since the late 1960s, and in the hills to the north, the renowned, co-operatively run **Centre for Alternative Technology** makes for one of the most interesting days out in Wales.

Small-time coastal resorts are sprinkled around the region, the pick of them being **Aberdyfi**, though many prefer to press on to **Tywyn** and ride the **Talyllyn Railway**, justly one of Wales' most popular narrow-gauge lines, running seven miles up the **Talyllyn Valley** to **Abergynolwyn** at the foot of Cadair Idris, and only a short distance from the dilapidated thirteenth-century **Castell-y-Bere** and the inland cormorant colony at **Craig yr Aderyn**.

A well-coordinated network of trains, steam rail lines and buses make **getting around** the area easy. The very useful, summer-only Dyfi Sherpa ticket (£8; ☎01286/679535), allows a circuit from Tywyn using the Talyllyn Railway to Abergynolwyn, the #30 bus to Machynlleth and the bus or mainline train back to Tywyn. Available from train stations and tourist offices, it can also be bought on the bus at Machynlleth.

Machynlleth and around

Shortlisted for Welsh capital in the 1950s and site of Owain Glyndŵr's embryonic fifteenth-century Welsh parliament, handsome **MACHYNLLETH** (pronounced Mah-hun-cthleth) has an air of importance hardly borne out by its population of a couple of thousand. Amongst its inhabitants are a sizeable number of people drawn to the area on the strength of its environmental and artistic reputation: "green" businesses thrive and sit comfortably alongside the town's more traditional status as the market place for the fertile lands of the Dyfi valley.

It is difficult to imagine a nation's capital consisting essentially of just two intersecting streets, but that is the basis of Machynlleth. The A489 enters the town from the east becoming the wide main street, **Heol Maengwyn**, busiest on Wednesdays when a lively **market** springs up out of nowhere. Heol Maengwyn comes to an end at a T-junction, under the fanciful gaze of a fussy **clock tower**, erected in 1873 by local landowner, the Marquess of Londonderry, to commemorate his son and heir's coming of age.

Glyndŵr's partly fifteenth-century **Parliament House** (Easter–Sept daily 10am–5pm; other times by arrangement on ☎01654/702827; free) sits halfway along Heol Maengwyn, a modest looking black-and-white-fronted building concealing a large interior. Displays chart the course of Glyndŵr's life, his military campaign, his downfall, and the 1404 parliament in the town, when he controlled almost all of what we now know as Wales and even negotiated international recognition of the sovereign state. The sorriest tales are from 1405 onwards, when tactical errors and the sheer brute force of the English forced a swift retreat and an ignominious end to the great Welsh uprising.

Opposite the Parliament House, a path leads into the landscaped grounds of **Plas Machynlleth**, the elegant seventeenth-century mansion of the Marquess of Londonderry. Its solitude is entirely intentional: in the 1840s the Marquess bought up all the surrounding buildings and had them demolished, and rerouted the main road away from his grounds. The gracious house is now home to **Celtica** (*www.celtica.wales.com*, daily 10am–6pm, last admission 4.40pm; £4.95) which sets out to be both a resource for all matters Celtic and an evocation of the Cymric spirit. The latter is attempted in the theatrical "Celtic Experience", a populist series of audiovisual tableaux and dioramas tracing the Celts over the last 3000 years. While successfully painting a picture of a modern, living Celtic race, its rather pointed omission of non-Celtic aspects of Welsh society is questionable: there isn't a black face anywhere, for instance. It also falls into the archetypal Welsh trap of conjuring up a mystical, lyrical past only to spill into romantic sentimentality, aided by the use of some particularly mawkish special effects. Nevertheless, it is a spirited show, and the final rousing chorus of *Yma o Hyd* ("We're Still Here") is satisfactorily uplifting to tempt you upstairs for the more substantial exhibitions, past the wonderful *Tree of Life* glass etching on the stairs. A mixture of serious study centre and Celtic museum-cum-gallery, there's enough to keep you occupied for a good couple of hours. Exhibits

OWAIN GLYNDŴR

No name is so frequently invoked in Wales as that of Owain Glyndŵr (*c.* 1349–1416), a potent figurehead of Welsh nationalism ever since he rose up against the occupying English in the first few years of the fifteenth century.

Little is known about the man described in Shakespeare's *Henry IV, Part I* as "not in the roll of common men". There seems little doubt that the charismatic Owain fulfilled many of the mystical medieval prophecies about the rising up of the red dragon. He was of aristocratic stock, and had a conventional upbringing, part of it in England of all places. His blue blood – he was directly descended from the princes of Powys and Cyfeiliog – furthered his claim as Prince of Wales, and as a result of his status, he learned English, studied in London and became a loyal, and distinguished, soldier of the English king, before returning to Wales and marrying a local woman.

Wales in the late fourteenth century was a turbulent place. The brutal savaging of Llywelyn the Last and Edward I's stringent policies of subordinating Wales had left a discontented, cowed nation where any signs of rebellion were sure to attract support. Glyndŵr became the focus of the rebellion through a parochial problem: his neighbour in Glyndyfrdwy, the English Lord of Ruthin, seized some of his land and when the courts failed to back him, Glyndŵr took matters into his own hands. With four thousand supporters and a new declaration that he was Prince of Wales, he attacked Ruthin, and then Denbigh, Rhuddlan, Flint, Hawarden and Oswestry, before encountering an English resistance at Welshpool. However, whole swaths of north Wales were his for the taking. The English king, Henry IV, dispatched troops and rapidly drew up a range of severely punitive laws against the Welsh, even outlawing Welsh-language bards and singers. Battles continued to rage, with Glyndŵr capturing Edmund Mortimer, the Earl Marcher, in Pilleth in June 1402. By the end of 1403, he controlled most of Wales.

In 1404, Glyndŵr assembled a parliament of four men from every *commot* (community) in Wales at Machynlleth, drawing up mutual recognition treaties with France and Spain. At Machynlleth, he was also crowned king of a free Wales. A second parliament in Harlech took place a year later, with Glyndŵr making plans to carve up England and Wales into three as part of an alliance against the English king: Mortimer would take the south and west of England, Thomas Percy, Earl of Northumberland, would have the Midlands and North, and Glyndŵr himself Wales and the Marches of England. The English army, however, concentrated with increased vigour on destroying the Welsh uprising, and the Tripartite Indenture was never realized. From then on, Glyndŵr lost battles, ground and castles and was forced into hiding; dying, it is thought, in Herefordshire. The draconian anti-Welsh laws stayed in place until the accession to the English throne of Henry VII, a Welshman, in 1485. Wales became subsumed into English custom and law, and Glyndŵr's uprising became an increasingly powerful symbol of frustrated Welsh independence. Even today, the shadowy organization that surfaced in the early 1980s to burn the holiday homes of English people and English estate agents dealing in Welsh property has taken the name Meibion Glyndŵr, "The Sons of Glendower". More prosaically, the figure of Glyndŵr, his trademark double-pointed beard to the fore, can usually be seen gracing Welsh pub signs of inns called the Prince of Wales – a far better option than the various playboys and whingers who, by dint of being the first-born son of the reigning British monarch, have occupied the title ever since.

cover areas as diverse as artwork, language, history, craft, politics, design and culture, and include spoken recordings of six Celtic languages – Welsh, Irish Gaelic, Scottish Gaelic, Manx, Cornish and Breton – as well as some fascinating memorabilia from the Welsh expat community in the USA. Visitors can also use various high-tech gizmos and work on the Internet.

Back into town, past the clock tower and up Heol Penallt, is **Y Tabernacl** (Mon–Sat 10am–4pm; ☎01654/703355; free), a beautifully serene old chapel converted into a cultural centre. Its main status is as the expanding home of the **Wales Museum of Modern Art**, and to that end, it hosts an ongoing programme of temporary exhibitions, including some from its own growing collection. Y Tabernacl's bar is undoubtedly Machynlleth's trendiest drinking hangout, and the centre is also the place to go for films, theatre, comedy, concerts of every musical hue and the August Gŵyl Machynlleth festival, which combines classical and some folk music with theatre and debate.

Machynlleth is a natural home for modern art, if only thanks to the sheer profusion of art and craft practitioners in the area. To see local work in a more commercial setting than at Y Tabernacl, don't miss the superb **Spectrum Gallery** (Mon–Sat 10am–5.30pm), in a beautiful blue-fronted house on the main Heol Maengwyn. A UK leader in ceramics, the Spectrum also deals in exquisite examples of sculpture, prints, posters and paintings.

Practicalities

The **train station** is a five-minute walk up the Heol Penallt/Doll from the clock tower. Most **buses** leave from the bus depot opposite, while the **postbus** services which loop inland pick up from outside the Spar supermarket on Heol Maengwyn at 7.20am and 3.55pm. You can **rent bikes** from Greenstyles Cycles, 4 Heol Maengwyn (☎01654/703543) at £8–12 per day, £16 for a tandem. The **tourist office** (daily: Easter–Sept 9.30am–6pm; Oct–Easter 10am–5pm; ☎01654/702401, *machtic@powys. gov.uk*) is next to the Parliament House on Heol Maengwyn. If you're after information of a more "alternative" ilk, try wholefood Siop y Chwarel, near the clock tower on Heol Maengwyn, or the Ian Snow craft shop opposite.

Accommodation is plentiful. There's the revitalized grandeur of the *Wynnstay Arms* (☎01654/702941; ③), on Heol Maengwyn, and the earthier *Glyndŵr Hotel* (☎01654/703989; ②) towards the station on Heol Doll. Central, serviceable B&Bs include the Maenllwyd (☎01654/702928; ①) on Newtown Road, the eastward extension of Heol Maengwyn, and the slightly cheaper Gwelfryn (☎01654/702532; ①), at 6 Greenfields, off Bank Street behind the central Dragon garage. Further out, there's the friendly Cwm Dylleth (☎01654/702684; ②) a mile and a half southeast at Forge; luxurious country-house accommodation and fine modern cuisine at *Ynys-hir Hall* (☎01654/781209, fax 781366; ⑥), close to the Ynys-hir Nature Reserve (see p.290) at Eglwysfach, six miles southwest on the A487; a campsite three miles north near the Centre for Alternative Technology at *Llwyngwern Farm* (☎01654/702492); and a **youth hostel** (see p.296) five miles away at Corris. There's also a tap-in-a-field campsite nearer town at *Plas Forge* (☎01654/703228), a mile and a half out on the mountain road to Dylife.

There are plenty of **cafés**, **restaurants** and **pubs** in the town, including a great wholefood shop and café on Heol Maengwyn, Siop y Chwarel, owned by the Centre for Alternative Technology. Lunch is good at the otherwise bland *White Lion* on Heol Pentrerhedyn, near the clock tower, but better at the more upmarket *Wynnstay Arms*, which also serves surprisingly reasonable evening meals. Less formal, but very good for food, is the *Dyfi Forester Inn* on Heol Penallt. The *Glyndŵr Arms* on Heol Doll features local music at the weekends, but the liveliest pub in town is a bikers' haunt, the *Skinners Arms* on Heol Penallt. The bar at Y Tabernacl (see above) is also very popular, and, if you've got your own transport, seek out the excellent pub food at the old-beamed *Penrhos Arms* in the village of Cemmaes, five miles east of Machynlleth.

Centre for Alternative Technology and Corris

Since its foundation in the middle of the oil crisis of 1974, the **Centre for Alternative Technology** (CAT), or *Canolfan y Dechnoleg Amgen* (daily 10am–5pm, displays open to 7pm in summer; £6.90 summer, £4.90 winter, discounts to those arriving by bike or public transport), just over two miles north of Machynlleth off the A487, has become one of the biggest attractions in Wales. In just twenty-five years, seven acres of a once-derelict slate quarry have become an almost entirely self-sufficient community, generating eighty percent of its own power from wind, sun and water. But this is no back-to-the-land hippie commune. Right from the start, the idea was to embrace sustainable technology – much of the on-site equipment was developed and built here, reflecting the centre's achievements in this field – and, most importantly, to promote its application in urban situations.

Whole houses have been constructed to showcase energy-saving ideas and to demonstrate how homes can be built with minimal skills and local materials. Composting toilet systems and a natural reed-bed filtration system produce superbly rich soil, much needed for the organic gardens, and drinkable water. Many of the hands-on exhibits are self-explanatory, but the ebullient fifty-strong staff – many living communally and all receiving identical (very low) wages – are happy to explain the concepts.

All this earnest education is leavened with flashes of pzazz. A water-balanced **cliff railway** (April–Oct) whisks the visitor 200ft up to the main site from the car park, a "mole hole" – a human-sized earth tunnel with authentic sounds and textures – forces an appreciation of insect life, and a new "transport maze" confuses and loses all except those who answer various options correctly to demonstrate their understanding of sound transport policy. It's also a beautiful site, sensitively landscaped using local slate and wood, and you can easily spend half a day sauntering around. There's plenty for kids to do, including a new straw-bale children's theatre, the wholefood restaurant turns out delicious organic food, and the excellent bookshop stocks a wide range of alternative literature.

Primarily, though, this is a living community which exists more to educate by example than entertain. A new environmental information centre, using the latest in database technology, is being built in a round earth building, and residential courses are offered (details from CAT, Machynlleth, Powys SY20 9AZ; ☎01654/702400, *www.cat.org.uk*), the most popular being a guide to building your own energy-efficient home. However, even a brief visit to the CAT will fascinate and inspire.

Corris

The spirit of the Centre for Alternative Technology is carried higher up the valley to **CORRIS**, a small slate-mining settlement which, after decades of decline, is beginning to reform itself. Almost thirty years of self-help have finally borne fruit with the opening of the **Corris Railway and Museum** (mid-July to Aug daily 11am–5pm; late May to mid-July & Sept daily 2–4pm; other times by appointment; ☎01654/761624; £1) which once moved slate and passengers from the main line at Machynlleth to the quarries at Corris. The line closed in 1948 when the bridge over the Dyfi was washed away, and since 1970, volunteers have raised money to rebuild the track. By summer 2000, two-thirds of a mile of track should be operational, initially with diesels and later with Welsh-built steam locos – however, progress is slow and its likely that the date might change again.

Elsewhere, there's the Corris Craft Centre on the A487, a former slate mine now home to **King Arthur's Labyrinth** (daily 10am–5pm; £4.50), a rather contrived 45-minute tour based around the ancient Welsh stories of The Mabinogion. Led by someone dressed as a monk, the boat trips into the various dank caverns that comprise the labyrinth are fun, but the half-baked son et lumière tableaux, hampered by poor sound and visuals, dilute the power of the magical tales.

The run-of-the-mill Craft Centre also houses the local **tourist office** (Easter–Oct daily 10am–5.30pm; ☎01654/761244, *corris.tic@gwynedd.gov.uk*) – staff can point you down the hill to the *Canolfan Corris* **youth hostel** on Old Road (March–Oct & weekends Nov–Feb; ☎ & fax 01654/761686; ①). Occupying a former village school, the hostel is an ecologically-minded concern, with large subdivided dorms, some family rooms and tent space; you can cook for yourself or have very reasonable, healthy meals made for you. Alternatively, you'll find **B&B** rooms and **bar meals** at the *Briach Goch Hotel* (☎01654/761229; ②) on the A487.

Aberdyfi

On a blustery winter's day, the battened-down Victorian seafront terraces of **ABER-DYFI**, at the mouth of the Dyfi Estuary on its northern shore, can seem almost suicidally forlorn. But in the summer, the streets come alive and Aberdyfi is transformed into an understated and likeable resort, whose sheltering horseshoe of mountains, dotted with a pleasing jumble of houses, provides a mild climate for the summer crowds drawn by the sandy beach and water sports. There's a rather sporadic rental service of canoes and sailboards on the beach, but there isn't much else to do here: swimming is possible, although the sea water was none too clean until a new sewage pipeline to the treatment station at Tywyn improved matters considerably. If you've got your own windsurfing or sailing equipment, you can become a temporary member of the Dovey Yacht Club (☎01654/767640) on the wharf.

In the mid-nineteenth century, the town, with its seamlessly joined eastern neighbour **Penhelig**, built shallow-draught coastal traders for the inshore fleet, a past remembered in the small historic and **maritime display** in the tourist office, Wharf Gardens (see below). Sticking to outdoor pursuits, there's a pleasant coastal walk east to the wooded **Picnic Island** starting at The Green, a manicured lawn in Penhelig. The path follows the inappropriately named Roman Road, a relatively modern path cut into the low coastal cliffs and crossing a couple of short bridges to well-sited rest spots on promontories. Appetite whetted, you might like to take in the fourteen acres of rock and water gardens, mature trees, heathers and woodland wild flowers which comprise **Plas Penhelig Gardens** (April to mid-Oct Wed–Sun 2.30–5.30pm; £1.95), immediately behind the *Penhelig Arms*.

Practicalities

Aberdyfi is served by two equally convenient **train** stations, the request-only Penhelig, half a mile east, and Aberdyfi, half a mile west of the **tourist office** at Wharf Gardens (Easter–Oct daily 10am–6pm; ☎01654/767321), near where the #29 **bus** stops.

The best **budget accommodation** here is the friendly, non-smoking *Cartref Guest House*, Penrhos (☎01654/767273; ①) near Aberdyfi train station, and the summer-only *Brodawel*, on Tywyn Road (☎01654/767347; ②), opposite the members-only golf course a mile north of town; both do evening meals for under a tenner. Also good are *Sea Breeze*, 6 Bodfor Terrace (☎01654/767449; ①), along the waterfront in town, and *Ceunant*, Aberdyfi Road (☎01654/767264; ①), a welcoming cheapie three miles east towards Machynlleth. Penhelig is also home to a couple of top-class small **hotels**. The *Penhelig Arms Hotel* (☎01654/767215, fax 767690; ④), near Penhelig train station, is particularly noted for its excellent restaurant with extensive wine list, while the Edwardian *Plas Penhelig Country House Hotel*, a mile up the road behind (closed Dec to mid-March; ☎01654/767676, fax 767783; ⑤), is justifiably proud of its magnificent oak-panelled public areas, seven-acre estuary-front gardens and traditional table d'hôte menu.

Lighter **meals** are offered at the good-value *Old Coffee Shop*, 13 New St (closed Jan), built into the cliff behind the *Britannia Hotel*, with home-made cakes and inexpensive lunches, and the *Grapevine Restaurant*, 1 Chapel Square (☎01654/767448), where you can get bistro-type fare. In the evening, the *Dovey Inn* on Sea View Terrace has the best bar meals and, along with the *Britannia* – where the highlight is sunset on the upstairs terrace – the liveliest atmosphere.

Tywyn and the Talyllyn Railway

Despite four miles of sandy beach, **TYWYN** ("the strand"), three miles north of Aberdyfi, is really only of interest as a base for the Talyllyn and Dysynni valleys (see pp.298–300). It's a traditional sort of seaside resort, but without the range of things to do that you'd expect from many such places. At the east end of the long High Street, the Norman nave of the **Church of St Cadfan** (daily 9am–5pm, later in summer, church tour Wed 5pm) houses one of the town's few real sights – the five-foot-high **St Cadfan's Stone** bears the earliest example of written Welsh, dating back to around 650 AD.

Tywyn's saving grace is the **Talyllyn narrow-gauge railway** (April–Oct daily and late December; ☎01654/710472; £8.50 return), which belches seven miles inland through the delightful wooded Talyllyn Valley to Nant Gwernol. From 1866 to 1946, the rail line was used to haul slate from the Bryn Eglwys quarry near Nant Gwernol to Tywyn Wharf station, then just four years after the quarry's closure, rail enthusiasts took over the running of services, making this the world's first volunteer-run railway. The round trip (at a maximum 15mph) takes two hours, but you can get on and off as frequently as the schedule allows, taking in some fine broadleaf **forest walks**. The best of these starts at Dôlgogh Falls station, where three trails (maximum 1hr; leaflet 30p) lead off to the lower, mid- and upper cascades. At the end of the line, more woodland walks take you around the site of the old slate quarries. In mid-August each year, the schedule is disrupted by the "Race the Train" event, when runners attempt to beat the train on its thirteen-mile trip to Abergynolwyn and back. Some do.

The **Narrow-Gauge Museum** (open when trains are running; 50p) at Tywyn Wharf station boasts half a dozen locos and some oddball rolling stock culled from the ruins of other lines – including a shunter from the Guinness brewery in Dublin – but equally venerable machinery still works the line. Of the original Talyllyn rolling stock, two steam engines and all five of the oak and mahogany passenger carriages still run up to Nant Gwernol.

Practicalities

The three main roads in Tywyn – the High Street, Pier Road and the Aberdyfi road – meet at the **train station**, which also acts as the main **bus** stop. The **tourist office** is in front of the Leisure Centre on High Street (Easter–Oct daily 10am–1pm & 2–6pm; ☎01654/710070), Pier Road makes for the beach, and the Aberdyfi road heads south past the Talyllyn narrow-gauge train station (Tywyn Wharf) two hundred yards away.

Decent **accommodation** can be found at the *Ivy Guest House*, opposite the tourist office on High Street (☎01654/711058; ①), or the cheaper, non-smoking *Glenydd Guest House*, 2 Maes Newydd (☎01654/711373; ①), two hundred yards from the beach off Pier Road. For something a little more luxurious, try the *Corbett Arms Hotel* (☎01654/710264; ②), on Corbett Square, just a little further up the main street from the parish church. Of the many **campsites** in the area, the handiest is *Ynysmaengwyn Caravan Park* (April–Sept; ☎01654/710684), a mile out on the Dolgellau road.

The moderately priced *Proper Gander* on High Street (☎01654/711270) serves the best **food** in town – imaginative lunches, teas and great desserts all day, as well as à la carte evening meals from Wednesday to Saturday. The *Tredegar Arms* is the most welcoming of the High Street **pubs**, and includes a decent new restaurant. There's occasional live music and functions at the *Corbett Arms* (see above).

The Talyllyn and Dysynni valleys

The **Talyllyn and Dysynni valleys** form a two-pronged fork pointing southwest towards the sea. The handle is formed by the Talyllyn Valley, which starts at the northeast by Minffordd and is followed by the Dysynni River (Afon Dysynni) as far as Abergynolwyn. Here the valley splits into two, some ancient geological upheaval having forced the river to abruptly switch its course north, forming the Dysynni Valley and leaving its original course beside the Talyllyn Railway all but dry. Although a quick tour around the sites won't take more than a day, the area is monumentally beautiful, with superb lowland or mountain walking (particularly on Cadair Idris) and some good accommodation – in all, the valleys are an ideal choice for a relaxing couple of days spent exploring.

The Talyllyn Valley is served by the #30 bus, running from Tywyn to Abergynolwyn, continuing to Minffordd (where you can catch #2 to Dolgellau) and Machynlleth. The Talyllyn narrow-gauge railway runs from Tywyn to Abergynolwyn station half a mile short of the village, or to Nant Gwernol, just past the village but off the road. **Accommodation** is scattered throughout the two valleys, but the only **restaurants** are those attached to hotels. Campsites tend towards the simple: farmers' fields with or without showers.

The Talyllyn Valley

From Tywyn, the road up the **Talyllyn Valley** runs parallel to the Talyllyn Railway (see overleaf), meeting it at Dolgoch Falls, the site of some wooded walks and the *Dolgoch Falls Hotel* (March–Oct; ☎01654/782258; ③), where moderately priced meals are available. You'll find cheaper accommodation half a mile further on at a superb farmhouse B&B, *Tan-y-Coed-Uchaf* (March–Oct; ☎01654/782228; ②), just two miles short of the twin valleys' largest settlement, **ABERGYNOLWYN**. The town is comprised of a few dozen quarry workers' houses, two pubs – including the *Railway Inn* with the best range of real ales for miles around – and the wonderful *Riverside Guesthouse and Café* on Cwrt (☎01654/782235; ①), which serves all-day breakfasts, full meals for residents, and also has a limited number of bargain riverside **tent sites**. It's worth bearing in mind that Abergynolwyn is the valleys' only real settlement, so stock up here at the village shop if you're hiking and camping.

The Dysynni Valley branches northwest here, but the Talyllyn Valley continues northeast past the basic *Cedris Farm* **campsite** (☎01654/782280), a mile northeast of Abergynolwyn, and two miles further on to the serene **Tal-y-Llyn Lake** (Llyn Mwyngil). The chief interest here is the fifteenth-century **St Mary's church** on the southern shores of the lake, a fine example of a small Welsh parish church, unusual because of its chancel arch painted with an alternating grid of red and white roses, separated by grotesque bosses.

The lake itself is frequently stocked with brown trout and, occasionally, it's the resting place of migratory sea trout and salmon. The classy, angling-oriented *Tynycornel* hotel (☎01654/782282, fax 782679; ⑥) issues fishing permits (£15 per day), as well as renting boats with outboard engines (£18) and tackle (£10); it also boasts a sauna, mountain bikes for guests and an excellent but expensive restaurant open to non-residents. On a tighter budget, try the nearby sixteenth-century *Pen-y-Bont* (☎01654/782218, fax 782666; ③), next to the church, which offers a good bar, an affordable restaurant and £12-a-day **mountain bikes** for rent.

It's a further two miles northeast to the start of one of the best routes up Cadair Idris (see box, opposite) from the hamlet of **MINFFORDD**. It's a tiny settlement, made up of only the informal *Minffordd Hotel* (March–Nov; ☎01654/761665, fax 761517; ④), an eighteenth-century farmhouse and coaching inn that's open to non-residents for traditional British dinners (Thurs–Sat), and two low-cost **campsites**: *Cwmrhwyddfor Farm*

WALKS ON CADAIR IDRIS FROM MINFFORDD

Note: The OS Outdoor Leisure 1:25,000 map no. 23, "Cadair Idris & Bala Lake/Llyn Tegid", is highly recommended for all these walks, although the OS Landranger 1:50,000 "Dolgellau" map will do.

The steepest and most dramatic ascent of Cadair Idris follows the **Minffordd Path** (6 miles; 5hr; 2900ft ascent), a justifiably popular route that makes a full circuit around the rim of **Cwm Cau**, probably the country's most dramatic mountain cirque.

The path starts just west of the *Minffordd Hotel* at the junction of the A487 and the B4405. From the car park, follow the signs along an avenue of horse chestnuts and up through the woods, heading north. You will reach a fork: take the left path that wheels around the end of Craig Lwyd into Cwm Cau, and before you reach the lake, fork left and climb onto the rim of Cwm Cau, following it round to **Penygadair** (2930ft; see also p.304), the highest point on the massif. Here, there's a circular shelter and a tin-roofed hut originally built for dispensing refreshments to thirsty Victorians, and now affording none-too-comfortable protection from wind and rain.

The shortest descent follows the summit plateau northeast, then down to a grassy ridge before ascending gradually to **Mynydd Moel** (2831ft), from which you get a magnificent view down into a cwm containing the waters of Llyn Arran. The descent starts beside the fence which you cross just before the summit – you follow the fence south all the way to fork below Cwm Cau described above.

On a good day, an **extended route** (9 miles; 7hr; 2900ft ascent) makes a more pleasurable descent and leaves your knees in better shape for the next day's walk. This follows the ridge around to **Gau Graig** (2240ft), finally dropping off the northernmost of the two spurs and swinging east to the road. Follow the A487 southwest until the old road branches right, then follow this parallel to the main road right back to Minffordd.

(☎01654/761380), half a mile northeast, and *Dôl Einion* (☎01654/761312), a couple of hundred yards southwest. *Dolffanog Fach* (☎01654/761235; ②), a seventeenth-century farmhouse B&B with a snooker room, is just under a mile to the southeast near the north end of Tal-y-Llyn Lake.

The Dysynni Valley

The **Dysynni Valley** has more to offer in the way of sights, even though a lack of public transport makes it difficult to get to. A mile and a half northwest of Abergynolwyn, a side road cuts northeast to the hamlet of **LLANFIHANGEL-Y-PENNANT** and the scant ruins of the native Welsh **Castell-y-Bere** (unrestricted access; CADW), a fortress built by Llywelyn ap Iorwerth (Llywelyn the Great) in 1221 to protect the mountain passes. After being besieged twice in the thirteenth century, this castle – one of the most massive of the Welsh castles – was consigned to seven centuries of obscurity and decay. Like so many of the native fortresses, Castell-y-Bere seems to rise almost imperceptibly out of the rock upon which it was built. With large slabs of the main towers still standing, there's still plenty to poke around, but it's primarily a great place just to sit or picnic, with good views to Cadair Idris and Craig yr Aderyn (see overleaf). A few hundred yards beyond the castle, you'll come to the centre of Llanfihangel, where the thick-set little **church of St Michael** is well worth seeing. Sitting snug in its circular graveyard, the church contains a couple of interesting exhibits in its vestry. One is a fabulous 3-D map of the valley, some fourteen feet long and built to a scale of 1 foot to 1 mile from patchwork and cloth. There are also some exhibits centred on one Mary Jones, including photos from 1921 detailing the unveiling of her monument, which can be found a little further up the lane at the ruined **Tyn-y-ddôl** (unrestricted access). Jones' fame rested with her 1800 Bible-buying walk to

Bala (see box on p.260), an event commemorated by a plaque in the remains of the house. The saintly image of the young Mary contrasts somewhat with local second- and third-hand memories of her as a rather cantankerous old bat. Tyn-y-ddôl marks the beginning of a path (10 miles; 7hr; 2900ft ascent) up Cadair Idris, though a longer and far less exciting one than those described in the box overleaf. Just beyond Tyn-y-ddôl, the lane peters out at *Gwastadfryn Farm*, complete with a very basic, but very beautiful, riverside **camping** field.

Three miles seaward from Tyn-y-ddôl, along the Dysynni Valley road, around thirty breeding pairs of cormorants colonize **Craig yr Aderyn** (Birds' Rock), a stunning 760-foot-high cliff four miles from the coast. As the sea has gradually withdrawn from the valley, the birds have remained loyal to their home, making this Europe's only inland cormorant nesting site. Watch them return in V-formation at dusk from the scant remnants of an Iron Age fort on top of Craig yr Aderyn, reachable via a path (2 miles; 1hr; 750ft ascent) from two miles west of Abergynolwyn – conveniently, the *Llanllûyda* **campsite** (☎01654/782276) is at the start of the path. Choughs and peregrine falcons share the rock in winter, and the occasional red kite may be seen at any time of year. On the other side of the rock, and with some superb views towards it, there's another decent camping option at *Glanywern* (☎01654/782247), a mile along the lane to Llanegryn.

A few hundred yards from the rock, next to the river bridge on the lane from Craig yr Aderyn to Llanegryn, a track cuts off to *Peniarth Uchaf* (☎01654/710804, fax 712044; ③), a wonderful, very formal guesthouse set in expansive grounds. Two miles further along this lane towards the sea, you meet the coast road (at this stage 2 miles inland) at **LLANEGRYN**, where the little church on a hill half a mile northwest of the village (open daily) has an unexpectedly beautifully carved rood screen, probably carved in the fifteenth century, which is said to have been carried overnight from Cymer Abbey (see p.303) after its dissolution.

Just over two miles west of Llanegryn, where the northbound A493 swings dramatically around to hug the coast, you come to the hamlet of **LLANGELYNIN**. A track descends seawards off the main road to another ancient church (open daily): a mainly eleventh-century building on the foundations of an eighth-century structure, and bare but for a few basic pews and a horse bier. Just outside the porch is the grave of Abram Wood, patriarch of Y Teulu Wood, a clan of Romanies who settled in Wales at the beginning of the eighteenth century.

Northern Cadair Idris and the Mawddach Estuary

In 1824, Wordsworth found the Mawddach "a sublime estuary". Some years later, John Ruskin concurred, deeming the waterside road he followed here "the most beautiful walk in the world". Romantic hyperbole perhaps, but these broad tidal flats gouging deep into the heart of the mid-Wales mountains create dramatic backdrops from every angle. With the sun low in the sky and the tide ebbing, the constantly changing course of the river trickles silver through the golden sands.

But the colour of the sands isn't just an illusion: they really do contain gold, though not enough for gold-mining company Rio Tinto Zinc, who thankfully abandoned their plans to dredge for the stuff in the early 1970s. Spasmodic outbursts of gold fever still occasionally hit the region's main town, **Dolgellau**, but most people are content to come here for some excellent walking up Cadair Idris and along the estuary, or to hit the beaches. The low-key **Fairbourne** and shoddy but relatively alive **Barmouth** are the main lures.

Fairbourne

The tiny, decaying resort of **FAIRBOURNE**, on the southern side of the Mawddach Estuary, was developed in the late nineteenth century as the country estate of the chairman of the McDougall's flour company. It sports one of the finest beaches in Wales and great views along the coast and across the estuary. Mr McDougall would undoubtedly be dismayed at the state of the town today, but it does have one attraction, the steam-hauled **Fairbourne Railway** (Easter–Sept 9 daily; £4.25 return), with a gauge of just one foot (31cm). The railway makes a pleasant alternative route across the estuary to Barmouth, starting across the road from the **train station** and running a mile to a connecting **passenger ferry** (Easter–Oct; £1 single, £1.70 return) which takes you the rest of the way. Midway between Fairbourne and the ferry's departure point, a halt on the railway line boasts a name to outdo even Llanfair PG on Anglesey (see p.425). No doubt hopeful that a ridiculously contrived station name might bring moribund Fairbourne the same kudos and visitors, it has been officially named Gorsafawddacha'idraigodanheddogleddollônpenrhynareurdraethceredigion ("The station on the Mawddach with dragon's teeth on the north Penrhyn Drive on the golden Cardigan sands"). If only to show how tortuously overblown the name is, the "dragon's teeth" are a set of grim concrete defences left over from World War II. And that's about as good as Fairbourne gets.

Dolgellau

Its distance from England and its historical position in the heartland of Welsh nationalism should make **DOLGELLAU** (pronounced Dol-gethl-aye) the Welshest of towns, but the town's architecture draws more from nineteenth-century England: a series of small grey squares – all with English names – clustered around the solid granite neo-Georgian facades of Eldon Square. That said, Dolgellau's dark architecture has its fans in those who find the unity of its appearance a pleasant contrast to the higgledy-piggledy nature of so many comparable Welsh market towns. The old county town of Meirionethshire, Dolgellau is still an important focal point for the highland hill farmers of the area.

It is a much older town than appearances suggest, lying at the junction of three Roman roads which converged on a now-vanished military outpost. It was here that Owain Glyndŵr assembled the last Welsh parliament in 1404, and later signed an alliance with Charles VI of France for providing troops to fight against Henry IV of England. Seventeenth-century Quakers sought freedom from persecution here, and in the 1860s, Dolgellau became the focus of numerous **gold rushes**, drawing wave after wave of prospectors to pan the estuary or blast levels into Clogau shale or mudstone sediment under the Coed y Brenin Forest. The quartz veins yielded some gold, but in quantities too small to make much money.

As the most convenient access point to the southern reaches of the Snowdonia National Park, Dolgellau is a decent and enjoyable base today. As well as offering some wonderful walks, notably an easy stroll along the Mawddach Estuary and a strenuous hike up Cadair Idris, Dolgellau offers plenty of evening diversions in the form of good pubs and restaurants and a fair bit of live music, none more so than during the superb annual **Sesiwn Fawr** (see p.303).

Arrival, information and accommodation

Dolgellau has no train station but is well served by **buses** from Bala, Barmouth and Machynlleth, which all pull into Eldon Square. The building on the square known as Tŷ

Meirion houses the **tourist office** (Easter–Oct daily 10am–1pm & 2–6pm; Nov–Easter Mon & Thurs–Sun 10am–5pm; ☎01341/422888), along with the Quaker Interpretive Centre (see opposite).

Though there is some commendable **accommodation** in Dolgellau itself, there are more appealing options scattered around the district, some so close to Cadair Idris that you can start your hike at the back door.

HOTELS AND GUESTHOUSES

Aber Café, Smithfield St (☎01341/422460). Very friendly B&B above a decent café. ①.

Borthwnog Hall, three miles west of Dolgellau on the A496, towards Bontddu (☎01341/430271, fax 430682). Small country house with its own art gallery superbly located on the northern shores of the Mawddach Estuary, with log fires and great meals. Take the #94 bus. ④.

Clifton House Hotel, Smithfield Square (☎01341/422554). Good-value hotel built in an ex-police station and jail – the basement cells are used as a restaurant. ②.

Dwy Olwyn, Coed y Fronallt, Llanfachreth Rd (☎01341/422822). Peaceful guesthouse in land-scaped gardens. A 10min walk from the centre – cross the Big Bridge and turn right. ①.

George III Hotel, Penmaenpool, four miles west of Dolgellau (☎01341/422525). Superb seven-teenth-century hotel right by the Mawddach Estuary (bus #28). Some rooms are in former train sta-tion buildings and the restaurant (see opposite) is excellent. ④.

Ivy House, Finsbury Square (☎01341/422535). Licensed guesthouse a few yards southeast of Eldon Square, with a restaurant and cellar bar. ②.

Penmaenuchaf Hall, Penmaenpool, four miles west of Dolgellau (☎ & fax 01341/422129). Grand house formerly home to a Lancashire cotton magnate and now operating as a classy hotel, with beautiful decor, a full-size billiard table and free angling for trout and salmon. It's pricey for one night but very competitive for short breaks. ④.

Tan-y-Fron, Arran Rd (☎01341/422638). Non-smoking B&B with en-suite rooms and an associated campsite, a 10min walk east along Arran Road. Closed Dec & Jan. ①.

Tŷ Isaf Farmhouse, Llanfachreth (☎01341/423261). Small, comfortable seventeenth-century guesthouse in three acres of grounds close to the Precipice Walk. Great £15 communal dinners and generous breakfasts. ③.

Tŷ Nant, Cader Rd, Islawrdref, three miles southwest of Dolgellau (☎01341/423433). Simple, com-fortable B&B, with a campsite, perfectly sited right at the foot of the Pony Path. ①.

Tyddyn Mawr Farmhouse, Islawrdref, three miles southwest of Dolgellau (☎01341/422331). Eighteenth-century farmhouse on the slopes of Cadair Idris at the foot of the Pony Path. Great value at the low end of this category with all rooms en suite. ②.

HOSTELS AND CAMPSITES

Bryn-y-Gwyn Campsite, Cader Rd (☎01341/422733). A basic tents-only site less than a mile south-east of Dolgellau.

Caban Cader Idris, Islawrdref, three miles southwest of Dolgellau (☎01248/600478). Twenty-bed bunkhouse at the foot of the road leading up to *Kings YHA hostel*. Beds at £6 a night. ①.

Kings YHA hostel, Penmaenpool, four miles west of Dolgellau (March–Oct; ☎01341/422392, fax 422477). Large country house a mile up a wooded valley off the #28 Tywyn bus route (last bus around 7pm). This is an ideal base for the Pony Path up Cadair Idris. ①.

Plas Isa, Lion St (☎01341/440666 or 01766/540569). Great 24-bed town centre hostel, with bedding provided and two kitchens and a games room on site.

Tan-y-Fron Campsite, Arran Rd (☎01341/422638). Well-appointed and reasonably priced camping and caravan site next to the B&B.

Tŷ Nant, Cader Rd, Islawrdref, three miles southwest of Dolgellau (☎01341/423433). Simple field campsite (£2 per person) with pay-to-use shower facilities shared by a simple bunkhouse. £4 gets you a bunk space (bring your own mat and bedding) and the use of a gas cooker, pots and pans.

Vanner Abbey Farm (☎01341/422854). Attractive camp and caravan site by Cymer Abbey.

The Town

Dolgellau's only central diversion is the **Quaker Interpretive Centre**, above the tourist office (see opposite), which uses a series of explanatory panels to tell of the local Quakers' (the Society of Friends) well-recorded sufferings before the 1689 Act of Toleration that put a stop – at least legally – to persecution for their pacifist Nonconformist views, non-attendance at church and non-payment of its tithes. At a trial in Bala in 1679, this last sin earned a group of Friends a prison term, a further encouragement to those thinking of following the two thousand Welsh Quakers who had already fled to the United States and started the Pennsylvania towns of Bangor, Bryn Mawr and others. The building also houses a **national park exhibition**.

Around Dolgellau

Gold frenzy hit Dolgellau long before its heyday in Victorian times: flecks of gold were discovered in the Mawddach silt by the Romans, while the thirteenth-century Cistercian monks based at **Cymer Abbey** (daily: April–Oct 9.30am–6pm; Nov–March 9.30am–4pm; £1.20; CADW), two miles north of Dolgellau, were given "the right in digging or carrying away metals and treasures free from all secular exaction". The fine location at the head of the Mawddach Estuary is typical of this austere order, but unfortunately the surrounding caravan site mars the effect of the remaining Gothic slabs. A path beside the abbey makes an alternative approach to the Precipice Walk (see box overleaf).

Precious metal was also the *raison d'être* for the town of **BONTDDU**, four miles west along the A496 towards Barmouth, the source of gold used in royal wedding rings for the Queen and Charles and Di. You can't visit the site, as it's still in operation, so the only gold you'll see now is in the springtime blooms at **Farchynys Cottage** (May–Sept Tues, Wed & Thurs 11am–5pm; £1) in the four acres of established garden and natural woodland.

There's more tranquillity a few miles southwest of Dolgellau at **Cregennan Lakes**, a serene local beauty spot set against a backdrop of brooding mountains. For something more boisterous, there's superb year-round pony trekking from **Abergwynant Trekking Centre** (☎01341/422377; £12 for 2hr), at Penmaenpool four miles west of Dolgellau on the A493.

Eating, drinking and entertainment

As with accommodation, most of Dolgellau's good **eating** takes place out of town, typically in the better hotels. Indeed, the only reason to hang around town in the evening is to take in rehearsals for one of the town's two **choirs**: the mixed Côr Gwerin y Gader, which meets at The Vestry, Tabernacle Chapel, Cader Road (Mon 8pm), and the male voice Côr Meibion Dolgellau, at Ysgol y Gader (Wed 8pm). The annual **Sesiwn Fawr** (literally "Big Session"; ☎01341/423355, *www.sesiwnfawr.demon.co.uk*) is just that: a long weekend of bands and musical shenanigans taking place in pubs and on open-air stages all over town, with some of Wales' better-known performers turning up for the crack. Taking place in mid-July, this is undoubtedly Dolgellau's finest hour.

Bwyty Dylanwad Da, 2 Smithfield St (☎01341/422870). The best restaurant in town, with creative, affordable dishes and great desserts served in simple surroundings. Closed Feb.

Fronoleu Farm Restaurant, Tabor, a mile east of Dolgellau off the Arran road (☎01341/422361). Licensed restaurant in eighteenth-century Quaker farmhouse with live harp playing Tues, Thurs & Sat. Bar meals also available.

George III, Penmaenpool (see opposite). Superb spot for an afternoon drink, a bar meal or something gamey and expensive from the à la carte menu.

Penmaenuchaf Hall, Penmaenpool (see opposite). High-quality modern British cuisine in tasteful surroundings, though the service and food don't quite warrant the high prices. The £5 cream teas are well worth it, though.

WALKS AROUND DOLGELLAU

Note: No map is needed for the first three walks; the OS Outdoor Leisure 1:25,000 map of "Cadair Idris & Bala Lake/Llyn Tegid" is recommended for the fourth, although the OS Landranger 1:50,000 "Dolgellau" map will do.

TORRENT WALK

The attractive lowland **Torrent Walk** (2 miles; 1hr; 100ft ascent), follows the course of the Clywedog River as it carves its way through the bedrock. Stroll downstream past the cascades and through some gnarled old woodland that drips with antiquity. Bus #2 can take you the two miles east along the A470, from where it's a hundred yards or so down the B4416 (signposted to Brithdir) to a sign on the left-hand side marking the beginning of the walk.

PRECIPICE WALK

The not remotely precipitous **Precipice Walk** (3–4 miles; 2hr; negligible ascent) is very easy-going, simple to follow and has great views to the 1000-foot ramparts of Cadair Idris and along the Mawddach Estuary – best in late afternoon or early morning sun. The path makes a circuit around Foel Cynwch, starting three miles north of Dolgellau off the Llanfachreth road just near the Big Bridge. Bus #33 runs twice daily on Tuesdays and Fridays only, from Dolgellau to the car park by the start of the walk. From the car park turn left down a side road then left again up a track, following the signs all the way. On the shores of Llyn Cynwch, the path splits. Take the left fork along the shores then follow the contour around the bracken- and heather-covered Foel Cynwch back to the lake and return along the approach route. If you don't coincide with the bus, a path beside Cymer Abbey (see p.303) is the next best approach to this walk.

PENMAENPOOL–MORFA MAWDDACH WALK

Beside the Mawddach Estuary's broad sands, a disused rail line makes for easy going on the **Penmaenpool–Morfa Mawddach Walk** (8 miles one way; 3hr; flat), starting at the car park by the Big Bridge in Dolgellau and passing Penmaenpool on its way to Morfa Mawddach. The first two miles are the least interesting, so it makes sense to catch the #28 bus to the **RSPB Nature Information Centre** (Easter–May Sat & Sun noon–4pm; June to mid-Sept daily 10am–5pm; free) in an old rail signal box at Penmaenpool, just by a wooden toll bridge (daily 8am–7pm; cars 50p, pedestrians 5p) linking the two banks of the estuary. From there the path hugs the estuary bank all the way to Morfa Mawddach, from where you can walk across the bridge to Barmouth (see opposite) or catch the bus back to Dolgellau. Another good scheme is to take the bus to Morfa Mawddach and walk back to Penmaenpool.

PONY PATH

If the weather is good and you are well kitted out, don't miss the classic **Pony Path** (6–7 miles; 4–5hr; 2500ft ascent), a straightforward and enjoyable route up Cadair Idris which starts from the car park at Tŷ Nant, three miles southwest from Dolgellau along the Cadair Road. Turn right, then right again at the telephone box, following the path to "Cader Idris". Already, the views to the craggy flanks of the massif are tremendous, but they disappear as you climb steeply to the col, where you turn left on a rocky path to the summit shelter on **Penygadair** (2930ft; see also p.299). The descent is either by the same route or (with some care and considerable efforts to minimize erosion) by taking the first part of the Fox's Path down to Llyn y Gadair. From the summit, go northeast to a grassy plateau then north to a couple of cairns and down to Llyn y Gadair. By the lake, forsake the rest of the Fox's Path in favour of a less obvious route heading off from the northwest corner of the lake, eventually meeting the Pony Path again. Note that there are no buses up Cadair Road.

Stag Inn, Bridge St. Straightforward town-centre pub with good beer and a garden.
Tafarn Caetanws, Smithfield St. Good food and occasional live music and comedy in this great town-centre pub.
Tyn-y-Groes Hotel, Glanllwyd, four miles north of Dolgellau. Hospitable hotel in the Coed y Brenin forest. Good beer washes down fine bar meals or you can opt for the à la carte restaurant.
Y Sospan, Queen's Square (☎01341/423174). Dependable café/bistro behind the tourist office, serving good coffee, decent daytime meals and better dinners (booking necessary).

Barmouth and around

The best approach to **BARMOUTH** (Abermaw) is the 2253-foot-long rail bridge created for the nineteenth-century English Midlands sea-bathers who popularized the town; from the south, the bridge traverses over 113 rickety-looking wooden spans across the Mawddach River estuary. On the face of it, this tight little town, tucked into the shadow of steep cliffs and lapped by both estuary and sea, should be the jewel of the Cambrian coast, but years of shabby development have lumbered it with too many heavy buildings and charmless pleasure-beach attractions. Keep your eyes out to sea or make for the hills behind the town, though, and it's a fine stop for a night or two.

Barmouth was once a shipbuilding centre, and a maritime air lingers around the quay at the south end of town, departure point for a **passenger ferry** to Fairbourne (Easter–Oct; as frequently as custom demands; £1 single, £1.70 return) as well as several sea angling and sightseeing trips (enquire on the quay). In late June each year, the highly competitive **Three Peaks Race** starts here, a two-to-three-day amateur yachting event entailing navigation to Caernarfon, the English Lake District and Fort William in Scotland, and a run up the highest peak in each country.

The quay is also where you'll find the **RNLI Lifeboat Museum** (daily 10am–5pm; free), with its workaday exhibition of lifesaving paraphernalia; and the **Tŷ Gwyn Museum** (July–Sept Tues–Sun 10.30am–5pm; free), a medieval tower house where Henry VII's uncle, Jasper Tudor, is said to have plotted Richard III's downfall. First recorded in a poem around the middle of the fifteenth century, the house was thought to have been destroyed until renovations in the 1980s revealed its identity. It now contains displays on the Tudor dynasty, as well as a shipwreck museum.

On the hill behind, the **Tŷ Crwn Roundhouse** (same hours as Tŷ Gwyn museum) acted as a lockup for drunken sailors in the eighteenth century, and was reputedly built circular to prevent the devil lurking in any corners and further tempting the incarcerated mariners. It now houses some old photos of Barmouth.

Practicalities

Buses from Harlech and Dolgellau stop on Jubilee Road, near the **train station** and just a few yards from the **tourist office** (Easter–Oct daily 10am–6pm; ☎01341/280787, *barmouth.tic@gwynedd.gov.uk*).

In winter, the office displays a list of available **accommodation**, but in summer, there's no shortage. There are also loads of places to **camp**, the closest – and least afflicted with fixed caravans – being *Hendre Mynach*, Llanaber Road (March–Oct; ☎01341/280262), just off the beach a mile north of town. For something simpler, try *Cefn Ddu* (☎01341/430644), a cheap, tent-only site with showers, down by the estuary, just west of Bontddu.

HOTELS AND GUESTHOUSES
Awelon, Ffordd Gellfechan (☎01341/280254). Central and very friendly, this is the best of Barmouth's cheapies. ①.
Bay View, 6 Porkington Terrace (☎01341/280284). Not quite as much of a bargain as other places in town, but a dependable place to rest your head. ②.

WALKS FROM BARMOUTH

The best lowland walk on the Cambrian coast, the **Barmouth–Fairbourne Loop** (5 miles; 2–3hr; 300ft ascent) makes a superb circuit around Barmouth and Fairbourne, with fine mountain, estuarine and coastal views all the way. The route can be done with almost no walking at all using the rail line to Fairbourne, the Fairbourne narrow-gauge railway and the ferry across the mouth of the estuary, but walking allows for seemingly infinite variation. The route first crosses the rail bridge (30p toll) to Morfa Mawddach station, follows the lane to the main road, crosses it onto a footpath that loops around the back of a small wooded hill to Pant Einion Hall, then follows another lane back to the main road near Fairbourne. Turn north for 400 yards, then left down the main street of Fairbourne to the sea, walk north along the beach and you can catch the ferry back to Barmouth. Any desired extension to the walk is best done from Morfa Mawddach, where the route described meets the Penmaenpool–Morfa Mawddach Walk (see box, p.304). Follow it for a mile to Arthog where a small road and a mesh of paths lead up past waterfalls to the beautiful **Cregennan Lakes** (NT).

The **Panorama Walk** (10min) is more famous, but apart from the fine estuary view, its chief quality is its brevity, the viewpoint being only yards away from the nearest road. By taking in **Dinas Oleu** (Fortress of Light), the cliffs immediately above Barmouth, which became the National Trust's first property in 1895, it can be turned into a decent walk (3 miles; 2hr; 400ft ascent). Essentially the route follows Gloddfa Road opposite Woolworth's on High Street onto the exposed clifftops, where there is a map of the reserve. Go through the metal gate and follow the path past Frenchman's Grave to a road where you turn left to the Panorama Viewpoint. Return by the same route.

Bryn Melyn Hotel, Panorama Rd (☎01341/280556, fax 280342; ④), comfortable, traditional, mountainside hotel noted for its fine estuary views and proximity to the Cambrian Way walking route. ④.

The Gables, Mynach Rd (☎01341/280553). Ten minutes' walk north of town, a characterful place that's very welcoming to walkers. ①.

Holme Lea, 4 Marine Rd (☎01341/281419). Another pretty decent budget B&B. ②.

Llwyndû Farmhouse, Llanaber, two miles north of Barmouth (☎01341/280144, fax 281236). One of the finest farmhouse B&Bs in Wales, with en-suite rooms in the seventeenth-century farmhouse building – complete with mullioned windows and inglenook fireplace – and adjacent converted barn, plus delicious evening meals in the candlelit dining room. ④.

Wave Crest Hotel, 8 Marine Parade (☎01341/280330). Antique-furnished seafront hotel known for its excellent cuisine. ②.

EATING, DRINKING AND ENTERTAINMENT

Among the usual cheap cafés that populate every seaside resort, there are quite a few decent places to eat. The *Llwyndû Farmhouse* and *Wave Crest Hotel* (see above) both serve good meals to non-guests, or try *Brambles* on Church Street (☎01341/280038) for British and French evening meals and very popular Sunday lunches. Also on Church Street is the *Indian Clipper* (☎01341/280252), a great South Asian balti house which serves plenty of vegetarian dishes, while on the harbourfront you'll find the low-key *Anchor Restaurant*, with mammoth French sticks, pancakes and pavement tables, and the neighbouring *Isis*, good for pizza and vegetarian food.

The **entertainment** scene has less to offer, with only a couple of decent pubs and the odd pretty awful holiday-season club. Your best bets are the *Last Inn* on Church Street (☎01341/280530), a cosy bar in a former cobbler's shop where you can also get a good pub meal, and *Tal y Don* on High Street, a traditional and friendly pub with well-kept real ales.

Ardudwy

North of Barmouth, the coast opens out to a narrow coastal plain running a dozen miles towards Snowdonia and flanked by the heather-covered slopes of the Rhinog Mountains, five miles inland. This is **Ardudwy**, a land which Giraldus Cambrensis described as "the rudest and roughest of all the Welsh districts", a contention hard to reconcile with a fertile strip used as a fattening ground for black Welsh cattle on their way to the English markets, and now tamed by caravan sites and golf courses.

No modern road crosses the Rhinogs to the east, but until the early nineteenth-century building of coach roads, the existence of two mountain passes (see box p.309) made this a strategic and populous area, as the number of minor Neolithic burial chambers and small Iron and Bronze Age forts demonstrate. Further up the coast, the town of **Harlech** was built as one link in Edward I's chain of magnificent fortresses. It is the only sizeable town in the region, followed in importance by **Llanbedr**, from where a road runs west to the dune-backed camping resort on Shell Island, and another rises east, splitting into two delightful remote valleys.

Bus #38 services the coast from Barmouth to Harlech, then inland to Blaenau Ffestiniog. The Cambrian coast train line covers the same route to Harlech, from where it makes for Porthmadog on the Llŷn peninsula (see p.349).

Llanddwywe and Dyffryn Ardudwy

Two of the most accessible and impressive Neolithic sites in Ardudwy are in the contiguous twin villages of **LLANDDWYWE** and **DYFFRYN ARDUDWY**, five miles north of Barmouth. Turn right opposite the church in Llanddwywe and continue for a mile to get to **Cors-y-Gedol Burial Chamber** (unrestricted entry), a large capstone on deeply embedded uprights. It's currently unsignposted, but follow the path to the right at the far end of Ffordd Gors; the one straight ahead leads to the old drovers' bridge at **Pont Scethin** and the Roman Steps (see overleaf). More substantial than Cors-y-Geddol, the communal **Dyffryn Ardudwy Burial Chamber** (unrestricted entry; CADW) is signposted just off the main road behind the school in Dyffryn Ardudwy. Two supported capstones lie amongst a bed of small boulders, the base stones of a mound thought to have been a hundred feet long. Finds from a dig here in the 1960s – including pottery, finely polished stone plaques and bones – are on display at the National Museum in Cardiff.

If you're travelling by train, get off at Talybont, walk north to visit the two sites and rejoin the line at Dyffryn Ardudwy, a walk of three miles in all. Just beyond Dyffryn Ardudwy station is the southern entrance to the **Morfa Dyffryn National Nature Reserve**, a coastal dune system stretching up to Shell Island (see overleaf) notable for its flora, particularly the marsh helleborine. This is a fragile zone and permission for access must first be obtained from the Countryside Council for Wales (☎01248/372333). Follow the path from Dyffryn Ardudwy station through the caravan parks and the dunes to the splendid, vast **beach**. A section of shore a few hundred yards to the north serves as a popular nudist area.

There's a great place to **stay** on the main road in Dyffryn Ardudwy: *Glan y Wern* (☎01341/247580; ②) offers attractive rooms in the main house or cottage annexe, and organic breakfast – with ingredients from the garden – cooked by a former chef at the Centre for Alternative Technology. Delicious evening meals are available, as are pottery and t'ai chi classes.

The latest "Dolgellau" OS map shows several routes with public foot access over the moors to the east. Most are ancient drovers' tracks and excellent for long lonely walks, especially if you're equipped with Shirley Toulson's *The Drovers' Roads of Wales* (see Contexts, p.487). The longest and most challenging of the tracks forms part of the old Harlech-to-London road and crosses the tiny and remote Pont Scethin, a favourite with postcard and calendar photographers.

Llanbedr and around

LLANBEDR, three miles north of Dyffryn Ardudwy, is home to more Neolithic sights. There are two imposing **standing stones** at the northern end of the village, in the field to the south of the petrol station; sadly, though, they and an oak tree are incarcerated behind a rusty fence. The taller one, about ten feet high, is shaped like a vast arrowhead. Across the road from the stones is the parish **church of St Peter**, which contains an ancient stone grooved with a spiral pattern, a common design from other pre-Christian sites. Other than that, its YHA **hostel**, *Plas Newydd* (☎01341/241287, fax 241389), right in the centre and open from April to October, makes Llanbedr a reasonable place to stay, as do the *Victoria Inn* (☎01341/241213; ④) with its beer garden, good bar meals and à la carte dinners, and the excellent *Llew Glas Brasserie* (☎01341/241555).

Though Llanbedr itself offers limited excitement, there are plenty of things to do in the area. A lane forks off the main road in the village centre, snaking its way alongside the babbling Afon Artro, past the train station and RAF airfield to **Shell Island**, or Mochras, two miles away (£4 per car in summer, £3 in winter). A peninsula at anything other than high tide, you reach the island by a tidal causeway, then you can swim, sail, examine the wild flowers or scour the beach for some of the two hundred varieties of shell found here. The Shell Island complex houses a restaurant, deservedly popular for Sunday roast lunch, and forms the centrepiece of the huge caravan-free **campsite** (☎01341/241453, fax 241501), which spreads its way along the beach from the harbour down to the vast dunes of Morfa Dyffryn. Although it can get crowded during the school summer holidays and warm bank holiday weekends, at any other time, you're virtually guaranteed solitude amongst quite spectacular scenery, with some of the best sunsets in north Wales. At low tide you can see a line of rocks in the sand leading out towards Ireland, known as Sarn Badrig (St Patrick's Causeway) and traditionally thought to be the road to a flooded land known as "The Low Hundreds", whose church bells still ring from below the water. Some imagination may be needed to hear this, but you can easily pick out what is probably a glacial lateral moraine, particularly from the top of the Rhinogs, from where it often appears to divide the ocean into two shades of blue.

East of Llanbedr, a narrow road follows the Afon Artro six miles to the waters of **Llyn Cwm Bychan**, deep in the heather and angular rocks of the Rhinog range. There's a basic **campsite** at the head of the lake, and paths up to the **Roman Steps** – most likely a medieval packhorse route, made of flat slabs cutting through the range – onto Rhinog Fawr (see box, opposite). Branching off the Cwm Bychan road, an even narrower and more picturesque road leads to **Cwm Nantcol**, the next valley south, where you can park at the ancient farm of **Maes-y-garnedd**, the birthplace of Colonel John Jones, brother-in-law of Oliver Cromwell and signatory to Charles I's death warrant, and a starting point for the Rhinog walks. There is no public transport up either valley.

North of Llanbedr the A496 climbs gently for a mile or so to **Chwarel Hên Slate Caverns** (Easter to mid-Oct daily 10am–5pm; £3.10) at Llanfair, a small slate quarry visited on a self-guided underground tour that doesn't hold a candle to those in Blaenau Ffestiniog. A few yards further on, a small road branches down to the hamlet of **Llandanwg**, a great place to get out onto the dunes, with a small, typically locked church that has to be periodically dug out of the sand by youth scheme workers so that the occasional service can be held. From the top road in Llanfair, a lane to the right

WALKS ON THE RHINOGS

The northern Rhinogs offer some surprisingly tough walking. At under 2500ft, they're hardly giant monliths, but the typically large, rough, gritstone rocks hidden in thick heather make anything but the most well-worn paths hard going and potentially ankle-twisting. Additionally, Rhinog Fawr is completely within the Rhinog National Nature Reserve and, while no permit is needed, the thin soil and fragile nature of the environment demand that you don't stray from the paths. The reward for your efforts are long views across Cardigan Bay, a good chance of stumbling across a herd of feral goats and a strong sense of achievement. The two walks described here start at the head of different valleys (see opposite), but share a common summit, that of Rhinog Fawr. Ambitious walkers might try combining the two (10 miles; 7hr; 3700ft ascent), using paths that only approximately follow those marked on the OS Landranger #124 Dolgellau map or the Outdoor Leisure #18 map of Harlech, Porthmadog & Bala.

CWM BYCHAN WALK #1

The **Cwm Bychan walk** (5 miles; 3–4hr; 1900ft ascent) starts at the car park in Cwm Bychan, following signs up through a small wood then out onto the open moor and up to the misnamed **Roman Steps**. These guide you up to a pass, Bwlch Tyddiad, giving views east to Bala and beyond. Continue a couple of hundred yards past a large cairn to a smaller one signalling a much less well-defined path leading south and steeply up. Beyond Llyn Du, the terrain gets steeper still, and you may have to use your hands to finally reach **Rhinog Fawr** (2362ft). The standard route is then to retrace your steps, but in good weather you can descend the same way you came for a few hundred yards and seek out a line running northwest from the shoulder towards Gloyw Llyn. From there, with some effort, you can pick up a path by following the obvious watercourse along a small stream to the head of Llyn Cwm Bychan.

CWM BYCHAN WALK #2

The second walk (6–7 miles; 5–6hr; 2900ft ascent) starts by the farmhouse at the head of Cwm Nantcol and makes a fairly rugged circuit over Rhinog Fawr and Rhinog Fach. Follow the track north from the car park to the house, into the fields and over the stile, then turn northeast and walk gradually towards the base of the rocky southwest ridge, following the white marker posts. Eventually, the path turns north to a cairn on the skyline, then east following more cairns up the ridge to the summit trig point of **Rhinog Fawr** (2362ft).

To approach Rhinog Fach you first have to make an arduous descent into Bwlch Drws Ardudwy (The Pass of the Door of Ardudwy). In 1773 Thomas Pennant found "the horror of it far exceeding the most gloomy idea that could be conceived of it. The sides seem to have been rent by some mighty convulsion into a thousand precipices." That might be a bit overstated, but describing the route between these precipices is all but impossible. From the summit of Rhinog Fawr head southeast towards a couple of cairns, then with Rhinog Fach ahead of you keep left, descending on whatever looks like it has had the most use. Eventually you'll reach the col, where you cross the stone wall and start on a fairly clear line up **Rhinog Fach** (2236ft). Explore the summit ridge to get the best views either way, then descend to Cwm Nantcol by first walking to a rocky ledge overlooking Llyn Hywel to the south. From here you should be able to see a scrappy path running very steeply down to the lake on the right-hand edge of the ledge. You'll have to use your hands at times, and there are sections of scree, but you're soon on a clear path that skirts north around the base of Rhinog Fach towards Bwlch Drws Ardudwy. When you reach the path through the pass, turn left and follow it back to Cwm Nantcol.

ascends into spectacular hill country, a crisscross of dry stone walls, sheep and pre-historic relics. Midway between Llanfair and the chapel at Rhiwgoch, on the left side of the road, you'll find the remains of **Muriau'r Gwyddelod** (The Irishmen's Walls), a series of Bronze Age hut circles dotted around a mossy field.

Harlech

One of the undoubted highlights of the Cambrian Coast is charming **HARLECH**, three miles north of Llanbedr. Clinging to a rocky outcrop, the time-worn castle alone dramatically raises Harlech above its neighbours, and the town behind commands one of Wales' finest views: over the Morfa Harlech dunes across Cardigan Bay and beyond to the Llŷn (see p.348), and north to the jagged peaks of Snowdonia (see p.315). The castle's bulky intactness, and its seemingly impregnable position, dominate the surroundings, but don't miss the narrow streets and buildings of this small, friendly town, cloaking the hill behind the fortress. With some superb places to stay, eat and drink, together with wonderful walking country behind and superb beaches in front, Harlech is an excellent option for a few nights' sojourn.

Arrival, information and accommodation

Harlech's **train** station is on the main A496 under the castle. Most **buses** call both here and on High Street, a few yards from the **tourist office** in Gwyddfor House (Easter–Oct daily 10am–6pm; ☎01766/780658). Theatr Ardudwy (☎01766/780667), on the main road, occasionally puts on a decent play and has the only cinema in the district. There's **accommodation**, in town and around, to suit all pockets, and a reasonable summer-only **campsite**, *Min y Don* (☎01766/780286), only three minutes' walk towards the beach (left out of the station then first right).

HOTELS AND GUESTHOUSES
Aris Guesthouse, 4 Pen y Bryn (☎01766/780409). Friendly guesthouse with a great view, just above the town – past the *Lion Hotel*, then second left. ①.
Byrdir, High St (☎01766/780316). Reliable small hotel with some en-suite rooms and meals available, fifty yards from the tourist office. Closed Nov. ②.
Castle Cottage, Pen Llech (☎01766/780479). Cosy informal hotel with the trappings of a place charging twice as much, and consequently often booked well ahead. Excellent meals and a comfortable bar. Closed Feb. ③.
Gwrach Ynys Country Guesthouse, Ynys, Talsarnau, two miles north of Harlech (☎01766/780742, fax 781199). Comfortable and justifiably popular country house on the coastal flats with en-suite rooms, good home-cooked meals and plenty of advice on local walks. Open March–Oct. ③.
Maes-y-Neuadd, Talsarnau, three miles north of Harlech (☎01766/780200, fax 780211. Substantially modernized country-house hotel, parts of which date from the fourteenth century. The expensive meals have garnered all manner of accolades. ⑦.
St David's Hotel on the A496 (☎01766/780366, fax 780820). A rambling pile of a hotel on the main road into town next to Theatr Ardudwy. Decent enough rooms, with all facilities, if in a slightly sterile atmosphere. ④.
Tremeifion, Talsarnau, three miles north of Harlech (☎01766/770491). Luxury, non-smoking vegetarian guesthouse in three acres of grounds. B&B and half-board deals are available for a few more pounds, the latter including evening meals made almost entirely from organic produce, and served with organic wine. ③.
Tyddyn-y-Gwynt, two miles above the town (☎01766/780298). Farmhouse with standard rooms, run by friendly local people. Take the road past the *Lion Hotel*, head straight at the crossroads and turn left at Bryn Gwyn Cottage. ①.

The Town

Although blessed with some of the coast's best beaches, it is the substantially complete **castle** (June–Sept daily 9.30am–6pm; April–May & Oct daily 9.30am–5pm; Nov–March Mon–Sat 9.30am–4pm, Sun 11am–4pm; £3; CADW), squatting on its 200-foot bluff, that is Harlech's showpiece. Intended as one of Edward I's Iron Ring of monumental fortresses (see p.408), construction of Harlech castle began in 1283, just six months after the death of Llywelyn the Last. It was built of a hard Cambrian rock, known as Harlech grit, hewn from the moat where sheep now peacefully graze. One side of the fortress was originally protected by the sea – the waters have now receded, though, leaving the castle dominating a stretch of duned coastline.

The castle has seen a lot of action in its time: it withheld a siege in 1295, was taken by Owain Glyndŵr in 1404, and the youthful, future Henry VII – the first Welsh king of England and Wales – withstood a seven-year siege at the hands of the Yorkists from 1461 to 1468, when the castle was again taken. It fell into ruin, but was put back into service for the king during the Civil War, and in March 1647 it became the last Royalist castle to fall.

The first defensive line comprised the three successive pairs of gates and portcullises built between the two massive half-round towers of the **gatehouse**, where an exhibition now outlines the castle's history. Much of the outermost ring has been destroyed, leaving only the twelve-foot-thick curtain walls rising up 40ft to the exposed battlements, and only the towering gatehouse prevents you walking the full circuit. The inner ward was never completed but corbels and inset fireplaces give clues to the original domestic functions.

Outside the castle, a modern equestrian **statue** by Ivor Roberts depicts a scene from The Mabinogion, recalling a semi-mythical era long before Edward's conquest. The heroic giant and king of the British, Bendigeidfran (Brân the Blessed), ruled the court at Harlech, which needed to ally itself with the Irish. Bendigeidfran's sister Branwen (White Crow) married the king of Ireland and bore him a son, Gwern, but war soon broke out and Gwern was killed. Sorrowful uncle and dead nephew are **The Two Kings** of the sculpture's title.

Although there are no specific sights in town aside from the castle and the obligatory cluster of attendant craft shops, Harlech is a cheerful enough place in which to wander, admiring the splendid views in all directions. Reachable via Beach Road, which shoots off the main road through Harlech, directly below the castle, the town's **sand dunes** and **beach** are superb. On the way to the sands, you'll brush past the rather snooty **Royal St David's golf course**, venue of many a championship.

Eating and drinking

Castle Cottage, High St (☎01766/780479). Limited choice two- and three-course dinner menu featuring the likes of smoked haddock in leek sauce. Very good, informal service, cosy surroundings and moderate prices. Wed–Sat only in winter, but Sun lunch served in summer.

Hung Yip, High St. Straightforward but good, cheap Chinese meals.

Lion Hotel. About the liveliest pub in Harlech, with hand-pumped ales and good home-cooked bar meals. Just up from the central crossroads.

Plâs Café, High St (☎01766/780204). Licensed café and restaurant with a good range of inexpensive to moderate food and one of the finest views around. Sit in the glass-fronted dining room, or the garden if the weather is fine.

Yr Ogof, High St (☎01766/780888). Highly commendable bistro-style place a few yards north of the centre, with bentwood chairs and a good-value range of inventive vegetarian and meaty dishes.

travel details

Unless otherwise stated, frequencies for trains and buses are for Monday to Saturday services; Sunday averages 1–3 services, though the main routes are more frequent and some routes have no Sunday service at all.

Trains

Aberdyfi to: Barmouth (8 daily; 30min); Machynlleth (8 daily; 20min); Porthmadog (6 daily; 1hr 20min); Pwllheli (6 daily; 1hr 40min); Tywyn (8 daily; 5min).

Aberystwyth to: Birmingham (7 daily; 3hr); Borth (9 daily; 12min); Machynlleth (6 daily; 30min); Shrewsbury (7 daily; 2hr).

Barmouth to: Aberdyfi (8 daily; 30min); Harlech (6 daily; 30min); Machynlleth (8 daily; 1hr); Porthmadog (6 daily; 45min).

Harlech to: Barmouth (6 daily; 30min); Birmingham (5 daily; 4hr 15min); Machynlleth (6 daily; 1hr 20min); Porthmadog (7 daily; 20min).

Machynlleth to: Aberdyfi (8 daily; 20min); Aberystwyth (9 daily; 30min); Barmouth (6 daily; 55min); Birmingham (7 daily; 2hr 30min); Harlech (6 daily; 1hr 20min); Porthmadog (6 daily; 1hr 45min); Shrewsbury (7 daily; 2hr).

Tywyn to: Aberdyfi (7 daily; 5min); Barmouth (7 daily; 25min); Harlech (6 daily; 1hr); Machynlleth (7 daily; 30min); Porthmadog (6 daily; 1hr 10min).

Buses

Aberaeron to: Aberystwyth (hourly; 40min); Carmarthen (5 daily; 1hr 30min); Lampeter (7 daily; 35min); New Quay (hourly; 20min).

Aberdyfi to: Machynlleth (4–6 daily; 25min); Tywyn (4–6 daily; 10min).

Aberystwyth to: Aberaeron (hourly; 40min); Borth (hourly; 25min); Caernarfon (1 daily; 2hr 40min); Cardigan (5 daily; 2hr); Carmarthen (1 daily; 2hr 35min); Devil's Bridge (2 daily; 40min); Dolgellau (5 daily; 1hr 25min); Machynlleth (5 daily; 45min); New Quay (hourly; 1hr); Ponterwyd (7 daily; 30min); Pontrhydfendigaid (1 daily; 55min); Tregaron (3 daily; 1hr); Ynyslas (5 daily; 30min).

Barmouth to: Bala (8 daily; 1hr); Blaenau Ffestiniog (4 daily; 1hr); Dolgellau (8 daily; 20min);

Harlech (9 daily; 25min); Llangollen (7 daily; 1hr 50min); Wrexham (7 daily; 2hr 20min).

Cardigan to: Aberaeron (6 daily; 1hr 10min); Aberporth (hourly; 25min); Aberystwyth (5 daily; 2hr); Carmarthen (hourly; 1hr 30min); Cilgerran (8 daily; 10min); Drefach Felindre (hourly; 30min); Newcastle Emlyn (hourly; 25min); New Quay (hourly; 1hr).

Dolgellau to: Aberystwyth (5 daily; 1hr 25min); Bala (9 daily; 35min); Barmouth (8 daily; 20min); Llangollen (8 daily; 1hr 30min); Machynlleth (6 daily; 35min); Porthmadog (6 daily; 50min); Tywyn (6 daily; 50min).

Fairbourne to: Dolgellau (6 daily; 20min); Tywyn (6 daily; 35min).

Harlech to: Barmouth (9 daily; 25min); Blaenau Ffestiniog (4 daily; 35min).

Lampeter to: Aberaeron (7 daily; 35min); Carmarthen (8 daily; 1hr 10min); Llanddewi Brefi (Mon 1 bus, Tues, Thurs & Fri 4 buses; 25min); Pontrhydfendigaid (Tues 3 buses; 50min); Tregaron (Mon 1 bus, Tues, Thurs & Fri 4 buses; 30min).

Machynlleth to: Aberdyfi (4–6 daily; 25min); Aberystwyth (5 daily; 45min); Corris (10–20 daily; 12min); Dolgellau (6 daily; 35min); Llangollen (6 daily; 2hr 55min); Tywyn (4–6 daily; 35–45min).

New Quay to: Aberaeron (hourly; 20min); Aberporth (hourly; 40min); Aberystwyth (hourly; 1hr); Cardigan (hourly; 1hr).

Tregaron to: Aberystwyth (3 daily; 1hr).

Tywyn to: Aberdyfi (4–6 daily; 10min); Abergynolwyn (4 daily; 15min); Corris (4 daily; 30min); Dolgellau (6 daily; 50min); Fairbourne (6 daily; 35min); Machynlleth (4–6 daily; 35–45min).

CHAPTER FIVE

SNOWDONIA AND THE LLŶN

What the coal valleys are to the south of the country, the mountains of **Snowdonia** (Yr Eryri) are to the north: the defining feature, not just in their physical form, but in the way they have shaped the communities within them. Trapped between the brash coastal resorts in the north and the thinly inhabited hill tracts of mid-Wales to the south, this mountainous kernel is north Wales' crowning glory, a tightly packed bundle of soaring cliff faces, jagged peaks and plunging waterfalls.

Snowdonia is the heart – and undisputed highlight – of the massive **Snowdonia National Park** (Parc Cenedlaethol Eryri), an 840-square-mile area which extends north and south, beyond the bounds of Snowdonia and this chapter, to encompass the Rhinogs, Cadair Idris (see pp.309 and 299 respectively) and 23 miles of superb Cambrian coastal scenery. It is this concentrated section, little more than ten miles by ten, that most people mean when they refer to Snowdonia: staggeringly beautiful and home to Wales' highest mountain, **Snowdon** (Eryri), where winter snows cling to 3000-foot peaks well into April.

Not surprisingly, the massif is the region's focus, and there are enough mountain paths to keep even the most jaded walking enthusiast happy for weeks. But Snowdonia isn't all walking. Small settlements are dotted in the valleys, making great bases or places to rest. Chief among them are **Betws-y-Coed** and **Llanberis**, the latter linked to Snowdon's summit by mountain rail, while others, like **Beddgelert** and **Blaenau Ffestiniog**, are former mining or quarry towns still brimming with interest.

West of here, the mountain landscape bleeds gently into the softer contours of the **Llŷn peninsula**, which juts into the Celtic Sea at a near right angle to the Cambrian Coast. Linked to Snowdonia by the magnificent, narrow-gauge **Ffestiniog Railway**, its first settlement is the harbour town of **Porthmadog**, best-known these days for its proximity to the Italianate dream village of **Portmeirion**. The Welsh castle at Cricieth and the museum devoted to Lloyd George a couple of miles away are amongst the good

---

ACCOMMODATION PRICE CODES

Throughout this guide, hotel and B&B accommodation is priced on a scale of ① to ⑨, the number indicating the **lowest price** you could expect to pay per night in that establishment for a **double room in high season**. The prices indicated by the codes are as follows:

① under £40	④ £60–70	⑦ £110–150
② £40–50	⑤ £70–90	⑧ £150–200
③ £50–60	⑥ £90–110	⑨ over £200

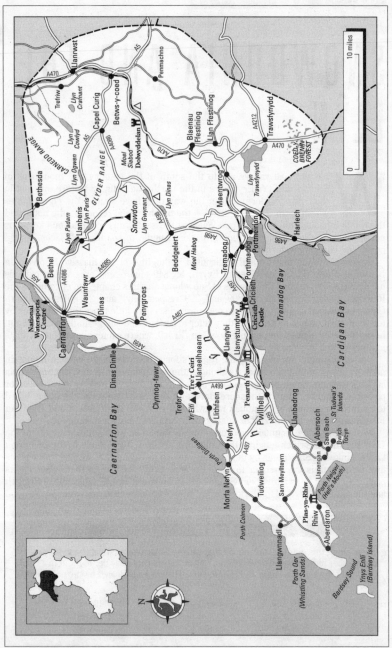

reasons to pause before Wales ends in a flourish of small coves around **Abersoch** and **Aberdaron**. Finally, roads loop back along the Llŷn to the tip of the north coast where **Caernarfon**, the heart of one of the most nationalist, Welsh-speaking areas in the country, is overshadowed by its mighty castle.

Getting around

Getting to the fringes of Snowdonia from elsewhere in Wales is not a problem: mainline **trains** run along the coast to nearby Bangor, while the Conwy Valley line branches at Llandudno Junction, penetrating to Betws-y-Coed and on to Blaenau Ffestiniog. Here, you can transfer to the useful and highly scenic Ffestiniog Railway for Porthmadog – the latter is also a stop on the Cambrian Coast line, shuffling daily around the coast to Pwllheli and to the heart of the Llŷn. There are frequent **bus** services from Llandudno and Conwy up the Conwy Valley to Betws-y-Coed, useful buses to Llanberis from Caernarfon and Bangor, and good connections from Porthmadog to Beddgelert and Blaenau Ffestiniog. Within Snowdonia (with the exception of the poor service in the Ogwen Valley), towns are linked every one to two hours by Sherpa minibuses. Pwllheli is the main transport hub for the Llŷn, with buses to most parts of the peninsula leaving from near the train station.

Routes and times are all fully detailed on the free *Gwynedd Public Transport Maps and Timetable*, available from tourist offices and bus stations. Current **discount fares** include the **Gwynedd Red Rover** (£4.20), good for one day's bus travel anywhere within Gwynedd and Anglesey. Arriva Cymru buses offer rover tickets valid for one day (£5), three days (£10) and five days (£15) – as many local bus companies are now owned by Arriva, these can work out to be cost-effective. If you intend to travel by both bus and train (including journeys on the Ffestiniog Railway), there's the **North & Mid Wales Rover**, available from any staffed train station: a one-day pass costs £17.30; three days in any seven costs £26.30, and five days in any ten is £40.90.

Roads throughout the region are well surfaced but also well travelled, making cycling less appealing than it might seem; however, there are a few new **cycle tracks**, and some quieter roads on the Llŷn and the bridleways through forests such as Coed y Brenin near Blaenau Ffestiniog (see p.348).

SNOWDONIA

To Henry VIII's antiquarian, John Leland, **SNOWDONIA** seemed "horrible with the sight of bare stones"; these days, it's widely acclaimed as the most dramatic and alluring region in Wales, a compact, barren land of tortured ridges dividing glacial valleys where the sheer faces belie the fact that the tallest peaks only just top three thousand feet. It was to this mountain fastness that Llywelyn ap Gruffydd, the last true Prince of Wales, retreated in 1277 after his first war with Edward I; it was also here that Owain Glyndŵr held on most tenaciously to his dream of regaining the title for the Welsh. Centuries later, the English came to remove the mountains; slate barons built huge fortunes from Welsh toil and reshaped the patterns of Snowdonian life forever, as men looking for steady work in the quarries fled the hills and became town dwellers.

From the late eighteenth century, Snowdonia became the focus for the first truly structured approach to geological research. Early proponents of this new science pieced together the glacial evidence – scoured valley walls, scalloped mountainsides and hanging valleys – to come up with the first reliable proof of the last Ice Age and its retreat ten thousand years ago. These pioneers produced the rock-type classifications familiar to any students of the discipline: Cambrian rock takes its name from the Roman name for Wales, Ordovician and Silurian rocks from the Celtic tribes, the Ordovices and the Silures.

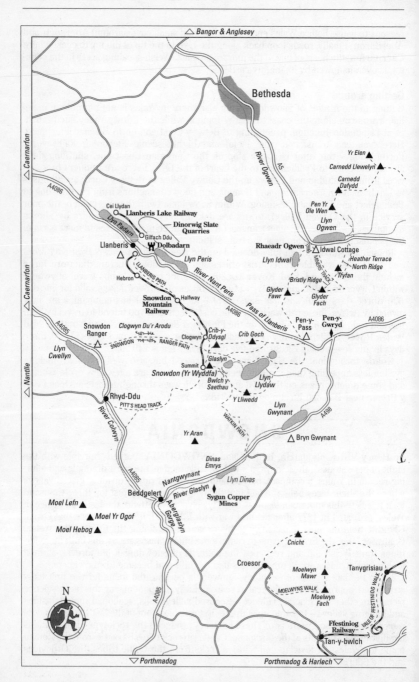

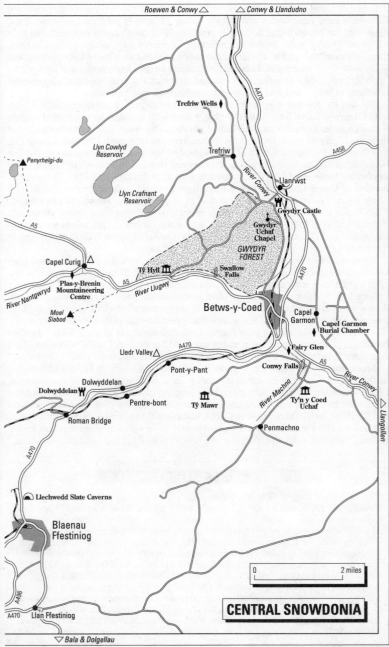

A470

Trefriw Wells ♦

Llyn Cowlyd
Reservoir

Trefriw

A458

River Conwy

Llanrwst

Llyn Crafnant
Reservoir

Penyrhelgi-du

♨ Gwydyr Castle

A5

Gwydyr
Uchaf
Chapel

*GWYDYR
FOREST*

Capel Curig △

Tŷ Hyll 🏛   Swallow
Falls

A470

Plas-y-Brenin
Mountaineering
Centre

A5

River Llugwy

Betws-y-Coed

River Nantgwryd

Capel
Garmon   Capel Garmon
Burial Chamber ♦

Moel
Siabod

Fairy Glen ♦

Lledr Valley △   A470

Conwy Falls   A5

River Conwy

Pont-y-Pant

River Machno

Llangollen ▷

Dolwyddelan

Tŷ Mawr 🏛   Ty'n y Coed
Uchaf 🏛

Dolwyddelan ♨

Pentre-bont

Roman Bridge

Penmachno

A470

▲ Llechwedd Slate Caverns

Blaenau
Ffestiniog

0   2 miles

A498

CENTRAL SNOWDONIA

A470   Llan Ffestiniog

▽ Bala & Dolgellau

© Crown copyright

Botanists found rare alpine flowers, writers produced libraries full of purple prose, and Richard Wilson, Paul Sandby and J.M.W. Turner all came to paint the landscape. Soon, those with the means began flocking here to marvel at the plunging waterfalls and walk the ever-widening paths to the mountaintops. Numbers have increased rapidly since then, and today, thousands of hikers arrive every weekend for some of the country's best walks over steep, exacting and constantly changing terrain. In recognition of the region's scientific importance, as well as its scenic and recreational appeal, Snowdonia became the heartland of Wales' first, and still largest, national park (see box below).

The last Ice Age left a legacy of peaks ringed by cwms – huge hemispherical bites out of the mountainsides – while the ranges were left separated by steep-sided valleys, a challenge for even the most fly-footed climber. The most striking monument, and understandably the clear focus, is **Snowdon**, reached by superb climbs and a cog railway from the former slate town of **Llanberis**. But the other mountains are as good or better, often far less busy and giving unsurpassed views of Snowdon. The **Glyders** and **Tryfan** are particular favourites and best tackled from the **Ogwen Valley**. The walkers' hamlets of **Capel Curig** and **Pen-y-Pass** have a suitably robust atmosphere, though many more prefer the comforts of the nearby Victorian resort, **Betws-y-Coed**. Elsewhere, settlements tend to coincide with some enormous mine or quarry. Foremost among these are **Beddgelert**, where the former copper mines are open to the public, and **Blaenau Ffestiniog**, the "Slate Capital of North Wales", where one of the mines has opened its caverns for underground tours.

If you're serious about doing some **walking** – and some of the walks described here are serious, especially in bad weather (Snowdon gets 200 inches of rain a year) – you need a good map, such as the 1:50,000 OS Landranger #115 or the 1:25,000 OS Outdoor Leisure #17. Walking conditions are often posted on the doors or notice boards of outdoor shops and tourist offices, but you should always consult the local mountain weather forecast before setting out. There are also premium-rate phone weather forecasts: Weathercall (☎0891/505315) providing an up-to-date summary of north Wales' weather conditions and a forecast for the next few days, and Mountaincall (☎0891/505330) which concentrates on hill-country conditions in the Snowdonia National Park.

Accommodation inside the Snowdonia National Park is strictly limited, and most is on the fringes. The main exception is Betws-y-Coed, a village packed with guesthouses, all of them filling up early during the busy summer season. Elsewhere in Snowdonia are B&Bs, hostels, bunkhouses and basic campsites, mostly geared towards walkers and climbers. In all, there are seven **YHA hostels** within ten miles of Snowdon's summit, and a further half-dozen other budget places. Even with a medium-sized backpack, walking from one to another makes a welcome change from the usual circular walks.

SNOWDONIA NATIONAL PARK

The oldest and largest of Wales' national parks, **Snowdonia National Park** (*Parc Cenedlaethol Eryri*) was set out in 1951 over 840 square miles of northwest Wales – all the way from Conwy to Aberdyfi – to encompass the Rhinogs, Cadair Idris and 23 miles of the Cambrian coast. Jagged mountains predominate, but the harsh lines come tempered by broadleaf lowland woods around calm glacial lakes, waterfalls tumbling from hanging valleys and complex coastal dune systems. However, you won't find total wilderness: 25,000 people, predominantly Welsh-speakers, live in the park, and another fourteen million people come here each year to tramp almost 2000 miles of designated paths. In apparent contradiction to its name, the national park is 75 percent privately owned by the Forestry Commission and National Trust. However, trespass isn't usually a problem as long as you keep to the ancient rights of way that conveniently cross private land where needed. Many of the most popular areas are National Trust land where access is unrestricted.

Betws-y-Coed and around

Sprawled out across a flat plain around the confluence of the Conwy, Llugwy and Lledr valleys, **BETWS-Y-COED** (pronounced Betoos-ah-Coyd) should be the perfect base for exploring Snowdonia. Its riverside setting, overlooked by the conifer-clad slopes of the **Gwydyr Forest**, is undeniably appealing, and the town boasts the best selection of hotels and guesthouses in the region, but after an hour mooching around the outdoor equipment shops and drinking tea you are left wondering what to do. None of the serious mountain walks start from here, and, while there are a couple of easy strolls (see box, p.322) up river gorges leading to the town's two main attractions, the **Conwy Falls** and **Swallow Falls**, these can get depressingly busy in the height of summer. That said, its much-touted role as "the gateway to Snowdonia" means it is hard to avoid. One particular peculiarity that you can hardly fail to miss, though, is that despite its genteel pretensions, Betws-y-Coed is something of a magnet for **bikers**, who can usually be seen roaring around the vicinity on souped-up machines and downing beer enthusiastically in the local pubs.

The quieter valleys in the vicinity can often be a lot more appealing than the town itself. The rail line from the coast comes up the **Conwy Valley** past **Llanrwst**, five miles north of Betws-y-Coed, a town graced by a fine bridge attributed to Inigo Jones and a couple of beautifully decorated chapels. The train continues south from Betws-y-Coed up the **Lledr Valley**, a wonderfully scenic journey passing the lonely **Dolwyddelan Castle**, on its way to the slate town of Blaenau Ffestiniog. Further to the southeast, a minor road leads to **Penmachno** and the house of William Morgan, who first translated the Bible into Welsh. Walkers bound for the high hills will be heading west beside the **Llugwy River** to the mountain centre of Capel Curig and beyond to Llanberis and the Ogwen Valley. Most of the land around Betws-y-Coed and along the Conwy Valley was part of the Gwydyr Estate owned by the Wynn family, descended from the kings of Gwynedd and the most powerful dynasty in the region until the male line died out in 1678; several place names are reminders of the family's might.

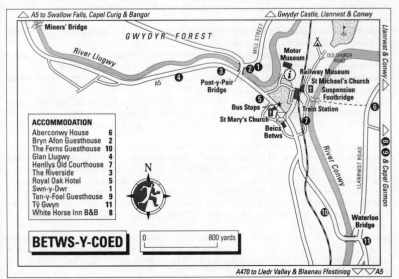

ACCOMMODATION

Aberconwy House	6
Bryn Afon Guesthouse	2
The Ferns Guesthouse	10
Glan Llugwy	4
Henllys Old Courthouse	7
The Riverside	3
Royal Oak Hotel	5
Swn-y-Dwr	1
Tan-y-Foel Guesthouse	9
Tŷ Gwyn	11
White Horse Inn B&B	8

BETWS-Y-COED

0   800 yards

© Crown copyright

Llanrwst is the largest town in the district and operates as a hub for the local **bus** system. Some services terminate here, requiring a change onto buses to Betws-y-Coed and Penmachno or Trefriw, Rowen, Conwy and Llandudno. If you are only planning to stop at Llanrwst and then the coastal resorts, **trains** from the station at the north end of town are faster and more comfortable.

Arrival and accommodation

Betws-y-Coed is arranged in a flat triangle bounded by the Conwy and Llugwy rivers and the A5, which forms the town's High Street, running west from the Waterloo Bridge to the Pont-y-Pair bridge. Access is easy, either by train or bus from the north coast, or by car along the A5 from Llangollen, and frequent buses continue towards the peaks around Snowdon. The **train station** is just a few paces across the grass from the **tourist office** in Royal Oak Stables (daily: Easter–Oct 10am–6pm; Nov–Easter 9am–1pm & 2–4pm; ☎01690/710426), where displays give a quick overview of conservation work in Snowdonia. You can also get lots of local information by visiting the Betws-y-Coed Web site (*www.betws-y-coed.co.uk*). **Buses**, which fan out to Penmachno, the Ogwen Valley, Llanberis, Conwy and Llandudno, stop outside St Mary's Church on the main street.

Accommodation

Betws-y-Coed has plenty of **accommodation**, but has to cope with an even larger numbers of visitors pushing prices up in the summer. Expect to pay a pound or two more than in other towns in Snowdonia, and don't be surprised to find the places listed below full if you arrive late in the day. There are two nearby **youth hostels**, at Capel Curig and in the Lledr Valley. The closest **campsite** is *Riverside Caravan & Camping Park* (Easter–Oct; ☎01690/710310), right behind the station. Walkers and climbers who want direct access to the mountains need to make for Capel Curig (see p.327) or Llanberis (see p.332).

Aberconwy House, Llanrwst Rd (☎01690/710202). Friendly Victorian guesthouse overlooking the Llugwy Valley. To get there on foot, cross the suspension bridge behind the train station; by car, take the A470 towards Llanrwst. ②.

Bryn Afon Guesthouse, Mill St (☎01690/710403). Popular if fairly standard guesthouse just over the Pont-y-Pair bridge from the main road. ②.

The Ferns Guesthouse, Holyhead Rd (☎01690/710587). Licensed non-smoking guesthouse reachable via an easy walk across the footbridge into town. All rooms are en suite. ②.

Glan Llugwy, on the A5 towards Capel Curig, 300 yards beyond Pont-y-Pair (☎01690/710592). One of the cheapest B&Bs around, with TVs in rooms. ①.

Henllys Old Courthouse, Old Church Rd (☎ & fax 01690/710534). Non-smoking guesthouse in a former Victorian magistrates courthouse, with comfortable single rooms in the old holding cells and views over the River Conwy. Healthy breakfasts and very good dinners served. March–Oct. ④.

Penmachno Hall, Penmachno (☎01690/760207). Superior country guesthouse with stylish, comfortable rooms, on the edge of Penmachno and right by the entrance to Tŷ Mawr Wybrnant. The hospitable hosts offer good meals made with garden vegetables, and often join you for dinner. ④.

The Riverside, Holyhead Rd (☎ & fax 01690/710650). The cheapest place for bed and continental breakfast, above the restaurant of the same name a few yards towards Capel Curig from the Pont-y-Pair bridge. Pleasant non-smoking rooms, some with baths, and restaurant discounts for guests. ①.

Swn-y-Dwr, Mill St, just past *Bryn Afon* (☎01690/710648). Popular, non-smoking guesthouse, over the Pont-y-Pair bridge. ②.

Tan-y-Foel, Capel Garmon (☎01690/710507, fax 710681). With eight acres of grounds, extensive views, a heated indoor pool and superb dinners for around £25, this sixteenth-century farmhouse ranks as the best small country hotel in the district. Take the A470 towards Llanrwst then turn right after two miles. Non-smoking. ⑥.

Tŷ Gwyn, on the A5, half a mile east of the town centre and just over Waterloo Bridge (☎01690/710383). Cosy old coaching inn with wood-beamed rooms, a bar that is hard to leave and some top-notch food. There are a couple of cheaper rooms, but you'll need to book well ahead. ②.

White Horse Inn, Capel Garmon (☎ & fax 01690/710271). Pleasant rooms just over a mile east of Betws-y-Coed, above a 400-year-old village inn with a popular bar and restaurant (see p.323). ③.

The Town

The settlement of Betws-y-Coed is first recorded during the fifth or sixth century, when a monastic cell was founded, earning the town its name of the "oratory in the forest". Apart from some lead mining, it remained a backwater until 1808, when road improvements brought the Irish Mail this way. As part of the A5 construction, Telford completed the graceful cast-iron **Waterloo Bridge** (Y Bont Haearn) in 1815, complete with spandrels that utilize the emblems of the four countries of the then newly-formed United Kingdom (English rose, Scottish thistle, Irish shamrock and Welsh leek). The bridge and new road gave far quicker access to the district, luring landscape painters David Cox and J.M.W. Turner, who in turn alerted the leisured classes to the town's beauty. Anglers keen to exploit the richly stocked pools came too, but it was the arrival of the train line in 1868 that really lifted Betws-y-Coed's status from coaching station to genteel resort, an air the town vainly tries to maintain. It's mainly a centre for walkers today, although there are a few sights worth seeking out. At some point, all camera-wielding visitors end up at the **Pont-y-Pair Falls**, a low cataract where the waters of the River Llugwy thunder over assorted boulders and funnel under the adjacent Pont-y-Pair ("Bridge of the Cauldron"). Relaxing on the stone slabs which surround the falls, it's hard to generate much enthusiasm for the fourteenth-century **St Michael's church** (key from the Railway Museum, or the tourist office in winter), most interesting for the twelfth-century font and a carved effigy of an armoured knight, whose inscription identifies him as Gruffydd ap Dafydd Goch, the grandson of Llywelyn ap Gruffydd's brother, Prince Dafydd. St Michael's obscure isolation, tucked away down the lane behind the train station, was one of the reasons why the rather plain **St Mary's** parish church was newly constructed on the main road in 1873.

Adjoining the train station, the **Conwy Valley Railway Museum** (Easter–Oct daily 10.15am–5.30pm, Nov–Easter Sat & Sun 10.30am–4.30pm; £1) is a fairly dull collection of memorabilia and shiny engines, slightly enlivened by a model of a Welsh slate quarry and the opportunity for kids to take a short ride on a miniature train or tram. If internal combustion interests you more than steam, the **Motor Museum** (Easter–Oct daily 10am–6pm; £1.50), a couple of hundred yards away behind the tourist office, is a marginally better bet. The half-dozen classic bikes and fifteen cars on display change frequently, but expect the likes of a 1934 Bugatti Straight 8 and a Model T Ford.

Activities

The most leisurely thing to do in Betws-y-Coed is to join a **guided walk** from outside the tourist office (5–6hr; May–Sept Thurs–Sun 10am; £3.50). For the more ambitious, Snowdonia Mountain Guides (☎01690/710720), contactable through the Climber and Rambler shop opposite Pont-y-Pair bridge, run day-courses in **guided mountain walking** (£32), **scrambling** (£37–42), **rock climbing** (£32–45), **abseiling** (£32–35) and **gorge walking** (£32), and longer excursions at all levels; prices include use of all specialized equipment.

Mountain bikes can be rented from Beics Betws (☎01690/710766) on Church Hill at the top of the road beside the post office, with information on routes through the Gwydyr Forest obtainable from the tourist office (£2). The nearest **horse riding** is at Ty Coch Farm (2hr £15; ☎01690/760248), seven miles south of Betws-y-Coed in

Penmachno. **Anglers** with a rod licence and their own tackle can try hooking salmon and sea trout on stretches of the Conwy right in town (£18–24 for 24hr; mid-March to mid-Oct Mon–Fri) and brown and American brook trout on Llyn Elsie in the hills just south (£13 a day). For details and permits contact Mr Parry (☎01690/710232) at the Tan Lan bread shop next to the post office. A decent walk, combined with a swim on a warm day, can be had by trekking west along the Llugwy for the best part of a mile to the **Miners' Bridge**, a vertiginous sloping footbridge across a series of low falls and plunge pools. It's a wonderfully refreshing place to take a dip, with the rocks providing great diving boards.

Eating and drinking

For a town so geared to tourism that it's hard to turn around without knocking some-one's cream tea onto the floor, there are surprisingly few places to **eat**. Guesthouses offering meals will often be your best bet, although most of the **pubs** serve snacks and basic meals as well as beer.

The Buffet Coach Café, The Old Goods Yard. Basic café serving home-made snacks inside (or outside) a converted 1940s railway carriage at the station.

Dil's Diner, Station Approach (☎01690/710346). Greasy spoon café beside the train station, a great place for breakfast or to fill up after a day in the hills. It often closes at around 5pm in winter, but stays open till around 9pm or 10pm in summer.

The Riverside, Holyhead Rd (☎ & fax 01690/710650). One of the town's best restaurants, small and convivial with an imaginative menu of well-prepared food and a good wine list. Not too expensive, either.

WALKS FROM BETWS-Y-COED

The best two walks from Betws-y-Coed follow narrow river gorges. Neither is circular, so unless you plan to hitch back to your base, consult bus timetables first to avoid a long wait for the infrequent services.

The **Conwy Gorge walk** (3 miles; 1hr 15min; descent only) links two of the district's best-known natural attractions, **Fairy Glen** and the **Conwy Falls** (see opposite), by way of a cool green lane giving glimpses of the river through the woods. The best approach is to forgo the forty-minute walk from Betws-y-Coed along the A5 towards Llangollen, and instead take the #49 bus (five times daily) to the *Conwy Falls Café*. After viewing the falls, walk a hundred yards back along the road towards Betws-y-Coed, then follow a path parallel to the river through the trees. After about half an hour, you'll see the gate to Fairy Glen on your left. Returning to the main path, continue to the *Fairy Glen Hotel*, where you can cross the river by Beaver Bridge, turn right and follow a minor road a mile back to town.

The car park on the north side of the Pont-y-Pair bridge marks the beginning of the **Llugwy Valley walk** (6 miles; 2hr 30min; 600ft ascent), a forested path following the twist-ing and plunging river upstream to Capel Curig. With the A5 running parallel to the river all the way, there are several opportunities to cut short the walk and hitch or wait for the bus back to Betws-y-Coed. Less than a mile from Pont-y-Pair, you first reach a ford where the Roman road Sarn Helen crossed the river, then pass the steeply sloping **Miners' Bridge**, which linked miners' homes at Pentre Du on the south side of the river to the lead mines in the Gwydyr Forest. The path follows the river on your left for another mile – though path maintenance sometimes means you have to cut up into the pines – to a slight-ly obscured view of **Swallow Falls**. Detailed maps available from the tourist office in Betws-y-Coed show numerous routes back through the Gwydyr Forest, or you can con-tinue half a mile to the road bridge by Tŷ Hyll and follow the right bank to Capel Curig, passing the scant remains of the Caer Llugwy, a Roman fort, and a couple more treacher-ous rapids: The Mincer and Cobden's Falls.

The Stables, *Royal Oak Hotel*, High St (☎01690/710219). The town's hottest bar, with good beer and bar food, and jazz on summer Thurs.

Tŷ Gwyn, on the A5 (see p.321). The best place to eat in town, whether you want a pub meal or table d'hôte. Menus usually include game and local fish, as well as good vegetarian dishes and delectable desserts. Prices are inexpensive to moderate.

White Horse Inn, Capel Garmon (see p.321). An excellent evening retreat, with cosy bars, good beer, home-cooked bar meals and a restaurant serving fine, moderate to expensive country cooking from Wed to Sun.

Conwy Falls, Fairy Glen and Penmachno

None of the attractions of Betws-y-Coed can compete with getting out to the gorges and waterfalls in the vicinity, and walking is the ideal way to see them (see box opposite). The final gorge section of the River Conwy, a couple of miles above Betws-y-Coed, is one of the most spectacular things to see, the river plunging fifty feet over the **Conwy Falls** into a deep pool. After slotting £1 in the turnstile beside the *Conwy Falls Café* (reached by the #49 bus five times daily), you can view the falls on the right and a series of rock steps to the left, originally cut as a kind of primitive fish ladder which is now superseded by a tunnel through the rock on the far side.

After carving out a mile or so of what kayakers regard as some of north Wales' toughest whitewater, the Conwy negotiates a staircase of drops and enters the **Fairy Glen**, a cleft in a small wood which takes its name from the Welsh fairies, the Tylwyth Teg, who are said to be seen hereabouts. A short lane from the Beaver Bridge beside the *Fairy Glen Hotel* leads to a car park, from where a short path (20min each way; 50p) leads to the glen, on the A470 to Blaenau Ffestiniog.

Penmachno

The River Machno merges with the Conwy just above the Conwy Falls at the end of its short run down through the small village of **PENMACHNO** from the surrounding hills. Just above the confluence, the waters once provided the motive power for the **Penmachno Woollen Mill** (daily 10am–5pm; free), where panels on the weaving process and half a dozen ageing looms producing uninspired patterned cloth feebly attempt to lure you into the shop.

The mill shares its car park with **Tŷ'n y Coed Uchaf** (April–Sept Thurs, Fri & Sun noon–5pm; Oct Thurs, Fri & Sun noon–4pm; £2; NT), a 35-acre smallholding reached along a twenty-minute path. Along with Tŷ Mawr Wybrnant (see below) and vast tracts to the east, the property was part of the fabulously rich Penrhyn Estate until 1951, when the land was gifted to the government in lieu of capital taxes. Twenty thousand acres of agricultural land now make up the Ysbyty Estate, where the National Trust is endeavouring to maintain the rural community partly by funding projects to replace dry-stone walls and re-lay hedges in the traditional manner. Pick up the free leaflet available in the car park to find some fine examples of both walls and hedges, which protect ancient fields rich in wild flowers and insect life that are threatened on agricultural land elsewhere.

The estate's centrepiece is its nineteenth-century Welsh **farmhouse** and outbuildings. Although inhabited until 1990, the house had not been structurally altered since 1916; electricity and gas were never connected and there was no piped water, nor even an indoor toilet. Careful restoration has been undertaken in the three small rooms, only slightly erasing the ghosts of generations of past tenants whose fine rustic furniture still fills every corner. A coal range shoehorned into an inglenook, a Welsh dresser arrayed with patterned plates and prim ornamentation lend a slightly formal air partly displaced by the short, personal guided tour.

Five miles on, and two and a half miles beyond Penmachno village at the end of a long drive, stands the isolated little cottage of **Tŷ Mawr Wybrnant** (times and prices as for Ty'n y Coed Uchaf). Here, Bishop William Morgan, the man who first translated the Bible into Welsh (see p.391), was born in 1545 and lived until his teenage years when he decamped to Gwydyr Castle to pursue his education. The original cottage was altered markedly over the years but has now been restored to something like its six-teenth-century appearance: all bare stone and beams, with a gaping fireplace support-ing a huge, sagging beam dating back to the thirteenth century. Star attraction is the collection of Bibles and prayer books, including a Morgan original. Despite this, virtu-ally the only people who come here are those wanting to pay homage to the man who not only furthered Protestantism in Wales but probably saved the language.

The Llugwy Valley: Swallow Falls and the Gwydyr Forest

The **Swallow Falls** (a mistranslation of *Rhaeadr Ewynnol* or "foaming cataract") lie two miles west of Betws-y-Coed along the A5 towards Capel Curig. Close proximity to the road and obvious photogenic qualities make it one of the region's most-visited sights, but it is no more than a straightforward, pretty waterfall with the occasional mad kayaker scraping down the precipitous rock. Pay your 50p and you can walk down to a series of viewing platforms.

Less than a mile beyond, the road crosses the river passing **Tŷ Hyll** (Easter–Oct daily 9.30am–5pm; Nov–Easter Mon–Fri variable hours; 75p), known as the "Ugly House" for its chunky appearance. Decked out with period furniture and surrounded by a forest full of easy paths, it is also the headquarters of the Snowdonia National Park Society, an environmental campaigning group which lobbies to preserve the region's ecological and social integrity.

From here, a small side road climbs north into the evergreens of the **Gwydyr Forest**, an area best explored by mountain bike but pleasant enough on foot. Starting from a lakeside parking area a mile or so northeast of Tŷ Hyll, the **Miners' Trail** (3 miles; 2hr; minimal ascent) gives a focus to a forest walk, though you would have to be pretty keen on defunct lead workings to get much out of it. From Tŷ Hyll, the A5 fol-lows the River Llugwy upstream past a number of roadside cataracts – most notably opposite *Cobden's Hotel* – and on to Capel Curig.

The Lledr Valley

The train line up the Conwy Valley from Betws-y-Coed follows the twists of the beauti-ful **Lledr Valley** to Blaenau Ffestiniog, the river flowing through deciduous and pine forests that give way to the smooth, grassy slopes of the Moel Siabod before the route bores through over two miles of slate – the longest rail tunnel in Wales. Take this trip while you can: the line is endangered by privatization and the recent closure of its prin-cipal funder, the Trawsfynned nuclear power station.

The A470 runs parallel to the river from Betws-y-Coed to Blaenau Ffestiniog. Four miles south of Betws-y-Coed, you come to Pont-y-Pant station, where the Roman road Sarn Helen crosses the river on a clapper bridge and follows its banks to Dolwyddelan. The Lledr Valley **YHA hostel** (March–Oct; ☎01690/750202, fax 750410), across the river from the station, is an ideal starting point for a walk up Moel Siabod (see box, p.328) and also accommodates **campers** for half the adult rate.

A mile further on is **DOLWYDDELAN**, a village well placed for the southern approach to Moel Siabod and only a mile east of lonely **Dolwyddelan Castle** (daily: April–Oct 9.30am–6pm; Nov–March 9.30am–4pm; £2; CADW), commanding the head of the valley. Llywelyn ap Iorwerth ("the Great"; see p.444) may well have been born here, since his father was reputedly responsible for its construction at the end of the twelfth century. The strategic site, on the important route from Aberconwy to the north and Ardudwy to the south, was soon turned against him when Edward I took the castle, refortified it and used it to further subdue the Welsh. By the end of the fifteenth century, it had become redundant and lay abandoned until the Wynns of Gwydyr treated it to a suitably Victorian reconstruction, complete with fanciful battlements and a new roof. Today, it shelters only a small exhibition on native Welsh castles, but affords a panoramic view of Snowdonia from between its castellations.

If you want to stay around here, the castle custodian runs the neighbouring *Bryn Tirion Farm* B&B (☎01690/750366; ①), a **campsite** and, from October to March, a **bunkhouse**, for which you need your own sleeping bag. Back in the centre of Dolwyddelan, *Elen's Castle Hotel* (☎01690/750207; ①) has both rooms and bunkhouse accommodation, and serves good, inexpensive bar food and pricier meals. The best **pub** is the cosy, welcoming *Y Gwydyr*, on the main road in Dolwyddelan, where Sunday lunch is served during the summer.

The Conwy Valley: Capel Garmon, Llanrwst and Trefriw

Fed by the water of the Machno, Lledr and Llugwy rivers, the Conwy River leaves Betws-y-Coed along its broad pastoral corridor to the sea at Conwy (see p.405) flanked on the left by the bald tops of Snowdonia's northern and eastern bulwark, the mighty Carneddau range. More manageable hills lie to the east, where Neolithic dwellers left their mark at the **Capel Garmon Burial Chamber** (unrestricted access; CADW), a heavily reconstructed, but hugely atmospheric, multichambered communal burial site built between 2500 and 1900 BC. The site – actually only some rough stones lining a series of linked pits, with a central chamber covered by an enormous capstone – is a five-minute signposted walk across farmland two miles southeast of Betws-y-Coed, half a mile south of the tiny hilltop village of **CAPEL GARMON**. Views of Snowdonia from the burial chamber – or, indeed, the village cemetery just up the road – are magnificent. There's top-notch refreshment in the village at the excellent *White Horse Inn* (see p.321 & 323).

Llanrwst and around

Five miles north of Betws-y-Coed, **LLANRWST** is the largest and most economically important town in the valley. Not particularly striking, nor especially large, it does have a working-town feel – it was once the largest wool market in north Wales, and had a spell as a centre for harp manufacture in the eighteenth century. Llanrwst still retains its Wednesday and Friday livestock markets, and a general one each Tuesday. All roads – and many of the area's prodigious numbers of biker visitors – converge on the central **Ancaster Square**, lined with some cheerfully unpretentious pubs and the odd eaterie.

Inigo Jones is said to have spent his early years here, so it isn't entirely unlikely that the great seventeenth-century architect was at least partially responsible for the town's most noted sight, the slender humpback **Pont Fawr** (Big Bridge), which is popularly attributed to him. It undoubtedly bears Jones' mark: three graceful arches and beautifully proportioned symmetry, combined with engineering techniques that were extremely advanced for their time. The bridge carried all the cross-river traffic in the area before the building of Telford's bridges at the estuary of the Conwy and upstream at Betws-y-Coed, and its single lane still struggles in summer. On the other side of Pont Fawr is the **Tu Hwnt i'r Bont**, a photogenic ivy-clad former courthouse that dates from the fifteenth century – it's now owned by the National Trust and open as a tearoom.

Claims that Jones also had a hand in the design for **Gwydyr Chapel** (open daily), accessed down a little lane round the corner from Ancaster Square, are harder to verify. He was certainly known to landowner Richard Wynn – Jones' father and grandfather were tenants on the Wynn estate – who in 1633 commissioned the elaborate chapel to be attached to the Church of St Grwst. A riot of alabaster, carved memorials and seventeenth-century brasses set off a huge stone coffin, said to be that of Llywelyn ap Iorwerth ("the Great"). The beautiful rood screen in the main body of the church was salvaged when the former Maenan Abbey, Wales' largest Cistercian house, was dissolved by Henry VIII. Its paltry remains can be seen in the grounds of the expensive *Maenan Abbey Hotel*, two miles to the north of Llanrwst.

Half a mile away across the river from the chapel is Richard Wynn's ancestral home, **Gwydir Castle** (March–Oct daily 10am–5pm; £3), actually a low-slung manor house begun in 1492 on the site of a fortified house a century older. Despite substantial additions in the sixteenth and nineteenth centuries, with parts plundered from the post-dissolution Maenan Abbey, the ivy- and wisteria-covered building is a fabulous model of early Tudor architecture. Its core is a three-storey solar tower, whose windows relieve the gloom of the great halls, each with enormous fireplaces and stone-flagged or heavy timber floors. Most of the original fittings and superb Tudor furniture were sold off in 1921 by the then owner, the Earl of Carrington, and much of the rest of the house was ruined in a fire a few months later. A major restoration of the house is well underway, and, in line with its baronial nature, the furnishing is kept simple – tapestries cover the solid stone walls, a few tables and chairs are scattered about and there's some fine painted glass. The effect is of effortless domestic simplicity, a welcome change from the overblown nature of many comparable dwellings. Fortunately, some of the original furnishings have been tracked down, including the heavily carved oak panels, Baroque doorcase and fireplace, and abundant gilded Spanish leather of the magnificent Dining Room. This was initially installed by Richard Wynn around 1642 and again attributed to Inigo Jones. The complete set was bought during the 1921 sell-off by American newspaper magnate William Randolph Hearst and shipped across the Atlantic. New York's Metropolitan Museum acquired it in 1956 and kept it boxed up for forty years until it was sold back to the castle in 1996. While you're here, don't miss the treats outdoors, where the **Dutch Garden**, with its fountain, peacocks and Cedars of Lebanon dating back to 1625, is the main attraction – on fine days at least. Since its owners have made two splendid bedrooms available to bed and breakfast guests (☎ & fax 01492/641687; ④), Gwydir represents one of the best opportunities in Wales to stay in an authentic castle which still maintains the air of a family home.

A few hundred yards from his home, Richard Wynn built his own private **Gwydir Uchaf Chapel** (key from the adjacent Forestry Commission office, Mon–Fri 8.30am–5pm; free; CADW) in 1673. The plain exterior is in striking contrast to the unashamedly Baroque interior, with its roof beams cut into angelic figures. The inward-facing pews are unusual, but it is the painted ceiling which is really outstanding, depicting the Creation, the Trinity and the Day of Judgement.

Ancaster Square is linked by Denbigh Street to the main **train station. Buses** stop on Watling Street, which branches off midway along Denbigh Street. Since it's so close to Betws-y-Coed, few people choose to stay in Llanrwst, but if you're looking for something a little less twee, it's a good bet for a night. There is decent **accommodation** at Gwydir Castle (see above) and, in town, along Main Street, where comfortable rooms and a friendly welcome are on offer at *Pickwick's* (☎01492/640275; ②), above the tearooms of the same name. Opposite here, the *Eagles Hotel* (☎01492/640454; ③) offers almost 200 gourmet sandwiches and moderately priced **meals** in addition to the affable rooms. Alternatively, there are a couple of decent places to eat in Ancaster Square: try the non-smoking *La Barrica* bistro, especially good for daytime snacks and evening speciality menus. For light meals, cross Pont Fawr to the *Tu Hwnt i'r Bont Tearooms* (see overleaf; Easter–Oct), or pick up picnic requisites from the well-stocked Blas ar Fwyd delicatessen, 25 Station St, at the north end of town. For no-nonsense **drinking**, try the lively *Pen-y-Bryn Hotel* on Ancaster Square, complete with a beer garden, or the *Tafarn Newydd* on Denbigh Street.

Trefriw and Llyn Crafnant

Judging by the brochures scattered all over north Wales, you would think that the only thing in the small village of **TREFRIW**, two miles north of Llanrwst, is the **Woollen Mills** (Easter–Oct Mon–Fri 9.30am–5.30pm; free). It isn't, but its demonstrations of late-nineteenth-century weaving methods, using power from the stream outside, certainly make for a more compelling visit than other mills around north Wales.

In the second century, Romans garrisoned in the now barely discernible camp of Canovium on the banks of the Conwy were the first to make a fuss over the restorative properties of the iron-rich waters of **Trefriw Wells** (Easter–Oct daily 10am–5.30pm; Nov–Easter Mon–Sat 10am–5pm, Sun noon–5pm; £2.65), a mile and a half north of the village. A robust pair of gentlemen's and ladies' bathhouses, complete with slate tubs, were built around 1700, but the spa vogue didn't get into full swing until the Victorian era when health-seekers flocked upriver from Conwy. The wells waned along with the fashion, but are open again for interesting, if laboured, twenty-minute self-guided tours during which you can sample the waters – they taste a little like sucking a rusty nail, but their invigorating, curative powers are extolled by the numerous testimonials kept in the cafe. A signposted road back in the village close to the woollen mills leads three miles southwest to **Llyn Crafnant**, a calm reservoir hemmed in by mountains, and one of the more popular local beauty spots. Alternatively, take the steep lane south of the village towards the neighbouring lakes of **Llanrhychwyn** and **Llyn Geirionydd**. There are numerous other small pools in the vicinity, many bordered by forest, and it's a lovely area for a picnic, a gentle walk or a swim. If you want to **stay** hereabouts, there are a couple of pleasant B&Bs in Trefriw village, including *Crafnant Guest House* (☎01492/640809; ①) and the lovely *Hafod Country Hotel* (☎01492/640029, fax 641351; ②).

Capel Curig and the Ogwen Valley

Tantalizing glimpses of Wales' highest mountains flash through the forested banks of the Llugwy as you climb west from Betws-y-Coed on the A5. But Snowdon, the mountain which more than any other has become a symbol of north Wales for walkers, mountaineers, botanists and painters alike, eludes you until the final bend before **Capel Curig**. This tiny walkers' village makes a perfect base for the two valleys which plunge westwards deep into the mountains. The A4086 follows Nant Gwryd southwest to the Snowdon massif (see p.336) while the A5 prises apart the Carneddau and Glyder ranges to the northwest, forging through the **Ogwen Valley** to tatty **Bethesda**, home to one of Wales' last surviving slate quarries.

As you cross the watershed between the Llugwy and Ogwen rivers, the frequently mist-shrouded Carneddau range to the north glowers across at the Glyder range and its triple-peaked **Tryfan**, arguably Snowdonia's most demanding mountain. This forms a fractured spur out from the main range and blocks your view down the valley, the twin monoliths of Adam and Eve that crown Tryfan's summit picked out on the skyline. The courageous or foolhardy make the jump between them as a point of honour at the end of every ascent. West of Tryfan, the road follows a perfect example of a U-shaped valley, carved and smoothed by rocks frozen into the undersides of the glaciers that creaked down **Nant Ffrancon** ten thousand years ago.

Capel Curig

The tiny, scattered village of **CAPEL CURIG**, six miles west of Betws-y-Coed, competes with Llanberis (see p.332) to be Wales' major centre for outdoor enthusiasts. There is scarcely a building here which isn't of some use either as inexpensive

A WALK FROM CAPEL CURIG

Note: the 1:50,000 OS Landranger #115 or the 1:25,000 OS Outdoor Leisure #17 are recommended for this walk.

If you approached Capel Curig from the west, you won't have looked twice at the rounded grassy back of **Moel Siabod** (2862ft), but its eastern aspect is another matter – a challenging ridge rising up to afford a magnificent summit view of the Snowdon Horseshoe.

The mountainous section of the **east ridge walk** (5 miles; 4hr; 2200ft) is circular and brings you back into the Llugwy Valley. The route starts from opposite the YHA hostel in Capel Curig, crossing the concrete bridge and following the right bank downstream past the falls by *Cobden's Hotel* to the Pont Cyfyng road bridge (30min), an alternative starting point for the walk. Taking the road south, turn right on the second path signposted to Moel Siabod. The path quickly rises out of the valley and keeps to the left of the mountain, past a disused slate quarry and across some boggy land, before the long scramble up the east ridge. Once found, the path is fairly clear, but it weaves around outcrops where a moment's inattention could be perilous. The summit is flat and uninteresting, so once you've admired Snowdon, turn northeast and follow the craggy summit ridge which eventually starts to drop across grass to the moors below, soon rejoining your ascent route for the hike back to Pont Cyfyng.

An alternative, if you are prepared to carry all your gear or chance the public transport system to get back to Capel Curig, is to approach the summit by the route described, then retrace your steps down the ridge, and descend through the pine forest above Dolwyddelan into the Lledr Valley (see p.324).

accommodation, a mountain-gear shop or just a place to replenish the body. Foremost among them is **Plas-y-Brenin: The National Mountaineering Centre** (☎01690/720214, *www.pyb.co.uk*), a quarter of a mile along the A4086 to Llanberis from the town's main road junction. Built around a former coaching inn and hotel, the centre now runs nationally renowned residential courses in orienteering, canoeing, skiing and climbing. Daily mountain weather forecasts are available from reception. If you're just passing through and don't have your own equipment, the two-hour abseiling, canoeing and dry-slope skiing sessions held during July and August (£8) may be of interest. Kids who want a full-day taster of canoeing, skiing and abseiling can be left on the "All Day Adventure" (£18), though adults are welcome too. There is also a state-of-the-art climbing wall (daily 10am–11pm; £2), a dry ski slope (daily 10am–9pm; prices vary) and the opportunity to hear talks or watch slide shows of recent expeditions (usually Mon–Thurs & Sat 8pm; free). Plas-y-Brenin doesn't rent out **mountain bikes**; for those you'll need to visit Clogwyn Mountain Bikes (☎01690/720210; £14 a day) at A5 Services petrol station half a mile along the A5 from the junction.

Despite Capel Curig's popularity, the only major walk from here is up Moel Siabod (see box above), but the village acts as a base for the Ogwen Valley and Snowdon. The road to the valley runs four miles southwest past **Dyffryn**, the farm written about by Thomas Firbank (see Books, p.483), to the *Pen-y-Gwryd Hotel* (see p.340). The A498 continues south to Beddgelert, past the best view of Snowdon's east face, while the A4086 branches west to Llanberis, passing Pen-y-Pass, the start for the best-known Snowdon walks.

Practicalities

The only **buses** servicing Capel Curig are the #19b and #96, which run between Llandudno, Llanrwst and Llanberis, the #97A from Betws-y-Coed to Porthmadog and the #65, which links Bangor, Bethesda and Llanrwst. If none suit, you can always walk the six miles along the Llugwy River from Betws-y-Coed (see box, p.322).

Once here, there are plenty of **places to stay**, though none is especially luxurious. Best are *Bron Eryri* (☎01690/720240; ②) is a comfortable and welcoming B&B half a mile outside the village towards Betws-y-Coed, while the wonderful *Bryn Tyrch Hotel* (☎01690/720223; ②) is also on the A5 but closer to the main road junction. There's also limited accommodation, mostly dorms, at the Plas-y-Brenin mountaineering centre (see opposite), while cheaper options include *Llugwy Guesthouse* on the A4086 (☎01690/720218; ③) and the simple yet comfortable *Bryn Glo* (☎01690/720215; ③), a mile towards Betws-y-Coed. The cheapest option in the village is the **YHA hostel** (mid-Feb to mid-Dec; ☎01690/720225, fax 720270), 500 yards along the A5 towards Betws-y-Coed.

During the day, walkers tend to patronize either the *Pinnacle Café*, grafted onto the post office and general store at the main road junction, or the *Snowdonia Café*, next to the YHA: both serve substantial portions at low prices. In the evenings, most retire to the warm and lively bar at the *Bryn Tyrch Hotel* (see above). The inexpensive **meals** here are huge, and predominantly vegetarian – indeed, this is one of the very few establishments in the whole of Snowdonia to make any real attempt to please vegans. Everyone who isn't at the *Bryn Tyrch* heads for the bar at Plas-y-Brenin.

The Ogwen Valley

Five miles west of Capel Curig the gentle **Ogwen Valley** fills with the waters of Llyn Ogwen, a post-glacial lake formed behind time-compacted moraine left by the retreating ice. At its western end stands **IDWAL COTTAGE**, the only settlement in the valley and so small it isn't named on most maps. Comprising just a mountain rescue centre, a snack bar and a YHA hostel clustered around a car park, the main reason to come here is to make some of Wales' most demanding and rewarding hikes (see box overleaf), or start the easier twenty-minute walk to the magnificent, classically formed cirque, **Cwm Idwal**.

The evidence of glacial scouring is so clear here that you wonder why it took geologists so long to work out the process that created these hollowed faces and scored rocks. In 1842, Darwin wrote of his visit with the geologist Alan Sedgewick eleven years earlier, recalling that "neither of us saw a trace of the wonderful glacial phenomena all around us". The cwm's scalloped floor traps the beautifully still **Llyn Idwal**, which reflects the precipitous grey cliffs behind, split by the jointed cleft of Twll Du, the **Devil's Kitchen**. Down this channel, a fine watery haze runs off the flanks of **Glyder Fawr**, soaking the crevices where early botanists found the rare arctic-alpine plants (see Contexts, p.465) that were the main motivation for designating Cwm Idwal as Wales' first **nature reserve** (NT) in 1954. More common species carpet the reserve in early summer but have to compete with grazing sheep who destroy all but the comparatively luxuriant fenced-off control areas. Geomorphologists pay more attention to the twisted rocks beside the Devil's Kitchen, one of the few places where you can see the downfolded strata of what is known as the Snowdon syncline, evidence that the existing mountains sat between two much larger ranges some 300 million years ago. To their left, the smooth inclines of the Idwal Slabs act as nursery slopes for budding rock climbers: they're also good for some half-hearted "bouldering" for the ill-equipped.

An easy, well-groomed path leads up to the reserve from the car park, where the *Idwal Cottage* café (daily 8.30am–5pm; later on summer weekends) will sell you a nature trail booklet for 75p. A five-minute walk down the valley from the car park, the road crosses a bridge over the top of **Rhaeadr Ogwen** (Ogwen Falls), which cascades down this step in the valley floor. Before you put your camera away, look under the road bridge, where you'll see the simple mortarless arch of a bridge, part of the original packhorse route that followed the valley before Telford pushed the Holyhead road through.

Practicalities

Depending on the season and school holidays, two or three daily **buses** run along the valley between Betws-y-Coed and Bangor; three or four more run east from Idwal Cottage in summer, but they are usually inconveniently timed. A footpath parallel to the fast and busy road follows a five-mile-long packhorse route that runs the length of the valley from Capel Curig to Idwal Cottage. **Accommodation** in the valley is lim-

---

WALKS FROM OGWEN: THE GLYDERAU AND THE CARNEDDAU

Note: The OS Outdoor Leisure 1:25,000 map #17 ("Snowdon & Conwy Valley") is highly recommended for all these walks. The 1:50,000 Landranger #115 also covers the whole area.

THE GLYDERAU

"Tourists" climb Snowdon, but mountain connoisseurs almost invariably prefer the sharply angled peaks of the **Glyderau**, with their challenging terrain, an entertaining high-level jump, cantilevered rocks and views back to Snowdon. The sheer number of good walking paths make it almost impossible to choose one definitive circular route. The individual sections have therefore been defined separately giving the greatest flexibility. **All times given are for the ascents**: expect to take approximately half the time to get back down.

Tryfan

If you've got the head for it, the **North Ridge of Tryfan** (3002ft) (1 mile; 1hr–1hr 30min; 2000ft ascent) is one of the most rewarding scrambles in the country. It's not as precarious as Snowdon's Crib Goch, but you get a genuine mountaineering feel as the valley floor drops rapidly away and the views stretch further and further along it. The route starts in the lay-by at the head of Idwal Lake and goes left across rising ground, until you strike a path heading straight up following the crest of the ridge to the summit. Anyone who has seen pictures of people jumping the five-foot gap between Adam and Eve, the two chunks of rhyolitic lava which crown this regal mountain, will wonder what the fuss is about until they get up there and see the mountain dropping away on all sides. In theory the leap is trivial, but the consequences of overshooting would be disastrous.

There are two other main routes up Tryfan. The first follows the so-called **Miners' Track** (2 miles; 2hr; 1350ft ascent) from Idwal Cottage, taking the path to Cwm Idwal then, as it bears sharply to the right, keeping straight ahead and making for the gap on the horizon. This is **Bwlch Tryfan**, the col between Tryfan and Glyder Fach, from where the **South Ridge** of Tryfan (800 yards; 30min; 650ft ascent) climbs past the Far South Peak to the summit. This last section is an easy scramble. The second route, which is more often used in descent, follows **Heather Terrace** (1.5 miles; 2hr; 2000ft ascent), which keeps to a fault in the rock running diagonally across the east face. The start is the same as for the north ridge, but instead of following the ridge, you cut left, heading south until you arrive between the South and the Far South peaks. A right turn then starts your scramble for the summit.

Glyder Fach

The assault on **Glyder Fach** (3260ft) begins at Bwlch Tryfan, reached either by the Miners' Track from Idwal Cottage or by the South Ridge from Tryfan's summit. The trickier route follows **Bristly Ridge** (1000 yards; 40min; 900ft ascent) which isn't marked on OS maps but runs steeply south from the col up past some daunting-looking towers of rock. In good conditions, it isn't that difficult, and saves a long hike southeast along a second section of the **Miners' Track** (1.5 miles; 1hr 30min; 900ft ascent), then west to the summit, a chaotic jumble of huge grey slabs that many people don't bother climbing up, preferring to be photographed on a massive cantilevered rock a few yards away.

ited. Two and a half miles west of Capel Curig, the *Williams Barn*, Gwern Gof Isaf Farm (☎01690/720276), has a self-catering bunkhouse and cheap **campsite**, or there's the smaller *Gwern Gof Uchaf* campsite, a mile further west, and the *Idwal Cottage* **YHA hostel** (March–Oct; ☎01248/600225, fax 602952), at the western end of Llyn Ogwen, five miles from Capel Curig. The only other amenity in the valley is the café (see p.329).

Glyder Fach
From Glyder Fach, it is an easy enough stroll to **Glyder Fawr** (3280ft) (1 mile; 40min; 200ft ascent), reached by skirting round the tortured rock formations of **Castell y Gwynt** (the Castle of the Winds) then following a cairn-marked path to the dramatic summit of frost-shattered slabs angled like ancient headstones.

Glyder Fawr is normally approached directly from Idwal Cottage, following the **Devil's Kitchen Route** (2.5 miles; 3hr; 2300ft ascent) past Idwal Lake, then to the left of the Devil's Kitchen, zigzagging up to a lake-filled plateau. Follow the path to the right of the lake; then, where paths cross, turn left for the summit.

A **southern approach** to Glyder Fawr (3 miles; 2hr 30min; 2100ft ascent) leaves from beside the YHA hostel at Pen-y-Pass (see p.340), following a "courtesy path" marked by red flashes of paint. It rises steeply behind the hostel heading northwest, but turning north for the summit to avoid straying onto the screes on the flanks of the neighbouring mountain, Esgair Felen.

THE CARNEDDAU RANGE

The appearance of the **Carneddau Range** could hardly be in greater contrast to the jagged edges of the Glyders. These peaceful giants, which present the longest stretch of ground over three thousand feet in England and Wales, form a rounded plateau stretching to the cliffs of Penmaenmawr on the north coast. The sound of a raven in the neighbouring mist-filled cwms, and the occasional wild pony, can often be your only company on inclement days, but in fine weather the easy walking and roof-of-the-world views make for a satisfying day out. Though the tops are fairly flat once you're up there, getting to them can be a hard slog. The start from Idwal Cottage is the most strenuous, requiring a long push up the shaley south ridge from the stile beside the road bridge at the foot of Ogwen Lake. If you can, avoid this in favour of the fine **Carneddau loop** (9 miles; 5hr; 3500ft ascent), starting from the lay-by at the head of the lake near Tal y Llyn Ogwen farm and taking in the range's four mighty southern peaks. The path keeps to the right of the farm, then follows boggy land by a stream towards its source, Ffynnon Lloer, before turning left up the east ridge of **Pen yr Ole Wen** (3212ft), with its magnificent view down into Nant Ffrancon and back to Tryfan. In clear weather, you can see the route running north past Carnedd Fach, past what looks to be a huge artificial mound, to **Carnedd Dafydd** (3425ft). After a short easterly descent, the path skirts the steep Ysgolion Duon cliffs, then climbs over stones to the broad, arched top of **Carnedd Llywelyn** (3491ft), the highest of the Carneddau and surpassed in Wales only by two of Snowdon's peaks, Yr Wyddfa and Crib-y-ddysgl. For little extra effort, enthusiasts can conquer **Yr Elen** (3152ft), a short distance to the northeast, but most will be content with the easterly descent to **Craig yr Ysfa**, a sheer cliff which drops away into the vast amphitheatre of **Cwm Eigiau** to the north. Continuing with care, skirt around the north of Ffynnon Llugwy reservoir and climb to the grassy top of **Penyrhelgi-du** (2733ft), from where there is a steady broad-ridged descent to the road near Helyg. The mile-long trek back west to the starting point is best done on the old packhorse route running parallel to the A5, and linked to it occasionally by footpaths.

If you are considering one-way walks, several other possibilities present themselves, the most appealing of which is the full ridge walk from here linking up with the Roman road which links Rowen to Aber (see p.412).

Llanberis and Snowdon

Mention **LLANBERIS**, ten miles west of Capel Curig, to any mountain enthusiast and **Snowdon** immediately springs to mind. The two seem inseparable, and it's not just the five-mile-long umbilical of the **Snowdon Mountain Railway** (see p.337), Britain's only rack and pinion railway, that bonds the town to the summit, nor is it the popular path running parallel to the tracks (see box, p.338). Llanberis is the nearest you'll get in Wales to an alpine climbing village, its single main street thronged with weather-beaten walkers and climbers decked out in Gore-Tex and Fibrepile, high fashion for what is otherwise a dowdy town. Most are Snowdon-bound, others are just making use of abundant budget accommodation and the best facilities this side of Betws-y-Coed.

At the same time, Llanberis is very much a Welsh rural community, albeit a depleted one now that slate is no longer being torn from the flanks of Elidir Fawr, the mountain separated from the town by the twin lakes of Llyn Padarn and Llyn Peris. The quarries, which for the best part of two centuries employed up to three thousand men to chisel out the precious slabs, closed in 1969, leaving a vast staircase of sixty-foot-high terraced platforms as a testament to their labours. At much the same time, proposals were tabled for a power station to be built on the former quarry sites. Environmentalists – as often as not the same middle-class English second-home owners who had pushed property prices beyond the means of the local people – were incensed that this fragile spot on the fringes of the national park could be desecrated. The people of Llanberis, still reeling from the closure of the quarries, had no such qualms. In the end both parties were pacified: the project went ahead underground.

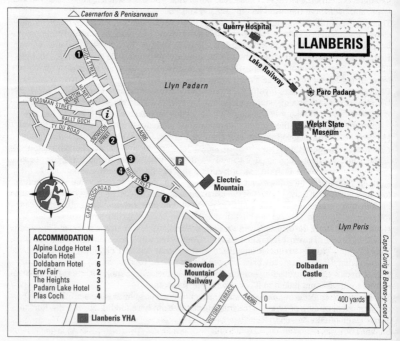

© Crown copyright

Arrival, information and accommodation

With no train or National Express services, the easiest way to get here is on **bus #77** from Bangor, bus #88 from Caernarfon or the summer-only Sherpa buses #19 or #95. All stop along High Street outside either of the two outdoor equipment shops, both just a few steps from the town's **tourist office**, 41a High St (Easter–Sept daily 10am–6pm; Oct daily 10am–4pm; Nov–Easter Wed–Sun 10am–4pm; ☎01286/870765, *llanberis.tic@ gwynedd.gov.uk*).

There's a wealth of low-cost **accommodation** and **campsites** in or close to town, as well as up at Pen-y-Pass (see p.340). Luxurious places are harder to find, so if you have your own transport and don't mind being a few miles further from the mountain, you might prefer to stay in places listed under Caernarfon (see p.365) or Bangor (see p.413).

Hotels and guesthouses

Alpine Lodge Hotel, 1 High St (☎ & fax 01286/870294). Traditional and friendly licensed guesthouse with comfortable rooms, all with private facilities, and bunkhouse accommodation let on a B&B basis. Rooms ②.

Dolafon Hotel, High St (☎ & fax 01286/870933). Appealing, well-priced B&B in its own grounds, with spacious, comfortable rooms and delicious evening meals. ②.

Dolbadarn Hotel, High St (☎ & fax 01286/870277). Reasonable rooms in a former coaching hotel that's one of the oldest buildings in the village, now operating its own pony trekking centre. ②.

Erw Fair, High St (☎01286/872400). Large house with nicely decorated rooms, all with TVs, and hearty breakfasts with locally made sausages. Rates drop dramatically in winter. ②.

Graianfryn, Penisarwaun, three miles northwest of Llanberis (☎01286/871007, *www.veg. ndirect.co.uk*). An exclusively vegetarian and vegan wholefood, non-smoking B&B in a Victorian farmhouse. Home-grown vegetables are used in the three-course evening meals. ①.

The Heights, 74 High St (☎01286/871179, fax 872507). B&B catering primarily to the walking and climbing set, with comfortable rooms and dorms (see "Hostels" below). Downstairs is the liveliest bar and restaurant in town, and a climbing wall. ②.

Padarn Lake Hotel, High St (☎01286/870260, fax 870007). One of Llanberis' larger, full-facility hotels with lake views from some of the spacious and pleasant rooms, and a restaurant and a couple of bars downstairs. ③.

Plas Coch, High St (☎01286/872122, fax 872648, *www.plascoch.ndirect.co.uk*). Pleasant, low-cost B&B with some mountain-view rooms. The inexpensive evening meals, with traditional Welsh and vegetarian options, are excellent. ①.

Hostels, bunkhouses and campsites

Cae Gwyn Campsite, Nant Peris, 2 miles southeast of Llanberis (☎01286/870718). Fairly basic water-and-showers campsite towards Pen-y-Pass, almost opposite the *Vaynol Arms* pub. Budget-minded climbers and mountain bikers make up the bulk of the clientele.

Gallt-y-Glyn, half a mile northwest of Llanberis on the Caernarfon road (☎01286/870370). Reasonable six-berth dorms in the annexe of a traditional hotel. There are no self-catering facilities but breakfast is included and bar meals are available. Take the #88 bus, and a sleeping bag and towel.

Gwastadnant B&B, Bunkhouse and Camping, three miles east of Llanberis, beyond Nant Peris (☎01286/870356). The closest accommodation to Pen-y-Pass with a pleasant and friendly B&B (①), a bunkhouse with self-catering facilities and three-tier bunks at £4–5 a night and a small campsite across the road.

Hafod Lydan Campsite, Capel Goch Rd. A couple of quid-a-night site in a farmer's field, with no showers, a quarter of a mile beyond the *Llanberis YHA hostel*.

The Heights (see "Hotels and guesthouses" above). Accommodation in eight-bed dorms with bedding and towels provided but no self-catering facilities. Bed only £9, B&B £12.

Jesse James' Bunkhouse, Buarth y Clytiau, Penisarwaun (☎01286/870521). The original bunkhouse, large, clean, non-smoking and efficiently run for thirty years by a mountain guide. Beds are £7.50 a night, and you'll need a sleeping bag and towel. Separate and slightly more luxurious self-contained accommodation (①) is also available. Take the A4086 two miles towards Caernarfon, turn right onto the B4547 and continue for a mile.

Llanberis YHA hostel, Llwyn Celyn (☎01286/870280, fax 870936). Well-appointed but not especially atmospheric YHA hostel, a 700-yard uphill slog along Capel Goch Road off High Street.

Pritchard's Camping, Nant Peris (☎01286/870494). Pretty much identical to *Cae Gwyn Campsite*, but 200 yards closer to Llanberis.

Rhydau Duon Farmhouse, Brynrefail, two miles northwest of Llanberis (☎01286/870744). A small rural group-activity centre with a friendly communal feel and a range of bunkhouse and B&B (②) accommodation. Canoeing and rock-climbing instruction is also available. Take the B4547 towards Bangor, first right into Brynrefail, cross the river then second right.

The Town and around

One dramatic tower and assorted scattered remains are all that is left of thirteenth-century **Dolbadarn Castle** (unrestricted access; CADW), perched on its rock between Llyn Peris and Llyn Padarn where it guards the entrance of the Llanberis Pass. Its construction, though undocumented, is usually attributed to Llywelyn ap Iorwerth ("the Great"), though its circular keep is more redolent of a Norman Marcher fort than a native Welsh castle. Close up, there's not a lot to look at, but, viewed across Llyn Padarn and framed by the grey crags of the Pass behind, it is easy to see why both Richard Wilson and Turner came to paint it.

The road opposite the Mountain Railway terminus, at the east end of town, runs a few yards past the castle to the grounds of the **Parc Padarn** (Llyn Padarn Country Park; unrestricted access), where lakeside oak woods are gradually recolonizing the discarded workings of the defunct **Dinorwig Slate Quarries**, formerly one of the largest slate quarries in the world. Equipment and engines which formerly hauled materials up inclined tramways have been partly restored and punctuate the paths which link the levels chiselled out of the hillside.

The fort-like complex of buildings at the base of the main tramway was once used as the quarry's maintenance workshops, but now houses the **Welsh Slate Museum** (Easter–Oct daily 9.30am–5.30pm, *www.nmgw.ac.uk*; £3.50). The fifty-foot-diameter water wheel that once powered cutting machines through a cat's cradle of lineshafts, countershafts and flapping belts still turns, but no longer drives the machinery. Though most of the equipment dates back to the early part of the twentieth century, it was still in use until the quarries closed and is quite familiar to the former quarry workers who demonstrate their skills at turning an inch-thick slab of slate into six, even eight, perfectly smooth slivers. The slate was delivered to the slate-dressing sheds by means of a maze of tramways, cranes and rope lifts, all kept in good order in the fitting and repair shops. As you pass through, look out for the scales used to calculate the price each rock cutter would be paid for his work, before the typical deductions for the amount of rope and gunpowder he used to extract the diverse types of slate. Some of these are displayed nearby and range from mottled burgundy and bottle green to every shade of grey. A recent addition to the museum is a set of four slate workers' cottages transported to the site from nearby Tanygrisiau and now kitted out in the style of different historical periods.

To keep everything in working order, the craftsmen here operate an ageing foundry, producing pieces for the scattered branches of the National Museum of Wales, as well as repairing the rolling stock which plies the adjacent **Llanberis Lake Railway** (July & Aug 4–11pm daily; March–June & Sept to early Oct 3–6pm daily except Sat; £4.20 return). The original railway, which from 1843 to 1961 transported slate and workers between the Dinorwig quarries and Port Dinorwig on the Menai Straits, was sold for scrap. Enthusiasts subsequently relaid a tame two-mile stretch to Pen-y-llyn along the shores of Lake Padarn. The smoking tank engine takes about forty minutes for the round trip, and although there's nothing much to do at the other end, you can at least catch a different train back and break your journey halfway at the **Cwm Derwen Visitor Centre** (open when trains are running; £1) which illustrates the history of the woodland that spreads up the slopes behind the rail tracks. You're really better off just walking slowly around the old slate workings and through the ancient woodlands of Coed Dinorwig, making for the period-furnished **Quarry Hospital** (May–Sept 10am–4.45pm; £1), where the resident surgeon patched up gruesome injuries from gunpowder blasts and falling rock.

In 1974, five years after the quarry closed, work began hollowing out the vast underground chambers of the **Dinorwig Pumped Storage Hydro Station**. Unlike most power stations, this is a net drain on the national grid, able to instantly produce electricity to cope with the early-evening increase in demand. Within ten seconds it can be wound up to its maximum power output (1800 Megawatts), achieved by letting the contents of the Marchlyn Mawr reservoir rapidly empty through the turbines into Llyn Peris; then, when the demand lessens, pumping it up again. If you can bear the thinly disguised electricity industry advertisement which precedes it, there's an hour-long minibus tour down through rock-hewn tunnels to the powerhouse below. For this, you need to call at **Electric Mountain** (April–Sept daily 9.30am–5.30pm, Oct–Dec daily 10.30am–4.30pm, Jan–March Thurs–Sun 10.30am–4.30pm, *www.electricmountain.co.uk*; £5;) by the lake on the A4086, which bypasses the town centre. Tours depart every half-hour or so; while you wait you can visit the Mammoth Exhibition: tolerably interesting displays on glaciation and its effect on Snowdonia's geology, flora and fauna which are centred on a replica of a huge woolly mammoth.

Eating, drinking and entertainment

While Llanberis isn't spilling over with good places to **eat**, it does have something to suit all pockets. Pretty much all there is lies on High Street, where you'll find a couple of likeable **pubs**. To broaden the choice, Bangor and Caernarfon are both only eight miles away.

Arthur's Café, next to *Dolafon Hotel*, High St. Basic café with no-nonsense dishes, including a good Welsh rarebit.

Gwynedd Restaurant, *Gwynedd Hotel*, High St (☎01286/870203). Hearty portions of good basic meals cooked well.

The Heights, 74 High St (☎01286/871179). Excellent-value pizza, meat, vegetarian and vegan meals, and one of the liveliest bars in town. Full of climbers and walkers.

Pete's Eats, 40 High St (☎01286/870358). Outdoor types flock here for top-value basic meals of gut-splitting proportions and a few more delicate dishes. Summer Mon–Fri & Sun to 8pm, Sat till 9pm; winter Mon–Fri till 5pm, Sat & Sun till 8pm.

Prince of Wales, 38 High St. Ordinary local pub which comes to life on Saturday night when you can join in with the Welsh singing led by the resident electric-organist.

Vaynol Arms, Nant Peris, two miles east of Llanberis. Cosy pub, the only one before Pen-y-Gwryd, with good beer and a convivial atmosphere. Full of locals midweek, and climbers and campers from across the road at weekends. The food is also well worth trying.

Y Bistro, 43–45 High St (☎01286/871278). The best restaurant for miles around, offering expensive but generous two-, three- and four-course set meals, all served with canapés on home-made bread. Booking recommended. Closed Sun.

Activities

By far the most popular activity around Llanberis is simply getting out on foot. This is principally on Snowdon (see box, p.338), whose vast, steep-sided cwms have become the summer playground for rock athletes picking their way up impossibly sheer faces.

If you're not equipped or confident enough to go **climbing** or **scrambling** by yourself, engage the services of one of the many mountain guides based around Llanberis: Gwynedd Mountaineering Services, Pant y Celyn, 13 Stryd y Ffynnon, Llanberis (☎01286/871128), and High Trek Snowdonia, Tal y Waen, Deiniolen (☎01286/871232) both offer good packages.

When inclement weather forces climbers in off the crags, the keen ones make straight for the bouldering room in *The Heights* (£1; see p.333), or the huge indoor climbing wall at **Beacon Climbing Centre**, three miles west from Llanberis in Waunfawr (Mon–Fri 11am–10pm, Sat & Sun 10am–10pm; ☎01286/650045; £4).

With so many precipitous mountains, Llanberis is ideally suited for **paragliding**. The longest-standing operator is Enigma: The Snowdonia School of Paragliding, 1 Stryd-y-Llyn, Cwm-y-Glo (April–Oct; ☎01248/602103) which offers solo flights from £45 and offer tandem flights – where you are effectively a passenger strapped to an instructor – from £30; Snowdon Gliders: The Mountain Paragliding Centre, Cefn yr Ynys, Mynydd Llandegai (☎ & fax 01248/602581), is comparable.

If you're looking for something less specialized, Padarn Water Sports and Activities Centre, Bryn Du, Tydu Road (☎01286/870556 or 870494), offers the broadest range of both **water sports** and land-based activities, mostly but not entirely oriented towards groups, with half-day courses in canoeing, abseiling, climbing and orienteering starting at £18; gear rental is also available.

As well as being one of the most popular walking routes up Snowdon, the **Llanberis Path** (see box overleaf) is designated a bridleway, making it, the Snowdon Ranger Path and the Pitt's Head Track to Rhyd-Ddu, open for **cyclists**. A voluntary agreement exists restricting access to and from the summit between 10am and 5pm from June to September, but otherwise these paths are open. Unfortunately, there is no bike rental in Llanberis, so you'll have to pick one up in Caernarfon (see p.367) or Betws-y-Coed (see p.321). You can also take a **horse** up onto Snowdon's lower slopes (£10 an hour, £40 a day) from The Dolbadarn Pony Trekking Centre at the *Dolbadarn Hotel* on High Street (☎01286/870277).

Snowdon

The highest British mountain south of the Scottish Grampians, the **Snowdon** massif (3650ft) forms a star of shattered ridges with three major peaks – Crib Goch, Crib-y-ddysgl and Y Lliwedd – and the summit, **Yr Wyddfa**, crowning the lot. If height were its only quality, it would be popular, but Snowdon also sports some of the finest walking and scrambling in the park, and in the winter, the longest season for ice climbers and cramponed walkers. Its Welsh name, Eryri, is derived from either *eryr* (land of eagles) or *eira* (land of snow); since the eagles have long gone, the latter is more appropriate, with winter snows a feature well into April.

Some hardened outdoor enthusiasts dismiss Snowdon as overused, and it certainly can be crowded. A thousand visitors a day press onto the postbox-red carriages of the Snowdon Mountain Railway (see opposite), while another fifteen hundred pound the well-maintained paths to make this Britain's most-climbed mountain. Opprobrium is chiefly levelled at the train for its mere existence, and at the abominable concrete-bunker summit **café** for selling the country's highest pint of beer. But at least there's a warm place for walkers to rest, and those unable to walk up have the chance of seeing the mighty **views** over most of north Wales – and even across to Ireland on exceptionally clear days.

There is no longer a tumulus on the top of Snowdon, but the Welsh for the highest point, Yr Wyddfa, means "The Burial Place" – near proof that people have been climbing the mountain for millennia. More recently, early ascents were for botanical or geological reasons – 500-million-year-old fossil shells can be found near the summit from when Snowdon was on the sea bottom – but the Welsh naturalist Thomas Pennant came up here mainly for pleasure, and in 1773, his description of the dawn view from the summit in his *Journey to Snowdon* encouraged many to follow. Some were guided by the Snowdon Ranger from his house on the south side (now a YHA hostel), but the rapidly improving facilities in Llanberis soon shifted the balance in favour of the easier Llanberis Path, a route later followed by the railway. This remains one of the most popular routes up, though many prefer the three shorter and steeper ones from the Pen-y-Pass car park at the top of the Llanberis Pass. By far the most dramatic, if also the most dangerous, is the wonderful Snowdon Horseshoe, which calls at all four of the high peaks.

Legends, painters and poets

From the departure of the Romans until the tenth century, Welsh history comes down to us leavened with equal measures of myth, and populated with the shadowy figures of Arthur, Gwrtheryn (Vortigern) and Myrddin (Merlin). Glastonbury in England lays a powerful, though not incontestable, claim to being the location of Arthur's court and burial place, but his British (as opposed to Anglo-Saxon) blood gives him a firm place in Welsh hearts; and in Wales, Snowdon is always held to be his home. It was on top of Dinas Emrys, the seat of Gwrtheryn's realm at the foot of the south ridge near Beddgelert, that that most potent symbol of Welsh independence, the **Red Dragon**, earned its colours. The Celtic king, Gwrtheryn, was trying to build a fortress to protect himself from the Saxons but each night the earth swallowed the building stones, a phenomenon that Myrddin divined to be due to two dragons sleeping underground: one white, the other red. When woken, they engaged in an unending fight which Myrddin pronounced to symbolize the Red Dragon of Wales' perpetual battle with the White Dragon of the Saxons.

Arthur's domain was higher up the mountain. Llyn Llydaw aspires to being the pond where Bedivere threw King Arthur's sword, Excalibur, while thirteen hundred feet above, Bwlch-y-Saethau (The Pass of the Arrows) was where a wayward arrow mortally wounded Arthur, while on the point of vanquishing his nephew Modred. The remains of Carnedd Arthur, just below Bwlch Ciliau on the Watkin Path (see box, p.339), are claimed as his burial site, but it is probably a fairly modern cairn. Another burial place is that of one of Arthur's victims, Rhita Gawr, whose now-vanished tumulus gave Snowdon's highest point, Yr Wyddfa, its name.

Throughout the eighteenth and nineteenth centuries, anywhere with Arthurian associations proved an irresistible magnet for all manner of writers and painters. Thomas Gray added to both the mystery of the place and its Celtic symbolism in his ode *The Bard*, in which the last Welsh bard hurls himself off the summit while fleeing Edward I's marauding army, but the painter Richard Wilson had already beaten him to the task. His *Snowdon from Llyn Nantlle* had already planted the pre-Romantic seeds from which grew a vast, and still growing, body of work capturing the mountain's changing moods from every conceivable angle. Two of the best places to see some of the classic artwork inspired by Snowdonia are the National Trust information centre in Beddgelert (see p.342) and the National Museum in Cardiff (see p.102).

The Snowdon Mountain Railway

The **Snowdon Mountain Railway** (mid-March to Oct 6–25 trains daily; summit return £15; ☎01286/870223, *www.SnowdonRailway.Force9.co.uk*) was completed in 1896, and carriages – some dating back to the nineteenth century, and pushed by seventy-year-old steam locos – still climb to the summit in just under an hour. The three-thousand-foot, mostly one-in-eight struggle up five miles of the most heavily maintained track in Britain follows the shallowest approach to the top of Snowdon. It starts at the eastern end of Llanberis opposite the *Royal Victoria Hotel*, and climbs past the summertime swimming hole at Bishop's Falls to the summit **café**, designed in 1936 by Portmeirion architect Clough Williams-Ellis on what must have been a rough Monday morning. The café currently has a licensed bar and a post office where you can buy a "Railway Stamp" (10p) to affix to your letter – along with the usual Royal Mail one – thereby entitling you to use the highest postbox in the UK and enchant your friends with a "Summit of

---

WALKS ON SNOWDON

Note: The OS Outdoor Leisure 1:25,000 map #17 ("Snowdon & Conwy Valley") is highly recommended for all these walks.

LLANBERIS PATH
The easiest and longest route up Snowdon, the **Llanberis Path** (5 miles to summit; 3hr; 3200ft ascent), following the rail line, is widely scorned by the sort of serious hiker who wouldn't use the railway or take tea at the summit café. The path starts opposite the *Royal Victoria Hotel* and out of sight of the summit, which gradually comes into view as you rise towards the midway point and **Clogwyn Du'r Arddu** (The Black Cliff, or "Cloggy" to its friends), an ominous sheet of rock which frames a small lake. Today, climbers sprint up the face, which caused an early exponent to lament, "No breach seems either possible or desirable along the whole extent of the west buttress. Though there is the faintest of faint hopes for a human fly rather on the left side." The path next passes Clogwyn station, from where you get a great view down onto the Llanberis Pass. This soon disappears from sight as the path gets steeper, passing the low remains of stables where mule trains used to rest. **Bwlch Glas** (Green Pass) is marked by the "Finger Stone" where the Snowdon Ranger Path (see opposite) and three routes coming up from Pen-y-Pass join the Llanberis Path for the final ascent to **Yr Wyddfa**. Llanberis Path is the route used by the annual **Snowdon Race** which takes place on the second Saturday in July, with the leading runners recording times of only a little over an hour for the combined ascent and descent.

THE MINERS' TRACK
The **Miners' Track** (4 miles to summit; 2hr 30min; 2400ft ascent) is the easiest of the three routes up from Pen-y-Pass. Leaving the car park, a broad track leads south then west to the former copper mines in Cwm Dyli. Dilapidated remains of the crushing mill perch on the shores of Llyn Llydaw, a tarn-turned-reservoir with one of the worst eyesores in the park, an above-ground pipeline slicing across Snowdon's east face to the power station in Nantgwynant. Skirting around the right of the lake, the path climbs more steeply to the lake-filled Cwm Glaslyn, then again to Upper Glaslyn, from where the measured steps of those ahead warn of the impending switchback ascent to the junction with the Llanberis Path.

PIG TRACK
The stonier **Pig Track** (3.5 miles to summit; 2hr 30min; 2400ft ascent) is really just a shorter and steeper variation on the Miners' Track, leaving from the western end of the Pen-y-Pass car park and climbing up to **Bwlch y Moch** (the Pass of the Pigs), which gives the route its name. Ignore the scramble up to Crib Goch (part of the Snowdon Horseshoe) and traverse below the rocky ridge looking down on Llyn Llydaw and those pacing the Miners' Track, content that you're already 500ft up on them. They'll soon catch up, as the two tracks meet just before the zigzag up to the Llanberis Path.

SNOWDON HORSESHOE
Some claim that the **Snowdon Horseshoe** (8 miles round; 5–7hr; 3200ft ascent) is one of the finest ridge walks in Europe. The route makes a full anticlockwise circuit around the three glacier-carved cwms of Upper Glaslyn, Glaslyn and Llydaw. Not to be taken lightly, it includes the knife-edge traverse of **Crib Goch**. Every summer's day, dozens of

Snowdon – Copa'r Wyddfa" postmark. In bad weather, trains terminate at Clogwyn station, a thirty-minute walk from the top.

Times and type of locomotive vary with demand and season, but whether hauled by steam or diesel, the full round trip takes two and a half hours, with half an hour on top. You can only book on the day, and in summer tickets are frequently sold out by 11am. If you walk up by one of the routes detailed in the box below, you can still take the train

---

people find themselves straddling the lip, empty space on both sides, and wishing they weren't there. In winter conditions, an ice axe and crampons are the minimum requirement. The path follows the Pig Track to Bwlch y Moch, then pitches right for the moderate scramble up to Crib Goch. If you balk at any of this, turn back. If not, wait your turn, then painstakingly pick your way along the sensational ridge to **Crib-y-ddysgl** (3494ft), from where it is an easy descent to Bwlch Glas and stiffer ascent to Yr Wyddfa. Having ticked off Wales' two highest peaks, turn southwest for a couple of hundred yards to a marker stone where the Watkin Path (see below) drops away to the east. Follow it down to the stretched saddle of **Bwlch-y-Saethau** (Pass of the Arrows), then onto the cairn at Bwlch Ciliau from where the Watkin Path descends to Nantgwynant. Ignore that route, continuing straight on up the cliff-lined northwest ridge of **Y Lliwedd** (2930ft), then descend to where you see the scrappy but safe path down to Llyn Llydaw and the Miners' Track.

SNOWDON RANGER PATH

Many of the earliest Snowdon climbers engaged the services of the Snowdon Ranger, who led them up the comparatively long and dull but easy **Snowdon Ranger Path** (4 miles to summit; 3hr; 3100ft ascent), on the now unfashionable south side of the mountain. The path starts from the *Snowdon Ranger YHA hostel* (see p.342) on the shores of Llyn Cwellyn, five miles northwest of Beddgelert. To the left of the hostel, a path leads up a track then ascends, steeply flattening out to cross sometimes boggy grass, eventually skirting to the right of the impressive Clogwyn Du'r Arddu cliffs (see Llanberis Path, opposite). This is another steep ascent which eventually meets the Llanberis Path at Bwlch Glas.

PITT'S HEAD TRACK

The **Pitt's Head Track** (4 miles to summit; 3hr; 2900ft ascent) has two branches, one starting from Pitt's Head Rock, two and a half miles northwest of Beddgelert, the other from the National Park car park in Rhyd-Ddu, a mile beyond that. They join up after less than a mile's walk across stony, walled grazing land, and after crossing a kissing gate continue to the northwest up to the stunning final section along the rim of Cwm Clogwyn and the south ridge of Yr Wyddfa.

WATKIN PATH

The most spectacular of the southern routes up Snowdon, the **Watkin Path** (4 miles to summit; 3hr; 3350ft ascent), is also the one with the greatest height gain. From Bethania Bridge, three miles northeast of Beddgelert in Nantgwynant, the path starts on a broad track through oaks opening up to long views of a series of cataracts. Ascend beside these to a disused inclined tramway where the track narrows before reaching the natural amphitheatre of Cwm Llan. The ruins of the South Snowdon Slate Works only temporarily distract you from **Gladstone Rock**, at which, in 1892, the 83-year-old Liberal statesman, then in his fourth term as British Prime Minister, officially opened the route. A narrower path wheels left around the base of Craig Ddu, then starts the steep ascent past Carnedd Arthur to Bwlch Ciliau, the saddle between Y Lliwedd (see Snowdon Horseshoe opposite) and the true summit (Yr Wyddfa), then turning right for the final climb to the top. The Watkin Path can be easily turned into a loop by descending the top section of the Pitt's Head Track then continuing down Bwlch Main to the saddle and cutting east into Cwm Llan and down.

down. Standby tickets back to Llanberis (£7) are sold at the summit if there are seats, but round-trippers get priority.

The Llanberis Pass and Pen-y-Pass

The steady Llanberis Path which grinds up Snowdon's gentlest ascent may be the most popular single route up the mountain, but more walkers start from the lofty saddle at the top of the **Llanberis Pass**, the deepest, narrowest and craggiest of Snowdonia's passes, running five miles east from Llanberis itself. At its head is the YHA hostel, café and car park which make up **PEN-Y-PASS**, the base for the Miners' Track, the Pig Track and the demanding Snowdon Horseshoe (see box, p.338). These all leave from the car park, while a route up Glyder Fawr (see box, p.331) follows a "courtesy path" to the west of the hostel.

Frequent #19 and #95 Sherpa **buses** travel daily to Pen-y-Pass, the latter being the recommended approach from the Llanberis side even if you have a car, since the Pen-y-Pass car park is almost always full and costs £5. Use the free "park and ride" facility at the bottom of the pass close to the *Vaynol Arms*.

The only **accommodation** at Pen-y-Pass is the YHA **hostel** (Jan–Oct; ☎01286/870428, fax 872434), open from 1pm each day, with free parking, plus videos on climbing and kayaking. A mile east is the nearest **pub** with accommodation, the *Pen-y-Gwryd Hotel* (Jan & Feb weekends only; ☎01286/870211; ②), a wonderfully rustic place with ageing furniture, magnificent Edwardian bathrooms, an outdoor sauna, and a lot of muddy boots in the bar. Amongst others, the first successful expedition up Mount Everest in 1953 stayed at the hotel while doing final equipment testing, and took time out to sign the ceiling: Edmund Hillary, Chris Bonnington, Doug Scott and Portmeirion designer Clough Williams-Ellis are all there. The Everest team also brought back a piece of the mountain, which now sits in pride of place on the bar. If you stay, expect a congenial though somewhat regimented atmosphere and lots of plain home cooking.

Beddgelert and around

Almost all of the prodigious quantity of rain which falls on Snowdon spills down the valleys on its south side: either into the Glaslyn River in Nantgwynant or the Colwyn River in Nant Colwyn. At their confluence, just before they jointly crash down the bony **Aberglaslyn Gorge** towards Porthmadog, the few dozen hard grey houses making up **BEDDGELERT** huddle together in some majestic mountain scenery. It's a curiously enchanting place, its front gardens bursting with award-winning flower beds and with plenty of places to mooch, eat and drink. When (and if) the Welsh Highland Railway (see p.371) project reaches completion, Beddgelert will be the principal halt between Caernarfon and Porthmadog.

If you tire of the view from the village, it's easy enough to get out on one of the longer walks described in the box opposite. A shorter and more celebrated excursion takes you four hundred yards south, along the right bank of the Glaslyn, to the spot that gives the village its name, **Gelert's Grave** (bedd means "burial place"), where a railed-off enclosure in a field marks the final resting place of Prince Llywelyn ap Iorwerth's faithful dog, Gelert, who was left in charge of the prince's infant son while he went hunting. On his return, the child was gone and the hound's muzzle was soaked in blood. Jumping to conclusions, the impetuous Llywelyn slew the dog, only to find the child safely asleep beneath its cot and a dead wolf beside him. Llywelyn hurried to his dog, which licked his hand as it died. Sadly, the story is an all-too-successful eighteenth-century fabrication, conjured up by a wily local publican to lure punters – something it has succeeded spectacularly in doing ever since. The real source of the name is probably the grave of Celert, a sixth-century British saint who is supposed to have lived hereabouts, possibly near **Dinas Emrys**, a wooded mound a mile up Nantgwynant on the A498, where Vortigern's fort once stood and, legend has it, dragons once fought (see p.337).

There's little enough to see now, except for the red-brown stain on the hillside opposite identifying the **Sygun Copper Mine** (daily 10am–5pm; £4.75), whose ore drew first the Romans, then nineteenth-century prospectors. The dilapidated remains of what was once the valley's prime source of income have now been restored and made safe for the cool (9°C) 45-minute guided tour up through the multiple levels of tunnels and galleries, accompanied by the disembodied voice of a miner telling of his working life. After the tour, you are free to potter around the ore-crushing and separation equipment, or ask the guide to point you over the hill towards the foot of the Aberglaslyn Gorge (see box, below).

WALKS FROM BEDDGELERT

As you might expect for a village sited at the southern point of the Snowdon massif, there are a couple of ascents of Snowdon starting near Beddgelert, listed in the Snowdon box (see p.339). Otherwise the following walks are the best ones to do from the village; all are covered by OS 1:25,000 #17 "Snowdon & Conwy Valley" and 1:50,000 #115 "Snowdon" maps.

THE ABERGLASLYN GORGE
An easy walk following the short but very picturesque **Aberglaslyn Gorge** (4 miles; 2hr 30min; 600ft ascent), and returning to the copper mines (see above) on a path up Cwm Bychan between Mynydd Sygun and Moel y Dyniewyd. Take the right bank of the river, past Gelert's Grave, crossing over the bridge onto the track-bed of the Welsh Highland narrow-gauge rail line. This gently graded path then hugs the left bank for a mile down to Pont Aberglaslyn, with the more adventurous Fisherman's Path just below it providing a closer look at the river's course through chutes and channels in sculpted rocks. From the road bridge at Pont Aberglaslyn – the tidal limit before The Cob was built at Porthmadog (see p.351) – you can retrace your steps, follow the A498 back on the far bank, or head north up Cwm Bychan on a path near the exit of the disused railway tunnel. It is about a two-mile valley walk to the copper mines from where a track follows the left bank of the River Glaslyn to Beddgelert. You can do the walk in reverse by setting off from the top level of the copper mines at the end of the guided tour; ask the guide for directions.

MOEL HEBOG
From Beddgelert, you are unlikely to have missed the lumpish **Moel Hebog** (Bald Hill of the Hawk; 2569ft) to the west of the village. It forms the highest point on a fine panoramic **ridge walk** (8 miles; 5hr; 2800ft ascent) which also takes in the lesser peaks of Moel Lefn, and Moel yr Ogof (Hill of the Cave), named after a refuge used by Owain Glyndŵr when fleeing the English in 1404, after his failed attempt to take Caernarfon Castle. The final forest section can be a bit disorientating, even in good weather, so make sure you have your compass.

Start half a mile northwest of the centre of Beddgelert on the A4085, where Pont Alyn crosses the river to Cwm Cloch Isaf Farm. Follow the signs to a green lane, which soon leads up onto the broad northeast ridge, all the time keeping left of the Y Diffwys cliffs. The summit cairn is joined by two walls, the one to the northwest leading down a steep grassy slope to Bwlch Meillionen, from where you can ascend over rocky ground to Moel yr Ogof, or descend to the right, then skirt left in a probably fruitless attempt to locate the difficult-to-find Glyndŵr's Cave. From the top of Moel yr Ogof, it's a clear route north to Moel Lefn, then down to a cairn from where you can plan your descent. The easiest line is to Bwlch Cwm-trwsgl, near the highest point of the Beddgelert Forest, where a stile over a wire fence leads into the forest. Both the maps detailed above show a clear, though not always easy-to-follow, route to the *Beddgelert Forest Campsite*, where you turn right and tramp a mile along the A4085 to Beddgelert.

Practicalities

Beddgelert sits on two **bus** routes: the #95 Caernarfon Sherpa and the #97A between Betws-y-Coed and Porthmadog. All stop near the road bridge over the Colwyn River, the effective centre of town and just a few yards away from the excellent **National Trust Shop and Information Centre**, Llywelyn Cottage (April–Oct daily 11am–5pm, July & Aug 11am–6pm; ☎01766/890293), a seventeenth-century former inn. There's a good exhibition within of the artists drawn to Snowdonia's landscapes, as well as inter-active stuff on the National Trust in the area. It's also the nearest thing in the village to a tourist office. You can **rent bikes** from Beics Beddgelert (☎01766/890434) at the *Beddgelert Forest Campsite* (see below).

Accommodation

Bed and breakfast **accommodation** is abundant. Most of the houses near the bridge and along the Caernarfon road let rooms, though if you're wanting to make an early start on the Snowdon walks you'll find the hostels better sited.

HOTELS AND GUESTHOUSES

Ael-y-Bryn, Caernarfon Rd (☎ & fax 01766/890310). Central guesthouse with good views and inex-pensive, home-cooked evening meals. ①.

Beddgelert Antiques and Tea Rooms, Waterloo House (☎01766/890543). Three attractive en-suite rooms above the restaurant and tearooms, directly opposite the bridge. ②.

Colwyn (☎01766/890276). Central 300-year-old cottage guesthouse with comfortable en-suite rooms. A separate two-person self-catering cottage is also let by the week. ②.

Plas Colwyn (☎01766/890458). Non-smoking guesthouse by the bridge, with inexpensive home-cooked evening meals served in the licensed restaurant. ②.

Royal Goat Hotel (☎01766/890224, fax 890422). Large central hotel with upmarket, sporty lean-ings – fishing, horse riding and golf available to guests – and a residents-only bar. ④.

Sygun Fawr Country House, three-quarters of a mile northeast off the A498 (☎01766/890258). This partially sixteenth-century house in its own grounds is the pick of the local hotels; a sauna and good evening meals add to the pretty bedrooms, most with wonderful mountain views. Closed Jan. ③.

Tanronnen Inn (☎01766/890347, fax 890606). Likeable pub on the south side of the river bridge with seven pleasant en-suite rooms and a good range of food. ④.

HOSTELS AND CAMPSITES

Beddgelert Forest Campsite (☎01766/890288). Excellent and reasonably priced campsite a mile out on the Caernarfon road. Here you can brush up your compass work via the site's orienteering course in the forest before testing it on the hills. Open all year.

Bryn Dinas Bunkhouse, Nant Gwynant (☎01766/890234). Fully self-catering £6-a-night bunkhouse, right at the foot of the Watkin Path (see box p.339) three miles northeast of Beddgelert on the A498. A sheet and blankets are supplied.

Bryn Gwynant YHA hostel (☎01766/890251, fax 890479). Beautifully sited hostel in Nantgwynant, four miles northeast of Beddgelert on the A498. There's also a campsite where you can use the hostel's facilities for half the adult rate. Daily March–Oct, phone for other times.

Cae Du Camping (☎01766/890595). Simple, summer-only site less than a 10min walk towards Capel Curig on the A498.

Snowdon Ranger YHA hostel, Rhyd Ddu (☎01286/650391, fax 650093) Former inn five miles northwest of Beddgelert on the Caernarfon road at the foot of the Snowdon Ranger Path (see Snowdon box, p.339). April–Oct.

Eating and drinking

Beddgelert Antiques and Tea Rooms, Waterloo House (see "Accommodation", above). (☎01766/890543). Attentive service, cosy surroundings, this boasts good daytime tearooms and an evening menu rich in game.

Lyn's Café and Tea Garden, Church St (☎01766/890374). Decent tearooms with garden seating, offering substantial daytime meals and moderately priced dinners.

Prince Llewelyn, Smith St. Convivial atmosphere around the fire or out in the sun, in a central pub serving good real ales.

Riverside Garden Restaurant (☎01766/890551). Central restaurant with a waterside terrace serving hearty breakfasts, moderately priced meals and cream teas.

Tanronnen, on the south side of the bridge. Cheery pub with decent beer and bar meals (see opposite).

Blaenau Ffestiniog and around

Snowdonia's most southerly major settlement, **BLAENAU FFESTINIOG** cowers at the foot of stark thousand-foot mountains thickly strewn with discarded heaps of splintered slate. *Blaenau* means "head of the valley", in this case the lush Vale of Ffestiniog, a dramatic contrast to this seemingly forbidding place. Blaenau Ffestiniog attracts some of Snowdonia's worst weather, and when clouds hunker low in the great cwm and rain sheets the grey roofs, grey walls and grey paving slabs it can become a terrifically gloomy town, unlike anywhere else on earth. Fortuitously, this is a great place to be in the rain – on days when every tourist office in north Wales is packed with wet visitors wondering what to do, Blaenau Ffestiniog is at its most dramatic, and besides, its slate mine will keep you dry.

Thousands of tons of slate per year were once hewn from the labyrinth of underground caverns below the town, but these days, only two mines manage to keep ticking over, one of them aided by the income made from site **tours** (see overleaf). It sometimes feels as though little has changed here since the late 1960s, the last time the mines were really profitable, but the loss of a steady income has hit the town hard: its population has dropped to less than half its 1910 peak of 12,000, unemployment is high, almost all the Nonconformist chapels are just discarded shells, and *Ar Werth* (For Sale) signs have sprouted everywhere. For now, the town's economy leans on tourism, generated by its mine tour and the fact that it's the junction of two of the finest train journeys in the country: the narrow-gauge **Ffestiniog Railway** which winds up from Porthmadog (see p.351), and the Lledr Valley rail line to Betws-y-Coed (see p.319).

Arrival and accommodation

By **car**, Blaenau Ffestiniog is most dramatically approached from the north along the Lledr Valley, climbing over the Crimea Pass between the Manod and Moelwyn mountains and plunging down into the town's shattered landscape. The **train station** on the High Street serves both the Ffestiniog line from Porthmadog and main-line train

---

THE CURSE OF THE RHODODENDRON

It is against the pervasive greyness of Blaenau Ffestiniog that Snowdonia's **rhododendron** invasion is most evident. Come in June and July, and many of Snowdonia's valleys are a riot of lilac and purple blooms. There's no doubting their aesthetic appeal, but these choking mats of foliage rank high on ecologists' hate lists. In their native Himalayas they grow into trees, but in Britain, where they've spread from the cultivated gardens of grand houses, they've become a noxious weed. Native flora can't compete with the dense canopy which cuts out so much sunlight that nothing can grow underneath – a major threat to native birds and insects which thrive in more open scrub. Volunteer action groups periodically target particular areas, blitzing a valley by digging out all the plants, but the rhododendron is proving difficult to contain.

services from Betws-y-Coed. The **tourist office** (April–Oct daily 10am–6pm; ☎01766/830360) is a little further up High Street, at Isallt, across the road from the *Queen's Hotel*. **Buses** stop either in the car park around the back, or outside *Y Commercial* pub on High Street.

Many of Blaenau Ffestiniog's visitors ride the train up from Porthmadog, visit a slate mine and leave, and this is reflected in the limited range of **accommodation**. There are good hotels, like the upmarket *Queen's Hotel*, right by the station at 1 High St (☎01766/830055, fax 830046; ③); otherwise, try *The Don*, a functional B&B at 147 High St (☎01766/830403; ①), or the plusher *Afallon*, almost a mile south of the tourist office on Manod Road (☎01766/830468; ①). A mile or so south along Manod Road (the A470), *Cae Du* (☎ & fax 01766/830847; ②) is a comfortable, seventeenth-century beamed farmhouse, beautifully situated at the end of a long drive. Five miles further south at Gellilydan there's *Tyddyn Du* (☎01766/590281; ②), an old farmhouse with a separate cottage suite reached on bus #35. The nearest **campsites** are *Bryn Tirion* four miles north in the Lledr Valley (see p.325) and *Llechrwd* (☎01766/590240), a similar distance southwest in Maentwrog.

The Town and mine tour

It is difficult to get a real feeling of what slate means to Blaenau Ffestiniog without a visit to the town's only remaining visitable slate mine, which presents entertaining and informative insights into the rigours of a miner's life. It's a mile or so north of town on the Betws-y-Coed road and reachable via bus #140, which runs hourly when the mine is open.

Although it's quite a pricey trip, a visit to the **Llechwedd Slate Caverns** (daily: March–Sept 10am–5.15pm; Oct–Feb 10am–4.15pm; single tour £6.95, both tours £10.50) is a must. For starters, this was the setting for the first ever Welsh language film, *Y Chwarelwr* (The Quarrymen) in 1935. You can walk around the reconstructed Victorian mining village, watch slate being split, shaped and engraved, and have a drink at *The Miners Arms* pub for nothing, but to visit some of the 25 miles of tunnels and sixteen working levels, you need to take one of two tours.

By way of a small train, the **Miners' Tramway Tour** takes you a third of a mile along one of the oldest levels, cut in 1846, disembarking a couple of times to admire the enormous Cathedral Cave and the open-air Chough's Cavern – both tilted at 30° to follow the slate's bedding plane – as you are plied with facts on slate mining. The awe-inspiring scale of the place justifies going on the tour even without the unconvincing tableaux of Victorian miners at work chained high up in the tops of the caverns. On the more dramatic **Deep Mine Tour** you're bundled onto specially designed carriages and lowered to one of the deepest parts of the mine down a 1-in-1.8 incline – Britain's steepest underground inclined railway. After donning waterproofs and headgear, you head off into the tunnels, guided by an irksome taped spiel of someone pretending to be a Victorian miner. That said, the content is good, concentrating on the working and social life of the miners who never saw daylight in winter, taking their breaks in a dank underground shelter known as a caban. The long caverns angling back into the gloom become increasingly impressive, culminating in one filled by a beautiful opalescent pool.

Alongside all of its largely deceased kin, the Llechwedd quarry employed the **Ffestiniog Railway** (see p.351) for the first leg of its journey to markets around the world, dispatching its dressed and packed product down to the ships at Porthmadog, thirteen miles away. Whether you're heading to Porthmadog or just want to ride the train, it is well worth considering doing part of the journey on foot (see box, p.346).

THE WELSH SLATE INDUSTRY

Slate is as much a symbol of north Wales as coal is of the south: it too peaked around the beginning of the twentieth century and shaped society throughout the period of British mass industrialization, drawing thousands from the impoverished hills to the relative wealth of the new towns which sprang up around the quarries.

Slate derives its name from the Old French word *esclater*, meaning "to split" – a perfect description of its most highly valued quality. Six hundred million years ago, what is now north Wales lay under the sea, gradually accumulating a thousand-foot-thick layer of fine-grained mud. In the collision zone of converging continental plates, the deposits were subject to immense pressures which caused the massive folding and mountain-building; the shale then metamorphosed into the purplish Cambrian slates of the Penrhyn and Dinorwig quarries (see p.417 and p.334) and the hundred-million-year-younger blue-grey Ordovician slates of Ffestiniog.

The Romans recognized the potential of the substance, and used it as roofing material for the houses of Segontium (see p.369), and Edward I used it extensively in his Iron Ring of castles around Snowdonia (see box, p.408). But it wasn't until around 1780 that Britain's Industrial Revolution took hold, leading to greater urbanization and a demand for roofing slates. As cities grew during the nineteenth and early twentieth centuries, millions of tons of slate were shipped around the globe, primarily for use as a cheap and durable roofing material. Hamburg was reroofed with Welsh slate after its fire of 1842, and it is the same material that still gives that rainy-day sheen to interminable rows of English mill-town houses.

By 1898, Welsh quarries – run by the English, like the coal and steel industries of the south – were producing half a million tons of dressed slate a year, almost all of it from Snowdonia. At Penrhyn and Dinorwig, mountains were hacked away in terraces, sometimes rising 2000ft above sea level, with teams of workers negotiating with the foreman for the choicest piece of rock and the selling price for what they produced. They often slept through the week in damp dormitories on the mountain, and tuberculosis was common, exacerbated by slate dust. At Blaenau Ffestiniog, the seams required mining underground rather than quarrying, but conditions were no better; miners even had to buy their own candles, their only light source. Few workers were allowed to join *Undeb Chwarelwyr Gogledd Cymru* (The North Wales Quarrymen's Union), and in 1900, the workers in Lord Penrhyn's quarry at Bethesda went out on strike. For three years they stayed out – one of Britain's longest ever industrial disputes – but failed to win any concessions. Those who got their jobs back were forced to work for even less money as a recession took hold, and although the two World Wars heralded mini-booms as bombed houses were replaced, the industry never recovered its nineteenth-century prosperity, and most quarries and mines closed in the 1950s.

Welsh slate was firmly established as the finest in the world at the 1862 London Exhibition, where one skilled craftsman produced a sheet 10ft long, 1ft wide and a sixteenth of an inch thick – so thin it could be flexed. Slate is now produced worldwide, and although none beats the quality of north Wales' output, this is little compensation as the region struggles to compete with inferior but cheaper Spanish slate. Until recently, the Snowdonia National Park Board insisted on local slate for roofing, but pressure from the European Union now forces them to accept slate "equivalent in colour, texture and weathering characteristics". The last criterion is a moot point, as the Spanish industry is barely thirty years old, but in the meantime, slate is being shipped from Spain while Welsh slate lies in the ground and unemployed quarrymen kick their heels. The quarries which do survive produce relatively small quantities, much of it used for floor tiling, road aggregate or an astonishing array of ashtrays and coasters etched with mountainscapes. More memorable are the roadside fences made from lines of broken, wafer-thin slabs, the beautifully carved slate fire surrounds and mantelpieces occasionally found in pubs and houses, as well as Westminster Abbey's memorial to Dylan Thomas which is made entirely of Penrhyn slate.

WALKS FROM BLAENAU FFESTINIOG

The following two walks can both be done from Blaenau Ffestiniog, but involve a fairly dull first mile easily avoided by catching the Ffestiniog Railway or driving to the reservoir at Tanygrisiau.

The gentler walk down into the **Vale of Ffestiniog** (4–5 miles; 2–3hr; descent only) follows the train line to its 360° loop, through sessile oak woods and past several cascades all the way to Tan-y-Bwlch. It is easy going, has some great views south to the Rhinogs (see p.309) and west to the Glaslyn estuary, and includes a ride back on the train; check the times at Tanygrisiau station and buy your ticket when you start to ensure a place on the return train. From the station, turn right past the Tanygrisiau information centre then take the second left – not the road beside the reservoir but the next one following the footpath signs. Cross the train line, then pass a car park on your left before turning left down a track and skirting behind the powerhouse. The path then sticks closely to the train line, occasionally crossing it. Even when there are several paths, you can't go far wrong if you keep the train lines in sight. The *Grapes* pub at Maentwrog, half a mile from Tan-y-Bwlch, is a great place to while away the time until the next train (or the one after that).

The second walk, a circuit of the peaks of **Moelwyn Mawr**, **Moelwyn Fach** and **Cnicht** (13 miles; 7hr; 4000ft), is tougher, longer and best left for a fine day. Even then, navigation isn't always easy, and you need both the Landranger #115 "Snowdon" map and the Landranger #124 "Dolgellau" map; the Outdoor Leisure 1:25,000 maps #17 ("Snowdon & Conwy Valley"), and #18 ("Harlech, Porthmadog & Bala") are better still. These factors make this far less popular than either Snowdon or the Glyders, but given the right conditions it can be a great walk past masses of old slate workings up onto some respectably lofty tops with panoramic views of southern Snowdonia.

From the station in Tanygrisiau, turn right past the information centre, then follow the road as it doubles back north away from the reservoir. After a couple of hundred yards, turn left at a T-junction onto a track up to a car park. Follow the footpath signs past the disused quarries in Cwmorthin, swinging west up to Bwlch-y-Rhosydd (not named on Landranger map), a small plateau strewn with slate waste and long-discarded slate-built workshops. The route from here up **Moelwyn Mawr** (2526ft) starts behind the largest building and heads south up an old incline, skirting left around a quarry and eventually reaching the northeast ridge route to the summit. From here, the route to **Moelwyn Fach** (2333ft) is straightforward, heading south down a generally easy ridge to Bwlch Stwlan then up the west ridge.

From Moelwyn Fach, turn west and follow the ridge to the hamlet of Croesor. If you have transport this makes a good starting point, cutting three miles off the walk since you avoid the stretch from Tanygrisiau to Bwlch-y-Rhosydd and back.

A road to the left of the disused chapel in Croesor leads to a stile from where the route up **Cnicht** (2260ft) is clearly signposted. From this angle, you're looking along the southwest-to-northeast ridge line of the mountain, giving it the triangular shape which earns it its rather fanciful "Matterhorn of Wales" nickname. The climb up is not particularly difficult, but it is steep in places. A series of almost equally high summits then give way to a shallow descent towards Llyn yr Adar. Just before the lake, a path cuts right and makes a gradual undulating southeast descent back to Bwlch-y-Rhosydd, from where you retrace your steps to Tanygrisiau.

About a mile down the track, the train stops at Tanygrisiau station, a short walk from the powerhouse for the **Ffestiniog Pumped Storage Power Station**, with a mildly diverting **information centre** (mid-July to Aug daily 10am–4.30pm, Easter–June, Sept & Oct closed Sat; free) and hour-long **guided tours** (hourly on the half-hour; £2.75) around rows of humming machinery and up to the Stwlan Dam, a buttressed structure in the hills above, visible throughout the Vale of Ffestiniog, that holds back the upper reservoir.

Eating, drinking and entertainment

Good **food** isn't especially abundant in Blaenau Ffestiniog, though *Penny's Café Restaurant*, 36 High St, does simple all-day breakfasts and snacks, and the decent *Lakeside Café*, by the information centre at Tanygrisiau, serves Welsh specialities. For something more substantial you're limited to the moderate *Myfanwys*, 4 Market Place (℡01766/830059) or the tasty dishes at the *Queen's Hotel* (see p.344). Most locals frequent the *Grapes* at Maentwrog, four miles south down the A496, a pub with a game-rich restaurant, *Flambard's* (℡01766/590208), and massive bar meals – leave room for the desserts if you can.

The *Wynnes Arms*, a short walk south of *Afallon* guesthouse, is Blaenau Ffestiniog's best traditional **pub**, though the newer *Queen's Hotel* has rapidly gained a dedicated clientele. About the only other thing to do in the evening is to listen to a **male voice choir**. The Brythoniaid choir rehearses at Ysgol y Moelwyn on Wynne Road near the hospital (Thurs 7.30pm); Côr Meibion y Moelwyn uses the Old Salem Chapel in Rhiw, half a mile north of the tourist office on the A470, then left as the road narrows (Tues & Fri 7.30pm).

Llan Ffestiniog, Trawsfynydd and Coed-y-Brenin

Blaenau Ffestiniog is surrounded by slate waste on three sides. The fourth drops away into the bucolic **Vale of Ffestiniog**, best explored using the Ffestiniog Railway (see p.351), or on the first walk described in the box opposite.

Heading south from Blaenau Ffestiniog, the A470 runs through the village of **LLAN FFESTINIOG** (Ffestiniog on maps, just Llan locally), three miles away, broadly following the remains of the old Great Western Railway route which ran across the broad open moors of the Migneint to Bala. **Walks** from Llan's former station run parallel with the old railway down into the wooded valley of the Afon Cynfal: follow the signposts to the lovely Rhaeadr Cynfal waterfalls, below a great rock known as Huw Llwyd's Pulpit, after a local seventeenth century wizard and bard. Rusted rails run as far as the greatest blot on the National Park's landscape, the defunct and hideously ugly **Trawsfynydd Nuclear Power Station**, a further four miles south. Trains removed the last of the fuel rods in 1995, but it's going to take 130 years to safely clear and landscape the area. In the meantime, cursory nature trails have been created around the plant and a visitor centre dispenses half-truths and irrelevant "facts". Both are best avoided. A far more edifying walk can be found just over a mile to the east, where a small lane off the A470 bumps down to the **Tomen-y-Mûr Roman fort**, straddling the trans-Wales route known as Sarn Helen. This bleak, inhospitable place must have been a difficult posting for any Roman soldier, more used to comparatively metropolitan comforts. The "tomen", or motte, from which the place takes its name, is a Norman addition to the site. Nearby are the scant remains of a Roman amphitheatre.

A mile or two south, the main road bypasses the low-key village of **TRAWSFYNY-DD**, best noted for its connection as the home of Ellis Evans, the poet awarded the Chair at the 1917 National Eisteddfod, held some six weeks after he had been killed in action in the Flanders trenches of World War I. His bardic pseudonym, Hedd Wyn ("beautiful peace"), became the title of a Welsh-language movie about his life and death, which was nominated for the foreign language Oscar in 1994. A statue of Evans stands in the village main street (which was also the set for much of the film), and the Eisteddfod Chair – draped in black and empty, as it was when it was awarded in 1917 – still sits in the family farmhouse down the road.

With the eastern flanks of the Rhinogs (see p.309) on the right, the A470 continues south to Dolgellau, past the **Rhiw Goch Ski Centre** (daily 9.30am–10pm), where two-hours' dry-slope skiing costs £12 and you can rent a self-catering log cabin

(☎01766/540219 or 540555), and through **Coed y Brenin** (The King's Forest). Economics dictate that this vast plantation comprises row upon row of pines, but there is the occasional patch of deciduous wood, including some lovely ancient oaklands, a few fine waterfalls and even the remains of various gold mines that have come and gone over the centuries. The best way to see all this is to drop in to the **visitor centre** at the northern end of the forest, just off the main road (Easter–Nov daily 10am–5pm; Dec–Easter Sat & Sun 11am–4pm; £1 per car) and pick up information on the terrific **cycle trails** throughout the forest, which penetrate into some of the loveliest parts. If you haven't brought a bike, you can hire one from the centre. There are also **orienteering** trails and a decent café on site.

THE LLŶN

An undulating spur from Snowdonia's mountainous heartland, the **Llŷn** takes its name from an Irish word for "peninsula", an apt description for this most westerly part of north Wales, which, until the fifth century, had a significant Irish population and which still maintains an atmosphere not unlike parts of western Ireland. The Llŷn's cliff-and-cove-lined finger of land juts out south and west, separating Cardigan and Caernarfon bays, its hills tapering away along the ancient route to **Aberdaron** where pilgrims sailed for **Ynys Enlli (Bardsey Island)**. Ancestors of those last Irish inhabitants may have been responsible for the numerous hillforts and cromlechs found on the Llŷn, particularly the hut circles of the **Tre'r Ceiri** hillfort. But these days, it's the beaches, rather than the prehistoric remains, that lure people to the south-coast family resorts of **Cricieth**, **Pwllheli** and **Abersoch**, and unless you want to rent windsurfers or canoes, it's preferable to make for the much quieter coves punctuating the north coast or press on along the narrow roads that dawdle down towards Aberdaron.

The Llŷn is approached through one of two gateway towns linked by the A487, an effective boundary between Snowdonia proper and the peninsula. **Porthmadog**, nestling into the crook of the elbow formed by the Cambrian coast and the Llŷn, is primarily of interest for its proximity to the private dream village of **Portmeirion**, reached on Wales' finest narrow-gauge train line, the **Ffestiniog Railway**. The Llŷn's northern coast comes to an abrupt end at the mouth of the Menai Strait, guarded by the awesome fortress that forms the centrepiece of **Caernarfon**, a good base for both the Llŷn and central Snowdonia.

Not even Snowdonia feels more remote than the tip of the Llŷn, and nowhere in Wales is more staunchly Welsh: road signs are still bilingual but the English is frequently daubed out; on the Llŷn proper, Stryd Fawr is used instead of High Street, and in most local shops you'll only hear Welsh spoken. There are pockets that are being bought up by English second-home owners and other immigrants, many of whom make no attempt to learn the language, and something like twenty percent of all houses on the Llŷn are either holiday homes or weekend retreats. But the peninsula remains defiantly Welsh, nearly eight decades after the meeting in Pwllheli that saw the formation of the Welsh nationalist party, Plaid Cymru. It is also a stronghold of the shadowy **Meibion Glyndŵr**, or "Sons of Glendower" (see Contexts, p.459), whose incendiary tactics remain legendary despite a quiet spell of late.

The Llŷn's bountiful caravan parks can seem unappealing to campers and often only accept families and couples, but a local ruling allows anyone with a field to run a **campsite** for one month a year, and through the summer they spring up everywhere. **Trains** and National Express **buses** both serve Cricieth and Pwllheli, leaving an extensive network of infrequent buses to cover the rest. Better still, the peninsula's quiet narrow lanes through rolling pastoral land are ideal for cycling, and you can **rent bikes** in Pwllheli and Porthmadog (see p.358 & opposite). If you want to do a little walking on the peninsula, check out the *Llŷn Footpath Network* package (£1.75), containing eight linear walks which can all be made circular by bus using the timetable included. It's a nice idea, but incompletely executed, so with a head for maps – the OS 1:25000 Explorer #12 and 13 are best – you may be better off devising your own walks.

Porthmadog and around

The Vale of Ffestiniog and Beddgelert's Glaslyn River meet the sea at Tremadog Bay, where the Cambrian coast (see Chapter Four) makes a sharp left to become the south side of the Llŷn. The bustling town of **PORTHMADOG** drapes itself around the northern shore of Traeth Bach, the mountain-backed common estuary, sadly making little of its wonderful position. It was once the busiest slate port in north Wales but now only rates as a pleasant enough town to use as a base for a couple of nights. Two things it does make a fuss about are the Italianate folly of **Portmeirion**, two miles east of the town, and the wonderful **Ffestiniog Railway** that originally carried down slates from Blaenau Ffestiniog through thirteen miles of verdant mountain scenery to Porthmadog-made schooners for export.

Arrival, information and accommodation

The main-line **train** station and the Welsh Highland Railway station (see p.371) are at the north end of the High Street; the Ffestiniog station is located down by the harbour, about half a mile to the south. In between, the helpful **tourist office** is at the southern end of High Street (Easter–Oct daily 10am–6pm; Nov–Easter daily except Tues 10am–5pm; ☎01766/512981, *porthmadog.tic@gwynedd.gov.uk*). A little further up High Street are the stops for both National Express **buses** from Chester, Liverpool and Manchester, and local bus services. Note that Dolgellau buses go inland through Coed-y-Brenin: take the train if you want to stick to the coast. There's **bike hire** from K K Cycles at 141 High Street (☎01766/512310), where a day's pedalling will set you back £8.

While limited budgets are well catered for, there's not much really decent **accommodation** without pressing on to Criccieth (see p.354) or Harlech (see p.310), unless you're prepared to splash out for a night at the swanky *Hotel Portmeirion*.

Hotels and guesthouses

Golden Fleece Inn, Tremadog, a mile north of Porthmadog (☎01766/512421). The best bet for pub accommodation with pleasant rooms above an excellent bar. ②.

Hotel Portmeirion, Portmeirion (☎01766/770000, fax 771331, *www.portmeirion.wales.com*). Elegant individually designed suites in the hotel or in serviced cottages throughout Portmeirion village. The more expensive suites will strain your credit, but it is worth asking about deals on low-season, midweek and weekend breaks. The most atmospheric of the cottages are often booked months in advance for popular times. Tennis and a heated outdoor pool. ⑥.

Mrs Jones, 57 East Ave (☎01766/513087). Very comfortable guesthouse near the train station. ①.

Mrs Williams, 12 Snowdon St (☎01766/512635). One of the town's best-value B&Bs. ①.

The Royal Sportsman, Avenue Rd (☎01766/512015, fax 512490, *www.royalsportsman.co.uk*). About the best hotel in the town, near the train station. ④.

Skellerns, 35 Madog St (☎01766/512843). The cheapest guesthouse around, near the Ffestiniog train station a 2min walk north from the tourist office. ①.

Treforris, Garth Rd (☎01766/512853). Large house overlooking the harbour to the west. Take Bank Place off High Street then left onto Garth Road – a 15min walk in all. ①.

Yr Hen Fecus, Lombard St (☎01766/514625). Relaxed and pleasant B&B above a deservedly popular restaurant (see p.354). ②.

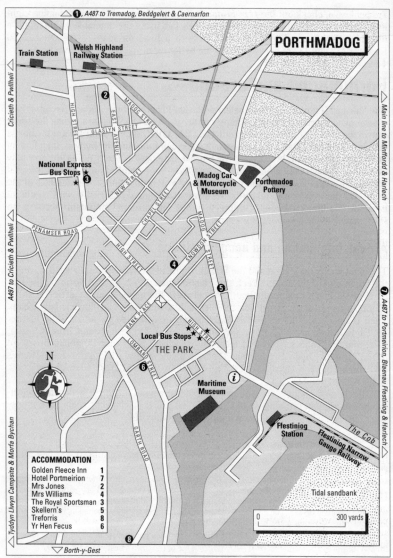

PORTHMADOG

△ ❶ A487 to Tremadog, Beddgelert & Caernarfon

Train Station

Welsh Highland Railway Station

◁ Criccieth & Pwllheli

Main line to Minffordd & Harlech ▷

❷

HIGH STREET

EAST AVENUE

MADOC STREET

GLASLYN STREET

National Express Bus Stops ★ ❸

NEW STREET

CHAPEL STREET

Madog Car & Motorcycle Museum

Porthmadog Pottery

◁ A497 to Criccieth & Pwllheli

PENAMSER ROAD

HIGH STREET

MADOC STREET

SNOWDON STREET

❹

❺

△ ❼ A487 to Portmeirion, Blaenau Ffestiniog & Harlech ▷

BANK PLACE

Local Bus Stops ★★

HIGH STREET

THE PARK

LOMBARD STREET

❻

Maritime Museum

ℹ️

N

GARTH ROAD

Ffestiniog Station

Ffestiniog Narrow Gauge Railway

The Cob

◁ Tydyn Llwyn Campsite & Morfa Bychan

Tidal sandbank

ACCOMMODATION	
Golden Fleece Inn	1
Hotel Portmeirion	7
Mrs Jones	2
Mrs Williams	4
The Royal Sportsman	3
Skellern's	5
Treforris	8
Yr Hen Fecus	6

0   300 yards

❽

▽ Borth-y-Gest

© Crown copyright

Bunkhouse, self-catering and campsite

Eric's Bunkhouse, Prenteg (☎01766/512199). Two miles north of Porthmadog on the A498 to Beddgelert, opposite *Eric Jones' Café* (see p.353), this is a rock climbers' bunkhouse where you can get a mattress for around £3 a night and a flasher one next door with kitchen and shower for a fiver.

Hotel Portmeirion (see overleaf). The hotel also runs fully equipped luxurious self-catering accommodation (two to eight people) let by the week, or half-week in winter. Four-berth cottages cost from £300 to £500 a week.

Tyddyn Llwyn, Black Rock Rd (☎01766/512205). High-standard family campsite on a grassy hill-side with all facilities and a bar on site. A 15min walk along the road to Morfa Bychan following Bank Place southwest off High Street. March–Oct.

The Town and around

Porthmadog would never have existed at all without the entrepreneurial ventures of a Lincolnshire MP named William Alexander Madocks, who named the town and its elder brother Tremadog, a mile to the north, after both himself and the Welsh Prince Madog, who some say sailed from the nearby Ynys Fadog (Madog's Island) to North America in 1170. In 1805, Madocks fancied he could get himself some good grazing land by draining a thousand acres of estuarine mudflats here; he bought Ynys Fadog, built an earth embankment, then started on Tremadog. The towns prospered and, buoyed by their success, Madocks embarked on a project to enclose a further 7000 acres by sealing off the Glaslyn estuary with a mile-long embankment known as The Cob, southeast of present-day Porthmadog. Madocks died before the project came to fruition, but the Glaslyn River was rerouted and soon scoured out a deep watercourse close to the north bank, ideal for a slate wharf. This was the first of several which, boosted by the completion of the Ffestiniog Railway in 1836, spread along a waterfront thick with orderly heaps of slate and the masts of merchant ships. The boom time has long since slowed, and slate traffic had ceased by the middle of the twentieth century – today, only a few dozen pleasure yachts grace the harbour.

The waterfront is still the most interesting place to wander, not least because the last surviving slate shed contains the recently refurbished **Maritime Museum** (Easter & June–Sept daily 10am–6pm; £1). Amongst the obligatory ships in glass cases, panels tell of the town's shipbuilding role and its importance in carrying slate around the world.

Just across the harbour, the Ffestiniog Railway (see below) begins its ascent, but Porthmadog has a second narrow-gauge line, the far less interesting **Welsh Highland Railway** (Easter & mid-May to Sept 6–8pm daily; £1.75), running from just near the train station along a mile of track. Plans are afoot to rebuild the railway all the way to Beddgelert and Caernarfon, though it's a venture not without its controversies and problems (see p.371).

On rainy days, you're best off heading for the northeastern end of Snowdon Street, where you can throw a pot, paint a plate or dip a candle at the **Porthmadog Pottery** in Snowdon Mill (Mon–Fri 9.30am–5pm; July & Aug daily), or admire the bodywork on show next door at the **Madog Car & Motorcycle Museum** (Easter–Oct Mon–Sat 10am–5pm; £1.75). The gleaming collection of exclusively British bikes and cars, from the 1920s through to the mid-1960s, includes a lovely belt-driven 1924 Sunbeam and a 1948 water-cooled Scott Flying Squirrel.

All the sand and water around Porthmadog might leave you hankering for a swim. **Black Rock Sands**, three miles west at **MORFA BYCHAN**, is the best beach, a two mile long swath of golden sands with sublime views down to Harlech and up to the peaks of Snowdonia. It's also a popular boy racers' spot, as it's possible to drive a car straight on to the beach. The #96 bus goes there in summer, or there's a Cricieth-bound footpath along the coast starting on Lôn Cei (Quay Lane) at the back of the harbour and reaching Black Rock Sands by way of **BORTH-Y-GEST**, a small former boat-building village enveloping a picturesque harbour a mile south of Porthmadog. There's nothing to do here but enjoy the estuary views and eat at the waterfront *Sea View Restaurant*, really more a pleasant café.

The Ffestiniog Railway

Without a doubt, the **Ffestiniog Railway** (Easter–Oct 4–10 times daily; Nov–Easter mainly weekends; return to Blaenau Ffestiniog £13.80; return to Tan-y-Bwlch £8.40) ranks as Wales' finest narrow-gauge rail line, twisting and looping up 650ft from Porthmadog to the slate mines at Blaenau Ffestiniog, thirteen miles away. The gutsy little engines make light of the steep gradients and chug through stunning scenery that ranges from broad estuarine expanses to the deep greens of the Vale of Ffestiniog, only fading to grey on the final approaches to the slate-bound upper terminus at Blaenau Ffestiniog.

When the line opened in 1836, it carried slates from the mines down to the port with the help of gravity, horses riding with the goods, then hauling the empty carriages back up again. Steam had to be introduced to cope with the 100,000 tons of slate that Blaenau Ffestiniog was churning out each year in the late nineteenth century, but after the slate-roofing market collapsed between the wars, passengers were carried instead until the line was finally abandoned in 1946. Most of the tracks and sleepers had disappeared by 1954, when, encouraged by the success of the Talyllyn Railway (see p.297), a bunch of dedicated volunteers began to reconstruct the line, only completing the entire route in 1982.

Leaving Porthmadog, trains cross The Cob then stop at Minffordd, an interchange point for the Cambrian coast main-line and the mile-long walk to Portmeirion (see below). A mile further on, Penrhyn station presents the possibility of a four-mile walk through the woods of Coed Llyn y Garnedd to either the third station, Plas Halt, from where it is a short stroll to *The Grapes* pub at Maentwrog (see p.346), or the nearby fourth station at Tan-y-Bwlch. Short **nature trails** spur off from Tan-y-Bwlch, as does the longer Vale of Ffestiniog walk (see box p.346) which passes Dduallt station by the spiral on its way to Tanygrisiau, the start of the Moelwyn/Cnicht walk (see p.346). You can get on and off as frequently as the timetable allows, and the journey is included in the North and Mid Wales Rover ticket (see Basics, p.29); you must pay £2 each way for bikes, but call first to confirm that there's room for them. Sit on the right of the carriage going up to get the best view of the scenery.

At the Ffestiniog Railway's imposing station in Porthmadog's High Street, a small but interesting **museum** (open when trains are running; free) presents the history of the line and exhibits some of the original rolling stock, including horse wagons.

Portmeirion

The other main lure of Porthmadog is the unique Italianate private village of **PORT-MEIRION** (daily 9.30am–5.30pm; £4; *www.portmeirion.wales.com*), set on a small rocky peninsula in Tremadog Bay, three miles east near Minffordd. You can visit the village by train: both the main-line and Ffestiniog trains, as well as buses #1 and #2, stop in Minffordd, from where it is a signposted 25-minute walk to Portmeirion. You can also walk from Porthmadog in an hour following the footpath parallel to the Ffestiniog line across The Cob.

Perhaps best known as "The Village" in the 1960s British cult TV series *The Prisoner*, Portmeirion is the brainchild of eccentric architect Clough Williams-Ellis and his dream to build an ideal village which enhances rather than blends in with the surroundings, using a "gay, light-opera sort of approach". The result certainly is theatrical: a stage set with a lucky dip of unwanted buildings arranged to distort perspectives and reveal tantalizing glimpses of the sea or the expansive sands behind. Ironically, a project of such warped genius would be impossible today, as one of the buildings razed in the construction of the *grand projet* was the native Welsh castle, Castell Deudraeth, and no planning authority – let alone the tourist boards who promote Portmeirion as if their very lives depended on it – would countenance such an action now.

In the 1920s, Williams-Ellis began scouring Britain for a suitable island – he believed only an island could provide the seclusion for his project – but having found nothing he could afford, was gratified to be offered a piece of wilderness four miles from his home, Plâs Brodanw, at Garreg (see opposite). A Victorian house already on the site was turned into a hotel, the income from which providing funds for Williams-Ellis's "Home for Fallen Buildings". Endangered buildings from all over Britain and abroad were broken down, transported and rebuilt, every conceivable style being plundered: a Neoclassical colonnade from Bristol; Siamese figures on Ionic columns; a Jacobean town hall; a Buddha; and the Italianate touches, a Campanile and a Pantheon. Williams-Ellis designed his village around a Mediterranean piazza, piecing together a scaled-down nest of loggias, grand porticoes and tiny terracotta-roofed houses, and painting them in pastels: turquoise, ochre and buff yellows. Continually surprising, with hidden entrances and cherubs popping out of crevices, the ensemble is wildly eclectic, yet never quite inappropriate.

Long-term structural considerations were evidently not foremost in Williams-Ellis's mind during the construction and the place soon fell into a state of tattiness, but a recent programme of renovation has ensured that Portmeirion is again looking spruce. More than three thousand visitors a day come to ogle in summer when it can be a delight; fewer in winter when it is just plain bizarre. And for one weekend in September, Portmeirion hosts *The Prisoner* convention when fans book the place out to re-enact scenes as best they can – though, as much of the series was shot in the studio, the juxtaposition of Portmeirion's buildings doesn't match that of The Village.

Sometimes dismissed as the grandest folly of all and a symbol of Britain's fascination with eccentrics, Portmeirion at least supports Williams-Ellis's guiding principle that natural beauty and profitable development needn't be mutually exclusive. Architectural idealism aside, it was always intended to be self-sustaining, much of the finance coming from the opulent waterside *Hotel Portmeirion* (see p.349). In the evening, when the village is closed to the public, patrons get to see the place at its best: peaceful, even ghostly. The hotel also takes up many of the cottages that make up the village, so much of your time will be spent outside, or popping into the shops selling *Prisoner* memorabilia or gaudy Portmeirion pottery. Guests and visitors can eat at the expensive hotel-restaurant (see overleaf), but most will be content with a couple of cafés – better still, bring a picnic and find a spot on the easy paths that lace the dell and its cloak of exotic forest.

Clough Williams-Ellis's talents are also in evidence four miles northeast of Portmeirion at his ancestral home **Plâs Brodanw** (daily 9am–5pm; £1.75), near Garreg, where whimsical topiary creates a formal, yet not quite manicured, setting for a solid Welsh stone house. The house itself is closed to the public, leaving only the gardens and some of the grounds, visited by following the "To the Tower" sign opposite the entrance. A ten-minute woodland walk brings you to the outlook tower, with expansive views of Porthmadog and the Moelwyns.

Eating, drinking and entertainment

Allport's, cnr of Snowdon and Madoc sts. Ordinary-looking fish-and-chip shop deemed the "Best in Wales" in 1995.

Australia Inn, High St. Lively town centre pub with regular karaoke nights and discos.

Brodanw Arms, Llanfrothen, five miles northwest of Porthmadog. Slate-floored traditional inn known locally as *Y Ring* and currently the only pub anywhere near Porthmadog with live entertainment. Saturday night usually sees live music and occasional comedy, while Thursday and Sunday are typically the preserve of local folkies. Real ales, pool tables, a beer garden, kids' play area and decent bar meals should please just about everyone.

Eric's Café, Prenteg, a mile east of Tremadog on the A498. Good, solid standard food wolfed down by climbers of the Tremadog crags across the road. There's a good notice board, a small stock of climbing gear and guidebooks for sale, and Eric runs an indoor climbing wall across the road (£1.75). Usually open to 6pm, later on summer weekends.

The Golden Fleece Inn and Bistro, Tremadog. An ancient coaching inn on Tremadog's main square with a cramped "cave bar" serving inexpensive meals around the fire or out in the courtyard. There's a blackboard bistro menu in the moderately priced restaurant out the back.

The Harbour Restaurant, High St (☎01766/512471). Not surprisingly, seafood dominates the menu in this simply decorated but very good restaurant. Open daily in summer, Thurs–Sat in winter.

Owen's, 71 High St. Sturdy and unremarkable daytime café; good for breakfasts and the like.

Passage to India Tandoori, 26a Lombard St (☎01766/512144). Typical curry restaurant menu disguises the fact that this is one of the best such places around. It's across the park, west of the High Street.

Portmeirion Restaurant, *Hotel Portmeirion* (☎01766/770000). Delightful, expensive hotel restaurant with views across the Traeth Bach sands. Inventive modern cuisine employs local game and seafood. Jacket and tie are required in the evening, and reservations are advisable.

The Ship, Lombard St. Popular pub noted for its good beer, its bar meals and the highly praised but reasonably priced Cantonese- and Peking-style restaurant upstairs.

The Ship and Castle, High St. Make up your own mind as to whether this youthful pub with lively jukebox lives up to its local moniker, "The Shit and Hassle".

Yr Hen Fecus, Lombard St (☎01766/514625). Imaginative, moderately priced eating, including some decent vegetarian dishes, served in café-style surroundings. Unlicensed, so bring your own booze.

Cricieth and around

Twenty years ago, seeing defaced road signs around north Wales was an everyday occurrence, as nationalists made their point about monoglot English instructions with the help of paint. Nowadays, with most signs bilingual, only the occasional bit of daubing can be seen. **CRICIETH**, five miles west of Porthmadog, is a case in point – official signs still tend to spell the name with a double C in the middle, which is a sound produced by the English alphabet, not the Welsh, where one C suffices. Consequently, signs hereabouts generally have a splash of colour or a whited-out gap through their middle, as the offending extra letter gets ritually removed. In a country so seemingly haphazard about place-name spelling, such pedantry might come as a surprise to visitors.

Cricieth, however, has depended on the English for its growth, and it's still smarter and more anglicized than its neighbouring towns. When sea-bathing became the Victorian fashion, English families descended on Cricieth's sweeping sand and shingle beach. Aided by the rail line, they built the long terraces of guesthouses that grew up behind the beach, which subsequently decayed and were reborn in recent years as retirement homes. These days, beach-bound holiday-makers go further west, leaving a quietly amiable resort which curiously abounds with good places to stay and great restaurants, making it a convenient touring base for the peninsula and Porthmadog.

There's not much to see or do here, though, apart from visiting David Lloyd George's childhood home a mile or so to the west at Llanystumdwy (see p.356), and the battle-worn **Cricieth Castle** (April–Sept daily 10am–6pm; £2.20; unrestricted free access at all other times; CADW), dominating the coastline with what remains of its twin, D-towered gatehouse. The castle was started by Llywelyn ap Iorwerth in 1230, but strengthened and finished by Edward I, who took it in 1283, and by his successors. During his 1404 rebellion, Owain Glyndŵr grabbed it back, only to raze it and leave little remaining besides a plan of broken walls and the gatehouse. It is a great spot to sit and look over Cardigan Bay to Harlech or down the ripples of the Llŷn coast in the late afternoon, but leave time for the fairly workaday exhibition on Welsh castles and a wonderful animated cartoon based on the twelfth-century Cambrian travels of Giraldus Cambrensis (see box opposite) in the ticket office. If all you want are glorious views, come out of hours or clamber up the neighbouring hill behind Marine Terrace. The view there is just as good and is set off by the hulking castle.

Just down from the castle towards the beach, don't miss the impressive community-run **Chapel of Art** (*Capel Celfyddyd*; April–Oct Tues–Sun 10am–6pm; winter call for

GIRALDUS CAMBRENSIS AND HIS JOURNEY THROUGH WALES

Through his books *The Journey Through Wales* and *The Description of Wales*, Norman-Welsh **Giraldus Cambrensis** (Gerald of Wales or Gerallt Cymro) has left us with a vivid picture of life in Wales in the twelfth century. Gerald worked his way up the ecclesiastical hierarchy, but failed to achieve his life-long goal, the bishopric of St David's, mainly because of his reformist ideals.

Gerald's influence in Wales made him the first choice when **Baldwin**, the Archbishop of Canterbury, needed someone to accompany him on his 51-day tour around Wales in 1188, preaching the cross and recruiting for a third Crusade that was designed to dislodge the infidel leader Saladin from Jerusalem. Three thousand signed up for the Crusade on Baldwin's circular tour from Hereford in England across south Wales, up the Cambrian coast to Caernarfon, along the north coast and back down the Marches, during which time he said Mass in each of the four cathedrals: Llandaff, St David's, Bangor and St Asaph, the first Archbishop of Canterbury to do so.

During the tour, Gerald amassed much of the material for his books, where he sensitively portrayed the landscape and its people, commenting that "the Welsh generosity and hospitality are the greatest of all virtues", parrying "If they come to a house where there is any sign of affluence and they are in a position to take what they want, there is no limit to their demands." But on the whole, he shows sympathy for the Welsh, coming up with a conclusion that has an oddly contemporary ring: "if only Wales could find the place it deserves in the heart of its rulers, or at least if those put in charge locally would stop behaving so vindictively and submitting the Welsh to such shameful ill-treatment".

details; donation requested), a nineteenth-century chapel that has been beautifully restored to house exhibitions – many are culled from amongst the thriving local artistic community, although those from further afield get a look in too. It's also a venue for year-round concerts and classes – call ahead to see what's on (☎01766/523570, *www.the-coa.org.uk*) – and a good place to check out happenings in the vicinity. Outside, the front of the chapel has been relandscaped with an International Pottery Path, opened on 31 December 1999, comprised of hundreds of pottery tiles sent by artists the world over.

If you're here during the third week of June, you might want to attend the week-long **Cricieth Festival** of jazz and classical music, which takes place at various venues around town: call ☎01766/522680 for information and bookings.

Practicalities

Both National Express **buses** from the north Wales coast, and frequent local buses from Porthmadog and Pwllheli stop at Y Maes, the open square at the centre of town flanked by The Green. At the time of writing, a portakabin on Y Maes is also the temporary home of the **tourist office** (May–Sept Mon–Sat 10am–6pm, Sun 2–6pm; ☎01766/523633). **Trains** on the Cambrian coast line stop at the station, a couple of hundred yards west. For such a small town, good **restaurants** are surprisingly abundant in Cricieth and offer the best range of eating on the peninsula.

Hotels and guesthouses

Bron Eifion Country House Hotel (☎01766/522385, fax 522003). Beautiful Victorian country house full of carved Oregon pine and set in five acres nearly a mile west of the centre of town. ⑤.

Craig-y-Môr, West Parade (☎01766/522830). Well-appointed rooms, some with excellent sea views, and home-cooked meals for around £12. Closed Nov–Feb. ②.

Moelwyn, 27–29 Mona Terrace (☎ & fax 01766/522500). Unfussy en-suite rooms with sea views and TVs. Above one of the best restaurants in town, with discounted meals for guests. Closed Dec–March. ②.

Muriau, Lôn Fel (☎ & fax 01766/522337, *www.smoothHound.co.uk/hotels/muriau.html*). Excellent-value seventeenth-century gentleman's residence with a congenial, if slightly formal atmosphere, large tasteful rooms overlooking formal lawns and £12 evening meals. ③.

Mynydd Ednyfed, Caernarfon Rd, a mile north on the B4411 (☎01766/523269). Luxurious country-house hotel with cheerful, floral but not over-fussy rooms and a strong sporting bent. There's a tennis court, gym and solarium on site, and shooting and fishing catered for. Classy, moderately priced food, too. ④.

Seabank Hotel, Marine Terrace (☎01766/522255). One of Cricieth's cheapest waterfront guest-houses, 200 yards west of the castle and with a good bar. ③.

Hostel, bunkhouse and campsites

Budget Accommodation, 11 Marine Terrace (☎01766/523098). Hostel-style accommodation in twin rooms for £9 per person right on Cricieth seafront below the castle. Open May–Sept.

Mynydd Du (☎01766/522533). Simple campsite a mile towards Porthmadog on the A497. April–Oct.

Tyddyn Morthwyl Farm and Caravan Park (☎01766/522115). Not the closest but the nicest campsite, on the Caernarfon road, a little over a mile north of Cricieth. A bargain price (£3 per person) includes hot showers and there's a spacious bunkhouse in converted farm buildings for £5 a night. Book ahead and bring a sleeping bag.

Eating and drinking

Blue China Tearooms, Marine Terrace. The pick of the bunch for daytime coffee and cake.

Bron Eifion Country House Hotel (see overleaf). Expensive, innovative and highly rated cuisine; strong on steak and seafood.

Bryn Hir Arms, Stryd Fawr. Pleasant, if slightly chintzy, pub with decent, cheap food until 9pm.

Granville's, 28 Stryd Fawr. Bright and cheerful café-cum-restaurant, good from breakfast snacks right through to evening dinners. A good fixed price menu at £6.95 for a three-course lunch or early dinner. Open daily 9.30am–9pm.

Lion Hotel, The Green. Popular town pub with a good beer garden and live and varied entertainment on Tues and Sat evenings.

Moelwyn (see overleaf). International menu with superb seafood and a comprehensive wine list in airy non-smoking surroundings with great sea views. Three-course Sun lunches for £9.

Mynydd Ednyfed, Caernarfon Rd (see above). Tasty, carefully presented and moderately priced food in a country-house hotel a mile north of town.

Poachers Restaurant, 66 Stryd Fawr (☎01766/522512). Highly commendable French-style café-restaurant with a three-course dinner for under £8 if you eat before 7pm (not Sat).

The Prince of Wales, Stryd Fawr. The best of the town's pubs: a multi-room local with a couple of guest beers, inexpensive bar meals and live music most Tues evenings.

Tir-a-Môr, 1–3 Mona Terrace (☎01766/523084). Even amongst such stiff competition, this is undoubtedly the pick of the town's restaurants: not strictly Italian, but with a large range of reasonably priced Italian-influenced dishes, many using fresh local ingredients, and an extensive wine list. It is just downhill from the square in the centre of town. Evenings only, closed Sun.

Llanystumdwy

Though born in Manchester, the Welsh nationalist, social reformer and British Prime Minister David Lloyd George (1864–1945) lived in his mother's home village of **LLANYSTUMDWY**, a mile west of Cricieth, until 1881, when he was nearly eighteen. He grew up in Highgate House, the home of his uncle, the village cobbler, which is now part of the **Lloyd George Museum** (Easter–May Mon–Fri and bank holiday weekends 10.30am–5pm; June Mon–Sat 10.30am–5pm; July–Sept daily 10.30am–5pm; Oct Mon–Fri 11am–4.30pm; £3). A fairly pedestrian collection of gifts, awards and caskets honouring Lloyd George with the freedom of various cities illustrate the great man's popularity, and the museum's displays are full of anecdotes and little-known facts about him, with weighty and hagiographic explanatory panels and a couple of short films giving a broad sweep of his life.

The video presentations demonstrate some of his talent as a witty and powerful orator, but only hint at the figure described by Churchill as "a man of action, resource and creative energy, [who] stood, when at his zenith, without a rival". Read between the lines to get a sense of the betrayal felt by many Welsh nationalists as his interest turned from the politics of Wales to those of Westminster.

Rustic late nineteenth-century beds and dressers furnish Lloyd George's wooden-floored two-up, two-down house, in a garden laid out much as it would have been in Lloyd George's day. Before ambling through the garden, walk down the path towards the River Dwyfor, beside which Lloyd George is buried under a memorial – a boulder and two simple plaques designed by Portmeirion designer Clough Williams-Ellis (see p.352). Bus #3 runs from Porthmadog and Cricieth, through the village on its way to Pwllheli.

Pwllheli and around

The undoubted "capital" of the Llŷn peninsula, **PWLLHELI** (pronounced something like "Poothl-heli") is a strange place: not quite a seaside resort, despite its best efforts, neither yet a town that makes much of its illustrious history. Its principal function, for locals and visitors alike, is as the area's major market place and transport hub, and, as such, you're likely to find yourself here at some point. That being said, after faintly twee Cricieth, full of English émigrés and craftspeople, or the braying yachties' heaven of Abersoch, there's something refreshingly real about Pwllheli, where the absolute defining feature is its Welshness. Even in the height of summer, you'll hear far more Welsh spoken here than English. It was at the *Maesgwyn Temperance Hotel* (now a pet shop on Y Maes, marked with a plaque) during the National Eisteddfod in August 1925 that six people, three from *Byddin Ymreolwyr Cymru* (the Army of Welsh Home Rulers) and three from *Y Mudiad Cymreig* (The Welsh Movement) met to form Plaid Cymru (see Contexts, p.456). Pwllheli also has one of the few exclusively Welsh-language bookshops in the country, *Llên Llŷn* , on Y Maes, owned by writer Alun Jones.

Despite the fact that the town appears largely Victorian, Pwllheli's market charter dates back to 1355. Each Wednesday, the latter-day incarnation of the weekly **market** breaks out just yards west of the train station and tourist office, on the central square of Y Maes – a great time to idly browse and eavesdrop on the *Cymraeg* chatter of youngsters and rainhat-clad old ladies alike. From Y Maes, Ffordd-y-Cob leads south, past the spruce new **marina** (☎01758/701219), home of numerous yachts and the local sailing club (☎01758/614442). Not so long ago, this was the hub of Pwllheli's considerable shipbuilding and fishing industries, now dwindled to nothing. Continue down Ffordd-y-Cob to Pwllheli's ghostly **West End**, a Victorian seaside development that stretches along a promenade backed by pastel-shaded villas, some of which are in chronic states of disrepair. Although the **beach** is clean enough, with great views over to the Rhinog mountains of Snowdonia and down to St Tudwal's islands, the net effect of the place is dispiriting, as it succeeds in being neither lively and resort-like nor wild and remote.

In such a Welsh corner of the land, it is perhaps ironic that Pwllheli's status and fame has been preserved in the last half-century thanks to the nearby presence of a vast holiday camp, formerly one of the mainstays of the Butlin's empire. The camp, three miles east of town, is rather down-at-heel these days, having been jettisoned by Butlin's and now rather sporadically open as **Hafan-y-Môr** (details ☎01758/612112) and pitched firmly at the kids' market.

Practicalities

The town spreads out from Y Maes, the central square where National Express and local **buses** pull in. The **train station**, northern terminus of the Cambrian coast line, stands a few yards to the east, opposite the **tourist office**, Sgwar yr Orsaf/Station Square (April–Oct daily 10am–6pm; Nov–March Mon–Wed & Fri–Sat 10am–4.30pm; ☎01758/613000, *pwllhelitic@gwynedd.gov.uk*). You can **rent mountain bikes** during the summer at £10 a day from Llŷn Cycle Centre, 2 Ala Rd (☎01758/612414).

The best of the local **accommodation** is scattered around Pwllheli, but in the centre, try *26 Stryd Fawr* (☎01758/613172; ①), with TVs in all rooms, or, bang opposite, the better-appointed *Bank Place* (☎01758/612103; ①). Better still, the *Victoria Hotel* on Embankment Road (☎01758/612843; ①) is a cosy pub with nine comfortable rooms. Four hundred yards away by the beach is the commendable *Llys Gwyrfai*, 14 West End Parade (☎01758/614877; ①), a comfortable guesthouse with sea views, en-suite rooms and home-cooked meals. The best place to stay in the vicinity, though, is *Plas Bodegroes* (March–Oct; ☎01758/612363, fax 701247; ⑥), a very swish Georgian country house set in parkland at Efailnewydd, two miles northwest of Pwllheli on the A497, and serving superb meals. Non-smokers are well catered for at *Hen Ficerdy* (March–Oct; ☎01758/612162; ②), a mile northeast of Pwllheli on the A499 in Abererch (turn left at the chapel), a former country vicarage with great views of Cardigan Bay; or try *Gwynfryn Farm*, just over a mile north of Pwllheli (☎ & fax 01758/614324; ①), a working organic dairy farm-cum-B&B with comfortable rooms, self-catering units and a low-cost, high-summer **campsite**. The farm is up Gaol Street, left of the Salem Chapel – branch left, then straight on until the entrance is signposted on the left. Other campsites include the expensive *Hendre Caravan Park*, Efailnewydd (March–Oct; ☎01758/613416), a mile northwest on the A497.

If you have the money, *Plas Bodegroes* (see above; dinner only and closed to non-guests on Mon) could present you with the best **eating** you'll experience in Wales. Five smallish courses of innovative, beautifully presented food with wine won't give you much change out of £40, but expect to be well pleased. Diners with lighter purses can eat moderately priced Italian food at *Pompei*, 53 Stryd Fawr (☎01758/614944), Spanish at the appealing *Tapas Restaurant*, 6 Lower Ala Rd (☎01758/614069), or basic classics from steak to fish at the inexpensive *Mariner Bistro* on Station Square. For all day breakfasts, including good veggie options, *Boadawen Café* on Y Maes is a good choice.

For **drinking**, Pwllheli's best bet is the 400-year-old *Penlan Fawr*, 3 Penlan St, where there's occasional live music, and summer barbecues in the beer garden. There are a few working mens-type clubs around town where you'll sometimes find live bands, often Welsh – check at the tourist office or on posters around town. In the last week of May, Pwllheli's annual **festival** sees concerts, drama and bands around the town.

Penarth Fawr and Llangybi

Travelling east from Pwllheli along the A497, signposts after a couple of miles point down a tiny lane inland towards **Penarth Fawr** (April–Oct daily 9.30am–6.30pm; Nov–March Mon–Sat 9.30am–4pm, Sun 2–4pm; free), a compact fifteenth-century hall-house built to a common standard for the Welsh gentry. Constructed in 1416, the aisle truss hall was originally heated only by a huge central hearth, replaced in the seventeenth century by the large fireplace you see today. Alterations at that time included the insertion of an upper floor – a dismantled beam from this work is on display and bears the date 1656. Adjoining the house is a lovely pottery gallery and café run by the custodians who live at Penarth Fawr – examples of their potting and bookbinding skills are on display. These days, the bookbinding business specializes in producing fake TV and film accessories – you can see Bergerac's false passport and a notebook and the Holy Grail from the movie *Indiana Jones and the Last Crusade*.

A couple of miles due north, but reached only along some tortuously confusing lanes, is the charming little village of **LLANGYBI**, a mysterious spot best known for its **healing well**, Ffynnon Gybi. St Cybi, a sixth-century Cornish saint and healer, was believed to have discovered the curative properties of the waters bubbling up out of the ground here, although, like many such wells, it is more likely that it was already known about and venerated in the pre-Christian era. In the eighteenth century, the well was encased in spa buildings, the ruins of which still stand today. As a spa, Llangybi water was said to cure warts, lameness, blindness, rheumatism and other disorders. Once you've had your fill of this bucolic spot, carry on up the hill, through the woodland behind for the ascent of Garn Bentyrch, a fabulous place for great views over the Llŷn. To reach the well, go through the village churchyard and over the stile on the wall in the far left corner, crossing the field ahead and down to the stream.

Llanbedrog

A couple of miles in the other direction from Pwllheli, off the road to Abersoch, is **LLANBEDROG**, a delightful village with a wonderful beach, great walks and one of the most impressive arts centres in north Wales. Until it was washed away in storms in 1927, a little tram railway, built to connect the village with Pwllheli's West End, disgorged holiday-makers into **Plas Glyn-y-Weddw** (Wed–Mon 11am–5pm; £2; *www.oriel.org.uk*), one of Wales' oldest public art galleries. Solomon Andrews, the Cardiff entrepreneur who built the West End in Pwllheli, had bought the Victorian Gothic mansion in 1896 and turned it into a genteel centre for the arts, establishing pleasure gardens and staging legendary tea dances. But the place had originally been built in 1856 for Lady Elizabeth Jones Parry as a dower house following the death of her husband (Glyn-y-Weddw means widow's glen), who rejoiced in the name of Sir Lovegod Parry Jones Parry. In the end, she never spent a night at the house, preferring to go there weekly for the day. It's an astonishing building: all rooms peel off a spectacular galleried hallway under a huge stained-glass window and a gorgeous hammerbeam oak roof, topped with a lantern. Don't miss the two sixth-century basalt columns in the hallway windows, once of Llanor church and latterly returned to the area from the Ashmolean Museum in Oxford. The exhibitions combine pieces from the gallery's permanent collection with touring works, often with a Welsh theme. The whole operation is most impressive, and, to cap it all, there's a lovely conservatory tearoom in which to sit and gaze out at the sea.

It's a short stroll from Glyn-y-Weddw down to Llanbedrog's charmingly old-fashioned beach, backed by a set of dilapidated beach huts. From here, you can take a walk up through the wooded glen at the southern end of the beach and onto the headland (Mynydd Tir-y-Cwmwd) towering above. Until 1999, a huge Tin-Man statue had stood near its summit, itself the replacement for an 8-foot ship's figurehead that was placed there in 1919. The Tin Man, victim of vandalism and rust, has been removed for restoration, and it is hoped that he – or a suitable replacement – will soon grace Tir-y-Cwmwd once again.

Back by the entrance to Glyn-y-Weddw, Llanbedrog's parish **church of St Pedrog** is well worth exploring. The church was used as stables by Oliver Cromwell during the Civil War, and fragments of medieval glass, broken by Cromwell's troops and now in the west window, are supposed to have been returned only in the nineteenth century after they had been unearthed buried on the beach. It's said that during the Civil War, villagers removed the glass and the church's elaborate screen for safe-keeping beyond the high tide mark, where they remained for a couple of hundred years.

Otherwise, Llanbedrog is home to a **field archery and shooting range** at the Llanbedrog Archery Centre (daily 10am–dusk; archery £17 a session, shooting £25hr; by appointment on ☎01758/740810), just off the A499, and you can go pony trekking with Llanbedrog Riding Centre, Abersoch Road (☎01758/740267). The village is also blessed with two of the finest **pubs** in the area, both serving tasty and inexpensive meals: the *Glyn-y-Weddw Arms* at Tŷ Du on the A499; and the friendly *Ship Inn* at Bryn-y-Gro, half a mile further on, which has a very popular summertime beer garden. With so many diversions and such good drinking options, you might be tempted to **stay** hereabouts: try the lovely *Penarwel Country House*, above the main road on the north side of the village (☎01758/740719; ③). Slightly cheaper and in the village proper, there's the *Eiriador* guesthouse (☎01758/740899; ②) on Lôn Pin. Also near the village centre is the plush *Refail Caravan & Camping Park* (☎01758/740511).

Abersoch and around

After the distinctly Welsh feel of Pwllheli, **ABERSOCH**, seven miles southwest along the coast, comes as a surprise. This former fishing village pitched in the middle of two golden bays has, over the last century, become a largely anglicized resort, catering to comfortably-off boat owners. Abersoch now ranks as one of the country's major dinghy-sailing centres, the odd foreign entrant to the numerous regattas throughout the summer lending a mildly cosmopolitan air to the place and fuelling its haughty opinion of itself.

Such high self-esteem isn't really justified, but at high tide, the harbour is attractive, and the long swath of the town beach is a fine spot even if it is barely visible under the beach towels at busy times. A short walk along the shore shakes off most of the crowds, but a better bet is to make for three-mile-long **Porth Neigwl** (Hell's Mouth), two miles to the southwest, which ranks as one of the country's best surf beaches – beware of the undertow if you're swimming. Around town, the needs of yachties and surfers are catered for with a couple of chandlers and more surf shacks than anywhere north of the Pembrokeshire coast. Sun-seekers should head a mile north to a fine stretch of beach backed by *The Warren* holiday park.

Bus #18 can take you to **Llanengan**, a short walk from the beach of Porth Neigwl, where you can also visit the gorgeous twin-aisled fifteenth-century **St Engan's Church** (instructions for obtaining the key are inside the porch), with its two altars and two rood screens, integral parts of decoration that have been little changed by the eighteenth- and nineteenth-century reformist zeal that altered most other churches. Llanengan is also home to the *Sun Inn* (see opposite), a cosy pub serving great bar meals, and with a pleasant beer garden.

Practicalities

Buses from Pwllheli make a loop through the middle of Abersoch, stopping by the **tourist office** on Lôn Pen Cei (Easter to mid-Sept daily 10.30am–5pm; ☎01758/712929). To continue to Aberdaron by bus, you have to take a Pwllheli-bound service as far as Llanbedrog, then change onto the #17.

There is no shortage of **places to stay** in Abersoch, the cheapest being *Trewen*, Lôn Hawen, just off Lôn Sarn Bach (☎01758/712755; ①), and *Ganllwyd*, Gwydryn Drive (☎01758/713590; ①). On Lôn Sarn Bach are the excellent *Tŷ Draw* (☎ & fax 01758/712647; ②); the smart *Angorfa Guest House* (closed Dec; ☎01758/712967; ②), and the comfortable, very professional *Neigwl Hotel* (☎01758/712363, fax 712544; ④).

The smartest place in town is the upmarket *Riverside Hotel* (☎01758/712419, fax 712671; ④), overlooking the harbour and well-reputed for its excellent food. Two and a half miles south of Abersoch, the road through Sarn Bach and Bwlchtocyn goes to the luxurious *Porth Tocyn* country-house hotel (Easter to mid-Nov; ☎01758/713303, fax 713538; ⑤), with an outdoor pool and great views of Cardigan Bay.

For more basic accommodation, you'll have to head out into nearby villages. Almost all the **campsites** around Abersoch are family-oriented places, so groups need to look especially responsible to be admitted. There are a couple of rather prim sites just over a mile south in Sarn Bach: continue to the simple *Bryn Cethin Bach*, Bwlchtocyn (☎01758/712285), nearly two miles south, for a rather more relaxed regime. Nearly two miles west of Abersoch, there's a lovely new **bunkhouse**, *Sgubor Unos*, at *Tanrallt Farm* (☎01758/713527; ①) in the hamlet of Llangian, where you can also hire a bike to explore the winding local lanes.

Abersoch is increasingly well supplied with decent **places to eat**, including *Mañana* on Lôn Pen Cei, a casual Mexican-Italian-influenced café-cum-restaurant, *Champers* bistro in the *Vaynol Arms*, Lôn Sarn Bach (☎01758/712776), and the restaurant at *St Tudwal's Inn* (☎01758/712539). The moderate *Neigwl Hotel* (see opposite) produces consistently good four-course meals in decent quantities, while *Porth Tocyn* (Easter to mid-Nov; see above), dishes up top-class five-course meals and a Sunday buffet lunch. For **snacks**, take afternoon tea at Oriel Fach, Stryd Fawr, or load up on wholefood quiche and pasties at *The Tasty Food Shop* on Lôn Pen Cei. **Drinking** is best done at the *Sun Inn* at Llanengan, an ancient pub about a mile southwest of Abersoch, also serving great bar food; the *Vaynol Arms* on Lôn Pen Cei; and *The Brig* in the *Harbour Hotel* on Lôn Sarn Bach.

If baking on the beach isn't active enough, you might fancy trying your hand at **water sports**: rent a sailboard or kayak at the town beach or *The Warren*, or windsurfers, surfboards and wet suits from Abersoch Watersports, Lôn Pont Morgan (☎01758/712483) by the harbour. The West Coast Surf Shop (☎01758/713067, *surf@westcoastsurf.demon.co.uk*) on Lôn Pen Cei will provide information on surfing events, competitions and parties, as well as being the base for the Abersoch Ocean Adventures school for surfing, windsurfing and related activities. Throughout the summer, fishing trips can be organized through the Craft and Angling Centre, The Harbour (☎01758/712646).

Aberdaron and around

Travelling through undulating pasture to the small lime-washed fishing village of **ABERDARON**, two miles short of the tip of the Llŷn, you really feel that you are approaching the end of Wales. Now comprising just a few dozen houses, this pleasantly laid-back village was little more than an inn and a church during the millennium from the sixth century, when it was the last stop on a long journey for pilgrims to Ynys Enlli or Bardsey Island (see p.363), tucked away around the headland. Just back from the water, the fourteenth-century stone *Y Gegin Fawr* (Great Kitchen) served as the pilgrims' final gathering place before the treacherous crossing, and now operates as a café; the twelfth-century **church of St Hywyn** on the cliffs behind the stony beach still serves its original purpose, and was ministered by Wales' greatest living poet, R.S. Thomas (see box overleaf), until he retired in 1978.

In the early years of his retirement, Thomas lived five miles east of Aberdaron in a cottage in the grounds of **Plas-yn-Rhiw** (April–Sept daily except Tues noon–5pm; £3.20; NT), a Regency manor house on Tudor foundations at the western end of Porth Neigwl. The slate-floored, stone-walled Plas-yn-Rhiw was derelict when bought in 1938 by Thomas' friends, the moneyed Keating sisters, and restored with the help of

R.S. THOMAS

The reclusive poet R(onald) S(tuart) Thomas is something of a Welsh anti-hero. Born in Cardiff in 1913, he was ordained into the Church in Wales at the tender age of 23, and spent all of his working life as a minister, in some of the rural parishes of mid-Wales, in Caergybi/Holyhead and, most famously, for his last couple of working decades as the parish priest in Aberdaron, the last parish on the fiercely Welsh Llŷn peninsula. He has remained in the area through his retirement.

Thomas' first volume of poetry, *The Stones of the Field*, was published in 1946. He remained a virtual unknown despite two more volumes, and it was not until 1955 that recognition started to come with the publication of his fourth tome, *Song at the year's turning: Poems 1942–1954*, which included an introduction by John Betjeman. Since then, the Thomas' output has been consistent and regular, with some of his better-known collections including *The Bread of Truth* (1963) and *Not that he brought Flowers* (1968). A good starter anthology of his work – *Selected Poems* – is published by Bloodaxe.

The poetry of R.S. Thomas is dark and spartan, illuminated with regular shafts of vision and clarity. Common themes include religion (and Christianity in particular), rural and pastoral strands and the eternal poetic topic of love in human relationships. However, it's in his Welsh-themed work that Thomas most savagely and thrillingly hits the mark. A belligerent advocate of Welsh as a language and culture (even if he most commonly writes in English), he is nonetheless gloomy about its direction and future, as this short extract from *A Welsh Testament* (1961), dealing with the contradictory emotions of his birthright nationality, demonstrates:

> *I never wanted the drab rôle*
> *Life assigned me, an actor playing*
> *To the past's audience upon a stage*
> *Of earth and stone; the absurd label*
> *Of birth, of race hanging askew*
> *About my shoulders. I was in prison*
> *Until you came; your voice was a key*
> *Turning in the enormous lock*
> *Of hopelessness. Did the door open*
> *To let me out or yourselves in?*

Portmeirion architect Clough Williams-Ellis, whose offbeat touch is evident in the flattened arches and a Gothic doorway rescued from a castle being demolished. Unlike most National Trust mansions, this is a manageable and relaxed place, filled with rustic furniture like a 1920s oil stove used by Honora Keating until her death in 1981, and the same sister's accomplished watercolours. All the rooms are interesting, but the upstairs sitting room is perhaps most notable for its six-foot-thick wall containing a fireplace, a spiral staircase and a window nook overlooking gorgeous gardens almost overgrown with fuchsias, hydrangeas, roses and wild flowers.

Having made your way out as far as Aberdaron, it's an idea to use the village as a base for exploring the narrow lanes at the end of the peninsula that lead to the National Trust property around **Mynydd Mawr**, the hill overlooking Bardsey Sound. A minor road weaves west to Braich-y-Pwll, two miles west of Aberdaron, from where a short path heads down the cliffs to the ruins of St Mary's church, the crossing point at the end of the Pilgrim's Way. The road continues from here to the top of Mynydd Mawr, from where the medieval patchwork of ancient fields which make up the tip of the Llŷn are clearly visible.

Alternatively, head two miles north to the clean, safe and secluded bay of **Porth Oer**, known as "Whistling Sands" for the white sands which squeak as you walk on them. The infrequent #10 bus runs here from Pwllheli and Aberdaron in the summer.

Practicalities

Without your own transport, the only way to get to Aberdaron is to catch the infrequent #17 **bus** from Pwllheli. **Accommodation** is fairly limited. The cheapest option is *Brynmor* (☎01758/760344; ①), a hundred yards up the road to Porth Oer; the central *Ty Newydd Hotel* (☎01758/760207; ⑤) is the most comfortable. A mile or so north of Aberdaron, *Pennant* (☎01758/760610; ①) makes a good base, especially since you can **rent bikes** there: coming from Pwllheli, turn right at the bottom of the hill, right again after fifty yards, then continue straight on until you see the sign. Continuing on the same road for half a mile and forking right, you come to a very good non-smoking guesthouse, *Carreg Plas* (☎01758/760308; ②). The nearest of many decent **campsites** is *Dwyros*, up the hill on the way to Mynydd Mawr; a little further afield, the seasonal *Mur Melyn* (no phone), midway between Aberdaron and Porth Oer off the eastbound B4413, is quieter. Tap-in-a-farmer's-field sites abound, including a couple of good ones along the road to Rhiw, a fine one overlooking Porth Neigwl, just below Plas-yn-Rhiw, and a couple more on the approach road to Mynydd Mawr.

For light **meals**, try the tearooms at the back of Hen Blas Crafts in the middle of the village. For bar snacks and full dinners, there's the *Ty Newydd Hotel* (see above).

Ynys Enlli (Bardsey Island)

Bardsey Island or **Ynys Enlli** (The Island of the Currents) rises out of the ocean two miles off the tip of the Llŷn, separated from it by a strait of churning, unpredictable water. This national nature reserve has been an important pilgrimage site since the sixth century, when Saint Cadfan set up the first monastery here: three visits were proclaimed equivalent to one pilgrimage to Rome. Legend claims Bardsey as "The Isle of Twenty Thousand Saints", most likely remembering not saints, but vast numbers of pilgrims who came to die at this holy spot. By the twelfth century, Giraldus Cambrensis was already claiming that "the bodies of a vast number of holy men are buried there", and that "no one dies there except in extreme old age, for disease is almost unheard of". Numerous other stories tell of the burial place of Myrddin (Merlin) and the former Bishop of Bangor, St Deiniol, but the only hard evidence is the remaining **bell tower** of the thirteenth-century Augustinian Abbey of St Mary and a few Celtic crosses scattered around it. After the Dissolution of the Monasteries in 1536, piracy became the focus of the island's economy for over a century, gradually giving way to agriculture and fishing.

Interesting though the abbey ruins and subsequent buildings are, most visitors come to watch **birds**, as there are a dozen or so species of nesting sea birds here – Manx shearwaters, fulmars, guillemots – and an astounding number of vagrants that turn up after being blown off course by storms. Few other people bother to make the journey, since **boats** are dependent on tides, winds and a viable load of passengers; contact the Bardsey Island Trust (☎01758/730740) which often runs a Saturday boat from Pwllheli (£15), or private operator Elwyn Evans, who runs trips from Porth Meudwy, a tiny cove half a mile south of Aberdaron, giving three hours on Bardsey (daily April–Oct; ☎01758/730654; £15). There are a few cottages rented by the week from the Trust, but no other facilities on the island.

The north Llŷn coast

Sprinkled with small coves and sweeping beaches between rocky bluffs, the **north Llŷn coast** is a dramatic contrast to the busier south. It has few settlements of any size, leaving quieter beaches – Porth Towyn by Tudweiliog and Traeth Penllech by Llangwnnadl – accessible via the #8 and #10 buses from Pwllheli and a short walk.

However, the services, even at the best of times, are infrequent and badly-timed, meaning that you're far better off with your own car or bike – the north Llŷn coast is particularly suited to cycling. Amenities are also thinly-scattered hereabouts – a few campsites dotted around, and the odd shop and pub in a village.

Nefyn and Porth Dinllaen

The only settlements of any size on the north coast are a pair of villages overlooking beautiful sweeping bays. **NEFYN** is the larger, but it doesn't have a lot to recommend it. Holiday-makers bring the most trade now, but you can learn about the village's herring-fishing past in the mildly diverting **Maritime Museum** (July–Sept Mon–Sat 10.30am–4.30pm; £1) inside St Mary's Church. The neighbouring village of **MORFA NEFYN**, a mile to the west, and the adjacent shoreline hamlet of **PORTH DINLLAEN**, both benefit from having lost the 1839 battle to become the terminus for ferries to Ireland. A single Parliamentary vote swung the decision in favour of Holyhead (see p.430), thus saving the tiny hamlet of Porth Dinllaen – recently bought lock, stock and a mile of beach by the National Trust – from that town's fate, and leaving a pristine sweeping bay and the popular waterside *Tŷ Coch Inn*, a refreshing place after a day on the beach. To get there, walk a mile west along the beach from Morfa Nefyn or walk the path across the golf course.

The smartest option for **accommodation** is the welcoming *Caeau Capel Hotel* on Rhodfár Môr in Nefyn village (☎01758/720240; ③), although you might prefer to be down the road in the more amenable Morfa Nefyn. If so, the best B&B there is *Llys Olwen* in the village centre (☎01758/720493; ①). There's also the summer-only *Greenacres* **campsite** along the road between the two villages.

Tre'r Ceiri, Trefor and Nant Gwrtheyrn

By far the most impressive prehistoric remains on the Llŷn are those of **Tre'r Ceiri** or "Town of the Giants" (unrestricted access) hillfort, five miles east of Nefyn, just beyond the village of **Llithfaen**. Crowning the entire rounded top of the second-highest of the three Yr Eifl mountains, the hillfort is a massive tumble of rocks, mostly formed into the waist-high walls of about 150 dry-stone hut circles, huddling together from the wind and encircled by a rampart twelve feet high in places. Archeological evidence indicates summer habitation here since the Bronze Age, but the huts are probably only a couple of thousand years old. Locals refer to them as *Cŷtiau Gwddelod* or "Irishmen's Huts", possibly recalling the Irish immigrant population on the Llŷn in the first few centuries AD, when five hundred people lived on this inhospitable site. Today, the ruins command a stunning view over the whole peninsula. The infrequent #14 bus from Tudweiliog passes the base of the main path up, which heads up from near a lay-by on the B4417 a mile west of **Llanaelhaearn**, itself reached by the hourly bus #12 from Pwllheli. The steep path makes for a saddle, then bears right, reaching Tre'r Ceiri in under an hour.

If you climb Tre'r Ceiri, you'll see how steeply and suddenly the mountains of Yr Eifl fall away to the sea in the north. Far below is the cluster of stone cottages at **TREFOR**, an old slate-quarrying port that has a distinctly ghostly feel to it. Due west of the village, a footpath bumps down to the beach, affording stunning views over the cliffs where Yr Eifl meets the sea. There's also a decent **hotel** with accompanying **bunkhouse** here in the shape of the *Plas yr Eifl* (☎01286/660781; ③). Two miles south along the coast, more old slate quarries and a derelict pier can be seen in **Nant Gwrtheyrn** (Vortigern's Valley), so named because it's supposed to be the final resting place of the Celtic chieftain Vortigern, who was responsible for inviting the Saxons to Britain after his magician, Merlin, had seen the struggle of the two dragons – the red of the ancient Britons and the white of the Saxons. Vortigern should be pleased to know that his valley is now doing its best to atone for his apparent mistake in keeping the ancient British language alive by way of the impressive **Nant Gwrtheyrn National Language Centre** (☎01758/750334), in a couple of rows of converted granite quarry cottages at the bottom of the valley. Reached down a narrow track from Llithfaen, three miles east of Nefyn, the centre holds residential courses entirely in Welsh, runs a café and has explanatory leaflets (£1) for its three-mile **nature trail**. If you're keen on acquiring some Welsh beyond the basics, this is about the best bet there is.

Clynnog Fawr

The last worthwhile stop on the #12 bus route to Caernarfon is **CLYNNOG FAWR**, a place abounding in ancient spiritual connections. The large early sixteenth-century **Church of St Beuno** (generally 10am–dusk) is built on foundations laid by Saint Beuno in the sixth century. This monastic settlement would have been an important stop for pilgrims heading for Ynys Enlli (see p.363), bringing a significant income to the parish and probably paying for the construction of such an impressive medieval church. The present interior combines spartan, monastic touches such as whitewash and limestone flags with wealthier flourishes like the fine hammerbeam roof with ornamental bosses, lovely choir stalls and the imposing chancel with well-worn misericords. Dating from around the eighth century, St Beuno's stone, a boulder used either as a prayer stone or a boundary marker, can be seen in the chapel adjacent to the bell tower, and, about two hundred yards south of the church, on the other side of the main road, **St Beuno's well** still bubbles forth. From the church, a lane heads seawards – the left-hand turn at its fork leads to the spectacularly-situated **Clynnog dolmen**. Lying beneath the peaks of Bwlch Mawr and Gyrn Goch, it's a perfect little cromlech, topped with a wonderfully-hued capstone in which 110 cup marks can be seen.

If you fancy **staying** in Clynnog Fawr, a good option is the pleasant *Bryn Eisteddfod Hotel* (☎01286/660431; ②) in the middle of the village. There's also a B&B and bunkhouse on the other side of the mountain in the shape of *The Old School* at Bwlch Derwyn, Pant Glas (☎01286/660701; ②), where you can get inexpensive **meals**.

Caernarfon and around

It was in **CAERNARFON** in 1969 that Charles, the current heir to the throne, was invested as Prince of Wales, a ceremony which, rather ironically, reaffirmed English sovereignty over Wales in the midst of one of the most nationalist of Welsh-speaking regions. Since 1282, when the English defeated Llywelyn ap Gruffydd, the last Welsh Prince of Wales, the title has been bestowed on heirs to the English throne, usually in a ceremony held either at Windsor Castle or in Westminster Abbey in London. However, in 1911, the machinations of Lloyd George – MP for Caernarfon, Welsh cabinet minister and future Prime Minister – ensured that the investiture of the future King Edward VIII would take place in the centre of his constituency: a paradoxical move for a nationalist, considering the symbolic implications.

By the time it was Charles's turn, nationalist activism was on the rise and two of the more militant cadres of the so-called Free Wales Army tried to blow up the Prince's train, succeeding only in killing themselves. That day, July 1, is now commemorated by a march through the streets of Abergele, near where the accident happened, led by their successors Meibion Glyndŵr, the Sons of Glendower (see p.459). Charles' 25-year commemorative return visit in the summer of 1994 was less than triumphant, a low-key affair most significantly characterized by the local constabulary ruling that the local joke shop risked committing a public-order offence by selling "wingnut" ears and Prince Charles masks.

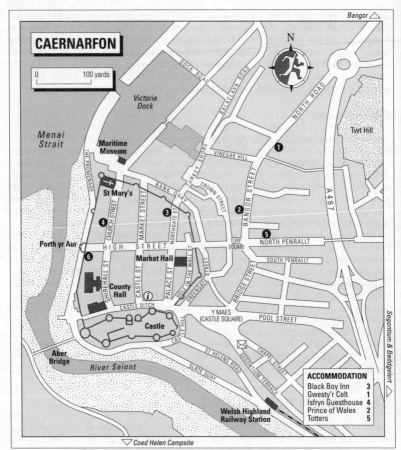

© Crown copyright

Caernarfon is a town where ardent support for Plaid Cymru guarantees the party a seat in Westminster, and where the local dialect is barely intelligible even to other Welsh-speakers. It is also the county town of Gwynedd, a suitable title for what is one of the oldest continuously occupied settlements in the country, once the site of the Romans' most westerly legion post. Segontium, on the outskirts of town, was the base of Maximus, the Spanish-born pretender to the imperial throne who was declared Emperor by his British troops in 383 AD, only to undertake an unsuccessful march on Rome. The remains of Segontium are about as impressive as Maximus' march, but, with its awesomely powerful castle and intact town walls, Caernarfon is an appealing place. However, though the town is one of north Wales' most popular tourist honeypots, there's surprisingly little to see or do once you've poked round the castle: you can only walk a small section of the town wall, and the rest of Caernarfon, ripped through by a dual carriageway, has a fairly modern feel. It even fails to exploit its magnificent setting, where the tidal mouth of the River Seiont meets the Menai Strait: buses have been allowed to clog the central square, and the prime waterside at the foot of the castle is lined by a huge car park. That said,

Caernarfon's position at the point where the Llŷn joins the north coast, and its good bus connections to Llanberis and Snowdonia make the town a decent base for a couple of days, and there are some diverting sights in the area. There's something of an edge to deeply individualistic Caernarfon which, when approached sensitively, could well provide you with some of the more memorable encounters of a Welsh tour.

Arrival, information and accommodation

With no main-line train station, the hub of Caernarfon's public transport system is Y Maes (Castle Square), where both National Express and local **buses** arrive right under the walls of the castle, just a few steps from the **tourist office**, Oriel Pendeitsh, Stryd y Castell/Castle Street (Easter–Oct daily 10am–6pm; Nov–Easter daily except Wed 9.30am–4.30pm; ☎01286/672232, *caernarfon.tic@gwynedd.gov.uk*). **Bike hire** is available from Beics Castell at 33 Stryd Fawr/High Street (☎01286/677400) – as two of the region's best cycle tracks (see p.370) emanate from Caernarfon, renting a bike is a particularly good idea here.

In terms of **accommodation**, central Caernarfon can provide something decent for all pockets, and there are some lovely farmhouse B&Bs in the near vicinity too. A couple of these – *Ty-Mawr Farm* and *Tŷ'n Rhos* – are in Llanddeiniolen, halfway between Caernarfon and Bangor see p.413). The town is well equipped with **campsites**: *Cadnant Valley* (March–Oct; ☎01286/673196) is twenty minutes' walk east of town near the start of the A4086 to Llanberis, and *Coed Helen* (March–Oct; ☎01286/676770), with only five tent sites among the caravans, is slightly closer on foot – cross the Seiont River by the footbridge by the castle and turn left. To get there by car, follow the signs from the road junction a mile south of town. The *Snowdonia Parc* pub (☎01286/650409; see p.369) on the southern side of the nondescript village of Waunfawr, four miles southeast of town, also has a year-round campsite.

Hotels, guesthouses and hostels

The Black Boy Inn, Northgate St (☎01286/673023). Characterful but bathless low-beamed rooms in what is said to be the town's oldest building (bar the castle). Newer en-suite accommodation also available. ②.

Chatham Farmhouse, Llandwrog, four miles south of Caernarfon just beyond Saron (☎01286/831257). Attractive and welcoming country guesthouse with a fine inglenook fireplace and nice decorative touches. The evening meals are made with organic vegetables from the garden and you can bring your own wine. ②.

Gwesty'r Celt Hotel, Bangor St (☎01286/674477, fax 674139, *www.nwi.co.uk/celticroyal*). Smart and very high standard town-centre hotel, known by most as the *Celtic Royal*. The rather formal restaurant is good, and there's an excellent leisure suite complete with decent-sized indoor pool. ⑥.

Hafoty, Rhostryfan (☎01286/830144, fax 830441, *www.accomodata.co.uk/310898.htm*). Small and highly rated B&B in a modernized eighteenth-century farmhouse with well-appointed rooms and a great view of Caernarfon Castle. Take the A487 south through Bontnewydd up the hill to the T-junction where you turn left and follow the signs. ③.

Isfryn Guesthouse, 11 Church St (☎01286/675628). Good-value B&B in the centre; book ahead in summer. Moderately priced three-course evening meals available. ①.

Pengwern Farm, Saron, three miles southwest of Caernarfon (☎ & fax 01286/830500). Friendly, top-quality, non-smoking B&B with en-suite rooms in a rural setting, and farm-fresh evening meals. Take the A487 south across the river then turn right towards Saron – *Pengwern* is just over two miles down on the right. Feb–Nov. ②.

Plas Tirion Farm, Llanrug, 3 miles east (☎01286/673190). Smart and welcoming Welsh farmhouse B&B, furnished with exquisite antiques. ③.

Prince of Wales, Bangor St (☎01286/673367, fax 676610). Town centre pub with good, if quite basic, rooms with private or shared bathroom, and some fine food on offer. ①.

Seiont Manor, Llanrug, 3 miles east of Caernarfon on the A4086 (☎01286/673366). Rustic building remodelled into the region's finest hotel, complete with indoor pool, sauna and use of mountain bikes. Superb, though pricey, French food. ⑤.

Totters, Plas Porth Yr Aur, 2 High St (☎01286/672963). Caernarfon's only backpacker hostel, but one of the best in Wales. Centrally located, with clean dorm rooms and some lovely communal spaces, including a great fourteenth-century cellar kitchen. Beds with linen go for £9, and guests can borrow bikes.

The Town

In 1283, Edward I started work on **Caernarfon Castle** (June–Sept daily 9.30am–6pm; April–May & Oct daily 9.30am–5pm; Nov–March Mon–Sat 9.30am–4pm, Sun 11am–4pm; £4.20; CADW), the strongest link in his Iron Ring (see p.408) and the decisive hammerblow to any Welsh aspirations of autonomy. Until Beaumaris Castle was built to guard the other end of the Menai Strait, Caernarfon was the ultimate symbol of both Anglo-Norman military might and political wrangling. With the Welsh already smarting from the loss of their Prince of Wales, Edward is said to have rubbed salt in their wounds by justifying his own infant son's claim to the title, having promised them "a prince born in Wales who could speak never a word of English", and subsequently presenting them with the newborn baby that had arrived after his pregnant wife had been forced to take up residence in the castle. The story is almost certainly apocryphal, since Edward's son, though born at Caernarfon, wasn't invested until seven years later.

Edward attempted to appease the Welsh in the building of his castle by paying tribute to aspects of local legend. The Welsh had long associated their town with the eastern capital of the Roman Empire: Caernarfon's old name, Caer Cystennin, was also the name used for Constantinople, and Constantine himself was believed to have been born at Segontium. Edward's architect, James of St George, exploited this connection in the distinctive limestone and sandstone banding and polygonal towers, both reminiscent of the Theodosian walls in present-day Istanbul. The other legend to influence the castle was the medieval **Dream of Macsen Wledig**, in which the eponymous Welsh hero (the Roman legionnaire Maximus) remembers "a fair fortress at the mouth of a river, in a land of high mountains, opposite an island, and a tower of many colours at the fort, and golden eagles on the ramparts". When it came to finishing off the turrets in 1317, Edward III perfected the accuracy of this description by adding eagles – also, ironically, the standard of Owain Gwynedd. These are weathered almost beyond recognition now, but the rest of the castle is in an excellent state of repair, thanks largely to Anthony Salvin's nineteenth-century reconstruction, carried out after Richard Wilson and J.M.W. Turner had painted their Romantic images of it.

As a military monument of its time, the castle is supreme, and it still commands a brooding, imperious presence. It was taken once, before it was finished, but then withstood two sieges by Owain Glyndŵr with a complement of only 28 men-at-arms. Entering through the **King's Gate**, the castle's strength is immediately apparent. Between the octagonal towers, embrasures and murder-holes face in on no fewer than five gates and six portcullises, and that's once you have crossed the moat, now bridged by an incongruous modern structure. Inside, the huge lawn gives a misleading impression, since both the wall dividing the two original wards and all the buildings which filled them crumbled away long ago. The towers are in a much better state, and linked by such a honeycomb of wall-walks and tunnels that a visit can be an exhausting experience. The most striking and tallest of the towers is the King's Tower at the western end, whose three slender turrets adorned with eagle sculptures give the best views of the town. To the south, the Queen's Tower is entirely taken up by the numbingly thorough **Museum of the Royal Welch Fusiliers** (sic), detailing the victories of Wales' oldest regiment through collections of medals, uniforms and a brass howitzer captured from the Russians at the Battle of the Alma in 1854. Crossing the upper ward from here, you pass the site of the original Norman motte, now covered in Dinorwig slate as part of the dais for the investiture of the Prince of Wales. Displays on the most recent ceremony, and others since the pageant was moved here in 1911, are presented in the **Prince of Wales Exhibition** in the Northeast Tower, just beyond the dais.

There are a few decent **walking tours** of Caernarfon available, the best being the Magical History Tour (£4; ☎01286/677059). Otherwise, it's an interesting town in which to wander. You'll find some fine seventeenth- and eighteenth-century buildings in the knot of streets wedged into the rectangle of **town walls**, which are almost as complete as those at Conwy (see p.405), but so boxed-in by modern buildings that they're far less striking. The castle forms one side of the town walls, but you can only walk a very short section, at the end of Market Street (Stryd y Farchnad) close to the Chantry of St Mary, the restored fourteenth-century church built into a corner of the town wall on Church Street (Stryd yr Eglwys). Just outside the walls, Victoria Dock is home to a **Maritime Museum** (Easter & June to mid-Sept daily 11am–4pm; £1) based in and around the *Seiont II* steam dredger, which is gradually being renovated, and the *Nantlys*, the last ferry to ply the Menai Strait. The only way to get out on to the Strait these days is on either the *Snowdon Queen* or the *Queen of the Sea* (June–Sept daily; ☎01286/672772), pleasure crafts which make forty-minute excursions (£4) from the quay below the castle. From the marina, St Helen's Road (Ffordd Santes Helen) leads to a small terminus station of the **Welsh Highland Railway** (see box, p.371), which currently only shuffles out as far as Dinas (return £3.80), three miles south, but which will eventually run all the way to Porthmadog.

A ten-minute walk along the A4085 Beddgelert road brings you to the western end of the Roman road from Chester, a location commemorated by the **Segontium Roman Fort and Museum** (April–Oct Mon–Sat 10am–5pm, Sun 2–5pm; Nov–March Mon–Sat 10am–4pm, Sun 2–4pm; £1.25; CADW). The Romans occupied this five-acre site for three centuries from around 78 AD, though most of the remains are from the final rebuilding after 364 AD. The ground plan is seldom more than shin-high and somewhat baffling, making the museum and displays in the ticket office pretty much essential.

Eating, drinking and entertainment

Caernarfon boasts a number of low-key and likeable **restaurants** which may well be the focus of your evening's entertainment, as there is little else except for a smattering of **pubs** and one nightclub. For organized nightlife, though, you're best off following the local example and heading ten miles north to Bangor (see pp.413–418); however, for something a little nearer, bus #95 to Beddgelert and Llanberis will drop you right outside the excellent *Snowdonia Parc* pub (☎01286/650409) on the southern side of the nondescript village of Waunfawr, four miles southeast of town. Beer is brewed on site, and the pub hosts numerous nights of live music and entertainment.

The *Caernarfon and Denbigh Herald*, which comes out on Thursdays, has **gig** information for both Bangor and Caernarfon. For news of alternative social occasions, check out the notice boards in the old **Market Hall** on Palace Street, home to a number of interesting shops and stalls.

Restaurants, cafés and pubs

Anglesey Arms, The Promenade. The sea wall outside makes this the best pub for soaking up the afternoon sun, though it also rates with good real ales and decent bar meals.

The Black Boy Inn (see p.367). The closest Caernarfon comes to an old-fashioned British pub, with a choice of two low-beamed bars and the best bar meals in town.

Caffi Maes, Y Maes. Good daytime café for snacks and breakfasts.

Courteney's, 9 Segontium Terrace (☎01286/677290). Eclectic range of excellent food and good wines served in a small room which is often full, especially at weekends. Closed Mon & Tues lunch and all day Sun.

Floating Restaurant, Slate Quay (☎01286/672896). Very good eaterie in a boat moored below the castle; particularly worth trying for locally-caught fish dishes.

The Gatehouse Restaurant, 20 Palace St (☎01286/674333). Licensed daytime café serving a good range of hearty dishes and good coffee. Turns into a pizza restaurant in the evening.

The Harlequin, Market Hall. Cheery daytime café upstairs in the Market Hall, with good coffee, toasted sandwiches, omelettes and varied vegetarian and meat dishes.

Paradox, Ffordd Santes Helen (☎01286/673100). Industrial-themed nightclub in an old bonded warehouse near the castle.

Prince of Wales, Bangor St. Occasional live music and regular karaoke nights in this cheerful and friendly local pub that also has rooms (see p.367).

Stone's, 4 Hole in the Wall St (☎01286/671152). Simply decorated brick-walled place serving moderately priced bistro-style meals. The roast pheasant is good, and there's a choice of four vegetarian dishes. Closed Sun.

Tafarn Yr Albert, 10 Segontium Terrace. Bustling local where you might catch a Welsh-language band on a Saturday night.

Y Goron Fach, Hole in the Wall St. A good range of cask ales in a friendly setting, with cheap bar snacks available and a small beer garden.

Around Caernarfon

One of the most enjoyable ways to get out into the Caernarfon surrounds is to follow either of two **bike paths** along the route of a disused railway: Lôn Las Menai, accessed from Victoria Dock and running north for four miles to Y Felinheri (Port Dinorwig) and thence via lanes to Bangor. In the other direction and leaving town alongside the line of the restored Welsh Highland Railway on Ffordd Santes Helen, Lôn Eifion heads twelve miles south to Bryncir, and then via lanes to Cricieth. **Bike hire** in town is detailed on p.367.

North of Caernarfon

Three miles northeast of Caernarfon, just west of the village of Bethel on the B4366, the **Greenwood Centre** (mid-March to Aug daily 10am–5.30pm; Sept and Oct daily 10am–5pm; £3.75) sets out to celebrate the life of trees, something it does admirably well. On the fringe of a copse of managed woodland, a large barn has been built using ancient methods and forty tons of green Welsh and English oak trees, its gargantuan beams held together with pine struts and wooden pegs. Tree and forest ecology is explored through a blend of the scientific, the spiritual (due attention is paid to Celtic tree spirits and the like) and the sensory: you're invited to punch the bark of a redwood to see how soft it is, identify aromatic woods from their smell and try out an Ethiopian wood pillow. Outside, visitors can turn wood on a foot-operated lathe, try shooting a longbow or simply amble around the wildlife pond, arboretum and forest nursery.

A couple of miles due west at Llanfairisgaer, the shores of the Menai Strait hold **Plas Menai: The National Watersports Centre** (☎01248/670964, or 670597 for the 24hr brochure request line), a predominantly group-oriented complex with two- to seven-day courses in sailing, windsurfing, canoeing and powerboating.

South of Caernarfon

A much-touted but overrated outing south from Caernarfon is the **Caernarfon Air World** museum (March–Oct daily 9am–5.30pm, Nov–Feb Sat & Sun 10am–5pm; £4) at the grandly-named Caernarfon Airport, eight miles south of town at **DINAS DIN-**

THE WELSH HIGHLAND RAILWAY

The Welsh love affair with restoring railways to operate them as steam-driven tourist attractions may well have reached its zenith with the tangled tale of the Welsh Highland Railway (WHR or *Rheilffordd Eryri*). Confusingly, there are currently two steam railways operating under the name – both covering just a couple of miles, one from Caernarfon (see p.369) and one from Porthmadog (see p.351), also the southern terminus of the Ffestiniog Railway. Plans to reconnect the two lines, forming one of Britain's longest steam railways, running just over 25 miles, are well advanced, and it is currently hoped that the full route will be up and running by 2006. It has, however, been a tortuous – and highly contentious – struggle.

For starters, the tiny original WHR at Porthmadog resented the bigger Ffestiniog Railway, which had been behind the project at Caernarfon, as well as the plans to link the two and to reroute trains in Porthmadog down to the Ffestiniog Railway's terminus station by the harbour. It took years of squabbling for the two Welsh Highland Railways to agree to pursue their connection. Permission for the project finally came from the Department of Transport in the summer of 1999, with £4.3 million of lottery money, under the auspices of the UK Millennium Commission, also forthcoming. Farmers with land along the route (and the ramblers who regularly walked it), however, were not so pleased, and with much public support, the National Farmers Union launched an appeal for a Judicial Review, which was turned down by the High Court in November 1999. This didn't stop individual farmers from doing their best to obstruct work on the old track-bed where it ran across their land. The feats of engineering needed to reopen the old line are staggering: over 20 bridges must be rebuilt, popular walking and cycling paths have to be re-routed, the four tunnels down the Aberglaslyn Pass near Beddgelert (see p.340) need extensive work to ensure that they're safe and – in order to link up with the Ffestiniog Railway's terminus at Porthmadog Harbour – trains will have to run along the street in Porthmadog town, a considerable safety concern. And all this mostly in a National Park – small wonder that hackles have been raised.

Current hopes are pinned on an extension of the northern section of the WHR from Dinas to Waunfawr by the summer of 2000, and Rhyd-Ddu, beneath Snowdon, by 2001. Following this, the line will extend south to Beddgelert, the main stopping-off point of the route, and thence to meet the existing southern section of the WHR at Porthmadog by 2006. Whether such an ambitious timetable can be maintained – dates have continually slipped back as the project has hit more and more controversy – remains to be seen. Emotions in the area are very mixed about the possible benefits of the line – the Department of Transport made great play of its potential for locals as well as tourists, claiming that it would restore the missing link in a rail loop (main-line Bangor–Betws-y-Coed, Ffestiniog Railway Betws–Porthmadog) that somehow ignored the fact that the Bangor–Caernarfon rail line, an essential chain in that link, was removed in the 1960s and is now a cycle track. Furthermore, with the steep gradients and twisting route of the WHR, it's unlikely to be a journey fast enough to satisfy the needs of commuters. The project might well be going full steam ahead, but its controversies rumble on. For up-to-date information, check out the project's excellent Web site (*www.bangor.ac.uk/ml/whr*), or the site for the Porthmadog branch (*www.whr.co.uk*).

LLE (bus #91), where cases of model aeroplanes help to fill out a small hangar containing half a dozen examples of the real thing. A better reason to come out here might be the **flying lessons** (☎01286/830800; half-hour £42, 1hr £84), which will take you over spectacular scenery around Caernarfon and Snowdon. No previous flying experience is necessary. At the southern end of the vast flat Dinas Dinlle beach and affording great views over to Anglesey and down the Llŷn, there's a sizeable Roman and early British oval **hillfort**. The hill has suffered erosion by the sea, removing most of the archeological evidence, and has also been damaged by footsteps, so the path to the top is sometimes cordoned off. If it's not, and your visit coincides with low tide, you might be able to see Caer Arianrhod, a row of rocks named after the girl in The Mabinogion legend who gave birth to Lleu Llaw Gyffer, destined to become Lord of Gwynedd.

The Lôn Eifion bike path veers right to the **Inigo Jones Tudor Slateworks**, Groeslon (Easter–Sept Mon–Fri 9am–5pm, Sat & Sun 10am–5pm; Oct–Easter Mon–Thurs 9am–4.30pm, Fri closes 3.30pm; £2.95), on the A487 six miles south of Caernarfon, a collection of roadside sheds where slate has been fashioned since 1861, when the factory was started by one Inigo Jones, a local man apparently unrelated to the seventeenth-century architect. A large proportion of the inscribed slate plaques adorning public buildings around north Wales were cut here, ample excuse for an interesting calligraphy exhibition. Try your hand at chiselling out a few random chips of slate to appreciate the skill of the carvers here. A mile west, off the A499 near Llandwrog, the **Glynllifon Country Park** (daily dawn–dusk) is a predictable enough cluster of twinky craft workshops, waymarked trails and gardens gathered around the sombre shape of nineteenth-century Glynllifon Hall (not open to the public). For a decent walk, though, you're far better off on the beach at nearby Dinas Dinlle or in any of the hills round about.

travel details

Unless otherwise stated frequencies for trains and buses are for Monday to Saturday services; Sunday averages 1–3 services, though the main routes are more frequent and some routes have no Sunday service at all.

Trains

Betws-y-Coed to: Blaenau Ffestiniog (7 daily; 30min); Llandudno Junction (6 daily; 25min).

Blaenau Ffestiniog to: Betws-y-Coed (7 daily; 30min); Llandudno Junction (6 daily; 1hr); Porthmadog by Ffestiniog Railway (Easter–Oct 4–10 daily; 1hr).

Cricieth to: Porthmadog (7 daily; 10min); Pwllheli (7 daily; 15min).

Porthmadog to: Barmouth (7 daily; 45min); Blaenau Ffestiniog by Ffestiniog Railway (Easter–Oct 4–10 daily; 1hr); Harlech (7 daily; 20min); Machynlleth (7 daily; 1hr 40min); Pwllheli (6 daily; 25min).

Pwllheli to: Cricieth (7 daily; 15min); Porthmadog (6 daily; 25min).

Buses

Aberdaron to: Pwllheli (8 daily; 40min).

Abersoch to: Pwllheli (9 daily; 15min).

Beddgelert to: Caernarfon (6 daily; 30min); Llanberis (5 daily; 40min); Porthmadog (6 daily; 30min).

Betws-y-Coed to: Bangor (2 daily; 50min); Blaenau Ffestiniog (1 daily southbound only; 30min); Capel Curig (7 daily; 15min); Idwal Cottage (6 daily; 20min); Llanberis (3 daily; 40min); Llanrwst (3 daily; 10min); Penmachno (5 daily; 10min).

Blaenau Ffestiniog to: Caernarfon (roughly hourly; 1hr 20min); Harlech (4 daily; 35min); Porthmadog (hourly; 30min).

Caernarfon to: Bangor (every 20min; 30min); Beddgelert (6 daily; 30min); Cardiff (1 daily; 7hr 25min); Cricieth (3 daily; 40min); Llanberis (every 30min; 25min); Porthmadog (at least hourly; 45min); Pwllheli (every 30min; 45min).

Capel Curig to: Bangor (2 daily; 40min); Betws-y-Coed (7 daily; 15min); Idwal Cottage (6 daily; 10min); Llanberis (3 daily; 30min).

Cricieth to: Caernarfon (3 daily; 40min); Llanystumdwy (hourly; 5min); Porthmadog (hourly; 15min); Pwllheli (hourly; 20min).

Idwal Cottage to: Bangor (2 daily; 30min); Betws-y-Coed (6 daily; 20min); Capel Curig (6 daily; 10min).

Llanberis to: Bangor (8 daily; 40min); Beddgelert (5 daily; 40min); Betws-y-Coed (3 daily; 40min);

Caernarfon (every 30min; 25min); Capel Curig (3 daily; 30min).

Llanrwst to: Betws-y-Coed (3 daily; 10min); Conwy (every 30min; 40min); Llandudno (every 30min; 1hr).

Nefyn to: Pwllheli (roughly hourly; 15min).

Porthmadog to: Beddgelert (6 daily; 30min); Blaenau Ffestiniog (hourly; 30min); Caernarfon (at least hourly; 45min); Cricieth (hourly; 15min); Dolgellau (6 daily; 50min); Pwllheli (hourly; 40min).

Pwllheli to: Aberdaron (8 daily; 40min); Abersoch (9 daily; 15min); Caernarfon (every 30min; 45min); Chester (1 daily; 4hr); Cricieth (hourly; 20min); Manchester (1 daily; 5hr 30min); Nefyn (roughly hourly; 15min); Porthmadog (hourly; 40min).

CHAPTER SIX

THE NORTH COAST AND ANGLESEY

Wales' north coast, and its natural extension, Anglesey, encompass not only the geographical extremities of the country, but take in an area exhibiting the extremes of Welsh life. Walking around most of the brash seaside towns along the eastern section of the coast, only the street signs give any indication that you are in Wales at all: further west, there are places where English is seldom spoken other than to visitors. Scattered along the coast, dramatically situated castles work as a superb antidote to the low-brow fun-seeking of the resorts, while head inland and the stark plainness of border towns like Wrexham is tempered by the picture-perfect tranquillity of the rural Vale of Clywd.

Two major forces shaped the region into what it is today. In the thirteenth century, the might of English king Edward I all but crushed the Welsh princes and forced their armies out of the area. Edward set about building the Norman castles which finally hammered them into subjugation. Towns grew up around the early castles at **Flint** and **Rhuddlan**, but neither had town walls, leaving the now mostly ruined structures in isolation. The castle at **Conwy**, however, was surrounded by a "bastide" town, the castle's keepers and town's burghers dependent on one another. Conwy was entirely the preserve of the English, thereby economically and politically marginalizing the Welsh who retreated west, to Anglesey, where the English wielded less influence. As a response, Edward sited his final castle at **Beaumaris**, a supreme expression of the militarily advanced concentric design, protecting the entrance to the **Menai Strait**, the treacherous channel that separates the Isle of Anglesey from the mainland.

The second sweeping change came in the late nineteenth and early twentieth centuries, when the benefits of the Industrial Revolution finally loosened the shackles on English mill-town factory workers enough for them to take holidays. Beachfront towns sprang up, catering entirely to the summer visitors who arrived by the trainload to spend one week's annual leave promenading and dancing. The setup isn't too different today, but the ever-present automobile has all but taken over from the train, caravans are as

---

ACCOMMODATION PRICE CODES

Throughout this guide, hotel and B&B accommodation is priced on a scale of ① to ⑨, the number indicating the **lowest price** you could expect to pay per night in that establishment for a **double room in high season**. The prices indicated by the codes are as follows:

① under £40	④ £60–70	⑦ £110–150
② £40–50	⑤ £70–90	⑧ £150–200
③ £50–60	⑥ £90–110	⑨ over £200

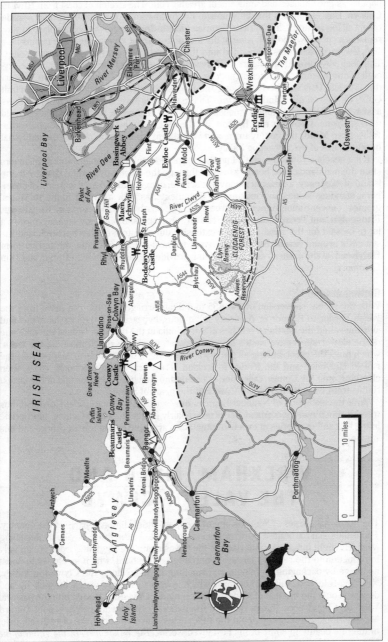

© Crown copyright

popular as guesthouses and amusement arcades rule. The stretch of coast from **Rhyl** to **Colwyn Bay** epitomizes this tatty image, the hallmarks of the shabby British seaside resort all too apparent. In contrast, Victorian **Llandudno**, always the posher place to stay, remains a cut above the rest, lying at the foot of the **Great Orme** limestone peninsula.

A few surprises come embedded into this matrix of bingo halls and caravan sites. The allegedly miraculous waters at **Holywell** have attracted the hopeful since the seventh century, while two different species of pilgrim make for either **Prestatyn**, to start the 170-mile Offa's Dyke Path along the English border, or for the National Portrait Gallery's collection at **Bodelwyddan**. To the south of here, the Vale Of Clwyd follows a pastoral valley, past Britain's smallest cathedral at **St Asaph**, to a pair of attractive old market towns, **Denbigh** and **Ruthin**. To the east, the Clwydian Range separates the valley from **Mold**, the county town, and **Wrexham**, a base for exploring the industrial heritage sites of the Clywedog Valley.

If it's beaches you want, you'll find that more discerning swimmers and windsurfers shun the mainland coast, heading instead through the university town of **Bangor** to the island of **Anglesey**, a pleasant patchwork of rural communities dotted with burial chambers, standing stones and mysterious alignments, as well as being home to Wales' greatest concentration of neolithic remains. The southwestern resorts of **Rhosneigr**, **Rhoscolyn** and **Trearddur Bay** are the favoured spots, though for scenery, there's a lot to be said for the coast along the extensive dune system of **Newborough** and the sea cliffs around **South Stack**, both great for bird-watching. Lastly, the ferries from **Holyhead**, at the western end of the island, provide the fastest route to Dublin and Dun Laoghaire.

Getting around

With the recent conversion of the A55 to a dual carriageway, you can drive from the Welsh border to Bangor or Anglesey in an hour, bypassing all the coastal towns and skirting round the northern reaches of Snowdonia in the process. Unless you take one of the slower alternative routes along the coast, you'll see much more on the **train**, which hugs the coast, linking all the resorts to Bangor, then across to Anglesey for the run to Holyhead and the ferries to Ireland. Travelling along the north coast, then changing onto the Conwy Valley line at Llandudno Junction, provides one of the fastest routes from England to Betws-y-Coed and the heart of Snowdonia.

With the exception of National Express **bus** services to Bangor and Holyhead, bus travel is much more piecemeal. Services are fairly frequent, detailed where appropriate in the text and in a series of excellent timetables available free at tourist offices and bus stations.

WREXHAM, MOLD AND
THE VALE OF CLWYD

The northeast corner of Wales is one of the most widely ignored parts of the country. Thousands skirt around it or drive through en route to the more obviously appealing west. The light industrial hinterland of the towns along the English border are an ugly introduction to the region's largest conurbation, **Wrexham**, which struggles to boost its image by packaging its mining and smelting heritage along the **Clywedog Valley**. Nearby **Mold** is a dull market town which seems to merely watch life tick by and deserves only the briefest of stops, but climbing the **Clwydian Range** into the pastoral **Vale of Clwyd** sees things improve dramatically. Nineteenth-century poet Gerard Manley Hopkins eulogized about the valley where he studied for the priesthood, celebrating its beauty in some of his best-loved works, *The Windhover, In the Valley of the*

Elwy and *Pied Beauty*. The gentle contours and minor sights take time to appreciate, something seldom afforded the valley by visitors to the largest towns, **Ruthin** with its fine set of medieval buildings, **Denbigh**, surmounted by its craggy castle, and the tiny city of **St Asaph**.

Wrexham, the Clywedog Valley and the Maelor

There's a curiously boisterous charm to **WREXHAM** (Wrecsam), the largest town (with extravagant hopes for future city status) in North Wales. It's not a classically pretty place, although some fine older buildings can still be seen nestling alongside the identikit chainstore developments that litter the town centre. Having long looked more to the industrial northwest of England than its own Welsh hinterland, Wrexham has the schizophrenic qualities of many border towns, although just because a place can't boast two lovespoon galleries and a Welsh tea towel emporium, it doesn't mean that it's not firmly, if rather enigmatically, Welsh. Wrexham's nationality is loudly and proudly revealed when the Welsh football team play international matches at the town's Racecourse Ground, home for the rest of the time of one of only three Welsh sides in the English Football League.

Wrexham's development stems from its status as the early medieval marketplace for the fertile lands around it; this led to growth as an administrative centre, and then as an early industrial town. With rich local seams of iron ore, coal and lead, mining was an inevitable development, acting as a considerable catalyst for the town's speedy growth both in size and importance. Two very contrasting areas on either side of the town demonstrate the various influences upon Wrexham's history. To the east, scooped out of England on three sides, is the **Maelor**, a lush agricultural land of pretty little villages and winding lanes. To the south and west is the far grittier and far more Welsh **Clywedog Valley**, which played a key role in the early part of the Industrial Revolution and whose sites have recently been rejuvenated as the town's chief attractions. Best of the bunch is the National Trust's splendidly evocative **Erddig Hall**.

The Town

Redevelopment funds have poured into Wrexham in recent years, and the cash injection is particularly evident in the freshly-landscaped squares that surround several gleaming new shopping malls on the fringes of the pedestrianized streets. They contain a predictable enough range of national chains; more interesting are the Edwardian arcades, two Victorian market halls and older, local traders around Chester Street and Bank Street, but the town centre's main draw is the imposing **St Giles' Church** (Easter–Sept Mon–Fri 10am–4pm; free), its Gothic tower gracefully rising above the kernel of small lanes at the end of Hope Street. Topped off with a steeple in the 1520s, the tower's five distinct levels, stepping up to four hexagonal pinnacles, is replicated at America's Yale University in homage to the ancestral home of the college's benefactor, Elihu Yale, whose tomb is here at the base. The engraved stone in the tower wall near Yale's grave came from the university, the one it replaced now holding up a replica tower there. The church's spacious interior is mainly of interest for the scant remains of the late-fifteenth-century wall painting of *The Last Judgement* above the entrance to the chancel, though the abundance of Victorian and contemporary stained glass are more conspicuous. The church is approached through wrought-iron gates installed between 1718 and 1724 by famed Welsh ironworkers Robert and John Davies of Bersham, also responsible for the striking gates at Chirk Castle (see p.247).

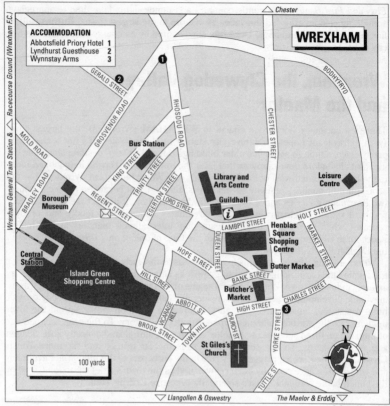

Hope Street leads up from near St Giles', swiftly becoming one of the town's main shopping thoroughfares as it turns into Regent Street. A five-minute walk along here brings you to the small but diverting enough **Wrexham County Borough Museum** (Mon–Fri 10.30am–5pm, Sat 10.30am–3pm; free). The central display room houses a ramshackle array of artefacts from the town's nineteenth-century boom years, along-side Roman nuggets and the remarkable remains of Bronze Age character Brymbo Man, who was unearthed from a local sandstone burial cist complete with his pottery beaker and flint knife. Two smaller galleries house temporary exhibitions, usually on local themes.

Practicalities

Wrexham has two **train stations**, half a mile apart. Chester, Chirk and Shrewsbury trains call only at Wrexham General on Regent Street, ten minutes' walk northwest of the centre along Hope Street. Services from Liverpool (change at Bidston on the Wirral line) call at General on request then at Wrexham Central, now incorporated into the Island Green shopping centre behind Hill Street, right in the middle of town. Part way along Regent

Street, King Street branches off north to the **bus station**, where infrequent National Express buses (tickets from Key Travel on King Street) arrive from Manchester, London and Glasgow and regular **local buses** leave to Chester, Llangollen and Mold. The **tourist office** is on Lambpit Street (April to mid-Oct Mon–Sat 10am–5pm; mid-Oct to March Mon–Sat 10am–4pm; ☎01978/292015, *tic@wrexham.gov.uk*), opposite the new Henblas Square shopping centre.

Accommodation

There's a reasonable choice of **places to stay** in Wrexham, most of them affordable if not very exciting. The nearest **campsite** is the pricey *Plassey Leisure Park* (☎01978/780277), nearly four miles south at Eyton, with tent and caravan facilities, a swimming pool and a microbrew pub. Better bets are *James Farm Caravan Park* (☎01978/820148) on the Llangollen Road in nearby Ruabon, or the racecourse campsite (☎01978/781009) at bucolic Bangor-on-Dee, four miles southeast of Wrexham.

Abbotsfield Priory Hotel, 29 Rhosddu Rd (☎01978/261211, fax 291413). Very comfortable hotel converted from an old priory. A 5min walk from the town centre – follow Regent Street towards Wrexham General, then turn right into Grosvenor Road. ③.

Grove Guesthouse, 36 Chester Rd (☎ & fax 01978/354288). Reasonably priced guesthouse with a couple of more expensive en-suite rooms. ①.

Littleton, 24 Bersham Rd (☎01978/352867). Comfortable B&B a 10min walk from central Wrexham with welcoming, garrulous hosts. ②.

Lyndhurst Guesthouse, 3 Gerald St, off Grosvenor Rd (☎01978/290802). Comfortable, central rooms, with a very warm welcome and good breakfasts. ②.

The Stableyard, High St, 4 miles southeast in Bangor-on-Dee (☎ & fax 01978/780642). Attractive rooms and superb meals in a former tavern, in an appealing, ancient village. ③.

Wynnstay Arms, Yorke St (☎01978/291010). Decent conversion of a large Georgian coaching inn, and conveniently close to town centre restaurants and bars. ③.

Eating and drinking

Though Wrexham isn't blessed with many great places to **eat**, the selection has improved in recent years. There are a few cheap cafés on Bank Street, a narrow passage off Hope Street, and around the markets. The **pubs** are also better, and while you're here, don't forget to sample Wrexham Lager, the UK's oldest lager, first brewed in 1882 using the town's naturally soft water supply.

Bumble, 2 Charles St. Café above a gift shop, good for sandwiches and more substantial meals. Closed Sun.

Chequers Wine Bar, 7–9 Church St (☎01978/290910). About the best place to eat in town, with moderately priced bistro-style meals served during the day in the downstairs café, and an upstairs wine bar open Thurs–Sat evenings.

Golden Lion, High St. Noisy pub serving a wide range of beers, including Wrexham Lager, as well as well-prepared bar meals.

Horse and Jockey, cnr of Hope and Priory sts. Thatched and characterful old cottage long since converted into a convivial low-beamed pub. Wrexham Lager is on tap and decent food is also on offer.

One to Five, Town Hill. Light and airy brasserie-cum-bar, serving some good snacks and full meals during the day. Chilled daytime ambience mutates into livelier evening sessions.

Plas Coch, Plas Coch Rd (☎01978/261470). Three-course meals for around a fiver, a 15min walk out past Wrexham General hospital.

The Stableyard (see above), Bangor-on-Dee. A better bet than any of Wrexham's establishments, with excellent à la carte dishes and a £17 three-course table d'hôte menu.

Yales Wine Bar, Hill St. The best bet in town for live bands or special entertainment; look out for posters around town advertising events.

The Clywedog Valley

The **Clywedog Valley**, which forms an arc around the western and southern suburbs of Wrexham, was the crucible of industrial achievement in the northern Welsh borders during the eighteenth century. Iron production boomed here, thanks to an abundance of ore deposits and cheap water power harnessed from the River Clywedog. As the Industrial Revolution forged ahead, however, coal became a more important energy source than water and factories moved closer to their raw materials, leaving the valley barely disturbed. Though considerable work is still being done, the emphasis is now on a series of modest attractions linked by the seven-mile-long **Clywedog Trail**. It is all a bit heavy on packaged heritage, but no less interesting for that, and you can see all the sights in one long, varied day, making use of the free *Clywedog Valley* leaflet available from tourist offices and any of the sites. With the exception of Minera and Nant Mill, all the sites are within a couple of miles of the centre of Wrexham, and can be visited on foot. The easiest way to see the whole valley from Wrexham is to catch the #10 or #11 bus to Minera, walk the full length of the trail to King's Mill, then catch the #31 the mile or so back into Wrexham.

The **Minera Lead Mines** (April–July & Sept Tues–Sun 10am–5pm; Aug daily 10am–5pm; £1), four miles west of Wrexham, is the latest to get the heritage treatment. There isn't a lot to see, and many of the surface workings are still incompletely excavated, but the engine house and a pithead derrick have been largely rebuilt, and there's a good patch of reconstructed ore-processing machinery by the small museum in the former ore house. You get a far better impression of the site's layout, though, by walking up onto the hill behind – a heather-clad moor on the fringe of a region known as World's End – and looking back on the valley which, in the eighteenth century, was covered with mines extracting galena, a silver-and-zinc-rich lead ore from the bottom of shafts over 1200ft deep.

From the lead mines, a path leads for almost a mile east along the River Clywedog to the wildlife and local history centre at **Nant Mill** (Easter–Sept Tues–Sun 10am–5pm; Oct–Easter Sat & Sun 10am–4pm; free), where you can pick up leaflets for nature trails leading to a very visible section of **Offa's Dyke** (see p.236) in the woods nearby. The Clywedog Trail runs through the wood to **Bersham Ironworks** (Easter–Sept

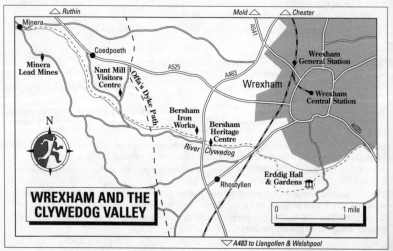

WREXHAM AND THE CLYWEDOG VALLEY

© Crown copyright

Tues–Sun 10am–5pm; £1), established in the seventeenth century and expanded by Cumbrian ironmaster John "Iron-Mad" Wilkinson who, in 1775, patented his new method for horizontally boring out cylinders. This produced the first truly circular, smooth bore, perfect for highly accurate cannons – hundreds were made here for the American Civil and Napoleonic wars – and the production of fine tolerance steam-engine cylinders. Engineer James Watt was a big customer: he produced steam engines which made water-powered sites unprofitable and eventually put Bersham out of business. After nearly two centuries of neglect, the remains are now being unearthed, revealing a broad area of mostly knee-high foundations around the centrepiece, the old foundry. This survived largely intact though it saw service as a corn mill and still retains its huge water wheel. The foundations really only serve to help you visualize the layout, which is better explained inside the old foundry and put in context ten minutes' walk away at the **Bersham Heritage Centre** (Easter–Oct Mon–Fri 10am–5pm, Sat & Sun noon–5pm; Nov–Easter closes 4pm; free), which has a room dedicated to Wilkinson.

Erddig Hall

Despite the closure of the ironworks, coal continued to be mined around Bersham until 1986. After World War II, coal tunnels were pushed under **Erddig Hall**, just south of Wrexham (April–Oct Mon–Wed, Sat & Sun house noon–5pm, 4pm in Oct; garden 11am–6pm, 5pm in Oct, July & Aug 10am–6pm; £6, "below stairs" & gardens only £4; NT), adding subsidence to the troubles of an already decaying building. Ever since the mansion was built in the late seventeenth century, its owners – all seemingly called Simon or Philip Yorke – maintained a conservative building policy which resulted in near decrepitude. Chief culprit was the fourth Simon Yorke, who inherited the estate in 1922 and did almost nothing, failing to install electricity, running water, gas or a phone and ignoring a chronic damp problem which had the Chinese hand-blocked paper peeling off the walls. The National Trust took charge in the 1970s, since when it has restored the house to its 1922 appearance and returned the jungle of a garden to its formal eighteenth-century plan.

The house itself isn't distinguished, but, as nothing was ever thrown away, the collection of fine furniture and portraits – including one by Gainsborough of the first Philip Yorke – is unusually complete. The real interest, however, lies in the servants' quarters, particularly the Servants' Hall, where specially commissioned portraits of eighteenth- and early-nineteenth-century staff members are accompanied by personalized dedications in verse written by a Yorke – a quite extraordinary display of benevolence. You can also see the blacksmith's shop, stables, laundry, the still-used bakehouse and kitchen.

Put an hour aside for the **walled garden**, saved from the worst excesses of the eighteenth-century landscaping craze despite the attentions of William Emes, a contemporary of Capability Brown, who worked on the surrounding parkland. Manicured box hedges delineate beds planted with pleached lime trees, the walls support some 150 species of ivy, and trained apple trees produce fruit celebrated during the Hall's annual apple festival in October.

To get back to Wrexham from Erddig Hall, head half a mile or so northeast to *Squire Yorke Inn*, from where it's about a mile along the road.

The Maelor

Although hardly ranking amongst Wales' most dramatic rural landscapes, the area of **The Maelor** (or "Maelor Saesneg", the "English Maelor"), to the immediate southeast of Wrexham, certainly warrants a leisurely amble. Historically a separated and remote outpost of Flintshire, this curiously shaped nodule of gentle agricultural land dotted with quiet villages protrudes into England, and the feel of the district is, indeed, very English – a place for picnics and gentle walks. The area's defining feature, certainly along its western edge, is the undulating River Dee, and the best place to appreciate the river is from the village of **BANGOR-ON-DEE** (Bangor-is-y-coed), some four miles southeast of Wrexham. From the second to the seventh century AD, this was the site of Britain's first, and most important, Celtic Christian monastery – the settlement grew to house some three thousand monks, but nothing of it remains these days. Otherwise, Bangor is a gently pleasing place to while away a few hours, whether admiring the seventeenth-century sandstone bridge, designed by Inigo Jones, or sampling one of the High Street pubs. Top choice is the *Stableyard* (☎01978/780642; ③), now a swish **restaurant** and excellent place to **stay**. Just off the B5069 Overton Road is Bangor-on-Dee **racecourse** (☎01978/781009), home of sporadic steeplechasing and race days nestled into a loop of the River Dee, as well as a decent campsite.

A couple of miles south of Bangor, **OVERTON** (Owrtyn) is the Maelor's prettiest village, its wide streets flanked by homely buildings of all ages, from almshouses to fine Georgian town houses and a succession of aged shop fronts. The village is best known as home to one of the "**Seven Wonders of Wales**", a grove of ancient yew trees surrounding the red-sandstone church of St Mary. These are believed to be up to 3,000 years old, considerably predating any Christian incursion on to the site, and suggesting that Overton was a notable **Pagan** place of worship.

Mold and around

MOLD (Yr Wyddgrug), ten miles north of Wrexham, enjoys a quiet, almost moribund existence disrupted only by the Wednesday and Saturday markets when stalls take the place of cars along the High Street. In truth, there's no great reason for a visit, though you may as well stop in on the way to **Ewloe Castle**, just four miles to the northeast or approaching the Clwydian Hills to the west.

The town was founded during the reign of William Rufus, though only a bowling green and a copse of beeches atop a mound mark the site of the motte-and-bailey fortifications on **Bailey Hill**, at the top of the High Street. The fort was built for the local Norman lord, Robert de Montalt, who probably gave the town its English name, essentially the same as the Welsh, meaning "The Mound". The commanding view over the River Alyn (Afon Alun) illustrates the strategic importance of the site, first taken by Owain Gwynedd in 1157 and again in 1199 by Llywelyn the Great, constantly shifting between Welsh and Anglo-Norman control until Edward I's hand came down hard on the region. Relative calm prevailed until a period during the Wars of the Roses, when private armies held sway. In 1465, after a skirmish in the town, local lord Rheinallt ap Gruffydd succeeded in capturing the Mayor of Chester and taking him back to the Tower in Nercwys, where he was presented with a pie containing the rope that would be his noose. A revenge party from Chester attempted to raid the Tower but was locked inside and the place subsequently torched by Rheinallt's men.

Henry VII's assumption of the throne, after his victory at the Battle of Bosworth, stamped some stability on the area. In gratitude for her son's victory, Henry's mother, Margaret Beaufort, commissioned the airy Perpendicular **St Mary's Church** on the site of a thirteenth-century church at the foot of Bailey Hill. The original oak roof carved with Tudor roses has been retained in the north aisle, as has a quatrefoil and animal frieze running below the small clerestory windows, though most of the rest was restored by Gilbert Scott in the nineteenth century.

Amongst the predominantly fifteenth- and sixteenth-century stained glass, one more modern, late-nineteenth-century window represents the town's meagre memorial to its most famous son (at least to English-speakers) and Wales' greatest painter, the eighteenth-century landscapist **Richard Wilson**, whose grave is by the church's north entrance. Having spent his childhood here, Wilson studied in Italy for six years, where he painted canvases from the Grand Tour, earning a good enough living to support himself back home while he concentrated on the subject for which he is best known: the mountains of Wales, typically dramatic scenes of Cadair Idris or Snowdon, often incorporating Latin elements into the Romantic panoramas. In the decades before John Ruskin's championing of Turner influenced critical taste, Wilson's style went undervalued, and though he co-founded the Royal Academy in 1768 and later won the acclaim of Ruskin, he died a pauper. The story goes that, in return for a few pints, he painted the two-headed sign for the *We Three Loggerheads* pub outside the Loggerheads Country Park (see below), the third loggerhead being the viewer.

Mold is no Welsh-language stronghold, so it seems ironic that it is **Daniel Owen**, a local tailor and nineteenth-century novelist, who should be commemorated by a statue, outside the library. "Not for the wise and learned have I written, but for the common people" is inscribed below the statue and it was his bluntly honest accounts of ordinary life that made him so unpopular with the Methodist leaders of the community. Writing only in Welsh, Owen became the most prominent writer of the late nineteenth century. A room full of his memorabilia takes up a sizeable portion of the small but effective **museum**, housed in the same building as the town's library and tourist office (hours as for tourist office below; free).

There's little else to see in Mold itself, but three miles west on the A494 (bus #B5), **Loggerheads Country Park** offers forest walks and nature trails with views of the Clwydian Range. Pick up more information at the **visitor centre** by the entrance (Mon–Fri 11am–4.30pm, Sat & Sun 10am–5pm; closes earlier in winter).

Practicalities

Mold has no train station, but regular **bus** services stop behind the cattle market east of High Street. From there it is a five-minute walk down King Street to Earl Road and the **tourist office**-cum-library (Mon & Tues, Thurs & Fri 9.30am–7pm, Wed 9.30am–5.30pm, Sat 9.30am–12.30pm or 4pm in summer; ☎01352/759331).

Accommodation isn't plentiful, but close to the centre you have a choice of the classy *Bryn Awel Hotel*, on Denbigh Road (☎01352/758622; ③), five minutes' walk north of the church, or *Glendale Lodge* (☎01352/754001; ②), just past Theatr Clwyd. The nearest **YHA hostel** (Easter, July & Aug only; ☎01352/810320) at Maeshafn, four miles southwest of Mold near Loggerheads Country Park, is an ageing affair with unusual three-tier bunks. You can camp here and use the facilities at reduced rates.

If you can't stretch to the moderately priced **meals** at *Chez Colette*, 56 High St (☎01352/759225), there are numerous cheap cafés nearby. *We Three Loggerheads* (see above) is the best of the **pubs** for both meals and drinking, while **entertainment** revolves around the region's major arts centre, Theatr Clwyd (☎01352/755114), a mile east on the A494. It suffered a funding crisis after its major patron, Clwyd County Council, was disbanded in 1996, but disputes between the succeeding councils have steadied to provide enough basic income for it to continue staging quality theatre and cinema – in 1996, it screened the world premiere of *August* starring Welshman Anthony Hopkins, for instance – aided by revenue from the good arts bookshop and café.

Ewloe Castle

Four miles northeast of Mold, **Ewloe Castle** (unrestricted access; CADW) makes an interesting diversion, if only to put Edward I's monstrous castles into perspective. Tucked in at the end of a wooded glen, Ewloe is so cloaked by sycamore and oak that you almost stumble into the ruins. An English stronghold which fell into Welsh hands around 1146, it was being fortified by Owain Gwynedd as an ambush castle when the Battle of Eulo took place in 1157. According to Giraldus Cambrensis, Henry II's "rash enthusiasm" hindered this first assault on Wales, and his push through the wooded pass resulted in the death of many of his men. In gratitude for his own life, the king contributed funds towards the building of Basingwerk Abbey (see p.394).

In 1210, Llywelyn ap Iorwerth ("the Great") built the apsidal Welsh Tower, and his grandson, Llywelyn ap Gruffydd ("the Last"), went on to add two wards, protected by a curtain wall and an outer ditch. However, Ewloe was never of great importance, and after the completion of Flint Castle at around 1283, it ceased to have any military significance at all.

Until preservation work was begun in the 1920s, local builders had helped themselves to the masonry, leaving just the shell at the head of a valley filled by the ancient woodland of **Wepre Park** (Parc Gwepra). The **visitor centre** (variable hours; ☎01244/814931) for both park and castle is ten minutes' walk from the latter, and a mile or so from Shotton train station, on the North Coast line, four miles southeast of Flint; walk towards the Somerfield supermarket, then turn left up Wepre Drive.

Hawarden

Immediately on the other side of Ewloe village from the castle is the interesting hilltop settlement of **HAWARDEN** (Penarlâg), whose commanding views over the Cheshire Plain and the Dee Estuary have made it a site of strategic importance for the past thousand years. By the busy village crossroads, a small door in an imposing castellated gateway leads into the rolling parkland (open daily until dusk) that surrounds the two Hawarden **castles**: one a stone tower on a mound, all that remains of Edward I's border fortress (free access), and the second a heavily gothicized eighteenth-century mansion (no access) that was renamed Hawarden Castle in the Victorian age. In 1839, William Ewart Gladstone, Britain's long-serving Liberal prime minister, married into the castle's resident family. He and his wife Catherine later made the castle their home, and both are buried in the village parish **church of St Deiniol**. The church, rebuilt by Sir Gilbert Scott in the mid-nineteenth century, stands quietly at the bottom of Church Lane, off the main street. Next door is the sumptuous **St Deiniol's Library**, a floridly extravagant neo-Gothic building constructed from a bequest after Gladstone's death. Britain's only residential library, St Deiniol's is open only to registered readers; for access, you'll need to make contact in advance (☎01244/532350, *deiniol.visitors@ btinternet.com*). Gladstone's legacy can also be seen in the memorial fountain that sits in the middle of the village's main crossroads. Heading east along the main street, a seventeenth-century **lock-up**, a small single cell built into a wall opposite a fine row of cottages is also worth a glance.

Hawarden is a decent, if quiet, place to base yourself for the night. The *Glynne Arms*, by the main crossroads, is an atmospheric old coaching inn that serves good **food** and **drink**. The best option for **accommodation** is the gorgeous Elizabethan *St Deiniol's Ash Farm* (☎01244/534215; ②), off Ash Lane on the north side of the village. The **train station** – on the line between Bidston and Wrexham – is a five-minute walk west of the main crossroads, and there are numerous daily **buses** from outside the *Glynne Arms* to Chester, Flint and Holywell.

The Vale of Clwyd

To the west of Mold, separated from the English Marches and the industry on Deeside by the soft contours of the broad-backed Clwydian Range, the wide and fertile **Vale of Clwyd** follows the sandstone course of the barely noticeable River Clwyd (Afon Clywedog) from Corwen on the A5 (see p.257) to the coast near Rhuddlan. Linked by quiet roads through a patchwork of small farms, three attractive towns of warm-hued stone sit on hillocks above the valley. None warrants more than a couple of hours' attention, but together they make a good day's diversion and a link between the north coast and the route up the Dee Valley towards Snowdonia (see Chapter Five).

Churches loom large in the valley. Britain's smallest cathedral dominates the village-sized city of **St Asaph**, at the valley's northernmost tip, but the structure is barely larger than the parish church in the ancient market town of **Ruthin**, thirteen miles south. Both these buildings and the ancient village church at **Llanrhaeadr**, midway between them, were modernized in the nineteenth century, but it is the last which remains the Vale's prime example of medieval ecclesiastical architecture. **Denbigh**, four miles south of St Asaph, is better known for its "hollow crown", the high-walled castle ruin which rings the top of the hill behind the town.

The old rail line from Corwen to Rhyl has long since gone, leaving regular **buses** along the A525 between Rhyl and Corwen as the primary transport route.

Ruthin

Though surrounded by modern housing and known primarily as a livestock market town, the centre of **RUTHIN** (Rhuthun), ten miles west of Mold, comprises an attractive knot of half-timbered buildings set between church and castle. The town is built on a commanding rise in the Vale of Clwyd, close to lands once held by Owain Glyndŵr, which made it ripe for the first push of his quest for dominion over all of Wales in 1400. The heavily restored red-stone **Ruthin Castle** (now open only as a hotel), dating from Edward I's first stint of castle-building, was then home to Lord de Grey of Ruthin, a favourite of Henry IV. Coveting a tract of land above Corwen held by Glyndŵr, de Grey used his influence with Henry to have Glyndŵr proclaimed a traitor and was given the land in return. He was thus the first to suffer when Glyndŵr crowned himself Prince of Wales and, with four thousand followers, launched an attack on Ruthin on September 20, 1400. The castle itself held, but the town was razed – though not until Glyndŵr's men had plundered the goods brought to the town's annual fair by the English. The castle went on to resist the Parliamentarians for eleven weeks during the Civil War, eventually falling to General Mytton in April 1646, after which it was destroyed. Over three hundred years later, in 1963, it was partially restored as the hotel that stands today (see overleaf), with Italian and rose gardens landscaped around the ancient moat and crumbling ruins. Strictly speaking, the grounds are open to residents and peacocks only, but you can wander through if attending one of the tacky medieval banquets or drinking in the panelled library bar.

Otherwise, time in Ruthin is better spent browsing the mixed bag of architectural styles around St Peter's Square, the heart of the town's medieval street plan. The north-east corner is dominated by the twin-aisled **St Peter's Church** (daily 9am–4pm or thereabouts), approached through a beautiful pair of 1728 iron gates wrought by the Davies Brothers, who also made the gates of St Giles church in Wrexham and those at Chirk Castle. Impressive though the church gates are, they are upstaged by the ceiling of the north aisle: here, 408 carved black oak panels meet at Tudor Rose bosses. This part of the building dates from the fourteenth century, when it was founded as a collegiate church, but Henry VII reputedly donated the ceiling, possibly from Basingwerk Abbey (see p.394), in gratitude to those who helped him take the English throne. The details can be hard to see, but a switch by the hymn board provides illumination for twenty seconds at a time, and the more intriguing designs – grotesque faces and floral and geometric designs – are reproduced on a panel opposite the door. One of the busts on the north wall is of Gabriel Goodman, who, in 1574, while Dean of Westminster, re-founded the **grammar school** that had been closed by Henry VIII forty years earlier; it still stands behind the church, next to the Christ's Hospital Almshouses, which Goodman built in 1590 as a gift to the town.

Goodman's birthplace in St Peter's Square, Exmewe Hall, is now occupied by a branch of Barclays bank, but outside sits an unimpressive chunk of limestone known as **Maen Huail**, testament to the darker side of King Arthur's character. The less-than-convincing story has Arthur and Huail, brother of a Welsh chieftain called Gildas, fighting over the attentions of a woman. Huail pierced Arthur's thigh, giving him a permanent limp, but promised never to mention Arthur's loss of face. Inevitably, though, Huail couldn't resist taunting him about it and an incensed Arthur had Huail beheaded on this stone.

Standing isolated on the other side of the square is one of the many half-timbered buildings around the town. Now the National Westminster bank, it was built in 1401 as a courthouse and prison and still retains under the eaves the barely visible stump of the **gibbet**, last used in 1679 to hang a Franciscan friar.

The most-photographed building in Ruthin isn't any of these, but the **Myddleton Arms pub**, built in 1657 in Dutch style and topped by seven dormer windows known as "The Eyes of Ruthin", an apt enough description of the higgledy-piggledy windows that stare blankly down on to the square.

Practicalities

Buses from Denbigh, Corwen and Mold all stop on Market Street, running between St Peter's Square and the valley's best **tourist office** (June–Sept daily 10am–5.30pm; Oct–May Mon–Sat 10am–5pm, Sun noon–5pm; ☎01824/703992), 300 yards away inside the Ruthin Craft Centre. **Bike rental** is available from Cellar Cycles (☎01824/707133) on Well Street. Ruthin is well provided with **accommodation**: top of the range is *Ruthin Castle Hotel* (☎01824/702664, fax 704924; ④), but the *Castle Hotel* (☎01824/702479; ②), a former coaching inn on the square, and the spacious thirteenth-century wood-panelled *Gorffwysfa* B&B, just around the corner on Castle Street (☎01824/702748; ①), are also very comfortable. Otherwise try *Moelfa* on Denbigh Road (☎01824/702468; ①), or *Ye Olde Cross Keys* (☎01824/705281; ②), five minutes' walk west along the B5105. Out of town on the disused Corwen to Rhyl line, the pleasant *Eyarth Old Railway Station* (☎01824/703643; ②), also serves decent meals; take bus #51 to Llanfair Dyffryn Clwyd, from where it's a half-mile walk. A mile south of Llanfair Dyffryn Clwyd and just off a small lane, *Plas Uchaf* (☎01824/705794; ②) is a superb rural B&B set in a beautiful hall-house dating from the early sixteenth century. You'll also need transport to get to the seventeenth-century *Three Pigeons Inn* (☎01824/703178; ③) in Graigfechan, a mile east of Ruthin on the A494 Mold road to Pentre, then three miles south on the B5429. It serves good beer and food, with Sunday barbecues in summer, and has live Welsh and Irish music most Saturday nights. There's a simple **campsite** (March–Oct) tucked in behind.

The range of good **food** in Ruthin itself is fairly limited. The *Bay Tree Café*, in the same complex as the craft centre and tourist office, is good for daytime wholefood snacks. Bar meals are available from the pubs around the square, including some good veggie and Cajun specialities at the *Castle Hotel*, and, round the corner, steaks, jacket potatoes and other pub standbys at *Ye Olde Anchor Inn* on Rhos Street. You can get a decent curry at *Spice Bangla* (☎01824/707277), tucked up an alley off Clwyd Street, or a wide range of seasonal Italian cuisine at *DaVinci's* (☎01824/702200), in Castle Mews off Well Street. If you've got plenty of cash, there's always the option of ersatz medieval banquets at the *Ruthin Castle Hotel* (see above; £29.50). As for more conventional **entertainment**, the *Castle Hotel* has a Thursday evening folk club, and is a decent place for a few pints any night. You might also catch some music at the *Eagles Hotel* on Clwyd Street.

If Ruthin's huddle of buildings becomes too claustrophobic, you might want to take one of the nearby **walks** along the Clwydian Range to Moel Famau and Foel Fenlli (see box opposite), or **horse riding** at the Star Farm Riding Centre (March–Nov; ☎01824/705929) at Llangynafal, four miles north of Ruthin.

WALK TO MOEL FAMAU AND FOEL FENLLI

Walks on Moel Famau and Foel Fenlli both start from Bwlch-Pen-Barras, a pass four miles east of Ruthin at the top of the B5429, once used for the main turnpike route over the Clwydian Range to Mold. The **Offa's Dyke long-distance path** (though not the Dyke itself) runs along these bald tops (*moel*, and its initial mutation *foel*, mean "bare mountain"), following the line of a Bronze Age trading route, past the remains of six Iron Age hillforts surrounding the tops and the Jubilee Tower. Proximity to Liverpool, Chester and Wrexham, and the relatively gentle terrain, make this a popular spot at weekends: stick to weekdays if possible. No public transport comes this way but you can walk two miles up the road from Llanbedr-Dyffryn-Clwyd (bus #B5 from Ruthin) to begin a walk at either of two car parks.

From the first car park (free), right at the top of Bwlch-Pen-Barras, you can make the steep climb southwards to the most impressive of the hillfort sites on 1800-foot **Foel Fenlli** (1 mile return; 40min; 500ft ascent). Excavations here uncovered 35 hut circles within earthworks three-quarters of a mile across. The height from ditch bottom to bank top reaches 35ft in places, with triple defences on the less easily defended eastern flank. Aerial shots make much more of this than is visible on the ground, but that doesn't detract from the walk.

From the same car park, a broad path leads a mile and a half north to the 1820-foot "Mothers' Mountain", **Moel Famau** (3 miles return; 1–2hr; 650ft ascent), the highest point in the range, topped by the truncated **Jubilee Tower**. The subject of many a disparaging remark when it was built in 1810 to celebrate George III's fifty-year reign, the top of this Egyptian-style structure was never completed. The planned pyramid was to rise to 150ft but was damaged in a storm in 1860 and only partially repaired in 1970. The ruins may not be much, but on a clear day the views over the Vale of Clwyd as far as Snowdon and Cadair Idris make it all worthwhile.

An alternative, less dramatic, approach to Moel Famau leaves a second car park (£1) half a mile or so down the eastern side of the pass, from where an easy blue-marked path (3.5 miles return; 2hr 30min; 900ft ascent) or slightly harder red path (2.5 miles return; 2hr; 900ft ascent) guide you through Corsican pine plantations up the southeastern flank to the tower.

Llanrhaeadr

Just off the A525, four miles north of Ruthin, **St Dyfnog's Church** seems much too large for the tiny hamlet of **LLANRHAEADR**. In the sixth century Saint Dyfnog established a hermitage here on the site of a healing well, and donations from pilgrims funded the building of the present church in 1533. Typically for the area it has twin aisles and, though heavily restored in 1880, drips with original features, including a glorious carved barrel roof with vine-leaf patterns and outstanding stained glass. The **Jesse Window**, at the east end of the north aisle, is considered to be one of the finest examples in Britain. Depicting the descent of Jesus through the House of Israel from Jesse, the father of King David, it draws you in to the Virgin and Child above the central light, surrounded by 21 of their bearded, ermine-robed ancestors, whose names are recorded in medieval Latin. The window is believed to be original, contemporary with the church, though it was removed and stored in an oak chest during the Civil War, which is when its companion in the south aisle is thought to have been destroyed. In the nineteenth century, fragments that may have belonged to it were found nearby and pieced together to form the west window.

Reached on the hourly #51 bus, Llanrhaeadr is an easy trip from Ruthin or Denbigh; or you can **stay** just across the road from the church at the *King's Head Inn* (☎01745/890278; ②), a well-preserved sixteenth-century coaching inn with a wide choice of food and a low-beamed bar.

Denbigh and around

The hilltop castle ruins dominating the Vale of Clwyd eight miles north of Ruthin herald **DENBIGH** (Dinbych), a former bastide town (see p.408) which tumbles down the hill towards its medieval centre. The glove-making industry for which the town was once famed has vanished, leaving it merely hosting Tuesday and Friday markets and servicing the sprawling postwar development on its outskirts.

The market takes place on the broad central section of the High Street, surrounded by a pleasing array of colonnaded medieval buildings. Thankfully, they haven't been over-restored and, together with the more modern structures in their midst, help retain a working town atmosphere. Beside *The Old Vaults* pub on the High Street, Broomhill Lane runs up past the crumbling **Burgess Gate**, the former northern entry to the town, to the vast grassy ward of the ruined **Denbigh Castle** (unrestricted access; CADW).

For a long time, the River Clwyd formed the border of England and Wales, guarded here by an unidentified castle built by Dafydd, brother of Llywelyn ap Gruffydd ("the Last"). This probably gave the town its name, meaning "small fort", though it's more imaginatively attributed to John Salusbury, a medieval knight said to have rid the town of a dragon, triumphantly returning with its head to cries of "Dim Dych!" (No More Dragon!). Dafydd's castle put up strong resistance, but eventually fell, allowing Edward I to erect castles here and at the other key sites of Rhuddlan and Ruthin. By 1282, only the outer defences – the town walls – had been started, under the charge of Henry de Lacy, Earl of Lincoln, who required each of his 63 burgesses to "find a man armed in Denbigh to guard and defend the town". This wasn't enough to repel a Welsh revolt in 1294, which though rapidly suppressed, goaded de Lacy into work on the castle proper, employing many of the concepts already implemented by Edward's architect, James of St George.

The most imposing piece of what remains is the **gatehouse**, its three octagonal towers enclosing an originally vaulted hall, making it one of the finest defensive structures of the era. Entrance is beneath a weathered statue of Edward I in a niche, flanked on the right by the Prison Tower, still showing evidence of five garderobes that discharge into a common cesspit, and the Porter's Lodge Tower on the left. From here, you can walk the only remaining section of the wall, extending as far as the Great Kitchen Tower with its two huge fireplaces. On the far side, the Postern Tower was heavily strengthened after 1294, as were the **town walls** that formed the outer ward branching off at the castle walls. Continue along the short section of wall walk (key from the tourist office) down to the **Goblin Tower** from where, at the end of a six-month-long siege in 1646, Charles I threw the castle keys onto the heads of the all-conquering Roundheads.

In 1563, Elizabeth I sold the castle to her favourite, Robert Dudley, Earl of Leicester, who in 1579 chose a site just below the castle for the church that he hoped would supplant St Asaph cathedral. It was never completed, but the shell still stands today as **Leicester's Folly**.

Back on High Street, the sixteenth-century County Hall contains the local library, the tourist office and a small **local history museum** (same hours as tourist office, see opposite; free) with its impressionistic modern mural of Denbigh running up the stairwell. There's also background on Denbigh's famous sons, such as Humphrey Llwyd, who, in the sixteenth century, drew up the first separate map of Wales, published posthumously in 1573. He is commemorated in the **St Marcella's Church** (usually closed), a mile east of the centre on Whitchurch Road. Here the cemetery contains the grave of the bard, satirist and playwright Tom o'r Nant or "Tom of the Dingle", who George Borrow casually refers to as "the Welsh Shakespeare". In his autobiography, Tom writes: "As soon as I had learned to spell and write a few words I conceived a mighty desire to learn to write; so I went in quest of elderberries to make ink."

Practicalities

All **buses** stop on the High Street, just along from the combined library, museum and **tourist office** in Hall Square (Mon, Wed & Fri 9.30am–7pm, Tues & Thurs 9.30am–5.30pm, Sat 9.30am–4pm; ☎01745/816313), where you can pick up some useful handouts detailing town walks. **Accommodation** in the centre is pretty much limited to *The Bull Hotel* (☎01745/812582; ②), just beside the tourist office, and *Cayo Guesthouse*, 74 Vale St (☎01745/812686; ①), a couple of hundred yards down the main St Asaph road. If you have your own transport, you should try one of the excellent rural B&Bs in the vicinity. *College Farm* (☎01745/550276; ②), at Penial three miles southwest of town on the B4501 is good, as is *Fron Haul Farmhouse*, in Bodfari, four miles northeast along the A543 (☎01745/710301; ①), which also serves good meals. People with dogs are particularly welcome at the friendly and comfortable *Berllan Bach*, Ffordd Las, three miles east at Llandyrnog, at the foot of the Clwydian Range (☎01824/790732; ②), where good country dinners go for under £15 – from the roundabout at the southern end of Denbigh, head east through Llanwfan, past the *Kinmel Arms*, then straight on for another half a mile. The most convenient **campsite** is the *Station House Caravan Park* (☎01745/710372) at Bodfari, reached on bus #14.

There are no outstanding **restaurants** in Denbigh, but you can eat well enough. *The Bull Hotel* provides straightforward bar meals, while the *Denbigh Balti House* at 53 High St (☎01745/815512) serves reliable Indian food. Otherwise, you're pretty much restricted to chips and kebabs from the town-centre takeaways. Finding a decent place to **drink** is no problem: *The Old Vaults* on High Street is good, or make for Back Row, behind High Street, for the *Y Llew Aur* (*The Golden Lion*) and *Y Llew Gwyn* (*The White Lion*). There's another *Golden Lion* five miles southeast at Llangynhafal, where the Saturday evening **Welsh singalongs** often draw local choral groups. Back in town, the *Hope & Anchor*, 94 Vale St, also has folk evenings every Saturday.

The Clocaenog Forest and Llyn Brenig

The high land to the west of the Vale of Clwyd is rolling sheep country, dissected by narrow lanes and the meandering streams which run off the bleak **Mynydd Hiraethog** moorland to the south. The peaty soil and challenging climate on this 1200-foot-high plateau support a delicate ecosystem with cottongrass, marsh marigold, the lilac-white cuckoo flower and the pink lousewort thriving amongst the heath, buzzards wheeling overhead and trout plucking at stoneflies and mayflies. But, as elsewhere in Wales, the evergreens are on the march and, over the last couple of decades, vast areas of "wasteland" have been planted with Sitka Spruce, Japanese Larch and Norwegian Spruce to form the **Clocaenog Forest**. At its heart lies the **Llyn Brenig** reservoir, used in conjunction with the waters of Llyn Celyn near Bala to control River Dee water levels, and providing modest opportunities for aquatic diversion. Few visitors penetrate this rather gloomy area, except to speed through on the A543, the fastest route from Denbigh to Betws-y-Coed and Snowdonia, but locals flock to the **Llyn Brenig Visitor Centre** (mid-March to Nov daily 10am–5pm; £1 per car), just off the B4501, principally for rainbow **trout fishing**. A permit will set you back £12 for the day and boats can be rented by the day (£18 on weekends; £15 on weekdays), for the morning (£11.50) or for an afternoon and evening (3pm onwards; £12.50); you can also rent **mountain bikes**. The two-mile lakeside drive north from here leads to the offices of Celtic Adventure: Brenig Watersports (April–Oct daily 9am–5pm; ☎01490/440408), from where you can rent kayaks, open canoes and windsurfers at reasonable rates, or launch your own craft for £3–4 per half-day. Windsurfing and canoeing courses run in summer for around £20 a day: they're mainly aimed at groups but you may be able to tag along. Landlubbers can entertain themselves nearby on the mile-long waymarked forest and moorland **nature trail**.

St Asaph

Five miles north of Denbigh, at the point where the valley opens out onto the north coast flats, a cluster of houses centred on a single main street ranks as Britain's second smallest city, **ST ASAPH** (Llanelwy). The city of St David's in Pembrokeshire is slightly less populous, but St Asaph boasts the country's smallest **cathedral** (open daily 8am–dusk); however, it's no bigger than many village churches, standing on a rise above the River Elwy (Afon Elwy) with its squat square tower at the crossing of a broad, aisled nave and a well-lit transept.

The town's Welsh name translates as "the church on Elwy River", a title which dates back to the sixth century when Saint Asaph succeeded the cathedral's founder, Saint Kentigern, as abbot in 570, and became its first bishop. Both are commemorated in the easternmost window in the north aisle of the cathedral. There is almost no record of the place from then until 1282, when Edward I's men stormed through and destroyed the church, leaving the incumbent bishop Anian II, whose effigy is in the south aisle, with the task of building the present structure. That too was attacked in 1402 by Owain Glyndŵr, but this time only the woodwork was lost and soon replaced.

From 1601 until his death in 1604, the bishopric was held by **William Morgan** (see box opposite), who was responsible for the translation of the first Welsh-language Bible in 1588. An octagonal monument in the churchyard on the south side of the cathedral commemorates the work of Morgan and his fellow translators, including William Salusbury and Gabriel Goodman (see p.385). This is Morgan's only memorial; his grave under the presbytery has been unmarked since Giles Gilbert Scott's substantial restoration in the 1870s.

Around a thousand Morgan Bibles were printed – one for every church in the land – of which only nineteen remain, one of them displayed in the north transept. The cathedral also has a handsome collection of psalter and prayer books in an alcove in the south transept, Elizabeth I's 1549 copy of *The Book of Common Prayer* only slightly pre-dating Salusbury's New Testament translation of 1567. Tucked into a recess in one of the columns opposite is an exquisite sixteenth-century ivory Madonna, said to have come from the Spanish Armada, and a plaque nearby commemorates native son and explorer, Henry Morton Stanley.

Contact the Dean in advance (☎01745/583597) for access into the crypt to view the cathedral **treasury**, which, alongside its collection of silverware, contains a Welsh–Greek–Hebrew dictionary compiled in the nineteenth century by Richard Robert Jones, usually known as Dic Aberdaron, a self-taught scholar who reputedly knew fifteen languages and smatterings of another twenty. The son of a fisherman, he was born in Aberdaron (see p.361) in 1780 and lived more or less as a tramp. His tombstone, in the churchyard of St Kentigern and St Asaph's Church at the bottom of the High Street, is engraved with a few lines by Ellis Owen which translate as:

A linguist eight times above other linguists – truly he was
A dictionary of every province.
Death took away his fifteen languages.
Below he is now without a language at all.

Practicalities

The A55 runs close by, but without your own transport you're reliant on local **buses**, which all stop right outside the cathedral. If you plan to **stay** in the region you may be better off at places listed under Denbigh (overleaf) or Rhyl (p.397), though you can get good central rooms with showers at the *Kentigern Arms* towards the bottom of the High Street (☎01745/584157; ②). A quarter of a mile away are the nicely furnished, non-

WILLIAM MORGAN AND THE FIRST WELSH BIBLE

Until 1588 only English Bibles had been used in Welsh churches, a fact which rankled Welsh-born preacher William Morgan, who insisted that "Religion, if it is not taught in the mother tongue, will lie hidden and unknown". This was the professed reason behind Elizabeth I's demand for a translation, though her subjects' disaffection could be most conveniently controlled through the church. Four clergymen took up the challenge over a period of 25 years, but it is Morgan who is remembered: working away in Llanrhaeadr-ym-Mochnant (see p.244), he so neglected his duties that he needed an armed guard to get to his services and was said to preach with a pistol at his side.

The eventual translation was so successful that the Privy Council decreed that a copy should be allocated to every Welsh church. Though it was soon replaced by a translation of the Authorized Version, Morgan's Bible differs little in style from the latest edition used in Welsh services today. More than just a basis for sermons, The *Welsh Bible* (*Y Beibl*) served to codify the language and set a standard for Welsh prose. Without it the language would probably have divided into several dialects or even followed its Brythonic cousin, Cornish, into history.

smoking *Chalet* (☎01745/584025; ①) and the plush *Plas Elwy* (☎01745/582263; ③), both on The Roe – across the river bridge then right.

Snacks, coffee and picnic supplies are available from the Farm Shop, halfway down High Street. For more substantial **meals**, make for the *Kentigern Arms* which, as well as being Denbigh's most appealing pub, serves inexpensive bar food and crispy pizzas; alternatively, walk across the High Street to the seventeenth-century former almshouse now operating as St Asaph's best restaurant, the moderately priced *Barrow Alms* (☎01745/582260).

THE NORTH COAST

Wales' northern seaboard elicits strong reactions. The ranks of detractors citing brash resorts at its eastern end are matched by files of advocates who swear by the low-cost charms of these same towns or who are drawn to the more highbrow attractions further west. Either way, the English borderlands and the interior of northeast Wales are poor preparation for the **north coast**, which peels away from England at **Deeside**, a wedge of former mining country between the salt marshes of the Dee estuary and the Clwydian Range which has its share of modest offerings. Amongst these are **Flint**, where you'll find the first link in Edward I's Iron Ring of castles, and understated **Holywell**, whose quiet attractions include St Winefride's Well, a pilgrimage site of varied fortunes during the last 1300 years.

The next 20-mile stretch of sand constitutes the ugliest piece of coastline in Wales, an endless stretch of cramped caravan parks – there's barely an arm's length between neighbouring caravans – packed each year with fun-seekers from Merseyside and the rest of northern England. The "amusements" liberally scattered along the promenades and beachfronts seem designed to keep you off the beaches: wise counsel even in the hottest weather since the sea here is none too clean. Of the resorts, **Prestatyn**, though uninspiring, is at least notable as the starting, or finishing, point of the Offa's Dyke long-distance path. **Rhyl** is the largest, loudest and tackiest, although it's full of good budget accommodation, and enjoys proximity to two inland attractions: the second of Edward I's castles at **Rhuddlan** and the National Portrait Gallery's Welsh outpost at **Bodelwyddan**. **Colwyn Bay** is smarter, but pales next to its far superior western neighbours, Conwy and Llandudno.

The great sweep of the north coast is interrupted by the **Great Orme**, a massive limestone hummock that rises above **Llandudno**, queen of the north Wales coast for over a hundred years. Neighbouring **Conwy** is more appealing still, packing more sights than the rest of the coast put together within the girdle of 700-year-old town walls which spur off from the mighty castle. The A55 expressway is held tightly to the coast by the northern fringes of Snowdonia's Carneddau range for the final fifteen miles to **Bangor**, home to north Wales' only university and consequently its liveliest town.

Deeside

The industrial hinterland that spreads over the border from Chester and licks the fringes of Mold and Wrexham can best be avoided by heading directly for **Deeside**, a narrow littoral flanking the River Dee where it broadens out into an expansive estuary. Its salt-soaked fields support huge numbers of waders and **wildfowl**, who come to feed on the sands and mudflats left by retreating tides. Plovers, oystercatchers and Europe's largest concentration of pintails winter here, pushing the population into six figures. The only designated viewing point is the RSPB's **Point of Ayr** site, two miles east of Prestatyn at the head of the estuary, the now-defunct colliery – the last to close in north Wales – and the offshore gas terminal discouraging all but the keenest of birders. The route there, along the A548 or the North Coast train line, passes an untidy string of largely uninteresting settlements. The crumbling castle remains at **Flint** should only detain you briefly, though you may want longer to pay homage to St Winefride and her healing waters at **Holywell**, especially if you're drawn to the adjacent minor collection of historic industrial buildings of the **Greenfield Valley Heritage Park**. A little further into Wales, there are two fine ancient sites of interest: the gorgeous carved Celtic cross of **Maen Achwyfaen** and **The Gop**, a mysterious prehistoric burial mound. By car, the easiest way to access Deeside is from the A55 expressway.

Flint

If you're travelling on the North Coast train line, be sure to take one of the regional services which stop at **FLINT** (Y Fflint), seven miles north of Mold, and spend the hour between trains rambling around the yellowish sandstone ruins of **Flint Castle** (unrestricted access; CADW), two minutes' walk over the footbridge from the station. Started in 1277 after the Treaty of Aberconwy, this was the first of Edward I's "Iron Ring" of fortresses (see p.408), standing sentinel over the coastal marshes of the Dee Estuary and the once-important shipping lanes into Chester. The ten-foot-thick pockmarked sandstone walls form a square with drum towers at all except the southeast corner, where a small moat and drawbridge separate the castle from the well-preserved Great Tower, or Donjon. Uniquely in Britain, this was intended as the castle's main accommodation and last place of retreat, and came equipped with its own well. Together with its large grassy outer ward and the adjoining town, the castle formed a unified enclave known as a "bastide" (see p.408). Though Conwy and Caernarfon subsequently received the same treatment, Flint can claim to be the first borough in Wales to receive its charter, in September 1284. Until then, towns didn't really exist in essentially rural Wales.

Perhaps Flint's greatest hour came in 1399 when Richard II was lured here from the safety of Conwy Castle and captured by Henry Bolingbroke, the Duke of Lancaster and future Henry IV. Shakespeare dramatized the event in *Richard II*, when in response to Bolingbroke's, "My gracious Lord, I come but for mine own", the defeated king replies, "Your own is yours, and I am yours, and all". Even Richard's favourite greyhound is said to have deserted him at this point.

During the Civil War, Flint remained Royalist until taken in 1647 by General Mytton, who so effectively dismantled it that only six years later it was practically buried in its own ruins. It was in this condition when Celia Fiennes found it on the brief – and generally displeasing – Welsh leg of her journeys around Britain between 1698 and 1712. She described Flint as "a very ragged place", and things haven't changed much. Unless you have come to spot some of the hundred thousand wintering waders on the Dee Estuary, you'll probably want to move on by the hourly **trains** or **buses** which leave from outside *The Raven* pub, a few yards north from the station along Holywell Street, the main coast road.

Holywell and around

A place of pilgrimage for thirteen hundred years, **HOLYWELL** (Treffynnon), just off the A55 four miles northwest of Flint, comes billed as "The Lourdes of Wales", though it doesn't really warrant such a comparison. Thankfully, there are no tacky souvenir stalls selling Virgin Mary lighters and the like; instead, Holywell is a quiet little town that modestly plays down its ancient appeal. Half a mile from the bus station at the far end of the High Street (turn right here and follow the signs), the source of all the fuss is **St Winefride's Well** (daily: mid-May to Sept 9am–5.15pm; Oct to mid-May 10am–4pm; 20p donation). A sacred spring possibly in use for thousands of years, the well was first recorded by the Romans, who used the waters to relieve rheumatism and gout. The Roman connection sheds considerable doubt on the veracity of local legends said to date back to 660 AD or thereabouts. The virtuous Winefride (*Gwenfrewi* in Welsh) was decapitated here after resisting the amorous advances of Prince Caradoc, and the well is said to have sprung up at the spot where her head fell. When Saint Beuno, her uncle, placed her head beside the body, a combination of prayer and the waters revived her, setting her on track for the rest of her life as an abbess at Gwytherin Convent near Llanrwst.

Richard I and Henry V provided regal patronage, ensuring a steady flow of believers to what became one of the great shrines of Christendom. After the Reformation, pilgrimages – now punishable by death – became more clandestine, and the well became a focal point of resistance to Protestantism. A century and a half later, the Catholic king of England, James II, came here to pray for a son and heir; the eventual answer to his imprecations threatened a Catholic succession and contributed to the overthrow of the House of Stuart.

Pilgrims spent the night praying in the Perpendicular **St Winefride's Chapel** (key from the ticket office; CADW), built around 1500 to enclose three sides of the well. Henry VII's mother, Margaret Beaufort, paid for the construction and earned herself a likeness amongst the roof bosses that depict the life of St Winefride in the ornate, Gothic fan-vaulted crypt that surrounds the well. With the gloom only cut by light from votive candles, she's not that easy to see now.

Though the site's importance has waned considerably, pilgrimages do still take place, mainly on St Winefride's Day, the nearest Sunday to June 22, when a couple of thousand pilgrims are led through the streets behind a relic, part of Winefride's thumb bone. The procession ends by the open side of the crypt where the spring – or at least the outflow of a pump installed after mine working disrupted the spring's source in 1917 – fills a calm pool capacious enough to accommodate the dozens of faithful who dutifully wade through the waters three times in the hope of curing their ailments, a rite also associated with the Celtic baptism by triple immersion. Immersion isn't limited to the procession: anyone, irrespective of their professed beliefs, can take the cure, though most choose to go in the summer "Curing Season", during which there are daily services.

Practicalities

Holywell doesn't have a train station, but a reasonable number of **buses** call at the bus station at the southern end of High Street. From here, head a hundred yards down High Street and turn left to get to the library on North Street, which serves as an unofficial **tourist office**, with librarians doling out leaflets and the like (Mon 9.30am–5pm, Tues, Thurs & Fri 9.30am–7pm, Wed 9.30am–1pm, Sat 9.30am–12.30pm; ☎01352/713157).

The few old pubs and coffee shops probably won't detain you overnight, but if you are **staying**, by far the best bet is the oak-beamed, partly sixteenth-century *Greenhill Farm* (March–Oct; ☎01352/713270; ②), reached by heading northeast from Winefride's Well on the B5121 for a few yards, then taking the second left opposite the *Royal Oak* pub. *Bryn Beuno Guesthouse*, on Whitford Street (☎01352/711315; ①), is also convenient: uphill from the well, turn right along a small bypass and continue for 300 yards. *The Springfield Hotel* (☎01352/780503, fax 780826; ③), just off the A55 expressway southeast of Holywell, caters mainly to business traffic but does have an indoor pool.

The best-value pub **meals** in town are those served at the *Royal Oak* on the B5121, which is also the best place to drink.

Greenfield Valley and Basingwerk Abbey

Trainloads of pilgrims used to arrive at Holywell by a steep branch which once ran off the North Coast line. From St Winefride's Well, a path follows a mile of the old line's bed towards the sea and passes a series of five ponds, the millraces between them providing power for the copper works and cotton mills whose remains now constitute the **Greenfield Valley** (Dyffryn Maesglas) **Heritage Park**. Most of this area is still being renovated and forms little more than a sideshow as you walk the mile down to **Basingwerk Abbey** (unrestricted access; CADW), where, in 1188, Archbishop Baldwin and Giraldus Cambrensis spent a night during their grand tour (see p.355). Most of the extant slabs of stonework are the remains of domestic buildings used by the abbot and twelve monks of the Savignac order, who lived in the abbey on its founding by Ranulph II, Earl of Chester, in 1131. Sixteen years later, the order merged with the Cistercians but went on controlling extensive lands in England and Wales until the Reformation when, in 1537, the abbey was dissolved and its spoils distributed around the region. There's a little more of the history in the **visitor centre** (April–Oct daily 10am–5pm; free), which is effectively the entrance to the **Greenfield Valley Farm and Museum** (same hours; £2), north Wales' collection of reconstructed buildings from around the region, many being saved from planned destruction. Particularly interesting are the Victorian school and the collection of agricultural buildings, the latter preserved as a working farm where you can feed the animals. Sunday afternoons are the best time to visit, when there are workshops, demonstrations and guided countryside walks.

Maen Achwyfaen and the Gop

If you've got your own transport, it's well worth making an excursion four miles west from Holywell to the stunning **Maen Achwyfaen**, the "Stone of Lamentation" (unrestricted access; CADW) and Britain's tallest **Celtic cross**. Though the shaft, incised with interwoven latticework, is over 10ft high and crowned with a wheel cross, this thousand-year-old cross is little celebrated and stands alone in a field. To get there, take the A5026 to the northwest of Holywell, turning right onto the A5151, following the third exit at the first roundabout and turning right at the junction. The #A19 **bus** runs past the cross from Holywell, but the long wait involved makes the journey less appealing.

Continuing further towards Prestatyn, there's another commonly neglected piece of ancient history in the shape of the **Gop**, Britain's second largest artificial neolithic mound after Silbury Hill in Wiltshire. Unlike Silbury, though, which was built on a flat floor, the Gop was constructed on top of an existing hill, crowning an already splendid viewpoint with a mysterious mound – prehistoric remains have been found both in the mound itself and in the caves directly below the hill. The Gop is a wonderfully atmospheric spot today, with vast views over the Clwydian hills and vales. Access is via a path from above the village of Trelawnyd, three miles further along the A5151 from the Maen Achwyfaen turning. In Trelawnyd village, take the steep lane signposted to Llanasa; the waymarked path to the Gop forks off just after the sharp bend on the edge of the village.

Prestatyn to Colwyn Bay

Almost all the vituperative comments aimed at the north coast land squarely on this heavily-populated twenty-mile stretch of amusement arcades, bingo halls, caravan sites and negligible beach. Of the resorts, the best known is **Rhyl** – big, brash and ballsy but with more gentle attractions nearby including one of Edward I's castles at **Rhuddlan** and the collection of Victorian portraits and furniture at **Bodelwyddan Castle**. There's little to keep you in **Prestatyn**, although it is significant as the starting point for the Offa's Dyke long-distance path, leaving the more architecturally coherent, if hardly exciting, **Colwyn Bay** as the nicest of the three main resorts.

If you happen to be passing on July 1, call in to **Abergele**, between Rhyl and Colwyn Bay, where supporters of the Free Wales Army march through the streets in memory of two martyrs to the cause (see p.365).

Prestatyn

Immortalized in the scabrous verse of Philip Larkin, **PRESTATYN**, nine miles north-west of Holywell, is a likeable enough market town, struggling to compete with its neighbours further along the coast by building new seaside attractions such as the pleasant **Festival Gardens** at Ffrith Beach, on the town's western side. At the Central Beach, an earlier example of seaside regeneration can be seen in the shape of the **Nova Centre**, a swimming and leisure complex (Mon & Tues, Thurs & Fri 5–8pm; Sat & Sun 10am–5pm; school holidays Mon–Fri 1–8pm, Sat & Sun 10am–5pm; £1.65). However, unless you're desperate to try every manner of aquatic activity, then you might find it more interesting to go next door to the **Offa's Dyke Path Centre** (Easter–Sept daily 10am–1pm & 1.30–5pm; winter weekends 10am–3pm), which also doubles up as the local **tourist office** (same hours; ☎01745/889092). Inside is an interpretive diagram of the 170-mile route of the Offa's Dyke Path from Prestatyn to Chepstow (see box, p.236) and a stack of leaflets for walkers. The more committed traditionally start at least ankle-deep in the water, then cross the beach past a stone pillar onto Bastion Road. The path then follows High Street, through the main shopping area, to the *Cross Foxes* pub, from where acorn-marked signs guide you up to the hills behind. The view to Snowdonia, Liverpool and, on a good day, Blackpool, makes up for the fact that you won't come across any of the Offa's Dyke earthworks until the path gets south of the River Dee, the route planners rightly preferring the Clwydian Ridge to the scrappy industrial towns of Trevor and Ruabon on the dyke's route.

Trains on the North Coast line stop in the centre of town, close to the bus station, and a fifteen-minute walk from the Central Beach and tourist office (see above) along Bastion Road. You'll probably want to continue along the coast rather than **stay** here, but the few **B&Bs**, all licensed and serving evening meals, are particularly convenient if you're preparing for (or recovering from) the long Offa's Dyke walk. From the station, turn towards the sea, then either right along the main A548 for *Roughsedge House*, 26–28 Marine Drive (closed Dec; ☎01745/887359; ②), or left to the equally good *Hawarden House*, 15 Victoria Rd (☎01745/854226; ①); *Traeth Ganol*, 41 Beach Rd West (☎01745/853594; ②), is further out, 100 yards left at the Nova Centre, but worth the effort. *Nant Mill Farm* (April–Nov; ☎01745/852360) is a simple grassy **campsite** a mile east along the A548.

Suhail Tandoori (☎01745/856829) serves moderately priced Indian **food** in a converted church near the station at 12 Bastion Rd, or try the filled baguettes and lasagne on offer at the inexpensive *Fredwinnie's Café Bistro*, 226 High St (☎01745/856844).

Rhyl and around

For raw and raucous seaside shenanigans, **RHYL** (Y Rhyl), three miles west of Prestatyn, is probably your best bet in Wales. The two-mile long Promenade, split self-consciously between the tarted-up eastern half and the down-at-heel western section, is a powerful assault on the senses: the sight of a thousand pulsing lights, the sound of bleeping and whooping arcade games and the ever-present smell of candy floss and vinegar on chips. Lots of money has boosted Rhyl in recent years, from EU initiatives, Welsh Office grants and some startling amounts of cash thrown at the place by Clwyd County Council before it was disbanded in 1996. There's no arguing, however, that Rhyl needed a serious injection of investment. Away from the seafront, paint-peeling boarding houses and grotty fun pubs tell the tale of a place that had been slowly disintegrating since the heyday of the British seaside resort some fifty years ago. These days, no one would claim that Rhyl is a sophisticated tourist destination: it is, however, as decent a place as any for a cheap, cheerful holiday blowout, especially if you're with kids. Bear in mind, though, that if bingo, beer, chips and arcades leave you as cold as the sea hereabouts, you'd be wise to steer clear of the place.

Starting at the eastern end, the slides and surfing-wave pool of north Wales' most popular tourist attraction, the **Sun Centre** (ring for times ☎01745/344433; £4.25), form the main lure. From here, continue westwards past more watery entertainment at the **Sea Life Centre** (daily 10am–5pm, closes 6pm in July and Aug; £4.95) with its tanks full of British marine life. Several coastal environments are re-created, but the star attraction is the perspex shark tunnel, where dogfish, basking sharks and various eels drift leisurely around you until the day's highlight: feeding time. Next to the Sea Life Centre is the new **Events Arena**, a circular amphitheatre of coloured bricks that plays host to all manner of concerts and outdoor extravaganzas in the summer season – check posters around town or ask at the tourist office to find out what's on. Continue west to the most eyebrow-raising piece of redevelopment on the front: the **Children's Village**, a garish splatter of (largely empty) candy-coloured huts and toddler rides near the 240-foot **Skytower**, a levitating observation platform on a huge concrete post. This is midway along the prom: compare the money that's been spent on this eastern section with what faces you to the west: a yawning great prom, untouched for decades, waiting for its share of cash. On the inland side of the road from the Skytower, a discreet entrance next to a large amusement arcade heralds the **Knights' Caverns** (May–Sept Mon–Fri noon–10pm, Sat–Sun 10am–10pm; £1.95), a cheesy romp through a bastardized version of ancient Welsh history that includes takes on King Arthur and the tales of The Mabinogion legend. It's worth the entrance fee, however, just for the display of medieval torture instruments such as a scold's bridle, leg crusher, knee splitter, manacles and chastity belts. Back above ground, at the western end of the long line of arcades, pubs and rock shops is the town's traditional fun fair, the **Ocean Beach Amusement Park**, the largest in North Wales.

Practicalities

The **train station** and **bus station** are adjacent, near the intersection of the A548 (Russell/Wellington Road) and the High Street. Rhyl is the area's major bus depot – services fan out all over north Wales and to northwest England, with National Express services running to all the major northern and Midlands cities of England. From the bus station, the High Street runs four blocks to the Promenade and the **tourist office** (April–Sept daily 9am–5pm; Oct–March Mon–Fri 9am–5pm, Sat 10am–1pm & 2–5pm; ☎01745/355068) in the heart of the sickly-hued Children's Village. If you want to rent a bike, try Hughes Cycles, 21 Bodfor St (☎01745/342012).

Competition has forced **B&B** prices down to some of the lowest in Wales: two central cheapies are *Stoneleigh Guesthouse*, 1 Morlan Park (☎01745/336344; ①), off Bath Street, running between East Parade and Russell Road, and the *Melbourne*, 8 Beechwood Rd (☎01745/342762; ①), off East Parade near the Sun Centre. Moving slightly upmarket, it's worth trying *Kilkee Guesthouse*, 50 River St (☎01745/350070; ②), and *Medeor Hotel*, 3 Elwy St (☎01745/354489; ②); both are off the right-hand side of Wellington Road, walking west from the tourist office. Despite the vast number of caravan parks in the area, the nearest **campsite** taking tents is either the *Henllys Farm Caravan and Campsite* (April–Oct; ☎01745/351208), three or four miles west of Rhyl, or, in the other direction, the *Nant Mill* (see "Prestatyn" opposite).

Decent **eating** places are almost as abundant as hotels. *Boswell's* on Bodfor Street (☎01745/355492) offers an eclectic range of inexpensive bistro food and a healthy wine and cocktail list. The reasonably priced *Indian Garden*, 41 Abbey St (☎01745/350092), is the best of the curry restaurants, while pricey *Barratt's*, 167 Vale Rd (☎01745/344138), tops them all with modern French cuisine in Rhyl's oldest house. The *Westminster Hotel*, on East Parade, has faint delusions of grandeur, but is worth trying for its restaurant and carvery, but on a sunny day you're better off at the beachfront *Splash Point*, twenty minutes' walk from the town centre on Hilton Drive (☎01745/353783), where you can enjoy monkfish cutlets or chicken burritos in the bar or conservatory or outside on the patio; this is also the ideal place for a **drink** on a warm afternoon or evening, but the beer is equally good at the more central and very lively *Caskey's*, 21 Vale Rd. Eclectic evening **entertainment**, often best out of high season, can be found at the Pavilion Theatre (☎01745/330000), next to the Sun Centre on the Promenade. Otherwise, there are plenty of diversions to keep you busy: bowling, laser fighting, discos, karaoke bars, late bars, pool and snooker halls, bingo, cinema, arcades – many at rock-bottom prices.

Rhuddlan

RHUDDLAN lies on the banks of a tidal reach of the Clwyd River (Afon Clywedog), which finally meets the sea at Rhyl, two miles to the north. The town itself seems little more than an insignificant suburb of Rhyl but for the diamond-shaped ruin of **Rhuddlan Castle** (May–Sept daily 10am–5pm; £2; CADW), a large and impressive hollow shell surrounded on three sides by a dry moat. Constructed between 1277 and 1282 by Edward I during his first phase of castle-building, Rhuddlan was designed as both a garrison and royal residence, and commands a canalized section of the then strategic river that allowed boats to service the castle and provided water for the huge stone-lined moat. **Gillot's Tower**, by the dockgate, provided protection for the supply ships. The massive towers behind were the work of James of St George, who was responsible for the concentric plan that allowed archers on both outer and inner walls to fire simultaneously. This had become irrelevant by 1648, when Parliament forces took the castle during the Civil War and demolished it.

When Giraldus Cambrensis visited Rhuddlan a hundred years before the construction of Edward's castle, he was put up by David ap Owain, son of Owain Gwynedd, at a castle which once stood on **Twt Hill** (unrestricted access), reached by a footpath to the south of the present castle, now just a low hump in a bow of the river.

Important though the castle was, Rhuddlan earns its position in history as the place where Edward I signed the **Statute of Rhuddlan** on March 19, 1284, consigning Wales to centuries of subjugation by the English that many insist still continues. The ceremony took place on the site of **Parliament House**, on the main street 200 yards to the north. A sign on the building cynically claims that the Statute secured Welsh "judicial rights and independence", despite the fact that Edward laid down the laws by which the Welsh should be governed, including the outlawing of the native language in any official capacity.

Rhuddlan is served by the frequent #51 **bus** from Rhyl or from the Vale of Clwyd and Bodelwyddan.

Marble Church and Bodelwyddan Castle: the National Portrait Gallery

Barrelling west along the A55 expressway towards the coast, the closest you come to Rhyl is the small village of **BODELWYDDAN**, four miles to the south. There is nothing of interest in the small town itself, but from miles around you can pick out the slender 202-foot limestone spire of **Marble Church**, a quarter of a mile to the east of Bodelwyddan, standing as a beacon over the flat coastal plain. The finely worked Gothic tracery of the spire is the most impressive feature; inside, the marble arcades that give the church its nickname and the repulsive, cherubic font are something of a letdown. Local architect John Gibson, the sole pupil of Sir Charles Barry, designed it in the 1850s, his choice of Scottish granite intended to bring to mind the home of Saint Kentigern, the first bishop of nearby St Asaph (see p.390) and, under his alternative name of Saint Mungo, the patron saint of Glasgow.

More samples of Gibson's sculptural work are displayed in the finest art showcase in north Wales, **Bodelwyddan Castle** (April–June, Sept & Oct daily except Fri 11am–5pm; July & Aug daily same hours; Nov–March Tues–Thurs, Sat & Sun 11am–4pm; £4.30, gardens £1), set amidst landscaped gardens on its hill, half a mile south of Bodelwyddan. Although crenellated and edged with turrets, the castle is substantially a nineteenth-century country mansion built on the site of a fifteenth-century house, its opulent Victorian interiors re-created during its restoration in the 1980s, after sixty years as a girls' school. Williams Hall, a wing of the building, now houses one of four provincial outposts of the **National Portrait Gallery**, specializing in works contemporary with the castle. Plans are afoot to link the gallery with the **Techniquest** hands-on science centre in Cardiff (see p.105), bringing loads of gizmos and gadgets to Bodelwyddan, so what is described here may well have changed before too long.

Most of the two hundred paintings are on the ground floor, approached through the "Watts Hall of Fame". This long corridor was specially decorated in William Morris style to accommodate not only a chair by Morris, but 26 portraits of eminent Victorians by G.F. Watts, among them Millais, Rossetti, Browning and Walter Crane. The Billiard Room leads off the corridor and through to the outstanding Dining Room. Two sensitive portraits here highlight the Pre-Raphaelite support for social reform: William Holman Hunt's portrayal of the vociferous opponent of slavery and capital punishment, Stephen Lushington; and Ford Madox Brown's double portrait of Henry Farell, prime mover in the passing of the 1867 Reform Bill, and suffragette Millicent Garrett. Works by John Singer Sargent and Hubert von Herkamer also adorn the room, which, like the others, is furnished with pieces from the Victoria and Albert Museum in London. The table and chairs originally belonged to one Alfred Waterhouse, who designed the superb walnut and boxwood grand piano.

More serious Victorians line the Library which leads on to the Ladies' Drawing Room where a beautiful Biedermeier sofa outshines the paintings of little-celebrated nineteenth-century women around the walls. The Drawing Room opposite serves as sculpture gallery, with a portrait of John Gibson looking down on his own images of Bacchus and Cupid. From the hall between these two drawing rooms, the Grand Staircase leads upstairs to a more detailed presentation of significant aspects of nineteenth-century portraiture. Portrait photography – including some wonderful portraits of a stern-faced Queen Victoria and her family – and works by female artists get generous coverage along with animal painters; Landseer in particular. The top floor is primarily reserved for temporary exhibitions, though there's also a fun, hands-on Victorian Extravaganza, with rooms devoted to sound transmission and reproduction, optical illusions and the moving image.

The entry fee entitles you to a taped audio tour of the ground floor, which introduces the key features but comes padded with wearisome dramatized anecdotes designed to enliven the experience. The machine has no fast-forward button, so turn the sound down and read through the *Visitor Guide* (£1.50) or the adequate information sheets in each room.

The rest of the castle and most of the grounds are given over to an expensive adults-only hotel complex open just to guests, though you can walk through the modest gardens, explore the small maze, and take tea in one of the cafés.

To get here, catch the #51 **bus** from Rhyl, Rhuddlan or anywhere in the Vale of Clwyd, bringing you within ten minutes' walk of both the castle and the church.

Colwyn Bay and Rhos-on-Sea

The A548 coast road west from Rhyl meets the A55 near the imposing nineteenth-century folly of Gwrych Castle (no access) and continues on to **COLWYN BAY** (Bae Colwyn). The hilly setting and unspoiled Victorian main street gives the place marginally more charm than its eastern neighbours, and the appeal is bolstered by an unspoilt old-fashioned seafront, complete with an adequate beach and a semi-operational pier. Along with many other British piers, Colwyn Bay's suffered three decades of neglect as Britons eschewed their seaside in favour of more glamorous Mediterranean resorts, but a small pier renaissance – 1996 was Britain's "Year of the Pier" – has engendered a number of restoration projects around the country. Colwyn Bay's fledgling but ambitious attempt has seen the opening of a number of shops and a bar on the first few yards of the ramshackle remains of this once-grand jetty. Running along the seafront and past the pier is a new cycle path – you can **rent bikes** from West End Cycles (☎01492/530269) at 121 Conwy Rd in Colwyn's West End – and it's worth riding one a mile inland and steeply uphill to the **Welsh Mountain Zoo** (daily: Easter–Sept 9.30am–6pm; Oct–Easter 9.30am–4pm; £5.95), a fairly traditional menagerie high in the woods behind the town, with Californian sea lions, "Chimpanzee World" and free-flying eagle displays touted as the main attractions. If you don't want to go by bike, hop on the free shuttle bus, which runs every twenty minutes (Easter to mid-Sept) between the zoo and the town's train station.

Colwyn Bay runs seamlessly west along the coast into **RHOS-ON-SEA**, a resort chiefly notable for the **Harlequin Puppet Theatre** on its Promenade (☎01492/548166), one of the very few remaining marionette shows in the British tradition, with an hour-long daytime family show. At Rhos Point, you'll find the minuscule **St Trillo's chapel**, some of which dates from the sixth century. It stands over an ancient healing well and is reputed to have been the launch point of Prince Madoc ap Owain Gwynedd's voyage to America in 1170 – Welshmen and women the world over like to claim that he was the first European to "discover" the New World, over three hundred years before Christopher Columbus.

Trains stop on the seafront, almost opposite the **tourist office** in Imperial Buildings, Princes Drive (July & Aug Mon–Sat 9.30am–5.30pm, Sun 10am–1pm; Sept–June Mon–Sat 9.30am–5pm; ☎01492/530478). Although you're probably better off staying in nearby Llandudno or Conwy, decent **accommodation** can be found in the shape of the friendly *Marine Hotel* on the Promenade (☎01492/530295; ②) or the *Bron Wylfa* B&B at 14 Woodland Rd East (☎01492/532320; ①), a short walk from the tourist office. There's also a **campsite** at *Dinarth Hall Farm* in Rhos-on-Sea (☎01492/548203). For **eating**, try the moderately priced, Provençal *Café Niçoise*, 124 Abergele Rd (☎01492/531555), with its two- or three-course *menu touristique*. There are a few decent **pubs** – try the *Red Lion*, on Abergele Road in Old Colwyn for a good selection of real ales, or the *Central Hotel* on the main Conwy Road for weekend musical entertainment. The historic *Rhos Fynach* pub in Rhos-on-Sea serves excellent food.

Llandudno

The twin limestone hummocks of the 680-foot **Great Orme** and its southern cousin the Little Orme provide a dramatic frame for the gently curving Victorian frontage of **LLANDUDNO**, Wales' most enduring archetype of the genteel British seaside resort. The core of the town occupies a low isthmus between two beachfronts, the less developed West Shore and Llandudno Bay where the older set of promenading devotees can be found huddled in the glass frontages of once-grand hotels. Despite the arrival of more rumbustious fun-seekers, Llandudno retains an undeniably dignified air but, as the coast's largest town, steers clear of retirement-home stagnation.

Llandudno's early history revolves around the Great Orme, where Saint Tudno, who brought Christianity to the region in the sixth century, built the monastic cell that gives the town its name. When the early Victorian copper mines looked to be worked out in

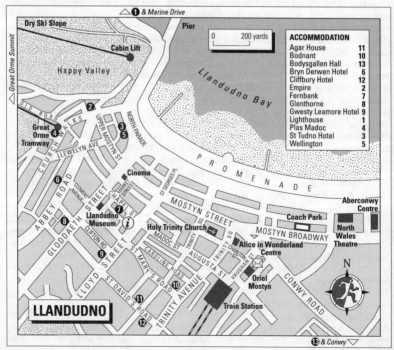

ACCOMMODATION
Agar House	11
Bodnant	10
Bodysgallen Hall	13
Bryn Derwen Hotel	6
Cliffbury Hotel	12
Empire	2
Fernbank	7
Glenthorne	8
Gwesty Leamore Hotel	9
Lighthouse	1
Plas Madoc	4
St Tudno Hotel	3
Wellington	5

the mid-nineteenth century, local landowner Edward Mostyn set about a speculative venture to exploit the growing craze for sea bathing with a seaside resort for the upper middle classes. Being MP for the constituency, and having the Bishop of Bangor in his pocket, he was able to tease through Parliament an enclosure act giving himself the rights to develop the land.

Work got underway around 1854 and the resort rapidly gained popularity until the end of the century, when Llandudno had become synonymous with the Victorian ideal of a respectable resort, drawing music stars such as Adelina Patti (see p.204) and Jules Rivière, the French conductor who sat in a gilded armchair facing the audience as he waved his bejewelled ivory baton. Mostyn Street, with its wrought-iron and glass verandas, was said to have some of the finest shops outside London, patronized by the titled guests staying in the hotels: Bismarck, Napoléon III, Disraeli, Gladstone, and Queen Elizabeth of Romania, who stayed here for five weeks in 1890 and is said to have given the town its motto *Hardd, haran, hedd*, meaning "beautiful haven of peace". It may have been just that in 1890, but today it is bustling, with some less-exalted emporia along Mostyn Street and fewer pretensions amongst the hotel owners.

Arrival, information and getting around

The forlorn **train station** at the corner of Augusta and Vaughan streets is only five minutes' walk down Augusta Street/Madoc Street from the **tourist office**, 1–2 Chapel St (Easter–Sept daily 9.30am–6pm; Oct–Easter Mon–Sat 9.30am–5pm; ☎01492/876413). Direct trains come from Chester, those from Bangor and Betws-y-Coed generally requiring a change at Llandudno Junction near Conwy. Chapel Street runs parallel to Mostyn Street, where **local buses** from Bangor, Betws-y-Coed, Conwy and Rhyl stop. Less than ten minutes' walk south, National Express buses pull in to the **coach park** on Mostyn Broadway.

The tourist office stocks a free map of Great Orme walking paths, though most people drive or use the tram or cableway (see p.403). Alternative **tours** for those in a hurry include Great Orme Tours' trips along Marine Drive and to the summit (April–Sept 3 daily; ☎01492/870870; £3.95) which leave from Prince Edward Square. Run by The Llandudno & Conwy Tour Company, open-top double-decker buses loop from Llandudno to Conwy and back (late May to mid-Sept at least hourly 10am–4pm; ☎01492/876606; £5.95). If you have more time and energy, you can **cycle** on bikes rented from West End Cycles, 22 Augusta St (☎01492/876891), across the road from the train station.

Accommodation

You may well want to stay a day or so in Llandudno, and with over 700 **hotels**, this isn't usually a problem, though in high summer (and especially bank holidays), booking ahead is wise. If you haven't made a reservation, your best bet for inexpensive accommodation, if all those listed below are full, is St David's Road, where there are almost a dozen high-standard, cheapish guesthouses.

Agar House, 17 St David's Rd (☎01492/875572). A suburban home offering a warm welcome, home-cooked dinners and an award-winning garden. ①.

Bodnant, 39 St Mary's Rd (☎01492/876936). Comfortable non-smoking guesthouse. ②.

Bodysgallen Hall, three miles south of town on the A470 (☎01492/584466). One of the top country hotels in Wales, set in a partly seventeenth-century house surrounded by 120 acres of terraced lawns and gardens. Antique-filled rooms, all beautifully decorated and festooned with flowers, in the house itself and in cottages in the grounds. ⑤.

Bryn Derwen Hotel, 34 Abbey Rd (☎ & fax 01492/876804). Sumptuous yet informal small hotel at the foot of the Orme, with huge Victorian rooms and terrific meals. March–Oct. ③.

Cliffbury Hotel, 34 St David's Rd (☎01492/877224). Excellent-value non-smoking hotel with well-appointed rooms. One of the best on this street. ①.

Empire, 74 Church Walks (☎01492/860555, fax 860791). Opulent, slightly over-fussy rooms with every conceivable convenience either in the main building, where the sauna and indoor and outdoor pools are located, or next door in the even better rooms of no. 72. ⑤.

Fernbank, 9 Chapel St (☎01492/877251). One of the cheapest and best equipped of a string of low-cost hotels just along from the tourist office. ①.

Glenthorne Hotel, 2 York Rd (☎01492/879591). Cheapest B&B in town, nestled under the Great Orme. ①.

Gwesty Leamore Hotel, 40 Lloyd St (☎01492/875552). One of the few guesthouses in Llandudno actually run by Welsh people. Friendly welcome and good facilities, including satellite TV. Closed Dec–Feb. ①.

The Lighthouse, Marine Drive, three miles north of Llandudno (☎ & fax 01492/876819). Fortress-like from outside but attractively furnished within, this lighthouse, 370ft above the Celtic Sea, is one of Wales' more unusual places to stay. ④.

Plas Madoc, 60 Church Walks (☎01492/876514). Exclusively vegetarian guesthouse, with great food and organic drinks on offer, well sited at the bottom of the Great Orme. ②.

St Tudno Hotel, 16 North Parade, just behind the pier (☎01492/874411, fax 860407). Superb, small seafront hotel hidden amongst others of much lower stature, with lavishly decorated rooms, excellent meals and "The Best Hotel Loos in Britain". ⑥.

The Wellington, 12 North Parade (☎01492/876709). Good-value seafront hotel with views across the bay from the front rooms, and good inexpensive meals. ②.

The Town

Much of Llandudno's daytime activity revolves around the Great Orme rising steeply to the north, but first-time visitors are inevitably drawn to the **pier** (open all year; free), jutting out into Llandudno Bay with views back to the limestone cliffs. Once the supreme expression of Llandudno's ornate Victoriana, it was partly destroyed by fire in 1994, but is back in operation, its neat wooden deck overrun in summer with kids clamouring to board the modest fairground rides and deckchair denizens cocking an ear to the taped sounds of some Wurlitzer maestro. Ice-cream and candy-floss outlets abound here, as a town ordinance bars the sale of such fripperies anywhere else on the waterfront. If you're interested in Llandudno's past, don't ignore the History Trail panels dotted around: they're unusually comprehensive and full of interesting nuggets. A leaflet from the tourist office maps them out for you.

From the pier, it's a leisurely ten-minute stroll along The Promenade, with its bank of regal four-storey terraced hotels, to Vaughan Street and the region's premier contemporary art gallery, **Oriel Mostyn**, at no. 12 (Mon–Sat 10am–1pm & 1.30–5pm; free), named after Lady Mostyn, for whom it was built in 1901. The gallery has no permanent collection, but its eight yearly shows are usually worth a browse, often featuring challenging works by artists of international renown with a particular leaning towards the current Welsh arts scene.

If you have kids to entertain, head down Charlton Street from the gallery to the **Alice in Wonderland Centre**, 3–4 Trinity Square (April–Oct daily 10am–5pm; Nov–March closed Sun; £2.95). Here, a twenty-minute taped tour guides you through the "Rabbit Hole", full of amateurish animated models of Mad Hatters and March Hares, and treats you to excerpts from Lewis Carroll's books. Lewis Carroll's association with Llandudno is tenuous but assiduously milked by the town's tourism machine. The writer never visited the town, but Alice Liddell, the inspiration for his books, did – her parents' holiday home now forms the core of the *Gogarth Abbey Hotel*, also on the West Shore. Aside from the child-oriented **Bodafon Park Farm** (daily 10am–6pm; £3.95 summer/£2.95 winter), off the end of Mostyn Avenue at the town's east end, the only other sight is the **Llandudno Museum**, 17–19 Gloddaeth St (Easter–Oct Tues–Sat 10.30am–1pm &

2–5pm, Sun 2.15–5pm; Nov–Easter Tues–Sat 1.30–4.30pm; £1.50), whose local history exhibits focus on pieces unearthed in local copper mines (see below), Roman artefacts and a rebuilt rural kitchen from Llanberis. Otherwise, Llandudno is a supremely easy place in which to wander: on a sunny day, join the ranks of folk on the seafront deckchairs or down on the beach, or head inland to explore the gracious shopping streets, clustered with the best upmarket and speciality **shops** in north Wales.

The Great Orme

The top of the **Great Orme** (Pen y Gogarth), an ancient mountain almost surrounded by the sea, ranks as the one spot in north Wales with comparable views to those from the far loftier summits in Snowdonia. In many ways they are superior, combining the seascapes east towards Rhyl and west over the sands of the Conwy estuary to the shores of Anglesey with the brooding, quarry-chewed northern limit of the Carneddau range where Snowdonia crashes into the sea. Take a short walk across the rounded top of the Orme to get away from the crowds around the summit car park – it's easy to find somewhere to admire the view as fulmars wheel on the thermals, but it's less easy to see the feral goats which roam all over the mountain.

Formed about 300 million years ago at the bottom of a tropical sea, this huge lump of carboniferous limestone was subject to some of the same stresses that folded Snowdonia, producing fissures filled by molten mineral-bearing rock. Though there are a few minor Neolithic sites dotted over the hill, it was in the Bronze Age that the settlement really developed, when the people began to smelt the contents of the malachite-rich veins, supplying copper – if current speculation turns out to be true – throughout Europe.

The Romans seemed to ignore the Orme's potential, leaving it to early Christian Celts like Saint Tudno. The Vikings later gave the place its name, which derives from Old Norse meaning "worm" or "sea serpent" – just how it might have appeared in the mist to those approaching by sea. Today it is favoured not just by day-trippers here for the view, but also by botanists drawn by the profusion of maritime species: goldilocks aster, spotted cats-ear and spiked speedwell.

Apart from walking, there are three other ways to explore the Orme. Traditionally the most popular is **Marine Drive**, a four-mile circuit cut into the rock high above the coastal cliffs, passing Pen-trwyn, a rock-climbing venue with several of Britain's trickiest limestone routes. You can freely walk or cycle around, or make the anticlockwise circuit from just near Llandudno's pier in your own vehicle (£1.50 toll summer 9am–8pm, winter 9am–4pm, otherwise free).

A separate route – Old Road – leads directly from Llandudno up to the cafés and bar at the **Summit Complex** (Easter–Oct daily noon–11pm; Nov–Easter Sat & Sun only, same hours). The road up to the summit runs parallel to the mile-long route of the vintage, San Francisco-style **Great Orme Tramway** (April–Sept 10am–6pm; Oct–March 10am–4pm; £3.80 return, £2.60 single), creaking up from the bottom of Old Road much as it has done since 1902. The third route starts at the base of the pier, close to the start of Marine Drive, where an Italianate colonnade flanks the short road to the **Happy Valley** formal gardens and the **Cabin Lift** (July & Aug daily 10am–5.30pm; Easter–June, Sept & Oct daily 10am–1pm & 2–4.20pm; £4.80 return, £4.30 single), which carries you up over the Orme to the Summit Complex, a mile away. At the start it swings over **Ski Llandudno** (variable hours, but generally 10am–6pm), where £12 will get you a couple of hours on the dry slopes (including all equipment), or for a quarter of the price you can make a couple of runs down a 700-yard-long snow-free **Toboggan Run**.

The Great Orme Copper Mines

From the tramway's halfway station, it's a five-minute walk to the long-disused **Great Orme Copper Mines** (Feb–Oct daily 10am–5pm; £4.20). The Victorians, who last mined the area, were aware of earlier workings, and until the late 1970s these were assumed to be Roman. Digs in the 1980s, however, uncovered 4000-year-old animal bones which had been used as scrapers up to 200ft down. This is one of the few sites in Britain where mineral veins were accompanied by dolomitization, a rock-softening process that permitted the use of the simple tools available in the Bronze Age. Ease of extraction led to this becoming the pre-eminent copper mine in Europe, and with more excavations continuing in the off-season, it may well turn out to have been the world's largest.

Hard hats are provided on the **guided tour**, which, after an explanatory video, takes you down through just a small portion of the tunnels. It's enough, though, to get a feel for the cramped working conditions and the dangers of rock-fall, and to see the burial site of one of three cats thought to have been ritually sacrificed by superstitious miners.

Eating, drinking and entertainment

Llandudno is blessed with the best choice of **restaurants** in north Wales, ranging from budget cafés to one of the most expensive places in the country. Most cluster at the foot of the Great Orme around Mostyn Street, where numerous **pubs** cater to most tastes. As the major town for the area, Llandudno's pubs can become chaotically crowded, particularly on weekend nights when the normally genteel atmosphere slides into raucous hedonism: if that's your bag, then head to the bars of Upper Mostyn Street.

Around the beginning of the twentieth century, all the best performers clamoured to play Llandudno, but today, you're lucky to get anything more than faded celebrities plying the resorts throughout the summer. However, with the new North Wales Theatre (see opposite) and the ten-day **Llandudno October Festival** of pop, jazz, opera and classical music (☎0800/872000), things are looking a little rosier. The tourist office can usually give you a good idea of what's on, but we've listed the most promising venues.

Restaurants and cafés

Bodysgallen Hall, three miles south of town on the A470 (☎01492/584466). Top-notch traditional and modern British fare in one of the best country hotels around. Table d'hôte with a selection of over 300 wines – very expensive.

The Garden Room Restaurant at the *St Tudno Hotel*, North Parade (☎01492/874411). One of Wales' best restaurants producing French-style meals prepared with fresh Welsh produce where possible. Three-course lunches are moderately priced, but in the evening you get the full five-course extravaganza.

Habit Tearooms, 12 Mostyn St. Rich home-made cakes and inexpensive light lunches are served in this bentwood-chair and pot-plant setting.

King's Head, Old Rd. Low-beamed pub offering substantial and tasty bar meals ranging from Welsh rarebit to noisettes of lamb.

Mediterranean Restaurant, 153 Mostyn St. Relaxed Greek/Italian/Spanish place serving well-prepared meze, pizza and pasta, and a Sunday lunch buffet for £5.

Number 1's Bistro, 1 Old Rd. One of Llandudno's finer low-key restaurants, with imaginative, moderately priced French-styled bistro meals served in a simple dark-wood and deep-burgundy furnished rooms. Closed all day Sun, and Mon lunchtime.

Richards, 7 Church Walks. There's a more formal restaurant upstairs, but the basement bistro is better, with a menu strong on seafood. The goat's cheese salad with plum dressing and the local mullet are particularly good.

Romeo's, 25 Lloyd St (☎01492/877777). Cheery Italian restaurant and pizzeria with fine calzone, excellent espresso and equally good traditional British dishes. Takeaways available.

Sandbach Café, 78a Mostyn St. Refined tearooms above a chocolate shop, with a good array of sandwiches, cakes and daily specials.

Bars and pubs

Annabel's, George's Place. Popular under-thirties hangout with a late licence, situated above a café.

The Carlton, 121 Mostyn St, cnr of Gloddaeth St. Lively town-centre pub with pool table, quiz nights, good beer and fine iron-and-glass verandas.

Cottage Loaf, Market St. Flag-floored pub built from old ships' timbers on top of an old bakehouse. Popular for lunchtime eating, and drinking all day.

Fat Cat, Upper Mostyn St. Frantic and fun café-bar with an eclectic clientele and heated pavement section for year round alfresco drinking and people-watching.

King's Head, Old Rd, by the bottom of the tramway. Llandudno's oldest pub, where Edward Mostyn and his surveyor mapped out the town. Interesting photos inside.

London Hotel, 131 Mostyn St. Despite the red telephone box inside and the Dick Whittington sign, this is a decent pub with good beer and a family room that turns into a piano bar at night.

Entertainment

Broadway Boulevard, Grand Theatre, Mostyn Broadway, cnr of Ty'n y Ffridd Rd (☎01492/879614). Llandudno's liveliest club, with a host of party nights.

North Wales Theatre (Theatr Gogledd Cymru), The Promenade (☎01492/872000). North Wales' premier live entertainment centre, this new 1500-seat theatre lures touring companies and occasional international acts.

The Palladium, Gloddaeth St (☎01492/876244). Llandudno's cinema, showing predominantly mainstream blockbusters; however, it's scheduled to close if plans for a multiplex cinema are realized.

Conwy and around

Since the completion of the A55 underground tunnel under the town and the subsequent reduction of traffic in the streets, **CONWY**, four miles southwest along the coast from Llandudno, has blossomed. Over the last few years, tarmac has been replaced with cobbles and shopfronts have been prettified, but despite the addition of an unnecessary and totally fake tall ship beside the quay, it has, for the moment, resisted becoming a heritage museum town. There's a huge amount to see and do here, all the same: a stunning early medieval castle and a complete belt of accompanying town walls enclosing some fascinating glimpses into the past of north Wales. The town remains one of the highlights of the north coast, its setting on the Conwy estuary, backed by a forested fold of Snowdonia, irresistible to painters and photographers ever since Englishman Paul Sandby published his *Views of North Wales* in 1776. Even if you're a little weary of castle-hopping, Conwy is still worth a stop, whether for the wondrous Elizabethan town house, Plas Mawr, the three estuary bridges or cutesy treats like Britain's smallest house.

In Sandby's day, the Conwy estuary still produced a good living for the families who had held mussel-gathering rights on the sands for centuries, a heritage which goes back long before the foundation of the Cistercian monastery of Aberconwy in 1172. The monastery, where Llywelyn ap Iorwerth ("the Great") died in 1240, was on the present site of the parish church of St Mary and All Saints, but a century later was moved eight miles upriver to Maenan, near Llanrwst, to make way for one of the toughest-looking links in Edward I's chain of fortresses.

Apart from a brief siege during the Welsh uprising of 1294, the bulk of events in Conwy's history occurred at the end of the fourteenth century: Richard II stayed at the castle on his return from an ill-timed trip to Ireland in 1399, until lured from safety by Bolingbroke's vassal, the Earl of Northumberland. Northumberland swore in the castle's chapel to grant the king safe passage, but Richard was taken to Flint (see p.392) and kept captive, Bolingbroke becoming Henry IV. Just two years later, on Good Friday

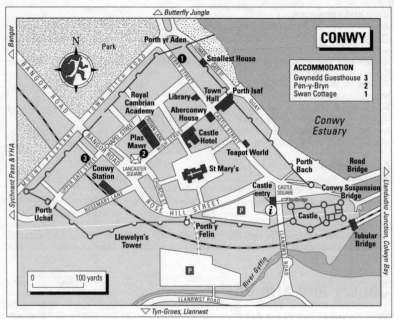

© Crown copyright

when the fifteen-strong castle guard were at church, two cousins of Owain Glyndŵr, Gwilym and Rhys ap Tudor, took the castle and razed the town for Glyndŵr's cause. Harry Hotspur, Chief Justice of north Wales, rushed from Denbigh (see p.388) to besiege the occupied fortress, eventually doing a deal: nine Welsh were to be handed over then hanged, drawn and quartered in return for the Tudors' freedom. After this, the castle fell into disuse, and was bought in 1627 for £100 by Charles I's Secretary of State, Lord Conway of Ragley, who then had the task of refortifying it for the Civil War. It held out until 1646, only surrendering to Mytton once the town had been taken. At the restoration of the monarchy in 1665, the castle was stripped of all its iron, wood and lead, and was left substantially as it is today.

Arrival and information

Llandudno Junction, less than a mile across the river to the east, serves as the main **train station** for services from Chester to Holyhead, as well as for trains heading south to Betws-y-Coed and Blaenau Ffestiniog; only slow, regional services stop in Conwy itself. National Express **buses** pull up outside the town walls on Town Ditch Road, as do the open-top double-deckers run by The Llandudno & Conwy Tour company (see p.401). Local buses to Bangor, Betws-y-Coed and Llandudno use the stops in the town centre, mostly on Lancaster Square or Castle Street.

Walking south from either Conwy station or the Lancaster Square bus stops, skip the Conwy Visitor Centre in favour of the **tourist office** (April–Oct daily 9.30am–6.30pm; Nov–March Mon–Sat 9.30am–4pm, Sun 11am–4pm; ☎01492/592248), which shares the same building and hours as the castle ticket office.

Accommodation

Although the Conwy region offers a fair range of **accommodation** – including the only town-centre YHA hostel in the vicinity – the choice is a bit thin right in the heart of town, and those without the transport to reach the less central places are advised to book ahead in summer.

Hotels and guesthouses

Castle Bank Hotel, Mount Pleasant (☎01492/593888). Licensed, non-smoking hotel with country-house atmosphere and excellent, moderately priced meals. A 10min walk from the town centre: turn first left outside the town walls on the Bangor road. Closed Jan. ③.

Church House, Llanbedr-y-Cennin, five miles south of Conwy (☎01492/660521). Fine, old two-roomed guesthouse with beautiful views. Get off the #19 bus in Tal-y-Bont and walk half a mile west. The *Olde Bull Inn* is nearby (see p.411). ②.

Glan Heulog, Llanrwst Rd (☎01492/593845). One of the best small guesthouses within easy walking distance of Conwy on the outskirts of town. Inexpensive meals are served. ①.

Glyn Uchaf, Conwy Old Rd, Capelulo, two miles west of Conwy (☎01492/623737). One of the best secluded B&Bs around, backing onto the hills just over Sychnant Pass. Good evening meals. ②.

Gwern Borter Country Manor, Barker's Lane, Rowen (☎01492/650360). Comfortable guesthouse on a Conwy Valley farm just north of Rowen (bus #19), with sauna, gym and pony trekking available and easy access to walks onto the nearby Carneddau range. Meals on request. ②.

Gwynedd Guesthouse, 10 Upper Gate St (☎01492/596537). About the cheapest central B&B and consequently often full. ①.

Henllys Farm, Llechwedd, 1.5 miles west of Conwy (☎01492/593269). Appealing guesthouse on a working farm. Turn up Upper Gate Street, bear left along St Agnes Road, then follow signs for Llechwedd – *Henllys* is on the right. Closed Dec–Feb. ②.

The Old Rectory, Llansantffraid Glan Conwy (☎01492/580611, fax 584555). Georgian-style country house, opulently furnished with antiques and fine paintings, overlooking the Conwy estuary, a mile up the Conwy Valley. Creative, expensive meals. Closed mid-Dec to Jan. ⑥.

Pen-y-Bryn, 28 High St (☎01492/596445). Well-appointed, welcoming, non-smoking B&B with private facilities in a central sixteenth-century building above tearooms. Closed Jan. ②.

Swan Cottage, 18 Berry St (☎01492/596840). Attractive, almost elegant rooms in a small, central B&B. The attic room has great estuary views. ②.

Hostels and campsites

Conwy Touring Park (☎01492/592856). A fully fixtured campsite taking tents, just over a mile south along the B5106 (bus #19). They operate a strict "families only" rule, so you'll have to look reasonably respectable to get in. Closed Nov–March.

Conwy YHA Hostel, Lark Hill (☎01492/593571). Brand-new hostel with double rooms (①) and small dorms in a converted 1960s building. A 10min walk from town up the Sychnant Pass road. Closed Dec to mid-Feb.

Pyllau Gloewen Farm, Tal-y-Bont, 6 miles south of Conwy (☎01492/660504). Conwy Valley farm with B&B facilities, a £7.50 a night bunk-barn suitable for walkers and backpackers and an adjacent camp and caravan site. Pick-up available from local train stations. ②.

Rowen YHA hostel, Rowen, a mile up a steep hill above the village (☎01492/650089). Simple but superbly set YHA hostel on the flanks of the Carneddau range, reached by turning right 50 yards past Rowen's pub. Hourly bus #19. Closed Sept–Easter.

The Town

Nothing within Conwy's core of medieval and Victorian buildings is more than two hundred yards from the irregular triangle of protective masonry formed by the town walls, which makes the town wonderfully easy to potter around and, though you'll get to see everything you want to in a day, you may well want to stay longer.

Conwy Castle

During their incursions along Wales' north coast, Edward I's Anglo-Norman ancestors had all but destroyed the castle at Deganwy, near Llandudno, but maintaining a bridge-head west of the Conwy River had always eluded them. Accordingly, once over the river in 1283, Edward set about establishing another of his bastide towns. He chose a strategic knoll at the mouth of the Conwy River and set James of St George to fashion a castle to fit its contours. With the help of 1500 men, James took just five years to build **Conwy Castle** (April, May & Oct daily 9.30am–5pm; June–Sept 9.30am–6pm; Nov–March Mon–Sat 9.30am–4pm, Sun 11am–4pm; £3.50; CADW), now entered through a ticket office and over a modern bridge.

Overlooked by a low hill, the castle appears less easily defended than others along the coast, but James constructed eight massive towers in a rectangle around the two wards, the inner one separated from the outer by a drawbridge and portcullis, and further protected by turrets atop the four eastern towers, now the preserve of crows. Strolling along the wall-top gallery, you can look down onto something unique in the Iron Ring fortresses, a roofless but largely intact interior. The outer ward's 130-foot-long Great Hall and the King's Apartments are both well preserved, but the only part of the castle to have kept its roof is the **Chapel Tower**, named for the small room built into the wall whose semicircular apse still shows some heavily worn carving. On the floor below, there's a small exhibition on religious life in medieval castles which won't detain you long from exploring the passages.

The rest of the town

Anchored to the castle walls as though a drawbridge, Telford's narrow **Conwy Suspension Bridge** (April–June & Sept–Oct daily except Tues 10am–5pm; July–Aug daily 10am–5pm; £1, £2.50 combination ticket with Aberconwy House; NT) was part of the 1826 road improvement scheme, prompted by the need for better communications

---

THE "IRON RING"

Dotting the north Wales coast, a day's march from each other, Edward I's fearsome **Iron Ring** of colossal fortresses represents Europe's most ambitious and concentrated medieval building project, designed to prevent the recurrence of two massively expensive military campaigns (see Contexts, p.444). After Edward's first successful campaign in 1277, he was able to pin down his adversary, **Llywelyn ap Gruffydd** ("the Last") in Snowdonia and on Anglesey. This gave him room and time enough to build the now largely ruined castles at **Flint**, **Rhuddlan**, **Builth Wells** and **Aberystwyth**, as well as to commandeer and upgrade Welsh castles, Edward's first attempt at subjugation.

Llewellyn's second uprising, in 1282, was also ultimately unsuccessful, and Edward, determined not to have to fight a third time for the same land, set about extending his ring of fortifications in an immensely costly display of English might. Together with the Treaty of Rhuddlan in 1284, this saw the Welsh resistance effectively crushed. The castles at **Harlech**, **Caernarfon** and **Conwy**, though nearly contemporary, display a unique progression towards the later, highly evolved concentric design of **Beaumaris**. All this second batch, including the town walls of Caernarfon and Conwy, were the work of the master military architect of his age, James of St George d'Espéranche, whose work is now recognized with **UN World Heritage Site** status.

Each of the castles was integrated with a **bastide town** – an idea borrowed from Gascony in southwest France, where Edward I was duke – the town and castle mutually reliant on each other for protection and trade. The bastides were always populated with English settlers, the Welsh permitted to enter the town during the day but not to trade and certainly not carrying arms. It wasn't until the eighteenth century that the Welsh would have towns they could truly call their own.

to Ireland after the Act of Union. Contemporary with his far greater effort spanning the Menai Strait (see p.421), Telford's bridge mimics the crenellations of the battlements above – an attempt to compensate for spoiling the view of the castle painted by J.M.W. Turner in 1802–03. The bridge was used until 1958, when the adjacent new road bridge was built, by which time the demands of modern traffic had inflicted tarmac, signs and street lighting on it. Once threatened with demolition, the bridge has now been restored to an approximation of its original state and is now a footbridge linking the town to the restored **tollhouse**, furnished as it would have been in around 1900. Note the c.1900 toll charges on the board outside.

The approach to the newer road bridge has created the only breach in the thirty-foot high **town walls** which branch out from the castle into a three-quarter-mile-long circuit, enclosing Conwy's ancient quarter. Inaccessible from the castle they were designed to protect, the walls are punctuated by 21 evenly spaced horseshoe towers, as well as twelve latrines bulging out from the wall-walk. At present, only half of the distance can be walked in two short sections, the closest and least appealing (castle opening hours only) over-looking a car park. Far superior views over the town to the castle and estuary behind open out from the section of wall which runs down from Porth Uchaf on Upper Gate Street to a spur into the estuary. Here, you come down off the walls by brightly rigged trawlers, mussel boats and the self-proclaimed **smallest house in Britain** (Easter–June & Sept to mid-Oct daily 10am–6pm; July & Aug daily 10am–9pm; 50p), which was built wedged between two terraces, one of them now demolished. The two tiny rooms combined are only nine feet high and five wide, the door taking up only a quarter of the frontage, so most will have to duck to get in, a problem encountered by the last resident and great-grandfather of the present guardian, a six-foot-three fisherman.

Porth Isaf, the nearby gate in the town walls, leads up Lower High Street to the fourteenth-century timber and stone **Aberconwy House**, Castle Street (April–Oct daily except Tues 10am–5pm; £2, £2.50 combination ticket with the Conwy Suspension Bridge; NT), the oldest house in Conwy and the town's sole surviving medieval building dating from around 1300. It was built for a wealthy merchant and saw service as a bakery, antique shop, sea captain's house and temperance hotel, somehow managing to survive numerous fires and equally destructive Victorian improvement. Its various incarnations are re-created in rooms furnished with a simple yet elegant collection of Welsh rural furniture on loan from the Museum of Wales. Tours start with an introductory video in the attic, winding up in a kitchen complete with fireside settle, pewter plates and a few hunks of stale bread.

Conwy's grandest residence is the splendid **Plas Mawr** (June–Aug Tues–Sun 9.30am–6pm; April–May & Sept Tues–Sun 9.30am–5pm; Oct Tues–Sun 9.30am–4pm; £4; CADW), just up the High Street at no. 20. One of the best-preserved Elizabethan town houses in Britain, Plas Mawr was built in a Dutch style for Robert Wynn of Gwydir Castle (see Llanrwst, p.325), who was one of the first native Welsh people to live in the town, returning to the area after living it up in the European courts. Elaborately demonstrating the trends in domestic building as the medieval age melted into the modern, the main part of the house dates from 1576, with additions such as the gatehouse, through which visitors enter, added some ten years later to augment the grand effect. The first room is the Great Hall, with its impressive plaster overmantel designed explicitly to woo the visitor with Wynn's noble credentials, most notably as a descendant of the Princes of Gwynedd. The plasterwork throughout is one of Plas Mawr's undoubted highlights, much of it relating to the powerful Wynn dynasty. The only exception to the unrelenting plaster egotism comes in the Great Chamber, where Wynn played down his own noble aspirations in the decor, presumably not to upstage visiting royalty. The tour concludes with a superb exhibition about Tudor and Stuart attitudes to disease and cleanliness, which manages to be compulsively gory, hilariously scatological and highly informative to boot.

For over a hundred years, Plas Mawr was home to the **Royal Cambrian Academy**, a group aiming to foster and further art in Wales. It's now located just behind Plas Mawr in a converted chapel on Crown Lane (Tues–Sat 11am–5pm, Sun 1–4.30pm; Sun 11am–5pm Aug & Sept; £1). At their best during the annual summer exhibition, the airy, well-lit galleries display work by the Academy members, almost all Welsh or working in Wales.

If you're suffocating on history and high art, there's light relief at **Teapot World**, across from Aberconwy House on Castle Street (Easter–Oct Mon–Sat 10am–5.30pm, Sun 11am–5.30pm; £1.50), which packs a thousand pots into one room. Clarice Cliff and the American Rockwood studio are well represented, while Wedgwood, majolica and Bauhaus pieces share space with Art Deco car and train forms, pots emblazoned with anti-slavery and suffragette slogans and items of lewd innuendo.

There's more featherweight entertainment ten minutes' walk north along Castle/Berry Street at the **Butterfly Jungle** (April–Sept daily 10am–5pm; Oct daily 10am–4pm; £2.95), a hothouse full of bougainvillea, hibiscus and oleander pollinated by some fifty breeds of tropical butterfly, most imported as chrysalises but several bred here.

If you're still stuck for something to do, **river cruises** on the *Queen Victoria* (30min; £2.80) or the *Princess Christine* (45min; £3.50) operate from the quay, and there's **pony trekking** from Pinewood Riding Stables (☎01492/592256) a mile up Sychnant Pass Road. During the school holidays, hour-long **ghost tours** (nightly 7.30pm; £2) start from the wishing well in Castle Square to trail around the town's spooked sites. You can book these at the tourist office, or just turn up.

Eating and drinking

For a popular tourist town, Conwy has relatively few **restaurants**, and if you want to sample some really excellent pubs, you've got to get a few miles out into the Conwy Valley. **Drinking** in town is fairly perfunctory, with nightlife being pretty limited to the odd pub gig. Most folk head into Llandudno or Bangor for anything with more of a pulse.

Restaurants and cafés

Alfredo's Restaurant, Lancaster Square (☎01492/592381). Good, low-cost pasta dishes and more expensive *secondi piatti* amongst the Chianti bottles.

Anna's Tearooms, 9 Castle St. Slightly pricey, but good-quality tearooms with a good lunchtime menu, located above the Conwy Outdoor Shop.

Austrian Restaurant, Conwy Old Rd, Capelulo, two miles west over Sychnant Pass (☎01492/622170). Worth making a journey for steaming, fair-priced helpings of goulash and paprika schnitzel. Closed Sun evening and all day Mon.

Edwards, 18 High St. Good deli with a decent salad bar, the place to stock up for picnics.

Pen-y-Bryn Tearooms, 28 High St. Small, non-smoking establishment with the best artery-hardening Welsh teas around and delicious lunches.

The Wall Place, Bishop's Yard, Chapel St (☎01492/596326). Licensed vegetarian establishment rapidly becoming one of Conwy's trendiest places, with indoor and outdoor seating and cheap, hearty wholefood staples, many of them vegan, and great fruit shakes. Live folk, jazz and Celtic music most Sat evenings for around £3. Closed evenings in winter.

Bars and pubs

Castle Hotel, High St. Decent bar in a town hotel that's a favourite amongst locals.

Groes Inn, Tyn-y-Groes, 2 miles south on B5106 to Llanrwst. Excellent bar meals and cask ales at an atmospheric fifteenth-century pub which claims to be the first licensed house in Wales.

Liverpool Arms, The Quay. Ordinary town pub, but its dockside location makes it a hot venue on warm evenings.

Malt Loaf, Rosehill St, opposite the station. Scruffily low-key pub, home to the town's folk club and attendant jumper-wearers.

Olde Bull Inn, five miles south in Llanbedr-y-Cennin. Quiet haven serving good bar meals.

Tŷ Gwyn Hotel, Rowen, 5 miles south of Conwy. Village pub in idyllic setting with friendly atmosphere and good garden.

Ye Olde Mail Coach, 16 High St. Spacious neo-olde-worlde pub serving good real ale and bar meals, and putting on occasional live music shows.

Around Conwy

With its marvellous setting and plentiful accommodation, Conwy is the ideal base for a couple of days spent exploring the Lower Conwy Valley and the coast around its estuary. It's easy to make a day-trip to Llandudno (see p.400), and there's a smattering of other attractive diversions within a few miles' radius. Thousands come here specifically to see **Bodnant Garden** beside the lower reaches of the Conwy, flowing down from Llanrwst and Betws-y-Coed. Conwy also acts as a base for the **Cambrian Way** long-distance walking path to Cardiff (see box, below). The guesthouses and restaurants mentioned in the text are all listed on p.407.

Sychnant Pass and Penmaenmawr

The best short walk from Conwy is on to **Conwy Mountain** (Mynydd y Dref) and the 800-foot Penmaenbach and Alltwen peaks behind, all giving great views right along the coast. Follow a sign up Cadnant Park off the Bangor road just outside the town walls, then take the road around until Mountain Road heads off on the right towards a hillfort on the summit. This group is separated from the foothills of the Carneddau range by the narrow cleft of **Sychnant Pass**, traversed by Old Conwy Road, which ducks away from the sea, making an alternative route west, and rejoins the A55 at workaday **PENMAENMAWR**, once a cheerful seaside resort but now sliced in two by the dual

---

THE CAMBRIAN WAY

The ultimate Welsh long-distance path, the **Cambrian Way** nips across the whole country, winding some 274 miles from Cardiff to Conwy. The main feature of the path is its sheer isolation, passing through some of Wales' most spellbinding natural upland scenery, as the route climbs over the Carneddau, the Glyders, the Snowdon massif, Cadair Idris and the Brecon Beacons before dropping down through the Valleys to Cardiff.

This is the most arduous long walk in Wales, and one of the most satisfying, requiring a high degree of commitment even from experienced walkers. Few people attempt to complete the whole walk in one bash, preferring to break it into manageable sections. Fit hikers might do it in two tough weeks but three or even four is more usual. Signposting is erratic en route – if you intend to try the whole path, or any of its sections, A.J. Drake's *The Cambrian Way: A Mountain Connoisseur's Walk* (see Contexts, p.487) is well worth acquiring.

The experience is undoubtedly heightened by spending nights under canvas atop the moors, but with fifteen YHA hostels scattered along the route and B&Bs selected from *Stillwell's National Trail Companion* (see p.487 in Contexts), much of the route can be completed with a roof over your head. Indeed, five hotel owners in Wales have grouped together to divide the path into five segments of six- to seven-day stages. Staying at the hotels, you will be bussed to and from easily walkable sections (around ten miles per day) and provided with electronic navigators, maps and even mobile phones. For details, and free information about the Way, contact the Cambrian Way Walkers Association's effervescent Nick Bointon at Llanerchindda Farm, Cynghordy, Llandovery, Dyfed SA20 0NB (☎01550/750274, fax 750300; see also p.150).

carriageway. To accommodate the new road, the gloomy shingle beach and promenade had to be completely remodelled – "Britain's first new promenade this century" was the vainglorious boast. If you see any photos of the original, you'll wish they hadn't bothered.

The road from Conwy, served by bus #71, passes the newly opened YHA hostel (see p.407) and the Pinewood Riding Stables before dropping into the hamlet of **CAPELULO**, a couple of miles short of Penmaenmawr. If you're armed with a decent map, Capelulo makes a good starting point for a walk across **Penmaenmawr Mountain**, an important source of stone for axe-making from around 3000 BC and still being quarried today. Not surprisingly, the area boasts several Neolithic remains, most notably the misnamed **Druid's Circle** (Y Meini Hirion) – marked on the map (grid reference 723746) simply as "Stone Circle" – on the hills behind Penmaenmawr. Of the thirty stones which originally composed the site, only ten survive in substantial form. Within the ring, archeologists found a buried cist containing a food vessel and the cremated remains of a child: possible evidence of a human sacrifice. Folklore has embellished the theme by naming one of the stones, its top scalloped into a cradle shape, the Stone of Sacrifice. Opposite, the Deity Stone is said to punish anyone who curses before it. Neo-druidic ceremonies still take place here from time to time.

Rowen and Aber Falls

Nine miles west of Conwy on the A55, the otherwise unremarkable *Aber Falls Hotel* signals a sideroad leading inland to the 100-foot **Aber Falls**. Though a torrent after a storm, it can be little more than a trickle in high summer and in the dead of winter can freeze enough to attract ice climbers. The road from the A55 runs a mile through a pretty oakwood valley to a car park at the start of a nature trail. This comprises several footpaths that lead to the Falls, two following the valley with its series of cataracts and cascades, the other cutting up into the pine forests and approaching across a scree slope.

The same road off the A55 continues for two more miles, ending on the northern slopes of the bare Carneddau. From here, a path (6 miles; 2–3hr; 600ft ascent) follows the low-level route of both a Bronze Age trackway and subsequent Roman road through the Carneddau range to Rowen. For much of the Roman occupation, this was the most important road in Wales, linking the legion's headquarters in Chester – where some of the sandstone paving originally came from – via the now barely visible fort at Canovium, located some two miles southeast of Rowen, to Segontium in Caernarfon (see p.369). The only walkable section these days is the stretch from Aber to Rowen, which, along the way, passes a burial chamber, a stone circle or two, evidence of prehistoric field systems and far too many power pylons.

The path emerges just behind the superbly set YHA hostel (see p.407) which, together with a post office, chapel, the lovely *Tŷ Gwyn* pub and a few houses, comprise the tiny mountainside hamlet of **ROWEN** (also spelt Roewen), one of the prettiest in the area. The #19 bus links Conwy with Rowen every two hours.

Bodnant Garden

During the months of May and June, the 160-foot laburnum tunnel flourishes and banks of rhododendrons are in full and glorious bloom all over **Bodnant Garden** (March–Oct daily 10am–5pm; £4.60; NT), Wales' finest formal garden and one of the most beautiful in Britain, eight miles south of Conwy. Laid out in 1875 around Bodnant Hall (closed to the public) by its then owner, English industrialist Henry Pochin, the garden spreads out over eighty acres of the east of the Conwy Valley. Facing southwest, the bulk of the garden – divided into an upper terraced garden and lower Pinetum and Wild Garden – catch the late afternoon sun as it sets over the Carneddau range, though the limited opening hours mean that visitors only experience this in October. Shrubs and plants provide a blaze of colour throughout the opening season, but autumn is a perfect time to be here, with hydrangeas still in bloom and fruit trees shedding their leaves. You'll need a minimum of two hours to fully appreciate the place. The #25 bus runs here from Llandudno every two hours, calling at Llandudno Junction, or it's a two-mile walk from the Tal-y-Cafn train station on the Conwy Valley line.

Bangor and around

After a few days travelling through mid-Wales or in the mountains of Snowdonia, **BANGOR** makes a welcome change. It's not big; but, as the largest town in Gwynedd and home to **Bangor University**, it passes in these parts for cosmopolitan. Although the students are the main reason for Bangor's vibrancy, the city has enough of an eclectic population of its own to keep the area's most active social life going all year round. Unlike Aberystwyth, however, where numerous summer visitors take up when the students have gone, Bangor relies more on its indigenous population for vacation-time entertainment, and therein lies one of the city's defining features: its staunch

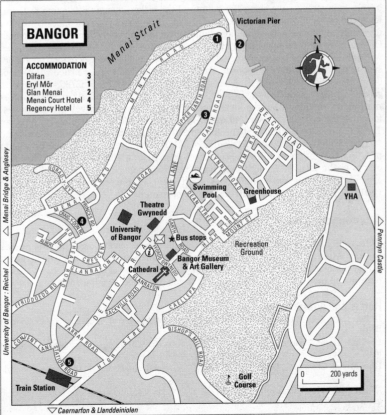

© Crown copyright

Welshness. The presence of a large non-Welsh student population inflames the passions of the more militant nationalists in this overwhelmingly Welsh-speaking area. Antagonism between students and locals seldom inflates to anything more than drunken slanging matches, but if you've just arrived from one of the largely English-speaking north coast resorts, you'll notice a dramatic change.

In the nineteenth century, the slate industry and road and rail projects brought some urbanization to Bangor. But for well over a millennium before that, the city was solely noted for its bishopric, founded as a monastic settlement by Saint Deiniol in 525 AD and thus the oldest continuous cathedral see in Britain, predating even Canterbury by some seventy years. At first, Saint Deiniol only cleared a space in the woods which became known as *Y Cae Onn* (The Ash Enclosure), later developing into the town's present name, a corruption of *bangori*, a type of interwoven wattle fence which presumably demarcated the monastic lands.

Arrival and information

All trains on the North Coast line between Chester and Holyhead stop at Bangor's **train station** on Station Road, at the bottom of Holyhead Road. From here, Deiniol Road, the town's main street, runs along the bottom of the valley, changing its name to Garth Road and continuing almost to the pier. The long High Street runs one block parallel to the south; to the north, the grandiose buildings of the university dominate the skyline. On the other side of them, **Upper Bangor** is home to some decent shops and pubs, as well as many student homes. National Express **buses** and local services stop on a short spur of Garth Road, almost opposite Theatr Gwynedd. The **tourist office** (April–Sept daily 10am–6pm; Oct–March Tues–Sat 10am–5pm; ☎01248/352786, *bangor.tic@gwynedd.gov.uk*) is yards away in the Town Hall on Deiniol Road. **Alternative information**, on anything from the local green scene to womens' and gay groups, is best found at the redoubtable **Greenhouse/Tŷ Gwydr** resource centre at 1 Trevelyan Terrace, opposite KwikSave at the top end of the High Street (Mon–Fri 9am–5pm; ☎01248/355821, *post@tygwydr.free-online.co.uk*). If nothing else, you should be able to pick up a copy of the monthly *Network News* from here, which has details of New Age events in the locality. Though you might be discouraged by the many hills in and around town, you can **rent bikes** from West End Cycles at 33–35 High St (☎01248/371158) or at the youth hostel (see opposite).

Accommodation

With its relatively low number of visitors, Bangor doesn't have a huge choice of **places to stay**. Most cheaper accommodation is at the northern end of Garth Road, about twenty minutes' walk from the train station. As usual, many of the better places are out of town and thoroughly inconvenient unless you have your own transport.

Hotels and guesthouses
Dilfan, Garth Rd (☎01248/353030). Marginally the best in a row of three serviceable, low-cost B&Bs. ②.

Eryl Môr Hotel, 2 Upper Garth Rd (☎01248/353789, fax 354042). Quiet, comfortable, fully licensed hotel with some rooms overlooking Bangor's pier and the Menai Strait. ②.

Glan Menai, Greenbank, Garth Rd (☎01248/352802). Good, no-frills budget rooms down towards the pier. ①.

Menai Court Hotel, Craig-y-Don Rd (☎01248/354200, fax 354512). Bangor's top hotel, with plush decor and well-appointed rooms, some with views of Snowdonia or the Menai Strait. ④.

Nant-y-Fedw, 2 Tre Felin, Llandegai (☎01248/351683). Extremely welcoming, very comfortable B&B with attractive gardens, en-suite rooms and good evening meals on request. The approach is unprepossessing, down a small turning a quarter of a mile past the entrance to Penrhyn Castle. Booked guests will be met from the train or bus. ②.

Regency Hotel, Holyhead Rd (☎01248/370819). Good-value small hotel noted chiefly for its proximity to the train station. ②.

Swn-y-Nant, Caernarfon Rd, three miles south of Bangor on the A4087 (☎01248/670792, fax 671140). Attractive rooms in a house that's ideal for kids. The obliging hosts cook lovely meals, keep geese and pigs, and will pick you up from town if you book ahead. ②.

Ty-Mawr Farm, half a mile east of Llanddeiniolen, five miles southwest of Bangor on the B4366 (☎01286/670147). Comfortable B&B on a working farm with views of Snowdonia and very good home-made food. Quality, well-equipped self-catering cottages also available short term outside the school holidays. The infrequent bus #77 (not Sun) stops within half a mile. ②.

Tŷ'n Rhos, Llanddeiniolen, five miles southwest of Bangor (☎01248/670489, fax 670079). Exceptionally good farmhouse accommodation which you'll need to book well in advance. Superb, moderately priced four-course meals. Bus #77 (not Sun). ⑤.

University of Bangor: Reichel, Ffriddoedd Rd (☎01248/372104). Clean, functional rooms available from late June to late Sept, and over the Easter holidays. ②.

Hostels and campsites

Bangor YHA hostel, Tan-y-Bryn (☎01248/353516, fax 371176). A large house signposted on the right of the A56, 10min walk east of the centre and reached either by walking along the High Street or taking bus #6 or #7 along Garth Road. Closed late Nov to late Dec.

Treborth Hall Farm (☎01248/364104). Cheap and cheerful campsite a couple of miles out of town (off the A487 between the two Menai Strait bridges), though easily walkable from Upper Bangor. Occasional bus #5 passes the entrance.

Tros-y-Waen Farm, off B4547 south of Pentir, 6 miles south of Bangor, towards Llanberis (☎01248/364448). Unremarkable farmhouse B&B surrounded by a quiet, low-cost (£4 per tent) campsite with hot showers and a good pub, the *Vaynol Arms*, within walking distance.

The Town

Straddling the hill that separates the town centre from the Menai Strait, the university takes up much of Upper Bangor. The shape of the college's main building is almost an exact replica of the **cathedral**, directly below on the other side of Deiniol Road (daily 11am–5pm; free), which boasts the longest continuous use of any cathedral in Britain, easily predating the town. Nowadays only a blocked-in Norman window gives any hint of the see's ancient origins. Though you won't want to spend a lot of time here, it's worth venturing into the spacious white-walled interior, particularly to see the sixteenth-century wooden **Mostyn Christ**, depicted bound and seated on a rock.

Little is recorded of the original cathedral until it was destroyed and subsequently rebuilt by the Normans in 1071. Archbishop Baldwin preached here in 1188 while raising support for the Third Crusade, when his chronicler, Giraldus Cambrensis, was shown a double vault by the high altar containing Owain Gwynedd and his brother Cadwaladr. Owain had been posthumously excommunicated by Archbishop Thomas for incest with his first cousin, and the Bishop of Bangor was asked to look for an opportunity to remove the body from the cathedral. He was probably reinterred in the churchyard, though many believe the body lies within the arched tomb in the south transept.

The earlier Norman building was heavily damaged by Vikings in 1073, by King John in 1211, a third time by Edward I in 1277 and then again by Owain Glyndŵr in 1402, the various reconstructions resulting in the present thirteenth- to fifteenth-century building, heavily restored by Gilbert Scott in 1866. Outside, there's a **bible**

garden with a collection of all the biblical trees, shrubs and flowers capable of withstanding the local climate.

Just over the road on Ffordd Gwynedd, the cathedral's Canonry now houses the **Bangor Museum and Art Gallery** (Tues–Fri 12.30–4.30pm, Sat 10.30am–4.30pm; free), where the standard regional museum fare and snippets of local history are enlivened by the refurbished traditional-costume section and the archeology room, the latter containing the most complete Roman sword found in Wales. The most insightful rooms are those devoted to a complete set of furniture from a moderately wealthy Cricieth farm, covering three hundred years of acquisitions, from brooding Welsh dressers to fine Italian pieces. Furniture also forms the basis of the museum's homage to Thomas Telford, whose favourite chair sits alongside a model of his bridge complete with the web of chains which were stripped off during strengthening in 1935, when they were found to be heavy and unnecessary. The art gallery downstairs has no permanent collection, its temporary displays concentrating on predominantly Welsh contemporary works.

Heading away from the centre, Telford's bridge is best appreciated if you walk out on to it, but you can also get a good look at it from Bangor's pristine **Victorian Pier** (50p at peak times, free otherwise), which reaches 1550 feet out into the Menai Strait – over halfway across to Anglesey. Built in 1896, the pier lay derelict for years; however, it's recently been restored and is blessed with just one token amusement pavilion. It's more a place just to sit and watch the world drift idly by on two shores than a traditional seaside pier. To get there, either follow Garth Road towards Conwy – a fifteen-minute walk – or work your way down from Upper Bangor along College Road, the latter route allowing a detour across a wooded hill known as Roman Camp. Recent digs here have failed to unearth any evidence at all of Roman occupation, but you do at least get a good view of the Strait.

Eating, drinking and entertainment

Bangor has few really good **restaurants**, though as befits a university town there are plenty of places to fill up reasonably well at modest cost. These are scattered around town, several clustering around the student bedsitland of Upper Bangor along Holyhead Road. High Street is the best zone for grazing or stocking up for a journey, with an abundance of cheap cafés, pasta and sandwich joints.

Restaurants and cafés

Fat Cat Café Bar, 161 High St. Breezy modern decor and a moderately priced menu – ranging from massive burgers to salmon-and-broccoli pasta quills – help pack this place out with students and locals.

Garden, 1 High St. Dimly lit Cantonese restaurant offering a broad but not overwhelming menu, and weekday lunchtime specials.

Greek Taverna Politis, 12 Holyhead Rd (☎01248/354991). Moderately priced souvlakia and *stifado* favourites and top-class Greek salads served around the fire, in the airy conservatory or outside in the courtyard. Cheaper meals at the bar and jazz every Mon.

Herbs Cookshop, 307–309 High St. Great daytime vegetarian café with an attached health-food shop and lots to take away. Closed Sun.

Mahabharat, 5–7 High St (☎01248/352802). The best of Bangor's curry houses with very good balti and tandoori dishes.

Menai Court Hotel, Craig-y-Don Rd (☎01248/354200). The restaurant of this classy hotel earns the plaudits of foodies for its traditional, expensive British and European dishes and its extensive wine list.

Tandoori Knights, 10 Holyhead Rd (☎01248/364634). All the usual tandoori and balti dishes in a restaurant that often looks closed when it isn't.

Pubs, entertainment and nightlife

Belle Vue, Holyhead Rd. Bangor's big student pub, right next to the university and heaving at the weekend.

The Nelson, Beach Rd. Reasonable wood-beamed pub with a reputation for good, inexpensive bar meals, tapas and sandwiches.

The Octagon, Dean St, off High St. Very mainstream town nightclub.

The Skerries, 374 High St. Lively pub with a decent pint, a relatively up-to-date jukebox and a young crowd.

Tafarn Y Glôb, 7 Albert St, Upper Bangor. If you've tried to learn any of the language, you can put it to good use at this traditional local where ordering in Welsh is pretty much *de rigueur*. For a pint of beer, try "Un peint o cwrw, os gwelwch yn dda".

Theatr Gwynedd, Deiniol Rd (box office ☎01248/351708). Along with its counterpart in Mold, Theatr Gwynedd is the most progressive art house in north Wales and is about your only chance of seeing contemporary plays or even slightly offbeat movies.

University Students' Union, Deiniol Rd (☎01248/353709). Fly posters around town almost all point you to the Students' Union, the venue for any touring rock/pop bands. Usually quiet over the summer break.

The Victoria Hotel, Telford St, Menai Bridge. The best bet for local live music, across the water in Menai Bridge (see p.422).

Y Castell/The Castle, Glanrafon. Big, new and studenty pub bang opposite the cathedral.

Penrhyn Castle

There can hardly be a more vulgar testament to the Anglo-Welsh landowning gentry's oppression of the rural Welsh than the oddly compelling **Penrhyn Castle** (April–June, Sept & Oct daily except Tues noon–5pm; July & Aug daily except Tues 11am–5pm; £5 with 50min recorded tour, £3 grounds & railway museum only; NT), two miles east of Bangor, which overlooks Port Penrhyn from its acres of isolating parkland. Built on the backs of slate miners for the benefit of their bosses, this monstrous nineteenth-century neo-Norman fancy, with over three hundred rooms dripping with luxurious fittings, was funded by the quarry's huge profits.

The responsibility falls ultimately on Caribbean sugar plantation owner, slave trader and vehement anti-abolitionist Richard Pennant, First Baron Penrhyn, who built a port on the northeastern edge of Bangor in order to ship his Bethesda slate to the world. But it was his self-aggrandizing great-great-nephew George Dawkins who inherited the 40,000-acre estate, added his ancestor's surname to his own, and with the aid of architect Thomas Hopper spent thirteen years from 1827 encasing the neo-Gothic hall in a Norman fortress complete with monumental five-storey keep.

Many would argue that the vulgarity doesn't stop with the owners but runs right through the fabric of the building, with the abundance of carved slate a further slap in the face to the workers. The decoration is glorious nonetheless, and fairly true to the Romanesque, with its deeply cut chevrons, billets and double-cone ornamentation. Hopper even looked to Norman architecture for the design of the furniture, but abandoned historical authenticity when it came to installing the central heating system, which piped hot air through ornamental brass ducts at the cost of twenty tons of coal a month.

Everything is on a massive scale and no more so than in the Great Hall with its pair of stained-glass zodiac windows by Thomas Willement. Three-foot-thick oak doors separate subsequent rooms: the Library, with its full-size slate billiard table, and the oppressive Ebony Room, which leads onto the Grand Staircase. Upstairs, the lightness of the original William Morris wallpaper and drapes around the King's Bed are in marked contrast to the Slate Bed, designed for Queen Victoria but declined by her in favour of the Hopper-designed four-poster in the State Bedroom. The family managed to assemble the country's largest private **painting collection**. Much of this remains, especially in the two dining rooms, where there's a Gainsborough landscape amongst the family portraits, Canaletto's *The Thames at Westminster* and a Rembrandt portrait.

Once Richard Pennant had built his port he needed some way of getting the slates down to it. His answer was a horse-drawn tramway, which opened in 1801 and remained in use – though using steam engines by this time – until 1962. Gleaming examples of rolling stock from this and the country's other private industrial railways are on display in the **Industrial Railway Museum** (same hours; entry with castle or grounds tickets), including Lord Penrhyn's luxurious coach linked to a quarrymen's car. Buses #5, #6 and #7 run frequently from Bangor to the gates, from where it is a mile-long walk to the house.

Vaynol Estate and Treborth Botanical Gardens

On the other side of Bangor from Penrhyn are a couple of sites of bucolic interest, both overlooking the ever-changing waters of the Menai Strait. Most gloriously, the National Trust-managed **Vaynol Estate** (*Glan Faenol*; unrestricted access) is a large, mixed landscape of woodland and open park running along the Strait to the west of the Britannia Bridge. Vaynol offers some charming waymarked walks and picnicking spots facing the gentle frontage of Plas Newydd, over the water on Anglesey (see p.426). Once the estate of the privately-owned Vaynol Hall (no access), which you pass on the way into the grounds, the parkland is noted for some curious follies, most obviously the round tower built to rival the Marquess of Anglesey's Column (see p.426) across in Llanfair PG on Anglesey. Access to Vaynol's car park and the walking trails is via the business park at the southern roundabout of the Britannia Bridge (A487/A5). Once inside Parc Menai, go down Ffordd y Parc and left into Ffordd y Plas, following the lane past Vaynol Hall and chapel.

There's another leafy treat at the southern end of the Menai Bridge, a mile back along the A487 towards Bangor. The **Treborth Botanical Gardens** (unrestricted access), owned and managed by the University of Bangor, is delightful: acres of springy lawns, wild grass areas, shrubs, bushes, exotic trees and ancient woodland, all set on the southern slopes of the Menai Strait. On selected open days (details ☎01248/353398), you can also see inside the extensive glasshouses. At other times, you can wander freely, as long as you respect the cordoned-off areas of experimental horticulture and keep to the obvious paths. Entrance is easiest through the Treborth Industrial Estate off the Menai Bridge access road.

ANGLESEY

Anglesey (Ynys Môn) is a world apart from Wales, let alone the rest of Britain. After the mountains and hemmed-in settlements of Snowdonia, this pastoral island, a green ripple of fields and farms, comes as a bit of a shock. At first glance, it can look comparatively dull, especially if you limit yourself to crossing the island on the A5, through lacklustre villages and past multiple roadworks that herald the building of the last part of the Trans-European Expressway, here the A55, destined to tear across Anglesey by 2002. Appearances can be deceptive, however, for there is plenty on Anglesey to see and do.

Signs and slogans dotted around the place announce Anglesey to be Mam Cymru, "The Mother of Wales", attesting to the island's former importance as the country's breadbasket. In the twelfth century, Giraldus Cambrensis noted that "When crops have failed in other regions, this island, from its soil and its abundant produce, has been able to supply all Wales", and while feeding their less productive kin in Snowdonia is no longer a priority, the land remains predominantly agricultural, with small fields, stone walls and white houses reminiscent of parts of Ireland and England. Linguistically and

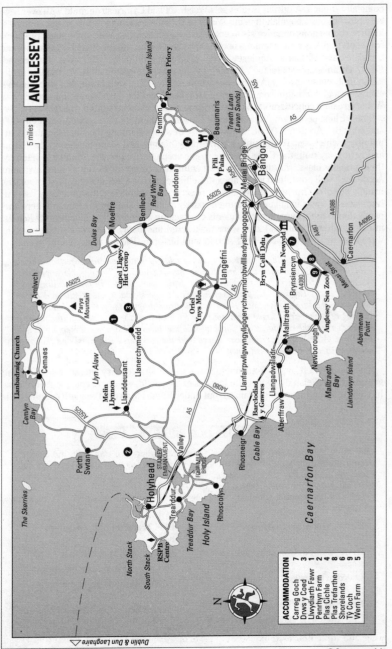

ANGLESEY

5 miles

Puffin Island
Penmon Priory
Penmon
Beaumaris
Traeth Lafan
(Lavan Sands)
Bangor
Pili Palas
Menai Bridge
Red Wharf Bay
Llanddona
Benllech
Moelfre
Dulas Bay
Capel Lligwy Hut Group
Langefni
Oriel Ynys Môn
Plas Newydd
Bryn Celli Ddu
Brynsiencyn
Anglesey Sea Zoo
Caernarfon
Menai Strait
Abermenai Point
Llanddwyn Island
Malltraeth Bay
Malltraeth
Newborough
Llanfairpwllgwyngyllgogerychwyrndrobwllllantysiliogogogoch
Llangadwaladr
Aberffraw
Barclodiad y Gawres
Cable Bay
Rhosneigr
Caernarfon Bay
Amlwch
Parys Mountain
Llyn Alaw
Llanerchymedd
Cemaes
Llanbadrig Church
Cemlyn Bay
Llanddeusant
Melin Llynnon
A5025
A5
A4080
Valley
STANLEY EMBANKMENT
FOUR MILE BRIDGE
Porth Swtan
Holyhead
Trearddur
Trearddur Bay
Holy Island
Rhoscolyn
The Skerries
North Stack
South Stack
RSPB Centre

Dublin & Dun Laoghaire

N

ACCOMMODATION
Carreg Goch 7
Drws y Coed 3
Llwydiarth Fawr 1
Penrhyn Farm 2
Plas Cichle 4
Plas Trefarthen 8
Shorelands 6
Tŷ Coch 9
Wern Farm 5

© Crown copyright

politically, though, Anglesey is intensely Welsh, a Plaid Cymru stronghold with over seventy percent of its population using Welsh as their first language – one of the country's highest proportions of native speakers. Most residents will at least understand the lines of one of Anglesey's most famous poets, Goronwy Owen, whose eulogy on his homeland translates as "All hail to Anglesey/ The delight of all regions/ Bountiful as a second Eden/ Or an ancient paradise". Judging by the numbers who flock to the island's necklace of fine sandy coves and rocky headlands, many agree with Owen, but just as many charge straight through from Bangor to **Holyhead** and the Irish ferries, missing out on Wales' greatest concentration of pre-Christian sites and some superb coastal scenery.

The earliest people on Anglesey were Mesolithic hunters who arrived between 8000 and 4000 BC. Around 2500 BC, a new culture developed among the small farming communities, which was responsible for the many henges and stone circles on the island and held sway until the Celts swept across Europe in the seventh century BC, led by their priestly class, the druids. In the centuries leading up to the Roman invasion, Anglesey – well positioned at the apex of Celtic sea traffic – became the most important druidic centre in Europe. The druids were so firmly established that Anglesey was the last place in Wales to fall to the Romans, partly thanks to the druidic strength here and partly due to the geographical problems of attacking an island. The bloodthirsty Roman invasion, when countless locals were massacred and many traces of druidic worship were forcibly trashed, came in 61 AD. Roman historian Tacitus recorded the scene:

Women were seen rushing through the ranks of soldiers in wild disorder, dressed in black, with their hair dishevelled and brandishing flaming torches. Their whole appearance resembled the frantic rage of the Furies. The druids were ranged in order, calling down terrible curses. The soldiers, paralysed by this strange spectacle, stood still and offered themselves as a target for wounds. But at last the promptings of the general – and their own rallying of each other – urged them not to be frightened of a mob of women and fanatics. They advanced the standards, cut down all who met them and swallowed them up in their own fires. After this a garrison was placed over the conquered islanders, and the groves sacred to savage rites were cut down.

The vacuum left by the Roman departure in the fifth century was soon filled by the greatest of all Welsh dynasties, the Princes of Gwynedd, who held court at **Aberffraw**. Initially, their authority was localized, but under Rhodri Mawr in the ninth century their

---

ANGLESEY'S RURAL B&BS

The island is so compact that, at least if you have your own transport, the choice of **accommodation** should be based on factors other than solely location. There are some excellent, moderately priced B&Bs and farmhouses, many of them relatively distant from any recognized sight, but no less appealing for it. Several of the better ones have been listed below and marked on the Anglesey map opposite; see the regional accounts for details.

Carreg Goch, near Llanfair PG (see p.426).

Drws Y Coed, Llanerchymedd (see p.433).

Llwydiarth Fawr, Llanerchymedd (see p.433).

Penrhyn Farm, Llanfwrog (see p.433).

Plas Cichle, Llanfaes, near Beaumaris (see p.423).

Plas Trefarthen, Brynsiencyn (see p.427).

Shorelands, Malltraeth (see p.428).

Tŷ Coch, Brynsiencyn (see p.427).

Tyddyn Goblet, Brynsiencyn (see p.427).

Wern Farm, near Menai Bridge (see p.422).

influence spread over most of Wales as he defeated the encroaching Vikings, earning thanks from Charlemagne for his efforts. Anglesey again fell to outsiders towards the end of the thirteenth century when Edward I defeated the Welsh princes, sealing the island's fate by building the last of his great castles at **Beaumaris**, by far the most absorbing town on the island.

Getting around the island is easy enough. The train line from Bangor crosses the Menai Strait, stopping at the station with the longest name in the world – usually abbreviated to **Llanfair PG** or Llanfairpwll – before continuing on to meet the ferries at Holyhead. The rest of the island is covered by a bus network thoroughly detailed in the free *Ynys Môn* public transport timetables.

Menai Bridge and the approaches

Two bridges – both engineering marvels of their time – link Anglesey to the mainland over the **Menai Strait**, a perilous fourteen-mile-long tidal race that in places narrows to two hundred yards wide, forcing the current up to eight knots as it rushes between Conwy and Caernarfon bays. The view from the mainland over to Anglesey is impressive enough, but outdone by the eastward vistas from the Anglesey shore, where you can look over the rocky mid-channel islets, some adorned with jetties and small houses, and backed by the heartland of Snowdonia.

For centuries before the bridges were built, drovers used the Strait's narrow stretches to herd Anglesey-fattened cattle on their way to market in England. Travellers had to wait for low tide to cross Lafan Sands, northeast of Bangor, then find a boat to take them across to Beaumaris, in foggy weather guided only by the sound of church bells. It's no surprise that the Irish MPs, needing transport to Westminster and a faster mail service, pushed for a fixed crossing.

The first permanent connection, in 1826, was Telford's graceful **Menai Suspension Bridge**, the world's first large iron suspension bridge, spanning 579 feet between piers and 100 feet above the water to allow high-masted sailing ships to pass. Almost everything about the project was novel, including the process of lifting the first 23-ton cable into place, which involved a pulley system and 150 men kept in time by a fife band. They celebrated their achievement by running across the nine-inch-wide chain from Anglesey to the mainland.

Robert Stephenson also made engineering history with his **Britannia Tubular Bridge** in 1850, which carried trains across the strait in twin wrought-iron tubes. It burned down in 1970, however, leaving only the limestone piers that now support the twin-deck A5/A55 road and rail bridge to Llanfair PG and Holyhead.

Nestling in the shadow of the older crossing, with a few private islands to break the view across the strait to the mainland, is the town of **MENAI BRIDGE** (Porthaethwy). A short bus ride from Bangor (#53 and #57), it's also little more than half an hour's pleasant walk from the town, with views from the bridge over to the fourteenth-century **Church of St Tysilio** (open mid-July to Aug) on Church Island, where the church's patron saint founded his cell around 630 AD. Topped by a Celtic cross war memorial, the island affords delightful views along the Strait and to both bridges. It can be reached through the woodland behind the car park on the approach to the Menai Bridge itself, or from the town along Belgian Walk, a causeway and waterside promenade so named because it was built by refugees during World War I.

There's little else of note in town, but if you have children to entertain, take the B5420 two miles northeast of the village to **Pili Palas** (mid-March to Oct daily 10am–5.30pm, Nov–Christmas Eve daily 11am–3.30pm; £4), a steamy walk-in butterfly house with up to seventy species, some as big as your hand. British butterflies that are becoming less common in the wild are bred for release here, a venture promoted in the educational material available for kids. An aviary and vivarium complete the setup.

Practicalities

If you plan to **stay** in Menai Bridge, be sure to book ahead at the welcoming, non-smoking *Bwthyn*, 5 Brynafon (☎01248/713119; ①), just off Beach Road (the approach to Belgian Walk) with a couple of nicely decorated en-suite rooms, and locally made sausages for breakfast. Two miles north of town, off the A5025, the beautiful *Wern Farm* (☎01248/712421; ②) is an excellent choice, with lots of little extras in a farmhouse that dates from the early seventeenth century. Back in town, the choice of **places to eat** is surprisingly good, the best being *Jodie's Bar & Bistro*, right by the bridge on Telford Road (☎01248/714864), with refreshingly original wine-bar food in the cosy main rooms or airy conservatory. Worthy alternatives include decent pub meals and superb beer at the very cosy *Liverpool Arms* on St George's Pier, and two highly rated, moderately priced Chinese places – the central *Sunshine* on Wood Street, and *Jade Village* on the A4080 near *Jodie's*. Another good reason to stay is one of the best live **music** venues in the region, the *Victoria Hotel* on Telford Road (☎01248/712309). Both Welsh- and English-language bands play here, particularly on Wednesdays and weekends, ranging from rock through folk and jazz to Cajun.

Beaumaris

The original inhabitants of **BEAUMARIS** (Biwmares) were evicted by Edward I to make way for the construction of his new castle and bastide town, dubbed "beautiful marsh" in an attempt to attract English settlers. Today the place can still seem like the small English outpost Edward intended, with a grand Georgian terrace (designed by Joseph Hansom, of cab fame) and more plummy English accents than you'll have heard for a while. Many of their owners belong with the flotilla of yachts, an echo of the port's fleet of merchant ships, which disappeared with the completion of the Menai bridges and subsequent growth of Holyhead.

Beaumaris is not only attractive, it boasts more sights than the rest of the island put together. This inevitably brings the crowds here in summer, though even then the evenings, when day-trippers have departed and overnighters are ensconced in their hotel restaurants, are peaceful.

Arrival and accommodation

With no trains, long-distance coaches or proper tourist office (the Town Hall, next to the *Bulkeley Hotel* on Castle Street, stocks leaflets and will advise on local amenities), Beaumaris seems poorly served, but it has a regular **bus** service to Bangor (#53 and #57; infrequent on Sun) and no shortage of decent **places to stay**. For tenters, the nearest **campsite** is Kingsbridge (☎01248/490636) not far from *Plas Cichle* (see opposite). **Bike hire** (Easter–Sept) is available from Beics Menai (☎01248/811200 or 713871) at the town's leisure centre, off Rating Row behind the castle.

Hotels and guesthouses

Bishopsgate House Hotel, 54 Castle St (☎01248/810302, fax 810166). High-standard, predominantly business-oriented hotel in an elegant Georgian town house with all the expected facilities and a good restaurant. Closed Jan. ④.

Hafan, Raglan St (☎01248/810481). Decent, and cheap, town centre B&B. ①.

Henllys Hall Hotel (☎01248/810412, fax 811511). Victorian country-house hotel, set in 25 acres of woodland walks, with sauna, sunbed, heated outdoor pool, croquet lawns and excellent country cooking. With an eye to the romantic weekend market, several rooms have four-poster beds. ④.

Penrhyn guest house, Penmon (☎01248/490435). The best option if you want to base yourself out on Anglesey's eastern edge, this no-frills, no-smoking B&B commands superb sea views. ①.

Plas Cichle, Llanfaes (☎01248/810488). The best of the local farmhouse B&Bs with lovely period furnished rooms in a substantial Georgian house a couple of miles from Beaumaris. The welcome is warm and you're encouraged to practise whatever Welsh you've picked up. Book well ahead in high summer. Closed Dec & Jan. ②.

Swn-y-Don, 7 Bulkeley Terrace (☎01248/810794). One of the best of the town B&Bs with antique-filled rooms and sea views. ②.

Ye Olde Bull's Head Inn, 18 Castle St (☎01248/810329, fax 811294). The best hotel in Beaumaris, this ancient and luxurious coaching inn was used as General Mytton's headquarters during the Civil War and, in more peaceful circumstances, by Dr Johnson and Charles Dickens.There's a fantastic restaurant on site (see p.425). ⑤.

The Town and around

While you can spend an hour or two mooching around Beaumaris's antique shops, enjoying the views across the Strait towards Bangor and along the coast to Llandudno's Great Orme from the stumpy pier, this shouldn't distract from the town's major attractions. There is little doubt that the **castle** remains central to Beaumaris, its water-filled moat and arrow-looped ramparts satisfying the British castle archetype more than any other in Wales. The law and order theme continues in the **courthouse** and **gaol**, both offering their own angle on Welsh subjugation. In good weather, a cruise out around **Puffin Island** or a wander along the nearby coastline close to **Penmon Priory** may suit better.

The Castle

Beaumaris Castle (June–Sept daily 9.30am–6pm; April–May & Oct daily 9.30am–5pm; Nov–March Mon–Sat 9.30am–4pm, Sun 11am–4pm; £2.20; CADW) is the most picturesque of Edward's gargantuan fortresses, built in response to Madog ap Llywelyn's capture of Caernarfon in 1294. Its architect, James of St George, produced a symmetrical octagonal form, his finest and most highly evolved expression of concentric design. Lacking the domineering majesty of Caernarfon, Conwy or Harlech, its low outer walls seem almost welcoming – until you begin to appreciate the defensive bent of its construction.

Sited on flat land at the edge of town, the castle is approached over a moat and through Moorish-influenced staggered entries at the huge towers of the Gate Next the Sea and the South Gatehouse. The moat originally linked the castle to the sea, now well over a hundred yards away, with a shipping channel allowing boats of up to forty tons to tie up at the iron rings hammered into a protective spur of the outer defences, **Gunner's Walk**. Supplies could be brought in, including the corn which was fed into the mill, still visible immediately below.

Despite over thirty years' work and ambitious plans for a lavish palace, the castle was never quite finished, leaving most of the inner ward empty and the corbels and fireplaces built into the walls never used. You can explore an unsatisfyingly short section of the **wall walk**, from which archers were able to fire simultaneously from the inner and outer defences, and wander through miles of internal passages in the walls, finding your way to the first floor of the **Chapel Tower** and the small but wonderfully resonant lime-washed chapel, immediately above a small display on "The Castles of Wales".

None of the castle's defences was able to prevent siege by Owain Glyndŵr, who held the castle for two years from 1403, although during the Civil War they did keep out General Mytton and 1500 Parliamentarian troops until the local Royalists were forced to surrender in 1646. At the restoration, the castle was returned to the Bulkeley family, only to be left to fall into ruin before twentieth-century restoration returned some of its glory.

The rest of the town

Almost opposite the castle stands the Jacobean **Beaumaris Courthouse** (Easter & June–Sept daily 11am–4.30pm; May Sat & Sun only; £1.50, joint ticket with gaol £3), built in 1614 and the oldest active court in Britain. It is now used only for the monthly Magistrates Court, but until 1971, when they were moved to Caernarfon, the quarterly Assize Courts were held here. These were traditionally held in English, giving the jury little chance to follow the proceedings and Welsh-speaking defendants none against prosecutors renowned for slapping heavy penalties on relatively minor offences. On session days you can go in to watch the trials, now conducted in Welsh, but won't be able to take the recorded tour or inspect *The Lawsuit*, a plaque in the magistrates' room depicting two farmers pulling the horns and tail of a cow while a lawyer milks it.

Many citizens were transported from the courthouse to the colonies for their misdemeanours; others only made it a couple of blocks to the **Beaumaris Gaol**, Steeple Lane (Easter & June–Sept daily 11am–5.30pm; May Sat & Sun only; £2.50 or £3 joint ticket with courthouse). When it opened in 1829, this was considered a model prison, its facilities including running water and toilets in each cell, an infirmary and, eventually, heating. Women prisoners did the cooking and were allowed to rock their babies' cradles in the nursery above by means of a pulley system. Advanced perhaps, but nonetheless a gloomy place: witness the windowless punishment cell, the yard for stone-breaking and the treadmill water pump operated by the prisoners. The least fortunate inmates were marched along a first-floor walkway through a door in the outer wall to the gibbet where they were publicly hanged. This was the fate of a certain Richard Rowlands, whose disembodied voice leads the recorded tour of the building and various displays on prison life.

Nearby on Church Street is the **Church of St Mary and St Nicholas**, the only building in Beaumaris approaching the age of the castle. Though ancient enough – started in the twelfth century and rebuilt around 1500 – its chief interest is the coffin in the porch, used as a horse trough for years but originally holding Joan, wife of Llywelyn the Great and daughter of King John of England. Further along Church Street, towards the sea, there's a **market square** full of local craft and art shops.

For a more light-hearted half-hour, visit the **Museum of Childhood Memories**, 1 Castle St (Easter–Oct Mon–Sat 10.30am–5.30pm, Sun 11am–5pm; £3), one man's personal collection amassed over the last thirty years and displaying over 2000 toys dating from the 1840s to around 1970. Highlights among this hoard of dolls, train sets and piggy banks are the musical instruments, an early TV, a stereoscopic viewer and a zoetrope designed in 1850, showing some of the earliest moving images.

Interesting as Beaumaris is, a fine day might be better spent **cruising** with Puffin Island Cruises (Easter–Sept daily 10am–5pm; ☎01248/810251; £4), based in a kiosk at the foot of the pier. From here (numbers permitting), you can book an hour-long excursion around, but not onto, Puffin Island (see opposite). Otherwise, the seafront is a pleasant enough place just to sit and admire the view over to Bangor and Snowdonia, or maybe catch the *Blue Peter II* lifeboat in action.

Penmon Priory

One of the earliest monastic sites in Anglesey was on the now uninhabited Puffin Island, four miles northeast of Beaumaris. In Welsh it goes by the name Ynys Seiriol, recalling the sixth-century saint who, on becoming head of the Augustine **Penmon Priory** (unrestricted access; CADW), moved the island community the three-quarters of a mile to Penmon. Saint Seiriol soon became known as the White Saint, not for his unblemished purity, but because his weekly walk to Llanerchymedd to meet Saint Cybi involved journeying with his back to the sun in both directions. Cybi, journeying into the sun from present-day Holyhead, was dubbed the Tawny Saint.

The priory's original wooden buildings were razed by the Danes in the tenth century, but their replacements, the twelfth-century church and the thirteenth-century south range of the cloister, are still standing. Only the church is in good repair and still used, the serene lime-washed nave housing an unusual Norman pillar-piscina – a font gouged from the plinth of a pre-Norman cross still used for Sunday services – and the Penmon Cross, moved here to prevent a thousand years of Welsh weather completely scouring off its plait and fret patterns. There's more patterned stonework in the south transept, approached through a magnificent chevron- and chequerboard-patterned arch. The church's site was chosen for its proximity to the refreshing waters of **St Seiriol's Well**, which now feeds a calm pool and is reached by either the path behind the church, or another opposite the distinctive domed dovecote, built around 1600 to house one thousand pairs of birds.

Three-quarters of a mile beyond the dovecote (£1 toll for cars in summer), a short strait separates Black Point, the easternmost point of Anglesey, from **Puffin Island**, now a nesting point for razorbills, guillemots and puffins, all once permissible food during Lent. Before retiring to the café in the car park at Black Point, take a walk around the headland or past the quarries, where James of St George cut fossil-ridden limestone for Caernarfon and Beaumaris castles, and Telford and Stephenson found the footings for their bridges. The rock was once part of a single mass that included the Great and Little Ormes, eight miles to the east on the mainland.

Getting here is no problem, as the frequent #57 Bangor–Beaumaris **bus** continues to Penmon roughly hourly.

Eating and drinking

There's no need to go hungry in Beaumaris which, for a small place, has a good selection of daytime cafés and several more substantial **restaurants**.

Chez Silvia, inside the *Bulkeley Hotel* on Castle St (☎01248/810415). One of the more refined places to relax over a coffee and admire the sea views. The cakes and coffee are good and the prices modest. You can also try the bar snacks – mainly posh sandwiches and spuds – or the more upmarket restaurant, with a five-course fixed price menu at £17.50.

Cottage Restaurant, 10 Castle St (☎01248/810946). The pick of the mid-range restaurants with an imaginative menu of meat and vegetarian dishes and good lunchtime specials, served in a room which partly cantilevers over the street.

Sailor's Return, Church St. Town pub best known for its excellent bar meals and therefore not too smoky for eating at lunchtimes.

Y Gragen Gocos/The Cockleshell, 13 Castle St (☎01248/810623). Wonderful seafood concoctions in a very cosy restaurant.

Ye Olde Bull's Head Inn (see p.423). Beaumaris's top restaurant in the plush wood-beamed rooms of its best hotel. Its immaculately prepared traditional dinners are worth saving up for. They also offer the option of cheaper brasserie food, mainly seafood, meat and pasta dishes.

Llanfairpwllgwyngyllgogerychwyrndrobw-llllandysiliogogogoch and the south coast

When Robert Louis Stephenson wrote "to travel hopefully is a better thing than to arrive" he might have been thinking of **LLANFAIR PG**, the village with the longest place name in Britain and little else but for a wool shop and a small train station bearing the famed sign **Llanfairpwllgwyngyllgogerychwyrndrobwllllandysiliogogogoch**. Sadly, "St Mary's Church in the hollow of white hazel near a rapid whirlpool and the Church of St Tysilio near the red cave" is no authentic Welsh tongue twister; simply the fabrication of a Menai Bridge tailor in the 1880s, who added to the original first five syllables in an attempt to draw tourists – as indeed it has.

Coming from Bangor, half a mile before the town you'll probably notice the bronze figure atop the 91-foot-high Doric **Marquess of Anglesey's Column**. The apocryphal story has him declaring to Wellington, on having a leg blown off at Waterloo, "Begod, there goes me leg", to which Wellington drily replied, "Begod, so it do". There hadn't been much love lost between them since the Marquess ran off with Wellington's sister-in-law some years previously. Between 10am and 6pm you can climb the 115 steps up to the Marquess (£1) and share his view across the strait to Snowdonia. His replacement leg is on show at Plas Newydd, close to Bryn Celli Ddu: two good reasons to spend time in the area.

Practicalities

The main reason to stop in Llanfair PG itself is to visit the **tourist office** by the station (Mon–Sat 9.30am–5.30pm, Sun 10am–5pm; closes 5pm Oct–Easter; ☎01248/713177), the only one worth its salt on the island. **Trains** continue from Llanfair PG to Rhosneigr and Holyhead, but to visit the rest of the **south coast** you're reliant on the hourly #42 **bus** that passes Plas Newydd and Bryn Celli Ddu, Brynsiencyn and Newborough on its way to Aberffraw and Llangefni (see p.436). No bus continues along the south coast, bus access to Rhosneigr being on the infrequent #25 from Holyhead and the #45 from Llangefni which runs slightly more often. There are several good **places to stay** along the south coast, the closest to Llanfair PG being the *Sarn Faban* (☎01248/712410; ①), a peaceful country B&B half a mile out on Penmynydd Road – follow the road opposite the *Tŷ Gwyn* pub, bear left where the road curves right and it's on the right. *Carreg Goch*, on the A4080 a mile west of Plas Newydd and Bryn Celli Ddu (☎01248/430315; ②), is also pleasant and convenient.

Bryn Celli Ddu

One of the island's most significant prehistoric sites, **Bryn Celli Ddu** (unrestricted access; CADW), the "Mound of the Dark Chamber", was built by Anglesey's late Neolithic inhabitants four thousand years ago, one and a half miles south of today's Llanfair PG. Several seasons of digs have shown it to be an extensive religious site, but today all you can see is a well-proportioned henge and stone circle, later built over to turn it into a passage grave under an earthen mound. Go inside, and in the last chamber you'll find an impressive, smooth monolith under a rather less than impressive supporting concrete beam. Even less awesome, the replica entrance stone outside – the original, along with disinterred bones and arrowheads, was whisked off to the National Museum in Cardiff – was inexplicably cast out of what looks like cream pebbledash. You can still get an idea of its carved spiral patterns, however. Niggles aside, Bryn Celli Ddu is an atmospheric spot, overlooked one way by a vast natural rock that may have been its precursor as a place of worship and, to the other, by the purple mountains of Snowdonia. The #42 bus passes within half a mile, as does the #4 (only when it goes to nearby Llanddaniel Fab); otherwise it's an hour-long walk from Llanfair PG.

Plas Newydd

A mile and a half along the road from Llanfair PG to Bryn Celli Ddu is the approach to **Plas Newydd** (April–Oct Sat–Wed noon–5pm; gardens open an hour earlier; £4.20; NT). Though now owned by the National Trust, the house remains, as it has been since the eighteenth century, the home of the marquesses of Anglesey. A house had stood on this site since the sixteenth century, but it was the First Marquess's huge profits from Parys Mountain (see p.434) and other ventures that paid for its transformation by James Wyatt and Joseph Potter into a Gothic mansion in the late eighteenth century.

Potter designed the pleasing, castellated stable block that almost upstages the modest-looking three-storey house with incongruous Tudor caps on slender octagonal turrets.

Inside, the Gothic Hall, with its Potter-designed fan-vaulted ceiling, leads to the longest and most finely decorated room in the house, the Music Room, originally the great hall. All available space is covered with oil paintings, including one of the First Marquess and another of Lady Paget, his first wife, both by John Hoppner. Despite the Gothic start, Wyatt was given free rein in the rest of the house, and there's a transition to the Neoclassical on entering the Staircase Hall with its cantilevered staircase and deceptively solid-looking Doric columns, actually just painted wood. Predominantly dull paintings line the stairs and the length of the gallery. Several monarchs and most family members are represented, those of the Sixth Marquess and his sister being the work of Rex Whistler, who spent two years here in the 1930s. Persevere through another half a dozen rooms, including Lady Anglesey's pink-and-white bedroom and a former kitchen containing a Whistler exhibition, to reach what is Plas Newydd's glory and Whistler's masterwork, in understandably the most popular room in the house. A whole 58-foot-long wall of the Rex Whistler Room is consumed by the magnificent trompe l'oeil painting of some imaginary seascape seen from a promenade. At first it seems utterly incongruous but you are soon drawn into the fantasy, your position seeming to shift by over a mile as you walk along, altering your perspective on the mountains of Snowdonia and a whimsical composite of elements. Portmeirion (see p.352) is there, as are the Round Tower from Windsor Castle and the steeple from St Martin-in-the-Fields in London. Whistler himself appears as a gondolier, and again as a gardener in one of the two right-angled panels at either end, which appear to extend the room further.

A few rooms further on you'll find a **Cavalry Museum**, where the prize exhibit is the world's first articulated leg, a synthesis of wood, leather and springs, designed for the First Marquess who lost his leg at Waterloo. All in all, you'll need to allow a couple of hours for a good look around, and a little longer to take in the Neolithic cromlech located in grounds landscaped by Humphrey Repton in the early nineteenth century. Recover in the former milking parlour, now an excellent tiled tearoom serving tasty snacks and light meals.

Anglesey Sea Zoo and Brynsiencyn

Facing Caernarfon across the Menai Strait, seven miles southwest of Llanfair PG, **Anglesey Sea Zoo** (daily: March–Oct 10am–5pm; Nov–Feb 11am–3pm; ☎01248/430411, *www.nwi.co.uk/seazoo*; £4.95), is one of the most absorbing attractions on Anglesey. Local sea conditions are simulated in wave tanks, and in shallow pools where plaice and turbot, camouflaged against the shingle bottom, are barely visible from the catwalks above. They haven't entirely got away from glass-sided tanks, but most are large and the contents chosen to depict specific environments: tidal flats, quayside and wrecks amongst them. In keeping with the buildings' previous functions as an oyster hatchery and lobster breeding farm, the zoo uses aquaculture to give the lobsters a much greater chance of survival once released into the wild. The schedule of the #42 **bus** allows for a three-hour visit (Mon–Sat), with Llanfair PG as your base. The nearest village is unremarkable **BRYNSIENCYN**, two miles to the north. Between the Sea Zoo and Brynsiencyn, *Plas Trefarthen* (☎01248/430430; ②) is a large, grand Georgian **B&B** in two hundred acres of farmland with magnificent Strait views, a relaxed atmosphere and an acclaimed opera-singing owner, Marian Roberts. Alternatively, try the *Tyddyn Goblet* (☎01248/430296; ②), a characterful farmhouse just off the A4080, and the small, very welcoming *Tŷ Coch* (☎01248/430227; ②). All serve first-class home-made **food**, or you can relax at the end of the road past the Sea Zoo at the *Ferryhouse Café* or *Mermaid Inn*, both with outdoor seating.

Newborough and Malltraeth

Three miles southwest of the Sea Zoo, the end of the Menai Strait is marked by Abermenai Point, a huge sand bar backed by the 600-acre **Newborough Warren** (unrestricted access), one of the most important dune systems anywhere in Britain. As its name suggests, rabbits are common here, as are the otherwise rare thick-horned Soay sheep, Britain's oldest native breed. Since 1948, much of the land has been clad in Corsican and Monterey pine, a commercial operation with ecological benefits – the trees stabilize the ground and provide habitats for goldcrests, warblers and rare native red squirrels, justifying the Warren's designation as a national nature reserve. Three main walking trails, none more than an hour or two's stroll and all very well marked, weave through the pines to **Llanddwyn Island**, a glorious peninsula of rocky coves and sandy beaches. If idling on the splendid sands gets dull, you can wander over the "island" to the Tûr Mawr (Great Tower), built in 1800 to warn the ships in Caernarfon Bay, and subsequently supplanted by the disused lighthouse, built in 1873 in the style of an Anglesey windmill, a row of restored cottages and a thirteenth-century church ruin dedicated to the patron saint of lovers in Wales, Saint Dwynwen. In the fifth century, after her abortive affair with Welsh prince Maelon, Dwynwen became a nun at Llanddwyn and requested that hopeful lovers who make a supplication to God in her name should receive divine assistance.

Entry to the Newborough Warren section of the reserve is from a free car park down a short track from the roundabout where the A4080 bends north. The main walk from here is out to Abermenai Point (2 miles), but be careful, as rapid tidal changes can quickly cover the broad sandy approach. To get to the reserve's main entrance (and Llanddwyn Island), continue north along the A4080 for half a mile to **NEWBOROUGH** (Niwbwrch), a town of limited appeal founded by Edward I to rehouse villagers displaced during the building of Beaumaris. From here, a signposted toll barrier (have a couple of pound coins handy) leads to a second car park. Alternatively, get the #42 **bus**. A couple of hundred yards back along the A4080 from the roundabout, the **Anglesey Model Village** (Easter–Oct daily 10.30am–5pm; £1.75) is a fun way of passing an hour, with 1:12 scale models of Anglesey landmarks and a model railway.

From 1945 until his death in 1979, the estuarine beaches to the north and around **MALLTRAETH** were the haunt of **Charles Tunnicliffe**, who spent much of his days meticulously producing beautifully detailed wildlife drawings. Birds were always his chief subject, and throughout his fifty-year career he produced thousands of intricate illustrations for other people's works as well as six books of his own, including *Shorelands Summer Diary*, largely researched around Newborough and named after his house in Malltraeth which is now run by a keen birder as a pleasant **B&B** (☎01407/840396; ②). It's located just off the A4080: cross the bridge in the village, turn left at the lay-by, then left again in front of the chapel. Examples of Tunnicliffe's work form a significant part of the Oriel Ynys Môn exhibition in Llangefni (see p.436).

Around Aberffraw

The area around Newborough and tiny **LLANGADWALADR**, three miles northwest, was once the seat of the great ruling dynasty of the Princes of Gwynedd who, from the seventh-century reign of Cadfan until Llywelyn ap Gruffydd's death in 1282, controlled northwest Wales, and frequently much of the rest of the country, from this now-quiet corner of Anglesey. Relatively recent finds of the foundations of a great hall are still being uncovered at Llys Rhosyr, near Newborough, but, for the moment, the most substantial evidence lies in **Llangadwaladr Church** (usually closed except for Sun mornings; key from the Rectory, 1 Maes Glas, Bethel; ☎01407/840190). When the church was built in the thirteenth century, a memorial plaque, carved in Latin around 625 AD, was incorporated into an inside wall. It reads "Cadfan the King, wisest and most renowned of all kings". Llangadwaladr village takes its name from Cadwaladr, Cadfan's grandson, who subsequently ruled from **ABERFFRAW**, a mile and a half west (bus #42), where the countryside centre, **Llys Llewelyn** (Whitsun to early Sept Tues–Sat and bank holiday Mon 11am–5pm, Sun 1–5pm; free), has a few explanatory boards on the court and times of the Princes of Gwynedd, and a little information on the flora and fauna of the Anglesey coast. It's also the place to pick up a key for Barclodiad y Gawres (see below) – the tearoom has one if the centre is shut.

CABLE BAY (Porth Trecastell), two miles northwest of Aberffraw, was the eastern terminus of the first telegraph cable to Ireland, though it is now better known for its good sandy beach, popular with surfers and kayakers. On the headland to the north stands the heavily reconstructed remains of the 5000-year-old **Barclodiad y Gawres** burial chamber. Though more obviously dramatic than nearby Bryn Celli Ddu (see p.426), it is more difficult to see, as CADW have perversely seen fit to keep it locked at all times – to get inside, ask at the Llys Llewelyn centre or the Wayside Shop in Llanfaelog for the key, and bring a torch. Without artificial light, you won't really see the stones carved with chevrons and zigzag patterns that the burial chamber shares with Newgrange and other Boyne Valley sites seventy miles across the water in Ireland. Barclodiad y Gawres faces the westward ocean, and it's a fabulous place to catch a good sunset. Bus #25 from Holyhead and Rhosneigr passes by.

Rhosneigr

The weekday roar of fighters from the nearby RAF Valley airfield deafens you long before you reach **RHOSNEIGR**, two miles further north along the coast, an otherwise peaceful Edwardian seaside resort. Rambling over consolidated dunes which back a series of small bays, Rhosneigr remains justifiably popular with English holiday-makers after almost a century of patronage, although space on the beach is these days contested by the dozens of devoted windsurfers who flock here when the wind is right. It is the sort of low-key place you might feel like stopping in for a day or two: if so, you can rent boards and rig from Funsport, 1 Beach Rd (☎01407/810899; £25 a day/3hr beginner's course) and take to the sea or the small Maelog Lake, safer when the wind is offshore.

There's central **accommodation** at *Bryn Maelog* on Chelford Close off the main Maelog Lake Road (☎01407/810285; ②); *Minstrel Lodge* on Station Road (☎01407/810970; ②); and *White Gables B&B* on Maelog Lake Road (☎01407/810863; ②), which welcomes pets and rents **bikes** (£10 a day). There's a **campsite**, *Shoreline Camping* (☎01407/810279), right by the **train station**, a mile north of the clock tower that marks the centre of the town. Rhosneigr has several decent **places to eat**, including *The Honey Pot* on The Square (winter closed Sun; ☎01407/810302), with both an inexpensive bistro and a moderately priced restaurant; the *Bistro* on High Street (☎01407/810295), where you can bring your own alcohol; and *Bee Bee's* ice-cream and coffee bar, also on High Street, selling the delicious "Denbigh Farmhouse" ice cream found in discerning outlets all over north Wales.

Holy Island

Holy Island (Ynys Gybi) is blessed with Anglesey's best scenery and cursed with its most unattractive town. The spectacular sea cliffs around **South Stack**, and the Stone Age and Roman remains on **Holyhead Mountain** are just a couple of miles from downbeat **Holyhead**, whose ferry routes to Ireland and good transport links mean you'll probably find your way there at some stage. In many respects, you can taste Ireland hereabouts without even getting on the ferry. The rough stone walls, prehistoric tumps and stones, ragged bays and whitewashed farms that characterise Holy Island are very redolent of the west of Ireland, with a similarly laid-back atmosphere to further the sensation.

This hourglass of land adjoins Anglesey's west coast at two points. The more ancient and picturesque approach turns off the A5 at Valley (Dyffryn), crosses the very short Four Mile Bridge and passes the fine beaches at **Rhoscolyn** and **Trearddur Bay** before reaching Holyhead. Most traffic takes the road or rail routes directly to the ferry terminal at Holyhead over the 1200-yard-long Stanley Embankment, built by Telford while working on the A5. Along the way he constructed distinctive octagonal toll-houses, used until 1895 when the A5 was Britain's last major toll road. A couple have been converted to houses and one, at the northern end of the Stanley Embankment, now operates as the *Tollhouse Tearooms*.

Getting to Holyhead itself is no trouble, as trains and a fair number of Anglesey's buses go there. Rhoscolyn and South Stack can be reached from Holyhead by the #23 and the #22 respectively. The #4 bus to Holyhead from Bangor and Llangefni is the only really useful service to Trearddur Bay.

Holyhead

HOLYHEAD (Caergybi) is a place of dilapidated shopfronts and high unemployment, the local council's valiant attempts to brighten its image with maritime remnants such as anchors and buoys sprinkled around the streets, somehow only making it even more depressing. In 1727, Swift found it "scurvy, ill-provided and comfortless", while a century or so later, George Borrow called it "a poor, dull, ill-lighted town", and, apart from the scurvy and the lighting, little has changed. Fortunately, recent modifications to the ferry terminal combined with the reasonably well-integrated train and ferry timings mean you shouldn't need to venture into the town proper, but if you do get stuck, there are a couple of things to see.

The town's recent relandscaping has only really worked along the Newry Beach seafront, to the immediate west of the ferry terminal. As well as great views over Britain's longest breakwater (7860ft – nearly 1.5 miles), you'll find, tucked down in the old lifeboat station, the spirited and interesting **Holyhead Maritime Museum** (Easter–Oct Tues–Sun 1–5pm; main exhibition £2). Dating from 1858, the building has been well adapted, with the free section (a tearoom and shop) including some panels that provide stimulating nuggets of the town's history. The fee-paying part is even better: lots of beautiful models of the boats that have plied the Ireland route over the centuries, haunting memorabilia of local maritime disasters and – bizarrely – some modelled whale's eardrums. These, in their natural state, show a passing resemblance to the shape of a human head and face. For no apparent reason, two on display here have been decorated to portray Mussolini and Hitler. There's also a temporary exhibition gallery, usually showing work of a seafaring bent.

The town's Welsh name indicates that this was the site of a Roman fort – an outpost of Segontium – and home of the sixth-century Saint Cybi. Cybi's cell was built in the protection of the Roman walls and is now marked by the partly thirteenth-century **Church of St Cybi** (June–Sept Mon–Sat 11am–3pm). Both walls and church have undergone substantial reconstruction, the church gaining stained glass by Edward Burne-Jones and William Morris. Next door, the tiny chapel housed the town's first free school. Views from here of the massive ferries and port activity are pleasantly surreal.

The **Breakwater Country Park** (daily 9am–dusk; free), a couple of miles west along Beach Road, is another of the better ways to pass the time if you miss your boat. On the site of an old brickworks that was used to build the town's vast breakwater, it still holds the remains of a couple of kilns but is primarily a place to enjoy a bracing clifftop walk to the foghorn station on North Stack (an hour or so return), or on to South Stack (see opposite), an hour's walk beyond.

Practicalities

The **train station**, local and National Express **bus stops** and **ferry terminal** are handily clustered together at the entrance to Holyhead and linked to the town by a pedestrian bridge to London Road. Inexplicably, the **tourist office** (Easter–Sept daily 10am–6pm, Oct–Easter Mon–Sat 10am–5pm; ☎01407/762622) has been moved from the complex and is now situated a mile short of town in a windswept portakabin, bang opposite the aluminium smelting works on the A5 Penrhos Beach Road. Staff are hopeful – desperate, even – for eventual relocation back to the ferry terminal. More alternative info on esoteric local happenings can be found at Ogof y Tylwyth Teg at 88 Market St. The needs of late-arriving ferry passengers has fostered a bunch of poor **B&Bs** (particularly avoidable are those along the A5 into the town), so it's worth searching off the main road for a decent place to stay, particularly along Walthew Avenue, running up from Beach Road, where *Glan Ifor*, no. 8 (☎01407/764238; ①), and *Orotavia*, no. 66 (☎01407/760259; ①), are both simple but cosy and perfectly serviceable. Nearby *Hendre*, on Porth-y-Felin (☎01407/762929; ②), is the best of the bunch, a very welcoming former manse with inexpensive evening meals, while the most comfortable **hotel** in town is the *Boathouse* on Beach Road (☎01407/762094; ④), with a good restaurant and bar. If you've got your own transport, head three miles out of town along Walthew Avenue to *Tan-y-Cytiau* (☎01407/762763; ②), a country house nicely set in three acres of grounds on the slopes of Holyhead Mountain; there's also a self-catering cottage sleeping seven in the grounds.

Fast **food** is the staple diet in Holyhead, but you can still eat well; the *Boathouse Hotel* (see above) does succulent fish and seafood dishes, the budget *Omar Khayyam Tandoori,* 8 Newry St (☎01407/760333), serves the tastiest curries for miles around, and the *Castle Bakery*, 83 Market St, is one of the more appealing cafés. For **drinking**, head again to the *Boathouse* (see above), the old-fashioned *George Hotel* on Stanley Street or crawl around the half-dozen bars on Market Street, starting with *The Seventy-Nine* at no. 79, which also does good daytime food. The best pub for occasional **gigs** is the *Britannia Inn* on Thomas Street, by the car park. The multipurpose Canolfan Ucheldre (☎01407/763361), a former convent chapel on Millbank, above the town centre, is Anglesey's premier centre for the **performing arts**; there's usually an art exhibition on here, too.

Holyhead Mountain and South Stack

The northern half of Holy Island is ranged around the skirts of **Holyhead Mountain** (Mynydd Twr) which rises 700ft to the west of Holyhead. Its summit is ringed by the remains of the seventeen-acre Iron Age **Caer y Twr** (unrestricted access; CADW), one of the largest sites in north Wales. It seems to have only been used during times of war, as digs haven't unearthed any signs of permanent occupation, just a six-foot-high drystone wall enclosure around the ruins of a Roman beacon. In an hour or so you can pick your way up rough tracks from the Holyhead side, but the best approach is by bus #22 or your own transport to the car park at **South Stack** (Ynys Lawd), two miles west of Holyhead. A path (45min) leads from the car park to the top of Holyhead Mountain, though you'll find most people walking the few yards to the clifftop, RSPB-run **Ellin's Tower Seabird Centre** (Easter–Sept daily 11am–5pm; free). From April until the end of July, binoculars and closed-circuit TV give an unparalleled opportunity to watch up to 3000 birds – razorbills, guillemots and the odd puffin – nesting on the nearby sea cliffs while ravens and peregrines wheel outside the tower's windows. When the birds have gone, rock climbers picking their way up the same cliff face replace them as the main interest. A twisting path, with over four hundred steps, leads down from the South

---

Stack car park to a suspension bridge over the surging waves, once the keeper's only access to the now fully automated pepper-pot **lighthouse** (Easter–Sept daily 11am–5pm; £2), built in 1809. Views on to the cliffs are stupendous as you climb down to the island and, once there, you'll find exhibitions on local wildlife and can take a tour of the lighthouse itself. Tickets are issued at the *South Stack Kitchen*, a café-cum-interpretive centre a hundred yards back down the lane.

William Stanley, who named Ellin's Tower (Tûr Elin) after his wife, did most of the excavation work on the **Cytiau'r Gwyddelod** hut circles (CADW), across the road from the RSPB Ellin's Tower car park. The name translates as the "huts of the Irish" – a common name for any ancient settlement – but evidence from excavations reveals little more than that the builders were late Neolithic or early Bronze Age people. The visible remains comprise nineteen low stone circles – some up to ten yards across – though there seem to have originally been fifty buildings, formed into eight distinct farmsteads separated by ploughed fields.

Trearddur Bay and Rhoscolyn

At the pinch of Holy Island's hourglass shape, a couple of miles south of Holyhead, the scattered settlement of **TREARDDUR BAY** (Bae Trearddur) shambles across low grassy hills, around a deeply indented bay of the same name that's punctuated by rocky coves. There's no centre to speak of, but it's a much pleasanter base than Holyhead; it even has a good, clean swimming beach sporting a rare European Blue Flag. Watersports equipment can be rented from Splash Watersports (☎01407/860318).

If you can afford it, the best **place to stay** is the *Trearddur Bay Hotel*, Lon Isallt (☎01407/860301, fax 861181; ⑥), overlooking the main bay and with a heated indoor swimming pool, a wonderful restaurant and decent bar meals for those whose pockets aren't quite so deep. On the southern side of the bay, along Ravenspoint Road, is the cheaper *Seacroft Hotel* (☎01407/860348; ②) and, a mile further on, the *Tyn Rhos Campsite* which, though packed with caravans, takes **tents** as well.

At the southern tip of the island, a mile or so south of Trearddur Bay, a lane runs down to **RHOSCOLYN**, another scattered seaside settlement, though much smaller and even more appealing. With a couple of exquisite sandy beaches, lots of rocky outcrops and some delightful coastal walking, this is the ideal place to spend a couple of relaxing days. If you fancy something racier than a walk or a swim, you can hire watersports gear from the limited selection at *The Outdoor Alternative* (☎01407/860469), a relaxed, simple **campsite** a few yards from the beach which also operates a **self-cater-**

ing hostel during school holidays (essentially Easter & Aug). Meals are available on request and staff can organize rock-climbing and kayaking supervision, and point you to some of the best walks around. A few minutes away are the *Old Rectory* (closed Jan & Feb; ☎01407/860214; ③), a Georgian country house with outstanding views of the sea, and the *White Eagle*, a good pub with a beer garden. Just short of the beach car park, the pleasant *Glan Towyn* (☎01407/860380; ②) offers B&B and self-catering accommodation. Back at Four Mile Bridge, where the Rhoscolyn lane turns off, there's a lovely little B&B and daytime café at *Y Gegin Fach* (☎01407/740317; ①).

Northern and inland Anglesey

The **northern and eastern sides of Anglesey** tend to be quieter than the south and west; the settlements are clustered behind the sheltered coves which, with the odd rocky headland, make up an appealing (if seldom dramatic) coast. This is primarily family holiday country, though its more thinly-spread host of caravan sites make it much less oppressive than the north Welsh coast. None of the resorts is especially notable in its own right but they are all well spaced, making cycling between them, or walking the coastal path, an ideal way to get around.

Relying on **buses** is possible, though less rewarding. From Holyhead, the #61 runs to Cemaes and Amlwch, where you can pick up the #62 and #63 to Moelfre, Menai Bridge and Bangor. The #32 links Amlwch to Llanerchymedd and Llangefni. **Accommodation** is detailed under the appropriate town account, but if you are exploring the coast with your own transport you might want to head inland to stay at one of the farmhouses near Llanerchymedd, all of which serve wholesome, hearty dinners. *Drws Y Coed* (☎01248/470473; ②), a comfortable, non-smoking B&B on a working farm a mile and a half east and *Llwydiarth Fawr* (☎01248/470321, fax 470540; ③), a spacious, secluded Georgian mansion half a mile north on the B5111, are both recommended.

The northwest coast to Cemaes

The main A5025 leaves the environs of Holyhead to follow the island's perimeter clockwise. There are plenty of good sandy beaches down the lanes to the left, although the first few come with the rather uninspiring view of Holyhead. Overlooking one such beach, Porth Penrhyn Mawr, and beyond the village of **LLANFWROG**, is the lovely farmhouse B&B of *Penrhyn Farm* (☎01407/730134, fax 730496; ②). A couple of miles inland, you might be tempted to swing off the main road for **LLANDDEUSANT**, where a signpost points you to **Melin Llynnon** (Easter–Sept Tues–Sat 11am–5pm, Sun 1–5pm; £2), Anglesey's only remaining working windmill. At one time, fifty-odd such mills were studded all over Anglesey, grinding away to feed all of north Wales; travelling around the island today, over thirty can still be seen, their sailless stumps either rotting away in field corners or converted (some imaginatively) into barns and houses. Only Melin Llynnon, which lay derelict for fifty years, survives in anything like its original form. Renovated and restored under the guidance of Lincolnshire millwrights, it is now white-painted, canvas-sailed and once again producing flour. Everything in the mill is wind-powered, even the hoists that lift the grain through trapdoors, and almost extinct milling skills have had to be relearnt by modern millers who now demonstrate the process and sell the result – in bag and cake form – from a good on-site café.

Back along the coastal drag, the highlight of the northwest coast is gently understated **PORTH SWTAN** (Church Bay), a diffuse settlement gathered loosely around a sandy cove of the same name. The beach is superb: a picturesque sweep of sand backed by yellow rocks that date from the pre-Cambrian era, some 570 million years ago. At the southern end of Porth Swtan are a couple of low-key **campsites**. Otherwise, village amenities consist of the wonderful *Lobster Pot* restaurant opposite the beach car park

(☎01407/730241), where you can see the live lobsters in storage tanks, and, up the hill by the spired church that gives the area its English name, the warm and welcoming *Church Bay Inn*. Views from here down the coast are uplifting.

From here, the coast dives and ripples northwards, much of it through National Trust land, before veering east at **Carmel Head** (Trwyn y Gader). The NT have also preserved much of the seascape and inland lagoon of **CEMLYN BAY**, three miles east. Here you'll find a summertime colony of terns on the lagoon, offshore seabirds and a curious black shingle spit separating the lake from the sea. Just try not to look eastwards too often: the brooding bulk of the ageing **Wylfa Nuclear Power Station** sits squat and ugly on the next headland.

If you can similarly ignore Wylfa, the harbourside village of **CEMAES**, a couple of miles east, is a charming spot. Energy is certainly a feature of the place: as well as the nuclear menace on one side, there's the 24-tower **Rhyd-y-Groes Windfarm** on the other. Between the two, Cemaes has one of the most attractive harbours on the north coast and a good selection of accommodation and food to boot. Once a major port, Cemaes now serves only the odd trawler and boatloads of yachties drawn by a broad sweep of beach and the most northerly pub in Wales, *The Stag* on High Street.

The headland that forms the eastern side of the bay is surmounted by the tiny and ancient **Llanbadrig Church** (May–Sept daily 10am–noon & 2–4pm), one of only two Welsh churches dedicated to St Patrick. The present structure is mainly fourteenth century, but the church's origins date back to the fifth century, when Ireland's patron saint is supposed to have been shipwrecked on the small island just offshore and made his way to a cave just below the site of the present church. The building was restored in the nineteenth century by Lord Stanley of Alderley, Bertrand Russell's grandfather, a Muslim who used Islamic imagery in the stained glass.

Cemaes is the most reliable source of **accommodation** along this stretch of coast, with the non-smoking *Treddolphin Guesthouse* (☎01407/710388; ①), 200 yards down Beach Road from *The Stag* (see above), while the *Woburn Hill Hotel* on High Street (☎01407/711388; ②) is the most central. Best of all, though, is the licensed Edwardian *Hafod Country House* (March–Oct; ☎01407/710500; ②), with en-suite rooms and excellent meals: it's at the roundabout on the A5025 at the top of High Street – turn inland towards Llanfechell and the house is half a mile along. *The Stag* serves up some of the best pub **food** around.

Amlwch and Parys Mountain

AMLWCH, five miles east of Cemaes, would be just another tiny fishing village but for **Parys Mountain** (Mynydd Parys) a mile or so inland, once the world's largest source of copper. The Ordovices, a great Celtic tribe who occupied north Wales in the Neolithic era, probably began to extract the ore, and the Romans certainly made use of it, but it wasn't until the eighteenth century that production levels reached industrial heights. During this period, Amlwch was a boomtown, almost in the Wild West tradition. Its population ballooned to six thousand by the late 1700s, making it Wales' second largest town, with some 1025 recorded alehouses to service the thirsty populace. Pollution had become a problem, but people noticed that the iron hulls of ships didn't corrode in the copper-laced harbour waters, fuelling a demand for protective copper sheathing that boosted the market for Parys copper. International competition in the early nineteenth century saw the town sink back into its role of a fishing port, although copper has been mined on Parys ever since. You can reach the ruined pumping mill on top of Parys Mountain by a path from the car park on the B5111, a mile south of town, just next to the premises of the one company still trying to squeeze a profit from the exhausted mountain. A waymarked trail leads around Parys' ravaged moonscape, made all the more bizarre by the derelict remains, multicoloured rocks, coppery pools of water and patches of scrubby heather and gorse. Back in town, in the Watch House by the spruced-up Amlwch Port, the local Industrial Heritage Trust have set up a small **exhibition** (Easter–Sept daily 10am–5pm; free) about Amlwch's remarkable past. They also run **guided walks** (£2.50; ☎01407/832277) on Parys Mountain.

Copper was once shipped out of Amlwch by rail along a now disused seventeen-mile line, which local enthusiasts hope to reopen as a steam-hauled tourist route by 2002. Currently, there's only the small **Lein Amlwch Museum**, in a former goods shed on Main Road (July to mid-Sept Tues–Sat 10.30am–7pm, Sun 10.30am–5pm; mid-Sept to June Tues–Sat 10.30am–4.30pm, Sun 12.30–4.30pm; £1.50), with a few model train layouts, railway memorabilia and a display on the history of the line.

After visiting so many ancient churches in Wales, **Our Lady Star of the Sea**, a couple of hundred yards along the A5025, to the west of Main Street, comes as something of a novelty. Built in the 1930s of reinforced concrete, the great parabolic ribs of what could be a giant toast rack are supposed to represent an upturned boat, complete with round portholes.

The handiest **accommodation** in Amlwch is at *Bron Arfor* (☎01407/831493; ②), right by the sea at the end of Ffordd Pen y Bonc, which runs opposite the library, and at the *Dinorben Arms*, High Street (☎01407/830358; ②), where you can also get filling pub **food**.

From Moelfre to Red Wharf Bay

MOELFRE has a reputation for shipwrecks, though wandering around the peaceful grey-pebbled cove on a sunny day it seems unlikely. An anchor behind the beach was salvaged from the shipwrecked *Hindlea*, which went down in October 1959, exactly a century after the 2700-ton *Royal Charter* foundered, with the loss of 450 lives and nearly £400,000-worth of gold. The dead are remembered by a memorial stone thirty minutes' walk north along the coastal path that starts at the end of the cove, past a small offshore cormorant colony.

The town's only other point of interest lies a mile west off the A5025, where the late Neolithic **Capel Lligwy Hut Group** (unrestricted access; CADW) forms the centre-piece of a site covering three thousand years of human occupation. A five-sided walled enclosure contains the foundations of several circular and rectangular buildings dated to the second and fourth centuries which, along with the hut group on Holy Island, give the best indication of how these people actually lived, rather than how they buried their dead. To the northeast of the main enclosure stands **Capel Lligwy**, a forlorn-looking twelfth-century church, and a short distance to the south is the **Lligwy Burial Chamber** with its 28-ton capstone. All are just a short stroll from the road. If you want to **stay**, try *Deanfield* (☎01248/410517; ②), 150 yards from the beach on the A5018 south of the village, or the farm **campsite** 500 yards inland from the beach, up the A5018, then along the signposted Ystad Nant Bychan.

Overlooking wide sands a couple of miles south of Moelfre is the east coast's principal resort, **BENLLECH**. Although the beach is excellent, and there are lots of B&Bs and hotels in the village, it's mainly a popular retirement centre for elderly English folk and thus lacking in appreciable stimulus. It is, however, a useful place to stock up before shipping out. Better on all counts is **RED WHARF BAY**, a mile southeast, a broad and appealing sweep of golden sand backed by the characterful, wooden-beamed *Ship Inn*, one of the best pubs on Anglesey. It is often crowded in summer, when you might want to wander down the road to *The Old Boathouse Café & Restaurant* for good meals and great ice-cream sundaes. Red Wharf Bay (Traeth Coch) itself is possibly the most beautiful beach on Anglesey – a huge sandy arc that never gets too crowded. The most popular end is at Red Wharf Bay village: for more solitude and bigger views, go to the other end, reached down narrow harepin lanes from the village of **LLANDDONA**.

Llangefni

About the only reason to come inland is to visit **LLANGEFNI**, Anglesey's low-key county town, and the **Oriel Ynys Môn** gallery (Tues–Sun 10.30am–5pm; £2), half a mile along the B5111 from the town centre. Examining various aspects of Anglesey life, from explanations of the numerous pre-Christian sites and the dynastic lines of the Princes of Gwynedd to exhibits about conservation and the Welsh language, Oriel Ynys Môn provides an excellent overview of the sheer variety of factors in the island's turbulent history. A corner of the gallery is devoted to a mock-up of Charles Tunnicliffe's Malltraeth studio (see p.428), from where he made many of his detailed wildlife paintings. Elsewhere are finds from archeological digs around the island (though the better ones are in the National Museum in Cardiff), including a well-worn sandstone head carved in the Iron Age.

It is easy enough to continue on from Llangefni, since it's only five miles west of Llanfair PG, and on the #4 bus route to Holyhead and Bangor; if you're stuck, you can **stay** comfortably a mile west of town at *Argraig* (☎01248/724390; ②) – take the B5420 west, then the B4422 south. There are several mainstream **cafés** on the main street, or try one of the wholefood or home-baked dishes on the blackboard menu at *The Whole Thing*, 5 Field St.

travel details

Unless otherwise stated frequencies for trains and buses are for Monday to Saturday services; Sunday averages 1–3 services, though the main routes are more frequent and some routes have no Sunday service at all.

Trains

Bangor to: Chester (20 daily; 1hr 5min); Colwyn Bay (20 daily; 25min); Conwy (7 daily; 20min); Holyhead (20 daily; 30–40min); Llandudno Junction (20 daily; 20min); Rhosneigr (6 daily; 25min); Rhyl (20 daily; 35min).

Colwyn Bay to: Llandudno Junction (30 daily; 6min); Rhyl (30 daily; 10min).

Conwy to: Bangor (7 daily; 20min); Holyhead (8 daily; 1hr); Llandudno Junction (8 daily; 4min).

Flint to: Chester (at least hourly; 15min); Llandudno Junction (at least hourly; 40min); Prestatyn (at least hourly; 15min).

Holyhead to: Bangor (20 daily; 30–40min); Chester (14 daily; 1hr 25min–1hr 40min); Llandudno Junction (20 daily; 1hr); Llanfair PG (7 daily; 30min).

Llandudno to: Llandudno Junction (at least hourly; 10min).

Llandudno Junction to: Bangor (20 daily; 20min); Betws-y-Coed (6 daily; 25min); Holyhead (20 daily; 1hr); Llandudno (at least hourly; 10min); Rhyl (30 daily; 20min).

Llanfair PG to: Bangor (7 daily; 10min); Holyhead (7 daily; 30min).

Prestatyn to: Flint (at least hourly; 15min); Llandudno Junction (at least hourly; 25min); Rhyl (at least hourly; 8min).

Rhosneigr to: Holyhead (7 daily; 10min); Llanfair PG (7 daily; 15min).

Rhyl to: Bangor (20 daily; 35min); Holyhead (7 daily; 1hr 10min–1hr 40min); Llandudno Junction (30 daily; 20min).

Buses

Bangor to: Beaumaris (every 30min; 25min); Betws-y-Coed (2 daily; 50min); Caernarfon (every 20min; 30min); Capel Curig (2 daily; 40min); Cardiff (1 daily; 7hr 45min); Holyhead (every 30min; 1hr 15min); Llanberis (every 30min; 25min); Llangefni (every 30min; 30min); Menai Bridge (every 30min; 12min).

Beaumaris to: Bangor (every 30min; 25min); Menai Bridge (every 30min; 15min).

Conwy to: Bangor (every 30min; 45min); Llandudno (every 30min; 20min); Llanrwst (every 30min; 40min); Rhyl (every 30min; 1hr 30min).

Denbigh to: Corwen (every 2hr; 1hr); Rhyl (every 30min; 40min); Ruthin (11 daily; 25min); St Asaph (every 30min; 15min).

Flint to: Holywell (every 30min; 10min); Mold (hourly; 30min).

Holyhead to: Amlwch (8 daily; 50min); Bangor (every 30min; 1hr 15min); Cemaes (8 daily; 40min); Chester (1 daily, 3hr 30min); Llanfair PG (every 30min; 1hr); Llangefni (every 30min; 45min); Menai Bridge (every 30min; 1hr 5min); Rhoscolyn (4 daily; 15min); Trearddur Bay (every 30min; 10min).

Llandudno to: Bangor (every 30min; 1hr); Llanrwst (every 30min; 1hr); Rhyl (every 15–30min; 1hr 10min).

Llanfair PG to: Bangor (every 30min; 15min); Holyhead (every 30min; 1hr); Llangefni (every 30min; 15min); Newborough (11 daily; 20min).

Mold to: Chester (every 30min; 50min); Ruthin (every 2hr; 45min).

Rhyl to: Llandudno (every 15–30min; 1hr 10min); Ruthin (10 daily; 1hr 10min); St Asaph (every 30min; 25min).

Ruthin to: Corwen (every 2hr; 30min); Denbigh (11 daily; 25min); Mold (every 2hr; 45min); Rhyl (10 daily; 1hr 10min); St Asaph (10 daily; 45min).

St Asaph to: Corwen (every 2hr; 1hr 15min); Denbigh (every 30min; 15min); Rhuddlan (every 30min; 15min); Rhyl (every 30min; 25min); Ruthin (10 daily; 45min).

Wrexham to: Chester (every 15min; 40min); Chirk (hourly; 40min); Llangollen (at least hourly; 35min); Mold (16 daily; 1hr).

Ferries

Holyhead to: Dublin (2 ferries daily; 3hr 30min; 4 catamarans daily; 1hr 45min); Dun Laoghaire (2 ferries daily; 3hr 30min; 4 catamarans daily; 1hr 40min).

PART THREE

THE
CONTEXTS

THE HISTORICAL FRAMEWORK

THE BEGINNINGS

Before the end of the last Ice Age around ten thousand years ago, Wales and the rest of Britain formed part of the greater European whole and the early migrant inhabitants eked out a meagre living on the tundra or a better one amongst the oak, beech and hazel forests in the warmer periods. Most lived in the southeast of Britain, but small groups foraged north and west, leaving 250,000-year-old evidence in the form of a human tooth in a cave near Denbigh in north Wales and a hand axe unearthed near Cardiff.

It wasn't until the early part of the **Upper Paleolithic age** that significant communities settled in Wales, those of the Gower peninsula interring the "Red Lady of Paviland" around 24,000 BC (see p.133). This civilization was far behind those of central France or northern Spain, and remained on Europe's cultural fringe as the melting ice cut Britain off from mainland Europe around 5000 BC. Migrating Mesolithic peoples had already moved north from Central Europe and were followed by **Neolithic colonists**, whose mastery of stone and flint working found its expression in over a hundred and fifty cromlechs (turf-covered chambered tombs) dotted around Wales, primarily Pentre Ifan in Mynydd

Preseli (see p.192), Bryn Celli Ddu (see p.426) and Barclodiad y Gawres on Anglesey (see p.429). Skilled in agriculture and animal husbandry, the Neolithic people also began to clear the lush forests covering Wales below 2000 feet, enclosing fields, constructing defensive ditches around their villages and mining for flint.

The earliest stone circles — more extensive meeting places than cromlechs — were built at this time and continued to spread over the country as the Neolithic period drifted into the **Bronze Age** around 2000 BC. Through their extensive trade networks, the inhabitants of Wales and the rest of Britain gradually adopted new techniques, changing to more sophisticated use of metals and developing a well-organized social structure. The established aristocracy engaged in much tribal warfare, as suggested by large numbers of earthwork forts built in this and the immediately succeeding period — the chief examples being at Holyhead Mountain on Anglesey and the Bulwalks at Chepstow.

THE CELTS

Celtic invaders spreading from their central European homeland settled in Wales in around 600 BC, imparting a great cultural influence. Familiar with Mediterranean civilization through trading routes, they introduced superior methods of metalworking that favoured iron rather than bronze, from which they forged not just weapons but also coins. Gold was used for ornamental works — the first recognizable Welsh art — heavily influenced by the symbolic, patterned **La Tène** style still thought of as quintessentially Celtic.

The Celts are credited with introducing the basis of modern Welsh. The original Celtic tongue was spoken over a wide area, gradually dividing into Goidelic (or Q-Celtic) now spoken in the Isle of Man, Ireland and Scotland, and **Brythonic** (P-Celtic) spoken in Wales and Cornwall, and later exported to Brittany in France. This highly developed language was emblematic of a sophisticated social hierarchy headed by **druids**, a ritual priesthood with attendant poets, seers and warriors. Through a deep knowledge of ritual, legend and the mechanics of the heavens, the druids maintained their position between the people and a pantheon of over four thousand gods. Most of these were variations of a handful of chief gods worshipped by the great British tribes: the

Silures and Demetae in the south of Wales, the Cornovii in mid-Wales and the Ordovices and Deceangli in the north. Great though the Celtic technological and artistic achievements were, the people and their pan-European cousins were unable to maintain an organized civic society to match that of their successors, the Romans.

THE ROMANS IN WALES

Life in Wales, unlike that in most of England, was never fully Romanized, the region remaining under legionary control throughout its three-hundred-year occupation. **Julius Caesar** made small cross-Channel incursions in 55 and 54 BC, kicking off a lengthy but low-level infusion of Roman ideas which filtered across to Wales. This flow swelled a century later when the emperor **Claudius** took the death of the British king Cunobelin (Cynfelyn) as a signal to launch a full-scale invasion in 43 AD which in four years swept across southern England to the frontier of south Wales. Expansionism fomented anti-Roman feeling along the frontier between the Lowland Zone (southern and central England) and the Highland Zone (northern England, Scotland and Wales). Traditionally insular Welsh hill tribes united with their Brythonic cousins in northern England to oppose the Romans, who proceeded to force a wedge between them. The Roman historian **Tacitus** recorded the submission of the Deceangli near Chester, giving us the oldest written mention of a Welsh land. The Romans, held back by troubles at home and with the East Anglian revolt of **Boudicca** (Boadicea), were limited to tentative dabbling in Welsh affairs, sending expeditionary forces against the Silures and the toughest nut, the druid stronghold of Anglesey. The obdurate nature of the Welsh on their back foot kept the Romans at bay until around 75 AD, when legionary forts were built at Deva (Chester, England) and Isca Silurium (Caerleon) to act as platforms for incursions west along specially built military roads.

By 78 AD, Wales was under Roman control, its chief fortresses at Deva, Isca Silurium and Segontium (Caernarfon) boasting all the trappings of imperial Roman life: bath houses, temples, mosaics and underfloor heating. Through three centuries of occupation, the Celtic people sustained an independent existence while drawing material comfort from the proximity of Roman cities and auxiliary forts. Elements of Roman life filtered into the Celtic culture: agrarian practices improved, a new religion was partly adopted from the newly Christianized Romans, the language adopted Latin words (pont for "bridge", ffenestr for "window") and the prevailing La Tène artistic style took on classical Roman elements.

The Roman Empire was already in decline when **Magnus Maximus** (Macsen Wledig) led a campaign to wrest control of the western empire from Emperor Gratian in 383 AD. Maximus' rule was short lived but Wales was effectively free of direct Roman control by 390.

THE AGE OF THE SAINTS

Historical orthodoxy views the departure of literate Latin historians, skilled stonemasons and an all-powerful army, as heralding the **Dark Ages**. In fact, a civic society probably flourished until a century later, when the collapse of trade routes was hastened by the dramatic spread of Islam around the Mediterranean, and Romanized society gave way to a non-classical but no less structured form of **Celtic society**.

For the next few centuries, **Teutonic barbarian tribes** were struggling for supremacy in the post-Roman power vacuum in southern and eastern England, having little influence in Wales, where the main dynastic kingdoms set to steer Wales' next seven hundred years were taking root. The confusion that surrounds the early years of these dynasties was further muddied in 1136, when Geoffrey of Monmouth published his *History of the Kings of Britain*, portraying **King Arthur** as a feudal king with his court at Caerleon. Victorian Romantics embellished subsequent histories, making it practically impossible to extract much truth from this period.

In the fifth century, the **Irish** (Gwyddyl), who had a long tradition of migrating to the Llŷn and parts of mid-Wales, attacked the coast and formed distinct colonies, but were soon expelled from the north by **Cunedda Wledig**, the leader of a Brythonic tribe from near Edinburgh, who went on to found the royal house of Gwynedd, consolidating the Brythonic language and ostensibly naming regions of his kingdom – the modern Ceredigion and Meirionydd – after his sons. In the southwest, the Irish influence was sustained; the kingdom of Dyfed shows clear Irish origins.

These changes took place against a background of increasing religious energy. Between the fifth and the sixth centuries the **Celtic Saints**, ascetic evangelical missionaries, spread the gospel around Ireland and western Britain, promoting the middle-Eastern eremitical tradition of living a reclusive life. Where their message took root, they founded simple churches within a consecrated enclosure, or Ilan, which often took the saint's name, hence Llanberis (Saint Peris), Llandeilo (Saint Teilo) and many others. In south Wales, **Saint David** (Dewi Sant) was the most popular (and subsequently Wales' patron saint), dying around 589 after a miracle-filled life, during which he made a pilgrimage to Jerusalem and established the religious community at St David's, which had become a place of pilgrimage by the twelfth century.

THE WELSH KINGDOMS

Towards the end of the sixth century the **Angles** and **Saxons** in eastern Britain began to entertain designs on the western lands. The inability of the independent western peoples to unify against this threat left the most powerful kingdom, Gwynedd, as the centre of cultural and political resistance, a position it has retained to this day. The weaker groups were unable to hold the invaders, and after the battle at Dyrham, near Gloucester in 577, the Britons in Cornwall were separated from those in Wales, who became similarly cut off from their northern kin in Cumbria after the battle of Chester in 616.

Though still geographically in a state of change, Wales could now be said to exist. At this point the racial mix in Wales was probably little different from that to the east where Saxon numbers were small, but Wales was held together by the people's resistance to the Saxons. The Welsh started to refer to themselves as **Cymry** (fellow-countrymen), rather than the Saxon term "Welsh", used by English-speakers today and which is generally thought to mean either foreigners or Romanized people. The construction of **Offa's Dyke** (Clawdd Offa) – a linear earthwork built in the middle of the eighth century to mark rather than defend the boundary between Wales and the kingdom of Mercia – gave the Welsh a firm eastern border and allowed them to concentrate on a gradual unification of the patchwork of kingdoms as their coasts were being harried by **Norse and Viking invaders**.

Rhodri Mawr (Rhodri the Great) killed the Viking leader off Anglesey, earning himself the formal thanks of the Frankish king Charles the Bald (Charlemagne), and helped the country's rise towards statehood through his unification of most of Wales. By this stage, England had developed into a single powerful kingdom for the first time since the departure of the Romans, and though the various branches of Rhodri's line went on to rule most of Wales down to the late thirteenth century, the princedoms were frequently forced to swear fealty to the English kings. Defensive problems were exacerbated by internecine struggles borne of the practice of partible inheritance that left each of Rhodri's sons with an equal part of Wales to control.

Rhodri's grandson **Hywel Dda** (Hywel the Good) largely reunified the country from Deheubarth, his power base in southwest Wales. He added Powys and Gwynedd to his domain, but his most valuable legacy is his codification, compilation and promulgation of the medieval **Law of Wales** (Cyfraith Hywel Dda) in around 930 at modern day Whitland (see p.154), then called Hendy Gwyn ar Daf, "the White House on the Taf". Regional customs were fashioned into a single legal system that was only abandoned under the 1536 Act of Union with England. The laws drew more from the tenets of folk law than state edict: farming was conducted communally, the bard was exempt from menial tasks, a husband did not have unrestricted control over his wife (as was the case in much of Europe), and if a family were destitute they were allowed to retain a cooking pot and their harp.

After Hywel's death in 950, anarchy and internal turmoil reigned until his great-great-grandson, **Gruffydd ap Llywelyn**, seized power in Gwynedd in 1039. He unified all of Wales, taking the coronation of the weak English king, Edward the Confessor, as an opportunity to annex some of the Marches in Mercia. Edward's successor, Harold, wasn't having any of this and killed Gruffydd, heralding a new phase of political fragmentation.

THE ARRIVAL OF THE NORMANS

In 1066, the **Normans** swept across the English Channel, killed Harold, the English king, and stormed England. Though Wales was unable to present a unified opposition to the invaders, the Norman king, William, didn't attempt to conquer Wales. The **Domesday Book** – his masterwork of subjugation commissioned in 1085 to record land ownership as a framework for taxation – indicates that he only nibbled at parts of Powys and Gwynedd. Instead, he installed a huge retinue of barons, the **Lords Marcher**, along the border to bring as much Welsh territory under their own jurisdiction as possible. Despite generations of squabbling, the barons managed to hold onto their privileges until Henry VIII's Act of Union over four hundred years later.

The payment of homage by **Rhys ap Tewdwr** (the king of Deheubarth), and **Gruffydd ap Cynan** (the king of Gwynedd) kept the Welsh borders safe until the death of William I in 1087. His son William Rufus made three unsuccessful invasions of Wales but finally left it to his Marcher lords (now numbering over 140) to advance from their castles into south Wales, leaving only Powys and Gwynedd independent. A lack of English commitment or resources allowed the Welsh to claw back their territory through years when distinctions between English, Normans and Welsh were beginning to blur. One product of this was the quarter-Welsh **Giraldus Cambrensis** (see p.355), who left a valuable record of twelfth-century life in Wales and his opinions on Welsh character. "They are quicker witted and more shrewd than any other Western people", he informs us, a quality which helped them form three stable political entities: Powys, Deheubarth and Gwynedd. The latter, led by **Owain Gwynedd** from his capital at Aberffraw on Anglesey, now extended beyond Offa's Dyke and progressively gained hegemony over the other two. Owain Gwynedd's grandson, **Llywelyn ap Iorwerth** (the Great), who earned his laurels through shrewd campaigning, progressively incorporated the weaker territories to the south into his kingdom and captured several Norman castles to reach the peak of the Welsh feudal pyramid. Manipulating the favours of the English king John, Llywelyn managed to extend his control over southern Powys before a fearful John led two devastating campaigns into north Wales. Llywelyn was humiliated and forced into recognizing John as his heir should Llywelyn's union with John's illegitimate daughter Joan not produce a son. Channelling

a now united Welsh opposition against John, Llywelyn struck back and won some degree of Welsh autonomy. Worried that his unified Wales would disintegrate on his death, Llywelyn engineered the smooth succession by commanding his princes to assemble at Strata Florida (see p.279) and pay homage not just to him (as was now his by right) but also to his son, Dafydd. This plan succeeded until after his death, when Wales began to disintegrate to the point where at Dafydd's death in 1246 the country had only nominal unity.

Most of the work of regrouping Wales around one standard fell to Llywelyn the Great's grandson and Dafydd's nephew, Llywelyn ap Gruffydd (Llewellyn the Last).

EDWARD I'S CONQUEST

By 1255, Llywelyn ap Iorwerth's grandson, **Llywelyn ap Gruffydd** (the Last), had won control of Gwynedd. During the next three years he pushed the English out of Gwynedd, then out of most of Wales. The English king Henry III was forced to respect Llywelyn's influence and ratified the **Treaty of Montgomery** in 1267, thereby recognizing Llywelyn as "Prince of Wales" in return for his homage. The English monarchy's war with the barons allowed Llywelyn time to politically consolidate his lands, which now stretched over all of modern Wales excepting Pembrokeshire and parts of the Marches. The tables turned when Edward I succeeded Henry III and began a crusade to unify Britain. Llywelyn had failed to attend Edward's coronation and refused to pay him homage – at the same time, Llywelyn's determination to marry the daughter of Simon de Montfort lost him the support of the south Welsh princes and some Marcher lords. Edward was a skilful tactician and with effective use of sea power had little trouble forcing the already weakened Llywelyn back into Snowdonia. Peace was restored with the **Treaty of Aberconwy**, which deprived Llywelyn of almost all his land and stripped him of his financial tributes from the other Welsh princes, but left him with the hollow title of "Prince of Wales".

Edward now set about surrounding Llywelyn's land with castles at Aberystwyth, Builth Wells, Flint and Rhuddlan (see p.408). After a relatively cordial four-year period, Llywelyn's brother Dafydd rose against Edward, inevitably dragging Llywelyn along with him. Edward didn't hesitate and swept through Gwynedd, crushing the revolt and laying the foundations for the remaining castles in his **Iron Ring**, those at Conwy, Caernarfon, Harlech and Beaumaris. Llywelyn, already battered by Edward's force, was captured and executed at Cilmeri (see p.228), after fleeing from the abortive Battle of Builth in December 1282. The **Statute of Rhuddlan** in 1284 set down the terms by which the English monarch was to rule Wales: much of it was given to the Marcher lords who had helped Edward, the rest was divided into administrative and legal districts similar to those in England. Though the treaty is often seen as a symbol of English subjugation, it respected much of Welsh law and provided a basis for civil rights and privileges. Many Welsh were content to accept and exploit Edward's rule for their own benefit, but in 1294, a rebellion led by **Madog ap Llywelyn** gripped Wales and was only halted by Edward's swift and devastating response. Most of the privileges enshrined in the Statute of Rhuddlan were now rescinded and the Welsh seemed crushed for a century.

OWAIN GLYNDŴR

Throughout the fourteenth century, famine and the Black Death plagued Wales. The Marcher lords appropriated the lands of defaulting debtors and squeezed the last pennies out of their tenants, while royal officials clawed in all the income they could from the towns around the castles. These factors and the pent-up resentment of the English sowed seeds of a rebellion led by the tyrannical but charismatic Welsh hero **Owain Glyndŵr**. Citing his descent from the princes of both Powys and Deheubarth, he declared himself "Prince of Wales" in 1400, and with a crew of local supporters attacked the lands of nearby barons, slaughtering the English. Henry IV misjudged the political climate and imposed restrictions on Welsh land ownership, swelling the general support Glyndŵr needed to take Conwy Castle the following year. By 1404, Glyndŵr, who already had control over most of western Wales and sections of the Marches, took the castles at Harlech and Aberystwyth, summoned a parliament in Machynlleth, and had himself crowned Prince of Wales, with envoys of France, Scotland and Castile in attendance. He then demanded independence for the Welsh Church from Canterbury and set about securing alliances with English noblemen who had grievances with Henry IV. This last ambitious move heralded Glyndŵr's downfall. A succession of defeats saw his allies desert him, and by 1408, when the castles at Harlech and Aberystwyth were retaken for the Crown, this last protest against Edward I's English conquest had lost its momentum. Little is known of Glyndŵr's final years, though it is thought he died in 1416, possibly in Herefordshire, leaving Wales territorially unchanged but the country's national pride at an all-time high.

THE TUDORS AND UNION WITH ENGLAND

During the latter half of the fifteenth century, the succession to the English throne was contested in the **Wars of the Roses** between the houses of York (white rose) and Lancaster (red rose). Welsh allegiance lay broadly with the Lancastrians, who had the support of the ascendant north Welsh Tewdwr (or Tudor) family. Through the early part of the wars, one Henry Tudor lived with his widowed Welsh mother, Margaret Beaufort, at the besieged Harlech Castle, escaping to Brittany when Yorkist Richard III took the English throne in 1471. Fourteen years later, Henry returned to Wales, landing at Milford Haven, and defeated Richard at the Battle of Bosworth Field, so becoming **Henry VII** and sealing the Lancastrian ascendancy.

Welsh expectations of the new monarch were high. Henry lived up to some of them, removing many of the restrictions on land ownership imposed at the start of Glyndŵr's uprising, and promoting many Welshmen to high office, but administration remained piecemeal. Control was still shared between the Crown and largely independent Marcher lords until a uniform administrative structure was achieved under Henry VIII.

Wales had been largely controlled by the English monarch since the Statute of Rhuddlan in 1284, but the **Acts of Union** in 1536 and 1543 fixed English sovereignty over the country. At the same time the Marches were replaced by shires (the equivalent of modern counties), the Welsh laws codified by Hywel Dda were made void, and partible inheritance (equal amongst all offspring) gave way to primogeniture, the eldest son becoming the sole heir. For the first time the Welsh and English enjoyed legal equality, but the break with native traditions wasn't well received. Most of the people remained poor, the gentry became increasingly anglicized, the use of Welsh was proscribed and legal proceedings were held in English (a language few peasants understood). Just as Henry VIII's decision to convert his kingdom from Catholicism to Protestantism was borne more from his desire to divorce his first wife, Catherine of Aragon, than from any religious conviction, it was his need for money, not recognition, which brought about the **Dissolution of the Monasteries** in 1536. Monastic lands were divided amongst the local gentry, but since Christianity had always been a ritual way of life rather than a philosophical code in Wales, Catholicism was easily replaced by Protestantism. What the Reformation did promote was a more studied approach to religion and learning in general. Under the reign of Elizabeth I, Jesus College was founded in Oxford for Welsh scholars, and the Bible was translated into Welsh for the first time by a team led by Bishop **William Morgan** (see p.391).

With new land ownership laws enshrined in the Acts of Union, the stimulus provided by the Dissolution hastened the emergence of the Anglo-Welsh gentry, a group eager to claim a Welsh pedigree while promoting the English language and the legal system, helping to perpetuate their grasp. Meanwhile, landless peasants continued in poverty, only gaining slightly from the increase in cattle trade with England and the slow development of mining and ore smelting.

THE CIVIL WAR AND THE RISE OF NONCONFORMISM

A direct descendant of the Tudors, **James I** came to the throne in 1603 to general popular approval in Wales. Many privileges granted to the Welsh during the Tudor reign came to an end, but the idea of common citizenship was retained, the Council of Wales remaining as a focus for Welsh nationalism. James, fearful of both Catholicism and the new threat of Puritanism – an extreme form of Protestantism – courted a staunchly Anglican Wales and curried the favour of Welsh ministers in the increasingly powerful Parliament. Though weak in Wales, Puritanism was gaining a foothold, especially in the Welsh borders, where William

Wroth and Walter Cradock set up Wales' first dissenting church at Llanfaches in Monmouthshire in 1639, to become the spiritual home of Welsh Nonconformism.

The monarchy's relations with the Welsh were strained by **Charles I**, who was forced to levy heavy taxes and recruit troops, but the gentry were mostly loyal to the king at the outbreak of the **Civil War**, which saw the Parliamentary forces installing **Oliver Cromwell** as the leader of the **Commonwealth**. The Puritan support for Parliament didn't go unnoticed, and after Charles' execution, they were rewarded with the livings of numerous parishes and the roots of Puritan Nonconformism spread in Wales. As Cromwell's regime became more oppressive, the Anglican majority became disaffected and welcomed the successful return of the exiled **Charles II**, and the monarchy was restored. Charles replaced many of the clergy in their parishes and passed the Act of Uniformity, requiring adherence to the rites of the Established Church, and so suppressing Nonconformity. The Baptists, Independents and Quakers who made up the bulk of Nonconformists continued to worship in secret, until **James II** passed the **Toleration Act** in 1689, finally allowing open worship, but still banning the employment of dissenters in municipal government; a limitation which remained in force until 1828.

THE RISE OF METHODISM

The propagation of the Nonconformist seed in this fertile soil was less a conscious effort to convert the populace from Anglicanism than to better educate the masses. The late seventeenth century saw a welter of new religious books in Welsh, but with most people still illiterate, religious observance remained an oral tradition. In 1699, the **Society for Promoting Christian Knowledge**, set about establishing schools where the Bible, along with reading, writing and arithmetic, were taught in Welsh as well as English. This met with considerable success amongst the middle classes in anglicized towns, but failed to reach rural areas where children couldn't be spared from farm duties. The next big reformist push came in 1731, when **Griffith Jones** helped organize itinerant teachers to hold reading classes in the evenings and in the quieter winter season, so farmers and their families could attend. Within thirty years, half the Welsh population could read. After Jones' death, **Thomas Charles** of Bala (see p.260) continued his work, establishing Sunday schools and editing the first Welsh Bible to be distributed by the **British and Foreign Bible Society**.

By the middle of the eighteenth century, a receptive and literate populace was ready for three eloquent figures of the **Methodist Revival**, all driven by a strong belief in a resurgent Welsh nation. In contrast to the staid Anglican services, the Methodists held evangelical meetings: **Howel Harris** took his preaching outside or into people's homes, **Daniel Rowlands** converted thousands with his powerful sermons, and **William Williams** became the most important hymn writer in Welsh history. Meanwhile, improved schooling brought about a literary revolution, Welsh reestablishing itself as the vehicle for a vast body of literature which today outweighs the number of speakers.

Until now, Methodism had worked within the framework of Anglicanism, but in 1811, the Calvinist Methodists broke away. As the gentry remained with the Established Church, Methodism associated itself with the spiritual and social needs of the masses, becoming a rallying point for the growing sense of disaffection with the traditional rule of the parson and squire. The chapel became the focus of social life, discouraging folk traditions as incompatible with the Puritan virtues of thrift and temperance. Political radicalism was also discouraged, perpetuating the stranglehold on parliamentary power exercised by the powerful landed elite, the Williams-Wynn, Morgan and Vaughan families in particular. Only property owners were eligible to vote and few were prepared to challenge established dynasties, even when the rare elections took place.

Human rights became an issue in 1776 with the publication of the American Declaration of Independence and a piece by the radical Welsh philosopher, **Richard Price**: *Observations on the Nature of Civil Liberty*. The subsequent calls for a greater degree of democracy – universal suffrage and annual parliaments – increased during the early days of the French Revolution, but little was actually achieved until the next century, when radical Nonconformists were able to exploit the increasing political consciousness of the working class.

WALES AND THE INDUSTRIAL REVOLUTION

Small-scale mining and smelting had taken place in Wales since the Bronze Age, but agriculture remained the mainstay of an economy with a dangerously limited diversity: meat, wool and butter being about the only exports. With the enormous rise in grain prices in the early nineteenth century, Welsh farmers began to diversify and adopted the more advanced English farming practices of crop rotation, fertilizing and stock breeding. Around the same time, acts of Parliament allowed previously common land to be "enclosed", the grazing rights often being assigned to the largest landowner in the district, which left the previous occupant with few or no rights to its use. Inevitably, this forced smallholders to migrate to the towns where ever more workers were required to mine the seams and stoke the furnaces, fuelling the **Industrial Revolution**. In the north, **John Wilkinson** started his ironworks at Bersham (see p.380) and developed a new method of boring cylinders for steam engines; while in the south, foundries sprang up in the valleys around Merthyr Tydfil, where methods of purifying iron and producing high-quality construction steel were perfected under the eye of English ironmasters. Gradually the undereducated, impoverished chapel-going Welsh began to be governed by rich, church-going, English industrial barons.

Improved materials and working methods enabled the exploitation of deeper coal seams, not just to supply the iron smelters but for domestic fuel and to power locomotives and steamships. As the rich veins of coal deep below the Rhondda valleys were exploited by Welshmen like Walter Coffin and George Insole, south Wales was transformed: rural valleys were ripped apart and quiet hamlets turned into long unplanned rows of back-to-back houses stretching up the valley sides, all roofed in north Wales slate from quarries dug by the Pennant and Assheton-Smith families.

Transportation of huge quantities of coal and steel was crucial for continued economic expansion, and the roads and canals built in the early nineteenth century were displaced around 1850 as the rail boom took hold. Great engineers made their names in Wales: **Thomas Telford** built canal aqueducts and successfully spanned the Menai Strait with one of Britain's earliest suspension bridges; **Isambard Kingdom Brunel** surveyed the Merthyr–Cardiff train line, then pushed the Great Western network almost to Fishguard; and **Robert Stephenson** speeded the passage of trains between London and Holyhead on Anglesey for the Irish ferry connection.

In mining towns, working conditions were atrocious, with men toiling incredibly long hours in dangerous conditions; women and children as young as six worked alongside them, until this was outlawed by the Mines Act in 1842. Pay was low and often in a currency redeemable only at the poorly stocked, expensive company (Truck) shop. The **Anti-Truck Act** of 1831 improved matters, but a combination of rising population, fluctuating prices and growing awareness of the need for political change brought calls for reform. When it came in 1832, the **Reform Bill** fell far short of the demands for universal suffrage by ballot and the removal of property requirement for voters. This swelled the ranks of the Reformist Chartist movement, and when a petition with over a million signatures was rejected by Parliament, the **Chartist Riots** (see p.75) broke out in northern England and south Wales. The Newport demonstration was disastrous, the marchers walking straight into a trap laid by troops, who killed over twenty men and captured their leader, **John Frost**. Chartism continued in a weakened form for twenty years, buoyed by the **Rebecca Riots** in 1839–43, when guerrilla tactics put an end to tollgates on south Welsh turnpikes.

1850 TO WORLD WAR I

During the latter half of the nineteenth century the radical reformist movement and religion slowly became entwined, despite Nonconformist denial of political intentions. Recognizing that their flock didn't share the same rights as Anglicans, the Nonconformists petitioned for **disestablishment** of the Church in Wales and began to politicize their message. In the 1859 election, tenants on large farms (the only ones permitted to vote) were justifiably afraid of voting against their landowners or even abstaining from voting, and the conservative landowning hegemony held. But as a consequence of the 1867 Reform Act, industrial workers and small tenant farmers got the vote,

finally giving a strong working-class element to the electorate, seeing **Henry Richard** elected as Liberal MP for Merthyr Tydfil the following year, the first Welsh member of what soon became the dominant political force. Bringing the ideas of Nonconformity to Parliament for the first time, he spoke eloquently on land reform, disestablishment and the preservation of the Welsh language.

The 1872 Secret Ballot Act and 1884 Reform Act, enfranchising farm labourers, further freed up the electoral system and gave working people the chance to air their resentment of tithes extracted by a Church that didn't represent their religious views. Although several bills were tabled in Parliament in the 1890s, the Anglican church was only disestablished in 1920. The Nonconformist Sunday Schools were meanwhile offering the best primary education for the masses, supplemented, after **Hugh Owen** pushed through the Welsh Intermediate Education Act in 1885, by a number of secondary schools. Owen was also a prime mover in getting Wales' first major tertiary establishment started in Aberystwyth in 1872 (the tiny St David's University College in Lampeter was already fifty years old by then), soon to be followed by colleges at Cardiff (1883) and Bangor (1884). Until they were federated into the University of Wales in 1893, voluntary contributions garnered by Nonconformist chapels supported the colleges. The apotheosis of "Chapel power" came in 1881 with the passing of the Welsh Sunday Closing Act, enshrining Nonconformism's three basic tenets: observance of the Sabbath, sobriety and Welshness.

THE RISE IN WELSH CONSCIOUSNESS

During the nineteenth century, Welsh language and culture became weakened, largely through immigration to the coal fields from England. English became the language of commerce and the route to advancement; Welsh being reserved for the home and chapel life of seventy percent of the population. But Welsh was still being spoken in Nonconformist schools when, in 1846, they were inspected by three English barristers and seven Anglican assistants. The inspectors' report – known as **The Treason of the Blue Books** – declared the standards deplorable, largely due to the use of the Welsh tongue, "the language of slavery". This unfair report did some good in fostering free, elementary education at "Board Schools" after 1870, though the public defence of Welsh that ensued failed to prevent the introduction of the notorious "Welsh Not", effectively a ban on speaking Welsh in school.

As the nineteenth-century Romantic movement took hold throughout Britain, the London Welsh looked to their heritage. The ancient tales of The Mabinogion were translated into English, the **Welsh Language Society** was started in 1885, eisteddfodau were reintroduced as part of rural life, and the ancient bardic order, the **Gorsedd**, was reinvented. But disestablishment remained the cause célèbre of Welsh nationalism which, despite the formation of the **Cymru Fydd** (Free Wales) movement in 1886, with its demands for home rule along the lines of Ireland, wasn't generally separatist. Perhaps the greatest advocate of both separatism and Welsh nationalism was **Michael D Jones**, who helped establish a Welsh homeland in Patagonia and campaigned vociferously against "the English cause" (see p.260).

By 1907 Wales had a national library at Aberystwyth, and a national museum was planned for Cardiff, by now the largest city in Wales and laying claim to being its capital – only officially recognized in 1955.

INDUSTRY AND THE RISE OF TRADE UNIONISM

The rise in Welsh consciousness paralleled the rise in importance of the **trade unions**. The 1850s were a prosperous time in the Welsh coal fields, but by the end of the 1860s the Amalgamated Union of Miners was forced to call a strike (1869–71), which resulted in higher wages. A second strike in 1875 failed and the miners' agent, **William Abraham (Mabon)**, ushered in the notorious "sliding scale" which fixed wage levels according to the selling price of coal. This brought considerable hardship to the Valleys, which became insular worlds with strictly ordered social codes and a rich vibrancy borne from the essential dichotomy of the chapel and the pub. Meanwhile, annual coal production doubled in twenty years to 57 million tons by 1913, when a quarter of a million people were employed. Similarly punitive pay schemes were implemented in the north Wales slate quarries where membership of **Undeb Chwarelwyr Gogledd Cymru** (The North Wales Quarrymen's Union) was all but outlawed by the slate barons. This came to a head in 1900 when the workers at Lord Penrhyn's quarry at Bethesda started one of Britain's longest-ever industrial disputes. It lasted three years but achieved nothing.

From 1885, the vast majority of Welsh MPs were Liberals who helped end the sliding scale in 1902 and brought in an eight-hour day by 1908. The start of the twentieth century heralded the birth of a new political force when **Keir Hardie** became Britain's first Labour MP, for Merthyr Tydfil.

THE TWO WORLD WARS

World War I (1914–18) was a watershed for Welsh society. Seeing parallels with their own nation, the Welsh sympathized with the plight of defenceless European nations and rallied to fight alongside the English and Scots. At home, the state intervened in people's lives more than ever before: agriculture was controlled by the state while food was rationed, and industries, mines and railways were under public control. The need for Welsh food and coal boosted the economy and living standards rose dramatically. Many were proud to be led through the war by Welsh lawyer **David Lloyd George** (see p.356), who rose to the post of Minister of Munitions, then of War, becoming Prime Minister by 1916; but by the time conscription was introduced, patriotic fervour had waned. Many miners, reluctant to be slaughtered in the trenches and resentful of massive wartime profits, welcomed the 1917 Bolshevik Revolution, and though Communism never really took hold, the socialist Labour Party was there to catch the postwar fallout.

Similar dramatic changes were taking place in rural areas, where Welsh farming was embracing new machinery and coming out of nearly a century of neglect. High wartime inflation of land prices and the fall in rents forced some landowners to sell off portions of major estates to their tenants in the so-called "green revolution", breaking the dominance of a rural landed gentry.

The boom time of World War I continued for a couple of years after 1918, but soon the Depression came. All of Wales' mining and primary production industries suffered, and unemployment reached 27 percent, worse than in England and Scotland, which both weathered the Depression better. The **Labour movement** ascended in step with the rise in unemployment, making south Wales its stronghold in Britain. Their stranglehold was challenged by Lloyd George's newly resurgent Liberal Party, but his Westminster-centred politics were no longer trusted in Wales and Labour held firm, seeking to improve workers' conditions: the state of housing was still desperate, and health care and welfare services needed boosting. The Labour Party effectively became the hope that had previously been entrusted to the chapels and later the Liberals.

A new sense of nationalism was emerging and, in 1925, champions of Welsh national autonomy formed **Plaid Genedlaethol Cymru** (the National Party of Wales) under **Saunders Lewis**, its president for ten years. In one of the first modern separatist protests, he joined two other Plaid members and set fire to building materials at an RAF station on the Llŷn, was imprisoned, dismissed from his post and spent the rest of his life immersed in the world of literary criticism, becoming one of Wales' greatest modern writers. Similar public displays and powerful nationalist rhetoric won over an intellectual majority, but the voting majority continued to fuel the Labour ascendancy in both local and national politics.

Some relief from the Depression came with re-armament in the lead-up to **World War II**, but by this stage vast numbers had migrated from south Wales to England, leaving the already insular communities banding together in self-reliant groups centred on local co-ops and welfare halls.

When war became inevitable, the Labour Party was committed to halting the Fascist threat along with most of Wales. As a result of the demands of the war, unemployment all but disappeared and the Welsh economy was gradually restructured, more people switching from extractive industries to light manufacturing, a process which continues today.

Plaid Cymru were less enthusiastic about the war, remaining neutral and expressing unease at the large number of English evacuees potentially weakening the fabric of Welsh communities. Their fears were largely ungrounded and the war saw the formation of a Welsh elementary school in Aberystwyth and Undeb Cymru Fydd, a committee designed to defend the welfare of Wales.

THE POSTWAR PERIOD

Any hopes for a greater national identity were dashed by the Attlee Labour government from 1945 to 1951, which nationalized transport and utilities with no regard for national boundaries, except for the Wales Gas Board. However, under the direction of Ebbw Vale MP, **Aneurin Bevan**, the postwar Labour government instituted the National Health Service, dramatically improving health care in Wales and the rest of Britain, and providing much-improved council housing.

The nationalized coal industry, now employing less than half the number of twenty years before, was still the most important employer at nationalization, but a gradual process of closing inefficient mines saw the number of pits drop from 212 in 1945 to 11 in 1989, and just one in 1999. Sadly, the same commitment wasn't directed at cleaning up the scars of over a century of mining until after 1966, when one of south Wales' most tragic accidents left a school and 116 children buried under a slag heap at **Aberfan** (see p.86).

In the rural areas, the price stabilization that followed the 1947 Agriculture Act brought some relief to financially precarious hill farmers, who were given further protection with the formation of the Farmers' Union of Wales in 1955. A more controversial fillip came from the siting of an aluminium smelter and two nuclear power stations in north Wales, dubious benefits soon eroded by the closure of much of the rural rail system following the Beeching Report in 1963. Despite the switch to light manufacturing and the improved agricultural methods, unemployment in Wales rose to twice the UK average, and women continued to be greatly under-represented.

After its postwar successes, the Labour Party remained in overwhelming control during the 1960s and 1970s, though Plaid Cymru became a serious opposition for the first time, partly due to Labour's reluctance to address nationalist issues. Attlee had thrown out the suggestion of a Welsh Secretary of State in 1946, and not until Plaid Cymru was fielding twenty nationalist candidates in the 1959 election did the Labour manifesto promise a cabinet position for Wales. The position of **Secretary of State for Wales** was finally created in 1964 by the Labour government, led by Harold Wilson, who also created the **Welsh Development Agency** and moved the Royal Mint to Llantrisant in south Wales. With Plaid Cymru's appeal considered to be restricted to rural areas, Labour was shocked by the 1966 Carmarthen by-election, when **Gwynfor Evans** became the first Plaid MP. It wasn't until 1974 that Plaid also won in the constituencies of Caernarfon and Meirionydd, and suddenly the Party was a threat, forcing Labour to address the question of devolution. By 1978 Labour had tabled the **Wales Act**, promising the country an elected assembly to act as a voice for Wales, but with no power to legislate or raise revenue. In the subsequent **referendum** in 1979, eighty percent of voters opposed the proposition, with even the nationalist stronghold of Gwynedd voting against.

MODERN WALES

In 1979, the Conservative (or Tory) government of **Margaret Thatcher** came to power, achieving an unprecedented 31 percent of Welsh votes. The 1979 referendum effectively sidelined the home-rule issue and Thatcher was able to implement her free-market policies with an unstinting commitment to privatizing nationalized industries. With 43 percent of the Welsh workforce as government employees, privatization had a dramatic impact. The number of jobs in the steel industry, manufacturing and construction all plummeted, doubling unemployment in five years. Despite this, the Tories held their share of the vote and, because of changes to constituency boundaries, increased their tally of MPs at the 1983 election, while Labour saw their lowest percentage since 1918.

Vast changes in employment patterns signalled the breakdown of traditional Valley communities and the labour movement was weakened by successive anti-union measures. None of this broke the solidarity of south Welsh workers during the year-long **Miners' Strike** (1984–85), after which women took a much greater proportion of the work now transferring out of the Valleys onto the south coastal plain. Living standards were still rising and the Welsh were now better off than ever before, but high unemployment and a large rural population meant that average income still lagged behind most areas of England, and despite free medical care, the Welsh remained in poorer health. As elsewhere in Britain in the second half of the

twentieth century, the Welsh have turned their backs on the established religions. The chapel has ceased to be the focal point of community life, and something like 4000 churches and chapels are due to close in the next twenty years.

During the 1980s, support for Plaid Cymru shifted back to the rural areas, the party holding three out of four Gwynedd constituencies after the 1987 election. At the same time, general enthusiasm for the Welsh language increased and a steady decline in numbers of Welsh-speakers was reversed. New Welsh-only schools opened even in predominantly English-speaking areas, learners' classes sprouted everywhere and in 1982, S4C, the first **Welsh-language television channel**, started broadcasting.

Until their overwhelming defeat in the general election of 1997 (when Wales – and Scotland – elected no Tory MPs at all), the Tories landed the country with a succession of variously disinterested, and usually English, Secretaries of State who did little to further the Welsh cause. The Labour party tried its best to show that it was different, even if, as a sop to "Middle England", a late clause was thrown in to the party's support for a devolved Welsh assembly that meant it was conditional on a referendum vote. When Tony Blair and "New" Labour won a huge majority in May 1997, the devolution process – the centrepiece of which was the creation of the first **National Assembly of Wales** for six hundred years – was put into practice, gaining an electoral endorsement from the Welsh people in the referendum only by the most slender of margins. Elections to the Assembly took place in May 1999, when a huge swing to Plaid Cymru denied the Labour party its assumed overall majority. Comprising 28 Labour members, 17 from Plaid Cymru, 9 Conservatives and 6 Liberal Democrats, the Assembly started business in the summer of 1999; however, it has no tax-varying powers and no right to pass primary legislation – a direct contrast with the more advanced set-up of the Scottish Parliament, which can do both. Its early days have been bumpy – public support is anything but assured, especially when the London-based Labour party is seen as explicitly manipulating events that most assume should be left to the politicians in Cardiff. This was starkly brought into focus when the architect of Labour's devolution package, Ron Davies, resigned as Secretary of State for Wales (and putative First Secretary of the Assembly), to be replaced from London by the deeply uncharismatic **Alun Michael**, never the popular choice in Wales. With Labour in a minority, the opposition parties successfully drove through a vote of no confidence against Michael in February 2000. This resulted in the installation of **Rhodri Morgan** – something of a Labour maverick and as popular in Wales as he is unpopular in London – as the First Secretary. This internal putsch gave the Assembly its first real sparks of independence and life, some eight months after it was established. Until then, most impressions of the Michael-led Assembly had focussed on its timidity and over-reliance on Westminster-style adversarial politics, but these are very early days. Whether it's window dressing or not, the upsurge in Welsh national consciousness (and confidence), spearheaded by the Assembly, is very real indeed and cannot be denied. Increasingly, polls show that people think of themselves as being Welsh before British, and Welsh popular culture – especially in music, literature and film – has boomed like never before.

Now that there is a junior legislature in Cardiff, and with much of UK-wide politics decided in the European Union parliament rather than London, a whole new axis of government is rapidly emerging. How this will develop is dependent on numerous vagaries – for starters, the success (or otherwise) of the euro, popular Europe-wide disenchantment with the faceless bureaucracy of the EU, the growth in multinational corporations and government, the London Labour government's centralizing tendencies, any potential English backlash against Welsh and Scottish devolution, and, most of all, how effective the new Cardiff Assembly is perceived to be. Falling between the two stools of outright self-determination and the British superstate as it does, the Assembly has already alienated many people at both ends of the nationalist spectrum, while the mainstream Welsh press have been typically feeble-minded in picking the wrong fights with the Assembly. The greatest hope, perhaps, is that the uprising in Welsh confidence, so admirably expressed outside of the party political hierarchies, will start to infect the political system. As teething troubles are overcome, and other devolving nations – Scotland, Catalunya and Lombardy, for instance – progress, it should be hoped that the Assembly will gradually increase its powers in accordance with the will of the Welsh people, and do so in a way that is genuinely progressive and Welsh, rather than smacking of hand-downs from London. It's an exciting time to be in Wales, for there is the undeniable feeling that it's all up for grabs, and that a new century will only hasten the process.

CHRONOLOGY OF WELSH HISTORY

250,000 BC	Earliest evidence of human existence in Wales.
9–8000 BC	End of last Ice Age.
6000 BC	Rising oceans separate Britain from Europe.
4000 BC	Agriculturalism becomes widespread in Wales.
2000 BC	Arrival of **Bronze Age** settlers from the Iberian peninsula colonizing Pembrokeshire and Anglesey, while the Gower was settled by people from Brittany and the Loire.
600 BC	**Celts** reach the British Isles: the Goidels settle in Ireland, the Brythons in parts of England and Wales.
43 AD	**Romans** begin conquest of Britain.
61	Suetonius Paulinus attacks north Wales and Anglesey.
78	Roman conquest of Wales completed as Agricola kills druids of Anglesey.
80–100	Caerleon amphitheatre built.
early 4thC	Roman departure from Wales.
early 5thC	**Cunedda Wledig** arrives from Scotland to conquer north Wales.
5th–6thC	**Age of Saints**.
c. 500	St Illtud arrives from Ireland, bringing Christianity and founding Llanilltud Fawr monastery.
c. 589	Saint David (Dewi Sant) dies.
615	Aethelfrith defeats Welsh at Bangor.
616	Battle of Chester – Wales isolated from rest of Britain.
768	Celtic Church accepts some of the practices and customs of the Roman Church, including its date for Easter.
c. 784	Offa's Dyke (Clawdd Offa) constructed.
844–78	**Rhodri Mawr** rules Gwynedd, later gaining most of the rest of Wales through inheritance and marriage.
C9th–10th	St David's accepts supremacy of Rome.
c. 900–50	Hywel Dda rules most of Wales.
late 10thC	Hywel Dda's unified Wales split into four independent principalities.
1039–63	**Gruffydd ap Llywelyn** reunites Wales.
1066	**Normans** invade Wales.
1067	Chepstow Castle started.
1090	First Norman castle at Cardiff.
1094	Normans repelled from Gwynedd and Dyfed.
1115	Norman bishop installed at St David's.
1143	Cistercians found Hendy-gwyn (Whitland) Abbey.
1180–93	St David's Cathedral built.
1188	Archbishop Baldwin (accompanied by Giraldus Cambrensis) recruits for the Third Crusade.
1196–1240	**Llywelyn ap Iorwerth** (the Great) rules as Prince of Gwynedd and later most of Wales.
1215	English barons force King John into signing Magna Carta. Limited rights for Wales.
1246–82	**Llywelyn ap Gruffydd** (the Last) intermittently rules large parts of Wales.
1267	**Treaty of Montgomery** signed by Henry III, ratifying Llywelyn ap Gruffydd's claim to the title "Prince of Wales".
1270–1320	Tintern Abbey built.
1276–77	**First War of Welsh Independence**.
1277	Llywelyn humiliated by signing **Treaty of Aberconwy**. Edward I begins Aberystwyth, Flint and Rhuddlan castles.
1282–83	**Second War of Welsh Independence**. Llywelyn's brother Dafydd rises up against Edward I.
1283	Caernarfon, Conwy and Harlech castles started.
1284	**Statute of Rhuddlan** signed by Edward I.
1294	Revolt of Madog ap Llywelyn.
1295	Beaumaris Castle started.
1301	Edward I revives title of "Prince of Wales" and bestows it on his son, Edward II.

1400–12	Third War of Welsh Independence. **Owain Glyndŵr**'s revolt.
1416	Owain Glyndŵr dies in hiding.
1471	Edward IV's Council of Welsh Marches at Ludlow.
1485	Accession of **Henry VII** to throne after landing from exile at Pembroke and beating Richard III at Bosworth.
1536–38	Henry VIII suppresses monasteries.
1536–43	**Acts of Union**: legislation forming the union of Wales and England. Equal rights but with a separate legal and administrative system conducted wholly in English.
1546	First book printed in Welsh: *Yn y Lhyvyr Hwnn*.
1571	Jesus College, Oxford (the Welsh college) founded.
1588	Translation of complete Bible into Welsh, chiefly by **William Morgan**.
1639	First Puritan congregation in Wales convened at Llanfaches, Gwent.
1642	Beginning of Civil War in England.
1644	**Battle of Montgomery**: first battle of Civil War on Welsh territory.
1646	Harlech and Raglan besieged during the Civil War. Harlech, the last Royalist castle, falls in 1647.
1660	Restoration of the monarchy.
1689	Toleration Act passed, allowing open, Nonconformist worship.
1707	Publication of Edward Lhuyd's *Archaeologia Britannica* initiates foundation of Celtic studies.
1743	Establishment of Welsh Calvinistic Methodist Church.
1759	Dowlais Ironworks started, followed by Merthyr Tydfil iron industry.
1782	Beginning of north Wales slate industry with the opening of Pennant's Penrhyn slate quarry at Bethesda.
1789	First **eisteddfod** for 200 years held at Corwen.
1793–94	Cardiff to Merthyr canal built.
1801	First census. Welsh population 587,000.
1811	Separation of Welsh Methodists from Church of England.
1832	Reform Bill passed in Westminster.
1839	**Chartist** march on Newport fails.

1839–43	**Rebecca Riots** close tollbooths on turnpikes.
1841	Taff Vale Railway built.
1845–50	Britannia Tubular Bridge built.
1859	Liberals win major victory in elections; tenants evicted for voting against their Conservative masters; Nonconformist revival.
1865	Michael D Jones founds Welsh colony in Patagonia.
1872	**University College of Wales** opens in Aberystwyth, followed by Cardiff (1883) and Bangor (1884).
1881	Passing of Welsh Sunday Closing Act.
1884	**Reform Act**. Farm labourers and small tenant farmers get the vote for the first time.
1885	**Welsh Language Society** founded.
1886	Tithe War in north and west Wales.
1893	**University of Wales** established.
1898	Foundation of **South Wales Miners' Federation**.
1900	Britain's first Labour MP, Kier Hardie, elected for Merthyr Tydfil.
1907	Founding of National Museum, Cardiff, and National Library, Aberystwyth.
1914–18	World War I.
1916	**David Lloyd George** becomes Prime Minister.
1920	Disestablishment of Church of England in Wales.
1925	Plaid Genedlaethol Cymru (Welsh Nationalist Party) formed.
1926	**Miners' strike** and General Strike.
1929–34	Great Depression.
1936	Saunders Lewis and colleagues burn building materials on the Llŷn.
1939–45	World War II.
1951	Minister for Welsh Affairs appointed.
1955	Cardiff declared capital of Wales.
1959	Welsh flag royally accepted as such.
1963	Cymdeithas yr Iaith Gymraeg (Welsh Language Society) formed.
1964	James Griffith, first cabinet-level Secretary of State for Wales, appointed.
1966	**Gwynfor Evans**, first Plaid Cymru MP, elected for Carmarthen. Aberfan disaster.

1967	**Welsh Language Act** passed. Limited recognition of Welsh as a formal, legal language.
1974	Local government reorganization, creating eight new counties in Wales.
1979	Referendum on Welsh Assembly. Eighty percent of voters come out against a separate parliament.
1982	Welsh-language TV channel S4C begins broadcasting.
1984–85	**Miners' strike**.
1992	Welsh Language Bill gives Welsh equal status with English in public bodies.
1993	Establishment of the Welsh Language Board.
1994	First Welsh film, *Hedd Wyn*, nominated for an Oscar.
1996	Another local government reorganization divides Wales into 22 unitary authorities.
1997	Referendum on Welsh Assembly. Only half the country vote, of whom 50.3 percent say yes, a majority of just 6000 nationwide.
1999	First **Welsh Assembly** elections. Assembly starts sitting.
	The Rugby World Cup takes place with Wales as the host nation.
2000	Rhodri Morgan takes over as First Secretary of The Welsh Assembly following Alun Michael's resignation.

TWENTIETH-CENTURY WELSH NATIONALISM

If any single event can be said to have given birth to Welsh nationalism in the modern sense, it was a meeting amongst Welsh academics at the 1925 eisteddfod in Pwllheli on the Llŷn peninsula. Led by gifted writer Saunders Lewis, the group metamorphosed into Plaid Genedlaethol Cymru, the National Party of Wales.

The Welsh identity had always been culturally rich, but was politically expressed only as part of the great Liberal tradition: in the dying years of the nineteenth century, Welsh Liberal MPs organized themselves into a loose caucus roughly modelled on Parnell's Irish parliamentarians and, although the Welsh group was without the clout or number of the Irish MPs, 25 or 30 MPs voting en bloc was serious enough to be noticed. **David Lloyd George** (1863–1945; Prime Minister 1916–22), fiery Welsh patriot and Liberal premier of Great Britain, had embodied many people's nationalist beliefs, although his espousal of greater independence for Wales came unstuck when, ever the expedient politician, he realized the potential difficulty of translating this ideal into hard votes in the industrialized, anglicized south of Wales. During Lloyd George's premiership, the Irish Free State

was established, drawing inevitable comparisons with the Home Rule demands being less stridently articulated in Scotland and Wales. But the Liberal Party was in sharp decline, nowhere more markedly than in the industrialized swath of southern Wales, where the populous and radical mining Valleys had deserted the Liberals in favour of new socialist parties. With the urban decline of a steadfast, fiercely pro-Welsh Liberal tradition, and the emergence of the two main parties as class-based warriors at either side of the political spectrum, Welsh nationalism – faced with a persistent slump in the Welsh language – was gradually honed into Saunders Lewis' embryonic political party.

Plaid Cymru – the "Genedlaethol" was soon dropped – had an inauspicious start electorally, polling a total of 609 votes in its first contest in 1929. Initially, the party acted more as a pressure group, focused inevitably on the issue of the decline in the Welsh language and inextricably suffused with a romantic cultural air that had little apparent relevance to party politics. As war loomed over Europe in the latter half of the 1930s, Plaid maintained a controversially pacifist stance, winning few new converts. Most sensationally, in September 1936, Saunders Lewis and two other Plaid luminaries, the Rev Lewis Valentine and D.J. Williams, set fire to the construction hut of a new aerodrome being built on the Llŷn peninsula as part of Britain's build-up to the war. They immediately reported themselves to the nearest police station, attracting huge publicity in the process. Interest in the ensuing trial electrified Wales, causing howls of outrage when the government decided to divert it from sympathetic Caernarfon to the Old Bailey in London. Even recalcitrant nationalist Lloyd George was outspokenly critical of the English decision. The three men were duly imprisoned for nine months, becoming Plaid's first martyrs.

Despite having dwindled throughout the rest of Britain, the prewar Liberal tradition was still strong with the rural majority of Wales, though by the 1951 election this had become just three parliamentary seats out of 36. The **Labour party** was now the establishment in Wales, winning an average of around sixty percent of votes in elections from 1945 to 1966.

National feelings of loss and powerlessness began to take a hold in postwar Wales as the Welsh language haemorrhaged from the country. Although Wales consistently voted Labour, the Conservatives, the most fervently unionist of British political parties, were in power for thirteen years from 1951. Labour's 1945–51 administration had tinkered with a few institutions to give them a deliberately Welsh stance, but the Conservatives – winning only six out of 36 Welsh seats in 1951 – had little time for specifically Welsh demands. Two Welsh Labour MPs, Megan Lloyd George, daughter of the great Liberal premier, and S.O. Davies, spearheaded new parliamentary demands for greater Welsh independence, presenting a 1956 petition to Parliament demanding a Welsh assembly that was signed by a quarter of a million people. Massive popular protests against the continued flooding of Welsh valleys and villages to provide water for England shook the establishment. The 1963 formation of the boisterous *Cymdeithas yr Iaith Gymraeg* (the **Welsh Language Society**) created many headlines and attracted a new youthful breed of cultural and linguistic nationalists to the fold. The ruling Conservatives offered token measures in an attempt to lance the rising boil of nationalism: a part-time Welsh Minister was appointed (although the job was always part of another, more important, ministerial brief), Cardiff was confirmed as capital and the Welsh flag authorized as official. The Labour party, meanwhile, was becoming more distinctively nationalistic, having formed a Welsh Council within the party, from where MPs, trade unionists and ordinary party members began to articulate the need for greater independence. In the **general election of 1964**, the party stood on a more nationalistic platform than ever before. As usual, they swept the board in Wales, and finally won throughout the UK as a whole. As promised in their manifesto, the post of **Secretary of State for Wales**, backed by a separate Welsh Office, was created, although with fewer powers than the Scottish equivalent which had existed since just after the war.

Wales presents a very different proposition from Scotland where early nationalist movements are concerned. Scotland is a far more recent arrival (1707) in the British Union than Wales and still maintains identifiably different education, judicial and legal systems, whereas Wales' are totally subsumed into the English framework. Scotland is also relatively isolated, 400 miles from London, but Wales lies immediately west of large English conurbations: Birmingham, Liverpool and Manchester. Nor is Scottish nationalism so wrapped in misty-eyed linguistic pride: Gaelic is so thinly scattered that, unlike in Wales, nationalism has far transcended the language issue. Scottish nationalism has gained acceptance in both urban and rural settings, appealing to fiery socialists in Glasgow as much as well-heeled Tories of Grampian. By contrast, Plaid Cymru's support, with a few occasional exceptions, has usually been drawn from the rural, Welsh-language strongholds of the west and north.

Despite these inherent drawbacks, it was Plaid Cymru who scored the first, and most dramatic, strike into Westminster. Veteran Labour MP for Carmarthen, Megan Lloyd George, died just a couple of months after the 1966 general election, precipitating a by-election won by charismatic Plaid president, Gwynfor Evans. For Wales, and for Scotland, two countries with a massive in-built majority for Labour and – for once – under a UK-wide Labour government, the nationalist parties provided a safe (and non-Conservative) repository for protest votes. Plaid Cymru and the Scottish National Party both soared in popularity in the wake of the Carmarthen result. Winnie Ewing, for the SNP, captured Hamilton from Labour in a 1967 by-election. Most dramatically, in the heart of socialist south Wales, Plaid ran the Labour government astonishingly close in two by-elections: in Rhondda West (1967) and Caerphilly (1968), the party saw swings of over 25 percent to cut Labour majorities of over twenty thousand to just a couple of thousand. From humble beginnings, it seemed that Plaid's time had come. Its traditional vote in the north and west was soaring, but, more importantly, Plaid was the only party threatening the dominance of Labour in the English-speaking industrial south. It appeared that the party had finally overcome its single-issue status around the Welsh language, and membership ballooned to forty thousand. Welsh nationalism reached new heights at the time of the Prince of Wales' theatrical 1969 investiture at Caernarfon, a gesture resented by many. The cause also gained its first casualties, when two extremist nationalists blew themselves up at Abergele in Clwyd whilst attempting to lay a bomb on the rail line where Prince Charles was due to travel. In some ways, this had a detrimental effect on

Plaid's cause, wrongly linking extremism with the more moderate and constitutional methods of the party.

Despite this, the **1970 general election** saw Plaid in more robust mood than had ever previously been justified. The astonishing results of the previous few years led them to believe that they could pick up a clutch of Westminster seats. Yet despite trebling their 1966 tally to 176,000 votes (11 percent of the poll in Wales), they failed to take any new seats and even lost their place in Carmarthen. The new Conservative government checked Plaid's progress, as protest votes could now safely go to the Labour party. Despite that, Plaid polled well in local elections, even taking control of Merthyr borough council. The Labour party, anxiously watching any inroads into their power base that Plaid could make, embarked on another measured programme of vaguely nationalistic proposals. Supporting bilingual road signs (daubing monoglot English signs was a practice of 1970s nationalists), briefly publishing a Welsh Labour party bilingual magazine, *Radical*, and drawing up plans for a watered-down Welsh assembly were hard-fought tenets of the new Labour party, although many traditionalists felt that these were pandering far too much to nationalist sentiment. The second 1974 election returned Gwynfor Evans in Carmarthen to join two other Plaid Cymru MPs elected in the February election. Plaid's parliamentary band of three was dwarfed by the enormous success of the SNP in Scotland, who had succeeded in getting eleven MPs to Westminster. Furthermore, Plaid's earlier success in the industrialized south had evaporated, and they lost their deposits in 26 of the 36 Welsh seats. Once again, they were a party geographically concentrated in the rural outposts of Wales.

The combined strength of the nationalist parties at Westminster, added to the wafer-thin and dwindling parliamentary Labour majority, meant that the political demands of devolution were high on the government's agenda, as they could ill afford to lose the support – and votes – of the SNP and Plaid Cymru MPs. The ruling Labour government dallied with devolutionary proposals, including setting up the **Wales Development Agency**, supporting the new Wales TUC (Trades Union Congress) and devolving the huge responsibilities of the Department of Trade and Industry in Wales to the Welsh

Office in Cardiff. As the Labour parliamentary majority became ever thinner, through the government losing a cache of by-elections, the nationalists' demands became more strident. Eventually, the Labour party put forward bills for Scottish and Welsh assemblies, subject to the result of referenda.

The devolution proposals were simple. Both Scotland and Wales were offered national assemblies, or as broadcaster Wynford Vaughan-Thomas put it, "after its long marriage with England, Wales was being offered, if not divorce, at least legal separation". Campaigning by both sides was fervent, but it was obvious from early on that many Welsh people were suspicious of the proposals. A large number of the eighty percent of the country who did not speak Welsh feared that a Welsh assembly would be the preserve of a new "Taffia", a *Cymraeg* elite. Both north and south Walians worried about potential domination by the other. People feared greater bureaucracy, particularly in the wake of the 1974 local government reorganization when a two-tier system of county and district councils had been imposed on Wales. A third tier, with few apparent powers, was not a terribly attractive proposition. On St David's Day 1979, the Welsh people voted and, by a massive margin (just one-fifth of the 59 percent who voted supported the measure), turned down the limited devolution on offer. In Scotland, the proposals also fell, although a slender majority had voted in favour, but not by the margin required in the bill.

The shock waves were great. Weeks later, the Labour government fell and **Margaret Thatcher**'s first Conservative administration was ushered in. Political nationalism seemed to have gone off the boil, and Plaid Cymru were back to just two MPs representing the northwestern constituencies of Meirionydd and Caernarfon. The early 1980s were dominated by swiftly rising unemployment and a collapse in Britain's manufacturing base. Nowhere was this more evident than in south Wales, where mines and foundries closed and the jobless total soared. Welsh nationalism was suffering an identity crisis, typified by Plaid Cymru's controversial 1981 rewriting of its own constitution to fight for an avowedly "Welsh socialist state", causing some of the more conservative, rural members to quit the party. Basing itself as a republican, left-wing party would, it was believed, bring greater fruit in the populated south. The nationalists suffered by implication from the activities of Meibion Glyndŵr (**Sons of Glendower**), a shadowy organization dedicated to firebombing English holiday homes in Wales. Plaid continued to plough a firmly constitutional and peaceful route to national self-determination, but many people assumed that the bombers received covert support amongst the party's ranks.

Gwynfor Evans might well have lost his Carmarthen seat in 1979, but he was single-handedly responsible for the most high-profile activity of Welsh nationalism in the early 1980s. The Conservative party had fought the general election of 1979 on a manifesto that included a commitment to a Welsh-language TV channel. When plans for the new UK Channel 4 were drawn up, this promise had been dropped. The Plaid Cymru president decided to fast until death, if necessary, as a peaceful protest. It did not take long before this action, gaining enormous publicity in the media, forced the Thatcher government to make a U-turn, and **Sianel Pedwar Cymru** (S4C) was born in 1982. Perhaps the Tories realized the political advantage of bringing Welsh nationalism into the legitimate fold, for the Welsh media industry, long accused of a nationalistic bent, dissipated many angry and impassioned arguments for national self-determination. Many of the most heartfelt radicals ended up in prominent positions within Wales' media.

Like so many other political affiliations and ideals in the 1980s, Welsh nationalism underwent something of a sea change during the decade. As the Labour party was routed in the 1983 election, precipitating a rightward slide for the rest of the decade and beyond, Plaid Cymru genuinely began to broaden its base as a radical, multilayered and mature political force with a firmly socialist and internationalist outlook. The party developed serious policies on all aspects of Welsh life, from traditional rallying calls of language and media to sophisticated analyses of economic policy, the Welsh legal framework and the country's role in the European Union and the wider world. But Welsh devolution – if not outright nationalism – ceased to be the preserve of Plaid Cymru alone. Two of the three UK-wide parties, Labour and, in particular, the Liberal Democrats, inheritors of the great Liberal tradition, evolved devolu-

tionary strategies for Wales, Scotland and, to a lesser degree, the regions of England. Each party created a semi-autonomous Welsh branch, with its own party conference, election broadcasts and manifesto. Even the Conservatives continued to devolve more governmental decision-making out to the Welsh Office in Cardiff, although this, ironically, strengthened the nationalist hand. Plaid and the other parties pointed out that a huge swath of government existed in Wales, overseen by no all-Wales authority, but run instead by unelected bodies, often made up of the government's friends, appointed from Westminster (Parliament) and Whitehall (the civil service). Their call for a Welsh assembly to oversee this vast array of public expenditure was consistently supported by huge majorities in opinion polls, and formed the basis of the Labour Party's manifesto for Wales throughout the 1990s.

Welsh nationalism in the 1990s looked increasingly outwards from a hitherto rather introspective corner that had always tended to focus on the big neighbour next door. Europe, in particular, was the great hope, particularly an evolving Europe of the Regions. Plaid Cymru had failed to get any Members of the European Parliament elected until 1999; until then, their only official entrant had been one of the three Welsh representatives on the EU **Council of the Regions**, a somewhat toothless body set up in 1994. However, lack of electoral success didn't stop Plaid from hitching its trailer to the great European juggernaut, and its policies through the 1990s breathlessly enthused about all matters European, something they have quietened down on a little since greater cynicism about the EU spread through Wales as it did throughout Britain. Nonetheless, many significant decisions are made in Brussels and Strasbourg rather than London or Cardiff, and to ignore the potential of a more devolved Europe would be hopelessly parochial – something Welsh nationalism has always needed to avoid.

The **1997 general election** changed everything. The Conservatives, tired and tetchy after eighteen years in government, were spectacularly swept from power, failing to keep any seats whatsoever in Wales. Labour – or "New" Labour as the party was styled under Tony Blair – won hugely, denting any further Plaid progress and keeping the nationalists, by now named bilingually as Plaid Cymru – The Party of

Wales – firm in their existing four seats (Ceredigion had been a surprise gain in 1992) but still on little more than one-tenth of the vote. However, it was always likely that Plaid would benefit more under a Labour government than a Conservative one, as they could reap substantial anti-Labour protest votes. This has proved to be the case – helped, it should be said, by the Blair government's own actions. New Labour's dilution of past socialist beliefs, and their framing of policies aimed at pleasing Middle England, has gone down particularly sourly in Wales. Added to this, Labour's election manifesto had contained an explicit commitment to a process of devolution, including referenda on a **Welsh Assembly** (*Cynulliad Cenedlaethol Cymru*) and a Scottish Parliament. Devolution was at the front of the new government's legislative queue, taking place within six months of their election. Scotland voted wholeheartedly for its parliament; in Wales, the proposals barely scraped through. Although this was potentially the first piece of self-government for Wales in 600 years, many nationalists felt that it fell far short of expectations and was not worth supporting. Plaid Cymru's own stance mirrored this ambivalence: initially unenthusiastic and only coming out for the Assembly in the latter stages of the campaign. Wales itself was firmly, and almost exactly, split by the devolution vote. The border areas and Pembrokeshire, true to their historical anglicization, voted no, while Plaid's west coast strongholds and the "Old" Labour bastions of the industrial Valleys were enthusiastic enough – just – to swing the ballot.

The strength of the "yes" vote in the industrial south of Wales was something of a harbinger to the campaign proper for the Assembly's sixty seats. Here, more than anywhere, Plaid Cymru achieved spectacular gains, taking Labour strongholds like Rhondda, Islwyn and Llanelli. The Plaid share of the vote was their highest ever, at nearly 30 percent, and it was enough to deny Labour – once the absolute party in Wales – an overall majority. Weeks later, in the first proportional representation elections for the **European Parliament**, Plaid did reach 30 percent, just two percent short of Labour, securing two out of the five Welsh MEPs.

However, it's too soon for Plaid Cymru to rest on its laurels. The party's two startlingly good results happened in very rarefied circumstances, and in both elections, many Labour voters simply stayed at home, disillusioned with the growing Thatcherite flavour of the Blair government in London and the recent back-room deals that had been stitched up to secure Alun Michael, Tony Blair's chosen man, the position of leader of the Welsh Labour party; he was later ousted in favour of Rhodri Morgan. Furthermore, many people who voted Plaid (obviously identifiable as the "most Welsh" of the political parties) in the first ever Welsh Assembly election would never consider doing so for Westminster. Getting nearer to a sniff of power has also had some discernible – some might say regrettable – effects on Plaid. In the run-up to the Assembly elections, rows broke out in the media about their support for Welsh independence, something that was perceived potentially to scare away their soft votes. Remarkably, they managed to contort themselves into claiming that this had never been on their agenda, and that their aim was for "self-determination" rather than independence. More hardheaded nationalists must have wept. At Gwynedd Council – the one place in which the party has exercised power for some years – a small rump of the ruling Plaid group have left to form an **independent nationalist grouping** that seems a little more in keeping with Plaid's fiery republicanism of fifteen years earlier. The mother party, meanwhile, in something of a mirror to the actions of Labour across Britain as a whole, has shoehorned itself into middling respectability, playing down or even casting aside policies which are assumed to frighten the average voter.

The way forward for Welsh nationalism is likely to be markedly different from the past few decades. In some ways, potential political fragmentation is a healthy sign of inherent Welsh democracy: once a nationalist outfit has (even if only slightly) seen its primary goal of self-determination achieved, real political differences start to emerge amongst the comrades. Plaid seem to be heading for a far more sober, Eurocentric vision of a devolved Wales; others will coalesce into new and revitalized groupings around different visions, outright independence included. The days of guerrilla-style bombing tactics against English-owned second homes are doubtless over, but many who spent years undertaking such campaigns in their youth are unlikely to feel represented by the pragmatic revisionism of the modern Plaid Cymru. Since the arrival of the Assembly, it's hard for even the most ardent of nationalists to argue that Wales' system of government is the most pressing issue facing the nation. With farming in utter crisis, one of the poorest standards of living in the UK and with the low-wage sector in old industrial areas of the south offering virtually the only jobs, there are plenty of meatier matters to chew. If the Assembly can be seen to be making a difference about these issues, its reputation will soar, and this in itself is surely the best argument for according it greater power.

At the beginning of the twenty-first century, it's safe to say that the majority of Welsh people are fairly happy with things as they are. The general sense of Welshness has been much augmented in recent years, as much by the Rugby World Cup and pop band Catatonia as by any politician. Now more than ever, organized nationalists are walking a tightrope – watering down the more extreme tenets of nationalism so as to retain those who voted for it the first time round, whilst simultaneously maintaining the fizz, the romance and the sheer commitment that has kept the flame of Welsh nationalism alive through some very dark times. Wales is more and more happily, and very easily, calling itself a nation. The question that still hangs in the air is simply this: to be a nation, does Wales really need to be a state?

NATURAL HISTORY OF WALES

A comprehensive account of Wales' landscapes, land use, flora and fauna would take several books to cover. What follows is a general overview of the effects of geology, human activity and climate on the country's flora, fauna and land management.

Wales is covered with a wide array of sites deemed to be of national or international importance, all seemingly with different designations. The three **National Parks** – Snowdonia, the Brecon Beacons and the Pembrokeshire Coast – comprise almost twenty percent of the country, with another couple of percent incorporated into the five **Areas of Outstanding Natural Beauty** (AONB): the Anglesey coast, the Llŷn coast, the Clwydian Range, the Gower peninsula and the Wye Valley. Smaller areas (from a few acres to large chunks of the Cambrian Mountains) with specific habitats such as lowland bogs or ancient woodlands are managed as **National Nature Reserves** (NNRs). Most are widely promoted, usually posted with information boards and threaded with easy, well-signed walking trails. All NNRs contain **Sites of Special Scientific Interest** (SSSIs; aka triple-SIs), a category including around another 700 locations in Wales singled

out for special protection. Most are on private land with no right of access.

It must be remembered that nowhere in Wales is untouched, almost every patch of "wilderness" being partially the product of human intervention, thoroughly mapped, mined and farmed. Nor is anywhere free from pollution: the conurbations of England are too close, nuclear power stations and factories dot the countryside and some of the seas are in a terrible state, not least from oil spills such as the 130,000 tonnes the *Sea Empress* leaked into the water around Milford Haven in 1996. That said, several clean-air-loving lichen species – found in few other places in Britain – abound in Wales.

GEOLOGY

Geologists puzzled over the forces that shaped the Welsh landscape for centuries before early nineteenth-century geologist **Adam Sedgwick** and his collaborator (and later rival) **Roderick Murchison** began to unravel the secrets. They were able to explain the shattered, contorted and eroded rocks that form the ancient peaks of Snowdonia, but fought bitterly over rock classification. By naming the **Silurian** rock system (400–440 million years ago) after one of Wales' ancient tribes, Murchison started a trend that continued with the naming of the earlier **Ordovician** system (440–500 million years ago) and the **Cambrian** system (500–600 million years ago), given the Roman name for Wales. Anglesey, the Llŷn and Pembrokeshire all have older **pre-Cambrian** rocks; those around St David's are some of the most ancient in the world.

Wales is packed with mountains, and several areas deserve brief coverage. Between 600 and 400 million years ago, **Snowdonia** was twice submerged for long periods in some primordial ocean where molten rock from undersea volcanoes cooled to form igneous intrusions in the sedimentary ocean-floor layers. Snowdon, Cadair Idris and the Aran and Arenig mountains are the product of these volcanoes, with fossils close to the summit of Snowdon, supporting the theory of its formation on the sea floor. After Silurian rocks had been laid down, immense lateral pressures forced the layers into concertina-like parallel folds with the sedimentary particles being rearranged at right angles to the pressure, giving today's vertically splitting sheets of **slate**, the classic metamorphosed product of these forces. It is known that the folded strata that rose above the sea bore no resemblance to today's mountains, the cliff face of Lliwedd on Snowdon showing that the summit was at the bottom of one of these great folds between two much higher mountains. One of these is now known as the **Harlech Dome**, a vast rock hump where the softer Silurian rocks on the surface all wore away and the Ordovician layers below were only saved by the volcanic intrusions, principally Snowdon and Cadair Idris. In between, the Ordovician rocks wore away, exposing the harder Cambrian sand and gritstones of the **Rhinog** range. In the very recent geological past from 10,000–80,000 years ago, these mountains were worked on by the latest series of **Ice Ages**, with glaciers scouring out hemispherical cirques divided by angular ridges, then scraping down the valleys, gouging them into U-shapes with waterfalls plunging down their sides.

Snowdonia is linked by the long chain of the **Cambrian Mountains** to the dramatic north-facing scarp slope of the **Brecon Beacons**, south Wales' distinctive east–west range at the head of the south Wales coal field. Erosion of the ancient Cambrian, Ordovician and Silurian rocks which once covered what is now northern Britain and much of the North Sea washed down great river systems, depositing beds of old red sandstone from 350–400 million years ago. These **Devonian** rocks lay in a shallow sea where the molluscs and corals decayed to form carboniferous limestone, which in turn was overlaid by more sediment forming millstone grit. Subsequent layers of shale and sandstone were interleaved with decayed vegetable matter, forming a band known as **coal measures**, from which the mines once extracted their wealth. The whole lot has since been tilted up in the north, giving a north to south sequence which runs over a steep sandstone ridge (the Brecon Beacons), then down a gentle sandstone dip-slope arriving at the pearl-grey limestone band where any rivers tend to dive underground into **swallow holes**. They reappear as you reach the gritstone, often tumbling over waterfalls into the coal valleys.

Erosion still continues today, slowly reshaping the landscape, hastened by the Welsh climate.

LAND SETTLEMENT AND USAGE

After the last ice sheet drew back from Wales, the few plant species which had survived on the ice-free peaks (known as nunataks) were in a strong position to colonize, producing an open grassland community more than 10,000 years ago. Birch and juniper were amongst the first trees, followed by hazel. Several thousand years later this had developed into a mixed deciduous woodland including oak, elm and some pine, and in wetter areas damp-loving alder and birch. The Neolithic tribes began to settle on the upland areas, using their flint axes to clear the mountain slopes of their forests. The discovery of bronze and later iron hastened the process, especially since wood charcoal was required for smelting iron ore, and so began the spiralling devastation of Wales' native woodlands. As the domestication of the sheep and goats put paid to any natural regeneration of saplings, more land became available for arable farming. Thin, acidic mountain soils and a damp climate made **oats** – fodder for cattle and horses – about the only viable cereal crop, except in Anglesey which, by the time the Romans arrived in the first century AD, was already recognized as Wales' most important corn-growing land. Cattle rearing was increasingly important on the lusher pastures, and even as late as the twelfth century, Giraldus Cambrensis tells us that "the whole population lives almost entirely on oats and the produce of their herds, milk, cheese and butter".

Giraldus lived at a time when the Normans were pushing into lowland Wales and acting as patrons of the monasteries. Until they were appropriated by Henry VIII in 1536, the seventeen Cistercian houses all kept extensive lands, cleared woods and developed sheep walks and cattle farms. With the Dissolution of the Monasteries, their lands became part of the great estates which still take up large tracts of Wales.

By contrast, the less privileged were still smallholders living simple lives. In the 1770s the travel writer Thomas Pennant noted in his *Tours in Wales* that the ordinary people's houses on the Llŷn were "very mean, made with clay, thatched and destitute of chimneys". The poor state of housing had much to do with the practice of *Tŷ unnos* (literally "one-night house"), supposedly a right decreed by Hywel Dda, in which building a house of common materials close at hand within 24 hours staked your claim on a plot of common land. The practice hadn't completely died out in the 1850s when George Borrow's guide observed, "That is a house, sir, built yn yr hen dull in the old fashion, of earth, flags, and wattles and in one night – the custom is not quite dead."

In the eighteenth century, **droving** reached its peak. Welsh black cattle, fattened on Anglesey or the Cambrian coast, were driven to market in England, avoiding the valley-floor toll roads by taking highland routes that can still be traced. Nights were spent with the cattle corralled in a halfpenny field (so called because this was the nightly rate per animal) next to a lonely homestead heralded by three Scots pines, which operated as an inn. It was a tough journey for men and cattle, but easier than for geese, whose webbed feet were toughened for the long walk with tar and sand.

At home, women ground the corn, aided by mills driven by the same fast-flowing mountain streams that later provided power for textile mills springing up all over the country. The Cistercians had laid the foundations of the **textile industry** for both wool and flannel, but it had generally remained in the cottages, with nearly every smallholding keeping a spinning wheel next to their harp. The same sort of damp climate that made Lancashire the centre of the world's cotton industry encouraged the establishment of a textile industry in Ruthin, Denbigh, Newtown, Llandeilo and along the Teifi Valley, but a lack of efficient transport made them uncompetitive.

The next major shift in land use came with a wave of **enclosure acts** from 1760 to 1820, which effectively removed smallholders from upland common pasture and granted the land to holders of already large estates. With the fashion for grouse shooting taking hold in the middle of the nineteenth century, large tracts of hill country began to be managed as heather moor, with frequent controlled fires to encourage the new growth that the grouse fed on. The people were deprived of their livelihood and access to open country was denied to future generations of walkers.

The mountain building processes discussed overleaf have left a broad spectrum of minerals under Wales. **Copper** had been mined with considerable success since the Bronze Age, and

was further exploited by the Romans, who dabbled in **gold** extraction. But it wasn't until the latter half of the eighteenth century that mining became big business, with a rapid expansion in both north and south Wales. **Slate** (see p.345) was hewn from deeper mines and higher mountainsides, while the northern ends of the south Wales valleys echoed to the sounds of the ironworks. The fortuitous discovery of iron ore, limestone for smelting and coal for fuelling the furnaces made the valleys the crucible of the iron industry, and iron stayed at the forefront here long after richer ore finds elsewhere.

Originally a service industry, **coal mining** soon took over and shaped the development of south Wales for over a century. Further west, the processing of Cornish **copper** financed the development of Swansea, while Llanelli devoted itself to **tin**.

FLORA

Wales supports 1100 of Britain's 1600 native plants, with ferns and other moisture-loving species particularly well represented.

Until five thousand years ago, birch, juniper, hazel, oak and elm covered the mountainsides, but devastating forest clearances and a wetter climate have left only a few pockets of native woodland in the valleys, their regeneration threatened by sheep grazing on fresh seedlings. **Pengelli Forest** in Pembrokeshire represents one of Wales' largest blocks of ancient woodland, comprising **midland hawthorn** and **sessile oak**, the dominant tree in ancient Welsh forests. Parts of the Severn and lower Wye valleys are well wooded, as is the Teifi Valley, where oak, ash and sycamore predominate. You can still occasionally see evidence of **coppicing** – an important and ancient practice common a century ago – where trees are cut close to the base to produce numerous shoots harvested later as small-diameter timbers. Under the canopy, **bluebells** and **wood sorrel** are common, and in the autumn look out for the dozens of species of **mushroom**, especially the delicious but elusive **chantrelle**, found mainly under beech trees.

A far greater area of Wales is smothered in gloomy ranks of **conifers** (predominantly sitka spruce), a product of the twentieth-century monoculture ethic. Forbidding to most birds and too shaded and acidic for wild flowers, they are the object of widespread criticism directed towards the Forestry Commission.

Perhaps the most celebrated of all Wales' plants are the **arctic alpines** that grow away from grazing sheep and goats amongst the high, lime-yielding crags and gullies of Snowdonia and the Brecon Beacons, their southernmost limit in Britain. Ever since the ice sheets retreated ten thousand years ago, the warmer weather has forced arctic alpines towards higher ground, where they cling to small pockets of soil behind rocks. Some get unceremoniously cleaned out by thoughtless climbers trying to push up novel routes, but in the main, their spread hasn't changed since they were discovered by seventeenth-century botanists such as Thomas Johnson and Welshman Edward Lhuyd, who found *Lloydia serotina*, a glacial relic more popularly known as the **Snowdon Lily** (though actually a spiderwort), that looks not unlike a small off-white tulip. In Britain, it is found only around Snowdon and then only rarely seen between late May and early June, when it blooms.

The exemplary habitat for arctic alpines is widely regarded to be **Cwm Idwal** in the Ogwen Valley, where you may get to see some of the more common species, in particular the handsome **purple saxifrage**, whose tightly clustered flowers often push through the late winter snows, later followed by the starry and mossy saxifrages and spongy pink pads of **moss campion**. The star-shaped yellow flowers of **tormentil** are typical of high grassy slopes, and you may also find **mountain avens**, distinguished by its glossy oak-like leaves, and, when it blooms in June, by its eight white petals. From June to October, purple heads of **wild thyme** cover the ground, providing food for a small beetle unique to Snowdonia.

Sheep prefer the succulent **sheep's fescue**, but competition for the juicier shoots leads to overgrazing and the growth of tough mat-grass which chokes out the **woolly-hair moss**, the **reindeer moss** and the **dwarf willow**, which can otherwise be seen in yellow bloom during June and July. Just below the wind-battered mountaintops are the early colonizing species; **alpine meadow grass**, **glacier buttercup**, **mountain sorrel** and **alpine hair grass** among them.

Poor acid soils on the igneous uplands foster the growth of lime-shy bracken, bilberry and purple **heather** – bell, ling, cross-leaved and Scottish are all found – which combine with decayed **sphagnum moss** in wetter areas to form peat bogs. Though generally less extensive than in upland bogs elsewhere in Britain, the Welsh wetlands still support the **bog asphodel** which produces its brilliant yellow spikes in late summer, often in company with the **spotted orchid** and less frequently the tiny **bog orchid**. Insectivorous plants are also found, such as the **butterwort** (both pale and common varieties) and the **sundew** (long-leaved and round-leaved), which both gain nutrients that their poor surroundings cannot provide by digesting insects trapped on the sticky hairs of their leaves.

Limestone uplands such as the Clwydian ridges and parts of the Brecon Beacons are more likely to host less rugged plants, like the **harebell** and the **rock rose**. Streams running off these uplands tumble down narrow valleys hung with ferns and mosses and sometimes scattered with the yellow-flowered **Welsh poppy**.

At sea level, the rivers spawn estuarine "meadows", which in summer are carpeted with bright violet **sea lavender**, followed by a mauve wash of **sea aster** after August. An unusual coastal feature is the dam-formed string of **Bosherston Lakes**, south of Pembroke, where the fresh water supports rafts of **white-water lilies**. Further west, the Pembrokeshire coast is a blaze of colour in early summer, with white-flowered **scurvy grass** and **sea campion**, yellow **kidney vetch** and **celandine**, and blue **spring squill**. **Water crowfoot** is found in fresh water near the coastal footpath, where you can also find the hemispherical lilac heads of **devil's bit scabious**. **Bluebells** and **red campion** cloak Pembrokeshire's islands, while the majority of species mentioned can be found in abundance in Newborough on Anglesey. Here, some of Wales' finest sand dunes are bound by **marram grass**, interspersed with **sea holly**, **sea bindweed** and the odd **marsh helleborine**.

BIRDS

With its long coastline, Wales, as you might expect, abounds in sea birds, and the profusion of islands and its position on the main north–south migratory route make several sites particularly noteworthy. This remains the case despite the massive *Sea Empress* oil spill that contaminated the waters around Milford Haven in early 1996. Wind and tides distributed the oil around the fragile breeding grounds of Pembrokeshire, and some 5000 common scoter were lost, but it could have been a lot worse. Most breeding birds hadn't yet arrived and the worst of the mess was cleaned up before they did.

The Royal Society for the Protection of Birds (RSPB), Sutherland House, Castlebridge, Cowbridge Road East, Cardiff CF11 9AB (☎029/2035 3000, *www.rspb.org.uk*), operates ten sites throughout Wales, half of them on the coast. The islands off the Pembrokeshire coast are incomparable for sea-bird colonies, the granite pinnacle of **Grassholm** (RSPB), 12 miles offshore, hosting the world's third-largest gannet colony with 30,000 pairs. Grassholm can only be visited by prior arrangement after mid-June, but the islands closer to the coast are more accessible (see p.178), **Skokholm** and **Skomer** between them supporting 6000 pairs of **storm petrels** and an internationally significant population of 140,000 pairs of the mainly nocturnal **Manx shearwater**, which spend their winter off the coast of South America. Burrows vacated by rabbits on the islands also provide nests for puffins, while **razorbills**, **guillemots** (known as *elegug* in Pembrokeshire) and **kittiwakes** nest on the cliffs. Since the eradication of the rats that previously deterred burrow-nesting birds (the chough, a rare, red-billed, red-legged member of the crow family, was the only species to remain), Manx shearwaters are also now colonizing **Ramsey Island**, a few miles north. A few pairs of choughs are also found on the important migration stopover, **Bardsey Island** off the Llŷn coast , and at the wonderful **South Stack Cliffs** (RSPB) on Anglesey which, especially from May to July, are alive with breeding guillemots, razorbills and puffins. Like much of the coast, **fulmars** and **peregrine falcons** are also present in respectable numbers, as are **cormorants** – though these birds usually nest only by the sea, Craig yr Aderyn, a cliff four miles inland from Tywyn, hosts a small population that is in decline.

The mudflats and saltings of Wales' estuaries provide rich pickings for wintering waders. The **Dee estuary** (RSPB), on the northern border with England, plays host to Europe's largest concentration of **pintail** as well as **oystercatchers**, **knot**, **dunlin**, **redshank** and many others. Numerous terns replace them in the summer months.

Central Wales represents one of Britain's last hopes for reviving the population of **red kites** which, like many other raptors, were traditionally persecuted by gamekeepers and suffered from the use of pesticides, which caused thinning of egg shells. The banning of DDT in the 1960s allowed numbers to increase, but there are still only 500 of these fork-tailed birds left, predominantly in the Elan Valley. However, as with the other persecuted species, the hen harrier, the peregrine falcon and the sparrowhawk, numbers are increasing. Perhaps one day the heights of Snowdonia may again resound to the cry of the eagle which gives the mountains their Welsh name, *Eryri*.

The high country supports larger populations of **kestrels**, usually seen hovering motionless before plummeting onto an unsuspecting mouse or vole, and golden-brown **buzzards** gently wheeling on the thermals on the lookout for prey which can be as big as a rabbit. Buzzards and peregrine falcons are as happy picking at carrion, but have to compete with sinister black **ravens**, that inhabit the highest ridges and display their crazy acrobatics, often banding together to mob the bigger birds.

Acidic heather uplands between one and two thousand feet provide habitats for the black and red **grouse**, whose laboured flight is in complete contrast to the darting zigzag of its neighbour, the **snipe**. On softer grassland, expect to find the **ring ouzel**, a blackbird with a white cravat, and the **golden plover**, a bird still common but being threatened, like many others, by the spread of conifer forests, which welcome little except wood pigeons and blackbirds.

After the gloomy pines, it is a delight to wander in relict stands of the ancient oak woodlands, and along the streams where the **dipper** and **kingfishers** flourish. On sheltered water you might also find shelduck, Canada geese and three species of swan.

MAMMALS

During the last interglacial period, Wales was warm enough to support hippos and lions, but humans, pressed for space by the expanding ice sheets, killed them off, leaving bears and boars which in turn were dispatched by human persecution. Some of the last beaver lodges in Britain dammed the Teifi in the twelfth century, while half a millennium later, wolves disappeared from the land. What remains is a restricted range of wild mammals topped up with semiwild and feral beasts: shy herds of **ponies** on the Carneddau in Snowdonia and on the Brecon Beacons are rounded up annually, deer occasionally stray from captive herds, and the **goats** in Snowdonia (on the Glyder and the Rhinog ranges especially) and on the Great Orme at Llandudno are descendants of domesticated escapees. Generally welcomed by farmers, they forage on the precipitous ledges, thereby discouraging sheep from grazing ventures beyond their capabilities. About the only other large land mammal are the soft-fleeced **Soay sheep** at Newborough Warren on Anglesey.

Though widely acknowledged as the scourge of wildlife, the spread of conifer plantations has seen a surge in the population of the elusive, stoat-like **pine marten**, which thrives in sitka spruce where its diet of squirrels is readily available. Both pine martens and the more common **polecats** are found in Snowdonia, in the ancient woodlands of Pengelli Forest on the slopes of Mynydd Preseli, in the relict beechwoods of the Brecon Beacons and the coastal dunes where they prey on rabbits. Trapped almost into oblivion in the nineteenth century, polecats have recolonized almost all of Wales and parts of western England over the last fifty years. **Foxes** are still torn apart by dogs in the name of sport but remain widespread, along with the **brown hare**, **stoat** and **weasel**, though the **badger** is rarer and still the subject of persecution through the cruel sport of badger baiting. **Rabbits** seem to be everywhere, and the North American **grey squirrel** has all but dislodged the native red squirrel from its habitat, though it still hangs on around Lake Vyrnwy and at Newborough on Anglesey. Of the smaller beasts, **shrews** and **wood mice** abound, and the island of Skomer has a unique subspecies of **vole**.

Otters almost became extinct in Wales some years back, but a concerted effort on the part of the Otter Haven Project has seen their numbers climbing in the Teifi and some of the rivers in Montgomeryshire. They remain an endangered species, and perhaps fortunately are seldom seen, but indicate their presence by their droppings.

The waters off the Pembrokeshire Coast around the Marloes peninsula and Skomer Island have been designated a **marine reserve**, though this doesn't cover the **grey seal** breeding colony on the west coast of Ramsey Island, where each year a couple of hundred white-furred pups are born. Sadly, marine pollution is being increasingly detected in the seals' blubber, a worrying sign too for the **dolphins** and **porpoises** inhabiting the coastline.

FISH, REPTILES AND INSECTS

Wales' clean, fast-flowing rivers make ideal conditions for the **brown trout**, a fish managed for sport throughout the country. In Wales, the damming of rivers has seldom cut off spawning grounds, but the fishable limit of the Conwy in particular has been extended by the introduction of a fish ladder around the Conwy Falls. **Salmon** are less common, found mainly in the Usk and the Wye, the latter being the only river where it is important as game fish. Along with **roach**, **perch** and other coarse fish, the depths of Bala Lake (Llyn Tegid) claim the unique silver-white **gwyniad**, an Ice Age relic not dissimilar to a small herring, said never to take a lure. Llyn Padarn in Llanberis also notches up a rarity with the freshwater **char**. Conditions for successful fish farming do not exist in Wales, but commercially viable beds of **cockles** still exist on the north coast of the Gower and families still own rights to musselling the sands of the Conwy estuary.

With Welsh red dragons dying out along with King Arthur, much smaller lizards and two species of snake are all that remains of Wales' reptiles. The poisonous, triangular-headed **adder** is sometimes spotted sunning itself on dry south-facing rocks, but, except in early spring when it is roused from hibernation, it frequently slithers away unnoticed. The harmless **grass snake** prefers a wetter environment and is equally shy. Easily mistaken for a snake, the **slowworm** is actually a legless lizard and is common throughout Wales, as are **toads** and **frogs** – though the rare **natterjack toad** is only found in a few locations.

As for **butterflies**, southern British species – the common blue and red admiral – are abundant in sheltered spots, but aim for the woodland reserves, found dotted all over the country, to find the **dark green fritillary** and its pearl-bordered and silver-washed kin. South Wales is particularly good for insect life, with Pengelli Forest home to the rare **white-letter hairstreak** as well as one of Britain's rarest dragonflies, the bright blue **southern damselfly**, while the Gower peninsula harbours populations of **marbled white butterfly** and the **great green bush cricket**, uncommon anywhere else in Wales. Lastly, Snowdonia has the unique and aptly named **rainbow leaf beetle**.

ECOLOGY AND THE FUTURE

With the smokestack industries now largely absent from Wales and the Valleys mostly devoid of working coal mines, nature (sometimes with the help of schemes to level and replant spoil heaps) is struggling to claw its way back. A verdure inconceivable thirty years ago now cloaks the hillsides, and already, the industrial remains are being cherished as cultural heritage; as much a valid part of the "natural" landscape as the mountain backdrops. If you need convincing, climb up to the disused slate workings behind Blaenau Ffestiniog or walk the old ironworks tramways around Blaenafon.

In other areas, much remains to be done to restore the ecological balance. The increasing commercialization of farming has led not just to the damaging application of pesticides and excessive use of nitrogen-rich fertilizers, but to the wholesale removal of **hedgerows** and **drystone walls**, ideal habitats for numerous species of flora and fauna. Conservation groups promote the skills needed to lay hedges and build dry-stone walls, but for every success, another chunk of farmland is paved over with a new bypass or a meadow is turned over to **conifers**.

The tax incentives which formerly encouraged vast expanses of spruce no longer apply, but economics still favour clear-felling a single species every thirty years or so. The largest forest owner, the Forestry Commission, is keen to shake off its monoculture image and aims to border its forests with a mix of broad-leaved trees and conifers of different ages.

Far from being areas where nature is allowed to take its course, the **national parks** can be their own worst enemies, attracting thousands of people a day. Some attempt is being made to control the effects of tourism through path management and the limited promotion of public transport, but this is more than outweighed by the increasingly aggressive promotion of these regions. Paradoxically, and for all the wrong reasons, **military zones** – Mynydd Eppynt and most of the Castlemartin peninsula, for example – have become wildlife havens away from the worst effects of human intervention.

Wind farms have become a contentious

issue in the mid-1990s. Initial enthusiasm for this clean energy has waned as local people complain about the constant drone of the generators, and conservationists battle it out over the relative merits of a nuclear power station that will take 130 years to decommission (as well as several millennia for the fissile material to become safe) and several forests of elegant windmills on top of hills. Friends of the Earth: Cymru, 26–28 Underwood St, London, N1 7JQ (☎020/7490 1555, *www.foe.org.uk*) stand firmly in favour of wind power, but have come up against the Campaign for the Protection of Rural Wales (CPRW), Tŷ Gwyn, 31 High St, Welshpool, Powys SY21 7YD (☎01938/552525, *www.cprw.org.uk*), one of Wales' main independent environmental groups, which is pushing for a ban on any new wind-farm developments favouring promotion of more efficient power usage.

Environmental groups are also keeping a weather eye on offshore **oil** and **gas** exploration, currently much under way off the Welsh coast, particularly in Cardigan Bay. Meanwhile in south Wales, reaction to the *Sea Empress* disaster hardened citizens' resolve to successfully resist the import of dirty but cheap Venezuelan orimulsion to fuel power stations.

One recent success has been the decision not to press ahead with the **Usk Barrage**, which was planned to create a freshwater lake on the outskirts of Newport by damming the estuary, forcing otters and other protected species to abandon the river. Things aren't as rosy on the shores of the Severn estuary nearby, where the construction of the second Severn crossing has engendered a new stretch of motorway across the environmentally rich Caldicot Levels, destroying several SSSIs.

The Snowdonia National Park Authority has recognized that sustainable management of farmland is not only ecologically beneficial, but that the landscape, with its character largely defined by past farming practices, is worth maintaining in its own right. In response it has set up the **Tir Cymen** (which loosely translates as "well-crafted landscape") scheme, a ten-year government initiative which pays participating farmers to maintain stone walls, slate fences, earth banks, traditional stone buildings and archeological features. Trial schemes are in place in the southern Snowdonian region of Meirionydd, Dinefwr in Carmarthenshire, and around Swansea and the Gower peninsula.

MUSIC IN WALES

Until very recently, mention of Welsh music conjured up images of miners in their Sunday best collectively raising the roof of their local chapel, and, despite the near-obliteration of the mining industry, male voice choirs remain a feature of Welsh rural life, with many choirs opening their practice sessions to the public. But Welsh music extends far beyond the dwindling chapels, into the country's village halls, clubs, festival sites and pubs, where Dylan Thomas' observation that "we are a musical nation" is often seen, and heard, to be true. In quieter venues, harp players repay their musical debt to ancestors who accompanied the ancient bards (traditional poets and storytellers), while modern folk draws directly from the broader Celtic musical tradition. Exponents of Welsh-language rock have traded in their dreams of commercial success for unabashed nationalism expressed through a multiplicity of styles from punk to hip-hop. Some bands sing in both English and Welsh, and there is a fast-growing scene in English-language Welsh rock, which has been one of the most dominant, and successful, musical genres in Britain through the late 1990s, thanks to the antics of bands like the Manic Street Preachers, the Stereophonics and Catatonia.

What follows is a general overview of the main styles and a run through the stars, both past and present.

FOLK

The word "folk" translates into Welsh as *gwerin*, but the Welsh word has a much wider meaning than its English counterpart, taking in popular culture as well as folklore. In a Welsh *gwyl werin* (folk festival), you're just as likely to encounter the local rock band as the local dance team, and the whole community will be there – not just committed specialists.

It's often said that the Welsh love singing but ignore their native instrumental music. Welsh folk song has always remained close to the heart of popular culture, with modern folk song-writing acting as the common carrier of political

WHERE TO GET INFORMATION

Taplas, the English-language bimonthly magazine of the folk scene in Wales, is the best source for current events. It's based at 182 Broadway, Roath, Cardiff CF2 1QJ (☎029/2049 9759).

Cymdeithas Ddawns Werin Cymru (Welsh Folk Dance Society) is also a useful source of events information, with an annual magazine and a twice-yearly newsletter, both bilingual. Contact the editor, 10 River View Court, Llandaff, Cardiff CF5 2QJ (☎ & fax 029/2055 5055, *www.welshfolkdance.org.uk*).

The **South Wales Echo** newpaper carries comprehensive daily listings of events in Gwent and mid- and South Glamorgan.

The **Museum of Welsh Life** at St Fagans, near Cardiff (see p.112), is a vibrant museum and a vital centre for research and collecting work (☎029/2056 9441).

Watch out on **posters** for the word *twmpath* – it's the equivalent of a barn dance or ceilidh and is used when Welsh dances are the theme of the night. Calling (dance instructions) could be in Welsh or English, depending on where you are in the country. A *Noson Lawen*, literally "a happy night", is most likely to be found in tourist hotels and usually offers a harpist, perhaps some dancers and a repertoire of Welsh standards.

FESTIVALS

For eisteddfodau, see main text.

Live at Llantrisant, mid-Glamorgan. Pub weekend staged by Llantrisant Folk Club, with limited space but a great party atmosphere. Late April.

Swansea Shanty Festival, West Glamorgan. Growing every year, the sea song and music take place on and around a tall ship in the marina. Early May.

Mid-Wales Festival, Newtown, Powys. The first big outdoor camping event, with an extensive guest list, has concerts at Theatr Hafren, and dances and sessions in most of the town's pubs. May.

Tredegar House Festival, Newport, Gwent. A laid-back and enjoyable weekend at the eighteenth-century country house, good for session players and dancers. Mid-May.

Gwyl Ifan, Cardiff. Welsh for "midsummer", the name of a Nantgarw dance is also the title of Wales' biggest and most spectacular dance festival, staged by Cwmni Dawns Werin Canolfan Caerdydd, with hundreds of dancers giving dis-

plays in Cardiff city centre, Cardiff Castle and St Fagans Folk Museum. Late June.

Gwyl Werin y Cnapan, Ffostrasol, Dyfed. The biggest folk event in Wales, hardly known outside the country, has a powerful line-up of bands from Wales and the rest of the Celtic world. Second weekend in July.

Sesiwn Fawr, Dolgellau, Gwynedd. Events indoors and in the streets. Third weekend in July.

Pontardawe International Festival, West Glamorgan – deservedly one of Britain's flagship folk events, with an ambitious line-up of international performers heading for the Swansea Valley town each year. Clever marketing policies and an excellent craft fair have brought local people pouring in as well as the long-distance festival-goers. Third weekend of August.

A number of smaller dance festivals also take place around Wales, including the **Cadi Ha** in Holywell in early May and **Gwyl Hydref** in Caernarfon on the first weekend of October.

messages and social protest, but traditional Welsh music and dance have had the difficult task of fighting back from near-extinction following centuries of political and religious suppression. Unlike their Celtic cousins in Ireland, Scotland and Brittany, folk musicians in Wales have learnt their tunes from books and manuscripts rather than from older generations of players, and unlike the Celtic music boom of the 1970s, bands concentrating on Welsh tunes remained virtually unknown, a situation that has improved markedly in recent decades.

This general lack of direction has meant that outside influences have had a considerable bearing on groups forming to play Welsh music, despite the common elements in the repertoire. Language has also been more of a divider in Wales than it has been in other Celtic countries – rock and folk are both great pillars of the Welsh language, but English-speakers have not received the same encouragement to explore their own folk culture within the Welsh framework.

The preservation and nurturing of Welsh-language songs, customs and traditions is vitally important, but the folklore of English-speaking Gower and south Pembrokeshire and the rich

vein of industrial material from the valleys is actually in much greater danger of disappearing.

HISTORY

The bardic and **eisteddfod** traditions have always played a key role in Welsh culture. Often the **bard**, who held an elevated position in Welsh society, was the non-performing composer, employing a harper and a *datgeiniad*, whose role was to declaim the bard's words. The first eisteddfod appears to have been held in Cardigan in 1176, with contests between bards and poets and between harpers, *crwth*-players (see p.472) and pipers. Henry VIII's **Act of Union** in 1536 was designed to anglicize the country by stamping out Welsh culture and language, and the eisteddfod tradition degenerated over the next two centuries.

The rise of **Nonconformist religion** in the eighteenth and nineteenth centuries (see "History", p.446), with its abhorrence of music, merry-making and dancing, almost sounded the death knell for Welsh traditions already battered by Henry VIII's assault. **Edward Jones**, *Bardd y Brenin* (Bard to the King), observed sorrowfully in the 1780s that Wales, which used to be one of the happiest of countries, "has now become one of the dullest". Folk music only gained some sort of respectability when London-based Welsh people, swept along in a romantic enthusiasm for all things Celtic, revived it at the end of the eighteenth century. As late as the twentieth century, old ladies who knew dance steps would pull the curtains before demonstrating them, in case the neighbours should see.

The **National Eisteddfod Society** was formed in the 1860s, and today, three major week-long events are held every year – the International Eisteddfod at Llangollen in July, the Royal National Eisteddfod in the first week

---

VENUES

In the Dyfed and Gwynedd heartland of the Welsh language, folk music can be heard in many of the same venues that stage rock events. The language is considered more important than musical categories, and the folk club concept is alien to Welsh-speakers, who never saw the need to segregate music that was a natural part of their cultural life. Folk clubs are found in the anglicized areas and only a few of them feature Welsh music. In the south, check for folk in the general programme at the Welsh cultural clubs in the area: *Clwb Ifor Bach* in Womanby Street, Cardiff (☎029/2023 2199); *Clwb y Bont* in Taff Street, Pontypridd, Mid-Glamorgan (☎01443/491424); *Clwb Brynmenyn* in Brynmenyn, Mid-Glamorgan (☎01656/725323); and *Clwb Y Triban*, Penallta Road, Ystrad Mynach, Mid-Glamorgan (☎01443/814491).

REGULAR FOLK VENUES IN SOUTH WALES

St Donats Arts Centre (☎01466/792151), in a delightful fourteenth-century tythe barn at Atlantic College near Llantwit Major, puts on major folk/roots guests as part of its regular programme.

Llantrisant Folk Club, Cross Keys, High Street, Llantrisant, Vale of Glamorgan (☎01443/226892). International guest list mixed with local sessions centred on Welsh tunes. Weekly, Wednesday.

Penarth Labour Club, Glebe Street, Penarth, Vale of Glamorgan. Guitar-oriented, with regular guests. Weekly, Thursday.

Heritage Folk Club, Llantwit Major Rugby Club, Vale of Glamorgan (☎01446/794461). Traditional folk night, with mainly local bands. Weekly, Thursday.

The Hostelry, Llantilio Crossenny, Monmouthshire. Beautiful fourteenth-century pub hosting lively gigs and sessions. Weekly, Thursday.

Four Bars Inn, opposite Cardiff Castle. Big-name international concerts staged by *Taplas* magazine. Monthly, Friday.

Pontardawe Folk Club, *Ivy Bush Hotel*, Brecon Road, Pontardawe, Vale of Neath. Mainstay of the Welsh folk scene, good for anything from very traditional stuff to modern folk-rock. Weekly, Friday.

Boat Inn, Penallt, Monmouthshire. Superbly informal nights in a wonderful pub. Monthly, last Tuesday.

Halfpenny Golf Club, *The Greyhound*, Llanrhidian, Gower (☎01792/850803). Smart clientele rub shoulders with the chunky jumper brigade. Weekly, Sunday.

Mullighan's Bar, St Mary Street, Cardiff. Irish sessions. Twice weekly, Sunday and Tuesday.

REGULAR FOLK VENUES IN NORTH WALES

ECTARC (the European Centre for Traditional and Regional Cultures) in East Street, Llangollen, Denbighshire (☎01978/861514). Regularly stages international concerts.

Theatr Clwyd Cymru, Mold, Flintshire (☎01352/755114). Monthly, first Tuesday.

The Bulkeley Arms, Beaumaris, Anglesey (☎01248/810415). Weekly, Monday.

The London Hotel, Llandudno, Aberconwy (☎01492/876740). Weekly, Sunday.

The Glangasfor, Rhyl, Denbighshire. Weekly, Friday.

The Lex Social Club, Wrexham. Weekly, Thursday.

The Heights, Llanberis, Gwynedd (☎01286/871179). Weekly, Tuesday.

Y Mount Dinas, Llanwnda, Gwynedd. Weekly, Thursday.

of August and the Urdd Eisteddfod, Europe's largest youth festival, at the end of May. The National and the Urdd alternate between north and south Wales.

Because competitions need rules, eisteddfodau have always tended to formalize Welsh culture, and such parameter-defining is naturally alien to the free evolution of traditional song and music. When Nicholas Bennett was compiling his 1896 book *Alawon Fy Nghwlad*, still one of the most important collections of Welsh tunes, he rejected a great deal of good Welsh dance music because it did not conform to the contemporary high-art notion of what Welsh music ought to sound like. Despite this frequently heard criticism, eisteddfodau have played a major role in keeping traditional music, song and dance at the heart of national culture.

THE HARP

Historically the most important instrument in the folk repertoire, the **harp** has been played in Wales since at least the eleventh century, although no instruments survive from the period before the 1700s, and little is really known about the intervening years. The only surviving music is the famous manuscript of **Robert ap Huw**, written about 1614 in a strange tablature that has intrigued music scholars: five scales were used, but no one has yet defined satisfactorily how they should sound. In recent years craftsmen have re-created the *crwth* (a stringed instrument which may have been either plucked or bowed), the *pibgorn* (a reed instrument with a cow's horn for a bell) and the *pibacwd* (a primitive Welsh bagpipe). Some groups have adopted these instruments, but their primitive design and performance means they rarely blend happily with modern instruments.

The simple early harps were ousted in the seventeenth century by the arrival of the **triple harp**, with its complicated string arrangement (two parallel rows sounding the same note, with a row of accidentals between them), giving it a unique, rich sound. The nineteenth-century swing towards classical concert music saw the invasion of the large **chromatic pedal harps** that still dominate today, but the triple, always regarded as the traditional Welsh harp, was kept alive by gypsy musicians who preferred to play something portable. A notable, and unique, Welsh harp performance that's well worth catching is the **Cerdd Dant**, where the harpist leads with one tune, accompanying soloists and groups take a counter-tune, and they all end up together on the final note.

MUSICIANS

Undoubtedly the most influential player of recent years is the triple harpist **Robin Huw Bowen**, who has revived interest in the instrument with appearances throughout Europe and North America, and has done tremendous work making unpublished manuscripts of Welsh dance music widely available through his own publishing company. In north Wales, the current pacemaker is **Twm Morys**, either with or without his band **Bob Delyn a'r Ebillion**, whose blend of contemporary Welsh and Breton influences veers over into the rock field: they have even won admiration from *Folk Roots* magazine in England. One of Wales' most well-known harpists, **Elinor Bennett** (coincidentally the wife of Plaid Cymru leader Dafydd Wigley), has been much in the ascendant of late, even being accorded the kudos of playing for rock supergroup Catatonia both on record and live.

New bands like **Y Moniars** are making a strong showing with young audiences in the north, with a raucous electric bass-and-drums approach to Welsh-language song; the father of Welsh folk, politician/songwriter **Dafydd Iwan**, remains as hugely popular and prolific as ever with his charismatic performances, and songwriter **Meic Stevens** is still producing good work on the borderlines of folk and acoustic rock. Musician **Tudur Morgan** has been involved in some notable collaborations, including working with Irish musician/producer Donal Lunny on *Branwen*, a song and music cycle based on the Welsh Mabinogion legend.

Singer/harpist **Sian James**, from Llanerfyl in mid-Wales, has produced two albums so far which have won the acclaim of Welsh- and English-speakers alike. One pacesetter among the women is **Julie Murphy**, born in Essex but now a fluent Welsh speaker, whose Welsh-language work alongside Breton singer **Brigitte Kloareg** in the band **Saith Rhyfeddod** has led to a promising bilingual collaboration with young English hurdy-gurdy expert **Nigel Eaton**. Another quality Welsh-language singer is Cardiff-based **Heather Jones**, who works solo and with fiddlers Mike Lease and Jane Ridout in the trio **Hin Deg**, who blend Welsh song with Welsh/Irish fiddle music.

RECORD COMPANIES

Cob Records at 1–3 Brittannia Terrace, Porthmadog, Gwynedd LL49 9NA (☎01766/512170) has an extensive mail-order business. The simplest way for international customers to pay is with Visa or MasterCard credit cards.

Cwmni Fflach at Llys-y-Coed, Heol Dinbych-y-Pysgod, Aberteifi, Ceredigion SA43 3AH (☎01239/614691) is a relative newcomer, with albums by Mabsant and Saith Rhyfeddod among its folk releases.

Sain, the major Welsh recording company, can boast a good number of folk albums and artists in its catalogue, available from Canolfan Sain, Llanddwrog, Gwynedd LL54 5TG (☎01286/831111, fax 831497, www.sain.wales.com).

Steam Pie, at 17 The Grove, Pontllanfraith, Gwent (☎01495/222173), has released albums by The Chartists, Huw and Tony Williams, The Milkshakes and other south Wales-based English-language artists.

RECORDINGS

Aberjaber *Aberjaber and Aberdaujaber* (Sain). Two albums by a defunct but extremely competent band formed by Cardiff jazz/roots/world musician Peter Stacey, Swansea harpist Delyth Evans and Oxford music graduate Stevie Wishart (viol and hurdy-gurdy), who experimented with Welsh and original instrumental music.

Ar Log *OIVIV* (Sain). Compilation CD of the last two studio albums.

Calennig Dwr *Glan* (Sain). Rocky Welsh dance sets and songs tinged with Breton and Galician influences.

Carreg Lafar *Hyn* (Sain). 1998 blast from this Cardiff-based Celtic folk outfit that was nominated for a US Grammy award.

Cilmeri *Cilmeri* (Sain). Long-defunct but well-respected north Wales six-piece, the first band to put a harder Irish-style edge on the music of Wales.

Delyth Evans *Delta* (Sain). Solo album of Celtic harp music by Aberjaber's harpist.

Dafydd Iwan ac Ar Log *Yma O Hyd* (Sain). Compilation CD of two great mid-Eighties albums which celebrated legendary joint tours around Wales by these performers.

Gwerinos *Seilam* and *Lleuad Llawn* (Sain). Two fine albums from Dolgellau-based folk funsters.

Sian James *Distaw* (Sain). Original, modern and traditional songs on harp and keyboard with spine-tingling vocals.

Mabsant and Eiry Palfrey *Mabsanta* (Sain). Live show by band and actress celebrating a Welsh Christmas in song and humorous verse.

Y Moniars *I'r Carnifal* (Sain). Debut album from this upfront young band.

Tudur Morgan *Branwen* (Sain). Project of songs and music based on The Mabinogion legend.

Pedwar Yn Y Bar *Byth Adra* (Sain). Four-piece, also now defunct, which arose from the ashes of Cilmeri and added American and other international influences to Welsh music.

Saith Rhyfeddod *Cico Nyth Cacwn* (Fflach). 1994 album by bagpipers Jonathan Shorland and Ceri Matthews.

Meic Stevens *Er Cof am Blant y Cwm* and *Mihangel* (Crai). The songwriter's most recent albums (1993 and 1998).

Robin Huw Bowen *Telyn Berseiniol fy Nghwlad* (Teires). Self-produced CD of dance music and airs for the triple harp.

Traditional Plygain parties *Carolau Plygain* (Sain). Few albums are available of Welsh "source" performances (the older generation who handed down their songs), but this Welsh Folk Museum-produced album of Christmas carols from mid-Wales is a gem.

Close-harmony songs in three or four parts were a feature of life in mid-Wales, where the *plygain* carol-singing tradition still survives at Christmas. Small parties of carol singers, each with their own repertoire, would sing in church from midnight through until the break of dawn on Christmas morning. The group **Plethyn**, which was formed in the 1970s to adapt this style to traditional and modern Welsh songs, still perform occasionally, and member Linda Healey was also involved in the *Branwen* project.

Wales' busiest band is probably **Calennig Dwr**, from Llantrisant in Mid-Glamorgan, who blend fiery Welsh dance sets with English-language songs from the Valleys and Gower. They tour regularly in Europe, America and New Zealand and have also helped to popularize Welsh dance with a punchy collection of *twmpath* tunes and upfront calling from **Patricia Carron-Smith**.

From the same town come Welsh-language band **Mabsant**, who have also travelled the world with their own tours in the States and Europe, and British Council tours to the Far East. Their strength lies in the powerful voice of **Siwsann George**, also a fine solo singer, and soulful sax work from **Steve Whitehead**.

The Hennessys, led by broadcaster, TV personality and songwriter Frank Hennessy, still have a huge and well-deserved middle-of-the-road following in the Cardiff area, twenty years after joining the procession of Irish-influenced trios on the folk circuit.

Huw and Tony Williams, from Brynmawr in the Gwent Valleys, are popular names on the British folk-club circuit whose following, like other English-language performers, is greater away from home than it is inside Wales. Huw's songwriting – notably songs like *Rosemary's Baby* – has been embraced by Fairport Convention and a string of other big-name performers, but he's best known in Wales for his Eisteddfod-winning clog dancing. Cardiff female trio **The Milkshakes** perform a cappella versions of pop hits.

DANCE

After a long period of religious suppression, **traditional dance** in Wales has been revived over the past fifty years. It plays a big part in the folk culture of Wales, and the top teams are exciting and professional in their approach. Dances written in recent years, often for eisteddfod competitions, have been quickly absorbed into the repertoire. **Cwmni Dawns Werin Canolfan Caerdydd**, Cardiff's official dance team, have taken their spectacular displays abroad – Texas and Japan are among the many trips they've made in their first 25 years. Their musicians are recommended as well. **Dawnswyr Nantgarw**, from the Taff Vale village that was the source of the country's romantic and raunchy fair dances, have turned Welsh dance into a theatrical art form: concise, perfectly drilled and very showy. **Dawnswyr Gwerin Pen-y-Fai**, from Bridgend, have an adventurous band full of good session players, while Anglesey-based **Ffidl Ffadl** also boast an excellent musician in fiddler **Huw Roberts**, formerly with the early 1980s bands **Cilmeri** and **Pedwar Yn Y Bar**. Dawnswyr Brynmawr also have a capable band who play for *twmpath* dances as **Taro Tant**. In the northeast, **Dawnswyr Delyn** are a competent and enjoyable troupe.

POP MUSIC IN WALES

The historic lack of international pop artists to emerge from Wales – long blamed on the music-industry dominance of London-based labels and media – has changed utterly in the past few years, at least for groups working in the English language. The growing profile of the **Manic Street Preachers**, who turned up on every "best of" list at the end of the twentieth century, spawned a much overdue interest in contemporary Welsh rock, as London A&R men descended on Cardiff and Newport in search of the next big thing. Bands like the **Super Furry Animals**, **Catatonia** and the **Stereophonics** were the main beneficiaries of what became rather ironically known as the "Cool Cymru" phenomenon. In some ways, this – like all record company-driven trends – has long since peaked, leaving a huge number of newer bands struggling hard for recognition. Undoubtedly, though, Welsh rock is taken a great deal more seriously than it was even ten years ago, and the sheer quality of new acts is remarkable for such a small country.

Many of the surging Welsh rockers hail from the country's anglicized southeast and speak little or none of the native language. Some profess support for Welsh and there is a relatively thriving scene in Welsh-language rock throughout the country. With rare exceptions, however, this does not generally make it into the mainstream and, consequently, many Welsh-language bands have turned their backs on commercial success, launching Welsh record labels and helping to stoke a less obvious, but perhaps just as exciting, buzz.

ENGLISH-LANGUAGE WELSH POP

The biggest, most enduring name in English-language Welsh pop is undoubtedly Sixties sex symbol **Tom Jones**, still pulling crowds around the world and still enough of a star to headline the spectacular 1999 **Voice of a Nation concert** in Cardiff Bay, to celebrate the opening of the National Assembly. Hailing from Treforest in south Wales, Jones' slick presentation and booming voice has seen him turn his love of black American soul music into an enduring career. Similarly, Cardiff-born singer **Shirley Bassey**, the daughter of a West Indian seaman, has carved out a hugely successful career since the mid-Fifties. In 1964 she sang the theme song to the James Bond movie *Goldfinger*, and in 1972 scored a major American hit with *Diamonds Are Forever*. Although these days records are rare, she still performs, most notably clambering into a stunning frock made of a giant Welsh flag both for the Voice of a Nation concert and the opening ceremony of the 1999 Rugby World Cup in her home city.

Cardiff musician-turned-record producer **Dave Edmunds**, whose first band Love Sculpture scored a UK hit in 1968, has had his hands on many a hit record since – both as a producer and a solo performer – during the Seventies and Eighties. Classically trained pianist **John Cale**, born in Garnant near Ammanford, went to America in 1963 and found fame with the **Velvet Underground**, one of the most influential avant-garde rock bands of the Sixties. He has since recorded solo and, more recently, has worked with the reformed Velvet Underground.

Other Sixties successes were **Amen Corner** with their 1968 hit *Bend Me Shape Me*. Amen Corner's singer, Andy Fairweather Low, went on to solo fame with the song *Wide Eyed and Legless*, a hit in 1975. Swansea's psychedelic-tinged rock outfit **Badfinger** had a brief flirtation with chart success in the late Sixties, whilst at a similar time, progressive rockers **Man** courted attention. Man are still going today after over 25 years and thirteen LPs. The rock band **Racing Car** also managed to sustain two hit LPs during the early Seventies, thanks mainly to the success of their single *They Shoot Horses, Don't They?*

In the 1980s, Welsh rock music was personified by Rhyl's rabble-rousing rock fundamentalists **The Alarm**, fronted by Mike Peters, who relaunched his solo career early in 1994. The band rode the stadium-rock wave of the mid-Eighties, their anthemic folk-punk sound bringing huge UK and American success and a career that spanned seven albums in eight years.

Rock ballad singer **Bonnie Tyler** achieved great commercial success from the late Seventies onwards, with a style described as that of a female Rod Stewart. In the mid-

Eighties she successfully teamed up with Meatloaf collaborator Jim Steinman. To a lesser extent, the New Romantic synth pop of **Visage** – with the big 1981 UK hit *Fade to Grey* – put a Welsh act in the pop charts, and later in the Eighties, the gentle pop sounds of **Scritti Politti** enjoyed some success. Other notable bands to emerge from Wales in the mid-Eighties were dreamy guitar popsters **The Darling Buds**, fronted by Andrea Lewis, and the whimsical, independently minded **Pooh Sticks**, whose upbeat guitar twang eventually saw them signed to RCA in 1992.

Possibly the most surprising – some would say ludicrous – Welsh success story of the Eighties was Fifties rock'n'roll impersonator **Shakin' Stevens**. As the name suggests, he mimicked Elvis' rubber-legged dance routine, and by covering old rock'n'roll standards and writing original songs that sounded like rock'n' roll standards, he sold millions of records, cashing in on Fifties musical nostalgia.

Most recently, south Wales rock nihilists the **Manic Street Preachers**, hailing from the small town of Blackwood in the Sirhowy Valley, have become the most successful Welsh band ever. Few would have predicted this from their early career of sneering bedsit-punk-meets-rock, topped with inflammatory statements such as "I laughed when John Lennon got shot", from the single *Motown Junk*. Released in 1991 on London-based independent Heavenly label, the record saw them courted by the big labels, eventually signing to Sony and producing a string of UK hit singles – notably *Motorcycle Emptiness*, the militant Welsh answer to Bruce Springsteen's *Born to Run* – and four LPs. It was the mysterious 1995 disappearance, and presumed suicide, of fractured, anorexic guitarist Richey James, that changed everything for the Manics. They returned as a three-piece, storming the charts worldwide with their anthemic album, *Everything Must Go* (1996), which spawned the huge hit singles *A Design for Life*, *Kevin Carter*, *Australia* and the title track. Their follow-up album, *This Is My Truth, Tell Me Yours* (1998) only continued the progress to megastardom, and included their first UK number one single, *If You Tolerate This, Then Your Children Will Be Next*. These weighty, faintly pompous, titles show how seriously they take their role as Wales' answer to Ireland's self-important stadium-rockers, U2.

By the time the Manics' star was firmly in the ascendant, the hunt was on for new Welsh talent. The now legendary Welsh bands compilation album, *Dial M for Merthyr* (1995), showcased the Manics alongside many who subsequently became huge: most obviously the Super Furry Animals, Catatonia and the Stereophonics. If there's anything that links these and other Welsh bands, apart from their country of origin, it is a tendency towards clever, zeitgeist lyrics, an assuredly Welsh loquaciousness and delight in the possibilities of language. The **Super Furry Animals**, whose fusion of Seventies psychedelia with Nineties

clubland quirkiness created a niche all of their own, have been perhaps the most informed: their three albums to date, mixing both Welsh and English, are a delight. From poignant ballads to thumping, raw rock, they have proved to be masters of many genres.

Cerys Matthews' talent for producing intelligent lyrics has also had much to do with the success of **Catatonia**, the band that she fronts (and utterly dominates). Hitting contemporary observations with unerring sweet perfection has thrown out some fine pop moments: from the pregnancy-test tale of *You've Got a Lot to Answer For* to their first huge hits, *Road Rage*

SELECTED RELEASES

The following records of English-language Welsh bands should be available at most high-street record shops in the UK.

The Alarm – including a live album and a singles collection, The Alarm released seven LPs between 1984 and 1991, including those recommended here.

Declaration (IRS). Debut LP full of catchy rock songs, establishing a simplistic formula they rarely veered from.

Strength (IRS). Second LP and another big hit.

Standards (IRS). Compilation LP from 1990.

Raw (IRS). Last LP, released in 1991, with a Welsh-language version released on Crai Records. The sound of a band ready to split.

Manic Street Preachers

Motown Junk (Heavenly). Essential first single. Total in-your-face punk rock.

Generation Terrorists (Sony). Debut double LP. Rock ballads meet punk ferocity and anti-establishment politics. A great rock record.

Gold Against the Soul (Sony). Second, more mature and darker LP. Straight-up rock with some rousing choruses. *From Despair to Where* – also released as a single – is a classic.

Everything Must Go (Sony). The most mainstream offering so far, spawning massive hits in the shape of its title song, *A Design for Life* and *Kevin Carter*.

This Is My Truth, Tell Me Yours (Sony). More gutsy anthems and a slightly more wistful tone than the previous album.

K Klass

Universal (Deconstruction/Parlophone). Debut LP from Wrexham dance act/remix team, featuring ex-Smiths guitarist Johnny Marr on one track.

Super Furry Animals

Fuzzy Logic (Creation). Highly acclaimed debut album containing the New Wave charge of *God! Show Me Magic*, the *West Coast Hometown Unicorn* and the jaunty, poppy hit *Something for the Weekend*.

Radiator (Creation). Rockier, harder follow-up album that didn't go down quite so well.

Guerilla (Creation). Altogether brighter and more accessible album, includes the stirring hit *Fire in my Heart*.

60ft Dolls

The Big 3 (Indolent). A fine debut album from Newport's pop-meets-garage-band newbies.

Joya Magica (Geffen). Fine album sadly released after the band had split up.

Dub War

Enemy Maker (Earache). Top dub-metal sounds.

Catatonia

Way Beyond Blue (Blanco y Negro). The first long-player, awash with critical acclaim on the back of its first single, *You've Got a Lot to Answer For*.

International Velvet (WEA). Wonderful follow-up, full of big hits and the new Welsh singalong anthem in the shape of its title track.

Equally Cursed and Blessed (WEA). More whimsical collection, with Cerys' lyrics getting intensely personal.

Which Says What?

Scardiff (Round Records). Jazz-inspired, cynical hip-hop from the underbelly of the capital city.

and *Mulder and Scully*. Catatonia probably benefited from their years of obscurity, ligging drunkenly around the Welsh circuit, for they are a mature crew, albeit one that is uncomfortably reliant on Cerys' strength and sanity – neither of which can be taken for granted in the dog-eat-dog world of rock stardom. As the pressures mount, they may well call it a day before very long – so be it, for they'll still leave one of the finest albums of the 1990s in the shape of *International Velvet* (1998), whose title track, with its verses in Welsh and its roustabout English chorus of "every day, when I wake up, I thank the Lord I'm Welsh" has become an unofficial national anthem.

More lyrical dexterity, combined with clean-cut guitar chords, are the hallmarks of the **Stereophonics**, three lads from Cwmaman in the Cynon Valley. Their rise has been meteoric – from highly competent pub-rockers to one of the country's favourite bands in less than a year. Their first album, *Word Gets Around* (1997) is jam-packed with classic bursts of three-minute genius, including hit singles *More Life In a Tramp's Vest*, *Local Boy in the Photograph* and *A Thousand Trees*. The follow-up, *Performance and Cocktails* (1999), includes their biggest hit to date, the fast and fabulous *The Bartender and the Thief.*

As the Welshpop bandwagon rolled by, on jumped many new acts, only to find themselves unceremoniously dumped by their record companies shortly afterwards when hoped-for sales failed to materialize. This was the fate of Newport's **60ft Dolls**, who churned out lusty, unreconstructed pop-rock, and the sublimely surreal **Gorky's Zygotic Mynci** from Carmarthen, hotly tipped for imminent stardom for years, but so far still waiting for it to happen. Although the Dolls are no more, Gorky's plough on, with a core of loyal – some would say fanatical – aficionados. Other south Wales outfits to watch out for include guitar popsters **Scuba**, mainstay of new Cardiff label FFVinyl, the chilled Celticism of **Dragonfall** and Rhondda rockers **Picture the Beautiful**, who scored a minor US hit with *Supermodel* in early 1999.

Though most of Wales' most successful rock has sprung from the anglicized south of the country, exponents from elsewhere have included Aberystwyth's larky, laddy **Murry the Hump**, named by Blur's Damon Albarn as one of the best new bands around, the sweetly sinister

WELSH-LANGUAGE RECORD LABELS

For an update of these labels' activities, contact:

Ankst Records, 106 Cowbridge Rd East, Cardiff CF1 9DX (☎029/2023 5453, fax 2023 5199).

Crai Records, Canolfan Sain, Llandwrog, Llandwrog, Gwynedd (☎01286/831111, fax 831497, *www.sain.wales.com*).

Cwmni Fflach Records, Llys-y-Coed, Heol Dinbych y Pysgod, Aberteifi, Ceredigion SA43 3AH (☎01239/614691, fax 614680, *www.westwales.co.uk/fflach*).

Ofn Records, Ein Hoff Le, Llanfaelog, Ty Croes, Gwynedd (☎01407/810742).

crooning of Snowdonia's **Melys**, and **Big Leaves**; the latter made considerable inroads into the Welsh language scene as Beganifs, but are now turning to the wider possibilities of singing in English.

But Welsh music isn't all guitars or misty, acid-fuelled weirdness. The thriving **dance music** scene, in all its fragmented glory, has a number of notable exponents. Trashcore colonialists **Dub War** hail from Newport, with their brand of dub-metal, combining trip-hop and hints of jazz with metallist basslines, a potent combination not a million miles from the sound of **Which says What?**, an outfit that grew out of former Cardiff heroes Shapeshifter. Rural west Wales is the base for dub gurus **Zion Train**, whose classic spliffed-up remakes of old new wave tracks have won many friends, and brought in whole posses of Welsh-based DJ talent in the rural parts of the country.

WELSH-LANGUAGE ROCK

Whilst English-language Welsh bands have usually enjoyed success by making their nationality an irrelevance, Welsh-language bands have purposely expounded their strong national identity. As a consequence, a unique, self-propagating Welsh-language rock scene has developed, albeit with a widespread lack of major commercial success. However, boundaries are becoming increasingly blurred: many bands choose to sing in both Welsh and English, and not for expedient purposes, but simply because that is the way most of their members use both languages. Of the bands mentioned above, the

Super Furry Animals, Catatonia, Gorky's Zygotyic Mynci, Big Leaves and Melys all regularly use Welsh in their songs.

The roots of this thriving, youthful and innovative scene owe much to a musical revolution whose shock waves emanated not from Cardiff or Newport, but from London. The **punk** explosion of 1976 kicked over many of rock's statues, partly thanks to the anarchic fervour of London bands like the Sex Pistols and The Clash (who made it to the south Wales town of Caerphilly on the ill-fated Anarchy Tour in 1976), but also by virtue of its strong DIY ethic.

Just as London-based labels like Rough Trade, Small Wonder and Cherry Red released records that major labels wouldn't, punk bands in Wales began putting out their own music as well. **Trynau Coch**, for instance, set up their own label, Recordiau Coch, attracting attention from the UK music press in the process.

It was in the Eighties, though, that the home-grown Welsh-language pop scene really began to consolidate itself. In 1983, Caernarfon punk band **Anhrefn** (Disorder) set up **Recordiau Anhrefn**, churning out what it called "dodgy compilations of up-and-coming left-field weirdo Welsh bands". This enthusiasm is a trademark of the Welsh-language rock scene. In fact, throughout the Eighties, any band that couldn't get some sort of record deal would simply press their own vinyl and sell their records at gigs. The market for the music was small, but the bands made up for it with their have-a-go attitude.

The scene was developing nicely, and in the early Eighties, Radio One DJ **John Peel** – to many, the standard-bearer for underground pop in the UK – became aware of the growing number of Welsh-language bands and began playing their records on air and inviting them in for sessions. This introduced Welsh music to a Europe-wide audience and proved an important catalyst to new Welsh bands. Peel still features occasional Welsh-language bands on his evening Radio One shows.

By the Nineties, Welsh-language pop music had established a solid infrastructure of bands, labels and venues. One of the most prolific, eclectic and innovative of these labels is **Ankst**. Started as a part-time venture in 1988, the label is now a full-time concern releasing Welsh-language pop of varied styles – best seen in their fantastically scabrous compilation albums,

including *S4C Makes Me Want To Smoke Crack*, which included tracks by Catatonia and professional Welsh weirdos **Rheinallt H Rowlands** and **Ectogram**. Ankst is also the home of multilingual dub-meets-punk twosome **Llwybr Llaethog**, and wild Welsh-language rappers, **Y Tystion**, whose album *Shrug Off Your Complex* is full of hilarious observation.

Another major promoter of Welsh-language pop is the Caernarfon-based **Crai Records**, a subsidiary of the more folk-oriented **Sain Records**. The label began life in 1989, and its current roster includes the back catalogues of original Welsh punks Anhrefn, folk-roots band Bob Delyn (see "Musicians", p.472), ex-Alarm vocalist **Mike Peters**, Celt rockers **Fernhill** and the Welsh outpourings of **Big Leaves**. Thier greatest achievement, though, has been the stunning **Crai Tecno** compilations, which have showcased some of Wales' harder-edged dance music.

Other home-grown labels promoting Welsh-language bands include the **Fflach** label in Aberteifi (Cardigan), Dyfed, with their subsidiary **Semtexx** specifically for heavy-rock bands. And in Ty Croes, Gwynedd, there's the **Ofn** label, releasing records by experimental, industrial Welsh-language innovators **Plant Bach Ofnus** (Timid Little Children) and the pop-oriented, electronic **Eirin Peryglus** (Perilous Plums). Finally, the new **R-Bennig** label is the home of trippy funksters **PicNic**.

The grassroots Welsh **gig circuit** is also healthy, with a lively local pub and club scene. The student unions of Lampeter, Bangor, Cardiff, Swansea or Glamorgan at Treforest universities also regularly put on Welsh bands. Other notable venues are *TJs* in Newport, *Sam's Bar* in Cardiff, the *Ship and Castle* in Caernarfon, *Gassy Jacks* in Cardiff, and the *Tivoli* in Buckley, near Mold. Welsh-language pop bands can also be found at the **National Eisteddfod**, although this is dominated by more traditional Welsh music.

Welsh-language bands have also been forging links in **Europe**. Bands like Anhrefn, U Thant, Fflaps, Ffa Coffi Pawb and Beganifs/Big Leaves have all taken Welsh-language pop to an international audience. Brittany and Prague have been particularly fertile grounds for Welsh pop and rock, and many Welsh-language bands have eagerly taken their music abroad without compromising their lyrical stance.

WELSH-LANGUAGE BANDS

Most major towns in Wales have a Welsh Shop (*Siop Gymraeg*), which will often stock an extensive Welsh-language music selection. Cob Records in Porthmadog (☎01766/512170) and Bangor (☎01248/353020) is also worth checking out, as is Spillers in The Hayes, Cardiff (☎029/2038 3848).

ANKST RECORDS

Various artists: *A.P. Elvis, the Fifth Anniversary Collection*. Featuring 15 tracks from the likes of Catatonia, Ian Rush, Ffa Coffi Pawb, Gorky's Zygotic Mynci, Fflaps, Beganifs and Datblygu. A great introduction to modern Welsh-language pop.

Gorky's Zygotic Mynci: *Tatay*. Debut LP from this young Carmarthen band, loved by John Cale and the UK music press. A strange but compelling brew of gentle balladeering and noisy guitars.

Various artists: *O'R Gad*. Another great Ankst collection, with 18 tracks.

Various artists: *Da! Da!* 1999 compilation, featuring the full range of Welsh music, including the punchy dub of Llwybr Llaethog, whose own album, *Mad!*, is also on Ankst.

Y Tystion: *Shrug off your Complex*. Clever, often bile-drenched, lyrical effort by the Welsh-language rappers.

CRAI RECORDS

Distributed by independent record distributors Revolver, so available in most independent stores and mainstream record shops throughout the UK.

Anhrefn: *Rhedeg I Paris*. The godfathers of Welsh-language rock, with an LP produced by Sex Pistols producer Dave Goodman. Raw and noisy.

Bob Delyn: *Gwbade Bach Cochlyd*. Recent release from one of Wales' most popular folk roots acts.

Mike Peters: *Back into the System*. Comeback single for the ex-Alarm vocalist, joined by all-Welsh band The Poets. It sees him taking a more acoustic path than previously.

Various artists: *Crai Tecno* and *Crai Tecno 2*. Compilation discs featuring new Welsh talent WwzZ, Acid Casuals and Plant o Wyddelwern.

Hen Wlad Fy Mamau: Wonderful 1995 sample of some of Wales' spunkiest current music-makers in a collection that ranges from steaming trip-hop, through lazy world dance beats to soulful soloists and Celtic harmonies.

OFN RECORDS

Eirin Peryiglus: *Noeth*. Electronic dance/pop music, released in 1992.

R-BENNIG RECORDS

Various artists: *Egnileniwm*. The full range of this distinctly esoteric label, from cutesy to just plain crazy, on this 1999 compilation.

PicNic: *PicNic*. Debut CD from this trippy Welsh-language dance act.

BOOKS

Where possible, we've given publishers in both the UK and US, in that order. If only one publisher is listed, the country of publication is included; if just a publisher is listed, the book is published in both the UK and US by the same company. Some of the books listed here are published by small local presses, and you're unlikely to find them outside Wales. However, you'll often be able to pick up rarer titles (and many of those listed here as out of print) by scouring independent or secondhand bookshops in Wales – Hay-on-Wye (see p.221) is particularly good for the latter.

TRAVEL AND IMPRESSIONS

Dannie Abse, *Journals from the Antheap* (o/p, UK). Abse's prose, more accessible than his poetry, succeeds in being wry, serious and provocative at the same time. Much of this volume deals with journeys in his native Wales, which he describes with verve and tongue-in-cheek humour.

George Borrow, *Wild Wales* (Gomer Press, UK). Highly entertaining, easy-to-read account of the author's walking tour of Wales in 1854 which says as much about Borrow and his ego as it does about Wales and the Welsh, who he treats with benign condescension.

Giraldus Cambrensis, *The Journey Through Wales* and *The Description of Wales* (Penguin). Two witty and frank books in one volume, written in Latin by the quarter-Welsh clergyman after his 1188 tour around Wales recruiting for the Third Crusade with Archbishop Baldwin of Canterbury. Both superb vehicles for Gerald of Wales' learned ruminations and unreserved opinions, *The Journey* breaks up the seven-week tour "through our rough, remote and inaccessible countryside" with anecdotes and ecclesiastical point-scoring, while *The Description* covers rural life and the finer and less praiseworthy aspects of the Welsh character, summing up with "you may never find anyone worse than a bad Welshman, but you will certainly never find anyone better than a good one".

Tony Curtis (ed), *Wales: The Imagined Nation* (o/p, UK, US). A wonderfully varied selection of essays and wry poetry on a great diversity of topics, including writers such as R.S. Thomas and Dylan Thomas, together with the representation of Plaid Cymru in Welsh and British media, Wales in the movies, images of Welsh women and the country's indigenous theatre. Learned, often funny, and extremely rich.

Daniel Defoe, *A Tour Through the Whole Island of Great Britain* (Penguin, UK). Classic travelogue opening a window onto Britain in the 1720s, with twenty pages on Wales.

Trevor Fishlock, *Wales and the Welsh* and *Talking of Wales – A Companion to Wales and the Welsh* (o/p, UK). These vivacious outsider's guides to living in Wales from the ex-Welsh correspondent of the London *Times* newspaper are rather dated now, but often found in secondhand stores. Both books touch on folklore, humour and politics, and paint an engaging picture of a nation perennially trying to define itself.

Heini Gruffudd, *Real Wales* (Y Lolfa, UK). An up-to-date, glossy but slim inventory of the country, taking in history and government, popular culture and a smattering of the Welsh language.

Jeremy Moore and Nigel Jenkins, *Wales, The Lie of the Land* (Gomer Press, UK). A gorgeous, glossy tome that combines the luscious photography of Jeremy Moore (often seen in the Wild Wales postcard series) and the musings of poet Nigel Jenkins. Spirited, passionate and a fine souvenir of contemporary Wales.

Jan Morris, *Wales: Epic Views of a Small Country* (a rewrite of her earlier *The Matter of Wales*) (Viking; Penguin). Prolific half-Welsh travel writer Jan Morris immerses herself in the country that she evidently loves. Highly partisan and fiercely nationalistic, the book combs over the origins of the Welsh character and describes the people and places of Wales with precision and affection. A magnificent introduction to a diverse, and occasionally perverse, nation.

H.V. Morton, *In Search of Wales* (Methuen, UK). Learned, lively and typically enthusiastic snapshots of Welsh life in the 1930s. A companion volume to his *In Search of England*.

Chris Musson, *Wales from the Air* (Royal Commission on the Ancient & Historical Mounuments of Wales, UK). Fascinating tour of the country via aerial photography and accompanying text, focusing on its historical development from pre-history to post-industry.

Thomas Pennant, *A Tour in Wales* (Gwask Carreg Gwalch, UK). First published in 1773, the stories from Pennant's horseback tour helped foster the Romantic enthusiasm for Wales' rugged landscapes.

Pamela Petro, *Travels in an Old Tongue* (HarperCollins, UK). An American woman comes to Wales to study, is bewitched by the place, attempts to learn Welsh and then sets off on a wild global pursuit of Welsh enclaves and speakers from Japan to Norway, Germany and Patagonia. Funny, informative and extremely perceptive about the language and its wider cultural significance.

Peter Sager, *Wales* (Pallas Athene). Not so much a travel guide as a 400-page celebratory essay on Wales, and especially its people, by a German convert to the cause of all things Welsh. A passionate and fabulously detailed book.

Meic Stephens, *A Most Peculiar People: Quotations About Wales and the Welsh* (University of Wales, UK). Fascinating and varied volume of quotations going back to the century before Christ and up to 2000. As a portrait of the nation, with all of its frustrating idiosyncrasies and endearing foibles, it is a superb example. Most tellingly, it is easy to see how the typical English attitude of sneering at the Welsh is rooted way back in history.

Edward Thomas, *Wales* (o/p). Lyrical and literary ponderings on the Welsh, and harsh put-downs on the English. Thomas' grandiloquent opinions, wrapped and couched in his assured and poetical English, are often maddening, but never dull.

George Thomas, *My Wales* (o/p). Glossy, ponderous coffee-table tome with selections of other writings and the musings of the ex-House of Commons Speaker as well. Fabulous photographs by Lord Snowdon are the main attraction in a book that's better as a souvenir than as a guide.

HISTORY, SOCIETY AND CULTURE

Jane Aaron et al (ed), *Our Sisters' Land: The Changing Identities of Women in Wales* (University of Wales, UK). A series of challenging and well-written essays that delve deep into male-dominated Welsh society, from the home to the political system. Includes personal testimonies and some startling facts about just how entrenched bigotry still is within much of the Welsh establishment.

Leslie Alcock, *Arthur's Britain* (Penguin; Viking). Info-laden assemblage of all archeological and written evidence on the shadowy centuries after the Roman occupation of Britain.

David Berry, *Wales and Cinema: The First Hundred Years* (University of Wales). Thorough examination of this small country's contribution to the big screen, both in terms of stars, directors and writers and its frequent role as subject and setting. From the sublime – some of the superb recent young movies kick-started by S4C – to the ridiculous – Hollywood's take on Wales for blockbusters like *How Green Was My Valley*.

Richard Booth, *My Kingdom of Books* (Y Lolfa, UK). Typically robust account autobiography by the man who made Hay-on-Wye the world's biggest secondhand bookshop. Amongst the self-deification is some interesting stuff on his tussles with authority and his semi-serious declaration of Hay as an independent country.

Julian Cope, *The Modern Antiquarian* (Thorsons, UK). Huge, bright tome detailing ex-Teardrop Explodes singer Cope's take on megalithic Britain, with a great gazetteer of hundreds of sites, including many in Wales. Intelligent, provocative and full of fabulous pictures.

Janet Davies, *The Welsh Language* (University of Wales). The most up-to-date history and assessment of Europe's oldest living language. Packed full of readable information, together with plans and maps showing the demographic and geographic spread of Welsh over the ages.

John Davies, *A History of Wales* (Penguin). Exhaustive run through Welsh history and culture from the earliest inhabitants to the late 1980s, reassessing numerous oft-quoted "facts" along the way. Translated from the original 1990 Welsh-language edition, this is clearly written and very readable, but, at 700 pages, it's hardly concise.

Alice Thomas Ellis, *A Welsh Childhood* (Collins Educational, UK). Wonderfully whimsical reminiscences of growing up in north Wales. Welsh legends and folk tales form a large part of the backdrop, fermenting excitedly in the young imagination of the popular novelist.

Gwynfor Evans, *Land of My Fathers* and *Welsh Nation Builders* (Y Lolfa, UK). Plaid Cymru's elder statesman first produced the former massive tome in Welsh, translating it into English for publication over twenty years ago. As a thorough and impassioned history, it's hard to beat, although the political viewpoint of the author is always apparent. The latter work engagingly assesses sixty of the greatest contributors to Welsh nationhood.

Geoffrey of Monmouth, *History of the Kings of Britain* (Penguin). First published in 1136, this is the basis of almost all Arthurian legend. Writers throughout Europe and beyond used Geoffrey's unreliable history as the basis of a complex corpus of myth.

P.H. Jeffery, *Ghosts, Legends and Lore of Wales* (Old Orchard Press, UK). Excellent, slim and low-cost – if rambling – introduction to Welsh mythology.

Philip Jenkins, *A History of Modern Wales 1536–1990* (Addison Wesley Longman; Pearson Education). Magnificently thorough book, placing Welsh history in its British and European contexts. Unbiased and rational appraisal of events and the struggle to preserve Welsh consciousness, with enough detail to make it of valuable academic interest and sufficient good humour to make it easily readable.

J. Graham Jones, *The History of Wales* (University of Wales, UK). The best step forward from our "Historical Framework" section (pp.441–452), this concise, easy-paced overview of Welsh life comes with a welcome bias towards social history.

John Matthews, *A Celtic Reader* (Thorsons). Selections of original texts, scholarly articles and stories on Celtic legend and scholarship. Sections on the druids, Celtic Britain and The Mabinogion. Assumes a deep interest on the part of the reader.

Elizabeth Mavor, *The Ladies of Llangollen* (Penguin; Trafalgar Square). The best of the books on Wales' most notorious and celebrated lesbian couple. This volume traces the ladies'

inauspicious beginnings in Ireland, their spectacular elopement and the way that their Llangollen home, Plas Newydd, became a place of pilgrimage for dozens of influential eighteenth-century visitors. A fascinating story, lovingly told.

Jan Morris and Twm Morys, *A Machynlleth Triad/Triawd Machynlleth* (Gwasg Gregynog, UK). Three-part saga in Welsh and English about Machynlleth, Glyndŵr's capital. Jan Morris evokes the town at the time of Glyndŵr, looks at the place today and imagines it "sometime in the 21st century" as the charmingly self-assured capital of an independent Wales. The book says much about Wales as a whole, is beautifully written and often very funny.

John Osmond (ed), *A Parliament for Wales* (o/p). Political contributors across the spectrum pitch in essays on how they see greater democracy in Wales working. A realistic, sober assessment of some burning contemporary issues.

Trefor M. Owen, *The Customs and Traditions of Wales* (University of Wales). Pocket guide to everything from outdoor prayer meetings to the curious Mari Lwyd, when men dress as grey mares and snap at all the young girls. Easy to read and fun to dip into.

George Thomas, *Mr Speaker* (o/p). The autobiography of Rhondda-born George Thomas, rich-toned ex-Speaker of the House of Commons, who died in 1997. From his humble beginnings, including the forceful discouragement of speaking Welsh at school, Thomas charts his fascinating career and is particularly interesting for his shattering recollections of the Aberfan disaster, and, when Secretary of State for Wales, the 1969 investiture of the Prince of Wales at Caernarfon.

Ned Thomas, *The Welsh Extremist* (Y Lolfa, UK). A good introduction to the political landscape that spawned the anti-English bombing campaigns. An evocative argument around the issues of oppression and emancipation.

Patrick Thomas, *Candle in the Darkness: Celtic Spirituality from Wales* (Gomer Press, UK). Tales from the "Age of Saints" in Wales, with particular focus given to the numerous Celtic saints who originated here.

Wynford Vaughan-Thomas, *Wales – A History* (o/p). One of the country's most missed broadcasters and writers, Vaughan-Thomas' masterpiece is this warm and spirited history of Wales. Working chronologically through the pre-Celtic dawn to the aftermath of the 1979 devolution vote, the book offers perhaps the clearest explanation of the evolution of Welsh culture, with the author's patriotic slant evident throughout.

Jennifer Westwood, *Albion: A Guide to Legendary Britain* (HCPA, UK). Highly readable volume on the development of myth in literature.

ART, ARCHITECTURE AND ARCHEOLOGY

Chris Barber and John Godfrey Williams, *The Ancient Stones of Wales* (Blorenge Books, UK). Comprehensive directory of standing stones and monoliths throughout Wales, together with some of the most potent legends and stories associated with them. Exhaustively researched, if a little difficult to use at times.

CADW, *Wales: Castles and Historic Places* (Wales Tourist Board, UK). General chat and rich colour photos of the major CADW sites around the country.

John Harvey, *The Art of Piety: The Visual Culture of Welsh Nonconformity* (o/p). Fascinating historical account of the stern-faced chapels which form an instant image of Wales.

Peter Lord, *Gwenllian: Essays on Visual Culture* (o/p). A well-illustrated and enthusiastic set of essays looking at the Welsh visual aesthetic in art from the eighteenth century (the Picturesque) to the present day.

Pevsner et al, *The Buildings of Glamorgan; The Buildings of Clwyd; The Buildings of Powys* (o/p). Magisterial series covering just about every inhabitable structure. This project was initially a one-man show, but later authors have revised Pevsner's text, inserting newer buildings but generally respecting the founder's personal tone. Volumes of Dyfed, Gwent and Gwynedd are yet to be published.

T.W. Potter and Catherine Johns, *Roman Britain* (British Museum Press; Harvard University Press). Generously illustrated account of Roman occupation, written by the British Museum's own curators.

LITERATURE

Leonora Brito, *Dat's Love* (Seren Books; Dufor). Best of the new black voices emanating from the UK's oldest ethnic minority community in Cardiff Bay. A spicy tale of love and life in a very Welsh cultural melting pot.

Michael Carson, *Stripping Penguins Bare* (Black Swan, UK). Hilarious and poignant semi-autobiographical account of a young gay man arriving at university in Aberystwyth in the pre-liberation 1960s.

Bruce Chatwin, *On the Black Hill* (Vintage; Penguin). This entertaining and finely wrought novel follows the Jones twins' eighty-year tenure of a farm on the Radnorshire border with England. Chatwin casts his sharp eye for detail over both the minutiae of nature and the universal human condition, providing a wonderfully gentle angle on Welsh–English antipathy.

Alexander Cordell, *Rape of the Fair Country; Hosts of Rebecca; Song of the Earth* (Blorenge, UK). Dramatic historical trilogy in the best-seller tradition, partly set in the cottages on the site of the Blaenafon ironworks during the lead-up to the Chartist Riots. *This Sweet and Bitter Earth* (Coronet) immortalizes Blaenau Ffestiniog in a lusty slate epic.

John Davies (ed), *The Green Bridge: Stories from Wales* (Seren; Dufor Editions). Absorbing selection of 25 short stories from a broad spectrum of Welsh authors writing in English during the twentieth century, including Dylan Thomas.

Thomas Firbank, *I Bought a Mountain* (John Jones, UK). One of the few popular books set in north Wales in which Anglo-Canadian Firbank spins an autobiographical yarn of his purchase of most of the Glyder range and subsequent life as a Snowdonian sheep farmer during the 1930s. Generous but patronizing observations about his neighbours and his wife mar an otherwise enjoyable, easy read.

Iris Gower, *Copper Kingdom; Proud Mary; Spinners' Wharf; Black Gold* (all Arrow, UK); *Fiddler's Ferry* (Century, UK); *The Oyster Catchers* (Corgi, UK) – the list goes on. Romantic novels by Wales' most popular author.

Emyr Humphreys, *The Gift of a Daughter* (Seren). Latest in a long line of mystical, well-placed novels by perhaps the greatest extant

Welsh novelist. In this one, the mood and land-scape of Anglesey is beautifully evoked.

Siân James, *Not Singing Exactly* (Hono, UK). Dazzling and diverse short-story collection from one of Wales' premier romantic novelists.

Glyn Jones, *The Island of Apples* (University of Wales). Set in south Wales and Carmarthen in the early years of the twentieth century, Jones artfully portrays a sensitive Valley youth's enthralment in the glamour of the district's new arrival.

Gwyn and Thomas Jones (trans), *The Mabinogion* (Everyman Paperback Classics). Welsh mythology's classic, these eleven orally developed heroic tales were finally transcribed into the *Book of Rhydderch* (around 1300–25) and the *Red Book of Hergest* (1375–1425). Originally translated by Lady Charlotte Guest between 1838 and 1849 at the beginning of the Celtic revival.

Lewis Jones, *Cwmardy* (Lawrence and Wishart, UK). Longtime favourite socialist novel, written in 1937 and portraying life in a Rhondda Valley mining community in the early years of the twentieth century. Followed by its sequel, *We Live*.

Russell Celyn Jones, *Soldiers and Innocents* (Abacus, UK). Tale of a soldier who deserts from Northern Ireland, kidnaps his five-year-old son and embarks on a voyage of self-discovery which takes him back to the Welsh mining com-munity where he grew up.

Richard Llewellyn, *How Green Was My Valley; Up into the Singing Mountain; Down Where the Moon is Small; Green, Green My Valley Now* (Penguin; Scribner). Vital tetralogy in eloquent and passionate prose, following the life of Huw Morgan from his youth in a south Wales mining valley through emigration to the Welsh community in Patagonia and back to 1970s Wales. A best-seller during World War II and still the best introduction to the vast canon of "valleys novels", *How Green Was My Valley* captured a longing for a sim-ple, if tough, life, steering clear of cloying sen-timentality.

Catherine Merriman, *State of Desire* (Pan, UK). Wry widow's tale, set against the backdrop of the mountains in the southeast Wales Valleys.

Caradoc Pritchard, *One Moonlit Night* (Penguin; New Directions). Dense, swirling tale of a young boy's emotional and sexual awakenings in an isolated north Wales vil-lage. Full-blooded Welsh prose at its most charged.

Kate Roberts, *The Living Sleep* and *Feet in Chains*, amongst others (Gomer Press, UK). Penned by one of the best-selling contemporary Welsh-language writers, these two novels, available in English translation, tell the tales of life in a north Wales slate village.

Ruth Janette Ruck, *Hill Farm Story* and *Along Came a Llama* (Business Innovations Research; Ulverscroft). Evocative stories about a farming area around Beddgelert.

Dylan Thomas, *Collected Stories* and *Under Milk Wood* (Everyman; W.W. Norton). Far better than buying any of the single editions, the *Collected Stories* contains all of Thomas' classic prose pieces: *Quite Early One Morning*, which metamorphosed into *Under Milk Wood*, the magical *A Child's Christmas in Wales* and the compulsive, crackling autobiography of *Portrait of the Artist as a Young Dog*. In all of Thomas' works, the language still burns bright in a uniquely robust way. *Under Milk Wood* is his most popular play, telling the story of a micro-cosmic Welsh seaside town over a 24-hour period. Reading it does little justice – far better, instead, to get a tape or record version of the play, and luxuriate in its rich poetry or, as Thomas himself described it, "prose with blood pressure".

Gwyn Thomas, *A Welsh Eye* (o/p). A partly autobiographical, partly anecdotal view of how it feels to grow up in a small Rhondda town; full of arcane and idiosyncratic wit and much more.

Alice Thomas Ellis (ed), *Wales – An Anthology* (o/p). A beautiful book, combining poetry, folklore and prose stories rooted in places throughout Wales. All subjects, from rugby and mountain climbing to contemporary descriptions of major events, are included in an enjoyably eclectic mixture of styles. Possibly the best introduction to Welsh writing.

John Williams, *Five Pubs, Two Bars And A Nightclub* (Bloomsbury). Very funny short story collection, firmly set in the twilight world of Cardiff's less salubrious drink-and-drugs dens. Something of an inspiration for the hit film *Human Traffic*.

POETRY

Dannie Abse, *Welsh Retrospective* (Seren, UK) and *Arcadia, One Mile* (Hutchinson, UK). Two recent collections from one of Wales' most prolific modern poets, showing his huge range of intellectual interests and warm, beguiling style of writing.

John Barnie, *The City* and *The Confirmation* (Gomer Press, UK). One of Wales' best contemporary writers, notable mainly for his combination of poetry and prose styles, narration and description. Evocative tales of wartime childhood and stifling parenting, leading to a poignant search for love.

Ruth Bidgood, *Lighting Candles* (Seren, UK). Light, elegiac verse inspired by the Welsh landscape. Bidgood's interweaving of climate, scenery and emotion is delicately done, producing fine and deceptively robust pieces that stand up as physical description, spiritual discussion or both.

Gillian Clarke, *Collected Poems* (Carcanet, UK). A good introduction to the nature-inspired and homely poetry of one of Wales' leading contemporary writers, now in her sixties.

Gladys Mary Coles, *The Glass Island* (Gerald Duckworth, UK). Breathtakingly cool and descriptive poetry, much of which is set in the Berwyn Mountains in Clwyd and the hills of north Wales. Coles' gently probing technique uses discoveries of random objects or sights to spark off musings about their history and derivation.

Gerard Manley Hopkins, *Collected Works* (Penguin; Viking). The religious poetry of this late-nineteenth-century Anglo-Catholic still bears scrutiny today. Much of his best work was inspired by Wales – "the loveable west" – and the metre and rhythm of the Welsh language that he strove to learn. Heartfelt and often profoundly sad, with an exquisite ability to marry the grandeur of the landscape with the intensity of his feelings.

Dafydd Johnson, *Iolo Goch: poems* (Gomer Press, UK). All of the surviving poems of Owain Glyndŵr's court bard are shown in translation and context. A fascinating insight into courtly medieval Wales at a time of great national resurgence.

David Jones, *The Anathémata* (Faber and Faber, UK). Once ranked with Ezra Pound and T.S. Eliot (who once declared him to be the finest poet then working in the English language), Jones has now been relegated to the footnotes of literary Modernism. A pity, because this long poem – a meditation on the history and mythology of Celtic-Christian Britain – is one of the most ambitious and intelligent pieces of writing to come out of Wales. A refreshing change from the emotive lushness of Dylan Thomas.

T. Harri Jones, *Collected Works* (Gomer Press, UK). Jones is one of Wales' most prolific twentieth-century writers, pumping out work firmly rooted in his native country. His passion and nationalism seems occasionally naive, although the *hiraeth* for Wales and its rootedness cannot fail to impress.

Robert Minhinnick, *Selected Poems* (Carcanet, UK). Overview of the recent career of one of Wales' brightest young writers: best when picking over his English-speaking south Walian youth in rich, impassioned imagery.

Meic Stephens (ed), *New Companion to the Literature of Wales* (University of Wales Press, UK). A customarily thorough volume of Welsh prose, spanning the centuries from the folk tales of The Mabinogion to modern-day writings. A succinct and entertaining collection.

Dylan Thomas, *Collected Poems* (Everyman; W.W. Norton). Thomas' poetry has always proved less populist than his prose- and playwriting, largely due to its density and difficulty. Many of his lighter poems resound with perfect metre and precise structure, including classics such as *Do Not Go Gentle Into That Good Night*, a passionate yet calm elegy to his dying father.

R.S. Thomas, *Selected Poems 1946–1968* (Phoenix Press; Everyman). A fierce, reclusive Welsh nationalist, Thomas' poetry tugs at issues such as God (he was an Anglican priest), Wales ("brittle with relics") and the family. His passion shines throughout this book, probably the best overview available of his prolific work.

Harri Webb (ed. Meic Stephens), *Collected Poems* (Gomer Press, UK). Fine collection of 350 works by a modern-day patriot and poet of biting satire and eloquent expression.

FOOD AND DRINK

CAMRA, *The Best Pubs in North Wales* (CAMRA, UK). A hundred or so top pubs with the emphasis on good beer, produced by the Campaign for Real Ale.

Gilli Davies, *A Taste of Wales* (Pavilion, UK). Lovely, glossy recipe book with some beautiful landscape photography. Dishes from all over Wales are featured, together with good write-ups on the history of Welsh regional food and drink.

Dave Frost and Barbara Rottner Frost, *Welsh Salad Days* (Y Lolfa, UK). Some good, hearty organic recipes and innovations from mid-Wales, rather spoiled by some distinctly purple prose about the land farmed by the authors.

Sarah and Ann Gomar, *Welsh Country Recipes* (o/p). Despite leaving out some of the traditional dishes, this bargain book makes amends with its broad scope of more ambitious Welsh recipes.

E. Smith Twiddy, *A Little Welsh Cookbook* (Appletree Press, UK). Slim hardback neatly covering the traditional Welsh staples: *bara brith*, *cawl*, Glamorgan sausages and *laver bread*.

WILDLIFE AND THE ENVIRONMENT

D. and R. Aichele, H.W. and A. Schwegler, *Wild Flowers of Britain and Europe* (o/p). Superb full-colour identification guide divided by flower colour and subdivided by flower form and habitat. Over 900 species covered but not Wales- or even UK-specific.

Douglas Botting, *Wild Britain: A Traveller's Guide* (Sheldrake Press; Interlink). Not much use for species identification but plenty of information on access to the best sites and what to expect when you get there. Excellent photos.

Collins Field Guides (HarperCollins). Series of thorough, pocket-sized identification guides. Topics include insects, butterflies, wild flowers, mushrooms and toadstools, birds, mammals, reptiles and fossils.

William Condry, *A Welsh Country Diary* (Gomer Press, UK). Over three hundred brief insights into the intricacies of Welsh country life – from the names of rivers to grass snakes in the garden – seen through the eyes of the longest serving contributor to *The Guardian's* "Country Diary" column.

Michael Leach, *The Secret Life of Snowdonia* (o/p). Beautifully photographed coffee-table delvings into the least visible natural sights of Snowdonia, from feral goats to the Snowdon lily and a close-up of a raven in its nest.

Les Lumsden and Colin Speakman, *The Green Guide to Wales* (Greenprint, UK). Eco-tourism Cambrian style. A now-dated pocket guide to how to get around Wales with the least damage to the environment and its people. Solid background section on green tourism and good for co-operative and community initiative contacts.

David Saunders, *Where to Watch Birds in Wales* (Christopher Helm; A. & C. Black). Enthusiasts' guide to Wales' prime birding locations, along with a bird spotting calendar and a list of English–Welsh–Scientific bird names. Not an identification guide.

Detef Singer, *Field Guide to Birds of Britain and Northern Europe* (HarperCollins, UK). Colour-coded sections based on birds' plumage, and 700 beautiful photos back up detailed discussion of behaviour and habitat.

Roger Thomas, *Brecon Beacons National Park – A Countryside Commission Guide* (Countryside Commission, UK). Superb book, going into huge detail on the beginnings and building of the Beacons, as well as the wildlife and flora that you can expect to see there today. Well-written and hugely informative, whilst remaining essentially personal and enthusiastic.

Martin Walters, *Wildlife Travelling Companion: Great Britain and Ireland* (o/p). One of the best amateur books on the flora and fauna of the British Isles, with a few full-colour pages to aid identification, and a region-by-region site guide. Twenty pages specifically on Wales, covering South Stack, Newborough Warren, Bardsey, Cadair Idris, Devil's Bridge, St David's Head, Skomer island and more.

OUTDOOR PURSUITS

Bob Allen, *On Foot in Snowdonia* (M. Joseph, UK). Inspirational and superbly photographed guide to the hundred best walks, from easy strolls to hard scrambles, in and around the Snowdonia National Park. Well-drawn maps, faultless instructions and a star rating for each walk help you to select your route. An essential guide, perfect but for its weight.

Pete Bursnall, *Mountain Bike Guide: Mid-Wales* (Ernest Press, UK). Easy-to-follow pocket guide to a score of biking routes with hand-drawn maps. Due to be followed by a north Wales edition.

Cicerone Guides, *The Mountains of England and Wales; Wales, The Ridges of Snowdonia; Hill Walking in Snowdonia; Ascent of Snowdon; Welsh Winter Climbs; Scrambles in Snowdonia* and others, various authors (Cicerone Press). Clearly written pocket guides to the best aspects of Welsh mountain activities.

Constable Guides, *Best Walks in Southern Wales; Best Walks in North Wales; Owain Glyndŵr's Way; A Guide to Offa's Dyke*, various authors (Constable, UK). More clearly written pocket guides to the best aspects of Welsh mountain activities.

A.J. Drake, *Cambrian Way: A Mountain Connoisseur's Walk* (o/p). Thorough and detailed lightweight guide to Wales' most demanding long-distance path by one of the original proposers of this three-week-long, 274-mile Conwy–Cardiff route along Wales' backbone.

Lawrence Main, *The Dyfi Valley Way* (o/p). Comprehensive guide to this long-distance path by one of its creators.

Terry Marsh, *The Mountains of Wales* (University of Wales; Hodder & Stoughton). A walker's guide to all 183 of the 600-metre peaks in Wales, giving step-by-step descriptions of one or more routes up them all with additional historical references and local knowledge.

Ordnance Survey National Trail Guides (Ordnance Survey). Large, paperback editions full of instructive step-by-step descriptions and additional side-walks from *Offa's Dyke North, Offa's Dyke South* and *Pembrokeshire Coastal Path*.

Ordnance Survey Pathfinder Guides. Softcover editions for large pockets covering *Pembrokeshire and Gower Walks, Snowdonia, Anglesey and the Llŷn Peninsula Walks* and *Snowdonia Walks* (Ordnance Survey). The 28 routes detailed in each are embellished with useful, if plodding, accounts of sights along the way.

W.A. Poucher, *The Welsh Peaks* (Constable; Trafalgar Square). The classic book on Welsh hill-walking, but fairly dated now; initially, it's also a little awkward to find your way around the 56 routes.

Stillwell's National Trail Companion (Stillwell). Excellent big-pocket directory of rea-sonably priced accommodation close to some of the more popular UK long-distance paths. Welsh routes include the Cambrian Way, Glyndŵr's Way, the Offa's Dyke Path, the Pembrokeshire Coast Path and the Wye Valley Walk.

Shirley Toulson, *The Drovers' Roads of Wales* with Fay Godwin and *The Drovers' Roads of Wales II: Pembrokeshire and the South* with Caroline Forbes; and *Walking Round Wales: The Giraldus Journey* (Whittet, UK). The first two are a pair of complementary books giving background material along with instructions on how to trace the routes along which Wales' characteristic black cattle were driven to market in England in the eighteenth and nineteenth centuries. The first book covers the northern two-thirds of Wales with superb shots in black-and-white by photography star Fay Godwin, the much more recent second book covers south Wales with more high-quality photos. *Walking Round Wales* is a very readable guide broken into thirty walks following the route around Wales taken by the twelfth-century clergyman Giraldus Cambrensis and enlivened by his own quirky accounts.

OTHER GUIDES

William Condry, *Snowdonia* (David & Charles, US). The best detailed approach to the region, this is a personal guided tour around the Snowdonia National Park, dipping into geology, natural history and industrial heritage. There's also Condry's *Wales* – as for Snowdonia, but covering the whole country.

David Greenslade, *Welsh Fever: Welsh Activities in the United States and Canada Today* (Barbara Hirsch, US). Essential companion for anyone searching out Welsh and Celtic roots in North America. Commentary on regions from Quebec to San Diego, along with accounts of a hundred individual sites of Welsh or Celtic interest.

Moira K. Stone, *Mid Wales Companion* (Anthony Nelson, UK). Wide-ranging though not terribly detailed look at life in the stretch of Wales from southern and eastern Snowdonia down to the Brecon Beacons. The town guides are perfunctory, and it is better for the examination of history (from transport to art), landscape influences and industry.

LANGUAGE

Welsh is spoken widely throughout the majority of the country and as a first language in many parts of the west and north. National TV and radio stations broadcast in it, road signs are written in both Welsh and English, Welsh-medium schools are everywhere, books in Welsh are published at a growing rate of around 400 every year and magazines and newspapers in the old language are mushrooming. The language's survival, and modest resurgence, is a remarkable story, especially considering the fact that the heart of English culture and its language – the most expansionist the world has ever seen – lies right next door.

In the families of Celtic languages, Welsh bears most similarity to largely defunct Cornish and defiant Breton, the language of the north-western corner of France. Scots and Irish Gaelic, together with defunct Manx, belong to a different branch of Celtic languages, and, although there are occasional similarities, they have little in common.

The language can be traced back to the sixth century. Through Celtic inscriptions on stones, a section of written Welsh in the eighth-century **Lichfield Gospels**, the tenth-century codified laws of Hywel Dda in neat Welsh prose and the twelfth- and thirteenth-century **Mabinogion** folk tales (believed to have been collated from earlier Welsh writings), it can be seen that Welsh was a thriving language in the centuries up to the Norman invasion of 1066. Moreover, the early language is still identifiable and easily comprehensible for any modern-day Welsh-speaker.

English domination since the Norman era has been mirrored in the fate of the Welsh tongue. The Norman lords were implanted in castles throughout Wales to subjugate the natives, with official business conducted in their native French. **Edward I** (1272–1307), who conquered Wales in 1284, was politically sensitive to the power of the language to define a nation, and is said to have promised the Welsh a prince, born in their own country who was unable to speak English. This promise was delivered when Edward made his pregnant wife take up residence in Caernarfon Castle, enabling the king to hold the newborn infant up as a non-English-speaking, Welsh-born prince.

Real linguistic warfare came with the 1536 **Act of Union** under Henry VIII. This stated that "from henceforth no Person or Persons that use the Welsh Speech or Language shall have or enjoy any Manner, Office or Fees within this Realm of England, Wales or other the King's Dominion, upon pain of forfeiting the same Office or Fees, unless he or they use and exercise the English Speech or Language". This only legitimized the growing practice of imposing English lords and churchmen on the restless, but effectively cowed, Welsh. Had it not been for **William Morgan**'s 1588 translation of the Bible into Welsh, it is likely that the language would have died. As it was, bringing written Welsh into the ordinary, everyday arena of the public ultimately ensured its survival.

The fate of the language became inextricably linked with its religious use. Right up until the early part of the twentieth century, Welsh was actively, even forcefully, discouraged in educational and governmental establishments, but new and Nonconformist religious movements from the seventeenth century onwards embraced the language. The **Industrial Revolution** brought mine owners and capitalists from England into the rapidly urbanizing southeastern corner of Wales, further diluting the language which was, nonetheless, upheld as the lingua franca in the growing numbers of chapels. In the first half of the nineteenth century, it is estimated that over ninety percent of the country's population spoke Welsh, with the remaining ten percent comprising those around the English border, in the small pocket of Pembrokeshire long known as "Little England Beyond Wales" and the wealthier classes throughout Wales, for whom English was part of their badge of status.

In 1854, **George Borrow** undertook his marathon tour of Wales and noted the state of the native tongue throughout. As a natural linguist, he had mastered Welsh and – in typically pompous declamatory fashion – fired questions at people he encountered as to their proficiency in both Welsh and English. The picture he paints is of poorer people tending to be monoglot Welsh, wealthier people and those near the border bilingual. Discouragement of Welsh continued in many guises, most notably in it being forbidden in schools in the latter half of the nineteenth- and early-twentieth-centuries. Anyone caught speaking in Welsh had to wear a "Welsh Not", a piece of wood on a leather strap, known as a *cribban*, that would only be passed on if someone else was heard using the language. At the end of the school day, the child still wearing the *cribban* was soundly beaten. There are still older people in Wales who can remember this barbaric practice, and it is hardly surprising that use and proficiency of the language plummeted. Figures are borne out by the official British census, the first of which was undertaken in 1851, when 90 percent of the country are recorded as speaking the language. Every decade, the figures dipped quite spectacularly – 49.9 percent in 1901, 37.1 percent in 1921, 28.9 percent in 1951 and 18.9 percent in 1981. Then, in 1991, for the first time ever, the percentage of Welsh speakers rose, still around the one-fifth mark but showing the most marked increase amongst the lower age groups, those most able to ensure its future.

The figure of 20 percent (ie half a million people), usually quoted as the current number of Welsh-speakers in Wales, is best seen in its geographical context. Considering the fact that nearly half of the nation's population live in the anglicized regions of Gwent and around Cardiff, the spread of the language becomes clearer. Although it is unusual to hear it regularly in the border counties, it is commonly understood throughout most of West Glamorgan, Carmarthenshire, the northern half of Pembrokeshire, right around Cardigan Bay up to Caernarfon, the Llŷn peninsula and Anglesey and in parts of inland Denbighshire, Montgomeryshire and Radnorshire. The north-western corner, centred on Snowdonia, Anglesey and the Llŷn peninsula, are the real strongholds of Welsh, reflected in these areas' steadfast political affiliation to Welsh nationalism.

If Welsh ended the twentieth century on a more upbeat note than could ever have been predicted thirty or so years ago (when it was believed to be dying out), it is largely due to those who campaigned to save it. The campaign dates back to the eisteddfod revivalists of the eighteenth century, although movements with a more political aim are a product solely of the twentieth century. The formation of **Plaid Cymru**, the Welsh National Party, in 1925 was largely around the issue of language, as indeed its politics have been ever since. In the early 1960s, concerns about the language reached a zenith in the 1962 radio broadcast entitled *Tynged yr iaith* (The Fate of the Language) by the Plaid founder member, Saunders Lewis. This became a rallying cry that resulted in the formation of *Cymdeithas yr Iaith Gymraeg* (the **Welsh Language Society**) the following year. One of the most high-profile early campaigns was the daubing of monoglot English road signs with their Welsh translations, including any town sign written solely in the anglicized format. As any visitor to Wales sees, nearly all signs are now in both languages. A 1967 Welsh Language Act allowed many forms of hitherto English officialdom to be conducted in either language, stating that Welsh, for the first time in over 400 years, had "equal validity" with English.

Bilingual road signs and tax forms are all well and good, but they could do nothing to stem the linguistic haemorrhage that Wales was threatened with. In the multinational, cross-media world of the late twentieth century, the keys to maintaining and promoting a language were in education and media, particularly television. Following the 1967 Act, **Welsh-medium education** blossomed, with bilingual teaching in all primary schools and for at least a year in all secondary schools. Many secondary schools, particularly in areas traditionally associated with the language, had Welsh as a compulsory subject for five years. Increasing numbers of schools all over the land educate their students in all subjects through the Welsh language. These trends have brought little but sneers from the English establishment, profiling loud complaints from numbers of parents, often English immigrants, who object to their children being "forced" to learn a "dead" language. Although there are still periodic rumbles of discontent, most have come round to the well-

WELSH VOCABULARY

Alban or **ab** Scotland
Amgeuddfa Museum
Ap (ab) Son of
Ar Agor Open
Ar Gau Closed
Ar Werth For Sale
Araf Slow
Bara Bread
Bore Morning
Bore da Good morning
Brecwast Breakfast
Bwrdd Table
Bws Bus
Cân Song
Cenedlaethol National
Crefft Craft
Croeso Welcome
Croglen Rood screen
Cromlech Literally "curved stone", generally used to refer to megalithic burial chambers
Cwm Glacially formed, cliff-backed and often lake-filled bowl in mountains. Also called cirque or corrie
Cyhoeddus Public
Cymdeithas Society
Cymraeg Welsh
Cymraes A Welshwoman
Cymreictod Welshness
Cymro A Welshman
Cymru Wales
Cymry The Welsh people
Da Good
Dewi Sant Saint David
Dim No (as an instruction), nothing

Diolch Thank you
Diwedd End
Druids Priestly class in pre-Roman Celtic culture, often including administrators and judges
Dŵr Water
Dydd Day
Dyn (ion) Man (men)
Eglwys Church
Eisteddfod Festival
Faint? How much?
Gorsaf Station
Gweddol Fair
Gwely Bed
Gwesty Hotel
Hafod Temporary summer house
Hanner Half
Heddiw Today
Heddlu Police
Heno Tonight
Heol Road
Hiraeth Longing, yearning
Hwyl Spirit
Iaith Language
Iawn Fine
Llech Slate
Llety Lodging place, B&B
Llew Lion (often found in pub names)
Lloegr England
Llwybr Path
Llyfr Book
Marchnad Market
Menyw Woman
Mihangel Michael, as in Llanfihangel

Milltir Mile
Neuadd Hall
Neuadd Y Dref Town Hall
Nofio To swim
Nos da Good night
Noson/noswaith Evening
Noswaith dda Good evening
Olaf Last
Os Gwelwch yn Dda Please
Pêl-droed Football
Pentref Village
Plaid Cymru The Party of Wales
P'nhawn da Good afternoon
Rhiniog Buttress
Saesneg English language
Sais Englishman
Sant Saint
Sarn Causeway
Senedd Parliament
Shwmae Hello
Siop Shop
Sir County, Shire
Stryd Street
Sut ydych chi? (formal) or **Sut ywt ti? (informal)** How are you?
Swyddfa Office
Swyddfa'r Post Post office
Tafarn Pub
Tocyn Ticket
Y, Yr or **'r** The
Yma Here
Ysbyty Hospital
Ysgol School

founded view that a bilingual education (which is, after all, what sixty percent of the world's children receive) actually helps children learn, increasing aptitude for other languages. At the other end of the educational spectrum, Welsh-language courses in the country's universities are growing in popularity and status, meaning

that, for pretty much the first time in Wales' history, it is possible to be educated in Welsh from nursery to degree level.

Paralleling Welsh-medium education has been the other modern cornerstone for developing a language – a growth in media. In the mid-1970s, a government report recommended

WELSH PLACE NAMES

The following list is of the most common words that you will see in town and village names. For a brief guide to pronunciation, see "Alphabet", overleaf.

Aber Mouth of a river; confluence of two rivers
Afon River
Bach Small, lesser
Bron Slope of a hill
Bryn Hill
Bwlch Mountain pass
Cadair Stronghold, chair
Caer Fort
Canol Centre
Cant Hundred
Capel Chapel
Carreg Stone
Cartref Home
Castell Castle
Clun Meadow
Clwyd Gate, perch
Coch Red
Coed Forest, woodland
Craig Rock
Cyntaf First
De South
Din or **dinas** Fort
Dros Over
Du Black
Dwyrain East

Fawr Big
Fferm Farm
Ffordd Road
Fforest Forest
Gardd Garden
Glas Blue
Glyn Valley
Gogledd North
Gorllewin West
Gwyn White
Gwyrdd Green
Hen Old
Isaf Lower
Llan Clearing, early church
Lle Place
Llwyd Grey
Llyn Lake
Llys Place, court
Maen Stone
Maes Field
Mawr Great
Melin Mill
Melyn Yellow
Merthyr Burial place of saint
Moel Bare or rounded mountain

Môr Sea
Morfa Coastal marsh
Mynydd Mountain
Nant Valley, stream
Newydd New
Nos Night
Pant Vale
Parc Park
Pen Head, top (as of a valley)
Plas Hall, mansion
Pont Bridge
Porth Port, gateway
Rhiw Hill
Rhyd Ford
Taf Dark
Tomen Mound
Traeth Beach
Tref Town
Twr Tower
Tŷ House
Uchaf Uppermost, highest
Uwch Higher
Wrth Near, by
Ynys Island

that the putative fourth national TV channel be bilingual in Wales, pulling together (and significantly increasing) periodic Welsh programming on other channels. When plans for Channel 4 were drawn up by the new Conservative administration under Margaret Thatcher in the early 1980s, this recommendation (and her own commitment to uphold this idea) had been dropped. A formidable campaign was launched by *Cymdeithas yr Iaith*, culminating in a hunger strike by Plaid Cymru leader, Gwynfor Evans. Margaret Thatcher, ever an astute politician, realized that creating a Welsh martyr could have dangerous ramifications and the government gracelessly capitulated, giving birth to **Sianel Pedwar Cymru** (S4C) in 1982. Together with the Welsh-language BBC Radio Cymru, S4C has sponsored and programmed enduringly popular Welsh learners' programmes and given the old language greater space than it has ever enjoyed before. Critics would like to believe that this is a false dawn, but this can easily be dismissed just by touring Wales and seeing the sheer number of Welsh-language classes on offer right across the country, including in some of the most anglicized of border towns. Welsh classes can invariably be found out of Wales too, in language centres across Britain, and universities in Europe and North America.

The Welsh language is both one of Wales' key strengths and its key drawbacks in the quest for some sort of national emancipation. There is still suspicion, occasionally bordering

RESOURCES FOR WELSH LEARNERS

Welsh language classes are held throughout Wales – a list can be obtained from the Welsh for Adults Officer at the Welsh Language Board (see below). Otherwise, there are rafts of publications, on paper and electronically, as well as TV and radio programmes and support groups for the Welsh learner. The list below is by no means exhaustive.

Acen, 1 Bridge St, Cardiff CF10 2EE (☎029/2066 5455, fax 2066 8810, www.acen.co.uk). S4C-originated company, now providing a multimedia Welsh course, together with a regular magazine and copious numbers of useful contacts.

Canolfan Iaith Nant Gwrtheyrn, Llithfaen, Pwllheli, Gwynedd LL53 6PA (☎01758/750334, fax 750335, www.marketsite.co.uk/wlc). Residential national language centre on the coast of the Llŷn peninsula (see Guide, p.462).

Cymdeithas Madog (North American Welsh Studies Institute), 5240 E Frances Rd, Mt. Morris, MI 48458, USA (www.madog.org). Annual residential language courses, plus a directory of resources.

Cymdeithas yr Iaith (Welsh Language Society), 15 Rhodfa'r Gogledd, Aberystwyth, Ceredigion SY23 2JH (☎01970/624501, fax 627122, www.cymdeithas.com). Campaigning and political organization dedicated to improving the status of the Welsh language.

National Language Unit of Wales, Welsh for Adults Officer, Welsh Joint Education Committee, 245 Western Ave, Cardiff CF5 2YX (☎029/2026 5009, fax 2057 5995, www.wjec.co.uk). Will provide a comprehensive guide to Welsh teaching provision.

Welsh Language Board/Bwrdd yr Iaith Gymraeg, 5–7 St Mary's St, Cardiff CF1 2AT (☎029/2022 4744, fax 2038 2879, www.netwales.co.uk/byig).

on hostility, towards the Welsh-speaking "elite" who are seen to control the media and local government in the country. Welsh nationalism is so defined by the language that Plaid Cymru has nearly always had great difficulty in applying its relevance to those who speak only English, particularly in the urban southeast. Nonetheless, the Welsh language seems to be facing the new millennium in greater heart than could ever have been expected only a few decades ago. The new **Welsh Language Board** was formed in 1994, and with the arrival of the **National Assembly** in 1999, with around half of its members proficient in Welsh, the language has gained a number of firm footholds in official life. It is nonsensical to believe that Wales can ever become a monoglot Welsh-speaking nation, but it does seem to be developing well as a model bilingual entity, in which there is room for both languages to thrive together.

ALPHABET

Although Welsh words, place names in particular, can appear bewilderingly incomprehensible, the rules of the language are far more strictly adhered to than in English. Thus, mastering the basic constructions and breaking words down into their constituent parts means that pronunciation need not be anywhere near as difficult as first imagined.

The Welsh **alphabet** is similar to the English, although with seven vowels instead of five, and a different collection of consonants. As well as the same five vowels (a, e, i, o, u), Welsh also has y and w. Most vowels have two sounds, long and short: a is long as in c**a**r, short as in f**a**t; e long as in br**e**r, short as in p**e**t; i long as in s**ea**, short as an t**i**n; o long as in m**o**re, short as in d**o**g; u roughly like a Welsh i; w long as in s**oo**n, short as in l**oo**k; y long as in s**ea** and short as in b**u**n or p**i**n.

Adjoining vowels are common in Welsh. Ae, ai, aw, ew, iw, oe, oi, ou, wy and yw are the usual forms and are pronounced as the two separate sounds, with, generally, the stress on the first.

There are no letters j, k, v, x and z in Welsh, except in occasional words appropriated and Cymrified from other languages. Additional Welsh consonants are ch, pronounced as in German or as in lo**ch**, dd, pronounced as a hard th as in **th**ose, ff and ph as a soft f as in **f**ive and si as in **sh**oe. The typically Welsh consonant that causes the most problem is the ll, featured in many place names such as **Ll**ango**ll**en. This has no direct parallel in English, although the tl sound in Ben**tl**ey comes close. The proper way

WELSH NUMBERS

1 un	13 un-deg-tri	200 dau gant
2 dau (fem. dwy)	20 dau-ddeg	300 tri chant
3 tri (fem. tair)	21 dau-ddeg-un	400 pedwar cant
4 pedwar (fem. pedair)	22 dau-ddeg-dau	500 pum cant
5 pump	30 tri-deg	600 chwe cant
6 chwech	40 pedwar-deg	700 saith cant
7 saith	50 pum-deg	800 wyth cant
8 wyth	60 chwe-deg	900 naw cant
9 naw	70 saith-deg	1000 mil
10 deg	80 wyth-deg	1,000,000 miliwn
11 un-deg-un	90 naw-deg	
12 un-deg-dau	100 cant	

to pronounce it is to place the tongue firmly behind the top row of teeth and breathe through it without consciously making a voiced sound. Single Welsh consonants are, for the most part, pronounced in similar ways to English. The exceptions are c and g, always hard as in **c**at and **g**ut (never soft as in ni**c**e or ra**g**e) and f, always pronounced as v as in **v**ine.

A further difficulty for those trying to recognize words is the Welsh system of word **mutation**, where a previous word can affect the beginning of a following one, principally to ease pronunciation. Prepositions commonly mutate the following word, turning an initial B into F or M, an initial C into G or Ngh, a D into Dd or N, F into B or M, G into C or Ngh, Ll into L, M into F, P into B, Mh or Ph, T into Th, D or Nh. Thus, "in Cardiff (Caerdydd)" is "y**ng Ngh**aerdydd" (note that the "yn" also mutates to ease pronunciation) and "from Bangor" is "o **F**angor".

GLOSSARY OF ARCHITECTURAL TERMS

Aisle Clear space parallel to the nave, usually with lower ceiling than the nave.

Altar Table at which the Eucharist is celebrated, at the east end of the church. When the church is not aligned to the geographical east, the altar end is still referred to as the "east" end.

Ambulatory Passage behind the chancel.

Apse The curved or polygonal east end of a church.

Arcade Row of arches on top of columns or piers, supporting a wall.

Bailey Area enclosed by castle walls.

Barbican Defensive structure built in front of main gate.

Barrel vault Continuous rounded vault, like a semi-cylinder.

Boss A decorative carving at the meeting point of the lines of a vault.

Box pew Form of church seating in which each row is enclosed by high, thin wooden panels.

Buttress Stone support for a wall; some buttresses are wholly attached to the wall, others take the form of a tower with a connecting arch, known as a "flying buttress".

Capital Upper section of a column, usually carved.

Chancel Section of the church where the altar is located.

Choir Area in which the church service is conducted; next to or same as chancel.

Clerestory Upper storey of nave, containing a line of windows.

Corbel Jutting stone support, often carved.

Crenellations Battlements with square indentations.

Crossing The intersection of the nave and the transepts.

Decorated Middle Gothic style, about 1280–1380.

Fan vault Late Gothic form of vaulting, in which the area between walls and ceiling is covered with stone ribs in the shape of an open fan.

Finial Any decorated tip of an architectural feature.

Gallery A raised passageway.

Gargoyle Grotesque exterior carving, usually a decorative form of water spout.

Hammerbeam Type of ceiling in which horizontal beams support vertical pieces that connect to the roof timbers.

Jesse window Stained-glass window depicting the descendants from Jesse (the father of David) down to Jesus.

Keep Main structure of a castle.

Lancet Tall, narrow and plain window.

Misericord Carved ledge below a tip-up seat, usually in choir stalls.

Motte Mound on which a castle keep stands.

Mullion Vertical strip between the panes of a window.

Nave The main part of the church to the west of the crossing.

Ogee Double curve; distinctive feature of Decorated style.

Oriel Projecting window.

Palladian Eighteenth-century classical style, adhering to the principles of Andrea Palladio.

Pediment Triangular space above a window or doorway.

Perpendicular Late Gothic style, about 1380–1550.

Pier Massive column, often consisting of several fused smaller columns.

Portico Colonnade, usually supporting a porch to the building.

Rood screen Wooden screen supporting a Crucifix (or rood), separating the choir from the nave; few survived the Reformation.

Rose window Large circular window, divided into vaguely petal-shaped sections.

Stalls Seating for clergy in the choir area of a church.

Tracery Pattern formed by narrow bands of stone in a window or on a wall surface.

Transept Sections of the main body of the church at right angles to the choir and nave.

Vault Arched ceiling.

INDEX